THE EDINBURGH COMPANION TO CHARLES DICKENS AND THE ARTS

Edinburgh Companions to Literature and the Humanities

These single-volume reference works present cutting-edge scholarship in areas of literary studies particularly those which reach out to other disciplines. They include volumes on key literary figures and their interaction with the arts, on major topics and on emerging forms of cross-disciplinary research.

For a complete list of titles in the series, please go to

https://edinburghuniversitypress.com/series/ecl

THE EDINBURGH COMPANION TO CHARLES DICKENS AND THE ARTS

EDITED BY JULIET JOHN AND CLAIRE WOOD

EDINBURGH
University Press

Edinburgh University Press is one of the leading university presses in the UK. We publish academic books and journals in our selected subject areas across the humanities and social sciences, combining cutting-edge scholarship with high editorial and production values to produce academic works of lasting importance. For more information visit our website: edinburghuniversitypress.com

© editorial matter and organisation Juliet John and Claire Wood 2024
© the chapters their several authors 2024

Published with the support of the University of Edinburgh Scholarly Publishing Initiatives Fund.

Edinburgh University Press Ltd
13 Infirmary Street
Edinburgh EH1 1LT

Typeset in 10/12 Adobe Sabon by
IDSUK (DataConnection) Ltd, and
printed and bound in Great Britain.

A CIP record for this book is available from the British Library

ISBN 978 1 4744 4164 3 (hardback)
ISBN 978 1 4744 4165 0 (webready PDF)
ISBN 978 1 4744 4166 7 (epub)

The right of Juliet John and Claire Wood to be identified as the editor of this work has been asserted in accordance with the Copyright, Designs and Patents Act 1988, and the Copyright and Related Rights Regulations 2003 (SI No. 2498).

CONTENTS

List of Illustrations	viii
Acknowledgements	x
1. Ahead of its Time: Dickens's Prescient Vision of the Arts *Juliet John and Claire Wood*	1

Part I: Novel Arts

2. Eighteenth-Century Cultures and the Novel *Paul Baines*	15
3. The Novel and the Arts of Modern Vision *Francesca Orestano*	29
4. Fanfiction *Maureen England*	47

Part II: Theatre and Drama

5. Clowns *Jonathan Buckmaster*	67
6. Melodrama *Carolyn Williams*	82
7. Amateur Theatricals *Mary Isbell*	97
8. Nineteenth-Century Stage Adaptations *Jim Davis*	114
9. Dickens and Drama *Gillian Piggott*	131

Part III: Performing Arts

10. Dance
    Goldie Morgentaler ... 151

11. Music
    Matthew Ingleby ... 164

12. Musical Theatre
    Sharon Aronofsky Weltman ... 180

13. Rap Music
    Melisa Klimaszewski ... 196

14. Puppets
    David Ellison ... 207

Part IV: Visual Arts

15. Illustration
    Julia Thomas ... 223

16. Caricature
    Brian Maidment ... 239

17. Landscape
    Malcolm Andrews ... 258

18. Photography
    Daniel A. Novak ... 272

19. High Art
    Jeremy Tambling ... 289

20. Architecture
    Ben Moore ... 303

Part V: Screen

21. Silent Dickens
    Joss Marsh ... 323

22. Twenty-First Century Television
    Christine Geraghty ... 341

23. Hollywood and British Cinema
    Barry Langford ... 356

24. Global Cinema
    Marty Gould ... 372

Part VI: National and International Dickens

25. Translations
    Klaudia Hiu Yen Lee ... 389

CONTENTS vii

26. Global Dickens 402
Michael Hollington

27. Education 416
Sarah Winter

28. Political Art and the Art of Politics 433
Dominic Rainsford

29. New Media and Cyberspace 448
Emma Curry

Part VII: Cultural Memory

30. Dickens and Shakespeare 465
Pete Orford

31. Dickensiana 480
Ryan D. Fong

32. Placing Dickens 496
Charlotte Mathieson

33. Commemoration 510
Claire Wood

Notes on Contributors 525
Index 533

ILLUSTRATIONS

Plates

1 John Orlando Parry, unpublished and unsigned pen drawing,
   'Starting for Cheltenham' (c.1835). Courtesy of Brian Maidment.
2 Marcus Stone, part issue title page for Charles Dickens's *Our Mutual
   Friend* (1864–5). Courtesy of the Charles Dickens Museum, London.
3 Robert Seymour, 'Repentance!!!', lithographed plate 9 for
   The Schoolmaster Abroad (London: McLean, 1834). Courtesy
   of Brian Maidment.
4 Day and Martin's Blacking Bottle. Courtesy of the Charles Dickens
   Museum, London [DH534_R3].
5 Hablot K. Browne ('Phiz'), 'Damocles', an illustration for Charles
   Dickens's *Little Dorrit* (1855–7). Courtesy of the Charles Dickens
   Museum, London.

Figures

7.1   Playbill for *Clari* (1833). Courtesy of the Charles Dickens Museum,
      London [F273].   102
12.1 Luke Fildes, 'At the Piano', an illustration for Charles Dickens's
      The Mystery of Edwin Drood (1870). Courtesy of the Charles
      Dickens Museum, London [F2806].   191
15.1 Hablot K. Browne ('Phiz'), 'Our Pew at Church', an illustration for
      Charles Dickens's *David Copperfield* (1849–50). Courtesy of the
      Charles Dickens Museum, London [F2994].   226
15.2 Hablot K. Browne ('Phiz'), Frontispiece for the final 'double' number
      of Charles Dickens's *The Pickwick Papers* (1836–7). Courtesy of the
      Charles Dickens Museum, London [F538].   228
16.1 George Cruikshank, 'The Nightingale Club', a wood-engraved
      illustration from *The Universal Songster* 1 (London: Jones, 1825).
      Courtesy of Brian Maidment.   240

LIST OF ILLUSTRATIONS

16.2 Robert Seymour, 'The Club', an engraving from *Sketches by Seymour* 5.4 (London: Carlile, March 1835). Courtesy of Brian Maidment.   241

16.3 Robert Seymour, 'Fisherman Dozing Against a Tree', in *Sketches by Seymour* 1.9 (Tregear, ?1834). Courtesy of Brian Maidment.   250

16.4 Robert Seymour, *The Heiress – A Farce in Six Plates*, plate 1 (McLean, 1830). Courtesy of Brian Maidment.   251

16.5 Robert Seymour, title page for *Pierce Egan's Book of Sports and Mirror of Life* (London: Tegg, n.d.). Chronicle/Alamy Stock Photo.   252

16.6 Pierce Egan, engraved title page to *Pilgrims of the Thames* (London: Strange, 1838). Courtesy of Brian Maidment.   253

20.1 Samuel Williams, after George Cattermole, 'The Child in her Gentle Slumber', an illustration for Charles Dickens's *The Old Curiosity Shop* (1840–1). Courtesy of the Charles Dickens Museum, London.   310

20.2 George Cattermole, 'At Rest', an illustration for Charles Dickens's *The Old Curiosity Shop* (1840–1). Courtesy of the Charles Dickens Museum, London [F513].   310

Table

4.1 Frequency of reference to and use of particular Dickens stories on AO^3, Fanfiction.net and Wattpad.   50

Acknowledgements

We would like to thank Jackie Jones, who first proposed a volume on *Dickens and the Arts*, as well as the editorial team at Edinburgh University Press – particularly Ersev Ersoy, Susannah Butler and Elizabeth Fraser – for their patience and care in stewarding this volume to completion. We would also like to thank the copy-editors and indexers for their help in preparing the volume for publication. The journey has been a long one, with many 'long and weary hills to climb', as *Nicholas Nickleby* puts it. Indeed, when we began it, we never envisaged that this project would extend through institutional and house moves, as well as a global pandemic. Our contributors, too, have experienced, in some cases, greater challenges. We are sincerely grateful to all the authors in this volume for bearing with us through these challenges and for the insight that they have brought to their topics; their collegiality and generosity have been second to none. One of our contributors, Jim Davis, is sadly no longer with us, passing away in late 2023. A true pioneer of nineteenth-century theatre studies, Jim's contribution to scholarship is enormous. We are grateful for the essay he generously contributed to this volume and know that readers will value it as much as we do. We send heartfelt condolences to Jim's family, friends and colleagues.

We would also like to thank our friends and colleagues at Royal Holloway, University of London, City, University of London, the University of Leicester and the wider scholarly community, as well as acknowledging the contributions made to indexing and illustration costs by the University of Leicester's Centre for Victorian Studies and School of Arts, and City, University of London. Thanks are due to the Charles Dickens Museum, London, too, especially to Louisa Price and Frankie Kubicki, who assisted with a number of the images.

Finally, we would like to thank our families – Calum, Iona, Hamish, Seren, Marc – for their love and support throughout.

1

AHEAD OF ITS TIME: DICKENS'S PRESCIENT VISION OF THE ARTS

Juliet John and Claire Wood

THE IDEA OF A BOOK DEDICATED to Dickens and the arts instinctively gives pause for thought – especially when other Edinburgh titles in this same series on, for example, Shakespeare, Virginia Woolf or Ezra Pound and the arts feel just right; consonant rather than, in the case of Dickens, vaguely dissonant. This dissonance sparked the curiosity which has driven this volume. When Dickens is widely – though not universally – cited as the greatest novelist in the English, if not any, language, and the 'number two' writer in English in the world after Shakespeare, why should the idea of scrutinising his relationship to that copious, resonant and, indeed, loaded concept of the arts seem unsettling or incongruous? One reason is that Dickens did not seem to engage much with the arts in his writings: his autobiographical novelist protagonist David Copperfield does not even mention his subject matter, focusing instead on his industrial efforts at learning shorthand and his commercial success, fulfilling his name Copperfield. It has been widely noticed that those artists who do appear in Dickens's novels are usually jobbing purveyors of popular art who work without noticeable talent for money. Dickens was averse to theorising about either his own work or other arts, famously telling G. H. Lewes, 'if readers cannot detect the point of a passage without having their attention called to it by the writer, I would much rather they lost it and looked out for something else.'[1] So notable is Dickens's apparent absence of engagement with the arts that the absence itself seems odd. Modernist discomfort with Dickens – though often simplified or exaggerated, as Francesca Orestano explores in this volume – is rooted in an elevated ideal of the arts with which Dickens seemed not to conform, and reinforced an idea of Dickens as somehow aesthetically lacking. While it is understandable that modernist writers might seek to distance themselves from Dickens and Dickens from their vision of the arts, less explicable is why Dickens himself went to such lengths to seem to disassociate himself from received ideas of the arts. Though, as this volume makes clear, he was well versed in a range of high and low arts, he was seemingly determined to embrace, if not the wrong side of the cultural track, metaphorically speaking, a different track. Our contention is that, far from being a philistine who had no interest in the arts, Dickens's apparent reticence in an industrial age where the value and function of the arts was uniquely important in public debate, masks a complex and sophisticated vision (if not theory) of the arts in the modern era, which is, and was, ahead of its time.

Dickens has given theorists of the arts and cultural value difficulty from his own day to the present: a roll call of those who have struggled to make Dickens 'fit' larger aesthetic frameworks and evaluations would include George Eliot, G. H. Lewes, Henry James, James Joyce, Theodor Adorno and F. R. Leavis, to name just a small sample, before postmodernism and critical theory worked to unpick some of the assumptions about cultural production which had rendered Dickens so often anomalous.[2] The reasons for this can be compressed into four broad areas: money/materialism; hierarchies of privilege; yardsticks of criticism or artistic judgement; the public good. There is an uneasy relationship between 'the arts' and all four areas, between Dickens and all four, and between Dickens and the arts understood via these frames, which are commonly invoked in discussions of the arts.

To first turn to money and materialism. There is a reason that defenders of the value of the arts and humanities not infrequently return to the Victorians and their 'sages'. The first age of industrialism was also the great age of the public intellectual in Britain: feeling the full force of intensified capitalism and watching machines reconfigure society, geography and the self, Victorian thinkers felt the need to articulate what made people more than machines and human relations more than a 'cash nexus', to use Thomas Carlyle's famous phrase.[3] However complex, varied and distinctive the writings of Thomas Carlyle, John Ruskin, John Stuart Mill and Matthew Arnold – to list the most obvious and vocal British worriers about the problems of their era – a vital thread in all their works is the elevating quality of the life of the mind, realised through the arts and/or a liberal education. The idea of an opposition between the capitalist and/or utilitarian values of the industrial marketplace and the ennobling, transformative force of the mind and the imagination lies at the core of the public philosophy of the industrial era and indeed structures much of the writing about the value of the arts today. The role of literature in the conversion of Mill away from the Utilitarian philosophy which had formed his education and belief system in many ways encapsulates the foundational idea in defences of the arts in all eras that the arts provide the soul of societies tending to soullessness. In Arnold's memorable phrase, culture provides 'sweetness and light'.[4] In Ruskin's worldview, 'the difference between a great and a common work of art' is that the latter is mechanistic whereas the former is not: 'Great art [. . .] does not say the same thing over and over again' but is characterised by 'imperfection'.[5] For Carlyle, literature is 'a branch of religion', shaped by the unconscious which is 'the sign of creation', whereas consciousness is a sign of 'manufacture'.[6] In 'the Age of Machinery', as he memorably describes the nineteenth century, 'Men are grown mechanical in head and in heart, as well as in hand.'[7]

Hard Times (1854) appears to provide an allegory for the industrial era, structured as it is around the core dialectic between the utilitarian world of numbers, machines and money, and the creative and emotional freedom of the circus performers. Famously dedicated to Thomas Carlyle, and F. R. Leavis's favourite Dickens novel (the one that earned Dickens an appendix in 'the great tradition' from which he had been excluded), *Hard Times* seems to secure Dickens's place in what Rick Rylance has called the 'idealist' tradition of cultural theory. Rylance's excellent 2016 book, *Literature and the Public Good*, identifies two main strands in writings which defend the value of literature in particular: 'the idealist', which emerges from 'the post-Romantic separation of the aesthetic and the economic in nineteenth-century thinking', and the 'integrationist'.[8] As Raymond Williams charts in *Culture and Society* (1958), the nineteenth century is a crucial juncture in the history and theory of culture: culture becomes associated with 'a body of values superior to the ordinary progress of society' and comes to be defined as 'a separate entity and a critical idea'.[9] Integrationist thinking about literature, culture and the arts, by contrast, accepts their integral position in the world of money and the market as both product and agent.

Though Leavis and others have been attracted to the ostensible idealism in *Hard Times*, how likely is it that the child of a man imprisoned for debt, whose own childhood and education were curtailed by a lack of money, would see the world of the arts as functioning outside and above the world of money?[10] This is a rhetorical question. On not much closer inspection, *Hard Times* is not a hymn to the healing powers of 'serious' art which ennobles in quite the sense implied by Leavis, nor is it a work of art which accepts such categories;[11] it includes an affectionate representation of circus performers who are obliged to work for money, and it is in this sense in keeping with many of Dickens's novelistic representations of the arts and artists. It is in other words, as integrationist as it is idealist in its representation of the arts, and indeed, as several recent critiques of the novel have demonstrated, it works to destabilise the seeming opposition between the utilitarian and creative worlds which is seemingly so bold.[12] As an author who diminished his own popularity on his first trip to the United States of America by campaigning for an international copyright law, who kept myopic watch over his own business dealings, and indeed made so much money from his reading tour of the States that the tour staff literally wallowed around in cheques, money was never something that Dickens felt able to rise above.[13] Nor did he wish to. Throughout his career, Dickens took pride in seeing, and indeed promoting, literary authorship as an honourable profession and literature as a serious art form. His concern was to ensure financial independence and respectability for authors, enabling them to eschew the patronage and poverty which were common conditions for artists and writers before and during his lifetime. In the 'Dignity of Literature' debate, he thus opposed Thackeray's satirical undermining of authorship and the literary community in *Pendennis* (1848–50) through the representation of the dedicated, unpretentious novelist David Copperfield, who needs to write to earn a living. Though David's silence on his subject matter is a little strange, as a riposte to Thackeray, David's model of authorship is explicable. As Florian Schweizer explains:

> *David Copperfield* was the first novel in which a young writer embarks on a literary career without falling into the usual traps for authors: he is not a victim of publishers or lionisers; he is not impoverished; he does not develop a lazy or overconfident attitude to his work; he does not neglect his duties towards his dependents. David is the exemplary professional writer of the Victorian age, endorsing and affirming Dickens's own status in the world.[14]

Dickens was a central figure in the commercialisation of literature in the nineteenth century which attended the rapid expansion of the book trade in this first age of mass culture, unembarrassed to champion both the financial rights and needs of authors and their status as serious artists. In an 1848 letter to Thackeray, he stated his hope 'of leaving the position of literary men in England, something better and more independent' than he had 'found it'.[15] He acknowledges his own influence in this respect – 'I do sometimes please myself with thinking that my success has opened the way for good writers' – and declares fervently his hope that 'when I die—that in all my social doings I am mindful of this honour and dignity and try to do something towards the quiet assertion of their right place'.[16] Dickens was in fact rarely quiet about these issues: haunted by both his own father's bankruptcy and by the penury of his predecessor Walter Scott, Dickens tried to help struggling authors of his acquaintance and to set up more institutionalised support systems, establishing with Edward Bulwer Lytton and other friends the Guild of Literature and Art (1851) to help authors, actors and artists who had fallen on hard times, and attempting a *'coup'* at the Royal Literary Fund.[17] In his very last public speech at the Royal Academy of Art banquet on 2 May 1870, a response to a toast to literature, he accepted 'on behalf of the brotherhood of Literature' and 'the sisterhood of Literature also', stressing the place of illustrations of literary works in the artworks exhibited and praising the 'patient labours' of writers for ensuring 'the place of truth upon these walls'.[18]

Dickens's view of money and the market as potential tools to free the writer from 'the shame of the purchased dedication, from the scurrilous and dirty work of Grub Street, from the dependent seat on sufferance at my Lord Duke's table [. . .] and from the sponging-house', is at odds with the anti-commercialism which has been the keynote of many of the most influential intellectual defences of the arts from the Romantic period to the present day.[19] Interestingly, very few of these have been written by novelists. Percy Bysshe Shelley's famous aphorism that poets were 'the unacknowledged legislators of the world', in 'A Defence of Poetry' (1821; 1840), captures the logic of this idealist line of 'defence': the poet is superior to others in intelligence and incisiveness but marginalised unjustly. Running through Shelley's defence is the language of hierarchy which is a common feature of philosophies of art and aesthetic theory: for example, Shelley maintains that 'Poetry is the record of the best and happiest moments of the happiest and best minds.'[20] Though Wordsworth and Coleridge's *Lyrical Ballads* (1798) aimed for a poetry which was written in 'language really used by men', High Romantic emphasis on genius and exceptionalism is evident in Wordsworth's unabashed claim that the poet is:

> endued with more lively sensibility, more enthusiasm and tenderness, who has a greater knowledge of human nature, and a more comprehensive soul, than are supposed to be common among mankind; a man pleased with his own passions and volitions, and who rejoices more than other men in the spirit of life that is in him.[21]

Carlyle's 'Hero as Man of Letters' is a variation on this theme. In the age of increased literacy and book production, 'Newspapers, Pamphlets, Books, these are the real working effective church of a modern country', argues Carlyle; yet somehow the Hero is doomed 'to travel without highway, companionless, through an inorganic chaos'.[22] The implied opposition between the material and the intellectual or spiritual laces idealist defences of the arts throughout the nineteenth century in educational and cultural treatises (Newman, Arnold), as well as more direct musings on the arts, in Tolstoy, aestheticism, through modernism. It is interesting that the visual arts of the early twentieth century – Futurism, Cubism, Dadaism – were quicker to reject the logic. As Rylance remarks of idealist literary argument, it 'oscillates between the twin poles of exaggerated heroics and utter irrelevance'.[23] And while postmodernism did much to deconstruct this opposition across the spectrum of the arts, it is interesting that idealist thought persists so markedly in one area today: attacks on the marketisation of higher education. While anyone who works in higher education can agree on the ills, the pre-market university was not a transcendent site of intellectual heroism, free of the cash-nexus; it was in fact a place of elitism and paternalism. Greater historicism in the campaign for the future of our universities would therefore move critique beyond objections to the new (the market) which are informed by an old logic (the intellect is good, the market is bad), to include objections to the old (a cultural clerisy built on normalised class, gender and racial privilege) and forge a future which improves on both models.

Dickens's philosophy of art in fact works to complicate in subtle ways the idea of an opposition between idealist and integrationist views of the aesthetic, though its most characteristic thrust is integrationist. The integrationist drive arises not just from the fact that he was a social reformer, nor from his overt desire to be 'acknowledged', to reverse Shelley's logic; nor did it arise only from his awareness that the economic and the aesthetic in life had never been separate, though there is truth in all these explanations. His integrationist beliefs about art are also political in a more sophisticated way than has been appreciated. Dickens was acutely aware that art had never been free of the 'cash-nexus', but that, in past times, art and artists had been utterly dependent on inherited hierarchies of privilege and the structures of power of church and state. Of the many definitions of 'the arts' in the *Oxford English Dictionary*, one is: 'Any of various pursuits or occupations in which creative or imaginative skill is applied according to aesthetic principles (formerly often defined in terms of "taste" [. . .]) the various branches of creative activity, as painting, sculpture, music, literature, dance, drama, oratory, etc.' Dickens's writings are riddled with an awareness that 'taste' and 'aesthetic principles', as Pierre Bourdieu has made clear more recently, are constructs of various forms of capital, whether social, cultural or economic.[24]

Idealist defences of the arts can be blind to the conditions of privilege which have enabled them. Furthermore, the hierarchical logic underpinning the idea of artist as hero or genius does not proffer, as proponents can assume, an alternative value system, free of sociological or materialist taint, but the occlusion of materialism and the market beneath other connected systems of capital distribution – class or education, notably. Another definition of art, according to a note in the *Oxford English Dictionary*, was not 'found in English dictionaries until the 19th cent.' This refers to 'the expression or application of creative skill or imagination [. . .], producing works to be appreciated primarily for their beauty or emotional power'. The increased prominence of this definition in the nineteenth century is no doubt the result of the idealist reaction against materialism. But in Dickens's works, perhaps because his perspective was that of an outsider to the clerisy, beauty and emotional power are only very rarely transcendent or 'other': and even then, transcendence, as in the works of Shakespeare, is the ordinary made extraordinary.

This is most obvious in *Pictures from Italy* (1846), a travelogue remarkable on first reading for Dickens's avoidance of the 'famous Pictures and Statues' which draw most travellers to Italy, but on closer inspection an extended meditation on the value and valuation of art, its conditions of production and its social function.[25] When visiting the Vatican, for example, he explains that when he finds 'heads inferior to the subject, in pictures of merit, in Italian galleries, I do not attach that reproach to the Painter, for I have a suspicion that these men were very much in the hands of the monks and priests' with their 'vanity and ignorance [. . .] who would be apostles' (146).

While it is easy to see why some have perceived an anti-Catholicism driving Dickens's critique, it is also possible to see criticisms like this as born of his dislike of inherited privilege and conditions of artistic production which undermine his ideal that art should foster community.[26] In Carrara, for example, the home of a distinctive marble used in the construction of the Pantheon and many Renaissance sculptures, Dickens's mind is gripped by 'the suffering and agony' of the 'cruel work' necessary to produce the marble which was the raw material of so many beautiful artworks; particularly in times before the railways, many quarry labourers were 'crushed to death' (105). John Keats's 'Ode on a Grecian Urn' (1819) undermines the idealistic maxim at its close, 'Beauty is truth, truth beauty', by the depiction of human suffering and violence on the urn itself. *Pictures from Italy* is less subtle and more political in the attention it draws to the suffering underpinning artistic labour, not the labour of the artist as hero, but that of those who may have died for an art from whose history they were erased:

> Standing in one of the many studii of Carrara, that afternoon—for it is a great workshop, full of beautifully-finished copies in marble, of almost every figure, group, and bust, we know—it seemed, at first so strange that those exquisite shapes, replete with grace, and thought, and delicate repose, should grow out of all this toil and sweat, and torture! (106)

Just as the production of art does not emerge from an ideal or transcendent realm, for Dickens, but from the world as it is, replete with hierarchies of privilege, the aspect of art's afterlife which seemed to interest him most was its relationship to the everyday or a culture that Raymond Williams might have called 'ordinary'.[27] Sally Ledger points out that, in *Pictures from Italy*, Dickens:

> immerses himself in the culture of the common Italian people. He tells us not – or not so much – about art and antiquity, but [. . .] about men in red caps playing bowls and the national game of Mora in Genoa [. . .] of peasant women washing clothes in the streets – Dickens is interested in contemporary Italian culture in its broadest sense.[28]

After praising 'the academy of Fine Arts' at Bologna, Dickens confesses that, even if the paintings there had not existed, 'the great Meridian on the pavement of the church of San Petronio, where the sunbeams mark the time among the kneeling people, would give it a fanciful and pleasant interest' (72). What Dickens likes about this is its integration into the city and its culture, its constructors less important than the effect of natural light on the floor. Though the construction of the unfinished church enables the effect, viewers do not need education or 'taste' to appreciate the wonder. Throughout *Pictures from Italy*, instead of the extended ruminations on famous buildings or artworks which might have been expected from a travelogue by a literary traveller, Dickens is absorbed by the art or culture of everyday life; in Naples, to give just one example, he observes a funeral, noting: 'Exhibitors of Punch, buffo singers with guitars, reciters of poetry, reciters of stories, a row of cheap exhibitions with clowns and showmen, drums, and trumpets, painted cloths representing the wonders within, and admiring crowds assembled without, assist the whirl and bustle.' All walks of life are here, 'and quiet letter-writers, perched behind their little desks and inkstands under the Portico of the Great Theatre of San Carlo, in the public street, are waiting for clients' (165).

What we would add to Ledger's astute observation about Dickens's interest in contemporary Italian culture is that he is as focused on critiquing the relationship between everyday culture and 'art and antiquity' as he is on opposing the two. The sight of letter writers in the 'public street' under the portico of a great theatre, for example, serves as an arresting visualisation of Dickens's awareness of the shifting nature of literary production in a more culturally inclusive era, as well as the entanglement of the arts in a 'great' history which lives alongside the everyday. Vitality, modernity and survival, to Dickens, come from the entwinement of art with the ordinary. It is not that Dickens is ignorant of high art or established culture, as contributors like Jeremy Tambling and Matthew Ingleby make clear, but he is also highly aware of the multiple hierarchies of privilege which attend the production and consumption of such art. Commenting on the opera in Naples, for example, he remarks with sarcasm that, 'Our English dilettanti would be very pathetic on the subject of the national taste, if they could hear an Italian opera half as badly sung in England as we may hear the Foscari performed, to-night, in the splendid theatre of San Carlo.' But Dickens's real praise is reserved for the 'shabby little San Carlino Theatre', not an opera house like its more famous neighbour but 'a rickety house one story high', originally a dialect theatre founded by a roving troupe of actors: 'for astonishing truth and spirit in seizing and embodying the real life about it', the San Carlino is 'without a rival anywhere' (177).

Dickens's scepticism about idealist or 'pure' definitions of the arts, 'appreciated primarily for their beauty or emotional power', is perhaps most obvious in his scathing critique of conventional art criticism or judgement. So many displays of taste or acts of criticism in Dickens are just that: displays or acts, purporting to depth, but in fact shallow signifiers of a privilege shorn of intellect or integrity. Moreover, derivative critical displays which are predicated on the idea of pure aesthetic response which is somehow transcendent in fact obscure the ideological work of the aesthetic, as Terry Eagleton might call it, or the role of the idea of the aesthetic in repressing the politics and ideology of its own production.[29] Harold Skimpole from *Bleak House* (1852–3) perhaps best exemplifies Dickens's scepticism about the possibility of a transcendent aestheticism which succeeds in divorcing itself from the material. In *Nicholas Nickleby* (1838–9), the myopic Shakespeare criticism of Mr Curdle is satirised: 'he was a great critic, and a very profound and most original thinker'.[30] Trying to impress Lord Verisopht, Mrs Wititterly goes into raptures: '"I'm always ill after Shakespeare," [. . .] "I scarcely exist the next day; I find the reaction so very great after a tragedy"', adding that she has been '"so much more interested in his plays, after having been to that dear little dull house he was born in!"'[31] The obvious object of Dickens's critique is the pretensions underpinning the use of Shakespeare as an empty signifier of cultural capital by the middle classes for their own social advancement, but it is also more specifically the ironic misuse of idealist appreciations of art for personal and social advancement.

Such exchanges are self-reflexive in a localised way, invoking Dickens's involvement in efforts to restore Shakespeare's birthplace and his frustration at the exploitation of authors who were public property but had little control over their works.[32] *Pictures from Italy*, by contrast, contains an extended 'social critique of the judgement of taste', to appropriate Bourdieu's subtitle, and of art criticism.[33] And, by implication, Dickens also proffers a critique of the category of the arts and the received ideas which so often inform it. As a cultural tourist, Dickens had what he called 'such a perverse disposition in respect of sights that are cut, and dried, and dictated' (70). What Dickens objects to is the circulation of normative judgements about art like a currency; they are standardised, brandished to signify social standing or membership of a clerisy, and leave no room for questioning or originality of thought. Of Leonardo's *The Last Supper*, he acknowledges that it is a 'wonderful picture', though one that has sustained damage from 'damp, decay, or neglect' and which has been blighted by inferior retouching. Dickens does not understand the reaction of 'an English gentleman' who 'was at great pains to fall into what I may describe as mild convulsions', because of small changes from the original, rather than accepting that it was still 'replete with interest and dignity' (96). The target here is the affectation of the aficionado who wishes to display his expert knowledge of the original which he fetishises to boost his own performed sensibility.

The Vatican brings out his most extended critique of pseuds masquerading as critics and the corrupting social and aesthetic effects of inauthenticity in art criticism. Though there are 'noble statues' and 'wonderful pictures' there, Dickens claims that it is not 'heresy to say that there is a considerable amount of rubbish there, too' (144). Critiquing the chain reaction whereby ordinary artworks are put into galleries because they are old, and then admired because they are in the gallery, Dickens lays bare the process by which someone who joins in with the general admiration 'may wear the spectacles of Cant for less than nothing, and establish himself as a man of taste for the mere trouble of putting them on'. Dickens cannot forfeit his 'natural perception of what is natural and true [. . .] in spite of high critical advice that we should sometimes feign an admiration though we have it not'. Part of the problem for Dickens is the 'indiscriminate [. . .] raptures in which some critics indulge', which are 'incompatible with the really great and transcendent works' (145). Interestingly, one hierarchy to which Dickens does not object is that which enables value judgements. Although he was aware of the sociological construction of taste, he did not share modern embarrassment, as Matthew Ingleby argues in this volume, about making aesthetic value judgements. And, indeed, he saw it as the role of criticism to discriminate. He 'cannot imagine [. . .] how the resolute champion of undeserving pictures can soar' to genuinely appreciate 'works of extraordinary genius': the conclusion is that he must be 'wanting in his powers of perception in one of the two instances, and, probably in the high and lofty one' (146).

Dickens's dislike of received ideas about art did not preclude value judgements in themselves, in other words, but judgements which were inauthentic. To a modern reader, such a caveat may seem contradictory as Dickens himself – or any 'authentic' commentator – will simply be swapping one scale of values for another in making aesthetic judgements. His defence, no doubt, would be that what he is opposed to is the commodification of critical judgement, whereby it is worn as a badge of social signification to replicate norms of acceptable taste, rather than allowing for discrimination, questioning or creativity in artistic response. Although Dickens accepted the market, he nonetheless believed that artistic value systems are, to borrow Helen Small's words on the value system of literature, 'different from [those of] monetary

AHEAD OF ITS TIME

wealth'.[34] In an extended passage on dandyism in *Bleak House* – 'of a mischievous sort, that has got below the surface' – Dickens makes one of the few mentions in his writings of 'the Fine Arts':

> There are also ladies and gentleman of another fashion [. . .] who have agreed to put a smooth glaze on the world, and keep down its realities. For whom every-thing must be languid and pretty. [. . .] Who are to rejoice at nothing, and be sorry for nothing. Who are not to be disturbed by ideas. On whom even the Fine Arts, attending in powder and walking backward like the Lord Chamberlain, must array themselves in the milliners' and tailors' patterns of past generations and be particu-larly careful not to be in earnest or to receive any impress from the moving age.[35]

Dickens's concern here is with nothing less than the erosion of the moral and ethi-cal self, a concern which grows with the later novels, and the potential of art to act as agent for good or ill. In *Little Dorrit* (1855–7), Henry Gowan is one of the few professional artists in Dickens's novels who is unambiguously corrupt: unlike others, he has no emotional or moral connection to the art he sells for money, or to other people. Like Skimpole, he uses the arts as a cynical vehicle of exploitation. While Skimpole poses as an idealist, Gowan is flagrant in his cynicism. Skimpole affects to believe in art as 'a body of values superior to the ordinary progress of society', to borrow Williams's description of the elevation of ideas of culture above the social in the nineteenth century, while Gowan's acceptance of the thoroughgoing commodifi-cation of art erases any association between art and the public good.[36]

For all the complexity of Dickens's attitudes to art, he was consistent, like George Eliot, Tolstoy and other nineteenth-century novelists, in his belief that art should and could work for the public good. His sense of the word 'good' embraces all three meanings of the word that recur in discussions of the value of art itemised by Rylance: 'a positive evaluative category'; 'a public benefit'; and 'a commodity' (goods).[37] In tandem with idealist defences of art as somehow 'superior' to the social realm and concern about the commodification of art in the first age of mass culture, another dis-tinctive thread of cultural commentary emerged with unique force in the nineteenth century: the belief that art could be socially transformative, indeed elevate society. In the vanguard of this strand of thought were novelists, whether George Eliot urging in *Adam Bede* (1859):

> do not impose on us any aesthetic rules which shall banish from the region of Art those old women scraping carrots with their work-worn hands [. . .]. In this world there are so many of these common coarse people, who have no picturesque sen-timental wretchedness! It is so needful we should remember their existence, else we may happen to leave them quite out of our religion and philosophy and frame lofty theories which only fit a world of extremes. Therefore, let Art always remind us of them.[38]

; or Dickens defending the truth of his representations, particularly of the underclass in the Preface to *Oliver Twist* (1841). Or Balzac defending his truth; or Tolstoy urging in *What is Art?* (1897) that art should not be detached from the moral and concern itself only with the beautiful.[39] Victorian novelists, however moralistic or sanctimonious some may seem to readers today, had a well-founded belief that their work made a difference. In an age of a rapidly expanding readership without the competition of the screen or the digital, literature in the nineteenth century was uniquely powerful.

In *Literature and the Public Good*, Rylance argues for a new 'literary humanitarianism', socially responsible and empathetic, which spreads 'the growing public good of the world'.[40] As a Victorianist, Rylance will know that this 'mission' represents a return to an earlier literary mission of the mainstream Victorian novelist. In *Pictures from Italy*, most pointedly, Dickens anticipates Eliot's objections to the picturesque, arguing for a 'new picturesque' 'as our duty', which does not keep out of view 'miserable depravity, degradation and wretchedness' (166, 165). Dickens ends the travelogue by celebrating 'the triumphant growth of peaceful Arts and Sciences' in Florence: 'Here, the imperishable part of the noble mind survives, placid and equal, when strongholds of assault and defence are overthrown; when the tyranny of the many, or the few, or both, is but a tale; when Pride and Power are so much cloistered dust' (186). This is the closest Dickens gets to a theory of the arts – and it is optimistic. Art outlives and uplifts the human sufferings from which it is made. Dickens's is a humanitarian vision of the arts.

It is crucial to this humanitarian aesthetic vision that it is inclusive. Dickens's sense of the arts is therefore capacious, encompassing the ordinary and the extraordinary, the material and the ideal. Culturally porous and always entertaining, it blends comedy and tragedy like a side of streaky bacon, to use his famous analogy.[41] This volume aims to stay true to Dickens's vision of the arts, which in many ways means that we are explaining it anew: as this essay has explored, Dickens's relationship to the idea of the arts is odd in that it has been so little considered or understood, even by Dickensians. Our impulse has been to resist assumptions that are 'cut and dried', to encourage new topics, to include both new and established voices, and rejuvenate our sense of both Dickens and the arts. Across the collection, contributors probe the ways in which Dickens engaged with, contributed to and was influenced by literary, theatrical and visual arts; explore adaptations and appropriations of Dickens's work across a broad range of art forms, from the nineteenth century to the present day; and introduce new lenses through which we might examine Dickens's relationship with the arts. This includes areas that have received little critical attention – such as dance, music, puppetry, and architecture – and some of the more surprising contexts in which Dickens has found a home, including fanfiction, rap music and cyberspace. In 'Amusements of the People' (1850), Dickens muses upon the 'curious' continuities between opera and melodrama: 'So do extremes meet; and so is there some hopeful congeniality between what will excite MR WHELKS, and what will rouse a Duchess.'[42] This was the conception of the arts that Dickens sought to bring to life and which this volume seeks to animate: an art that encompasses the popular and elite, grounded in the world in its fullest sense.

Notes

1. 'To G. H. Lewes (? 9 June 1838)', *The Letters of Charles Dickens*, ed. by Madeline House, Graham Storey et al., Pilgrim/British Academy Edition, 12 vols (Oxford: Clarendon Press, 1965–2002), I (1965), 403–4, 404. Hereafter *PLets*.
2. See George Eliot, 'The Natural History of German Life', *Westminster Review* 10 (1 July 1856), 51–79; G. H. Lewes, 'Dickens in Relation to Criticism', *Fortnightly Review* 11

AHEAD OF ITS TIME 11

(February 1872), 141–54; Henry James, '*Our Mutual Friend*', *Nation* 1 (21 December 1865), 786–8; Theodor W. Adorno, 'On Dickens' *The Old Curiosity Shop*: A Lecture', in *Notes to Literature*, ed. by Rolf Tiedemann, trans. by Shierry Weber Nicholson (New York: Columbia University Press, 1992), IV, 171–7; and F. R. Leavis, *The Great Tradition* (London: Chatto & Windus, 1948). On Joyce, see Francesca Orestano's essay in this volume.

3. See Chapter 6 ('Laissez-Faire') of Carlyle's *Chartism* (1840), where he describes '*Cash payment*' as 'the universal sole nexus of man to man'; in Chapter 7, 'Not Laissez-Faire', Carlyle famously wrote, 'Cash payment is the sole nexus; and there are so many things which cash will not pay! Cash is a great miracle; yet it has not all power in Heaven, nor even on Earth. "Supply and demand" we will honour also; and yet how many "demands" are there, entirely indispensable, which have to go elsewhere than to the shops, and produce quite other than cash, before they can get their supply!' Qtd in *Thomas Carlyle: Selected Writings*, ed. by Alan Shelston (London: Penguin, 1971), 151–230, 193, 199.

4. See Chapter 1 ('Sweetness and Light') of *Culture and Anarchy* (1869), ed. by J. Dover Wilson (Cambridge: Cambridge University Press, 1994), 43–71.

5. 'The Nature of Gothic' in *The Stones of Venice*, II (1853), in John Ruskin, *Selected Writings*, ed. by Dinah Birch (Oxford: Oxford University Press, 2004), 32–63, 47.

6. 'Characteristics' [1831], in *Critical and Miscellaneous Essays: Collected and Republished* (1839; 1869), 7 vols (London: Chapman & Hall, 1872), IV, 1–38, 20, 14.

7. 'Signs of the Times' [1829], in *Thomas Carlyle: Selected Writings*, 61–85, 67.

8. Rick Rylance, *Literature and the Public Good* (Oxford: Oxford University Press, 2016), 111.

9. Raymond Williams, *Culture and Society, 1780–1950* (London: Penguin, 1963), 96–7.

10. See Leavis, 'The Novel as Dramatic Poem (I): *Hard Times*', *Scrutiny* 14 (1946–7), 185–203; Ruskin, 'The Roots of Honour', in *Unto this Last* (1860), in *Selected Writings*, ed. by Dinah Birch, 140–53.

11. Leavis called the novel Dickens's only 'completely serious work of art' in 'The Novel as Dramatic Poem', 185.

12. See, for example, Tamara Ketabgian, *The Lives of Machines: The Industrial Imaginary in Victorian Literature and Culture* (Ann Arbor: University of Michigan Press, 2011).

13. See Juliet John, *Dickens and Mass Culture* (Oxford: Oxford University Press, 2010), Chapter 2 (74–102) on relations with America and the copyright debate and Chapter 4 (131–56) on the public readings and his fascination with the physicality of paper money and cheques (133–4 and n. 5).

14. Florian Schweizer, 'Authorship and the Professional Writer', in *Charles Dickens in Context*, ed. by Sally Ledger and Holly Furneaux (Cambridge: Cambridge University Press, 2011), 117–24, 122.

15. 'To William Makepeace Thackeray, 9 January 1848', *PLets*, V (1981), 227–8, 227.

16. Ibid.

17. See Schweizer, 123.

18. Charles Dickens, *The Speeches of Charles Dickens*, ed. by K. J. Fielding (Oxford: Clarendon Press, 1960), 420–1.

19. 'Presentation to Dickens and Banquet to Literature and Art: Birmingham (6 January 1853)', in *Speeches*, 154–1, 157.

20. *Classic Writings on Poetry*, ed. by William Harmon (New York: Columbia University Press, 2003), 351–74, 374, 371.

21. William Wordsworth, Preface (1802) to *Lyrical Ballads with Pastoral and Other Poems*, in *Lyrical Ballads*, ed. by Michael Mason (London: Longman, 1992), 55–93, 59, 71.

22. 'The Hero as Man of Letters' (1840), published in *Heroes and Hero Worship* (1841), in *Thomas Carlyle: Selected Writings*, 235–56, 242–3, 249.

23. Rylance, 83.
24. See Pierre Bourdieu, *Distinction: A Social Critique of the Judgement of Taste* (1979), trans. by Richard Nice (New York: Routledge, 2003).
25. Charles Dickens, *Pictures from Italy*, ed. by Kate Flint (London: Penguin, 1998), 5. Subsequent references are given in the text.
26. On anti-Catholicism, see Mark Eslick, 'Architectural Anxieties: Dickens's *Pictures from Italy*', *English: Journal of the English Association* 61 (2012), 354–64.
27. In 1958 Williams wrote 'Culture is Ordinary' (originally published in *Convictions*, ed. by Norman Mackenzie (London: MacGibbon & Kee, 1958), 74–92), which was a critique of elitist models of culture such as those represented in T. S. Eliot's *Notes towards the Definition of Culture* (1948).
28. Sally Ledger, '"God be Thanked: A Ruin!": The Embrace of Italian Modernity in *Pictures from Italy* and *Little Dorrit*', in *Dickens and Italy:* Little Dorrit *and* Pictures from Italy, ed. by Michael Hollington and Francesca Orestano (Newcastle upon Tyne: Cambridge Scholars, 2009), 82–92, 88–9.
29. Terry Eagleton, *The Ideology of the Aesthetic* (Oxford: Blackwell, 1990).
30. Charles Dickens, *Nicholas Nickleby*, ed. by Michael Slater (London: Penguin, 1978), 385, ch. 24.
31. Ibid., 430, ch. 27.
32. During his trip to the United States in 1842, Dickens made his dissatisfaction with the lack of protection afforded to authors by inadequate copyright laws particularly clear. Emily Smith's doctoral research (Royal Holloway, 2022) on Dickens and author tourism contains new and detailed insights on Dickens's involvement with the Shakespeare birthplace.
33. See Bourdieu.
34. Helen Small, *The Value of the Humanities* (Oxford: Oxford University Press, 2012), 162.
35. Charles Dickens, *Bleak House*, ed. by Norman Page (London: Penguin, 1971), 210–11, ch. 12.
36. Williams, *Culture and Society*, 91. Interestingly, Williams uses this phrase to describe Carlyle's thinking and to acknowledge Carlyle's contribution to 'the formation of the characteristic modern idea of the artist' as 'one of the main lines of criticism of the new kind of industrial society'.
37. Rylance, 131.
38. George Eliot, *Adam Bede*, ed. by Stephen Gill (London: Penguin, 1980), 224.
39. See Leo Tolstoy, *What is Art?* (1897), trans. by Aylmer Maude (Chicheley: Minet, 1971).
40. Rylance, 200.
41. Charles Dickens, *Oliver Twist*, ed. by Kathleen Tillotson (Oxford: Clarendon Press, 1966), 105–6, ch. 17.
42. Charles Dickens, 'The Amusements of the People (II)', *Household Words* (13 April 1850), in *Dickens' Journalism Volume 2: The Amusements of the People and Other Papers*, ed. by Michael Slater (London: Dent, 1996), 193–201, 201.

Further Reading

Matthew Arnold, *Culture and Anarchy* (1869), ed. by J. Dover Wilson (Cambridge: Cambridge University Press, 1994)

Juliet John, *Dickens and Mass Culture* (Oxford: Oxford University Press, 2010)

Rick Rylance, *Literature and the Public Good* (Oxford: Oxford University Press, 2016)

Leo Tolstoy, *What is Art?* (1897), trans. by Aylmer Maude (Chicheley: Minet, 1971)

Raymond Williams, 'Culture is Ordinary', in *Convictions*, ed. by Norman Mackenzie (London: MacGibbon & Kee, 1958), 74–92

Part I
Novel Arts

2

EIGHTEENTH-CENTURY CULTURES AND THE NOVEL

Paul Baines

The Eighteenth Century and 'the Novel'

WHAT DID 'THE EIGHTEENTH CENTURY' MEAN to Dickens? In *A Child's History of England* (1853) Dickens virtually stopped his narrative at 1688, as subsequent events 'would neither be easily related nor easily understood in such a book as this'. The final two pages, which skate through 150 years, inform the child that Anne was 'a popular Queen'; that, apart from the young chevalier and his 'romantic adventures', the Stuarts were 'a public nuisance'; and that the libertarian United States of America emerged in 1783. The Four Georges, whose court would occupy a sizeable sketchbook by William Makepeace Thackeray (1860), are indistinguishable ciphers before the 'much beloved' Victoria.[1]

The five volumes of Thomas Babington Macaulay's *History of England from the Accession of James II* (1848) suggested there was a good deal to recall, and other novelists found much to mine in the previous century's history. Thackeray's *The Luck of Barry Lyndon* (1844) revisited the mid-century as a ground for picaresque self-making; *The History of Henry Esmond* (1852) reimagined the reign of the 'popular' Queen Anne; *The Virginians* (1857–9) returned to the American War of Independence. As well as *The Four Georges*, Thackeray wrote lectures on *The English Humourists of the Eighteenth Century* (1853). Dickens, by contrast, set only two of his major novels in the eighteenth century, in both cases beginning in 1775 (when the American War started) and working towards historical rifts, as if drawn to some convulsive disjuncture.

In *Barnaby Rudge* (1841), much of London is destroyed in the Gordon Riots of 1780, together with an emblematically cosy pub and a haunted country house. The book takes a sceptical look at Britain as it headed into something resembling revolutionary upheaval. In imagining the history of 'fifty years before', Dickens paints a tainted milieu: poor roads, bad lighting, highwaymen, footpads. Using historical figures from that world – Richard Akerman, the keeper of Newgate Prison (destroyed in the riots), Lord Mansfield (whose books were burned) and the magistrate Sir John Fielding (half-brother of the novelist Henry) – Dickens presents an England defined almost purely by crime and punishment: looting, arson, murder, incarceration and

16   PAUL BAINES

execution. However, the uprising also delivers a pre-emptive strike against the governing *ancien régime*, as the real villain is the louche aristocrat Sir John Chester, based on Lord Chesterfield, whose posthumous *Letters* (1774) of suave advice to his natural son appalled and fascinated Dickens as much as they had disgusted Samuel Johnson.[2] Chester, father in this version of the feral ostler Hugh, hanged for his part in the riots which Chester has fomented for private reasons, is killed by the code of his own class, a duel, a form of poetic good-riddance, if not exactly justice.

In *A Tale of Two Cities* (1859), 'the best of times' like 'the worst of times' also commences in 1775, culminating now in the Terror of 1793–4. The pathology of the citizen mob (an issue for many 'Jacobin' novelists of the 1790s) is again analysed and individualised, but there is no sympathetic shading for the loathsome Monseigneur, this novel's exemplary aristocratic villain. This too was a world characterised (especially in England) by crime, as Chapter 1, 'The Period', recounts in detail. In the Revolution itself, prisons are again stormed (including the Bastille, always the symbol of French tyranny for eighteenth-century writers) and ancestral sins destructively revealed. Dickens's eighteenth century comes inevitably to its catastrophic end, its system of aristocratic privilege annihilated by the irresistible if criminal popular agitation it generated: two forces cancelling each other out with little to regret beyond the self-consuming violence itself.[3] The revolutionary years, beginning the sequence of agricultural, financial, industrial and technological shifts which made the England of 1850 so radically unlike that of 1750, constitute an impassable historical rupture. There is little pre-revolutionary peace to reimagine: Dickens the novelist is drawn to the point where the eighteenth century disintegrated.

Culture is not discontinuous, and Dickens the journalist bears fascinated witness to several kinds of precarious survival. *Sketches by Boz* (1836) and *The Uncommercial Traveller* (1860–9) register vestiges of the world of Addison, Gay and Hogarth. Astley's, a circus theatre founded in 1768, was thriving, a possible source for the circus in *Hard Times* (1854). But Vauxhall Gardens, a key locale of eighteenth-century pleasure and of fiction such as Fanny Burney's *Evelina* (1778) and Thackeray's *Vanity Fair* (1847–8), is tawdry by day, a modern disillusionment.[4] Queen Anne's churches, erected with pious optimism, are exhausted and ghostly, like the customer-free news-shop from George III's time, or coaching towns after the railways arrive.[5] But however moribund the eighteenth century's legacies were, it had bequeathed Dickens one successful type of popular entertainment that Dickens inherited gratefully: the cultural form we now call the novel. Two years before Dickens was born, a consortium of over thirty-five publishers produced a fifty-volume set called *The British Novelists*, with a substantial introduction by Anna Laetitia Barbauld, 'On the Origin and Progress of Novel-Writing'. At once a commercial and critical venture, *British Novelists* helped to ratify the corpus of the eighteenth-century novel for the nineteenth century.[6] The first fifteen volumes consist of Samuel Richardson (*Clarissa*, 1748; *Sir Charles Grandison*, 1753), followed by Daniel Defoe's *Robinson Crusoe* (1719) and Henry Fielding's *Joseph Andrews* (1742) and *Tom Jones* (1749). We have Johnson's orientalist fable *Rasselas* (1759), Walpole's proto-Gothic *Castle of Otranto* (1764) and its feminised re-tread, Clara Reeve's *The Old English Baron* (1777); mock-novels (Richard Graves's *The Spiritual Quixote*, 1773); sentimental fiction (Oliver Goldsmith's *Vicar of Wakefield*, 1766; Mackenzie's *Man of Feeling*, 1771); and Tobias Smollett's polyphonic epistolary ramble *Humphry Clinker* (1771).

There was no Sterne, but much varied fiction by women: Charlotte Lennox, Charlotte Smith, Fanny Burney, Ann Radcliffe, Elizabeth Inchbald and Maria Edgeworth, with conservative alongside radical texts.

'The novel' entailed generic variety, therefore, but the work of 'British novelists' had an identifiable origin and a progress. Barbauld was a respectable poet who had edited the correspondence of Richardson (1804): her collection resembled the canon-forming (though male-only) *Works of the English Poets* (1779–81), for which Johnson contributed 'Lives'. Dickens, however, rarely referred to himself as a 'novelist' and was sceptical about 'novel-writers' in *Sketches by Boz* before his own entry into the field.[7] He does not use the word 'novel' inside his own fictions much, except to imply further scepticism: the faddish melancholy of Mr Knag, in *Nicholas Nickleby* (1838–9), is exacerbated by the fact that he 'reads every novel that comes out; I mean every novel that—hem—that has any fashion in it, of course', as his daughter explains.[8] We find Mrs Wititterly reclining while Kate 'read aloud a new novel in three volumes, entitled "The Lady Flabella," which Alphonse the doubtful had procured from the library that very morning'; no surprise that 'there was not a line in it, from beginning to end, which could, by the most remote contingency, awaken the smallest excitement in any person breathing' (358–9, ch. 28). None of Dickens's own fictions bore the word 'novel' on the title page on first appearance: he preferred *Life and Adventures* or *Personal History*, titles aligned with masculine eighteenth-century models such as *The History of Tom Jones, a Foundling* or *The Adventures of Roderick Random*. Early male novelists, avoiding the aristocratic or feminine connotations of 'romance', would undergo any contortion to avoid the contaminations of 'novel', which was associated with the scandalous fictions of Aphra Behn and Eliza Haywood.[9] If, as Henry James put it, for the English, 'there was a comfortable, good-humoured feeling abroad that a novel is a novel, as a pudding is a pudding', Dickens was happier to call a pudding a pudding than a novel a novel, perhaps for similar reasons.[10]

The Paternal Bookroom

Dickens left plentiful evidence of a personal canon of eighteenth-century fiction, not least the famous passage in *David Copperfield* (1849–50) in which the adult narrator recalls the solace he had found as a lonely boy:

> My father had left in a little room up-stairs, to which I had access (for it adjoined my own) a small collection of books which nobody else in our house ever troubled. From the blessed little room, Roderick Random, Peregrine Pickle, Humphrey Clinker, Tom Jones, The Vicar of Wakefield, Don Quixote, Gil Blas, and Robinson Crusoe, came out, a glorious host, to keep me company.[11]

David remembers himself on 'a summer evening, the boys at play in the churchyard, and I sitting on my bed, reading as if for life' (ibid). Smollett populated the environment: 'I have seen Tom Pipes climbing up the church-steeple; I have watched Strap, with the knapsack on his back, stopping to rest himself upon the wicket-gate; and I *know* that Commodore Trunnion held that club with Mr. Pickle, in the parlor of our little village alehouse' (ibid.). In the novel this passage forms a kind of semi-public homage to influence; John Forster confirms that it corresponds exactly to Dickens's 'personal history' of reading, written before it was patched into the novel, where it forms a comforting alternative to Murdstone's brutal educational regimen.[12]

These texts, resonant throughout Dickens, have several things in common, one of which is the eighteenth century: *Don Quixote* would have been available to David only in English translations such as that by Peter Anthony Motteux (1700); Smollett translated Le Sage's *Gil Blas* in 1749. *The Arabian Nights* and *Tales of the Genii*, in which David also immersed himself, were inventions of the eighteenth-century translation industry (*Arabian Nights Entertainments* appeared from 1706, *Tales of the Genii* from 1764). They all lie before the revolutionary gulf: David is not reading the perfervid Gothic shockers of the 1790s. Another thing they have in common is masculinity: all the novels are by men, presenting male protagonists. It is a paternal library, the stamen only from Barbauld's anthology. Most offer some version of the foundling tale: a young male abandoned or otherwise bereft must overcome a series of Oedipal traps to become a self-supporting man. The template, overt in *David Copperfield* itself, is repeated from *Oliver Twist* (1837–9) to *Great Expectations* (1860–1).

These fictions formed a compact set of influences. In fiction as in biography, patrimony is the economic trace of fathers: Dickens had to pawn his father's actual books in 1824, though he re-equipped himself once financially secure.[13] Literary inheritance entailed primogeniture, to the exclusion of female begetters and heirs: Dickens toyed with calling his youngest son Oliver Goldsmith before settling on Henry Fielding, as an act of homage, in preparation for *David Copperfield* (perhaps also as a way of reversing the order of literary filiation); but none of his daughters was going to be called Ann Radcliffe Dickens.[14] Perhaps Esther Summerson's Copperfield-type narrative in *Bleak House*, and the semi-autonomous female narratives of Miss Wade and others, offer some acknowledgement of the women novelists of the past, but essentially this was a masculine club, as was the non-novelistic writing of the eighteenth century that Dickens referred to regularly: the comedies of Goldsmith and Sheridan, Gay's *The Beggar's Opera*, the prose of Addison, Swift and Johnson, the poetry of Pope, Gray and Goldsmith.

Dickens scarcely left an 'Art of Fiction', but his 1841 'Preface' to *Oliver Twist* did insert his writing into a recognisably eighteenth-century heritage, and he did leave significant comments on his predecessors, writing, for example, to Forster about inset stories in Fielding and Smollett during the composition of *Little Dorrit*.[15] An early review noted resemblances to Smollett, Fielding and Hogarth, to Dickens's pleasure.[16] Certain influences from eighteenth-century writing were always conscious and obvious: the energies and ironies of narration, satire against hypocrisy and power, situational comedy, characterisation by idiolect, gesture and physiognomy.[17] Forster felt that Pickwick's sojourn in prison encompassed both the 'minute reality' of Defoe's incarceration scenes and the social humour of *Peregrine Pickle*.[18] Dickens knew a good deal about the careers of these writers, particularly from Forster's *Life and Adventures of Oliver Goldsmith* (1848), which was dedicated to him and prompted the choice of his own future Boswell. When Forster was ill, he read Goldsmith to him.[19] Like these forebears he wrote in many formats (fiction, journalism, crime reportage, travel); like them he was often entangled in hard-to-break contracts with publishers and short of money. But he was, thanks to the bigger mass markets of an industrialised press, better at making money than they were: one way to outgrow paternal acres.

Patrimony constitutes one of the dominant motifs of Dickens's fiction; it is lost, found, risked on disappointing sons, discovered in surrogate fathers – real fathers often proving feckless, sometimes hostile, deranged, guilty of some hidden crime.[20] Dickens's less destructive patriarchs (Pickwick, Brownlow, Boffin, Mr Dick) are normally preserved from the economy of romance, acting more like benevolent uncles than powerful fathers (they have no biological children). There is a strong emphasis on professional self-making about the destinations of men: nobody simply evaporates into an already gentrified identity. Fathers must be left, or they must die. Aspiring novelists also have to transcend the stories their fathers left them. If *Copperfield* enacts the laying of David's ghosts, moments reimagined in order to rest for ever, the earlier stories must likewise be found a burial place. The passage in *David Copperfield* continues:

> They kept alive my fancy, and my hope of something beyond that place and time [. . .] and did me no harm; for whatever harm was in some of them was not there for me; *I* knew nothing of it [. . .] It is curious to me how I could ever have consoled myself under my small troubles [. . .] by impersonating my favorite characters in them – as I did [. . .] I have been Tom Jones (a child's Tom Jones, a harmless creature) for a week together. I have sustained my own idea of Roderick Random for a month at a stretch [. . .] (53, ch. 4)

The stories constitute an infantile, compensatory fantasy of self-direction. *Robinson Crusoe* was a boyhood favourite of many Victorian men, perhaps because it both promoted a colonisation of solitary space, and seemed uninterested in the problem of sexual desire. David does not understand what Tom Jones is doing in the bushes with Molly Seagrim.[21] Presumably he skipped the sexed-up 'Memoirs of a Lady of Quality' in *Peregrine Pickle*; he was lucky not to find Sterne on his father's shelf at all, or the intimate, sex-focused epics of Richardson (whom Dickens did not like).[22] The boyhood patrimony remains innocently locked in the coffin-room of the displaced father.

Decontamination is complex, however, and leaves vestigial traces. *Copperfield* is a 'personal history' indeed, but also borderline metafictional: this is not merely a nostalgic confession of boyish enthusiasm, for these readings are the origin of what will make David himself a writer, though his entry to a literary career begins, like Johnson's (and Dickens's), with parliamentary reports and journalism. David (or 'Daisy') becomes (suggestively) Scheherazade to the alpha-male Steerforth, entertaining him with stories from *Peregrine Pickle* – given its sexual profligacy, perhaps a hint on Dickens's part towards other sorts of desire (89–91, ch. 7). Seeing Micawber in prison is modulated through a scene in *Roderick Random*; David records 'the manner in which I fitted my old books to my altered life, and made stories for myself, out of the streets, and out of men and women' (163, ch. 11). But when he leaves his friends, about to discover Emily's catastrophic betrayal, he is relinquishing something else: 'I parted from them at the wicket-gate, where visionary Straps had rested with Roderick Random's knapsack in the days of yore' (436, ch. 31).[23]

The legacy of *Crusoe* can offer comfort but also a sense of separation. David is 'more solitary than Robinson Crusoe, who had nobody to look at him and see that he was solitary' (69, ch. 5); his first independent home reminds him of 'Robinson Crusoe, when he had got into his fortification, and pulled his ladder up after him' (347, ch. 24). As a legal clerk, he finds a case 'just twice the length of Robinson Crusoe' (377, ch. 26), a signal not only of the tediousness of the lawsuit but of the perhaps overextended nature of the fiction it is compared to. The avatar is then displaced altogether into 'My aunt sitting on a quantity of luggage, with her two birds before her, and her cat on her knee, like a female Robinson Crusoe, drinking tea' (482, ch. 34). It is a process of dissociation, via increasing incongruity. As quotations from the novel render it neutral, Dickens substitutes his own counter-examples: the 'Tempest' (ch. 55) which destroys the strong men Ham and Steerforth is a panoramic version of the one which wrecks Crusoe, narrated from David's position of masterful survivor.

Like most Victorians, Dickens officially avoided *Moll Flanders* (1722), Defoe's highly sexualised female adventure story; but the rumour that Emily 'wanted to be a lady' recalls ominously Moll's express wish to become 'a gentlewoman'.[24] Mr Peggotty's quest for the seduced and abandoned Emily is a sanctified version of similar paternal redemptions in Goldsmith's *The Vicar of Wakefield* and Mackenzie's *Man of Feeling*. In the reclamation of Martha, Dickens is fending off eighteenth-century templates for the fallen woman, like Hogarth's schematic *Harlot's Progress* (1732); it is possible he was unaware of the pleasanter career outcomes enjoyed by the prostitutes of John Cleland's *Fanny Hill* (1749).[25] The narrative manner, meanwhile, with its controlled sorting of memory and foreknowledge and its patiently intense moments of present-tense recall, reads like a reverse parody of *Tristram Shandy* (1759–67), channelling its hobby-horsical digressions into Mr Dick's unwriteable 'Memorial', another 'personal history' continually thwarted by some primordial psychosexual crippling (Charles I's head as symbolic castration), and replacing the fractal chaos inspired by Tristram's page-one mis-conception with the orderly comedy of 'Chapter 1: I am Born'.[26]

Novels are not the only eighteenth-century texts Dickens plays with in the book. Micawber embellishes his letters and speeches with quotations from Pope, Burns, Johnson, Gray and Goldsmith, among scraps of drama, melodrama and Shakespeare; it is comic, but also a sign of profligacy, a cheap inheritance easily wasted. When Creakle, transferred from the oppressive school to the panoptical prison, claims to have been Traddles's 'guide, philosopher, and friend' (827, ch. 61), a line from Pope's *Essay on Man* (1733–4, IV. 390) already used by Micawber (216, ch. 17), the hollow repetition is more pointedly malign. Dickens can appropriate and transform what he wants from Pope: Dora, her hair in curl-papers, romanced by a tutelary lapdog, is a miniature, infantilised version of Pope's Belinda – also a 'Sylph' at one point (379, ch. 26) – to be supplanted by the Victorian matron Agnes. But characters who quote snatches of Pope are normally suspect, using received wisdom rather than heartfelt language. People incarcerate themselves in eighteenth-century environments, like the petrific women in Steerforth's house, with its Georgian pictures and costumes (284, ch. 20). Dr Strong quotes the piously facile Isaac Watts (220, ch. 16), to a sceptical reaction from Wickfield; a further sign of his superannuated dotage (too old for a young wife) is his inability to complete the millstone replication of Johnson's *Dictionary* (that school-leaving gift straightforwardly hurled out of a coach window by Becky Sharp two years earlier).[27]

Displacing Defoe: Crusoe to Crime Writing

The eighteenth century thus offers a store of fictional models and literary motifs, to be outgrown by appropriation, transformation or skewed allusion as the style matures. These novels, of course, remained reference points for imaginative stimulus: in *Hard Times*, Sissy's lifeline reading is Defoe and Goldsmith, not books of arithmetic.[28] Innocent reading remains a sign of virtue. In *Martin Chuzzlewit* (1843–4), the forever guileless Tom Pinch experiences a momentary return to boyhood in a shop:

> where children's books were sold, and where poor Robinson Crusoe stood alone in his might, with dog and hatchet, goat-skin cap and fowling-pieces: calmly surveying Philip Quarll and the host of imitators round him, and calling Mr. Pinch to witness that he, of all the crowd, impressed one solitary footprint on the shore of boyish memory, whereof the tread of generations should not stir the lightest grain of sand.

As David will be, Pinch is drawn to 'Persian tales' and 'rare Arabian nights', perhaps in chapbook abridgements:

> Which matchless wonders, coming fast on Mr. Pinch's mind, do so rub up and chafe that wonderful lamp within him, that when he turned his face towards the busy street, a crowd of phantoms waited on his pleasure, and he lived again, with new delight, the happy days before the Pecksniff era.[29]

In an essay of 1853, Dickens declared:

> We have never grown the thousandth part of an inch out of Robinson Crusoe. He fits us just as well, and in exactly the same way, as when we were among the smallest of the small. We have never grown out of his parrot, or his dog, or his fowling-piece, or the horrible old staring goat he came upon in the cave, or his rusty money, or his cap, or umbrella.[30]

In 'Nurse's Stories', in *The Uncommercial Traveller*, Dickens expatiated on his love of returning in imagination to 'places to which I have never been', beginning with Crusoe's island.[31] For a few pages the island is remade in Dickens's elegiac mind's eye, with scenes from *Gil Blas, Don Quixote*, the *Arabian Nights* and *Gulliver's Travels*, deeply impressed before adult kinds of journey were required of him. In the fiction, however, the boyhood identification has to be modified or abandoned, if you are going to become Martin Chuzzlewit rather than Tom Pinch, or David the writer rather than David the reader.

Some of Dickens's comments on Defoe as a writer tended, indeed, towards disparagement, particularly concerning the *Farther Adventures*, which 'will not bear enquiry': in a letter of 1855, Forster records, Dickens berated Defoe for his lack of sentiment at the death of Friday: 'as heartless as *Gil Blas*, in a very different and far more serious way'. In the same letter Dickens called Defoe's female characters 'terrible dull commonplace fellows without breeches', and Defoe a 'dry and disagreeable article himself', lacking the necessary quality of humour.[32] (These perceptions throw a certain light on Dickens's own deathbed scenes and female characterisation.) Dickens had actually begun to render *Robinson Crusoe* eccentric as early as *The Pickwick Papers* (1836–7): Bob Sawyer's apparel makes him look 'something like a dissipated Robinson Crusoe'.[33] Characters high and low are thereafter readily and ludicrously associated with Crusoe. Quilp bases his two-house existence on Crusoe's; Clennam's early love for Flora is compared to Crusoe's saved money.[34] Captain Cuttle, a Smollett throwback, daily 'clapped on his glazed hat [. . .] with the solitary air of Crusoe finishing his toilet with his goat-skin cap', to defend himself against 'the savage tribe' (his landlady).[35] Mrs Sparsit, sneaking through the woods to spy on Louisa's supposed tryst with Harthouse, 'stood behind a tree, like Robinson Crusoe in his ambuscade against the savages'.[36] These are visual jokes, closer to pantomimic caricature than the novel itself, estranging an appropriated source. Swift likewise bequeaths Dickens two comic ideas in particular, 'Lilliputian' and 'Brobdingnagian', signalling cognitive surprise or abrupt recalibration of perspective, but which, stripped of satiric context, at once identify and defamiliarise points of origin.[37]

Eighteenth-century material in Dickens is simultaneously a matter of recognition (influence, homage) and distancing (loss, liberation). *Oliver Twist* purifies the foundling *topos* that underlies *Tom Jones*. The 'Progress' of the subtitle signals the spiritual journey of Bunyan's Pilgrim, and the 1841 'Preface' more or less identifies Oliver as an allegorical being, but the realism of the fiction recalls Fielding's later milieu. So Oliver is falsely accused, mercilessly beaten, expelled and abducted from places of safety, and destined for the gallows. Like Tom, Oliver will be reclaimed, in part because 'higher' blood outweighs illegitimacy. But Oliver remains incurably pre-pubescent, loving only the dead mother and her surrogates, while Tom is easily seduced by increasingly suspect women. Dickens presents the formative effects of childhood as few eighteenth-century novelists did (he learned from Wordsworth in this respect), but there are no effects of upbringing on Oliver, and he never reaches puberty: an ideal reader of *Tom Jones*.

What he is inoculated against is not just sex but the criminal eighteenth century, the mirror-world of Fielding the magistrate more than of Fielding the novelist. Dickens visited prisons wherever he went, but he also drew on the hellish chaos of Newgate in *Moll Flanders*, *Peregrine Pickle*'s Bastille chapters, and the Vicar of Wakefield working pious wonders in his gaol. Dickens observed court procedure before creating Justice Fang, but he also channels Justice Thrasher from Fielding's *Amelia* (1751), kingpin of the corrupt 'trading justices' of the period. Dickens also drew on the gallows satire of Gay's *Beggar's Opera* (1728) and Fielding's *Jonathan Wild the Great* (1743), which themselves drew on another eighteenth-century genre, true-crime writing: murder narratives, sensational trials, execution ballads, prints about George Barnwell (apprentice turned murderer, celebrated in George Lillo's 1731 play and in melodrama ever after, a regular in Dickens's list of criminal cult-heroes).[38] The prurient compilations known as the *Malefactor's Register* or *Newgate Calendar* were begun in 1773, reaching a hefty four volumes by 1826. Crime runs through Dickens's fiction, as through Defoe's, albeit with a significant increase in detective policing (thanks in part to Fielding's efforts as a magistrate), and greatly enhanced panoptic surveillance in the narrative method. Like Defoe, Dickens conceives of crime both as a social issue and as a study in character, as even the unfinished *The Mystery of Edwin Drood* (1870) shows, but the narration is always heavily controlled by external perspective and always avoids the confessional *Moll Flanders* mode.[39]

Oliver Twist was Dickens's protest against the effects of an emerging literary tradition which used earlier materials to detach crime from social causes and emotional effects, particularly the 'Newgate novels' which made psychological thrillers and glamorous romances out of famous eighteenth-century crimes: Bulwer Lytton's *Eugene Aram* (1832), Ainsworth's *Rookwood* (1834) and *Jack Sheppard* (1839), romancing a murderer, Dick Turpin, and a jail-breaking thief, respectively. *Oliver Twist* was an attempt to present in fiction a thoroughly-detailed criminal milieu – not that this stopped Thackeray from including it in his own attack on criminal romances in *Catherine* (1839–40), a satiric case history of a sensational murder from 1726, prompting Dickens's insistence in the 'Preface' to the third edition that his story represented an actual truth.[40] Dickens's effect is partly achieved through an elaborately-observed gazetteer of criminal London, as if Fielding's *Inquiry into the Late Increase in Robbers* (1751), with its underworld journey through night-cellars and thieves' dens, had rematerialised in a much later novel. (There is a fairly direct line from Fielding's invention of the Bow Street Runners, as Westminster magistrate, an office Dickens considered applying for, to the Metropolitan police force which superseded them just after *Oliver Twist* was published.[41]) Dickens does not simply present a scene of Hogarthian brutality, though Tom Idle's route to the gallows (*Industry and Idleness*, 1747) provides a crude narrative logic. His boys are already corrupted by literary depictions of crime: the Artful Dodger and his companions misread their criminal fortunes and misidentify their future appearances in what is clearly a rogue's gallery of the eighteenth-century highwayman-romance kind – a grim sociological channelling of the ironies of Gay's *Beggar's Opera*, where adults do much the same thing.

Relics and Fossils: The Eighteenth-Century Object

All the novels present a dynamic of escape from bequeathed modes of being, sometimes personified as a thwarting father, often linked to eighteenth-century models. Nicholas Nickleby, a sort of chaste Tom Jones, must elude the economic stranglehold of his haunted, murderous uncle. He must also protect his sister against Sir Mulberry Hawk, an embodied quotation of Richardson's Lovelace, or of Sir Hargrave Pollexfen, Richardson's own attempt to castrate the seducer-rapist of *Clarissa* (Sir Charles Grandison knocks Pollexfen's teeth out while foiling an abduction attempt).[42] Lovelace is killed in a duel; in *Nickleby*, Hawk is scarred by Nicholas in a cross-class fight, but a duel is still his downfall. He kills Lord Verisopht, a ridiculous last-gasp vestige of aristocracy, at that site of eighteenth-century literary elitism, Twickenham, then dies in exile. Dickens would continue to present sexual predators with an inherited sense of entitlement, and to defeat them by more domestic means, but they would not again be aligned with the aristocrats of eighteenth-century fiction.

The Old Curiosity Shop (1840–1) offers a brief dream-vision of something like a pre-contamination eighteenth-century landscape. To preserve Nell as a prepubescent handmaiden, protecting the senescent grandfather from the once-aristocratic vice of gambling, Dickens walks them away from the modern locus of vulture capitalism into what might once have been a pre-industrial countryside idyll.[43] A brief interlude in a travelling waxworks show, a benign survival from an earlier era of folk culture

24   PAUL BAINES

(chs 27–9) is ruined by card sharps, a less benign throwback.[44] The manufacturing town which prefigures the Coketown of *Hard Times* (chs 43–5) is a traumatising blot on the modern landscape: we are evidently not in *The Pickwick Papers* anymore. Eventually, the Schoolmaster guides them to a village which would have been recognisable to Thomas Gray's aunt – Stoke Poges with the lights on. (The Schoolmaster himself is resurrected from Goldsmith's rose-tinted *Deserted Village* (1770) before it was obliterated by enclosure.) But Gray's village has no future: Nell and her grandfather are simply consigned to death there, not writing elegy in their country churchyard, but becoming it.

Dickens's fiction features many relics from a previous era: novels, texts, customs, things, objects of power and fascination, sometimes even of security (Peggotty's upturned boat-home) but more often signs of blockage. A deadening hand reaches over characters: shops of 'curiosities', pre-industrial marine instruments, bottles, tresses of hair, wooden legs, manuscripts; houses about to collapse or burn; graveyards rural and urban. Jilted spinsters are frozen in time; eighteenth-century prisons still stand; ancient crimes haunt people. In its lightest guise, characters identify themselves by quoting eighteenth-century poetry: it is not a promising sign of Wopsle's theatrical abilities that he quotes William Collins's *The Passions, an Ode*.[45] Dick Swiveller's rootlessness is punctuated by snatches of old song; Eugene Wrayburn disengages himself in speech with half-remembered quotations from Addison, Pope, Farquhar and *The Mysteries of Udolpho* (1794). Young idlers are redeemable, but pompous civic hypocrites (Pecksniff, Podsnap, Sapsea) cannot relinquish their threadbare set of eighteenth-century commonplaces, an idiolect signalling moral inauthenticity. Others are fatally oblivious to their own status as parody quotations: in *Dombey and Son* (1846–8), Mrs Skewton, with her flirtatious fan and perpetual need to be assembled from a prosthetic kit, is a grotesque hybrid of Pope's Belinda and Corinna from Swift's 'A Beautiful Young Nymph Going to Bed'. Dombey's educational plan for Paul parodies Walter Shandy's comically doomed *Tristrapaedia*, now exemplifying an oppressive ideology which kills the child.

Dickens developed advanced techniques of allusion and appropriation, refashioning the revenants of the eighteenth century. *Bleak House* (1852–3), with its vast reach and split narrative, is unexampled among Dickens's models, but shows even greater variety of skewed quotation and adapted motif. Chesney Wold houses a gouty Tory aristocrat, Sir Leicester Dedlock (born around 1775), wilfully embedded in Pope's world of scandal, ancient hag-women and decayed sylphs, a museumised representative of a pre-industrial decorum, self-condemned to heirlessness. (We know the non-aristocratic Lady Dedlock is fertile, because, like Moll Flanders, she rediscovers her illegitimate child; unlike Moll Flanders, she must not control or survive the revelation.) The sequential code of sentimental gestures (tears, handkerchiefs, coins) was already open to parody in *The Man of Feeling*; in Dickens such behavioural clichés duplicate themselves in social intercourse until they are definitively unmasked as fraudulent in the selfish 'sensibility' of Skimpole. We cannot be sure that every caged bird in *Little Dorrit* or *The Old Curiosity Shop* intentionally alludes to Sterne's trapped starling, singing 'I can't get out', in *A Sentimental Journey* (1768); but Miss Flite's last-gasp release of birds endows the gesture with symbolism far weightier than Yorick's purchase of the bird, and we know this is a consciously grave rewriting because the story has already been cited, smugly, by Skimpole.[46] How far Dickens was always conscious of such gestures is open to question, but readers of eighteenth-century literature will find much in *Bleak House* that looks like a scaled-up version of something familiar. Mrs Snagsby's suspicions about Jo's parentage surely remind us of the false accusation that Partridge is Tom Jones's father; but that comic miscarriage of local justice is supplanted here by a nationwide system of conspiratorial surveillance. The toils of Chancery come from Scriblerian satire, ballooned into a self-sustaining bureaucracy (the Office is one definitively nineteenth-century aspect of Dickens's fiction). The polluted fog that envelops London has no ecological parallel in earlier fiction, but is rather a psycho-social version of Pope's anti-intellectual goddess Dulness, as the dark river that runs through the fiction channels Pope's Thames – not the 'silver' emblem of *Windsor-Forest* but the 'sable' one of *The Dunciad*, rendered with a panoramic, sustained gravity which itself makes a point about what Dickens thinks the novel can now do.

Escaping the Paternal Prison: The Last Novels

If the eighteenth century was ever the site of innocent boyishness, in Dickens's fiction it also featured as a compromised adult memory, a culture-mine of guilty patronage that fatally circumscribes its legatees. Laundering the inheritance involved play, parody, misquotation and rewritings, overt, covert, sometimes perhaps unconscious. The late novels overwrite earlier models with grand symbolism; they are also populated by ever more bizarre and playful throwaway allusions to earlier materials, perhaps a kind of celebration. Little Dorrit is born in the Marshalsea as Moll Flanders is born in Newgate, but her psychological imprisonment is a subtle affair compared to Moll's; her father's status there, meanwhile, is a self-circumscribing travesty of Primrose's gravitas in *The Vicar of Wakefield*, his deportment a low-rent Chesterfieldian pomp.[47] The Lammles trap themselves in a fortune-hunted marriage, having failed to absorb the lessons of the identical motif in *Moll Flanders*. Mrs General's 'face-setting' iambic line 'Papa, potatoes, poultry, prunes, and prism' is condemned to echo ludicrously the accoutrements of Belinda's already-silly dressing table, 'Puffs, powders, patches, bibles, billets-doux'. But Pancks's vengeful snipping off of the 'sacred locks' of the complacent, Johnson-quoting Patriarch, itself riotously plunders *The Rape of the Lock*'s main action.[48]

Our Mutual Friend (1864–5), which has a Lady Belinda in passing, presents also Lady Tippins, all fan, cosmetics and antiquated coquetry, another Georgian fossil randomly spouting Dryden, *Robinson Crusoe* and Mozart. Bella Wilfer, bedecked with curls, devoted to her mirror and her casket-laden dressing table, has committed herself to a cut-price Popean femininity from which redemption will be necessary.[49] Boffin, benign and oblique inheritor of the fickle, evasive patrimony which saturates this final plot, seems at one point almost hidden in eighteenth-century textuality: his spell inside an alligator in Mr Venus's body-parts shop is lifted from the Scriblerian farce *Three Hours after Marriage* (1717), where the disguise features in an adultery plot.[50] Boffin also builds a deceptive carapace (to re-educate Bella) by appearing in thrall to readings by another scrap text merchant and quotation-mangler, Silas Wegg, from heavyweight eighteenth-century wastepaper: Edward Gibbon's *History of the Decline and Fall of the Roman Empire* (1776–8), Charles Rollin's *Ancient History* (1730), the cobwebby *Lives* of Georgian misers.

26   PAUL BAINES

Our Mutual Friend recycles the already-recycled, to the verge of metafiction. Old texts are aligned with the dust-mounds which loom over the trap that is the paternal estate, a sedimentary waste dump, collective detritus to be carted away except for one magically retrieved golden item (naturally enough, a secreted document). Ultimately patrimony is textualised in wills, those powerful decrees of the father that cripple the lives of sons – in fiction as in life.[51] The last novel reinvents its hero's identity under a series of testaments capriciously rewritten by another absent, unregretted patriarch. Wegg, malign misreader of dead eighteenth-century literature and hobbled father-surrogate, blackmails Boffin with one, an embezzled fragment of castratory Oedipal intent. In a final gesture of sovereign novelistic play, he is out-texted by another one, already retrieved (in a Dutch bottle, like a cheap genie) from the mounds by Boffin, the legal inheritor and childless but benevolent substitute patriarch. But the inherited writings themselves might as well be interchangeable, as the father's scripts no longer matter: the point is the possibility of purifying the inheritance by a free action, the finding of the rightful inheritor who can come into his own.

Notes

1. *A Child's History of England*, 3 vols (London: Bradbury & Evans, 1853–4), III, 318–21, ch. 37.
2. *Boswell's Life of Johnson*, 2 vols (London: Oxford University Press, 1924), I, 177. Dickens elsewhere pictures a grace in working-class politeness that 'Lord Chesterfield could not have taught his son in a century'; *Hard Times*, ed. by Paul Schlicke (Oxford: Oxford University Press, 2006), 151, bk 2, ch. 6.
3. A point to some extent shared with Thackeray: see n. 40 below.
4. See 'Astley's' and 'Vauxhall Gardens by Day' in *Dickens' Journalism*, ed. by Michael Slater and John Drew, 4 vols (London: J. M. Dent, 1994–2000), I (1994), 'Scenes', ch. 11 and ch. 14; Vauxhall was sold in 1839 and finally closed in 1859.
5. See 'City of London Churches', 'The City of the Absent' and 'An Old Stage-Coaching House', published as part of *The Uncommercial Traveller* series in *All the Year Round* on 5 May 1860, 18 July 1863 and 1 August 1863. *Dickens' Journalism*, IV (2000), 105–15; 260–9; 269–77.
6. On the status of the collection, see Anne Toner, 'Anna Barbauld on Fictional Form in the *British Novelists* (1810)', *Eighteenth-Century Fiction* 24.2 (2011–12), 171–93. Dickens received a set of *Bentley's Standard Novels*, a later incarnation of the same idea, in 1837; Claire Tomalin, *Charles Dickens: A Life* (London: Viking, 2011), 77–8.
7. See the digs at 'fashionable novel-reading families' in 'Scenes', ch. 9; girls with 'some new novel in their reticule', 'Scenes', ch. 10; 'the licence of novel-writers' in respect of time, 'Tales', ch. 1; and similar instances in 'Horatio Sparkins', 'Tales', ch. 5. *Dickens' Journalism*, I. Dickens opens his 1846 travelogue by guying the conventions of 'a Middle-Aged novel'; *Pictures from Italy*, ed. by Kate Flint (London: Penguin, 1998), 8. Both 'novel' and 'novelist' settled into relatively modern usage in *Household Words* and *All the Year Round*.
8. *Nicholas Nickleby*, ed. by Paul Schlicke (Oxford: Oxford University Press, 1990), 167, ch. 18.
9. For the troubled identity of the form, see Brean Hammond and Shaun Regan, *Making the Novel: Fiction and Society in Britain, 1660–1789* (Basingstoke: Palgrave Macmillan, 2006), chs 1–3.
10. 'The Art of Fiction', *Longman's Magazine* 4 (September 1884); perhaps James noticed that Dickens often uses puddings as an emblem of robustly satisfying English food.
11. *David Copperfield*, ed. by Nina Burgis (Oxford: Oxford University Press, 1998), 53, ch. 4.

EIGHTEENTH-CENTURY CULTURES AND THE NOVEL

12. John Forster, *The Life of Charles Dickens*, ed. by J. W. T. Ley (London: Cecil Palmer, 1928), 6. For Dickens's interest in education outside school, see Juliet John, *Dickens and Mass Culture* (Oxford: Oxford University Press, 2010), 44–5.

13. Tomalin, 23. See Helen Small, 'The Debt to Society: Dickens, Fielding, and the Genealogy of Independence', in *The Victorians and the Eighteenth Century*, ed. by Francis O'Gorman and Katherine Turner (Aldershot: Ashgate, 2004), 14–40.

14. Tomalin, 217. In *Hard Times*, Gradgrind names his sons after the eighteenth-century economists Adam Smith and Thomas Malthus in a tragically humourless version of the gesture.

15. Forster, 626. An article, 'The Spirit of Fiction' in *All the Year Round* 18 (27 July 1867), 118–20, is perhaps by Dickens.

16. Tomalin, 97.

17. For a survey, see Monica Fludernik, 'Eighteenth-Century Legacy', in *A Companion to Charles Dickens*, ed. by David Paroissien (Malden, MA: Blackwell, 2008), 65–80.

18. Forster, 90.

19. Tomalin, 211, 253. Forster's biography of Dickens delayed his *Life* of Swift, unfinished at his death; his biographies of Defoe and Charles Churchill appeared in 1855.

20. See Anny Sadrin, *Parentage and Inheritance in the Novels of Charles Dickens* (Cambridge: Cambridge University Press, 1994).

21. On homoerotic desire in Dickens, which might be linked here to Crusoe's affection for the handsome Friday, see Holly Furneaux, *Queer Dickens* (Oxford: Oxford University Press, 2009).

22. Richardson was 'no great favourite of mine, and never seems to me to take his top-boots off, whatever he does'; 'To Edward Taggart, 28 January 1848', *The Letters of Charles Dickens*, ed. by Madeline House, Graham Storey et al., Pilgrim/British Academy Edition, 12 vols (Oxford: Clarendon Press, 1965–2002), v (1981), 20.

23. Dickens was fond of an old acquaintance 'forasmuch as we had made the acquaintance of Roderick Random together', in 'Dullborough Town' in *The Uncommercial Traveller* series (*All the Year Round*, 30 June 1860). *Dickens' Journalism*, iv, 138–48, 146.

24. Dickens wrote to Forster (*Life*, 96) in November 1837 commending Defoe's *History of the Devil*, which would be printed by Bohn with *Moll Flanders* in 1854; *Moll Flanders* was not in Scott's edition of Defoe (1809–10) but was in the Oxford edition (1840–1) and available clandestinely. For Moll's aspirations to resemble a 'gentlewoman' (prostitute), see Defoe, *Moll Flanders*, ed. by Paul A. Scanlon (Peterborough, ON: Broadview, 2005), 50–1.

25. Fanny marries her first love despite a prodigious sexual career, and nobody dies of syphilis. Dickens's Urania Cottage was a discreet version of the loudly sermonising Magdalen Hospital for the Reception of Penitent Prostitutes, founded in 1758; Tomalin, 203–9.

26. For Dickens and Sterne, see Valerie Purton, *Dickens and the Sentimental Tradition: Fielding, Richardson, Sterne, Goldsmith, Sheridan, Lamb* (New York: Anthem Press, 2012).

27. Thackeray, *Vanity Fair* (1847–8), ch. 1.

28. *Hard Times*, 52, bk 1, ch. 8.

29. *Martin Chuzzlewit*, ed. by Margaret Cardwell (Oxford: Clarendon Press, 1982), 64–5, ch. 5. *Philip Quarll*, a 'Robinsonade', appeared as *The English Hermit* (1727).

30. 'Where We Stopped Growing', published in *Household Words* on 1 January 1853, in *Dickens' Journalism*, iii (1998), 105–12, 108.

31. See *Dickens' Journalism*, iv, 171.

32. Forster, 611n.

33. *The Pickwick Papers*, ed. by James Kinsley (Oxford: Oxford University Press, 1998), 365, ch. 30.

34. *The Old Curiosity Shop*, ed. by Norman Page (London: Penguin, 2003), 377, ch. 50; *Little Dorrit*, ed. by John Holloway (Harmondsworth: Penguin, 1982), 191, bk 1, ch. 24; 351, bk 1, ch. 25.

35. *Dombey and Son*, ed. by Andrew Sanders (London: Penguin, 2002), 597–8, ch. 39.
36. *Hard Times*, 196, bk 2, ch. 11.
37. See *American Notes*, ed. by Patricia Ingham (London: Penguin, 2004), 57, 72, 82; for a more poignant Gulliverian encounter with slaves, see 154. See also *Pictures from Italy*, 18 and 71. The scene in bk 1, ch. 2 of *Hard Times* where Sissy cannot 'define' a horse is probably a twisted revenge against Swift's reasoning horses in Book 4 of *Gulliver's Travels*.
38. On engagement with melodrama, see John, *Dickens and Mass Culture*, ch. 6.
39. See Philip Collins, *Dickens and Crime* (Bloomington: Indiana University Press, 1962); and Juliet John, 'Twisting the Newgate Tale: Dickens, Popular Culture and the Politics of Genre', in *Rethinking Victorian Culture*, ed. by Juliet John and Alice Jenkins (Basingstoke: Palgrave Macmillan, 2000), 127–45.
40. *Catherine* was serialised in *Fraser's Magazine*, where Thackeray published several articles attacking the 'Newgate Novel' and attitudes to executions. See, for example, 'On Going to See a Man Hanged', *Fraser's Magazine* 22 (July–December 1840), 150–8.
41. The 'runners' appear in *Oliver Twist*, ed. by Kathleen Tillotson (Oxford: Oxford University Press, 1999), 235, ch. 30; see Tomalin, 182, and James Beattie, *The First English Detectives: The Bow Street Runners and the Policing of London, 1750–1840* (Oxford: Oxford University Press, 2014).
42. In *The Pickwick Papers*, ch. 49, an abduction plot forms an inset ghost-dream of the eighteenth century.
43. Charley Bates's escape to life as a Northamptonshire grazier in *Oliver Twist* is more successful but scarcely given substance.
44. For similar survivals, see Paul Schlicke, *Dickens and Popular Entertainment* (London: Unwin Hyman, 1988).
45. *Great Expectations*, ed. by Margaret Cardwell (Oxford: Oxford University Press, 1998), 96, ch. 13.
46. The birds are released as Richard dies, ch. 65; Skimpole's flippant reference ('I am not like the starling: I get out') comes in ch. 37: *Bleak House*, ed. by Nicola Bradbury (London: Penguin, 2003), 595. Sterne's book was among the childhood favourites in 'Where We Stopped Growing'.
47. *Little Dorrit*, 274, bk 1, ch. 19. He behaves like Addison's Sir Roger de Coverley; 480, bk 1, ch. 36.
48. *Little Dorrit*, 661, 866, 872, bk 2, ch. 15 and ch. 32; Pope, *Rape of the Lock*, I. 198; Belinda's lock is 'sacred' at IV. 133.
49. *Our Mutual Friend*, ed. by Michael Cotsell (Oxford: Oxford University Press, 1998), 38–43, bk 1, ch. 4; 471–2, bk 3, ch. 5; the ivory casket on the toilette, 778, bk 4, ch. 13, is redeemed in final marital harmony.
50. *Our Mutual Friend*, 580, bk 3, ch. 14.
51. For the last version of Dickens's own will (dated 12 May 1869), see Tomalin, 479 n. 25, and Michael Slater, *Charles Dickens* (New Haven: Yale University Press, 2009), 615–19.

Further Reading

Monica Fludernik, 'Eighteenth-Century Legacy', in *A Companion to Charles Dickens*, ed. by David Paroissien (Malden: Blackwell, 2008), 65–80

Juliet John, *Dickens and Mass Culture* (Oxford: Oxford University Press, 2010)

Valerie Purton, *Dickens and the Sentimental Tradition: Fielding, Richardson, Sterne, Goldsmith, Sheridan, Lamb* (New York: Anthem Press, 2012)

Helen Small, 'The Debt to Society: Dickens, Fielding, and the Genealogy of Independence', in *The Victorians and the Eighteenth Century*, ed. by Francis O'Gorman and Katherine Turner (Aldershot: Ashgate, 2004), 14–40

3

The Novel and the Arts of Modern Vision

Francesca Orestano

Dickens and Visibility, According to Italo Calvino

In *Six Memos for the Next Millennium* (1988) Italo Calvino selected five literary values that would stand the test of the future. These were lightness, quickness, exactitude, visibility and multiplicity. A sixth memo was yet *in mente dei*. Calvino's lectures emphasised that such values, or categories, belong to the classics as well as to popular literature, to the arts of the past as well as the present. It is my point that Dickens's art incorporates these values, not only as instances of modernity and promises for the future but as enduring elements of the art of narration.[1] I shall analyse them separately and then dwell on the response they obtain in the fictional discourse of some twentieth-century authors.

'Lightness', according to Calvino, creates 'harmony between the adventurous, picaresque inner rhythm [. . .] and the frantic spectacle of the world, sometimes dramatic and sometimes grotesque' (4). Such is the quality of much of Dickens's fiction. 'Quickness' entails a narrative time that can be either 'delaying, cyclic, or motionless' (35), but also includes repetition and digression; 'exactitude' demands:

1. A well-defined and well-calculated plan for the work in question;
2. An evocation of clear, incisive, memorable visual images;
3. A language as precise as possible [. . .]. (55–6)

In addition to these qualities, uncontestably present throughout Dickens's work as the response of his readers from the beginnings to present times suggests, Calvino adds to his categories of literary value 'visibility': 'If I have included visibility in my list of values to be saved, it is to give warning of the danger we run in losing a basic human faculty: the power to bring images into focus with our eyes shut' (92). Such ability to give verbal life to visual scenes, characters and objects inside a mental theatre has to be carefully preserved in contemporary and future literature, in as much as, Calvino maintains, in our time 'we live in an unending rainfall of images' (57). Speaking of remarkable literary models, Calvino adds:

> I followed the visionary and spectacular vein that pulses in the stories of Hoffmann, Chamisso, Arnim, Eichendorff, Potocki, Gogol, Nerval, Gautier, Hawthorne, Poe, Dickens, Turgenev, Leskov, and continues down to Stevenson, Kipling, and Wells. (95)

It is worth remarking that the name of Dickens, when associated by Calvino with 'visibility', places the writer among those authors who deploy images with a specific performative energy: besides being endowed with sharp retinal perception, Dickens gives ulterior substance to his vision by reading stories into images. Finally, the category of multiplicity entails the complexity of a fictional universe in which the value of exactitude is constantly challenged and countered by the value of frenetic distortion, and where fantastic and grotesque events spring from everyday reality. To sum up the 'five memos' for the next millennium selected by Calvino, one last quote seems relevant: 'I am accustomed to consider literature a search for knowledge' (26).

Knowledge indeed, in Dickens's epistemic universe, goes hand in hand with the techniques of the observer: both technically and metaphorically ocular perception mingles with vision, the real with the unreal, landscape with inscape.[2] Criticism has justly dwelt on Dickens's fascination with new kinds of visual tools popular in Victorian mass visual culture. Magic lantern slides, dissolving views, dioramas, panoramas and the stereoscope did chime in with the sharp focus on detail, and with the hallucinations, the inner cinema, the spectral quality inherent in ocular vision when, beyond the retinal datum, the world is seen with eyes wide shut.[3] Vladimir Nabokov in 1969 summed up the result of such combinations, arguing that between the magic lantern and the microscope there lies the golden section of art:

> There is, it would seem, in the dimensional scale of the world, a kind of delicate meeting place between imagination and knowledge, a point, arrived at by diminishing large things and enlarging small ones, that is intrinsically artistic.[4]

Visible Narration: Hogarth and Dickens

The comparison between Dickens and Hogarth – here deployed to analyse the borderline between image and word, but also the dawn of the modern in novel writing – is an early one. In 1837, Sydney Smith salutes the writer in these terms: 'The Soul of Hogarth has migrated into the Body of Mr Dickens.'[5] Another reviewer, Lister, repeats the comparison in 1838, adding that Dickens is a satirist who takes a practical view of life, but without Hogarth's cynicism and coarseness.[6] R. H. Horne follows the critical track in *The Spirit of the Age* (1844).[7] Hippolyte Taine again strikes the note of comparison: 'Dickens is gloomy, like Hogarth; but, like Hogarth, he makes us burst with laughter by the buffoonery of his invention and the violence of his caricatures.'[8] It is worth noting that Taine emphasises the relief, energy, precision and the passionate exactness of Dickens's descriptions, but also the boldness of style that

> attests the violence of the impression. [. . .] Excessive metaphors bring before the mind grotesque fancies. [. . .]. [H]is inspiration is a feverish rapture, which does not select its objects, which animates promiscuously the ugly, the vulgar, the ridiculous, [. . .] communicating to his creations an indescribable jerkiness and violence.[9]

Realism-cum-hallucination, according to Taine, may cause a disturbing lack of selection: 'the imagination of Dickens is like that of monomaniacs.'[10] There is indeed a passionate attention, both in Hogarth and Dickens, for kindred subjects, and for crowded places, situations and characters: urban London and its popular thorough-fares; daytime and night-time scenes; harlots and rakes; stages of cruelty; gin lanes and beer streets; elections; briberies; banks; judges; executions. But beyond the recognition of kindred subjects, Taine and George Eliot seem to suggest a common technique, or rather style, that dwells neither on realism nor on distortion, but feeds upon both: 'he scarcely ever passes from the humorous and external to the emotional and tragic, without becoming as transcendent in his unreality as he was a moment before in his artistic truthfulness.'[11]

Actually, in addition to kindred themes and style, between Hogarth's visual presentations of stages of a story in 'progress' and Dickens's serialised chapters (let alone the progress of *Oliver Twist* in 1837–9), there seems to be a similar philosophical project establishing a moral link between cause and effect.[12] The interstitial space calls for the readers' or spectators' imaginative response, to fill in the gaps in the montage. Eisenstein's awareness of such technique is well known and discussed.[13] In Dickens's illustrated books, both attitudes, the active creativity of the reader, and the passive stance of the image viewer, are in constant dialogue.[14] As suggested by Robert Patten, 'two competing systems of knowing and representing the world' are set in fruitful dialogue.[15] Token of this is also Dickens's counterpoint on names that suggest visually prominent qualities: Rakewell and Mary Hackabout have their counterparts in the Cheerybles, the Barnacles, the Veneerings, to name just a few. Such epistemological dialogue sustains in Dickens 'a remarkable fusion of modes. Realism, fantasy, symbolism, melodrama, terror, and comedy all exist together' constantly demanding the reader to move quickly from one kind of fictional base to another.[16] As argued by Andrew Mangham, naive realism was a style that troubled both Hogarth and Dickens: 'both men developed forms in which caricature, melodrama and exaggeration [are] crucial to the development of verisimilitude.'[17]

There is no doubt that Dickens knew Hogarth's work at first hand and owned a number of engravings: Leonée Ormond and Kate Flint have remarked on the relationship between Hogarth and Dickens, starting from the fact that: 'There were forty-eight Hogarth prints on the walls of Gad's Hill.'[18] Not only did Hogarth's engravings adorn Dickens's house: he liked to 'read' the scenes of the famous episodes to his guests.[19] As pointed out by Mark Bills, the Victorians' interest in Hogarth rested upon the moral element: Dickens's description of 'Gin-Shops' in *Sketches by Boz* (1836), as well as his comments on Cruikshank's series *The Drunkard's Children* (1848), testify to the revulsion and passionate reaction elicited by abject social conditions that chained together poverty and descent into vice.[20] In addition to this, and on a playful note, it is worth recalling *The Lazy Tour of Two Idle Apprentices* (1857) by Dickens and Wilkie Collins, where the two protagonists take their names after Hogarth, as Mr Thomas Idle and Mr Francis Goodchild.[21] In the nineteenth century, the first critical comparisons between Dickens and Hogarth seem to dwell on the moral parables imparted by their work: this is going to shift under the joint pressure of visual technology and end-of-the-century *Weltanschauung*. Spectacular progress in visual technology seems to relegate the black-and-white engraving to the arts of the past. The advent of photography, from 1835, with calotypes and daguerreotypes, Baxter's patented colour prints in 1839, biunials and triunials, and the stereoscope, would produce images of sharp realism. Made possible by technical reproduction, copies and cheap replicas were at once accurate and fascinating, but also immensely perplexing when modern visual tools caused a revision of acquired notions of ocular perception. A revolution of no lesser import occurs when Victorian values and the connection between morality and the arts end up in their divorce.[22] Partially ignited by Parnassian *l'art pour l'art* poetics and by British aestheticism, exploded by Darwinian notions of the descent of humankind into atavism, condemned by the sense of degeneration tainting the *fin de siècle*, the primacy of the moral mission of art is questioned everywhere – even in children's literature, with Alice's careless attitude to authority, religion, school and manners. Accordingly, critics and writers are going to view the Dickens–Hogarth relationship in a different light. Their relationship changes in several subtle ways. The reasons for local, contemporary satire in both artists are outdated: the public forget Victorian issues concerning legislation, ragged schools and administrative reform. While the satirical sting subsides, another element of composition has to be focused upon. Such element is caricature, a genre with a peculiar syntax.

Hogarth's *Satire on False Perspective* (1754), whose Inscription reads: 'Whoever makes a DESIGN without the Knowledge of PERSPECTIVE will be liable to such Absurdities as are shewn in this Frontispiece', was well known to Dickens. He even mentioned it in his piece on the Pre-Raphaelite painters, 'Old Lamps for New Ones' (1850), in order to criticise their apparent disregard for the laws of perspective.[23] Yet Dickens's idiosyncratic handling of perspective is well known: namely, his accurate use of it as an element of composition is both factual and symbolic. Perspective unfolds in a predictable way, like a long straight avenue, whenever he wants to indicate the safe unrolling of events, and a visible teleology; conversely, he shuffles background, middle ground and foreground, and thus the relative size of objects, whenever he intends to stage the uncanny, the absurd, the out-of-place. Such idiosyncratic use of perspective indicates the artist's intentional handling of artificial order, of visual selection and focus: it destabilises the traditional hierarchy of distances that set character at the centre of the fictional scene. Characters and objects shift from their respective assigned places: thus validating not only the study of their symbolic order discussed by Erwin Panofsky in his 1927 *Perspective as Symbolic Form*, but also Dorothy Van Ghent's analysis of things that, 'like animal pets, have adopted the disposition and expression of their masters. [. . .] The animate is treated as if it were a thing.'[24] Thing theory would dwell on such a quality.[25] And, as Van Gogh would remark, these aspects are not conducive to realism: 'There is no writer, in my opinion, who is *so* much a painter and a black-and-white artist as Dickens. His figures are resurrections.'[26] Such resurrections, that grotesquely bridge the physical divide between life and death, indeed take place in the modern novel.

Recipes for the Modern Novel

The apparent lack of selection in Dickens's style, matched by what appeared as a wilful plurality of fictional modes and voices, the elements of ambiguous realism and psychological import, were noted by his commentators, who, at first, celebrated the writer's *post-mortem* with critical contempt. Of course, there were followers who admired this quality: such is the position of George Gissing, who, besides writing *Charles Dickens: A Critical Study* (1898), shared with H. G. Wells 'a common debt to Dickens'.[27] Gissing, in particular, is the writer whose 'awareness of the darker side of London life, derives very largely from Dickens, though without the Dickensian exuberance and pervading fantasy'.[28] Despite these followers, the turn of the century is a fitful moment in Dickens's reception. G. H. Lewes in 1872 had defined Dickens 'a seer of visions' whose types amounted to a kind of universal experience individualised:

> Unreal and impossible as these types were, speaking a language never heard in life, moving like pieces of simple mechanism [. . .], these unreal figures affected the uncritical reader with the force of reality [. . .]. And the critic is distressed to observe the substitution of mechanisms for minds, puppets for characters.[29]

Thus the assessment of Dickens's work seems to inhabit the borderline where realism and grotesque distortion find a common ground, and infuse his writing with a heightened visibility:

> When he imagined a street, a house, a room, a figure, he saw it not in the vague schematic way of ordinary imagination, but in the sharp definition of actual perception, all the salient details obtruding themselves on his attention. He, seeing it thus vividly, made us also see it; and believing in its reality however fantastic, he communicated something of his belief to us.[30]

Together with judgements emphasising the visual element, critics who dwelt on character strove to understand the relationship between surface and depth. Thus E. M. Forster in *Aspects of the Novel* (1927) stated that despite his imperfect handling of character Dickens was capable of transmitting force. Focusing on Forster's distinction between 'flat' and 'round' characters, Bernard Bergonzi questioned the value of such evaluation:

> If, in fact, one regards Dickens, not as a striking but somehow second-rate talent (as it was not unusual to regard him in the 1920s, when Forster wrote), but as one of the great creative geniuses of our literature, then one will feel the need of a more adequate critical terminology. At best, the 'flat' versus 'rounded' distinction will be descriptive rather than evaluative.[31]

It is from such statements that one can envisage the difficulty experienced by writers and critics who were to evaluate Dickens and his lesson – indeed inimitable – and at once had to meet the demand of the new century to revitalise the art of fiction. Actually Dickens's influence can be seen as providing – simultaneously – inspiration and model for two opposite trends in twentieth-century fiction. One trend led the writer's interest towards the realm of psychology, and the materials of the psyche, repressed, lingering or erupting out of the dark within; the other trend generated a stark realism verging on expressionism, and on external style, devoid of all psychology, intent on comicality and bitter satire. Accordingly, both trends found their fertile hotbed in the cities of modernism,[32] at once realistic and spectral, in the 'make-it-new' statements of the avant-garde, but also in the hoarded accumulations of memory, powerfully moulding time and subject. In the future, these positions would mingle again under the label of magic realism; later on, they would merge in the postmodern novel; eventually, in neo-Victorian fiction where Dickens would be energetically resurrected.

Both trends, however, if viewed at the dawn of the twentieth century, bring to the fore T. S. Eliot's digestive, and rather bulimic, appreciation of the modernity of those artists endowed with a 'mechanism of sensibility that could devour any kind of experience' – 'the noise of the typewriter' and 'the smell of cooking'.[33]

From Dickens's Tramps to Wyndham Lewis's Dark Laughter

Elsewhere I have argued that Dickens's article on 'Tramps' in *The Uncommercial Traveller* (1860; 1868) opens a window on modernity.[34] Tramps would be fashionable at the beginning of the new century, socially embraced by Leslie Stephen's fellowship of Sunday tramps, and given a voice in the pages of *The Tramp: An Open Air Magazine*, edited by Douglas Goldring between 1910 and 1911. It is remarkable that, in 1910, the *Manifesto of Futurism* by Filippo Tommaso Marinetti appeared in *The Tramp*. Definitely an avant-garde magazine, with its violently modernist antics and the practical instructions on how to set up camp and live in a caravan, *The Tramp* reflects at once identity and changing cultural mores.

Among the contributors to *The Tramp*, Wyndham Lewis would soon emulate Marinetti's Futurism with his Vorticist manifesto. Lewis's first short stories, especially his 'Le Père François: A Full-length Portrait of a Tramp' (1910), revolve around tramps and their mobile universe, much in a Dickensian vein.[35] Tramps seem to provide Lewis with the right material for his literary experiments.

Like the microcosm of grotesque Dickensian types and caricatures in Katherine Mansfield's German pension (Mansfield another modern avowedly influenced by Dickens, albeit within the short-story dimension), Lewis's early stories are peopled with a gallery of innkeepers, *pensionnaires* and vagabonds.[36] The Dickensian mode is already present in Lewis's early novel *Mrs Dukes' Million* (composed between 1908 and 1910, published in 1977), to the extent that Mrs Dukes is seen by Ian Duncan as a descendant of Mrs Gamp, insofar as 'the use of Dickensian animation technique is so striking as to be imitative'.[37] The grotesque mode allows the writer to construct identity by means of external signs, mannerisms and idiolect, 'replacing identification based on hereditary or hierarchic models'.[38] Lewis's Père François descends in a direct line from Dickens's 'Tramps'. This 1910 story is included in his collection *The Wild Body* (1927), where tramps figure as early avatars of Lewis's modern characters, whose existence is shaped by his 'external style' pictorial technique. His types are indeed wild bodies, empty carapaces, marionettes without psychology or interiority, but possessed with a mechanical energy that equates them to human automata. These wild bodies are essentially caricatures and outrageously 'modernist': Lewis's theory of dark laughter has its roots in Dickens's work.

In his short-lived Vorticist magazine *BLAST*, Lewis would trace the lines of a theory of laughter at once implemented in his aesthetics of painting as well as in his poetics of the novel.[39] While addressing his BLASTS against the 'Gloomy Victorian Circus [. . .] Trundling out of Sixties – Dickensian Clowns – Corelli Lady Riders – Troups of Performing Gipsies', within the same issue, in his Vorticist drama *Enemy of the Stars* (1914), Lewis sets the scene in 'Some Bleak Circus', and his characters are 'Two Heathen Clowns – Grave Booth Animals – Cynical Athletes' that remind us of Sleary's circus in *Hard Times* (1854), presented by Michael Hollington as an avatar of modernity.[40]

In *The Wild Body* (1927) Lewis describes his theory of laughter as the artist's preference for the 'hard without' of the human body, the physical carapace of the human marionette – opposed to the 'dark within' of psychology – and, visually, as the choice for external style:

1. *The meaning of the Wild Body*
   First, to assume the dichotomy of mind and body is necessary here, without arguing it; for it is upon that essential separation that the theory of laughter here proposed is based [. . .].
2. *The root of the Comic*
   The root of the Comic is to be sought in the sensations resulting from the observations of a thing behaving like a person. But from that point of view all men are necessarily comic: for they are all things, or physical bodies, behaving as persons.[41]

Such reduction of humans to things would chime not only with the visual satire of Hogarth's descent, but also with the more recent discourse of thing theory.[42] Lewis's recipe for modern fiction and modern painting moulds his novel *Tarr* (1916–17) and his *Apes of God* (1930), as well as his pictorial Tyros and wild bodies, meant to excite dark laughter.

Typically, and mischievously, in *Men without Art* (1934), Lewis was quick in detecting the Dickensian influence in his contemporaries: he maintains that Joyce copies from Mr Jingle in *The Pickwick Papers* the thought-stream of Mr Bloom in *Ulysses* (1922); Hemingway models his low jargon on Dickens; the characters in Faulkner's *Sartoris* (1929) are 'a Dickensian company'.[43] D. H. Lawrence, instead, whose horizons were set well beyond the scenario of London and Londoners, is categorised by Lewis:

with those Columbuses who have set sail towards the El Dorados of the Unconscious, or, of the Great Within. [. . .] Dogmatically, then, I am for the great Without, for the method of *external* approach – for the wisdom of the eye, rather than that of the ear.[44]

The implications of Lewis's concept of external style would be later confirmed by the philosophical debate on the primacy of perception, from which visual studies would germinate. Within a different context, in the new art of the cinema, Dickensian moods and the physicality of his characters would be resurrected by the inimitable Chaplinesque marionette of the tramp, analysed by Gillian Piggott from a Dickensian perspective.[45]

1912: Joyce Celebrates Dickens

The year 1912 marked the first centenary of Dickens's birth, and on this occasion James Joyce composed an essay in Italian in which Dickens's survival as a fiction writer is discussed. I shall dwell on this article as containing a specific response to Dickens's fiction that includes a view of its influence on modern writers.

Joyce opens his argument by emphasising that the form of Dickens's writing is, in his opinion, irksome, cumbersome and altogether deplorable. Such form is 'prolissa, sovraccarica di osservazioni minute e spesso irrilevanti, puntualmente alleggerita a intervalli regolari dall'immancabile nota umoristica'.[46] Such prolixity, loaded with unnecessary details, punctuated by the comic note chiming at regular intervals, was in Joyce's opinion unconvincing, and for such reasons he argues that Dickens does not deserve a place among the major literary authors. For Joyce the arrival of 'ultra-modern' writers such as Tolstoj [*sic*], Zola, Dostoievsky [*sic*] on the British literary scene was the event that would generate a revolution in taste: their committed and rigorous realism seemed to consign Dickens to a sentimental past, stale and discoloured. Yet Joyce, by referring to Dickens as 'il grande Cockney', the great Cockney, removes him from the European context and places him much more favourably in the context of London, where his fiction is nourished by the life of the great metropolis. London, Joyce admits, is Dickens's kingdom, the source of his immense power.[47] And in such an urban context Dickens's fans proliferate and still cherish his writings. It would be interesting, Joyce wonders, to inquire about the response to Dickens in the anglophone world at large: yet, he concludes, Dickens deserves a place among the great 'creatori letterari' – literary creators.[48]

Dickens is so successful, Joyce argues, because like Hogarth he is a great caricaturist; like Goldsmith a great sentimentalist. His characters are types, usually marked by one single strong, deliberate, even exaggerated quality, but this indeed is what makes of him a truly popular author, and imprints his characters on popular memory. Dickens has moulded 'la lingua parlata' – the English spoken throughout the British Empire – like no other writer after Shakespeare. For these reasons Joyce assigns to Dickens 'un passaporto per l'immortalità' – a passport to immortality. While seemingly inconsistent with Joyce's previous criticism, this statement emphasises Dickens's role as creator of a modern language for the novel, and, I should argue, the conductor of a polyphony suggestive of complexity and dissonance, and of a kaleidoscopic multiplicity of perspective.

It is not difficult to trace in Joyce's assessment the indication that the root of modern novel writing coincides with a close focus on the city, and on urban life and experience:

> I colori, i rumori familiari, gli odori stessi della grande metropoli si fondono nella sua opera come in una possente sinfonia, in cui humour e pathos, vita e morte, speranza e disperazione, sono inestricabilmente intrecciati.[49]

Out of such colours, sounds, smells – whether in London or in Dublin – Joyce would compose his own symphony of modern life, *Ulysses*, finally agreeing with Dickens on the inexhaustible variety of types and tempos the metropolis offered to the modern novelist. London, Dublin or even Trieste in the fiction of Italo Svevo, and Paris for Marcel Proust, contain all the stories, myths, characters and types the modern artist needs to build his 'galleria'. 'Gallery' indeed is a keyword that points again to the graphic quality, the wide panopticon gaze and the Hogarthian 'visibility' of Dickens's fiction. In this essay, Dickens's fiction, although unfavourably contrasted against the work of Tolstoy or Dostoevsky, in the end obtains a passport to immortality owing to its magisterial handling of the modern city, whose map is viewed in all its complexity of layers, directions, intricacy.

1913–1927: Marcel Proust's *Recherche* and the Art of Memory

While setting the principal scene of his *magnum opus* in Paris, with forays to the countryside, to Combray, to Balbec or to Venice – locations evoked for their highly symbolic, oneiric quality – Proust is the artist who best represents the energy, power and sway of memory within the inner life of his characters. Critics have based their appreciation of Proust on this quality: within the context of this essay, Proust's art of writing incarnates those aspects that, in Dickens, mark the persistence of memory, the dreamlike and *déjà-vu* quality of some scenes, the obsessive nature of some *idées fixes*, the nightmares and the hallucinations awaiting the most common situations of everyday life. In a famous letter to John Forster from Lausanne, when composing *Dombey and Son* (1846–8), Dickens made a remarkable comment equating London to the magic lantern, and both as the powerful sources of his creative process.[50] In a similar way, resorting to the magic lantern as the source of inspiration, at once optical tool *and* source of frightening visions, Marcel Proust's *Du côté de chez Swann* (1913–27) opens with the narrator's perception of the colours and images traced by the magic lantern slides on the wall of his room:

> On avait bien inventé, pour me distraire les soirs où on me trouvait l'air trop malheureux, de me donner une lanterne magique, [. . .] à l'instar des premiers architectes et maîtres verriers de l'âge gothique, elle substituait à l'opacité des murs d'impalpables irisations, de surnaturelles apparitions multicolores, où des légendes étaient dépeintes comme dans un vitrail vacillant et momentané.[51]

The mechanical tool generates stained-glass Gothic images, apparitions, legends, terror:

> Au pas saccadé de son cheval, Golo, plein d'un affreux dessein, sortait de la petite forêt triangulaire qui veloutait d'un vert sombre la pente d'une colline, et s'avançait en tressautant vers le château de la pauvre Geneviève de Brabant.[52]

Golo, Ralph Nickleby, Tulkinghorn, Blandois/Rigaud, John Jasper: there is no limit to the transforming energy of which the magic lantern is at once instrument and symbol. And this transformative power communicates itself in the simplest way to portraits that vaguely suggest a resemblance; then to everyday objects that – as in *American Notes* (1842) – become crouching animals of prey, ugly dwarfs or other nightmarish presences; finally, it infects characters like Martin Chuzzlewit, or Mr Dombey, or Pip, who undergo a deep process of change, foregrounded by vision. The magic lantern, with the dissolving view mechanism, also models the notion of time, presenting to the eye whatever exists outside the regular chronology of experience, actually igniting a kind of *à rebours* process.[53] If these were not reasons sufficient to place Dickens at the fountainhead of Freudian fiction, there are gifts of vividness and humour in Proust for which 'we shall look in vain for anything like that outside the novels of Dickens'.[54] Remarking on the 'singular relief' into which the characters are thrown as soon as they begin to speak and act, Edmund Wilson maintains:

> And it seems plain that Proust must have read Dickens and that this sometimes grotesque heightening of character had been partly learned from him. Proust,

like Dickens, was a remarkable mimic: as Dickens enchanted his audiences by dramatic readings from his novels, so, we are told, Proust was celebrated for impersonations of his friends; and both, in their books, carried the practice of caricaturing habits of speech and of inventing things for their personages to say which are outrageous without ever ceasing to be lifelike to a point where it becomes impossible to compare them to anybody but each other.[55]

According to Wilson's comparison, there is yet another connection between Dickens and Proust: he remarks that their villains, albeit despicable, are amusing. Endowed with generous sympathy, both writers deal at once with humanity and monstrosity. Proust reminds us of Dickens also because of the comic violence of his incidents; the theatrical heightening of character; the strong impressions meted out by a simple gesture or just by a look. Wilson produces a list of comparisons, also remarking on the apparently loose structure of novels consisting of a well-planned succession of scenes.

Thus one may argue that Proust, one of the great novelists of the twentieth century, is also among those moderns who galvanise Dickens back to life. The energy for such resurrection comes from three factors: the value both writers assign to the comic treatment of character and society, often verging on theatricality and comedy; their expert handling of satire, whose bitterness is mitigated by their interest in human foibles, vices and sins; and, last but not least, the superior power that memory, whether freewheeling or repressed, holds upon their fictional scene. In Dickens we just need to listen to the great narrators of their own *temps perdu* – David Copperfield, Esther Summerson, Miss Wade, Pip, not to mention the role of memory for the entire Dorrit family – to realise that memory operates within the psychological chemistry of these characters by powerfully moulding their behaviour and thus the orderly unfolding of narration. Backwards and forwards, realism is not a monolith for Dickens or for Proust: eroded by small *madeleines* and striking minor details, exploded by shocks of recognition, their realism contains volumes of life experience, the passing of time as well as the archives of the past.

Virginia Woolf, a Passionate Reader

As a writer born to an intellectual family of the upper middle class, connected to the Thackerays, inured to Victorian codes of behaviour determined by rank, manners and gender, Virginia Woolf comes from a context in which Dickens is not a hero, but the representative of popular bad taste. Her first experiments in fiction date back to that period described as 'modernism' when the influence of the Bloomsbury group – mainly coming from Clive Bell and Roger Fry – causes her aesthetic revision of the visual arts, but such close tutoring will also bear its fruit in her ideas about fiction. Here the relationship between Woolf and Dickens becomes tighter, and deeper, especially because of her awareness of the dynamics of visual perception and the way the visible world comes to be expressed in words.

Thus, despite the prevailing critical opinion, that modernism meant 'the rejection as "anti-modern" of a whole mass of social material which had provided the focus of nineteenth-century fiction', to the extent that 'the world of human production explored in the work of writers like Dickens and Zola now largely disappeared',

THE NOVEL AND THE ARTS OF MODERN VISION

I suggest that this very world, with its many shades and seen from various perspectives, gave body and substance to much of twentieth-century fiction.[56]

Elsewhere I have argued that Dickens and Woolf are two Londoners, but the great metropolis is not just the geographical area in which they situate their fiction.[57] London is the symbolic world on which their stories are grafted; characters are seen, lost and found again; London is where East End and West End provide the co-ordinates for wealth and poverty, virtue and vice; London is where a polyphony of voices and languages are heard, so that in 1941, in front of the destruction of her world under the Nazi fire, Woolf writes in a last act of faith: 'Chaucer, Shakespeare, Dickens. It is my only patriotism.'[58]

In the context of this collection it is not only the fertile connection with London that has to be examined, but rather the ways in which the lesson imparted by Dickens still lives in Woolf's modern fiction. The fact that Woolf read Dickens throughout her life, often rereading his novels, is proved by a quick perusal of her diaries and letters. Here the element to be emphasised is Woolf's ample, panoramic view of literature in 1919:

> But oh, dear, what a lot I've got to read! The entire works of Mr James Joyce, Wyndham Lewis, Ezra Pound, so as to compare them with the entire works of Dickens & Mrs Gaskell; besides that George Eliot; & finally Hardy.[59]

No iconoclasm, no blasting and bombardiering here: in 1922 Woolf is again bent 'On Re-reading Novels' and welcomes the new recent editions of the Victorians novelists, commenting that 'in spite of the mischief-makers, the grand-children, it seems, get along very nicely with the grand-parents'.[60] To reread the unwieldy nineteenth-century novels is indeed a hard task for the modern reader, but if much pleasure is to be drawn from Flaubert's story 'Un cœur simple' (1877), 'there is no limit to be put upon the intoxicating effects of Meredith and Dickens and Dostoevsky, of Scott and Charlotte Brontë'.[61] Against the supreme craftsmanship of Flaubert's short story, Woolf wonders:

> Can we sharpen our impressions of a long and crowded novel in the same way? Can we make out that the masters – Tolstoy and Flaubert, and Dickens, and Henry James, and Meredith – expressed by methods which we can trace and understand the enormous mass and myriad detail of their books?[62]

The complaint against the loose baggy monsters of Victorian fiction, according to Henry James's description of some hefty three-decker crammed with unnecessary detail, is thus silenced. Woolf is after a new method of storytelling, and the year 1922, with the publication of *Jacob's Room*, marks her most direct attempt towards a modernist aesthetic. Yet her character, Jacob, is solidly planted in London, in Bloomsbury when he reads at the British Library, in Soho when he wanders at dusk.

In 1925 an essay on *David Copperfield* marks the recent publication of new editions of Victorian novels, cheap, well-printed, likened by Woolf to fresh strawberries. The occasion brings to the fore a reflection on Dickens's critics, his fans and readers, to whom he has become an institution, a monument:

> The rumour about Dickens is to the effect that his sentiment is disgusting and his style commonplace; that in reading him every refinement must be hidden and every

sensibility kept under glass; but that with these precautions and reservations, he is of course Shakespearian; like Scott a born creator; like Balzac, prodigious in his fecundity; but, rumour adds, it is strange that while one reads Shakespeare and one reads Scott, the precise moment for reading Dickens seldom comes our way.[63]

While on the one hand the fact that Dickens seems to have become an institution, and a repository of conventional virtues, seems to quench Woolf's enthusiasm, on the other hand her attention is caught by his fictional technique: 'We remodel our psychological geography when we read Dickens,' she maintains.[64] And there follows a closer look at his method, indeed at his apparent idiosyncrasies, which have to do with:

> the ardour, the excitement, the humour, the oddity of people's characters; the smell and savour and soot of London; the incredible coincidences which hook the most remote lives together; the city; the law courts; this man's nose; that man's limp; some scene under an archway or on the high road; and, above all, some gigantic and dominating figure, so stuffed and swollen with life that he does not exist singly and solitarily, but seems to need for his own realisation a host of others, to call into existence the severed parts that complete him [. . .]. This is the power which cannot fade or fail in its effect. The power not to analyse or to interpret, but to produce, apparently without thought or effort or calculation of the effect upon the story, characters who exist not in detail, not accurately or exactly, but abundantly in a cluster of wild and yet extraordinarily revealing remarks.[65]

Woolf dwells on the sources of Dickens's power like the sorcerer's apprentice, eager to unveil the recipes of such stories, of such characters. And beside these aspects, a third source of power must be reckoned: 'As a creator of character his peculiarity is that he creates wherever his eyes rest – He has the visualising power in the extreme. His people are branded upon our eyeballs.'[66] Such a comment has a specific value when proffered by one who was lectured by Roger Fry on the elements of significant form, and on the mastery of painters like Paul Cézanne, who draw the eye inside the dynamics of composition as resulting from line and masses. The qualities to which Woolf refers in this 1925 essay are, it is argued, primarily innate gifts such as a sharp visual perception, and as such they cannot be learned. Nevertheless, by insisting on Dickens's 'visualising power', Woolf reflects on Dickens's ability to make us see not only character, but composition, albeit punctuated by a crowd of details and sharp impressions, and crossed not by one, but by several perspective lines. Such plurality of viewpoints, occurring in unison or in contrast, allows the story to be told from the external side but also from inside out. This is the lesson that Woolf treasures throughout her intense activity as writer, reviewer, editor, when the impulse to write like a modern finds its counterpoint in her passionate respect for the excellence of past tradition.

The essay 'Phases of Fiction' (1929) takes a panoramic view of the history of the English novel, where Dickens does not reside with 'The Truth-Tellers', 'The Romantics', 'The Psychologists', 'The Satirists and Fantastics', 'The Poets', but with 'The Character-Mongers and Comedians'. Again, his ability to create character is deemed prodigious: characters serve as stationary points 'in the flow and confusion of the

THE NOVEL AND THE ARTS OF MODERN VISION 41

narrative'. Thus what may have seemed inappropriate, unstylish, uncouth, falls back into a view of life that amply excuses our writer for his baroque constructions: 'After all, is not life itself, with its coincidences and its convolutions, astonishingly queer?'[67]

> One after another his characters come into being, called into existence by an eye which sees once and for all; which snatches a woman's steel hair curlers, a pair of red rimmed eyes, a white scar and makes them somehow reveal the essence of a character; an eye gluttonous, restless, insatiable, creating more than it can use. Thus, the prevailing impression is one of movement, of the endless ebb and flow of life round one or two stationary points.[68]

In these statements one may seek the poetics of Woolf's fiction, the lines that she follows in her own production, inasmuch as she concludes that 'the most characteristic qualities of the novel [. . .] are the very qualities that are most incompatible with design and order'.[69] If style, arrangement, order, construction, are not essentially conducive to a good novel, then Dickens's wieldy books, albeit unique and inimitable, become all the more valuable.

In addition to this, one may argue that all through Virginia Woolf's works there are strange resurrections of characters, conditions, plots and moods used by Dickens. Her first novel, *The Voyage Out* (1915), is a progress-novel albeit without a happy ending; *Jacob's Room* (1922) portrays – sketches – more than 300 characters, swarming by day and night through the crowded streets of London; *Mrs Dalloway* (1925) inherits from Lady Dedlock the sentiments for a lost lover and her almost-lost daughter; *To the Lighthouse* (1927), like *Little Dorrit*, is divided into two parts, the past and the present that carries the load of past memories: both hinge around a 'Time Passes' device;[70] *The Waves* (1931) resonates with a polyphony of voices distinctly heard from the very infancy of the characters, like *A Holiday Romance* (1868); *Flush* (1933) is decidedly Victorian with its London scenario, enriched with the contrast between West and East End London, with the criminal kidnapping of the dog and Miss Barrett's courageous foray into the dangers of the East End, like Florence Dombey; *The Years* (1931) covers the time from 1880 up to 'The Present Day' offering a history of the past marked by a distinct polyphony of voices and of London sounds, in which ageing persons and indestructible objects emerge from the flux of time, often endowed with a spectral nature that resists dissolution and allows them to predict the present.

In Conclusion: 'Consistency?'

At the bottom of his list, Calvino traced with a very light hand, and in pencil, the word 'Consistency'. It was supposed to be the sixth memo for the next millennium. But it was not to be. One wonders whether consistency would really be part of his agenda, and whether he doubted of its value within the scenario of modern literature. The writers on which this essay focuses and the comparisons between their work and the work of Charles Dickens do not offer a panorama of 'consistency' as a prominent quality of modern fiction. Those who saw Dickens as a model and a source of inspiration still had a lot to debate, and, if there is one common attitude marking early twentieth-century reviews, essays and novel writing, this is the lack of consistency in evaluating Dickens's work. The debate between surface and depth, without and within, 'flat' and 'round' character, caricature and psychology, progress and memory, would affect the modern novel so that two tendencies, both arguably Dickensian, would operate simultaneously, and sometime be stereoscopically contrasted although in mutual disagreement.

In addition to these tendencies, there would be genres that Dickens consigned to future writers' exploitation: detective fiction, as T. S. Eliot suggested in 1927, had its foundation stone in *Bleak House* (1852–3).[71] Also Kafka's *The Trial* (1925) gestures back to *Bleak House*: legal fiction seems to have in Dickens one of its first interpreters, and a commentator fully aware of the absurd traps hidden within the universe of the law. Socially engaged fiction saw in *Hard Times* (1854) a memorable *ur*-text, as argued by G. K. Chesterton and later on, with some critical comments, by George Orwell.[72] Subsequently, magic realism drew its formula from the romantic side of familiar things, and placed a strong accent on visibility, perspective and its aberrations.[73] At the turn of the millennium, when neo-Victorianism and neo-Victorian novels became fashionable, Dan Simmons's *Drood* (2009), Matthew Pearl's *The Last Dickens* (2009), Tabish Khair's *The Thing about Thugs* (2012) – to mention just a few – welcome Dickens back, triumphantly, with his bright waistcoats and his dark aura, with the vivid and sombre London scene and its grotesque types.

The memos offered by Calvino are indeed valuable when we try to make sense of the immense and varied panorama of modern fiction in order to trace Dickens's presence in the next millennium. Among them, visibility seems to be – as the Hogarthian track here pursued suggests – the prominent quality of Dickens's writing, an astonishing gift, whether it envelops the outer surface of the human marionette, of crowds moving on the city map, or whether it plunges into a visionary inscape of memory, fear and desire. Dickens's artistic legacy, with its lightness and its heavy passages, its multiplicity often at odds with consistency, with the exactitude of detail and its cinematic technique allowing dramatic variations in montage and focus, posed a manifold challenge to twentieth-century novelists. For this reason, the writers considered in this essay performed the hardest task: besides coming to terms with the prejudice and criticism following upon the writer's death, they were able to mould the modern novel in creative ways while still looking back to Dickens's lesson, and to an intimidating wealth of narrative suggestions embedded in his oeuvre.

To conclude, I should go back to Virginia Woolf and her 1934 essay 'A Conversation about Art' where, dwelling on the art of Walter Sickert, the writer reflects on its essential quality, at once visual and discursive. In this essay shaped like a conversation, the dichotomy between painting and literature leads to a comparison between Sickert and Dickens. Both the writer and the painter are evoked by these same words: 'Think of his Venice, his landscapes; or of those pictures of music halls, of circuses, of street markets, where the acute drama of human character is cut off.'[74] The sentence applies to both artists, Dickens and Sickert, suggesting a future intermedia exchange between verbal and visual texts, but it applies especially to Dickens when Woolf maintains: 'The novelist, after all, wants to make us see.'[75] Such indeed is the quality that at first generated the frequent comparisons between Dickens's art and Hogarth's; later, visibility would strike novelists and critics as the very element of modern fiction, whether perception would proceed from an ocular source or from the psychological sounding of the spectral landscapes of subjectivity.

THE NOVEL AND THE ARTS OF MODERN VISION

Notes

1. Italo Calvino, *Six Memos for the Next Millennium*, trans. by Patrick Creagh (London: Random House, 1996). Subsequent references are inserted parenthetically in the text.
2. Jonathan Crary, *Techniques of the Observer: On Vision and Modernity in the Nineteenth Century* (Cambridge, MA: MIT Press, 1990).
3. Calvino, 92. In this context it is worth making reference to *Traumnovelle*, or *Rhapsody: A Dream Novel* (1926) by Austrian author Arthur Schnitzler, adapted in Stanley Kubrick's 1999 movie *Eyes Wide Shut*.
4. Vladimir Nabokov, *Speak Memory: An Autobiography Revisited* (London: Penguin, 2000), 130–1.
5. Philip Collins, 'Introduction', in *Charles Dickens: The Critical Heritage*, ed. by Philip Collins (London: Routledge, 1997), 1–26, 5.
6. [Thomas Henry Lister], from a review of *Sketches* (1st and 2nd Series), *Pickwick*, *Nickleby* and *Oliver Twist*, in *Edinburgh Review* (1838), in Collins, 71–7, 72.
7. R. H. Horne, *The New Spirit of the Age* (1844), in Collins, 198–202.
8. Hippolyte Taine, 'Charles Dickens: son talent et ses œuvres', *Revue des deux mondes* (1856), in Collins, 337–42, 340.
9. Ibid.
10. Ibid., 337.
11. [George Eliot], 'The Natural History of German Life', *Westminster Review* (1856), in Collins, 343.
12. John R. Harvey, 'Bruegel to Dickens: Graphic Satire and the Novels', in *Charles Dickens: Critical Assessments*, ed. by Michael Hollington, 4 vols (Mountfield: Helm Information, 1995), IV, 452–76, offers a close analysis of the similarities between Hogarth and Dickens.
13. See, for example, Grahame Smith, *Dickens and the Dream of Cinema* (Manchester: Manchester University Press, 2003).
14. Mary Elizabeth Leighton and Lisa Surridge, 'The Illustrated Novel', in *Dickens in Context*, ed. by Sally Ledger and Holly Furneaux (Cambridge: Cambridge University Press, 2011), 166–77.
15. Robert L. Patten, 'Serial Illustration and Storytelling in *David Copperfield*' (2002), cited in Leighton and Surridge, 166.
16. Harry P. Marten, 'The Structural Imagination of Dickens and Hogarth: Structure and Scene', *Studies in the Novel* 6.2 (1974), 145–64, 145; Marten argues that Dickens is 'a writer of carefully structured psychological-symbolic novels'.
17. Andrew Mangham, 'Dickens, Hogarth and Artistic Perception: The Case of *Nicholas Nickleby*', *Dickens Studies Annual* 48 (2017), 59–78.
18. Leonée Ormond, 'Dickens and Painting: Contemporary Art', *Dickensian* 80 (1984), 2–25 and 'Dickens and Painting: The Old Masters', *Dickensian* 79 (1983), 130–51; also see Kate Flint, *The Victorians and the Visual Imagination* (Cambridge: Cambridge University Press, 2000) and 'Visual Culture', in *Dickens in Context*, 148–57, 15.
19. Mark Bills, 'Dickens and the Painting of Modern Life', in *Dickens and the Artists*, ed. by Mark Bills (Florence: Watts Gallery and Yale University Press, 2012), 111–53.
20. Ibid.
21. On the subject, see Nathalie Vanfasse, *La Plume et la Route. Charles Dickens, écrivain voyageur* (Aix-en-Provence: Presses universitaires de Provence, 2017).
22. Francesco Marroni, *Victorian Disharmonies: A Reconsideration of Nineteenth-Century English Fiction* (Newark: University of Delaware Press, 2010). Also see *Strange Sisters: Literature and Aesthetics in the Nineteenth Century*, ed. by Francesca Orestano and Francesca Frigerio (Oxford: Peter Lang, 2009).

44 FRANCESCA ORESTANO

23. Charles Dickens, 'Old Lamps for New Ones', in *Dickens' Journalism*, ed. by Michael Slater and John Drew, 4 vols (London: J. M. Dent, 1994–2000), II (1997), 242–8, 247. The element of perspective in art composition and Dickens's reaction against Roman Baroque art are discussed in my chapter 'Against Reading: Dickens and the Visual Arts' in *Texts, Contexts, and Intertextuality: Dickens as a Reader*, ed. by Norbert Lennartz and Dieter Koch (Göttingen: V&R Unipress, 2014), 263–82.

24. Dorothy Van Ghent, 'The Dickens World: A View from Todgers' (1950), in *Charles Dickens: Critical Assessments*, IV, 53–66, 53.

25. On Dickens and 'thing theory', see Maria Teresa Chialant, 'The Dickens World, a World of Objects', in *Dickens's Signs, Readers' Designs: New Bearings in Dickens Criticism*, ed. by Francesca Orestano and Norbert Lennartz (Rome: Aracne, 2012), 33–52.

26. Vincent Van Gogh, 'From Two Letters' (1882–3), in *Charles Dickens: Critical Assessments*, IV, 431–3, 432. Also see Andrew Sanders, *Charles Dickens: Resurrectionist* (New York: St Martin's Press, 1982).

27. Bernard Bergonzi, *The Turn of a Century: Essays on Victorian and Modern English Literature* (London: Macmillan, 1973), 70. Bergonzi also remarks that Chesterton's two books on Dickens 'though they may seem a little dated now, contain – along with Gissing's – some of the first respectable criticism to be written about Dickens' (129).

28. Ibid., 53.

29. G. H. Lewes, 'Review of Vol. I of Forster's *Life*', *Fortnightly Review* (1872), in Collins, 569–77, 572.

30. Ibid., 571.

31. Bergonzi, 189–90.

32. Malcolm Bradbury, 'The Cities of Modernism', in *Modernism, 1890–1930*, ed. by Malcolm Bradbury and James McFarlane (London: Penguin, 1976), 96–104. Dickens cited on 97 and 99.

33. T. S. Eliot, 'The Metaphysical Poets', in *Selected Prose of T. S. Eliot*, ed. by Frank Kermode (London: Faber & Faber, 1975), 59–67, 64.

34. Francesca Orestano, '"Tramps": Dickens's Modern Rhapsody', in *Unsettling Dickens: Process, Progress, and Change*, ed. by Christine Huguet and Paul Vita (Wimereux: Éditions du Sagittaire, 2016), 157–92.

35. Wyndham Lewis, *The Complete Wild Body*, ed. by Bernard Lafourcade (Santa Rosa, CA: Black Sparrow Press, 1982), 277–83.

36. See Michael Hollington, 'Mansfield Eats Dickens', in *Katherine Mansfield and Literary Influence*, ed. by Sarah Ailwood (Edinburgh: Edinburgh University Press, 2015), 155–67 and Michael Hollington's essay on 'Global Dickens' in this collection.

37. Ian Duncan, 'Towards a Modernist Poetics: Wyndham Lewis's Early Fiction', in *Wyndham Lewis, Letteratura / Pittura*, ed. by Giovanni Cianci (Palermo: Sellerio, 1982), 67–85, 70.

38. Ibid., 71.

39. *BLAST* 1 (1914) <https://library.brown.edu/pdfs/1143209523824858.pdf> [accessed 1 March 2018], 19–20.

40. The quote is from *BLAST* 1, 55. Michael Hollington, 'Dickens and the Circus of Modernity', in *Dickens and Modernity*, ed. by Juliet John (London: Boydell & Brewer, 2012), 133–49.

41. *The Complete Wild Body*, 277–83.

42. Bill Brown, 'Thing Theory', *Critical Inquiry* 28.1 (2001), 1–22.

43. Geoffrey Wagner, *Wyndham Lewis: A Portrait of the Artist as the Enemy* (London: Routledge & Kegan Paul, 1957), 170, 276; Wyndham Lewis, *Men without Art*, ed. by Seamus Cooney (Santa Rosa, CA: Black Sparrow Press, 1987), 28; 48–50.

44. *Men without Art*, 105.

45. Gillian Piggott, 'Dickens and Chaplin: "The Tramp"', in *Charles Dickens, Modernism, Modernity*, ed. by Christine Huguet and Nathalie Vanfasse, 2 vols (Wimereux: Éditions

du Sagittaire, 2014) I, 187–210. Also by Piggott: *Dickens and Benjamin: Moments of Revelation, Fragments of Modernity* (Farnham: Ashgate, 2012).

46. James Joyce, 'Il centenario di Charles Dickens', in James Joyce, *Lettere e saggi*, ed. by Enrico Terrinoni (Milan: il Saggiatore, 2016), 806–9. Translation: 'prolix [form], loaded with unnecessary details, often irrelevant, and punctually made lighter, at regular intervals, by the unfailing note of humour'.

47. In recent years *The Reception of Charles Dickens in Europe*, ed. by Michael Hollington, 2 vols (London and New York: Bloomsbury, 2013), restores a balance between Dickens and his European readers, translators and followers.

48. 'Il centenario di Charles Dickens', 808.

49. Ibid., 807. Translation: 'The colours, the familiar sounds, even the smells of the great metropolis are fused together in his [Dickens's] work as in a powerful symphony, where humour and pathos, life and death, hope and despair, are inextricably mixed.'

50. 'To John Forster, [30 August 1846]', *The Letters of Charles Dickens*, ed. by Madeline House, Graham Storey et al., Pilgrim/ British Academy Edition, 12 vols (Oxford: Clarendon Press, 1965–2002), IV (1977), 612–13.

51. Marcel Proust, *Du côté de chez Swann* (Paris: Gallimard, 1954), 16. *Remembrance of Things Past, Swann's Way*, trans. by C. K. Scott Moncrieff (London: Chatto & Windus, 1922): 'Some one had had the happy idea of giving me, to distract me on evenings when I seemed abnormally wretched, a magic lantern [. . .]: in the manner of the master-builders and glass-painters of gothic days it substituted for the opaqueness of my walls an impalpable iridescence, supernatural phenomena of many colours, in which legends were depicted, as on a shifting and transitory window' (9).

52. Ibid., 16–17. Moncrieff's translation: 'Riding at a jerky trot, Golo, his mind filled with an infamous design, issued from the little three-cornered forest which dyed dark-green the slope of a convenient hill, and advanced by leaps and bounds towards the castle of poor Geneviève de Brabant' (10).

53. On the transformative power of the dissolving view, see Francesca Orestano, 'Charles Dickens and Italy: The "New Picturesque"', in *Dickens and Italy: Little Dorrit and Pictures from Italy*, ed. by Michael Hollington and Francesca Orestano (Newcastle upon Tyne: Cambridge Scholars Publishing, 2009), 49–67.

54. Edmund Wilson, 'Marcel Proust' [1931], in *Axel's Castle. A Study in the Imaginative Literature of 1870–1930* (London: Collins, 1969), 114.

55. Ibid., 115.

56. Peter Nicholls, *Modernisms: A Literary Guide* (London: Macmillan, 1995), 78–9.

57. Francesca Orestano, 'Two Londoners: Charles Dickens and Virginia Woolf', in *Dickens, Modernism, Modernity*, I, 71–94. In addition to Woolf, also Katherine Mansfield, Elizabeth Bowen and Christina Stead were influenced by Dickens: see Michael Hollington, 'Dickens among Women Modernist Writers', in *Dickens and Women ReObserved*, ed. by Edward Guiliano (Brighton: Edward Everett Root Publishers, 2020), 323–40.

58. *Leave the Letters Till We're Dead: Letters of Virginia Woolf, 1935–1941*, ed. by Nigel Nicholson and Joanne Trautmann (London: The Hogarth Press, 1980), 460.

59. *The Diary of Virginia Woolf, Volume 1: 1915–1919*, ed. by Anne Olivier Bell (London: Penguin, 1977), 247.

60. Virginia Woolf, 'On Re-reading Novels', in *The Essays of Virginia Woolf*, 6 vols, ed. Andrew McNeillie (London: The Hogarth Press, 1988), III, 336–46, 336.

61. Ibid., 341.

62. Ibid., 342.

63. Virginia Woolf, '*David Copperfield*', in *The Essays of Virginia Woolf*, IV, 284–9, 285.

64. Ibid., 286. In 1905, Woolf had reviewed for the *TLS* F. G. Kitton's *The Dickens Country*. But famously in this piece on 'Literary Geography' she had maintained that 'a writer's

country is a territory within his own brain; and we run the risk of disillusionment if we try to turn such phantom cities into tangible brick and mortar', thus setting literary geography against psychological geography. Virginia Woolf, 'Literary Geography', in *The Essays of Virginia Woolf*, I, 32–6.

65. '*David Copperfield*', 286–7.
66. Ibid., 287.
67. 'Phases of Fiction', in *The Essays of Virginia Woolf*, VI, 40–88, 56.
68. Ibid., 56.
69. Ibid., 83.
70. On *Little Dorrit* and the adoption of the stereoscope device, see Francesca Orestano, '*Little Dorrit*', in *The Oxford Handbook of Charles Dickens*, ed. by Robert L. Patten, John O. Jordan and Catherine Waters (Oxford: Oxford University Press, 2018), 245–59.
71. T. S. Eliot, 'Wilkie Collins and Dickens', in *Selected Essays*, New Edition (New York: Harcourt, Brace, 1950), 409–18. Michael Hollington, '"Patient Etherised upon a Table": T. S. Eliot's Dissection of Dickens', *Dickensian* 502 (2017), 139–49. Also, Osbert Sitwell in *Dickens* (London: Chatto & Windus, 1932) argues that Dickens is 'the originator of the modern "thriller," the father [. . .] to Sherlock Holmes and all the numerous subsequent tales of crime detected through coincidence [. . .]; an artist [. . .] with an extraordinary and personal technique' (15).
72. Gilbert Keith Chesterton, *Charles Dickens: A Critical Study* (London: Methuen, 1906), and George Orwell, 'Charles Dickens', in *Critical Essays* (London: Secker & Warburg, 1946), 7–56.
73. The mention of Dickens in relation to magic realism is to be found in Giuseppe Tomasi di Lampedusa who argues that the kingdom of Dickens is *magic realism*. A kingdom of infinite attractiveness, a kingdom governed with great difficulty. Tomasi adds that only Kafka can claim to rule over a similar kingdom, but laughter makes the one by Dickens the more attractive of the two. Giuseppe Tomasi di Lampedusa, 'Letteratura inglese', ed. by Nicoletta Polo, in *Opere*, ed. by Gioacchino Lanza Tomasi (Milan: Mondadori, 2006), 617–1421: 1113. See also Francesca Orestano, 'Magic Lantern, Magic Realism: Italian Writers and Dickens, from the End of the XIX century to the 1980s', in *The Reception of Charles Dickens in Europe*, I, 231–44.
74. Virginia Woolf, 'A Conversation about Art' (1934), revised version of 'Walter Sickert. A Conversation', in *The Essays of Virginia Woolf*, ed. by Stuart N. Clarke (London: Hogarth Press, 2011), VI, Appendix, 409–21, 416.
75. Ibid., 417. Woolf adds: 'All great writers are great colourists, just as they are musicians into the bargain; they always contrive to make their scenes glow and darken and change to the eye' (418).

Further Reading

Leon Litvack and Nathalie Vanfasse, eds, *Reading Dickens Differently* (Chichester: Wiley-Blackwell, 2020)

Francesca Orestano, 'Hogarth, Dickens, and the Progress of Vision', in *Enduring Presence: William Hogarth's British and European Afterlives*, ed. by Caroline Patey, Cynthia E. Roman, and Georges Letissier (Oxford: Peter Lang, 2021), II, 57–94.

Robert L. Patten, John O. Jordan and Catherine Waters, eds, *The Oxford Handbook of Charles Dickens* (Oxford: Oxford University Press, 2018)

Gillian Piggott, *Dickens and Benjamin: Moments of Revelation, Fragments of Modernity* (Farnham: Ashgate, 2012)

Grahame Smith, *Dickens and the Dream of Cinema* (Manchester: Manchester University Press, 2003)

4

FANFICTION

Maureen England

THE EXTRACT BELOW IS FROM THE opening chapter of fanfiction from the platform Archiveofourown.org (AO[3]):

> Jip landed with a rustle of brown feathers on the Ravenclaw table, and Arthur watched as Amelia extracted a roll of parchment from the creature's scaly grip. Probably just a petty love note from one of her admirers, he decided, and lost interest, his gaze wandering once again. This time, his eyes landed on a handsome seventh year Slytherin sat a few seats away.
>
> The seventh year winked at him, and Arthur looked away sharply, feeling, to his dismay, heat rushing to his cheeks. Dear god, wasn't that sort of behaviour a little too risky in public?
>
> kairoses, 'Veritaserum: A Hogwarts AU'[1]

The writer, kairoses, has created an open-ended two-chapter crossover piece set in J. K. Rowling's *Harry Potter* universe (1997–2007), which introduces characters from Dickens's novels as students and teachers at Hogwarts. Dickens's characters are mediated through their adapted use in the BBC series *Dickensian* (2015–16).[2] 'Veritaserum: A Hogwarts AU' does not announce its Dickens connection in the title, but it does list *Dickensian* in its search metadata, while the writer's profile includes a link to their Tumblr site dedicated to the series.[3] The conjunction of *Dickensian* and *Harry Potter* in the same piece is known as a 'crossover', in which characters from different fandoms interact with one another or enter the 'universe' or 'world' of another fandom. The writer has called the piece an 'AU' (alternative universe) for Hogwarts; in fact, it is an alternative universe for characters from *Dickensian* since they are placed in a different setting. Further enhancing the crossover element of this fiction is the fact that *Dickensian* itself is already an alternative universe (and crossover) for the Dickens characters within it.

The reuse and transposition of Dickens's characters from their respective novels to *Dickensian*, and then from *Dickensian* to Hogwarts, is indicative of the intermingled cultural memory practices at play in the online fanfiction community.[4] The barriers between established roles of author and reader set up by commercial publication are torn down in fanfiction. The readers have become writers just as the text has become malleable. The practice of fanfiction writers revisiting characters, settings and scenes contributes to the survival of various fandoms after their source material has ceased developing; by this I mean that numerous fanfiction writers revisit source material for new fanfiction and that sometimes the same source material is used for multiple standalone pieces by a single fan author.[5] This repetition is also at play in the social and written interactions of the fanfiction community. Interactivity (or communality) between text/user/community is the foundation of this study of Dickens in fanfiction. While standalone terms themselves, I list interactivity alongside communality. Interactivity alone implies a mutual exchange; by adding the idea of communality, the sense of a nonbinary relationship is included in these interactions.

I will explore three prominent internet platforms for fanfiction: Archive of Our Own (AO[3]), Fanfiction.net and Wattpad. After providing a brief overview of the first 100 works on each of these sites tagged with the metadata 'Dickens', I will examine several works in detail and look at how the communal response to Dickens's works in digital fanfiction has unconsciously addressed debate surrounding Dickens's 'place' within contemporary culture. Juliet John and others have indicated that digital Dickens projects in the recent past have failed to reach a popular mass audience much beyond that of academia unless those projects have had large budgets or connections to established media.[6] Yet while the relative anonymity of fanfiction sites makes it difficult to definitively ascertain the audiences for, and reach of, Dickens fanfiction across these three platforms, the variety of ways in which Dickens's work has been appropriated into fanfiction – especially via crossovers with popular film, television and celebrity fandoms – is a modern and developing way of addressing the idea of Dickens in popular arts.

It is important to note here that this chapter will examine Dickensian fandom only in terms of digital fanfiction. As Rebecca Williams notes, while fanfiction is 'undoubtedly a vibrant and fascinating aspect of fandom, it is important not to allow it to become a synonym for fan culture as a whole'.[7] The interactivity and user-created content of fanfiction varies in style and output from the interactivity of Dickens-focused social groups like the Dickens Fellowship, and again from the role-playing cosplay of Dickens Festivals.[8] Although it is beyond the scope of the present chapter, the similarities and distinctions between these various fan cultures are deserving of much wider consideration.

Repetition

In studying the use of a deceased author's texts, one might argue that the relationship between reader and text is unidirectional: while readers can interact with Dickens's text, he cannot respond or react in turn. In the use of Dickens's works, we find what Williams calls post-object fandom: 'when a fan object moves from being ongoing to dormant, yielding no new instalments.'[9] Unlike television series or more recent fandoms, Dickens has and always will be post-object. The continued interest in Dickens partly depends upon the repetition of his works in cultural memory. The now meme-like nature of Dickens's characters and plots allows fanfiction writers to build upon source material without needing to give their readers background knowledge.[10] As Rebecca Ward Black notes:

> Having a pre-existing setting or cast of characters to choose from makes it easier to focus on developing elements of the plot, and vice versa. In addition, if spelling and grammatical errors are significant enough to impede comprehension, readers can still follow the plot if they are somewhat familiar with the original media productions.[11]

Ward Black's discussion focuses on the value of fanfiction in literacy studies, but its pertinence lies in the usefulness of Dickens's cultural fame to fanfiction writers. While individual fandoms can rely on a certain amount of background knowledge, Dickens is all the more useful because of the awareness of his characters and stories in mass cultural memory. One does not need to identify as a fan to know the basic story of *A Christmas Carol* (1843) or identify characters such as Fagin. Indeed, Dickens's characters and stories appear so often in crossovers because they are familiar enough to require little or no exposition.

In the initial author's notes for 'Veritaserum', kairoses writes that the story will 'loosely follow the canon plot', designating *Dickensian* and not *Harry Potter* as the primary source. Several of the changes to Dickens's texts made by *Dickensian* are maintained in this AU; Miss Havisham's first name is Amelia, Arthur Havisham is gay and falling in love with Compeyson, and Jip belongs to Miss Havisham (this time appearing as an owl instead of a dog). However, knowledge of the differences between the BBC series and the Dickens novels is not necessary in order to follow the fanfiction; it is enough that one recognises the characters and can anticipate the heartbreak of Miss Havisham and the death of Jacob Marley. Details from Dickens's stories that *Dickensian* relies on in expanding the prequels of Miss Havisham, Nancy and Bill Sikes are also assumed in 'Veritaserum'. In fact, kairoses uses a ghost called Charles to hint at the fates of these three characters. Undoubtedly meant to be Charles Dickens, the ghost haunting the 'hall of prophets' tells Nancy: 'No hope, no hope, [. . .] Not for him, not for you.' Charles the ghost also hints at Miss Havisham's end when she asks after her fate. The fanfiction has been left incomplete and so we do not know if the prophecy of the authorial figure will be carried out as originally planned or if kairoses will subvert our expectations. In fact, though the ghost of Charles hints at bad endings for these three characters, he does not explicitly tell them or the fanfiction reader the details, thus avoiding spoilers if there are any readers unfamiliar with the characters. This simultaneously relies upon the reader's cultural memory of established characters to foreshadow the fanfiction while still leaving enough mystery intact to entice the fanfiction reader to continue reading. Significantly, Charles is given a prophetic role in the characters' lives yet is left unable to physically dictate authorial control. While some fanfiction rewrites endings and subverts established characterisations (as in gender-swapping stories or slash fiction), others rely on those already established to carry their story and indeed foster continued interest.[12]

Increasing familiarity with various metatextual elements of a story or character can create what Paul Davis defines as a 'culture-text'. In his discussion of *A Christmas Carol*, Davis explains that repeated elements of the story and characters within popular culture creates a shared cultural memory external to the original text. Davis explains:

> The text, *A Christmas Carol*, is fixed in Dickens's words, but the culture-text, the Carol as it has been re-created in the century and a half since it first appeared, changed as the reasons for its retelling change. We are still creating the culture-text of the Carol.[13]

A text becomes a culture-text when elements of it are repeated often enough to engrain it into cultural memory. As the Dickens text most adapted for the screen, it is unsurprising that *Carol* holds a prominent place in Dickens fanfiction, due to its existence in cultural memory. As illustrated in Table 4.1, *Carol* was the most referenced and reused of Dickens's novels in each of the three websites I examined. While this study of 300 works total was by no means exhaustive, since there were many more listings on each of the three sites, it indicates a general preference for Dickens's ubiquitous Christmas story.[14]

Table 4.1: Frequency of reference to and use of particular Dickens stories. Data was taken from the first 100 stories using the metadata 'Dickens' on AO[3], Fanfiction.net and Wattpad on 28 September 2018.

	AO[3]	Fanfiction.net	Wattpad	Total
A Christmas Carol	30	72	63	165
Great Expectations	22	6	16	44
A Tale of Two Cities	6	4	7	17
Nicholas Nickleby	10	0	0	10
Oliver Twist	4	1	4	9
David Copperfield	8	0	1	9
Bleak House	7	0	0	7
Other Dickens story	4	4	2	10
Dickens himself/use of his style	9	13	7	29

In contrast to the use of established characters to drive narrative in fanfiction, the use of *Carol* primarily centres on reshaping the plot to fit other fandom and pop culture figures. In these stories, it is the narrative structure, not the individual characters, which is repeated. The simplified narrative structural repetition of [protagonist] + [ghosts/spirits] = [life lesson] is used across a variety of fandoms. On Fanfiction.net alone, an adapted three-stave carol format (as opposed to Dickens's original five-stave novella) is used on characters from: television shows *Big Bang Theory*, *Bonanza*, *Supernatural*, *Lost*, *Hollyoaks* and *Law & Order: Special Victims Unit*; literary and film franchises such as *The Chronicles of Narnia*, *Twilight* and *Percy Jackson*; and even pop culture figures such as The Beatles. Ultimately, this use of *Carol* to facilitate other fandoms is indicative of John's suggestion that 'when people respond to Dickens today, they are responding not just to Dickens's texts but to a sense of a Dickens world which has been built up over time and across media'.[15]

While the use of *Carol* in fanfiction, particularly in crossovers, indicates its prominence in cultural memory, Dickens's characters in general are also useful to many fanfiction writers. Whether a writer wants to give Estella a first-person narrative about being Miss Havisham's instrument of revenge in *Great Expectations* or tell the tale of Em'ly and Steerforth's failed elopement in *David Copperfield* (1849–50), Dickens's established characters are perfect bases from which fanfiction writers can extend Dickens's stories.[16] In fanfiction terminology, this practice is called filling in the blanks (FIB). Unlike prequel or sequel writing, fanfiction that fills in the blanks usually takes place during the timeline of the original source but expands scenes or plots not covered directly. Filling in the blanks also develops minor characters or addresses relationships that are hinted at, but not overtly narrated, in the source. Given Dickens's vast array of minor characters, his source material is rich for FIB stories.

Dickens's existence in fanfiction enacts a feedback loop of cultural memory; his work is reread and adapted because we continue to reread and adapt it. This circular use/reuse/memory relationship is explained by David Brewer, who argues that literary 'characters came to seem more socially canonical and desirable as they came to seem more common and used by all, which in turn enhanced their value and publicity that much more'.[17] Repetition of a work or character itself creates extra-original context and subsequent repetition begins to create a 'boundless user-driven archive of material to be repurposed and refashioned to suit the tastes of its users'.[18] While any fan-created content can contribute to the post-original text, it is the novel art of fanfiction that adopts the most traditional repurposing of literature, by using text. Abigail Derecho writes about fanfiction as naturally archontic, or driven to develop into an archive, and indeed fundamentally driven by the archontic principle. She begins by explaining the term's origins in Derrida, noting 'the internal drive of an archive to continually expand' and arguing that the archive is never closed because of this drive.[19] Fan reactions and subsequent fan productions expand on the archive. As Francesca Coppa explains:

> The existence of fanfiction postulates that characters are able to 'walk' not only from one artwork into another, but from one genre into another, fanfiction articulates that characters are neither constructed or owned [and have] a life of their own not dependent on any original 'truth' or 'source'.[20]

Archontic texts, whether fan-produced or authorised, work in tandem with the 'original' or source to create the archive of the text, and it is in this dialogue that we find cultural memory. Deborah Kaplan explains, 'cumulatively, these formal and informal analyses come together to inform a community understanding of character in the source text'.[21] In other words, the analysis of character in source and archontic texts is not even a unidirectional conversation; rather, interpreting how readers have appropriated and remembered characters in fanfiction can help to better inform the original source.

As students at Hogwarts, kairoses places each Dickens character into a Hogwarts house – Gryffindor, Hufflepuff, Ravenclaw and Slytherin. The author makes a point of telling the reader which house each character is in by mentioning common rooms and house stereotypes. The assumption here is that the reader already knows about the qualities of each Hogwarts house. Thus, by remediating Dickens's characters through readers' background knowledge of Hogwarts, another level of characterisation is given to the original source. In *Dickens and Mass Culture* (2010), John writes of the 'portability' of Dickens:

> A distinctive feature of Dickens's mass cultural impact is his 'portability', the ability of his novels and indeed his image, even during his lifetime, to travel across various media and national boundaries, and after his death, across historical periods.[22]

It is because of this portability that Dickens sits so well in various fanfiction genres. Kaplan writes about this kind of textual reinterpretation: 'A large part of the fannish [*sic*] experience lies in analysing the source texts of fandom. Fans interpret these texts through discussion and formal analysis, but also through the creative act of writing fanfiction.'[23] By placing the two 'worlds' together, the writer is unconsciously or consciously analysing both in terms of one another. What if Dickens's world had magic? What was Hogwarts like in the 1800s? Both of these questions have possible solutions played out in narrative using recognisable characters and pre-established plot points.

The 'What if?' principle is a common starting point for much fanfiction and 'asking the question both unmakes one story and makes a new one possible'.[24] This new archontic knowledge works not only to reinforce background knowledge but also to subvert it. An ongoing piece on Wattpad, 'In the Land of Dickens', has Dickens's characters cohabiting one world much like *Dickensian* but with no reference to the BBC production. Indeed, while using Dickens's established characters, writer LaurenlJohnson changes much more about their source plots than *Dickensian* did. In her opening author's note, LaurenlJohnson verbalises the often-cited impetus for fanfiction, 'What if?':

> The world of Dickens is a place where nothing is impossible and everything can get a little crazy. What if Fagin wanted a better life? What if Bill Sykes [*sic*] had a soft side? What if Betsey Trotwood had a secret past? What is life like for Oliver as an adult? Life in the land of Dickens will never be the same again . . .[25]

This fanfiction writer uses the reader's established cultural memory as a foil for new characterisations. LaurenlJohnson comments on Dickens's originals by subverting their source characterisations: Bill Sykes has a 'soft' side and Oliver grows up. Expansion or reversal of the source material enables readers to discover something new about the characters. One possibility we discover is that, if Sykes was kinder to Nancy, perhaps they might have had a child together. In the ten published parts, LaurenlJohnson continues in this vein, including some plots paraphrased from the source text, writing other scenes that closely resemble Dickens's but changing some of the characters involved, and creating some entirely new episodes. When a reformed Sykes is officially hanged in part ten of 'In the Land of Dickens', the reader feels grief; in contrast, when Dickens's Sikes is accidentally hanged, the reader feels it is reparation for Nancy's gruesome murder (Nancy dies in childbirth in the Wattpad fanfiction). While the outcome for the two characters is ultimately the same, the interpretation of the characters in the original versus the fanfiction provokes different emotions in the readers.

While repetition is a vital reason why Dickens exists in cultural memory, it is not the direct replication of texts but rather the revisiting, reuse and reinterpretation of characters and stories that sees the original persist. As Karen Hellekson and Kristina Busse suggest, 'Rather than privileging a particular interpretation as accurate, we have learned from fandom that alternative and competing readings can and must coexist.'[26] Dickens exists in fanfiction because of various forms of repetition. Dickens, and indeed any fandom, is kept dynamic in cultural memory because of a community of users and the communality in fanfiction.

Interaction

When introducing the participatory nature of new media, Eggo Müller discusses how digital spaces have traversed the traditional roles of producers and consumers, 'to create empowering forms of communication and cultural participation'.[27] Fanfiction provides an interactive space that allows readers to assume the role of author and adjust the source text(s) to fit within their sphere of knowledge and/or interest. Within fanfiction, many levels of interaction create ever-expanding communal texts that are constantly reinformed by other fandoms, fanfiction writers and readers. These interactions change how we can view the original text as a static or complete text and turn 'the text into an event, not an art object'.[28] Rather than relying on solely the interpretation of the viewer, as in an art object, the continual interactions of both texts and producers (writers and readers) in fanfiction creates an ever-evolving event; fanfiction as an art form refuses to remain static even when based on post-object fandoms. In this section, I will explore the interaction between fanfiction writer and source text and how the interactions between fanfiction readers and writers create communal spaces which inform the cultural memory of the source.

The communal nature of reading and writing in fanfiction platforms subvert the outdated model of the omniscient author versus passive reader.[29] While fanfictions do have a posted author, and some do choose to note their implied copyright over their own original characters or the work itself, a sense of shared authorship is still implied on most platforms where commenting, reviewing, beta reading and requests for further instalments are encouraged. This shared authorship, whether it is between two or more fanfiction writers, fanfiction writer(s) and the source writer(s), or writer(s) and reader(s), creates a sense of communal ownership of the fandom and a shared responsibility in its longevity and/or demise. It is important to note here the legal implications of the term 'ownership' especially as it pertains to fanfiction – an art form that has long had murky relationships with copyright. In the case of Dickens's original work and other classic literary sources, the original text may be in the public domain: this means that the work is free for use/reuse/adaptation. In a legal sense, Dickens does 'belong' to the public. However, as we have seen, much Dickens fanfiction also references other media uses of Dickens which are not in the public domain.

With the proliferation of fanfiction and the increasing sophistication of fanfiction internet databases, authors of certain popular fandoms have had to answer questions about their position on fanfiction. Some published authors, such as Anne Rice and Diana Gabaldon, have statements on their websites regarding their policy against fanfiction.[30] Anne Rice is vehement: 'I do not allow fan fiction. The characters are copyrighted. It upsets me terribly to even think about fan fiction with my characters.'[31] Other writers approve of fanfiction and even admit to writing it, like Meg Cabot, but often ask that fanfiction writers acknowledge the source author.[32]

Dickens himself was vocal against those who pirated his works for financial gain. Addressing those who published serial piracies alongside his works in progress, Dickens stated to a friend:

> My general objection to the adaptation of any unfinished work of mine simply is, that being badly done and worse acted it tends to vulgarize the characters, to destroy or weaken in the minds of those who see them the impressions

I have endeavoured to create, and consequently to lessen the after-interest in their progress.[33]

Dickens was worried that the nature of serial publication would leave readers and pirates with avenues for expansion between each instalment and more particularly that these expansions would not be in line with his own plan for the plot or would alter the characters.[34] Dickens goes so far as to call plagiarisms of *The Pickwick Papers* (1836–7) 'libels' in *Master Humphrey's Clock* (1840–1) – itself a crossover, which reintroduced the characters of Pickwick and Weller – with the eponymous Master Humphrey noting that 'I condoled with [Samuel Pickwick] upon the various libels on his character which had found their way to print'.[35] The serial nature of Dickens's style of publication, while encouraging readers to revisit the story monthly (or weekly), displays the very same fluidity which governs many fanfiction writers. While Dickens abhorred the idea of unauthorised interaction with his text at all, let alone while the story was unfinished, fanfiction writers often post stories serially, actively encouraging reader response by inviting followers to post reviews and comments on each instalment, and sometimes letting the fans decide whether the story will continue at all. Fanfiction readers are thus given agency in the perpetuation of the story which re-enforces the interactivity of fanfiction. Hellekson and Busse observe the symbolic and empirical importance of 'work in progress' to fan communities:

> The source texts in many cases are serial, in progress, and constantly changing, as are the fan stories set in these universes. Fans' understanding of the characters and the universe the characters inhabit changes, just as scholarly understandings of fans and their relationship to one another, to the source text, and to the texts they generate is constantly being revised and rewritten.[36]

Not only is the work of fanfiction constantly being reinterpreted through the serialised nature of many sources of fandom (television shows, film series, etc.) but the relationships of fans to their source text is itself often a product of this serialisation. Fanfiction's ongoing interaction with iconic Dickens texts and characters creates a new serial relationship, one without end. John Kucich links Dickens's serial publishing with the success of his works, noting that:

> one effect of this form of publication was to intertwine the twists and turns of his plots with the rhythms of his readers' lives over a period of eighteen months, which did much to promote a sense of 'living with his characters'.[37]

Sarah Winter agrees: 'Numerous Victorian readers described their affectionate attachment to Dickens's novels and companionable friendship for Dickens's characters as personal ties developed through repeated readings and revisited in fond remembrance in later life.'[38] The regular publication of Dickens meant that not only were readers connected to his characters while they were reading, but the repeated revisiting of the same characters over that time period also created a meme-like associational memory. Winter writes about the contribution of associational memory to the overall cultural memory of Dickens:

People tend to care about and retain associations with fictional characters and plots that have unfolded in serial formats over time; these meanings associated with serial media become embedded in recollections of other significant events, both individual and collective, not just because of their significance to the individual but because of their capacity for accruing a shared cultural relevance over time.[39]

This 'shared cultural relevance' is seen in fanfiction crossovers and in Dickens fanfiction that draws upon Dickens's original texts and commercially produced adaptations for film and television.

A piece in AO[3] titled 'In the Quiet' by Rosa_Cotton is a fanfiction about the romance between Arthur Clennam and Amy Dorrit. In the author's notes, the author indicates that the story is inspired by both the original novel and the 2009 BBC adaptation of *Little Dorrit*. This work proves the influence of Dickensian cultural memory on fanfiction by using elements of the television serial as well as the book. The fanfiction is only six scenes covering the relationship between Arthur and Amy. One scene highlights the intimate moment when Arthur carries an unconscious Amy from her room in the Marshalsea to the awaiting carriage. The novel does not describe Arthur finding Amy and instead highlights how Amy is forgotten by her family. In contrast, the 2009 BBC adaptation brings the viewer into the scene in Amy's bedroom. 'In the Quiet' goes further into the relationship between the two characters and allows Arthur a moment to say goodbye which the other two versions do not; 'Pausing an instant before walking out into the daylight, he whispers, "Good bye, Amy," and kisses her.'[40] The fanfiction borrows from both previous versions by incrementally giving prominence to the Arthur/Amy storyline.

Another example of a fanfiction piece drawing upon multiple sources is 'An Eraman Christmas Carol', in which Dickens's story is retold as a crossover with the musical *Cats* (1981), while also using songs from *The Muppet Christmas Carol* (1992). This multi-crossover indicates the prominence of *Carol*'s adaptations in popular culture; the author, Eraman, writes in the author's note, 'Okay after watching a Muppet Christmas Carol [*sic*] this idea popped into my head.'[41] While Eraman, like many fanfiction authors, also gives an obligatory copyright disclaimer, the fact that the author has used their name in the title of the fanfiction means that not only are they borrowing from three established works but are also noting their own authorship status. Echoing Barthes's theory of the death of the author, Henry Jenkins writes of the audience's interpretative power to shape popular culture:

> Once television characters enter into a broader circulation, intrude into our living rooms, pervade the fabric of our society, they belong to their audiences and not simply to the artists who originated them.[42]

Fan studies is increasingly acknowledging communal ownership and resisting labels of 'infringement' and 'piracy'. Eraman's work indicates this shared ownership within fan culture. Outside of fan culture, however, it is this very sense of sharing against which many published authors protest. George R. R. Martin's vocal stance against fanfiction speaks of his need to retain control over the source material: 'I decide who gets to borrow my creations, and I review their stories, and approve or disapproval [*sic*] what is done with them. [. . .] No one gets to abuse the people of Westeros but me.'[43]

Legally, fanfiction is still lost in the 'grey area' of copyright law. Providing that no-one benefits economically from its writing and its online publication, fanfiction most often falls under the Fair Dealing exception to UK copyright law (Fair Use Doctrine in the United States of America). Both uphold the right to write transformative works if there is not economic infringement on the copyright holder. However, both also acknowledge that the law is not binding for every case; the UK governance states 'The relative importance of any one factor will vary according to the case in hand and the type of dealing in question.'[44] The US doctrine, while much more detailed in its definition of 'transformative', also points out that 'Courts evaluate fair use claims on a case-by-case basis'.[45] With the vast amount of fanfiction published and read on internet platforms, fanfiction writers legally rely on the impossibility of courts pursuing every work on a case-by-case basis. Indeed, the community of fanfiction writers creates a sort of strength-in-numbers which overwhelms copyright law.[46]

The writing and publication of fanfiction based on established media characters adds an additional level of authorship to the original author.[47] Thus, what we have is the primary author (original) and the secondary author (fanfiction writer). These levels can be extended when the fanfiction is based on another adaptation (or indeed another fanfiction). In 'Veritaserum', Dickens is a primary author, J. K. Rowling is another primary author, the writers of *Dickensian* are secondary authors, and kairoses is a tertiary author. The fanfiction work is impossible without this interaction between authors. This multi-level shared authorship is directly addressed in the practice of writing and posting author's notes (A/N) at the beginning or end (and occasionally the middle) of a fanfiction. Alexandra Herzog addressed A/Ns as a negotiation of authorial power in fanfiction. As Herzog explains, A/Ns function to both proclaim the authorial power of the fanfiction writer and fan community at large, at the same time as acknowledging the symbolic power of the author over the reader, often by dictating to the reader how the fanfiction is meant to be read.[48]

Fanfiction is often posted in stages, or chapter by chapter. This serialisation allows the readers to comment on, ask questions, praise or critique the fanfiction as it is being posted and often while it is being written. Sometimes, writers wait for feedback to write or post more of a story, waiting until they have a readership for the fanfiction. Louise Geddes and Valerie Fazel write: 'For the fanfic author, the communal aspect of the creative process is crucial.'[49] Fanfiction writers will sometimes address their readers with copyright remarks or disclaimers about literary and/or historical accuracy. Fanfiction writers will directly acknowledge the community in A/Ns, and the community can respond, often quickly, through commenting and messaging. Herzog writes of this shared agency that 'writers reach out to their audience and vice versa, understanding fan fiction to be a dialogic genre based on the integration of a vast variety of fannish voices'.[50]

Sometimes A/Ns address the fanfiction author's frustration with the writing process, a frustration not often addressed by more traditional authorial silence present in publishing completed books. By addressing these frustrations, the fanfiction author is inviting the readers into the immediacy of the writing process and including them by asking for their help, critiques or leniency in review. Before the second chapter of 'Veritaserum', kairoses posts a note about their frustration while writing this chapter:

Sorry about the long wait for the update! I rewrote this chapter quite a few times because it wasn't really working, and although I'm still not fully happy with it, I really want to continue with the story, so here it is!

The writer is inviting the reader into the working space; we are able to read the chapter, knowing that the writer reworked it a number of times and is still not satisfied. Some of this prologue is asking the readers their opinions on the outcome of the chapter. In stating this disclaimer, kairoses is also reiterating their amateur status. They are reminding the reader that this fanfiction is not a professional work; it is not professionally written, edited or published. This sharing of an unfinished work is similar to the collaborative editing space of a writers' workshop: 'fan authors assume an interactive dialogic learning space where they are able to communicate with and receive almost immediate response from readers via the internet.'[51]

The comments section, given either at the end of each chapter or the end of the work, is a space for readers to respond to the fanfiction writer. In the generally supportive atmosphere of fanfiction websites, emotive responses are the most common type of comment. For works in progress or unfinished works, readers often ask for further instalments in the comments section. In response to the first chapter of 'Veritaserum', RedDaisies wrote, 'Wonderfully done and perfect characterisation! Combined two of my favourite things into one masterpiece. I look forward to seeing what mischief my faves get up to :).'[52] The reader not only comments on the writing technique, 'perfect characterisation', but also applauds the fandom crossover and indicates that they will be waiting for more instalments. In this series of eleven comments for Chapter One, four were posted by readers on the same day that the chapter was posted on AO[3], and four are responses to those initial four readers by the author also on the same day. This time-stamping indicates the almost immediate interaction between author and reader on the site.

The interaction between reader and writer also affects the direction of the story. While the writer is not beholden to any suggestions from readers, particular interest from readers might shape the fanfiction. For example, two commenters on Chapter One of 'Veritaserum' note concern for the fate of the owl, Jip, given that, in the original, Jip the dog dies (while Jip dies in different ways in *Dickensian* and *David Copperfield*, his ultimate fate is still the same). In the fanfiction, Jip is mentioned only twice at the beginning, one reader comments, 'Slightly worried for Jip the owl considering the dog fate in the tv show', and another asks the writer, 'Please maybe let Jip live this time? Please? For me?'[53] This second comment is particularly interesting given the similar pleas from fans that Dickens received about Little Nell's fate in *The Old Curiosity Shop* (1840–1). In a letter to his publishers, Chapman and Hall, Dickens wrote, 'I am inundated with imploring letters recommending poor little Nell to mercy. —Six yesterday, and four today (it's not 12 o'clock yet) already!'[54]

The comments from readers on fanfiction sites are generally supportive and constructive. Because the realm of fanfiction is fairly insular,[55] these communities tend to be affirmative spaces. Ward Black talks of fanfiction platforms as 'affinity spaces' where 'people interact and relate to each other around a common passion, proclivity, or endeavor'.[56] One reason that comments and reviews are generally positive and constructive is that 'there is a wide range of valued expertise and forms of knowledge' and 'roles of "expert" and "naïve" are highly variable and contingent on activity and

58 MAUREEN ENGLAND

context'.[57] The online communities of fanfiction are filled with anonymous diverse audiences, with 'a range of ages, locations, socioeconomic groups, education levels, and linguistic backgrounds'.[58] These diverse groups of fans bond over their shared interest in a fandom and that same shared interest leads towards constructive feedback. This interaction between fans is, as John Fiske argues, sometimes more important than the fandom itself:

> Indeed, much of the pleasure of fandom lies in the fan talk that it produces, and many fans report that their choice of their object of fandom was determined at least as much by the oral community they wished to join as much by any of its inherent characteristics.[59]

Within the communality of fanfiction, readers and writers 'cease to be simply an audience for popular texts' which statically receives; friendships are formed, and analysis of source texts leads to a sharing of ideas and background which would not have happened had it not been for the fandom community.[60]

In one comment thread attached to a piece of *Dickensian* fanfiction, readers and the fanfiction writer discuss a slash relationship between Mr Jaggers and Amelia Havisham. The single chapter 'A Better Shape' by Verecunda is an alternative ending to the series and *Great Expectations* and begins with an author's note:

> A/N: I've just finished rewatching Dickensian, and I decided to give Amelia a happy ending. Because she deserved better.
>
> Disclaimer: This is fanfic of Dickens fanfic, so I own nothing, but I hope Charlie D. will forgive me for pinching some of his words for my own nefarious purposes.[61]

The author describes *Dickensian* as a work of fanfiction and is driven by the need to 'fix' Amelia's ending. This need is shared by the readers in the comments; TheMalhamBird writes, 'yes yes, this is excellent and also exactly how it happened :)',[62] and Verecunda replies, 'And yeah, this is obviously what happened. Don't listen to that Charlie Dickens, he doesn't know what he's talking about. :P.'[63] Through discussion, the fans decide that the fanfiction is the preferred ending and joke about their ending being the 'real' one. One reader, who admits to not knowing *Dickensian* or *Great Expectations* well, explains:

> And indeed, thank God for AUs, and canon divergence. I love missing scenes and what ifs too, but this fix-it story fixes everything for me just the way I like it and from now on this is the only ending I'll be happy with. I guess I could say, headcanon accepted![64]

When reader flowerdeluce uses the phrase 'headcanon accepted', they are telling the writer that they are accepting the fanfiction's interpretation of Jaggers's and Havisham's relationship as canonical. By saying this, the reader is also indicating that, should they write about Jaggers and Amelia, flowerdeluce will incorporate the romance into the new fanfiction. Collectively developing new endings from which characters can begin new lives is a way of extending a source text beyond its initial form. If, like both *Dickensian* and Dickens's works, that source is a post-object fandom, the continued writing and reading of fanfiction is a way to keep the fandom alive. By creating entirely new 'canon' paths for characters to explore, fanfiction writers and readers are moving the text beyond the interpretative.

When Dickens's texts were originally published, reading his stories often became a social act; they 'created a field of discourse, a common ground for communication. It was a source of shared symbols, images and phrases, a melodramatic meeting ground for social sentiment'.[65] This community is now reflected in fanfiction as an art form on the internet. Since their publication, the repetition of Dickens's stories and characters in adaptations, pirated versions and now fanfiction has led to a rich and continually adaptable life for Dickens's work in cultural memory. Even in digital fanfiction, readers and writers interact with one another to develop Dickens's stories and characters, leaving Dickens's place in this modern art form anything but static.

Cultural Memory

From George H. Lewes in 1872, to F. R. Leavis and Q. D. Leavis in 1970, to this very volume, perceptions of Dickens's literary standing have changed over time.[66] This debate resonates in interesting ways in discussions of the cultural value of fanfiction. The continued alignment of fanfiction with 'stealing' and copyright infringement has encouraged the assumption that all fanfiction is poorly written and far from a legitimate art form. Instead of the democratic notion of shared authorship within the fanfiction community, commercial producers have often labelled fanfiction writers as 'thieves' or 'pirates'. In a since deleted blog post, author Diana Gabaldon calls fanfiction 'immoral'.[67] Despite a thriving community on many websites and mobile applications, fanfiction is still considered to be 'other'.

What initially drove F. R. Leavis to exclude Dickens from *The Great Tradition* (1948) was 'Dickens's commercialism and the tailoring of his work to the mass market'.[68] It is a similar harnessing of the popular that has lowered fanfiction in many estimations:

> the mass is alienated, anonymous and of lower value than privileged individual thinking and action. The mass has always been interpreted as dangerous and unstable, and always a group that is 'other' than the people labelling.[69]

The dichotomy of 'mass' and 'institutional' reflected in the quote above is one that is carried through in many discussions of the value of fanfiction and indeed can be seen in discussions of Dickens's 'value'. The use of the term 'Other' is also significant; despite its growing popularity, those writing about fans and fanfiction still fight against the perception of the fan as marginal and 'Other'. Herzog notes the early positioning of the fan as 'stereotypical lone other' and Jenkins wrote his seminal *Textual Poachers* using 'poachers' to describe this otherness or 'cultural marginality and social weakness'.[70]

Shortly after Dickens's death, Lewes wrote of Dickens that he 'delighted thousands, that his admirers were found in all classes, and in all countries; that he stirred the sympathy of the masses not easily reached through Literature'.[71] Lewes is indicating a division between the mass cultural appeal of Dickens and those 'reached through Literature'. Even though Lewes is celebrating the cross-social appeal of Dickens, he is also recognising that there is indeed a general division, one that might lead to the very position of 'otherness' that fanfiction and fan studies is continuing to battle.

The use of Dickens in digital fanfiction is antithetical to many perceptions of Dickens, and indeed perceptions of fanfiction and online fan culture. Jenkins proposes the beginnings of fanfiction in the 1980s and 1990s as an act of resistance against official means of production, 'seeking to influence the text where they may [. . .] but also claiming the right to retell the stories in their own terms'.[72] With the increased use of fanfiction in studies of adolescent literacy and the broadening of the scope of fandoms with social media and the internet, fandoms and fanfiction are beginning to shift from a niche subculture to a common literary practice.[73] As Kirsten Pullen argues, 'stereotypes of the fan as a fringe obsessive will give way to views of the fan as a typical Internet user.'[74]

The integration of now canonical literature with amateur fanfiction, in the case of Dickens, disrupts an assumed distinction between cultural significance and general popularity. As David Inglis suggests, 'particular works, and in fact whole genres, can change their cultural standing over time.'[75] We should consider how the very existence of this fanfiction can contribute to our understanding of literary art and the placement of canonical authors in popular and digital culture. Rather than dismissing Dickens as culturally dormant, fanfiction writers have sought to redefine Dickens in modern cultural terms. One look through fanfiction sites will see multiple stories exploring homosexual relationships in Dickens.[76] Dickens's art is being focalised through modern experience and cultural norms in fanfiction and is as significant to popular digital culture as nineteenth-century literature.

Though, in his early work, Jenkins placed the early days of fanfiction in the late twentieth century, as the field of fan studies has grown in reputation and scope, fanfiction is being acknowledged more and more as a novel art that is not 'novel' at all. David Brewer (2005) and Elizabeth F. Judge (2009) have explored characters transformed from their original source texts in the eighteenth century.[77] While still straddling the line between copyright infringement and fair use, fanfiction's value as a cultural lens through which to view canonical literature like Dickens is perhaps a more than appropriate way to study 'the great popular entertainer'.[78]

Notes

1. kairoses, 'Veritaserum: A Hogwarts AU', *Dickensian* and *Harry Potter* crossover fanfiction, *Archive of Our Own*, 11 April 2016 <archiveofourown.org/chapters/13496146> [accessed 23 September 2018]. This fanfiction was chosen before recent discussions about J. K. Rowling.
2. Developed by the writer Tony Jordan, *Dickensian* ran for twenty episodes over a period spanning 26 December 2015 to 21 February 2016. The concept brought together characters from different Dickens novels and expanded the backstories of several, including Miss Havisham (given the name Amelia) and her brother, Arthur.
3. Tumblr is a social media platform which enables users to post and repost content as well as interact with other users through comments, questions and sharing material.

4. Cultural memory speaks of a collective cultural consciousness and memory. It combines the ideas of community identity through cultural nostalgia with the interactivity of new media. Cultural memory implies both institutional support and popular culture.

5. The term 'fan' is assumed to be a shortening of the term 'fanatic', which was often used in reference to overenthusiastic devotees of a religion or sport, while 'fandom' has been traced back to 1903. *OED* online, 'fan' n2; 'fandom' n3.

6. See Juliet John, 'Crowdsourced Dickens', in *The Oxford Handbook of Charles Dickens*, ed. by John O. Jordan, Robert L. Patten and Catherine Waters (Oxford: Oxford University Press, 2018), 756–73; Ben Winyard, '"May We Meet Again": Rereading the Dickensian Serial in the Digital Age', *19: Interdisciplinary Studies in the Long Nineteenth Century* 21 (2015), 1–21 <http://doi.org/10.16995/ntn.737>; and Emma Curry's chapter in this volume.

7. Rebecca Williams, *Post-Object Fandom: Television, Identity and Self-Narrative* (New York: Bloomsbury, 2015), 189.

8. 'Cosplay' is the practice of fans dressing in costumes (often partly or entirely hand-made) as characters from particular fandoms. See Nicolle Lamerichs, 'Stranger than Fiction: Fan Identity in Cosplay', *Transformative Works and Cultures* 7 (2011) <dx.doi.org/10.3983/twc.2011.0246> and Paul Mountfort, Ann Peirson-Smith and Adam Geczy, *Planet Cosplay: Costume Play, Identity and Global Fandom* (Bristol: Intellect, 2019). For a look at literary fandoms, see Holly Luetkenhaus and Zoe Weinstein, *Austentatious: The Evolving World of Jane Austen Fans* (Iowa City: University of Iowa Press, 2019) and Maureen England, 'The Pickwick Club Minute Book', *The Charles Dickens Museum* website, 30 August 2017 <https://dickensmuseum.com/blogs/charles-dickens-museum/the-pickwick-club-minute-book-the-social-media-of-the-victorian-age> [accessed 1 April 2020].

9. Williams, 2.

10. The term 'meme' was coined by Richard Dawkins in *The Selfish Gene* (1976); a 'meme' is a noun which is culturally derived, repeated and imitated. When I propose that Dickens's characters are 'meme-like', I mean that they are repeated and reused until integrated into the culture of the time.

11. Rebecca Ward Black, 'Convergence and Divergence: Informal Learning in Online Fanfiction Communities and Formal Writing Pedagogy', in *Mirror Images: Popular Culture and Education*, ed. by Diana Silberman Keller, Zvi Bekerman, Henry A. Giroux and Nicholas C. Burbules (New York: Peter Lang, 2008), 125–43, 133.

12. Slash is a form of fanart, usually fanfiction, in which two (or more) characters are imagined in sexual or romantic scenarios. Historically, slash was a term used when the characters borrowed were two (originally conceived) heterosexual men, with femslash being the equal term for female/female pairings. For more on slash, see April S. Callis, 'Homophobia, Heteronormativity, and Slash Fan Fiction', *Transformative Works and Cultures* 22 (2016) <dx.doi.org/10.3983/twc.2016.0708> and *The Darker Side of Slash Fan Fiction: Essays on Power, Consent and the Body*, ed. by Ashton Spacey (Jefferson, NC: McFarland, 2018).

13. Paul Davis, 'Retelling *A Christmas Carol*: Text and Culture-Text', *The American Scholar* 59 (1990), 109–15, 110.

14. This study is by no means definitive as the selection was not exhaustive. The pieces were selected as the first 100 from each site using the search criterion 'Dickens' with the populated results listed by relevance (according to the website algorithm). A more exhaustive study would explore the difference, for example, in the number of *Nicholas Nickleby* (1838–9) fanfictions on AO[3] versus the absence of any on the other two platforms. This is most likely because of the interest in slash fiction on AO[3] and the homosocial bond between the characters of Nicholas and Smike. After *Carol*, *Great Expectations* (1860–1)

and *A Tale of Two Cities* (1859) are likely to be the next most used Dickens novels because these texts are commonly read in schools.

15. John, 'Crowdsourced Dickens', 767–8.
16. Saudade do coracao, 'Estella' fanfiction, *Archive of Our Own*, 12 April 2012, <https://archiveofourown.org/works/1072151> [accessed 23 September 2018]; Selena, 'Selkie Bride' fanfiction, *Fanfiction.net*, 1 January 2018, <https://www.fanfiction.net/s/12782983/1/Selkie-Bride> [accessed 23 September 2018].
17. David A. Brewer, *The Afterlife of Character, 1726–1825* (Philadelphia: University of Pennsylvania Press, 2005), 14.
18. Valerie Fazel and Louise Geddes, '"Give me your hands if we be friends": Collaborative Authority in Shakespeare Fanfiction', *Shakespeare* 12.3 (2016), 274–86, 275.
19. Abigail Derecho, 'Archontic Literature: A Definition, A History, and Several Theories of Fan Fiction', in *Fan Fiction and Fan Communities in the Age of the Internet*, ed. by Karen Helleksn and Kristina Busse (Jefferson: McFarland, 2006), 61–78, 64.
20. Francesca Coppa, 'Writing Bodies in Space: Media Fan Fiction as Theatrical Performance', in *Fan Fiction and Fan Communities*, 225–44, 230.
21. Deborah Kaplan, 'Construction of Fan Fiction Character through Narrative', in *Fan Fiction and Fan Communities*, 134–52, 137.
22. Juliet John, *Dickens and Mass Culture* (Oxford: Oxford University Press, 2010), 15.
23. Kaplan, 135.
24. Juli J. Parrish, 'Metaphors We Read By: People, Process, and Fan Fiction', *Transformative Works and Cultures* 14 (2013) <dx.doi.org/10.3983/twc.2013.0486>
25. LaurenIJohnson, 'In the Land of Dickens' Charles Dickens fanfiction, *Wattpad*, last updated 26 September 2018 <www.wattpad.com/story/113890474-in-the-land-of-dickens> [accessed 11 October 2018].
26. Karen Hellekson and Kristina Busse, 'Introduction', in *Fan Fiction and Fan Communities*, 5–33, 8.
27. Eggo Müller, 'Formatted Spaces of Participation: Interactive Television and the Changing Relationship between Production and Consumption', in *Digital Material: Tracing New Media in Everyday Life and Technology*, ed. by Marianne van den Boomen, Sybille Lammes, Ann-Sophie Lehmann, Joost Raessens and Mirko Tobias Schäfer (Amsterdam: Amsterdam University Press, 2009), 49–63, 49.
28. John Fiske, 'The Cultural Economy of Fandom', in *The Adoring Audience: Fan Cultures and Popular Media*, ed. by Lisa A. Lewis (London: Routledge, 1992), 30–49, 40.
29. Larger discussions of the nature of authorship and reader response and the role of the author in modern literary criticism are too vast for the scope of this chapter. For an introduction to authorship and reader-response, interested readers can refer to: Roland Barthes, 'The Death of the Author' (1968), Michel Foucault, 'What is an Author?' (1969) and Wolfgang Iser, *The Act of Reading* (1980).
30. Diana Gabaldon's statement can be found on her website: Diana Gabaldon, 'Diana's Fan Fiction Policy', *Diana Gabaldon* <http://www.dianagabaldon.com/misc/dianas-fan-fiction-policy> [accessed 10 January 2019].
31. Anne Rice, 'Important Message from Anne on "Fan Fiction"', *Anne Rice: The Official Site* < http://annerice.com/ReaderInteraction-MessagesToFans.html> [accessed 10 January 2019].
32. Cabot writes in her official statement on fanfiction on her website: 'I don't have any problem with people writing fan fiction based on my books [. . .] so long as they don't try to pass it off as an original work.' Mag Cabot, 'Fan Fiction', *Meg Cabot* <https://www.megcabot.com/2006/03/114184067156643148/> [accessed 10 January 2019].
33. 'To Frederick Yates, 29 November 1838', *The Letters of Charles Dickens*, ed. by Madeline House, Graham Storey et al., Pilgrim/ British Academy Edition, 12 vols (Oxford:

Clarendon Press, 1965–2002). Subsequent citations: *PLets* followed by volume (year of publication), page. Here I (1965), 463.

34. For more on piracies of Dickens's work, see Adam Abraham, 'Plagiarising Pickwick: Imitations of Immortality', *Dickens Quarterly* 32 (2015), 5–20 and Paul Schlicke, 'Dickens and the Pirates: The Case of the Odd Fellow', *Dickensian* 100 (2004), 224–5.

35. Charles Dickens, *Master Humphrey's Clock in Three Volumes* (London: Bradbury and Evans, 1840), I, 51.

36. Hellekson and Busse, 7.

37. John Kucich, 'Dickens', in *The Columbia History of the British Novel*, ed. by John Richetti (New York: Columbia University Press, 1994), 381–405, 395.

38. Sarah Winter, *The Pleasures of Memory: Learning to Read with Charles Dickens* (New York: Fordham University Press, 2011), 110.

39. Ibid., 327.

40. Rosa_Cotton, 'In the Quiet', *Archive of Our Own*, 29 December 2015 <https://archiveofourown.org/works/5573949> [accessed 1 October 2018].

41. Eraman, 'An Eraman Christmas Carol' author's note, *Fanfiction.net*, last updated 25 December 2011 <www.fanfiction.net/s/7604755/1/An-Eraman-Christmas-Carol> [accessed 1 October 2018].

42. Henry Jenkins, *Textual Poachers: Television Fans and Participatory Culture* (London: Routledge, 1992, repr. 2013), 279.

43. George R. R. Martin, 'Someone is Angry on the Internet', *Not A Blog* Livejournal, 7 May 2010 <https://grrm.livejournal.com/151914.html?page=3> [accessed 10 January 2019].

44. Intellectual Property Office, 'Fair Dealing', *Exceptions to Copyright* (18 November 2014) <www.gov.uk/guidance/exceptions-to-copyright#fair-dealing > [accessed 17 January 2019].

45. U.S. Copyright Office, 'More Information on Fair Use', *U.S. Copyright Office Fair Use Index* (December 2018) <https://www.copyright.gov/fair-use/more-info.html> [accessed 17 January 2019].

46. For more about fanfiction and copyright, see Aaron Schwabach, *Fan Fiction and Copyright: Outsider Works and Intellectual Property Protection* (Farnham: Ashgate, 2011).

47. For this particular work, I will include the use of real people as authors of themselves and their media personas as their 'character'. This is based on the assumption that the fanfiction author does not personally know the celebrity.

48. Alexandra Herzog, '"But this is my story and this is how I wanted to write it": Author's Notes as Fannish Claim to Power in Fan Fiction Writing', *Transformative Works and Cultures*, 11 (2012) <doi.org/10.3983/twc.2012.0406> 2.1.

49. Fazel and Geddes, 4.

50. Herzog, 4.10.

51. Ward Black, 135.

52. RedDaisies, 'Veritaserum' comment, 30 January 2016.

53. Havishamble, 'Veritaserum' comment, 30 January 2016. SecretAgentCodenameBob, 'Veritaserum' comment, 30 January 2016.

54. 'To Chapman and Hall, 24 November 1840', *PLets*, II (1969), 153.

55. Fiske notes this insularity in discussing the relationship between commercialism and fanfiction, suggesting that 'because fan texts are not produced for profit, they do not need to be mass-marketed, so unlike official culture, fan culture makes no attempt to circulate its texts outside its own community' (40).

56. Rebecca Black, 'Digital Design: English Language Learners and Reader Reviews in Online Fiction', in *A New Literacies Sampler*, ed. by Michele Knobel and Colin Lankshear (New York: Peter Lang, 2007), 116–36, 117.

57. Ibid.

58. Ibid., 138.
59. Fiske, 38.
60. Jenkins, 24.
61. Verecunda, 'A Better Shape', author's note, *Archive of Our Own*, last updated 19 June 2016 <https://archiveofourown.org/works/7239973> [accessed 1 October 2018].
62. TheMalhamBird, 'A Better Shape' comment, 1 October 2016.
63. Verecunda, 'A Better Shape' comment, 1 October 2016.
64. Flowerdeluce, 'A Better Shape' comment, 21 January 2017.
65. Robert McParland, *Charles Dickens's American Audience* (Plymouth, MA: Lexington Books, 2012), 6.
66. George Henry Lewes, 'Dickens in Relation to Criticism', in *The Dickens Critics*, ed. by George H. Ford and Lauriat Lane, Jr (Ithaca: Cornell University Press, 1966), 54–74, 54. F. R. Leavis and Q. D. Leavis, *Dickens the Novelist* (Harmondsworth: Penguin Books, [1970]; 1972).
67. Diana Gabaldon, quoted in 'Novelist Diana Gabaldon Causes Fanfic Furor', *Teleread* (5 May 2010) <https://teleread.com/novelist-diana-gabaldon-causes-fanfic-furor/index.html> [accessed 1 April 2020].
68. John, *Mass Culture*, 18.
69. P. David Marshall, *New Media Cultures* (London: Arnold, 2004), 7.
70. Herzog, 4.11. Jenkins, 26.
71. Lewes, 57.
72. Jenkins, xxi.
73. Kirsten Pullen argues that 'The World Wide Web has opened up the boundaries of fandom, allowing more people to participate in fan culture, and designating more television programmes, celebrities and films as worthy of fan activity.' See 'Everybody's Gotta Love Somebody, Sometime: Online Fan Community', in *Web.Studies*, ed. by David Gauntlett and Ross Horsley (London: Arnold, 2000, repr. 2004), 80–91, 80.
74. Ibid., 83.
75. David Inglis, *Culture and Everyday* (London: Routledge, 2005), 84.
76. The more commonly explored relationships are between Pip and Herbert in *Great Expectations*, David and Uriah Heep in *David Copperfield*, and Nicholas and Smike in *Nicholas Nickleby*. The majority of the slash fiction was found on AO[3].
77. See Brewer, *Afterlife*, and Elizabeth F. Judge, 'Kidnapped and Counterfeit Characters: Eighteenth-Century Fan Fiction, Copyright Law, and the Custody of Characters', in *Originality and Intellectual Property in the French and English Enlightenment*, ed. by Reginald McGinnis (London: Routledge, 2009) 22–68.
78. F. R. Leavis, *The Great Tradition* (New York: George W. Stewart, 1950), 228.

Further Reading

Kristina Busse, *Framing Fan Fiction: Literary and Social Practices in Fan Fiction Communities* (Iowa City: University of Iowa Press, 2017)

Kristina Busse and Karen Hellekson, eds, *Fan Fiction and Fan Communities in the Age of the Internet* (Jefferson: McFarland, 2006)

Matt Hill, *Fan Cultures* (London and New York: Routledge, 2002)

Henry Jenkins, *Textual Poachers: Television Fans and Participatory Culture: 20th Anniversary Edition* (London and New York: Routledge, 2013)

Sheenagh Pugh, *The Democratic Genre: Fan Fiction in a Literary Context* (Bridgend: Seren, 2005)

Part II
Theatre and Drama

5

CLOWNS

Jonathan Buckmaster

LEAR   Dost thou call me fool, boy?
FOOL   All thy other titles thou hast given away; that thou wast born with.
KENT   This is not altogether fool, my lord.

–William Shakespeare, *King Lear*, Act I, Scene 4[1]

THIS FOOL-LADEN EXCHANGE ENCAPSULATES TWO of clowning's governing tenets: first, that everyone is born as a potential fool and second that the clown's frivolous nonsense contains profound truths. On 25 January 1838 William Macready revived the Fool in his Covent Garden production of *King Lear*, after an absence of over 150 years. Charles Dickens was an enthusiastic spectator, describing Priscilla Horton's Fool as giving 'as exquisite a performance as the stage has ever boasted', and identifying the clown's broader function by noting that Lear's 'love for the Fool is associated with Cordelia'.[2] Fool's resurrection came less than a year after the death of Covent Garden's most famous clown, Joseph Grimaldi, with whom Dickens was similarly enraptured. In his introduction to Grimaldi's *Memoirs* (1838) – a text which represents an act of literary necromancy correspondent with Macready's – Dickens wrote of his 'strong veneration for Clowns' and 'the ten thousand million delights of the pantomime'.[3] These two acts – the Fool's return to *Lear* and the posthumous publication of *The Memoirs of Joseph Grimaldi* – emblematise Dickens's conviction that what clowns tell us should continue to be told, a conviction which engendered some of his most imaginative and comical writing.

Dickens's conception of the clown was rich and varied in its antecedents and forms, drawing on figures from medieval drama, *commedia dell'arte*, and folk spectacle, but the Shakespearean clown and Grimaldi's pantomime clown were the most influential. Shakespeare collaborated with his comic actors to utilise the clown in a variety of functions – for diverting physical comedy, plot or character development, or philosophical moralising, according to the play's needs and the individual personalities of his comic performers.[4] He fully integrated an initially peripheral figure into his dramaturgy, deepening his characterisation and narrative function until reaching an apotheosis with Falstaff. Grimaldi was the pre-eminent clown of the London pantomime from 1800 to 1823, allegedly seen by an eight-year-old Dickens in the twilight of his career.[5] Grimaldi's clown usurped the centrality of Harlequin, who was the stock figure of the cunning and dextrous servant-hero, and transformed the rustic simpleton duped by everyone into an urban trickster who dominated the harlequinade, that popular anarchic revue of physical comedy, tricks of construction, playful satire and vicarious assaults on authority.

However, believing that 'Clowns that beat Grimaldi all to nothing turn up every day!', Dickens extended the clown's stage beyond the prescribed boundaries of the theatre or circus ring into all aspects of life, embracing not just those who wear the greasepaint, but anyone who displays 'clownish' traits such as excessive consumption or a propensity for slapstick violence.[6] Instead, his characters temporarily become clowns to point out the follies of others, puncture social pretence, provide wish fulfilment, or act as scapegoat for the readers' own follies. Dickens's imaginative engagement with this figure from popular entertainment means that the clown becomes a persistent presence, and the offices that the clown performs represent central themes within his work.

Yet despite Dickens's repeated assertion that the ritualised separation of the clown from society is illusory, literary criticism has focused on Dickens's professional clowns, whose rictus grins barely mask the degraded performer lurking underneath. For Joseph Butwin, Dickens uses the clown to represent artistic and professional failure, while others trace a gradual diminution in the quality and quantity of clowns – for Edwin Eigner, Micawber's emigration also signals the departure of Dickens's clowns.[7] Attention to the artistic and commercial disappointment of Grimaldi's memoirs has prompted pessimistic readings of the lives of both biographer and subject that highlight the fatal consequences of their shared compulsion to perform to adoring yet demanding audiences, in contrast to which only a few positive appraisals have appeared.[8]

Critics also use the clown as a touchstone for the tone of a particular work, as denoted by particular types of laughter. George Bernard Shaw asks readers of *Hard Times* (1854) to 'bid adieu now to the lighthearted and only occasionally indignant Dickens of the earlier books' as he is in 'passionate revolt against the whole industrial order of the modern world'.[9] While he may have cast off 'all restraint on his wild sense of humor', it is not for 'fun' – by *Little Dorrit* (1855–7), 'the fun was no fun to Dickens: the truth was too bitter'.[10] Instead, this unbounded laughter is felt to shock the laugher into a change of attitude, akin to Theodor Adorno's critical laughter that acts 'violently against reified structures' and acts as a bulwark to an 'uncritical use of laughter that simply concretizes social repression'.[11]

But closer examination reveals more complex patterns, and Dickens's imaginative engagements with the clown blended the carefree laughter with the scornful. Jacky Bratton and Ann Featherstone note how the clown's role 'is confined within the relatively stable, predictable relationships with the audience and the dramatist', and a number of universal features of clowning have been proposed.[12] In this chapter I will explore four interrelated tropes which are the most significant within Dickens's work: identity; patterned behaviour; magic; and the outcast.

Identity

[. . .] the portrait of Signor Jacksonini the clown, saying 'How do you do to-morrow?' quite as large as life, and almost as miserably.

–Charles Dickens, *The Mystery of Edwin Drood*[13]

The jester's *marotte*, the tiny replica of his head on a stick, symbolised one of his primary functions: to interrogate the nature of identity and reveal the folly underlying presupposed notions of a fixed, monolithic identity. As Mrs Jarley's waxworks neatly symbolise, Dickens's clowns perform the same role: to conciliate 'a great many young ladies' boarding-schools' she alters 'the face and costume of Mr Grimaldi as clown to represent Mr Lindley Murray as he appeared when engaged in the composition of his English Grammar'.[14] In this world where everyone dresses up and plays a part, the clown can quickly become the grammarian – and vice versa.

Dickens took particular aim at the pretensions of the middling classes and figures of authority, described by George Orwell as 'the cadging dowagers who live up mews in Mayfair, and the bureaucrats and professional soldiers'.[15] Alfred Jingle and Montague Tigg are two such 'cadging' tricksters who ingratiate themselves within society by allowing their identity to be contingent on circumstance. Jingle uses the power of 'assumption' (the 'assumption' of a role and the 'assumptions' made based on that role) to infiltrate the Pickwickians, borrowing Winkle's jacket to appear at a ball 'incog' and later reinventing himself as 'Sir Thomas Blazo'.[16] Tigg similarly metamorphoses from a parasitical scrounger into the respected head of the 'Anglo-Bengalee Disinterested Loan and Life Insurance Company', in a parodic version of the 'self-made' nineteenth-century entrepreneur.[17]

Rob Polhemus feels that Dickens ridicules not only 'all who assume moral superiority' but also 'the gullibility of those who take moral authority at face value' and the clown is an important agent in this process.[18] Dickens shares the joke with his audience, so that they can both relish the cunning performance and indulge in wicked laughter at those who are duped. The narrator reveals the artifices beneath Jingle's 'costume and appearance' when Pickwick cannot: Jingle's 'scanty black trousers displayed here and there those shiny patches which bespeak long service' and despite his efforts at concealment his 'dirty white stockings, [. . .] were nevertheless distinctly visible' (24–5, ch. 2). Dickens similarly intervenes in *Martin Chuzzlewit* (1843–4) when, after a lengthy and sumptuous description of Tigg's new business attire, he reminds us that 'The brass was burnished, lacquered, newly-stamped; yet it was the true Tigg metal notwithstanding' (408, ch. 27).

Tigg's new 'moral authority' is directly invested in his appearance, which has transformed from 'very dirty and very jaunty' to being 'the newest fashion and the costliest kind' (53, ch. 4; 407, ch. 27), and other Dickensian clowns also expose clothing as an unreliable signifier of identity. Joe Gargery, a Bergsonian clown who is 'comic in proportion to his ignorance of himself', visits Pip in an oversized suit and performs some grotesque comic business with his hat as he vainly searches for the 'proper' place to put it.[19] Later the mockery is turned on Pip by the tailor's servant who dons an improvised costume to burlesque Pip's gentlemanly pretensions and cause him great 'aggravation and injury'.[20]

Dickens also uses the clown to challenge the identity of an entire nation. In *American Notes* (1842), he mocks the gaudy ephemerality of American architecture when he observes that 'every thoroughfare in [Boston] looked exactly like a scene in a pantomime', to the extent that he 'never turned a corner suddenly without looking out for the clown and pantaloon'.[21] In *Chuzzlewit*, the clown reappears to puncture the gravitas of authoress Mrs Hominy's 'highly aristocratic and classical cap' which Dickens describes as 'so admirably adapted to her countenance, that if the late Mr Grimaldi had appeared in the lappets of Mrs Siddons, a more complete effect could not have been produced' (353, ch. 22).

General Fladdock's grand and bombastic entrance is similarly confounded by his inherent clownishness as he makes a slapstick tumble into the room:

> the General, attired in full uniform for a ball, came darting in with such precipitancy that, hitching his boot in the carpet, and getting his sword between his legs, he came down headlong, and presented a curious little bald place on the crown of his head to the eyes of the astonished company. (280, ch. 17)

Dickens skewers the showiness of military costume and, in exposing the top of Fladdock's head, recalls the jester within the king's 'hollow crown': 'Scoffing his state and grinning at his pomp' until he 'Comes at the last and with a little pin | Bores through his castle wall, and farewell king!'[22]

There is a grotesque dissonance between Fladdock's 'rather corpulent' body and 'very tight' uniform, which echoes Grimaldi's mockeries of military fashions (280, ch. 17). On one renowned occasion, he created a Hussar's boots from 'two black varnished coal-scuttles', heeled with 'two real horseshoes' and spurred with candlesticks, or donned 'a rattling, shiny uniform of saucepan lids and dish-covers'.[23] Fladdock's lack of bodily control and puppet-like motions embody Henri Bergson's comic trait of 'mechanical inelasticity', as 'he came up stiff and without a bend in him, like a dead Clown' with 'no command whatever of himself until he was put quite flat upon the soles of his feet, when he became animated as by a miracle' (280, ch. 17).[24]

While these dissections of identity generate much comic capital, they make clown's identity equally vulnerable. Dickens's discomforting exploration beneath the greasepaint reveals that clowns are just as keen to maintain an illusory identity as those they ridicule. 'Astley's' (9 May 1835) concludes with a troubling contemplation of how the show's fantastical clown (a being of 'light and elegance') can be reconciled with his daytime incarnation as one of the 'dirty shabby-genteel men in checked neckerchiefs, and sallow linen, lounging about [the stage door]', a group which reappears in the starving clown's narrative.[25]

Henry Mayhew's accounts of clowns demonstrate a jarring juxtaposition between an idealised clown's life and the reality. The street clown's daughter laughs at his costume, but he admits unromantically that 'I would rather see her lay dead before me [. . .] than she should ever belong to my profession.'[26] A comparable disparity exists between Jupe's clown persona and his offstage fatherhood, as, contrary to his expected role, he escapes into the fantasy world that Sissy creates from fairy tales in order to 'to cheer his courage' and avoid 'what did him real harm'.[27] In fact, Jupe doubly fails as a clown, prompting guilt rather than absorbing it – he cried when people wouldn't laugh, and:

> 'Lately, they very often wouldn't laugh, and he used to come home despairing [. . .] Sometimes they played tricks upon him; but they never knew how he felt them, and shrunk up, when he was alone with me.' (49, bk 1, ch. 9)

Although the injuries may be invisible to the audience during performance, Sissy reminds us that clowns nonetheless 'bruise themselves very bad sometimes' (24, bk 1, ch. 5). Thus when Dickens asks, 'Who entertains the entertainers?', the answer is never 'Themselves', a commonplace encapsulated in an apocryphal tale of Grimaldi's trip to the doctor when he felt unhappy, where he was advised by the doctor, who did not recognise him, to visit the theatre and watch himself perform.[28]

Patterned Behaviour

Mr Bumble [. . .] glanced complacently at the cocked hat; and smiled. Yes, he smiled. Beadles are but men: and Mr Bumble smiled.

–Charles Dickens, *Oliver Twist*[29]

Clowns also query the patterns which structure our lives and interactions with others. To facilitate this they use laughter to collect the audience into a *'communitas'*, a 'symbolic' social grouping 'in which the usual hierarchies [. . .] are supplanted by a sense of communal unity where equality is the norm'.[30] Astley's clown creates one such *communitas* by collapsing social boundaries; Boz knows as the stage is set 'we feel as much enlivened as the youngest child present', suspending his detached observer persona to 'actually join in the laugh which follows the clown's shrill shout' ('Astley's', 131–2).

The clown attempts to liberate us from the 'usual hierarchies' by manipulating or obstructing them from within. Dickens's clowns operate inside environments which function through structure and repetition, and through Dickens's comic imagination they playfully suggest a levelling randomness and disorderliness. The army is one such environment: as well as improvising costumes from domestic objects, Grimaldi burlesqued Falstaff's 'awkward squad' of ramshackle conscripts by fashioning a similar troop from junkyard scrap. Astley's clown, who claims to have served in the army, undermines the military ringmaster at every turn, 'making ludicrous grimaces at [him] every time his back is turned; and finally quitting the circle by jumping over his head, having previously directed his attention another way' ('Astley's', 133). In an act of clownish regeneration, he later reappears in *The Old Curiosity Shop* (1840–1) as 'the clown who ventured on such familiarities with the military man in boots' (299, ch. 39).

However, the legal profession is a more sustained target for Dickens's clowns. By *Bleak House* (1852–3), the readers' laughter at its fog-like insidiousness is embittered, but in earlier work the treatment is lighter. Dickens's clowns perform their comic set-pieces in the theatre of the law, the courtroom. In 'The Old Bailey' (23 October 1834), we meet 'a boy of thirteen' on trial for pick-pocketing, who disrupts the orderly proceedings with comic irreverence. He improvises his routine from the available materials, the court's own forms and ceremonies, claiming that 'all the witnesses have committed perjury' and hinting that 'the police force generally have entered into a conspiracy again' him', before sending 'a stout beadle' out to collect fifteen non-existent witnesses. He demonstrates his multiple identity when he blames his crimes on 'a twin brother, vich has wrongfully got into trouble, and vich is so exactly like me, that no vun ever knows the difference atween us'. His performance reaches a crescendo at sentencing, giving 'vent to his feelings in an imprecation bearing reference to the eyes of "old big vig!"', and as he is carried out congratulates himself 'on having succeeded in giving everybody as much trouble as possible'.[31]

The audience is a silent spectator of this performance, but when it is reprised at the Artful Dodger's trial in *Oliver Twist* (1837–9), Dickens registers the audience's laughter and draws them into a *communitas* of criminality with Dodger and his confederates:

> the Dodger [. . .] desired the jailer to communicate 'the names of them two files as was on the bench', which so tickled the spectators, that they laughed almost as heartily as Master Bates could have done if he had heard the request. (294, ch. 43)

Once again, the clown frames his retorts in the law's own language – 'Wery good. That's a case of deformation of character, any way' (294, ch. 43) – and similarly bows out in a moment of triumphant self-satisfaction, suffering himself 'to be led off by the collar; threatening, till he got into the yard, to make a parliamentary business of it; and then grinning in the officer's face, with great glee and self-approval' (296, ch. 43). Sam Weller's testimony in *Bardell* v. *Pickwick* also conjures laughter in the audience, as he knowingly plays with his status as a 'simple' servant. His disarmingly honest testimony under Buzfuz's cross-examination exposes the machinations of Pickwick's accusers.

As well as infiltrating the courts with mocking outsiders, Dickens also unpicks the garments of power and, recalling Grimaldi's impersonation of a drunken watchman, depicts authority figures who are no more than clowns dressed in the right costume. In *Oliver Twist*, he observes how 'there are some promotions in life, which, independent of the more substantial rewards they offer, acquire peculiar value and dignity from the coats and waistcoats connected with them' (239, ch. 37). The Bow Street officers Blathers and Duff recall Shakespeare's comic duo Dogberry and Verges; Blathers is 'a stout personage' with 'a round face' and his partner is 'a red-headed, bony man [. . .] with a rather ill-favoured countenance' (202, ch. 31). Rather than embodying stability and order, Duff is bumbling and awkward, turning even the simple task of sitting down into a distracting piece of comic business, seating himself 'after undergoing several muscular affections of the limbs; and forc[ing] the head of his stick into his mouth, with some embarrassment' (202, ch. 31). Like the constable's truncheon, the authority invested in their instruments of office is dissolved through imaginative transformation: Blathers plays 'carelessly with the handcuffs, as if they were a pair of castanets' (203, ch. 31).

Clown also disrupts the very fabric of the narrative itself, when, for example, he attempts to thwart the pantomime's romance plot. As Pickwick anxiously parleys with the stern patriarch Winkle Senior on behalf of Nathaniel, Bob Sawyer is possessed by Grimaldi's irreverent spirit and punctures the solemnity of proceedings. Sawyer 'whose wit had laid dormant for some minutes, placed his hands on his knees, and made a face after the portraits of the late Mr Grimaldi, as clown' (671, ch. 49), a gesture which could have upset the old man so much that he refused to assent to his son's marriage. Clown's disruptiveness can thus have a profound structural impact associated with comedy's wider destabilising power, as our pause for laughter arrests the narrative's forward momentum and fractures the novel's architecture. Orwell describes 'the *unnecessary detail*' as the 'outstanding, unmistakable mark' of Dickens's writing, which 'overwhelms everything, like a kind of weed [. . .]. Everything is piled up and up, detail on detail, embroidery on embroidery.'[32] For Orwell, the accumulated weeds and embroidery of such superfluous by-play weakens the novel's integrity in bursts of uncontrollable whimsy, making Dickens a writer whose parts are greater than his wholes, 'all fragments, all details – rotten architecture, but wonderful gargoyles'.[33]

However, if the unity of the novel is as illusory and constructed as the unity of the self, then, as Chesterton noted, the clown is merely pointing out pre-existing fissures and questioning secure notions of reality: in these 'magic accelerating growth[s]', 'Dickens saw something, whether in a man's notions or in his nose, which could be developed more than dull life dares to develop it.'[34]

Magic

Smike was called in, and pushed by Mrs Squeers, and boxed by Mr Squeers, which course of treatment brighten[ed] his intellects.

–Charles Dickens, *Nicholas Nickleby*[35]

Clowns also function as shamans, serving society's most primal psychological needs. Lucile Charles characterises the clown as an avatar to whom we temporarily 'lend [. . . our] own powers' and 'identify ourselves' so that we can 'experience imaginatively [that] which he concretizes before our eyes', and for James Caron, his creation of *communitas* enables the audience to 'symbolically shed all signs of status and acknowledge a common desire and a common fear'.[36] Hitherto, such elements are sublimated and contained within society's taboos but by holding 'the licentious thing in his hands' for our amusement, 'ritual clowns provide an institutionalized means for a traditional society to express collective laughter at taboos'.[37] From his tangential position, the clown can be 'objective at the same time that he has a most intimate and thoroughgoing relationship with the tabooed thing', and so can more closely scrutinise a society's self-fashioned myths and norms, such as those around sex and death.[38]

The clown's sexual play within traditional societies is direct, involving real body parts, but in more industrialised societies this is remediated into a symbolic form. One mechanism for this displacement is the consumption of food and drink, with Falstaff an example of a clown who satisfies different physical appetites on the same site: drinking 'a good sherris sack' 'warms [the blood] and makes | it course from the inwards to the parts extreme'.[39] Grimaldi similarly entertained audiences with superhuman feats of prodigious consumption, such as the draining of fountains and hyperbolic eating contests against other clowns.

Noah Claypole demonstrates this conflation in his comic *pas de deux* with Charlotte and some oysters, in homage to Grimaldi's duets with 'an oyster crossed in love'.[40] Noah strikes a suggestive pose, 'loll[ing] negligently in an easy-chair, with his legs thrown over one of the arms' and brandishes the phallic prop of 'an open clasp-knife'. His face is flushed with amorous desire, with 'a more than ordinary redness in the region of [his] nose, and a kind of fixed wink in his right eye', while he devours the oysters with 'remarkable avidity' and 'intense relish' (*Twist*, 184–5, ch. 50).

In *Pickwick*, Joe the Fat Boy similarly confuses these two types of fleshy pleasure when dining with Mary, in an unsettling tableau of displaced cannibalism and grotesque eroticism. During these *amours*, Joe devours a variety of foodstuffs and cannot separate his thoughts of Mary from those of eating. He speculates that 'we should have enjoyed ourselves at mealtimes' as a couple, and when she asks a favour he 'looked from the pie-dish to the steak, as if he thought a favour must be in a manner connected to something to eat'. He switches attention between his dinner and his companion in a manner that makes it unclear to which he is referring: he pauses, knife and fork hovering over the pie, to tell Mary how nice she looks, a compliment regarded as 'doubtful' because 'there was enough of the cannibal in the young gentleman's eyes' as he offered it (717, ch. 53).

While the clown's removed position gives him the latitude to engage in such outrageous behaviour with impunity, this means that he only apes sexual behaviour, rather than fully participates. Dickens's clowns never get the girl, ultimately stepping aside for the 'serious' lover after declaring their passion in comic fashion. Mr Guppy and John Chivery attempt to be genuine suitors, but only manage temporary performances for our amusement and both are rejected for more socially acceptable matches.

The clown's removal from the rhythms of ordinary life also detaches him from the biological processes of regular mortals. He dances along the margin between life and death during the course of his performance, until his 'death' at the end comes with the comforting knowledge that he will be resurrected tomorrow night. This mockery performs important cultural work, making death, in Polhemus's words, 'the property of the living'.[41] Bailey disappears in Chapter 42 of *Chuzzlewit*, presumed dead after being thrown from a carriage, only to return 'all alive and hearty' at the finale (760), and such a regeneration is also denoted in *Hard Times* when the vanished Jupe is replaced by another clown. Yet while this may please the audience (who must be amused), it does not console the orphaned Sissy, again exemplifying how the clown's function is incompatible with the performer's life offstage.

Slapstick violence becomes another site upon which Dickens plays out the ideological struggle between the need for amusement and the acknowledgement of a more troubling reality. In his memoirs, the clown James Frowde grimly observed that 'an audience are ever more ready to laugh at a fellow's misfortunes than wit or humour', and Dickens pointedly contrasts acts of violence with the satisfaction they elicit from the crowd: in a deliberately weighted juxtaposition of hyperboles, the 'gymnastic convulsions' of Astley's clown mimic 'the most hopeless extreme of human agony, to the vociferous delight of the gallery' ('Astley's', 132–3).[42]

Elsewhere, however, he obfuscates the reality of violence through a rhetoric of comedy: Polhemus notes that Dickens 'imagines and plays with fantasies of aggression [. . .] against children and parental figures', in which the clown 'bears the onus' so the audience can enjoy these fantasies liberated from the guilt and consequences they should conventionally bring.[43] Thus Bumble's cruel treatment of his young wards – such as when he gives Oliver 'a tap on the head, with his cane, to wake him up; and another on the back to make him lively' (24, ch. 2) or later 'threshed a boy or two, to keep up appearances' (49, ch. 5) – is recast as comedy through its denomination as 'parochial flagellation' (56, ch. 7).

The presence of the clown similarly muddles our compassion in *Nicholas Nickleby* (1838–9): Dickens wants to expose 'such offensive and foul details of neglect, cruelty and disease, as no writer of fiction would have the boldness to imagine' (4), but simultaneously invites the 'less interested observer' to laugh when, for example, Mrs Squeers stretches the boys' mouths with a giant spoon or Wackford knocks a crying boy back and forth (97, ch. 8). Even the beating of Smike, Dickens's primary sympathetic focus, is lightened by its epithet as a 'course of treatment' aimed at 'brightening his intellects' (95, ch. 8).

By making pain comical, the clown better prepares his audience to accommodate their own injuries, but potentially desensitises them too, so that they permanently treat violence as a game. In *A Tale of Two Cities* (1859), the double effect of his son's death and the frightening onslaught of the Terror desensitises the sinister wood-sawyer to the extent that he eventually treats violence as a clownish game:

> The wood-sawyer [. . .] pointed at the prison, and putting his ten fingers before his face to represent bars, peeped through them jocosely.
> [. . .] 'Ah! But it's not my business. My work is my business. See my saw! I call it my Little Guillotine. La, la, la; La, la, la! And off his head comes!'
> The billet fell as he spoke, and he threw it into a basket.
> [. . .] 'See here again! [. . .] And off *her* head comes! Now, a child. Tickle, tickle; Pickle, pickle! And off *its* head comes. All the family!'
> Lucie shuddered as he threw two more billets into his basket[44]

However, here Lucie rightfully resists the desensitisation and is shocked by this performance in which human bodies have been reduced to theatrical stunt props that are disposed of in a singsong mock execution.

Outcast

> 'Joe—damn that boy, he's gone to sleep.'
> 'No, I ain't, sir,' replied the fat boy, starting up from a remote corner, where, like the patron saint of fat boys—the immortal Horner—he had been devouring a Christmas pie.
>
> –Charles Dickens, *The Pickwick Papers* (370, ch. 28)

Bratton and Featherstone characterise the clown as 'at best an auxiliary, at worst a loose cannon, in the dramatic theatre', and although clowns operate alongside other dramatic elements, they are not reliant upon them.[45] Shakespeare's early clowns could be excised without material effect, while the later clowns hovered in a liminal 'othered' state between societies and worlds. As we saw, this outsider status – both enforced and cultivated – places him at a sufficient distance to judge society without respect for its rules. In *Twelfth Night*, Olivia reminds everyone that 'there is no slander in an allowed fool'.[46]

The original licensed clown was the 'holy fool', a natural simpleton privileged as God's mouthpiece, but clowns are also marginalised through other mechanisms, such as their association with the medieval Vice figure or their grotesque, hyperreal appearance. Dickens uses such tropes to grant his clowns the same licence.[47]

Bodily disproportion is the most physical marker of clown's marginality and further develops his lack of order. Clowns carry fat bellies, large noses or over-sized hairstyles, which provoke both laughter and alienating revulsion. *Pickwick*'s starving clown has a 'bloated body and shrunken legs', an imbalance accentuated by his 'glassy eyes, contrasting fearfully with the thick white paint with which the face was besmeared', 'the grotesquely-ornamented head, trembling with paralysis, and the long skinny hands, rubbed with white chalk'. They create a 'hideous and unnatural appearance', which pushes him outside the bounds of 'normality' and in recalling 'the most frightful shapes' of Holbein's *Dance of Death* places him in the hinterland between life and death (49, ch. 3).

Joe the Fat Boy's name indicates one dimension of his bodily grotesque, and Sam Weller's comic epithets alter him through a succession of different shapes – 'young twenty stun', 'young dropsy', 'opium-eater' and 'boa constructer' (365, 369, 374, ch. 28). This visual disorientation, which renders someone as multiple things simultaneously is also reflected in Dickens's description of Quilp, who is 'so low in stature as to be quite a dwarf, though his hands and face were large enough for a giant' (29, ch. 3).

The clown also signals his outsider status through location; although he orchestrates the temporary *communitas*, he only enters society at prescribed times (for example, festivals or show times). Sleary's circus is pitched on 'the neutral ground upon the outskirts of the town, which was neither town nor country', and the starving clown lives in a tenement room that resembles a stage-set, thus neither wholly inside nor outside the theatre (12, bk 1, ch. 3). Even then, there are margins within margins, Astley's clown is physically circumscribed apart from the audience within a 'hoop, composed of jets of gas' ('Astley's', 131). The Artful Dodger not only lives at the physical margins of London's topography, in the dirt of Saffron Hill, but also on the social margins within the criminal 'under-world'. Joe the Fat Boy lurks on the edge of scenes (on the outside of a coach, or behind the lovers' bower) and has to be summoned to centre stage.

Physical marginalisation often follows economic marginalisation: Mayhew's clowns catalogue a range of financial reward and the physical and mental consequences. The street clown, earning six shillings per week, displayed 'sunken eyes and other characteristics of semi-starvation, whilst his face was scored with lines and wrinkles, telling of pain and premature age', and relates how 'Most of the street clowns die in the workhouses'.[48] Despite his own belief in the clown's value, Dickens highlights similar privations. *Pickwick*'s clown is 'reduced to a state bordering on starvation', relieved only by borrowing from companions or performing at 'the commonest of minor theatres' (49–50, ch. 3). Before his disappearance, Jupe's precarious living was jeopardised by his failures (being 'short in his leaps and bad in his tumbling'), which drew the audience's disapproval (*Hard Times* 27, bk 1, ch. 6). While Grimaldi's farewell benefits demonstrate a general popularity, the *Memoirs* also highlights the audience's indifference to multiple injuries he suffered onstage, and how his final days were spent in modest circumstances.

However, Dickens's most persistent reworking of the marginalised comic outsider develops Shakespeare's device of the comic servant. Chesterton regards the comic servant as assuming superiority over his master 'in wit and satire and cunning, but not [. . .] in status or seriousness or dignity', and believes that Dickens 'is more really concerned to show that the tyrant is undignified than that the slave is dignified'.[49] However, by playing out the foibles and appetites that we all possess he also evokes a common humanity shared by master and servant. Figures such as Joe, Newman Noggs and the anonymous Yarmouth waiter in *David Copperfield* (1849–50) exhibit their clownishness by combining their servant's role with another clownish trope, such as unusual clothing, laziness or gluttony.

The outfit of Noggs is described as 'a suit of clothes (if the term be allowable when they suited him not at all) much the worse for wear, very much too small, and placed upon such a short allowance of buttons that it was marvellous how he contrived to keep them on' (*Nickleby* 24, ch. 2). Again, he is on the margins of the margins since he does not wear the traditional livery that could partially integrate him and adopts an outfit of threefold non-conformity. The magical impossibility of its tailoring continues in his hat, 'in which, by-the-bye, in consequence of the dilapidated state of his pockets, he deposited everything', which resembles Grimaldi's own pockets that became receptacles for live animals or strings of sausages (136, ch. 11).

Joe's brief scenes economically compress multiple clownish traits into their space, for example, during his reluctant service at a picnic, when 'roused from his lethargy', he is asked to:

> 'Come, hand in the eatables.'
> There was something in the sound of the last word which roused the unctuous boy. He jumped up, and the leaden eyes which twinkled behind his mountainous cheeks leered horribly upon the food as he unpacked it from the basket. (*Pickwick* 66, ch. 4)

He hangs 'fondly over a capon' until finally he 'sighed deeply, and, bestowing an ardent gaze upon its plumpness, unwillingly consigned it to his master' (66, ch. 4).

The Yarmouth waiter appears in a single scene at a coaching inn, a place more suited to transient rather than lasting encounters, yet this comic set-piece becomes memorable for the apparently artless ways in which this greedy servant traduces David into surrendering his dinner. First, he reports that someone died drinking the house ale, and therefore only he can risk the superhuman feat of drinking it: when he does, 'it didn't hurt him. On the contrary, I thought he seemed the fresher for it.'[50] He then explains how David's chops will offset any poisonous effects:

> 'Why, a chop's the very thing to take off the bad effects of that beer! Ain't it lucky?'
> So he took a chop by the bone in one hand, and a potato in the other, and ate away with a very good appetite, to my extreme satisfaction. He afterwards took another chop, and another potato; and after that, another chop and another potato.

He finally races David through his dessert using comically mismatched utensils, echoing Grimaldi's eating races with his fellow clowns:

> what with his table-spoon to my tea-spoon, his dispatch to my dispatch, and his appetite to my appetite, I was left far behind at the first mouthful, and had no chance with him. I never saw anyone enjoy a pudding so much, I think; and he laughed, when it was all gone, as if his enjoyment of it lasted still. (79, ch. 5)

A number of elements foreground this as a clownish performance, such as comic accumulation and the repetition of the chops and potato, but most crucial is David's amused reaction and pleasure in the waiter's enjoyment that builds as the performance unfolds.

The only physical trace left of Jupe is his 'white night-cap, embellished with two peacock's feathers and a pigtail bolt upright', an object which conjures the evocative memory of how he 'enlivened the varied performances with his chaste Shakespearean quips and retorts'. Apart from this fool's cap, though, 'no other portion of his wardrobe, or other token of himself or his pursuits, was to be seen anywhere' (*Hard Times*, 25, bk 1, ch. 6).

This is the essence of Dickens's clowns: they fill an imaginative space far greater than their allotted physical space. The figures I have explored are all characters popularly regarded as 'larger-than-life', who have made an indelible impression on readers' minds despite their limited impact on the plot and carry a memorability far beyond that merited by their small narrative territory. In a telling metaphor, Chesterton calls these figures 'superb supers who have nothing to do with the play, and who are the making of it', and they expand and optimise what Alex Woloch terms their 'character-space' – the intersection between a character's personality and the narrative which they inhabit.[51] Woloch plots these character-spaces on a spectrum which encompasses 'worker' characters, whose personality is entirely subsumed for the benefit of narrative, and 'eccentric' figures, whose characterisation overreaches their bounds and disrupts the narrative flow.[52] The 'character-space' occupied by clowns represents an interesting case study for Woloch's thesis.

As Bente Videbaek's comprehensive taxonomy suggests, the Shakespearean clown adopted a range of positions from minor functionary to major presences like the 'bitter Fool' or Falstaff.[53] Grimaldi's pre-eminence made the pantomime clown the central figure of the harlequinade, for which the fairy-tale plot was just a flimsy prelude. However, while no clown drives a Dickens novel in the same way and Dickens's clowns instead operate in the margins, their characterisation is closest to Woloch's 'eccentric' mode, whereby his use of heightened descriptive language and attention to physical detail means that local effect is privileged over structure. Dickens's clowns draw attention in-and-of-themselves, while simultaneously pulling the reader's focus centripetally away from the central characters and the novel's suprastructure, and out towards the margins.

Here Dickens engages in a dangerous balancing act: as E. M. Forster recognised, if you give such 'peripheral' characters too much freedom, they will dismantle the story, but too much circumscription means they do not thrive as credible presences within the novel.[54] Yet this is a common Dickensian method: when describing Dickens's interest in prop limbs, John Carey notes how, 'Like most of Dickens's imaginative ideas, the idea of separate legs is kept going by minor figures who have really no claim to be in the novel at all.'[55] Indeed, in taking such risks Dickens is playing the licensed fool himself, something that Orwell recognised when he noted how the 'English institutions' that Dickens attacked ('with a ferocity that has never since been approached') 'have swallowed him so completely that he has become a national institution himself'.[56] By using such magical, outcast figures to disrupt the narrative pattern of his work, Dickens audaciously challenges both the identity of its form and of its readers.

Notes

1. William Shakespeare, *King Lear*, ed. by G. K. Hunter (London: Penguin, 1996), I.4.146–9.
2. Charles Dickens, 'The Restoration of Shakespeare's Lear to the Stage', *The Examiner*, 4 February 1838, 5–6.

CLOWNS   79

3. Charles Dickens, *The Memoirs of Joseph Grimaldi*, ed. by Charles Whitehead (London: Bentley, 1846), xi, xii.

4. See Robert H. Bell, *Shakespeare's Great Stage of Fools* (New York: Palgrave Macmillan, 2011); Robert Hornback, *The English Clown Tradition from the Middle Ages to Shakespeare* (Woodbridge and Rochester, NY: Brewer, 2009); and Bente Videbaek, *The Stage Clown in Shakespeare's Theatre* (Westport, CT: Greenwood Press, 1996).

5. 'To the Sub-Editor of Bentley's Miscellany, [March 1838]', *The Letters of Charles Dickens*, ed. by Madeline House, Graham Storey et al., Pilgrim/British Academy Edition, 12 vols (Oxford: Clarendon Press, 1965–2002), i (1965), 382.

6. Charles Dickens, 'The Pantomime of Life', in *Dickens' Journalism*, ed. by Michael Slater and John Drew, 4 vols (London: J. M. Dent, 1994–2000), i (1994), 500–7, 503.

7. Edwin Eigner, *The Dickens Pantomime* (Berkeley: University of California Press, 1989), 171; Joseph Butwin, 'The Paradox of the Clown in Dickens', *Dickens Studies Annual 5* (1976), 116–32.

8. See Leigh Woods, 'The Curse of Performance: Inscripting the *Memoirs of Joseph Grimaldi* into the Life of Charles Dickens', *Biography* 14.2 (1991), 138–52. For positive (albeit) brief reappraisals, see Michael Slater, *Charles Dickens* (New Haven: Yale University Press, 2009), and Robert Douglas-Fairhurst, *Becoming Dickens* (Cambridge, MA: Belknap Press, 2011). For longer reassessments of the *Memoirs*, see Jonathan Buckmaster, '"A man of great feeling and sensibility" – The *Memoirs of Joseph Grimaldi* and the Tears of a Clown', *19: Interdisciplinary Studies in the Long Nineteenth Century* 14 (2012), 1–20 <http://doi.org/10.16995/ntn.602> and '"We are all actors in the Pantomime of Life": Charles Dickens and the *Memoirs of Grimaldi*', *Victorian Network* 3.2 (Winter 2011), 7–29.

9. George Bernard Shaw, 'Introduction to *Hard Times*', reprinted in Charles Dickens, *Hard Times*, ed. by Fred Kaplan and Sylvère Monod (London: Norton, 2001), 357–63, 359.

10. Ibid., 360; Shaw, 'Introduction to *Great Expectations*', reprinted in *Charles Dickens*, ed. by Harold Bloom (New York: Chelsea House, 2006), 59–70, 64–5.

11. Shea Coulson, 'Funnier Than Unhappiness: Adorno and the Art of Laughter', in *New German Critique* 100 (Winter 2007), 141–63, 143.

12. Jacky Bratton and Ann Featherstone, *The Victorian Clown* (Cambridge: Cambridge University Press, 2014), 1.

13. Charles Dickens, *The Mystery of Edwin Drood*, ed. by David Paroissien (London: Penguin, 2002), 154, ch. 14.

14. Charles Dickens, *The Old Curiosity Shop*, ed. by Norman Page (London: Penguin, 2000), 221, ch. 29. Subsequent references are inserted parenthetically in the text.

15. George Orwell, 'Charles Dickens', in *Shooting an Elephant and Other Essays* (London: Penguin, 2003), 49–114, 71.

16. Charles Dickens, *The Pickwick Papers*, ed. by Mark Wormald (London: Penguin, 2003), 34, ch. 2; 205, ch. 7. Subsequent references are inserted parenthetically in the text.

17. Charles Dickens, *Martin Chuzzlewit*, ed. by Patricia Ingham (London: Penguin, 2004), 408, ch. 27. Subsequent references are inserted parenthetically in the text.

18. Robert M. Polhemus, *Comic Faith: The Great Tradition from Austen to Joyce* (Chicago: University of Chicago Press, 1980), 106.

19. Henri Bergson, *Laughter*, trans. by C. Brereton and F. Rothwell (Rockville, MD: Arc Manor, 2008), 15.

20. Charles Dickens, *Great Expectations*, ed. by Edgar Rosenberg (London: Norton, 1999), 188, ch. 30.

21. Charles Dickens, *American Notes*, ed. by Patricia Ingham (London: Penguin, 2000), 34.

22. William Shakespeare, *Richard II*, ed. by Stanley Wells (London: Penguin, 1997), III.2. 160, 163, 169–70.

23. *The Times* (5 January 1813), 3; Gerald Frow, *Oh Yes It Is!: A History of Pantomime* (London: BBC, 1985), 78.
24. Bergson, 13.
25. Charles Dickens, 'Astley's' in *Sketches by Boz*, ed. by Dennis Walder (London: Penguin, 1995), 128–35, 134–5. Subsequent references are inserted parenthetically in the text.
26. Henry Mayhew, *London Labour and the London Poor*, 3 vols (London: Griffin, Bohn, and Company, 1861), III, 120.
27. *Hard Times*, 24, bk 1, ch. 5. Subsequent references are inserted parenthetically in the text.
28. Richard Findlater, *Joe Grimaldi: His Life and Theatre* (Cambridge: Cambridge University Press, 1978), 169.
29. Charles Dickens, *Oliver Twist*, ed. by Fred Kaplan (London: Norton, 1993), 22, ch. 2. Subsequent references are inserted parenthetically in the text.
30. James E. Caron, 'Silent Slapstick as Ritualizing Clowning: The Example of Charlie Chaplin', *Studies in American Humor* 3.14 (2006), 5–22, 6.
31. Charles Dickens, 'The Old Bailey', republished as 'Criminal Courts', in *Sketches by Boz*, 229–34, 232–4.
32. Orwell, 100, 102–3.
33. Ibid., 105.
34. Gilbert Keith Chesterton, 'Charles Dickens', in *The Great Victorians*, ed. by H. J. and Hugh Massingham (New York: Doubleday, Doran, 1932), 153.
35. Charles Dickens, *Nicholas Nickleby*, ed. by Mark Ford (London: Penguin, 2003), 95, ch. 8. Subsequent references are inserted parenthetically in the text.
36. Lucile Hoerr Charles, 'The Clown's Function', *The Journal of American Folklore* 58.227 (January–March 1945), 25–34, 32; Caron, 19.
37. Charles, 32; Caron, 6.
38. Charles, 32.
39. William Shakespeare, *2 Henry IV*, ed. by P. H. Davison (London: Penguin, 1996), IV.3.95, 104–5.
40. Findlater, 182.
41. Polhemus, 121.
42. Bratton and Featherstone, 122.
43. Polhemus, 121.
44. Charles Dickens, *A Tale of Two Cities*, ed. by Andrew Sanders (Oxford: Oxford University Press, 1998), 340–1, bk 3, ch. 5.
45. Bratton and Featherstone, 1.
46. William Shakespeare, *Twelfth Night*, ed. by M. M. Mahood (London: Penguin, 2015), I.5.88–9.
47. See Enid Welsford, *The Fool: His Social and Literary History* (London: Faber, 1968) and Sandra Billington, *A Social History of the Fool* (Brighton: Harvester Press, 1984).
48. Mayhew, 119, 121.
49. Chesterton, 150.
50. Charles Dickens, *David Copperfield*, ed. by Jeremy Tambling (London: Penguin, 2004), 78, ch. 5. Subsequent references are inserted parenthetically in the text.
51. Chesterton, 154; Alex Woloch, *The One vs. the Many: Minor Characters and the Space of the Protagonist in the Novel* (Princeton: Princeton University Press, 2003), 24.
52. Woloch, 25.
53. See Videbaek.
54. See E. M. Forster, *Aspects of the Novel* (London: Edward Arnold, 1958), 102.
55. John Carey, *The Violent Effigy: A Study of Dickens' Imagination* (London: Faber, 1991), 92–3.
56. Orwell, 50.

Further Reading

Jonathan Buckmaster, *Dickens's Clowns: Charles Dickens, Joseph Grimaldi and the Pantomime of Life* (Edinburgh: Edinburgh University Press, 2019)

David Mayer, *Harlequin in His Element: The English Pantomime, 1806–1836* (Cambridge, MA: Harvard University Press, 1969)

Jane Moody, *Illegitimate Theatre in London, 1770–1840* (Cambridge: Cambridge University Press, 2000)

David Robb, *Clowns, Fools and Picaros: Popular Forms in Theatre, Fiction and Film* (Amsterdam: Rodopi, 2007)

6

MELODRAMA

Carolyn Williams

NOT LONG AGO, DICKENS'S MANY USES of melodrama seemed cause for casual, uncritical dismissal.[1] After melodrama itself began to be taken seriously in the 1960s, however, Dickens's reliance on it began to be taken seriously as well.[2] Now that melodrama is better understood – and its profound importance well established – we can better evaluate Dickens's brilliant transformations of it.

The novels of Charles Dickens are melodramatic in so many ways that one essay cannot hope to do justice to the subject – for example, in familiar plot structures involving orphanhood, illegitimacy in the family, social and personal dangers to women, the plight of the poor, villainous deception, and the gross injustices of the law; in sudden revelations of familial and social identity that resolve the plot very close to its end; in familiar character types and quasi-allegorical character names; and in the invitation to recognise characters by visible physiognomic traits or individualised gestures, as well as identifying speech tics or styles of histrionic declamation. Unfortunately, his concentration on melodramatically 'external' signs has sometimes led critics of Dickens to underestimate his finesse in representing interiority.[3]

Dickens was finely attuned to other formal features of melodrama as well. The soundscapes of his novels make use of patterned music, speech, orchestrated silences and special 'sound effects'. He also theorised the melodramatically rhythmic oscillations between comedy and pathos, absorption and shock – as we shall see.[4] This essay will focus much of its attention on Dickens's deployment of melodrama's pictorial dramaturgy, particularly his use of the tableau. In the novel as well as on the stage, the tableau provides a moment of stillness; alerts the audience to the significance of the picture's formal composition; and condenses in one moment the past, present and potential future of narrative development. Occurring in the midst of dramatic movement and sound, the sudden stillness and silence of the tableau enthrals or fixates its spectator.[5] Dickens powerfully and frequently uses these moments of spectatorial fixation and astonishment. This essay will explore the ways Dickens expands on other dynamics of the tableau as well: as a technique for signalling and concentrating affect; as a fixed point after which movement resumes or a still point before an explosion; and as a 'point' in the serial structure of melodramatic narrative form.[6]

Dickens makes fun of melodramatic conventions, but he also deploys them without parody. Some critics, focusing on Dickens and melodrama, have noticed this seriocomic doubleness in his attitude towards the genre and its conventions.[7] So this essay will begin by asking how we might understand the relation between his parodies of melodrama and his non-parodic, non-ironic uses of it. Over the course of Dickens's career, his treatment of melodrama becomes less parodic, less separated out into cameo episodes or comic set pieces, and more fully integrated on all levels of the fiction. In short, Dickens's fiction is melodramatic through and through. This essay will argue that the fiction's saturation with melodrama is not only a strength but also a vital part of its 'realistic' dimension. The opposition of melodrama and realism is a false dichotomy, as many critics have recognised.[8] Certainly, that false dichotomy should be overcome in Dickens studies, where the two are always intertwined – as Dickens himself pointed out in Chapter 17 of *Oliver Twist* (of which more, below).[9]

Parody and Adaptation

Margaret Rose offers the best definition of parody: 'the *comic refunctioning* of pre-formed linguistic or artistic material'.[10] For Dickens criticism we must add 'theatrical' to her types of 'preformed [. . .] material'. The most concentrated comical treatments of melodrama are found in *Sketches by Boz* (1836), *The Pickwick Papers* (1836–7) and *Nicholas Nickleby* (1838–9) – though there are examples of comic refunctioning in the later novels as well. But we must move beyond Rose's definition to understand that in Dickens parody is not always comic; we must also attend to non-comic 'refunctioning of preformed linguistic, [theatrical,] or artistic material'. Parody is a mode of imitation, and Dickens imitates melodrama in a wide range of moods and tones, ranging from critique, distanced irony and fun-making to imitation in which the melodramatic and realistic dimensions of the fiction are mutually interpenetrative.

Even when Dickens uses melodrama without marking it as comic, we should see that he is yet engaging in a form of parody, in the sense that he is imitating melodrama and making it a part of his own more comprehensive purpose. For example, one might think that her response is conventionally melodramatic when Kate Nickleby demands of Sir Mulberry Hawk: 'Unhand me, sir, this instant!'[11] But no reader, I think, is likely to feel that Edith Dombey's imperious denunciation and dismissal of Carker is merely conventional, even though it closely resembles the melodramatic heroine's eloquent efforts to repel the rapacious villain in order to preserve her virtue. Neither of these is in the least bit comical; the character of Kate Nickleby is meant to be recognised as the stereotypical 'helpless girl' who 'should most have found protection' under her uncle's roof (237, ch. 19), while Edith Dombey rises above this stereotype altogether, even though she, too, is compromised and in danger of losing her reputation. Both employ the heroine's melodramatic attitude and her rhetoric. Should Edith Dombey's language and behaviour be regarded as a 'parody' of melodramatic conventions? Technically, yes. But this is not most readers' idea of parody. Dickens's villains offer another way to make the same point. Rigaud/Blandois in *Little Dorrit* (1855–7) is to some extent parodic, if only because his identity as villain is so blatantly conventional, even down to the twitching moustache. But Bradley Headstone and John Jasper are terrifying; their pathological violence is a 'given', as is conventional for the melodramatic villain, and yet these two are more lavishly psychologised, clearly in pain, confused and struggling with impulses they cannot understand. Should they be understood as 'parodies' of melodrama? Yes, because it is important to see that their behaviour remains conventionally villainous, even as their characters have been realistically deepened and rounded.[12]

These non-comical but still conventional uses of melodrama might better be called 'adaptations' or 'transformations', in order that we might focus on the fact that Dickens does not only imitate but also fundamentally changes familiar tropes, figures, plot devices and situations of melodrama, while still making their presence clear. Using the term 'adaptation' has the advantage of referring to a dominant characteristic of nineteenth-century theatre culture, while using the term 'transformation' emphasises Dickens's shaping force.[13] We should note, too, that adaptation is structurally similar to parody – in fact, parody might be seen as a subset of adaptation – since both are forms of originality that depend on imitation, citation, allusion, recirculation and recombination. Finally, it is important to remember that genre parody is characteristic of the novel itself, considered as a genre. Thus Dickens's uses of melodrama could be seen to mark his place in the history of the novel as a genre. His focus on the genre parody and adaptation of melodrama – as opposed, say, to the parody of allegory or romance, which had proved most salient to earlier novelists – shows a close attention to his own historical moment and becomes a marker of that moment in the history of novelistic realism. In his fiction melodrama becomes realism's primary 'other' as well as a component of it.[14]

Meanwhile, Dickens's use of parody provides us with important historical evidence about what melodrama was really like.[15] Parody always takes a present-tense stance, a contemporaneous and up-to-date point of view, casting its 'knowing' look at things that have passed or are passing out of style. This historical dimension of parody can be presented nostalgically or critically (or in both tonalities at once). Thus parody, especially in its comic form, preserves forms of culture that are passing away, while it also actively distances itself from them and pushes them further into the past. As a result, present-day phenomena, if subjected to parody, can seem suddenly defamiliarised. Especially early in his career, when writing about popular culture – including melodrama – Dickens uses parody in this way. In these early texts we can feel his obvious relish, not only for popular culture, but also for its conventional or 'generic' aspects. For example, in 'Amusements of the People' – two articles published in *Household Words* that describe visits to the theatre in 1850 – Dickens not only characterises spectators like 'Joe Whelks' with affectionate condescension, but also humorously represents melodramatic declamation, the strange practice of adding syllables to words in order to fill out the rhythm of the utterance, and thus this is still one place we can go to learn about that feature of melodrama.[16]

Amused condescension and sentimental affection are bound up with admiration in Dickens's analysis of how hard it was to make a living in the theatre – another good example of his historicising vein. Both *Nicholas Nickleby* and *The Old Curiosity Shop* (1840–1) focus on marginalised forms of entertainment whose very existence is tenuous during the present time of the novel's action, and on low, degraded and precarious performers. Yet in both these early novels – as later in *Hard Times* (1854) – these forms of entertainment also suggest a utopian world elsewhere, an alternative or supplement to the 'real world' of suffering and broken community, a place where the main characters can turn for solace and replenishment, and where the novel can turn for plot deferral that temporarily avoids but also supports the norms of realism.

In *Nicholas Nickleby*, comically historicising parodies of melodrama famously abound in the scenes involving the Crummles troupe, where Dickens dwells on its formulaic or clichéd and genre-specific conventions. He extends to his readers a playful invitation to indulge in the pleasures of recognising 'the generic'. The Crummleses enable Dickens to anatomise generic forms while making the point that the

MELODRAMA   85

family stock troupe is also an economic institution; as such, the ensemble of players represents a division of labour, each one with a specialist's 'line' of work (and thus the stereotypes are seen to have an economic rationale). Even the pony has his own line, 'drinking port-wine with the clown' (280, ch. 23). Mrs Crummles specialises in tragic and Gothic roles; she is most 'terrible' in her role as 'the Blood Drinker', which audiences could not tolerate because it was 'too tremendous'.[17] And Mr Crummles sometimes encroaches on the tragedians' prerogative by playing 'heavy' roles himself. Assessing his new friends in terms of their usefulness, Vincent Crummles identifies Smike as someone who would 'make such an actor for the starved business' (275, ch. 22). Here we see a clever twisting of parody with realist narrative, since Crummles imagines that Smike looks the stereotypical part of what we know Smike 'in reality' to be. Nicholas himself appears to the 'professional eye' of Mr Crummles as a collection of theatrical genres: 'There's genteel comedy in your walk and manner, juvenile tragedy in your eye, and touch-and-go farce in your laugh' (275, 277, ch. 22). When he tells Nicholas that he wants to 'bring him out' as 'a novelty', we can further see the intertwined relations of theatre and 'real life', for Nicholas would be merely a new actor filling the same recognisably generic roles.

Of course, nostalgic amusement is not Dickens's only response; he also vents his anger against the Victorian culture of adaptation. When Mr Crummles charges Nicholas to translate a French play into English, assuring him that 'invention' is beside the point, Nicholas responds merely with ironic surprise. But later, during his encounter with the 'literary gentleman' in Chapter 48 – supposedly based on W. T. Moncrieff – who had 'dramatised in his time two hundred and forty-seven novels as fast as they had come out', Nicholas acts out Dickens's own rage, comparing the literary gentleman's activity to blatant robbery (597–8, ch. 48). Here again we can see the doubleness of Dickens's attitude towards parody and adaptation; for his well-known anger at the lack of dramatic copyright protection cannot distract us from the fact that Dickens, like 'Bill Shakespeare', is also 'an adapter'. However, he adapts a genre (usually not a specific work), and thus he cannot be accused of theft.

The comic Crummles episodes are sequestered and separately set off within the novel, while more integrally adapted melodrama saturates its main plot. Scenes of Nicholas acting with the Crummles troupe alternate with scenes of Sir Mulberry Hawk and Lord Verisopht's villainous plot against Kate Nickleby, replete with her performance as the 'helpless girl'; her uncle's venal rationalisations; her mother's gullible assistance of the villains; and her enraged defiance. When Nicholas re-joins the main plot, he appears within it as the perfectly generic melodramatic hero in order to denounce his uncle in vehemently stilted manly eloquence, while Ralph stands 'fixed and immoveable', 'remain[ing] in the same attitude' throughout the scene – exhibiting the conventional attitude of the petrified spectator to Nicholas's melodramatic attitudes (245, 250, ch. 20). Those readers well versed in melodrama will hear the broad hint when Nicholas, thinking of Smike, wishes 'that [he] knew on whom [Smike] has the claim of birth' (247, ch. 20). That Ralph Nickleby is Smike's father will not be revealed until forty chapters later. So the pleasure of recognising that a melodramatic revelation of identity will come is heightened by the novelistic pleasure of knowing that the revelation will be postponed for a very long time.

Of course, Dickens anticipates me in all these points by making them himself. I am simply highlighting the notable technical achievement we can see during these

Crummles episodes: the systematic alternation or cross-cutting between melodrama played on the stage and melodrama in the 'real life' of the main plot. This is a perfect example of Dickens's thorough embrace of melodrama juxtaposed with comic parodies of it; here melodrama is seen to be both preposterous and realistic. The deft switch back and forth between these attitudes towards melodrama in *Nicholas Nickleby* might be seen as a further developed version of the melodramatic alternations the narrator had theorised in the famous 'streaky bacon' passage of *Oliver Twist*, to which we now turn.

Streaky Bacon: Melodramatic Alternations

The 'streaky bacon' passage that opens Chapter 17 of *Oliver Twist* has been frequently analysed, since it is Dickens's most explicit defence of melodrama *as a version of realism*, not the opposite of it.[18] Surely, the most important commentator has been Sergei Eisenstein, who makes Chapters 16–18 of *Oliver Twist* central to his analysis in 'Dickens, Griffith, and the Film Today', making clear the continuities between melodramatic alternations and basic montage structure.[19] In the present context, I want to show the full range of Dickens's engagement with – and extension of – the rhythmic melodramatic oscillations between tragedy and comedy, pathos and humour; and Chapter 17 itself provides a good example of Dickens's use of the melodramatic rhythm in his fiction:

> It is the custom on the stage, in all good murderous melodramas, to present the tragic and the comic scenes, in as regular alternation, as the layers of red and white in a side of streaky bacon.

The narrator gives several examples of this alternation between comic and tragic scenes: a hero, weighed down by cares, relieved suddenly by his squire singing a comic song; a heroine under threat, 'her virtue and her life alike in danger', interrupted by a funny chorus.

> Such changes appear absurd; but they are not so unnatural as they would seem at first sight. The transitions in real life from well-spread boards to death-beds, and from mourning-weeds to holiday garments, are not a whit less startling; only, there, we are busy actors, instead of passive lookers-on, which makes a vast difference.

With the pointed double meaning of 'actors', the narrator stresses the difference between spectatorship of 'mimic life' on the stage and the experience of 'real life', when no aesthetic distance protects one from absorption within an unfolding temporality whose shifts seem 'startling' and above all undesigned.

He concludes by pointing out that these 'sudden shiftings of scene' are well regarded in fiction as the evidence of 'an author's skill in his craft'. Thus, after the 'streaky bacon' passage has explained the technique of melodramatic alternation, the narrator interrupts his own commentary to shift the scene, returning to 'the town in which Oliver Twist was born', urging the reader to 'take it for granted' that there are 'good and substantial reasons' for his doing so (135, bk 1, ch. 17).

The narrative continues in a comic mode, offering the ridiculously pompous figure of Mr Bumble as a caricature. Soon, however, this parody gives way to the pathos of little Dick imagining his own impending death and wanting to leave a written record of his love to Oliver, 'after [he] is laid in the ground' (139, bk 1, ch. 17). The mood shifts again when Mr Bumble reacts to Dick with anger, and thus we are reminded that he is a villain, not merely a comic bumbler. Interpreting his own anger, Mr Bumble becomes a narrative theorist for a moment, angrily predicting that narrative coherence will emerge: furious because it seems that Dick and Oliver are in cahoots somehow – 'They're all in one story' – he blames 'that out-dacious' Oliver (139, bk 1, ch. 17). This comic malapropism, very much a characteristic of the low plots of melodrama, shows Mr Bumble's ignorance, to be sure, but does not return him to a comic modality. His villainy remains paramount because little Dick is meanwhile being locked in the coal-cellar for expressing the pathetic sentiments that Mr Bumble so wilfully misunderstood.

Of course, they are 'all in one story', and emphatically so, as we soon learn, when Mr Bumble goes to London and immediately happens to see Mr Brownlow's advertisement offering a five-guinea reward for information as to the whereabouts of Oliver Twist. As narrative coherence blatantly emerges, this coincidence raises our own fears. How will the child victim clear his name? The suspense is continued through a return to pathos at the end of the chapter, when the narrator represents Oliver's state of mind: 'Oliver's heart sank within him, when he thought of his good friends; it was well for him that he could not know what they had heard, or it might have broken outright' (143, bk 1, ch. 17).

Dickens's deft use of these melodramatic alternations – not only between comic and tragic scenes, parody and pathos, but also between low and high plots, danger and relief, immersion and suspension – help us see how he manages his profound interpenetration of melodrama and realism.

Transformations of Melodrama in *Bleak House*

I will use *Bleak House* (1852–3) and *Little Dorrit* as examples of Dickens's later transformations of melodrama, attending especially to plot structure, uses of the tableau, and the generalising, even allegorising, of melodramatic form. Each analysis ends by turning to novelistic effects that cannot be achieved in stage melodrama.

Esther's plot depends upon putting the familiar melodramatic figure of the orphan into play. Not only does the novel float the question of whether she is an orphan or not, illegitimate or not, but also stresses the generic aspect of the figure. Skimpole romantically suggests that she not be called 'an orphan' for she is 'a child of the universe'.[20] Paired against this too high Skimpolian absurdity, the novel provides a low comic parody as well, when Mrs Snagsby, in the 'ceaseless working of her mill of jealousy', feels that she 'knows' that Jo is Mr Snagsby's son (827–8, ch. 54). But Esther herself understands that something was 'wrong' in the circumstances of her birth, and the retrospectively narrating Esther presents herself as motherless at the beginning of the novel, even though she knows that her mother had still been alive at that time.[21] All this sets up the conventional expectation that a melodramatic revelation of familial identity will be forthcoming.

In the conventionally melodramatic maelstrom of estranged primal relations, *Bleak House* notably focuses on the relation of mother and daughter (rather than father and daughter or father and son, much more usual in melodrama).[22] Mother and daughter form a double figure, their secrets intertwined. Lady Dedlock's story would suggest the many fallen women of melodramas – except that she has not fallen, but has managed to rise. In other words, the novel does not explore the conventional plots of the melodramatic erring daughter or fallen woman, except insofar as Lady Dedlock must hide her past from her husband – but instead focuses on her as a mother, the object of Esther's quest. Thus Esther's odd combination of knowing and not-knowing allows for the plot of detection that culminates in the uncanny scene of recognition at the climax of the novel. Correlatively, the novel's two narrators – one autobiographical, the other objective or 'omniscient' – cleverly position Esther's psychic quest for self-recognition and her effort to 'bring the mother back to life' within the larger scope of social realism.[23]

When, after the long chase sequence, Esther comes upon a figure lying just outside the pauper's graveyard, she pulls back the figure's 'long, dank' hair – as if drawing back a curtain in a theatre, preparing us for the scene of recognition – and narrates the shocking, sudden realisation that 'it was my mother, cold and dead' (915, ch. 59). Here Dickens transforms the melodramatic tableau of recognition, bringing it close to Gothic horror, fully psychologised. Before her moment of recognition, Esther experiences a moment of misrecognition, as John O. Jordan shows, when she sees the shape as 'the mother of the dead child' – thinking that Lady Dedlock is Jenny, since she is disguised in Jenny's clothes – though, as Jordan further argues, the words could just as well refer to Esther herself.[24] Thus, this scene elaborates a two-step tableau of recognition, like a double-take, Esther's stunned registering of the sight itself only later followed by an understanding of what she sees. Jordan's reading makes it clear that this moment of misrecognition reflects uncannily on mother and daughter alike: Honoria Dedlock's sister had told her that her baby was dead, while Esther's sense of abandonment had internalised a mother who wished that she had never been born. Thus, in recognising her dead mother, Esther also recognises herself as 'dead' or deadened. So Esther's fleeting thought – that she sees 'the mother of the dead child' – is not a misrecognition after all, for her words are 'at once mistaken and yet truer than she knows'.[25] Thus, her quest throughout the novel has been for her own reanimation as well as her mother's – reminding us that reanimation of the static or frozen figure is a master trope of melodrama.[26] In the melodramatic tableau, the 'frozen' quality of the static posture is only metaphorical, but here it has been literalised; usually the stillness of the tableau leads to reanimation, but in this case it underscores the 'dead' in Dedlock. My addition to Jordan's powerful reading, in other words, is simply to remind us that the formal elements of melodrama – its 'body language', its frozen moments, and its forms of recognition – prefigure psychoanalysis.[27]

The tableau also figures in *Bleak House* as an image for the serial pictorialisation of the melodramatic plot. This dimension of pictorial dramaturgy is represented by the picture gallery at Chesney Wold – a conventional figure for the temporal unfolding of a plot about family lineage and inheritance. Drawn from Gothic melodrama, the portrait gallery at Chesney Wold memorialises a lineage that is in danger of dying out and identifies the house as a haunted repository of the past.

During his tour of Chesney Wold, Mr Guppy notices a resemblance between Esther Summerson and the portrait of Lady Dedlock.[28] In Guppy's reaction, as he stares 'absorbed', 'in a dazed state', fixated and immoveable before the portrait of

Lady Dedlock, Dickens offers a parody of the spectator at a tableau (110–11, ch. 7). The fact that Guppy recognises a likeness to Esther's features provides a clue for the reader, the significance of which Guppy himself is unable to grasp at the time. As it does with the figure of orphanhood, the novel includes parodic versions of the family portrait gallery as well, such as Mrs Bayham Badger's portraits of her dead husbands and the Divinities of Albion, or the Galaxy Gallery of British Beauty, hung up in the room of Mr Weevle (Tony Jobling) (206–8, ch. 13; 330–1, ch. 20). Since this room had been Nemo's room in the past, the suggestion of erotic yearning above one's station, here represented comically, seems also poignantly to reflect on Nemo/Captain Hawdon. In other words, these various picture galleries illustrate the novel's concentrated consideration of this figure for melodramatic narrative form as serial pictorialisation. If Mr Guppy's melodramatically fixated response is comic, the picture gallery at Chesney Wold itself is offered instead in the grandiose key of Gothic haunting.

After the scene in the picture gallery, a haunting political backstory of the Ghost's Walk emerges. Mrs Rouncewell, herself a loyal servant of the aristocracy, regards 'a ghost as one of the privileges of the upper classes' (112, ch. 7). She recounts the story of the Dedlocks during the English Civil War, telling of his wife's rebellion against Sir Morbury Dedlock's Royalist aims. This past Lady Dedlock lamed her husband's horses in order to weaken the Royalist forces, but, in a violent retaliatory incident, he lamed her in turn. For the rest of her life, she paced haltingly up and down on the terrace, vowing to 'walk here, until the pride of the house is humbled' (113, ch. 7). Thus is the fall of the House of Dedlock prefigured, a fall that is completed in our current story. Thus, too, while Mrs Rouncewell narrates, the reader understands that the novel as a whole engages a Gothic critique of the aristocracy by telling a tale of its sinking fortunes. However, Dickens again transforms our melodramatic expectations, for Sir Leicester, though oblivious as a 'master', is kind and loving as a husband; the wound Honoria Dedlock suffers is not at his hand. Jordan interprets the story of the Ghost's Walk as a 'national allegory' – the history of England framed as a history of repeated trauma, with the telling wound inscribed on a woman's body.[29] Like the mute pantomime figure in early melodrama, the ghost of the past silently 'speaks' the expressive body language that prefigures Freud's theorisation of hysteria.[30] In other words, through an aspect of the novel that we might be tempted to dismiss as 'merely' Gothic trappings, we can see, as Jordan points out, that the novel recalls a national and revolutionary past by which the present is still actively haunted.

In this novel, the historical and psychological dimensions of haunting are intertwined, melodramatic and realistic at once. Dickens generalises from the figure of the picture gallery to suggest not only the death of the family lineage, but also the death that must come to us all. The novel itself begins to seem haunted, when the narrator transports us into a future beyond the novel's frame, by imagining an empty house with 'no inhabitants except the pictured forms upon the walls' (639, ch. 40).[31] Soon enough, however, that emptiness is populated with a hypothetical future 'Dedlock in possession', who 'might have ruminated', while looking at the pictures: 'So did these [inhabitants] come and go [. . .] so did they see this gallery hushed and quiet, as I see it now' (639, ch. 40). Anchoring the complex narrative switch-backs in temporality – from present to future to that future's past – are the pictures on the wall. The thought of past beholders, and how difficult it would have been for them to believe that 'it could be, without them', as now it is, leads this future 'Dedlock in possession' to an even graver thought. Here is a quintessential example of the resources of narration accomplishing something that a staged melodrama would be hard-pressed to accomplish, even with all of its resources. Though, of course, novels often narrate what someone is thinking, here that someone thinking is purely imaginary, not really 'there' – a ghost from the future, not the past. Depending on the figure of the melodramatic picture gallery for this ghostly effect, the passage culminates in a delicate, evanescent and deeply moving conclusion, as the imaginary future Dedlock compares his leaving the picture gallery to dying: the pictured figures will, he imagines, 'so pass from my world, as I pass from theirs, now closing the reverberating door; so leave no blank to miss them, and so die' (639, ch. 40).

Melodramatic Form Writ Large: *Little Dorrit*

Fixated staring – the posture of the spectator when suddenly presented with a melodramatic tableau – is elevated and generalised to become a serious and overarching thematic structure in *Little Dorrit*, as we shall soon see. But let us begin in the comic mode by looking at a parodic treatment. The Dorrits are travelling in the Alps when they come upon the wealthy Mrs Merdle and her son, Edmund Sparkler. Sparkler had been in love with Amy's sister, Fanny Dorrit, back in London. Mrs Merdle opposed her son's attachment to Fanny at that time. However, in this scene, she pretends that she has never met the Dorrit sisters before:

> [Mrs Merdle] addressed a winning smile of adieu to the two sisters [. . .] whom she had never had the gratification of seeing before.
> Not so, however, Mr Sparkler. This gentleman, becoming transfixed at the same moment as his lady-mother, could not by any means unfix himself again, but stood stiffly staring at the whole composition with Miss Fanny in the foreground. On his mother's saying 'Edmund, we are quite ready' [. . .] he relaxed no muscle. So fixed was his figure, that it would have been a matter of some difficulty to bend him sufficiently to get him in the carriage door, if he had not received the timely assistance of a maternal pull from within. He was no sooner within, than the pad of the little window at the back of the chariot disappeared, and his eye usurped its place. There it remained [. . .] staring (as though something inexpressibly surprising should happen to a cod-fish) like an ill-executed eye in a large locket.[32]

Dickens clearly creates the first part of this scene on the model of the tableau, and he plays it for laughs. Our amusement depends on recognising the formal parody of a framed 'whole composition', with background and 'foreground', and, further, on our recognising Mr Sparkler's response as a parody of the melodramatic spectator's astonishment. Scenes of spectatorial astonishment are prevalent in Dickens's fiction – one of the most easily recognisable of his debts to the theatre.[33] Here Sparkler's mix of recognition and incomprehension is telling – like Mr Guppy's reaction to the portrait in *Bleak House* and like Esther's first sight of her dead mother – insofar as the spectator of a suddenly presented tableau first sees and only later understands the picture, in a two-step process that prioritises affect over cognition. The first response of the spectator is enthralment, dumb amazement, astonishment and fixation, the stillness of the tableau reflected by the beholder's frozen stance.

Dickens takes these matters a step further, using the tableau as a pivot-point within the unfolding temporality of the novel. At the end of this scene, in something like a shot/reverse shot, the narrative pulls away from its focalisation in Sparkler's point of view and adopts an objective visual stance towards Sparkler and his mother. Then the narrator stops the action with another picture, as they prepare to drive away. The second picture – a miniature, framed by the aperture at the back of the carriage, 'like an ill-executed eye in a large locket' – makes the shot/reverse shot structure clear. As Sparkler continues to stare at the Dorrits, we now look at Sparkler looking. With this shift in perspective, the initial parody tableau recedes into the narrative past, as another takes its place – and, indeed, as Mrs Merdle and Sparkler are released into the 'distance' of the narrative past. Narrative time here is punctuated with and built around a sequence of pictures, as it is in melodrama. Thus, when Sparkler's real-life eye is reframed as 'art' in the second parody tableau, the initial parody tableau seems to become, in narrative retrospect, an image of 'real life' receding into the narrative past. One might say that this narrative sequence confers a sense of realism on the Dorrit family group, whose pictorial composition had at first seemed merely parodic. Parody, in other words, paves the way for the realism of the scene to be perceived retrospectively.

This dynamic of fixated staring is 'writ large' in *Little Dorrit*. An inhuman figure of fixated staring opens the novel, setting its keynote, just as the 'implacable' fog sets the keynote in the opening of *Bleak House*, the sunlight in Marseilles as oppressive as the fog in London. With a similarly bleak passage of relentless parallelism, the narrator harps on 'staring, [. . .] staring, [. . .] staring', everything 'fixedly staring' in Marseilles, where 'a staring habit had become universal' (15, bk 1, ch. 1). Generalisation verges on allegorisation here, since the sun might have been imagined as the secularised form of the Providential eye; but Dickens does not imagine it that way. Bleak and unrelieved, the sun in Marseilles remains unpersonified. If this is a figure for narrative omniscience, it is an ominous one, part of Dickens's early conception of the novel as a story of 'Nobody's Fault', a vision in which even seeing the complexity of social problems in their full interrelatedness would not necessarily mean that blame could be ascribed or justice could be achieved. As it is, this stare seems implacable but indifferent; it lacks judgement or agency and seems to promise no engagement, no justice, no revelation. We can see this as an overarching narrative figure because of the many other ways Dickens meditates on staring and fixation in the novel.[34]

Throughout his fiction Dickens relies on the figure of fixated mutual staring between characters, in a plot device modelled on the tableau of recognition in melodrama. When two characters suddenly 'start' back and then stare fixedly at one another, they signal to the audience that something in their mutual past will be revealed in the future of narrative time. (One might recall the riveting scene in Thomas Holcroft's influential *A Tale of Mystery* (Covent Garden, 1802), when the mute hero and his enemy confront one another for the first time.)[35] But in this novel, fixation itself also becomes metaphorically central, as all readers of the novel have noticed. To take the most obvious example, the motif of fixation thematically joins the Dorrits to the Clennams, linking the two plotlines that will become one ('They're all in one story', as Mr Bumble's narrative theory would have it). The Dorrits are arrested or fixated and imprisoned for debt, while Mrs Clennam is arrested and fixated bodily, immobilised and self-imprisoned by her anger, guilt and fierce Christian judgement. In turn, her guilty fixation has caused a kind of arrested development in Arthur. Bureaucracy – represented by the Circumlocution Office – and Society itself (with a capital S) are also presented as moralised versions of arrest and stasis. Thus the static states of 'arrest' and fixated immobilisation gather much more thematic importance than Mr Sparkler's fixated stare at the parody tableau would at first suggest.

Fixation or arrest is the first step in the melodramatic dynamic of imprisonment and release, immobilisation and reanimation, which expands to become a model for expression in general. The secret of Arthur's true parentage bursts out in the end, of course. But the force of that outburst depends on the novel's heavy thematisation of arrest, fixation and immobilisation beforehand.[36] In other words, as we all know, melodramatic revelation depends on this dynamic of containment and release. I would urge us, despite years of training in the critique of this dynamic, to take it seriously within its historical and formal context. We should still see the melodramatic dynamic of containment and release as a post-revolutionary acting out of imprisonment and escape, even when, as here, it also becomes a model of expression in general.

Secrecy causes paralysis in Mrs Clennam, and expression is its cure. In this sense – again, as Peter Brooks has shown – melodrama is distinctly pre-psychoanalytic, and so is Dickens. We should hear the term 'expression' in its most dynamic and literal sense, as pressure forcing something outward: ex-pression. *Little Dorrit* is organised upon this model. After Merdle's suicide, for example, society gossip holds that his death was caused by 'Pressure', and 'there was 'a general moralising upon Pressure' (741, bk 2, ch. 25). Pancks – the novel's chief detective figure – puffs and blows, as if he were 'a little steam-engine with more steam than it knew what to do with' (407, bk 1, ch. 32). Mr Dorrit's rambling speech before he dies bespeaks his release from the effort towards socialised self-containment (676–9, bk 2, ch. 19). And when Affery begins to 'tell her dreams' – to tell what she saw that will expose the Flintwinches – she says she has 'broke out now' (799, bk 2, ch. 30). Here we see the pressure of containment leading to release clearly used as a figure for narrative revelation; as Rigaud says to Mrs Clennam, urging her to keep talking: 'Time presses, madame' (812, bk 2, ch. 30).

Because it has been fixed and contained under pressure, the melodramatic secret *will* burst out in the end. Mrs Clennam 'broke out vehemently' with the confession that she is 'Not Arthur's mother!' and with that 'explosion of her passion, and with a bursting from every rent feature of the smouldering fire so long pent up', she seizes the narrative and tells its backstory herself, while the fixated expression on her face was 'torn away by [the] explosion' (807, bk 2, ch. 30). As Dickens put it in his working notes for Chapter 30: 'Mrs Clennam's immobility [is] gradually and frightfully thawing' (905). A panoply of melodramatic effects – including 'thundering' sounds as the House of Clennam falls to the ground – reinforce the notion that something 'explodes' or 'bursts out' – the world outside matching the psychic pressure within (in typically post-romantic fashion, but also in typically realist fashion, with body and house positioned as analogous material structures). Therefore, most dramatically, Mrs Clennam runs *out* of the house as it explodes and crashes down, and thus, the narrator tells us, 'the mystery of the noises [that Affery heard inside the house throughout the novel] was *out* now' (827–8, bk 2, ch. 31, italics mine). Mrs Clennam, briefly on the loose and reanimated, must be punished and re-fixated: falling down and never moving or speaking again, 'she lived and died a statue' (827, bk 2, ch. 31). Thus, when the secrets come 'out', the plot is also 'Closing In', as the titles of Chapters 30 and 31 emphasise. What comes out, of course, had been intentionally put in. And this is perhaps the main flaw of the novel – that the existence of a secret is hypothesised so blatantly from the beginning. But this, too, should be regarded as part of Dickens's strategic use of melodrama, for once we know that a secret has been posited, we are held in suspense until it does finally 'come out'.

However, the novel both turns away from – and shows its thorough absorption of – melodrama in the end, and turns inward towards the intensities of novelistic narration and a scene of silent reading. In the first place, the melodramatic revelation of identity changes little in the social relations of the novel. The revelation that his true mother was a singer whose patron had been Frederick Dorrit reveals Arthur's low family origins – and thus he and Little Dorrit, their class affiliations now settled, are a good match. As in many (or most) realist novels – but perhaps especially in the Dickens world of social 'varnishings' and 'veneerings' – lowering in the social scale operates as a sign of the real. In the novel's 'very quiet conclusion', as Dickens describes it in his working notes (905), the novel repeatedly stresses that Arthur and Amy 'go down' into the city and finally disappear into its 'usual uproar' (860). Like the ending of *Middlemarch* (1871–2), the ending of *Little Dorrit* secures the novel's realism by stressing the way that the individual protagonists have been absorbed within a generalised urban complexity – their stories, then, emphatically reframed in the end as stories that would otherwise have remained untold, were it not for their novelisation.

Secondly, the novel turns away from melodrama because Amy Dorrit keeps the secret in the end. Though the secret has 'burst out', she emphatically recontains it. She promises that she will not tell Arthur about his parentage during Mrs Clennam's lifetime, and, since she eventually possesses the box of original documents, she can be sure that Arthur will not learn the truth, except perhaps 'in time to come', beyond the closing of the novel's frame (845, bk 2, ch. 33). Thus the secret, though materially existing in the form of written documents, is physically boxed up and packed away. And Little Dorrit's own secret – that she was materially cheated by the Clennams – will forever be locked away in her unselfish heart.

And finally, the dual need of this novel to recontain the melodramatic explosions (in the interests of realism) and to reassert its status as novel (rather than melodrama) explains the brilliant *mise en abyme* of reading built into the lengthy denouement. In the crucial scene, Mrs Clennam stands over her as Little Dorrit silently reads the documents that reveal the secret of Arthur's birth and the secret of the diverted inheritance. To be clear: we silently read about Little Dorrit's silently reading a summary account of the revelations that we have just read about over the last hundred pages of the novel's unfolding (822–3, bk 2, ch. 31). The explosions are over now, but the novel's 'very quiet conclusion' depends for its effect on the reader's memory of their melodramatic force. When melodrama and realism work together, sound and silence, action and picture – fixation and outburst – are dialectically interdependent. In this moving scene, Little Dorrit acts out the silent reading that can enfold the conventions of melodrama within novelistic narration.

Notes

1. For a good example, see Robert Garis, *The Dickens Theatre: A Reassessment of the Novels* (Oxford: Clarendon Press, 1965). He claims: it is not 'the bad, the melodramatic, the trashy Dickens who is a theatrical artist' (28).

2. The earliest contributions to the reclamation of melodrama were: Michael Booth, *English Melodrama* (London: Herbert Jenkins, 1965); Frank Rahill, *The World of Melodrama* (University Park: Pennsylvania State University Press, 1967); and Peter Brooks, *The Melodramatic Imagination: Balzac, Henry James, Melodrama, and the Mode of Excess* (New Haven: Yale University Press, 1976; repr. 1995). George J. Worth was the first critic to treat Dickens's melodrama seriously in *Dickensian Melodrama: A Reading of the Novels* (Lawrence: University of Kansas, 1978).

3. Cf. the distinction between 'flat' and 'round' characters as described by E. M. Forster in *Aspects of the Novel* (1927). While both 'flat' and melodramatic characters are said to be one-dimensional, my focus here is on the way melodramatic characters are defined audio-visually.

4. Juliet John has described this dynamic best: 'the emotional economy of melodrama is best figured as a series of waves'. *Dickens's Villains: Melodrama, Character, Popular Culture* (Oxford: Oxford University Press, 2003), 31.

5. This phenomenon of spectatorial enthralment or 'fixation' was first theorised by Diderot. See Michael Fried, *Absorption and Theatricality: Painting and Beholder in the Age of Diderot* (Chicago: University of Chicago Press, 1988), 92–4. This tradition of analysis is taken up by Brooks as 'The Aesthetics of Astonishment' in *Melodramatic Imagination*, 24–55.

6. Martin Meisel has called this pictorial narrative form 'serial discontinuity' in *Realizations: Narrative, Pictorial and Theatrical Arts in Nineteenth-Century England* (Princeton: Princeton University Press, 1983), 38.

7. See Worth, 23–5 and passim; Tore Rem, *Dickens, Melodrama, and the Parodic Imagination* (New York: AMS Press, 2002), 18–37 and passim.

8. See, for example, Jim Davis, 'Melodrama On and Off the Stage', in *The Oxford Handbook of Victorian Literary Culture*, ed. by Juliet John (Oxford: Oxford University Press, 2016), 686–701.

9. I develop this argument at greater length in 'Melodrama and the Realist Novel' in *The Cambridge Companion to English Melodrama*, ed. by Carolyn Williams (Cambridge: Cambridge University Press, 2018), 209–23.

10. Margaret Rose, *Parody: Ancient, Modern, and Post-Modern* (Cambridge: Cambridge University Press, 1993), 52. Italics in original.

11. Charles Dickens, *Nicholas Nickleby*, ed. by Mark Ford (London: Penguin, 1999), 237, ch. 19. Subsequent references are inserted parenthetically in the text.

12. For a different treatment of this question, see Chapter 4 of John, *Dickens's Villains*, 95–121.

13. Dramatic and melodramatic adaptations of Dickens's novels have been well covered elsewhere. See Anne Humpherys, 'Victorian Stage Adaptations and Novel Appropriations', in *Charles Dickens in Context*, ed. by Sally Ledger and Holly Furneaux (Cambridge: Cambridge University Press, 2011), 27–34; and H. Philip Bolton, *Dickens Dramatized* (Boston, MA: G. K. Hall, 1987).

14. Cf. Fredric Jameson, *The Antinomies of Realism* (London: Verso, 2013), which treats melodrama as dialectical other, especially in George Eliot's realism.

15. Evidence that early (silent) film also provides. See David Mayer, 'Melodrama in Early Film', in *English Melodrama*, ed. by Williams, 224–44.

16. On the style of melodramatic declamation, see also Rahill, 142 and Booth, 193–4.

17. Her role refers to Monk Lewis's *The Captive* (1803), which, as Lewis himself said, was 'much too terrible for representation'. On this reference and other specific historical references in *Nicholas Nickleby*, see Paul Schlicke, *Dickens and Popular Entertainment* (London: Unwin Hyman, 1985), 33–86.
18. Charles Dickens, *Oliver Twist*, ed. by Philip Horne (London: Penguin, 2002), 134–5, bk 1, ch. 17. Subsequent references are inserted parenthetically in the text.
19. Sergei Eisenstein, 'Dickens, Griffith, and the Film Today', in *Film Form: Essays in Film Theory*, trans. by Jay Leyda (New York: Harcourt, 1949), 195–255.
20. Charles Dickens, *Bleak House*, ed. by Nicola Bradbury (London: Penguin, 1996), 92, ch. 6. Subsequent references are inserted parenthetically in the text.
21. John O. Jordan emphasises the narrative and psychoanalytic effects of Esther's knowing retrospection. See 'Voice' in *Supposing Bleak House* (Charlottesville: University of Virginia Press, 2011), 1–25, especially 5 and 7–9.
22. I am indebted here to Carolyn Dever, *Death and the Mother from Dickens to Freud: Victorian Fiction and the Anxiety of Origins* (Cambridge: Cambridge University Press, 1998).
23. Hilary M. Schor, writing of *Bleak House* states: 'The attempt to bring the mother back to life [. . .] is the most powerful motive for fiction in every Dickens novel from *Oliver Twist* to this one.' *Dickens and the Daughter of the House* (Cambridge: Cambridge University Press, 1999), 122.
24. Jordan, 'Psychoanalysis', 44–66, especially 66, and 'Voice', 1.
25. Jordan, 'Voice', 1.
26. On stasis and movement figured in melodrama as deadness and reanimation, see Ellen Lockhart, 'Forms and Themes of Early Melodrama', in *The Melodramatic Moment, 1790–1820*, ed. by Katherine Hambridge and Jonathan Hicks (Chicago: University of Chicago Press, 2018), 25–42.
27. As Brooks has also argued; see 79–80 and 201–2.
28. Dickens uses a similar plot device in *Oliver Twist*, when a convalescent Oliver becomes fascinated by the portrait of a young woman, while Mr Brownlow notices with astonishment that Oliver looks just like her – his mother, as it will turn out (90–3, bk 1, ch. 12).
29. Jordan, 120–9.
30. For more on the mute figure, see my 'Stupidity and Stupefaction: *Barnaby Rudge* and the Mute Figure of Melodrama', *Dickens Studies Annual* 46 (2015), 357–76.
31. In what follows, I will be drawing on John Bowen's reading of this passage in 'The Passages of *Bleak House*', a lecture given on 2 August 2012 at the Dickens Universe in Santa Cruz, CA.
32. Charles Dickens, *Little Dorrit*, ed. by Stephen Wall and Helen Small (London: Penguin, 1998), 487, bk 2, ch. 3. Subsequent references are inserted parenthetically in the text.
33. For early evidence of this preoccupation in Dickens's work, see Christina Jen, 'Drop the Curtain: Astonishment and the Anxieties of Authorship in Charles Dickens's *Sketches by Boz*', in *Dickens Studies Annual* 49 (2018), 249–78.
34. For another reading of this opening allegorisation, see Jeremy Tambling, *Dickens' Novels as Poetry: Allegory and the Literature of the City* (London: Routledge, 2015), especially 'Staring in *Little Dorrit*', 145–59.
35. On the tableau and on 'starting' back as a sign of astonishment, see George Taylor, 'Melodramatic Acting', in *English Melodrama*, ed. by Williams, 114–16; see also Taylor, 'The First English Melodrama: Thomas Holcroft's Translation of Pixérécourt' in *The Melodramatic Moment*, ed. by Hambridge and Hicks, 137–50.
36. John Kucich explores this dynamic in *Excess and Restraint in the Novels of Charles Dickens* (Athens: University of Georgia Press, 1981): 'Dickens' novels generate a series of explosions, in which the energy of characters and narrators is repeatedly concentrated against rigid limits to thought and action' (1).

Further Reading

Juliet John, *Dickens's Villains: Melodrama, Character, Popular Culture* (Oxford: Oxford University Press, 2001)

Carolyn Williams, ed., *The Cambridge Companion to English Melodrama* (Cambridge: Cambridge University Press, 2018)

7

AMATEUR THEATRICALS

Mary Isbell

CHARLES DICKENS PERFORMED IN ALMOST ALL of the typical venues for amateur performance in the nineteenth century. In his early twenties, while living at his parents' home on Bentinck Street, he mounted private home theatricals. He also participated in the rich tradition of military theatricals: for his public debut in 1842, Dickens performed alongside and served as temporary stage manager of the 'Garrison Amateurs' of Montreal.[1] Later, when he and his significantly more notable troupe of amateurs wanted a venue larger than a private residence in 1845, they rented Miss Kelly's theatre with the intention of turning her public venue into a 'strictly private' one.[2] When these private performances gave rise to larger (though still ostensibly private) charity performances in 1846, Dickens's process became a model for other charity theatricals in the period. Amateurs were performing on public stages in America, England and its colonies long before Dickens, but his productions received such extensive press coverage that we can see them as a model for the aspirants to amateur fame who followed him. For example, the Prologue for an amateur performance to benefit the printing trade charities in 1846 explains that, "twas Boz who set the fashion' for benefit theatricals.[3] One account of charity performances from the 1880s includes a paragraph acknowledging Dickens as an unrivalled stage manager of 'probably the most perfect troupe of amateur actors' because 'in a notice however brief and restricted of Celebrated Amateur Actors, the omission of the name of the late Charles Dickens would be considered as showing but slight knowledge of the subject'.[4]

The major moments of Dickens's career as an amateur performer have been recovered and interpreted by countless biographers, from Forster to Tomalin.[5] Thus, this essay responds specifically to the seeming paradoxes in Dickens's involvement with amateur theatricals. While Dickens had great admiration for particular theatre professionals and briefly considered a career on the stage when he was twenty, he insisted that his own participation in the theatre remain amateur. Approaching this same contradiction through the traces of Dickens's efforts as a dramatist, Jacky Bratton suggests that Dickens's professional success as a novelist was an important factor in his decision to remain a theatrical amateur.[6] I explain Dickens's commitment to amateurism by introducing the concept of the 'deliberate amateur': an amateur keen to remain distinct from theatre professionals in an effort to preserve or recover the dignity of the art form. As his literary fame introduced him into more elite circles than his family's position would have made possible, Dickens cultivated his status as a deliberate amateur in the theatrical realm. This stance helps to explain why Dickens did not lend dignity to the less serious aspirants to amateur fame that he depicted in

Sketches by Boz (1833–6) and *Great Expectations* (1860–1). The 'dirty boys and low copying-clerks' in 'Private Theatres' are unrefined and the family in 'Mrs Joseph Porter' are embarrassingly concerned with social class. In *Great Expectations*, Mr Wopsle's performance in *Hamlet* exemplifies the boorishness of the amateur performer who seeks an audience before undertaking careful study. I argue that Dickens used his fiction to distance himself from this class of amateurs because he was committed to the elevation and prestige of the practice.

Amateur Theatricals in the Nineteenth Century

Until recently, very few literature or theatre scholars prioritised the study of amateur theatricals.[7] Michael Dobson's *Shakespeare and Amateur Performance: A Cultural History* (2011) signified a shift, and several critical articles, as well as a 2011 special issue of *Nineteenth-Century Theatre and Film* entitled 'Amateur Theatre Studies' point to an emerging field.[8] To this growing body of scholarship, I contribute a number of interpretive practices that allow us to understand how amateur theatricals participated in a distinct tradition, instead of dismissing these productions as derivative imitations of the professional stage.

Because they were performed outside the patent theatres and not reliant on ticket sales, amateur theatricals exhibit a range of theatrical conventions. Productions varied widely depending on the goals of performers and their relationships with their spectators. Most significantly, I argue, amateur productions are shaped by performers' conception of themselves *as* amateurs. To understand the significance of Dickens's productions, we have to understand the complexities of amateurism in the period, which requires careful attention to the textual and performative choices made by non-professional performers and managers to establish and protect their status as amateurs.

To this end, I draw a sharp distinction between deliberate amateurs, who work hard to distinguish themselves from professional theatre makers, and those who would rather not be called amateurs because they are inspired by professional actors or hope to perform on the professional stage. While the term 'amateur' was used in French from the early sixteenth century to describe a person who loves, cultivates or studies a certain thing or activity, the amateurs I discuss defined themselves according to the meaning that developed in French in the second half of the eighteenth century and entered English usage shortly after.[9] Just as the term 'professional' was coming into its current use, 'amateur' came to mean its opposite: a person who cultivates an art or science for his or her own pleasure, not to make a living.[10] This usage gave rise to a conceptual category that has had a profound impact on the way people engage in activities from athletic competition and botany, to photography and theatrical performance. The role of this concept of the amateur cannot be overstated. The nuances of the amateur/professional divide have prompted fascinating scholarship on the history of science, sport and the arts.[11] Careful consideration of the concept of amateurism reveals that our twenty-first century usage of the word differs significantly from its meaning in the nineteenth century. I argue that we can locate in Dickens's fictional representations of amateurs a source (one of many supplied by nineteenth-century novelists) of our own sense of 'amateur' today as meaning 'embarrassingly unskilled'. However, this notion of the amateur does not seem to inform the way Dickens viewed his own amateur theatrical activity.

Perceiving oneself as a deliberate amateur was not an automatically elitist act, but it did function in that way for many aristocratic amateurs early in the century. Aristocratic producers of private theatricals welcomed the label 'amateur' because they did not want to be mistaken for theatre professionals; calling oneself an 'amateur' was one way of distancing oneself from the derogatory designation of 'actor'. To participate in a private theatrical performance was, to this privileged set, an act of recovering art from the squalor and chaos of public theatres.[12] Deliberately calling oneself an 'amateur' while engaging in a theatrical performance emphasised that one performed for the love of theatre, not for necessary income. Emily Eden's account of an aristocratic amateur theatrical illustrates this idea. Eden, whose famous *Letters from India* chronicle her experience as 'first lady' to the governor general, Lord Auckland, from 1835 to 1842, also wrote letters before her departure that document her active social life in England's aristocratic circles. She writes this of a performance at Hatfield House in 1829:

> The whole evening has lowered my opinion of the merits of professional people. I went expecting the *gentlefolk* all tolerable sticks on the stage, awkward, affected, and only helped through an indulgent public, and I found I never had laughed more heartily, never had seen a play really well acted in all its parts before, and Lady S., whom I thought the least good, was only objectionable because she was like an actress on the real stage.[13]

Eden is delighted with the evening because her equals in rank and fortune create the performance; the only tarnish is the fact that an aristocratic lady too closely resembled a professional. To the elite in the late eighteenth and early nineteenth centuries, to see a play 'really well acted' is to see a play that depicts aristocrats performed by aristocrats.[14]

One will immediately recognise that Lady S., the amateur Eden criticises, does not need to earn a living; acting for love was a luxury for those with sufficient income and time. While Eden's understanding of deliberate amateurism automatically dismissed the value of 'the real stage', Dickens's assessment of the problems with professional theatres is far more nuanced. In 'Amusements of the People', published in *Household Words* on 30 March 1850, Dickens clarifies that the play and acting evident in 'the lower class of dramatic amusements' are disappointing because of the demands placed on underpaid actors by unruly spectators in overfilled theatres. He explains: 'Heavily taxed, wholly unassisted by the State, deserted by the gentry, and quite unrecognised as a means of public instruction, the higher English Drama has declined.' If, he writes:

> the actor's nature, like the dyer's hand, becomes subdued to what he works in, the actor can hardly be blamed for it. He grinds hard at his vocation, is often steeped in direful poverty, and lives, at the best, in a little world of mockeries. It is bad enough to give away a great estate six nights a-week, and want a shilling; to preside at imaginary banquets, hungry for a mutton chop; to smack the lips over a tankard of toast and water, and declaim about the mellow produce of the sunny vineyard on the banks of the Rhine; to be a rattling young lover, with the measles at home; and to paint sorrow over, with burnt cork and rouge; without

being called upon to despise his vocation too. If he can utter the trash to which he is condemned, with any relish, so much the better for him, Heaven knows; and peace be with him![15]

Though not explicitly offered as such, we have in this set of contradictions Dickens's rationale for remaining a deliberate amateur, a position that allowed him to escape the 'trash' without giving up his deep love for the stage.

I do not argue that Dickens's deliberate amateurism was motivated by the same elitism we see in Eden's commentary. The performance events he mounted, however, share many features with Hatfield House productions. Most nineteenth-century amateur productions were private occasions, but even when they were public, spectators knew performers personally or recognised them as members of the community in a capacity other than actor. This is the aspect of amateur theatre that J. Ellen Gainor links to the Provincetown Players' contributions to American Realism in the early twentieth century. Gainor refers to the Little Theatre Movement, a twentieth-century tradition with roots in amateur theatre practices, but the dynamic is the same. 'In a community where the identities of the actors are known to the audience', explains Gainor, 'it is impossible for the audience to "identify" with the characters, or for the production to convey an unfiltered mimesis, precisely because the audience will not suspend their knowledge of that duality – in fact, it is integral to their enjoyment of the art.'[16] This same effect was key to nineteenth-century amateur theatricals. I follow Jane Austen's lead and refer to it as an 'aggregate'. The narrator of *Mansfield Park* (1814) uses this term to describe the effect Fanny perceives as she watches Mary Crawford and Edmund Bertram rehearse a scene from *Lovers' Vows* (1798). When asked to evaluate the rehearsal, Fanny is described as feeling 'too much of it in the aggregate for honesty or safety in particulars'.[17] What Fanny observes is not a scene from the play, nor a conversation between Mary and Edmund, but a blend of the two. By 'aggregate', the narrator refers to the performance that results when a fictional play interacts with the personal lives of performers.

Austen's own involvement in private theatricals certainly helped her to describe the impact of the practice.[18] Her familiarity with typical selections for theatricals helped her to devise a scenario in which a rehearsal (not even an actual performance) could be tremendously meaningful to participants. Rather than perform any of a number of comedies or tragedies popular in the eighteenth-century repertoire, Austen had the amateurs at Mansfield Park choose *Lovers' Vows* (1798), a translation by Elizabeth Inchbald of August von Kotzebue's *Das Kind der Liebe* (1780). The play tells the story of a fallen woman, Agatha, and her reluctantly repentant seducer, the Baron, and includes a surprisingly unconventional love scene between the Baron's daughter, Amelia, and her tutor, Anhalt. British audiences of *Lovers' Vows* were scandalised by the depiction of an aristocratic lady, Amelia, actively pursuing her tutor, Anhalt.[19] This was the role that Mary Crawford assumed, and Fanny saw Mary and Inchbald's Amelia blending painfully into an aggregate heroine who would certainly seduce her cousin Edmund.

The effect of the aggregate hinges on a degree of intimacy between spectators and performers. We can understand aggregation as operating in every instance of embodied performance, professional or amateur, an effect of the 'ghosting' that Marvin Carlson has so thoroughly theorised.[20] Carlson uses ghosting to describe the way spectators' memories of previous performance events inform their experiences of a given production. A spectator of a professional performance will see in an actor's performance the combination of the character he depicts in that particular performance and all of the previous heroic, tragic and comic roles that the spectator has observed. But to a spectator of an amateur production, I contend, aggregation is in most cases a combination of the character performed and all of the traits the spectator has come to recognise as the performer's personal identity. Given this, we can think of amateur theatrical managers and performers as deliberately exploiting the aggregate. At times this means casting a play to match characters to performers so as to foster a more believable performance, but it can also mean deliberately casting a play incongruously (through cross-dressing, for example) for comic or other effects.

I contend that Dickens's thinking about amateurism was shaped by the aristocratic tradition of deliberate amateurism. His involvement with the Garrick Club further teases out the nuances. Named for David Garrick, the club was formed in 1831 to provide a place where 'actors and men of education and refinement might meet on equal terms'.[21] William Charles Macready and John Forster were founding members, and it was Forster who introduced Dickens to Macready in 1837, initiating the close friendship that would continue for decades to come. Dickens and Macready both had fraught relationships with the club, primarily due to conflicts with other members. However, their affiliation with a club founded to address the separate worlds of actors and 'men of distinction' suggests they were aware of the social divide; their friendship suggests a desire to reduce that separation. Within this context, Dickens's deliberate amateurism can be understood less as a snobbish superiority to professional actors and more a desire to mount productions on his own terms.

Dickens and Home Theatricals

One of Dickens's most discussed home theatricals was *The Frozen Deep*, produced in 1857 at Tavistock House. It was Dickens's final home theatrical before the dissolution of his marriage and the sale of the house in 1860. The cast of friends and family in the play rehearsed up to four times a week for three months, albeit pleasurably and with massive rehearsal dinners.[22] During that time the house was filled with carpenters who installed gas lines for elaborate lighting effects and constructed in the schoolroom a stage thirty-feet-deep, leaving an auditorium that could seat ninety.[23] But Dickens did not always plan lavish theatricals attended by 'the principal celebrities of law, literature, science, and the arts'.[24] Despite his efforts to erase all traces of his early experiments in stage management, we have a playbill (Figure 7.1) and enough correspondence to reconstruct a performance event at Bentinck Street on 27 April 1833.[25]

The aggregate would have functioned quite differently for the twenty-one-year-old Dickens performing at his parents' home than it did when he was hosting grand private theatricals at Tavistock House; the guest he was then probably most concerned with pleasing was Maria Beadnell, who he had been courting unsuccessfully for four years. The plays for this particular performance – *Clari*, *The Married Bachelor* and *Amateurs and Actors* – are typical for an amateur production: a long piece and two short farces.[26] Dickens seems to have pursued a thematic linking in his selection; all of the plays feature women running away with men to be secretly married or jilted by aristocratic rogues. Beyond the themes of female virtue and victimisation, two of the

Private Theatricals.

STAGE MANAGER, MR. CHARLES DICKENS.

ON SATURDAY EVENING, APRIL 27, 1833,

At Seven o'clock precisely. The performances will commence with

AN INTRODUCTORY PROLOGUE;

THE PRINCIPAL CHARACTERS BY

MR. EDWARD BARROW; MR. MILTON; MR. CHARLES DICKENS; MISS AUSTIN;
AND MISS DICKENS.

IMMEDIATELY AFTER WHICH WILL BE PRESENTED THE OPERA OF

CLARI.

The Duke Vivaldi	MR. BRAMWELL,
Rolamo, a Farmer, (Father to Clari)	MR. C. DICKENS,
Jocoso, (Valet to the Duke)	MR. H. AUSTIN,
Nicolo	MR. MILTON,
Geronio	MR. E. BARROW,
Nimpedo	MR. R. AUSTIN,
Pages to the Duke	MASTERS F. DICKENS & A. DICKENS.
Clari	MISS DICKENS,
Fidalma (her Mother)	MISS L. DICKENS,
Vespina	MISS AUSTIN,
Ninette	MISS OPPENHEIM.

CHARACTERS IN THE EPISODE.

The Nobleman	MR. HENRY KOLLE,
Pelgrino, a Farmer	MR. JOHN DICKENS,
Wife of Pelgrino	MISS URQUHART,
Leoda	MISS OPPENHEIM.

AFTER WHICH THE FAVOURITE INTERLUDE OF

The Married Bachelor.

Sir Charles Courtall	MR. C. DICKENS,
Sharp	MR. JOHN URQUHART,
Lady Courtall	MISS L. DICKENS,
Grace	MISS DICKENS.

TO CONCLUDE WITH THE FARCE OF

Amateurs & Actors.

David Duket, Esq. (a Musical Dramatic Amateur, who employs Mr. O. P. Bustle, and attached to Theatricals and Miss Mary Hardacre)	MR. H. AUSTIN,
Mr. O. P. Bustle, (a Provincial Manager, but engaged to superintend some Private Theatricals)	MR. BRAMWELL,
Wing, (a poor Country Actor)	MR. C. DICKENS,
Berry, (an Actor for the heavy Business)	MR. BOSTON,
Elderberry, (a retired Manufacturer, simple in wit and manners, and utterly unacquainted with Theatricals)	MR. J. DICKENS,
Timkins, (Elderberry's Factotum)	MR. R. AUSTIN,
Geoffry Muffincap, (an elderly Charity Boy, let out as a Servant at Bustle's Lodging)	MR. E. BARROW,
Miss Mary Hardacre, (a fugitive Ward of Elderberry's	MISS DICKENS,
Mrs. Mary Goneril, (a Strolling Tragedy Actress, and a serious evil to her Husband)	MISS OPPENHEIM

The Scenery by Messrs. H. Austin, Milton, H. Kolle, and Assistants.——The Band which will be numerous and complete, under the direction of Mr. E. Barrow.

J. & G. Nichols, Printers, Earl's Court, Cranbourn Street, Soho.

Figure 7.1 Playbill for *Clari* (1833). Courtesy of the Charles Dickens Museum, London [F273].

three plays also depict theatrical productions. The comic moments of these plays, in fact, turn on the demands placed on the managers of the productions.

Dickens's company in 1833 included six family members and ten friends, and it was the friends who were more difficult to manage as they had to travel to the house for regular rehearsals. Fred Kaplan includes in his biography the list of regulations Dickens's company members were expected to follow, written out and distributed by Henry Austin. One imagines Dickens eagerly occupying the managerial role here, knowingly alluding to common sources of conflict in amateur productions and attempting to banish them from his troupe:

> Mr Dickens is desirous that it should be distinctly understood by his friends that it is his wish to have a series of Weekly Rehearsals for some time, experience having already shown that Rehearsals are perhaps the most amusing part of private theatricals [. . .] 2. It is earnestly hoped that Ladies and Gentlemen who may have somewhat inferior parts assigned them in any piece, will recollect the impossibility of giving every performer a principal character, and that they will be consequently induced rather to consult the general convenience and amusement than individual feeling upon the subject [. . .] 3. [costume]. 4. [. . .] a punctual attendance at Rehearsals, and an early knowledge of the several parts, are most especially necessary. 5. It is proposed that a Rehearsal shall take place every Wednesday at 7 o'clock precisely—Charles Dickens, Stage Manager.[27]

Dickens's letter to Henry Kolle in April, in which he says, 'of course', he 'much regretted the absence of any Member of my company on the occasion of a Grand Rehearsal', suggests that not everyone heeded this mandate, but of course Kolle was playing only a small role.[28]

The plays selected were all available from John Cumberland, the publisher of acting editions that would eventually be bought out by T. H. Lacy in 1848.[29] Because the promptbook from the performance event is not extant, one cannot know the exact text Dickens used, but Cumberland's edition would certainly have served the purpose. The acting editions claim to replicate all of the business from the professional production. Though often used by amateurs, they do not modify the plays for amateur performance. The 'OPERA OF CLARI', announced on the bill, premiered at Covent Garden in 1823 as *Clari, or The Maid of Milan*.[30] The play tells the story of a peasant girl, Clari, who is seduced by the Duke Vivaldi, who promises marriage but instead holds her prisoner in his castle. Most interesting for Dickens's amateur production is the fact that the opera includes a play performed by strolling players. On Dickens's playbill, the characters of this play are listed as 'characters in the episode', and they map onto the plot of the opera. The nobleman in that episode, like Duke Vivaldi, lures away a young peasant girl, who represents Clari. When the Duke arranges for the play to be performed for Clari, she so identifies with the plight of the peasant girl that she leaps onstage and intervenes on the peasant girl's behalf. Just to ensure the audience grasps how very similar the two situations are, the song that Clari sings in her nostalgia for home, the now famous 'Home, Sweet Home', is the same tune the character in the play sings.[31] This similarity is what drives Clari to make a spectacle of herself at the climax of the play.

The revival of Richard Brinsley Peake's farce *Amateurs and Actors* in 1827, nine years after its debut at the Theatre Royal, Covent Garden, surely factored into Dickens's decision to add it to the bill of fare. The play was first performed at Covent Garden in 1818.[32] In it, the professional stage manager, Bustle, is a source of much comedy in his frenzied attention to all aspects of a private production. On the professional stage, Peake's play allowed professionals to comment on the craze for private theatricals, and this was not new. Helen Brooks describes a caricatured depiction of amateurs in the play *Private Theatricals* (1787) by James Powell in which Lady Grubb is so eager to see her name in the papers that she writes her own review.[33] The plot of *Amateurs and Actors* revolves around a private theatrical being arranged by a provincial manager, and the fact that the play returned to the stage some nine years after its original premiere signals continued public interest in the subject.

Amateurs and Actors does not actually mock amateurs so much as the professionals who manage and act alongside amateurs. The manager describes amateurs as 'liberal patrons, but barbarous murderers, of the Drama', but we never see these amateur performers – only the professionals, who are shown to create involuntary burlesque themselves.[34] The preface to the play explains that the professional actress, Mrs Mary Goneril, is 'not the first lady of high pretensions, who has burlesqued Shakespeare,—and probably without intending it'.[35] The underlying premise of the play betrays an anxiety that, if non-professionals begin acting, then one will not be able to tell the difference between actors and gentlemen. The play's humour pivots on a harried provincial (and professional) stage manager, Mr O. P. Bustle, who is pulled in all directions by his company of amateurs and actors. Adopted by Dickens, the play invites the amateurs to use the Bentinck Street home, which would inevitably be filled with theatrical activity and properties, as a set with similar characteristics.

Consider, for example, this scene of rehearsal between Mrs Mary Goneril (played by Miss Oppenheim), a professional actress who has been brought in to serve as the 'tragedy heroine' opposite Mr Wing (played by Dickens), a poor country actor who had just been relating a story about his wife, an actress from his company, who ran away with another actor who played 'our Harlequin'.[36] Mrs Mary Goneril, it turns out, is this runaway wife. Within Bustle's line introducing the two, the stage directions lay out the recognition:

> BUS. I must introduce you to each other—Mrs Goneril, give me leave to present—
> [*Wing comes forward*, R.] Mr Wing to you. [*She shrieks. Wing starts, and exit*
> R. *a la 'Stranger', Act 4. Scene last, and is pulled back by the skirts of his coat, by*
> *Bustle.*] Very well! bravo! a very natural tragedy outcry.[37]

Through asides, the spectators of this play are made to understand what Bustle does not know: that the two are husband and wife. The aggregate that their knowledge of one another creates during the rehearsal is the source of the scene's comedy. The reference in the stage directions is to *The Stranger* (1798), the English translation of August von Kotzebue's melodrama *Menschenhass und Reue* (1790), which features a scene of horrified recognition between estranged husband and wife. If well executed and recognised by the spectators of Dickens's production, it would have provided a reference to the professional stage. As they rehearse the balcony scene from *Romeo and Juliet*, Bustle finds Mrs Mary Goneril 'a little too affected', to which she responds that the scene 'is pathetic, and I ought to be affected'.[38] She speaks of her own situation, of course, not Juliet's.

A rehearsal or backstage play always involves a degree of self-reflexivity about the craft of acting – we see characters on stage assume roles and are reminded that what we are watching is artifice. It is not surprising, then, that playwrights would respond to the popularity of amateur theatricals with this trope. That Dickens selected plays with metatheatrical moments could suggest that he wanted to call attention to the artifice of his own production and laugh knowingly with the audience at their imperfections. And without money for a stage thirty feet deep, nor gas lines for special lighting effects, surely Dickens's early theatricals must have had their imperfections. But Dickens's managerial style also points to the pursuit of a production that would announce itself as deliberately, and proudly, amateur. What is interesting in *Clari* and *Amateurs and Actors* is the fact that all actors with on-stage roles in the play are actually professionals – no amateurs are shown performing. In other words, when members of Dickens's amateur theatrical troupe impersonated actors, they were impersonating professional actors, not amateur actors. It is just as likely, therefore, that these backstage plays were selected to allow amateurs to mock professionals. One can imagine Dickens, having recently decided against a career on the stage, playing a professional actor in a way that draws attention to the fact that he is *not* a poor country actor with an estranged wife. In other words, he could exploit the aggregate created by his performance to emphasise that he is a respectable man courting a proper young lady.

Dickens and Public Theatricals

Dickens's production at Bentinck Street in 1833 suggests that he may have already been positioning himself as a deliberate amateur in his home theatricals. His first production on a London stage in 1845, with a bill including Ben Jonson's *Every Man in His Humour*, provides ample evidence that he cultivated this position of superiority. This is most evident in his interactions with Fanny Kelly, whose theatre he rented for the production. And when the carefully publicised 'private' performance attracted attention, the amateurs were asked to repeat the play for a larger audience. In this 1845 production, I argue, Dickens discovered charity as a useful strategy for preserving his status as an amateur while performing for ever larger audiences. Drawing on Gilli Bush-Bailey's meticulously researched performance biography of Kelly, I argue that Dickens saw himself as (and, in many ways, was) Kelly's benefactor.

Fanny Kelly was a popular actress who started honing her craft at the age of seven, when she began acting alongside Sarah Siddons and other luminaries of the Georgian stage.[39] In 1835, when she retired from the Theatres Royal at the age of forty-five (because, in her words, 'my services ceased to be required'), she embarked upon an ambitious plan to develop a dramatic school and an adjoining theatre, where 'the youthful pupils of both sexes' would be afforded 'a fair proportion of the funds arising from their own exertions'.[40] This endeavour, supported financially by the Duke of Devonshire, was publicised as an effort to revive the stage as a dignified profession. It is useful to consider Kelly's dramatic school, an ambitious attempt to 'recall the Stage from a state of degradation',[41] alongside Dickens's formation of a troupe of gentleman actors, which positions Dickens alongside other deliberate amateurs who seek to distinguish their involvement with the dramatic arts from the work of professional actors. Bush-Bailey's work reveals that Kelly shared some of Dickens's criticisms of the professional stage in 1845.[42] The complex and contradictory nature of these criticisms prompted the two to respond in different ways.

The venue emerging from Kelly's plan, 'Miss Kelly's Theatre', had a less than impressive opening in 1840. The circumstances of the opening are complex and easily oversimplified – an issue that Bush-Bailey's careful research corrects.[43] One factor stands out as particularly relevant to this chapter. As Bush-Bailey explains, Kelly was courting audiences who preferred private amateur performances, but not quite hitting the mark: 'The intimacy of the house, its "comfort and elegance", evoke images of the private theatrical, rather than the commercial public venue.'[44] She goes on to suggest that 'it is hard to avoid the conclusions that Kelly is uncomfortably straddling two worlds here'.[45] I would suggest that, if Kelly was attempting to recreate the feeling of a private theatrical in a public venue while charging for seats and performing alongside actors-in-training, she was misunderstanding the primary appeal of amateur theatricals (most notably, the effect of the aggregate). If she were going to harness the commercial potential of the rage for private theatricals, the spectators would need to know the performers personally.

It is possible that Kelly was aware of this unique feature of private theatricals and incorporated it into her plan. It seems she might have considered theatrical amateurs as a possible source of income from the outset, as an 1840 announcement of the theatre in the *Theatrical Journal* describes it as 'for private performance and for public ones'.[46] By the time Dickens was ready to perform in a public theatre, five years after her theatre opened to lacklustre reviews, it would seem that Kelly's primary (and unfortunately very meagre) income came from renting the venue for private performances and supplying professional actors to join the amateurs. Bush-Bailey notes that the money Kelly received from Dickens for the use of her theatre was the only income she received in 1845 and 1846.[47] Though it certainly was not the goal of her theatre, the strategy Kelly scraped together – appealing to the desires of amateurs in an effort to stay afloat financially – has perhaps most in common with the much-maligned private theatres that Dickens mocked in *Sketches*. This comparison would probably have horrified Kelly; one wonders if it occurred to Dickens.

After the performance, Dickens and his amateur troupe performed in a private benefit for Kelly, positioning themselves even more explicitly as her benefactors: deliberate amateurs quite distinct from the professionals. By offering charity, or benefit, theatricals, amateurs expanded on the practice of benefit performances in commercial theatres, a notoriously corrupt system whereby poorly paid actors were appeased by carefully negotiated benefit nights from which they would take all or part of the profit.[48] Amateurs did not want to *appear* to be interested in making money, but there was nothing shameful about raising money for charity. Many amateur theatricals were probably organised out of purely benevolent motives, but I argue that whichever came first – the desire to maintain one's status as an amateur or the desire to raise money for charity – charity shielded performers from being perceived as professional. Some amateurs actually used charity to fund their hobby. This scheme was rarely acknowledged explicitly in the period, but Shirley Hodson states the case in a very straightforward manner in his guidebook for private theatricals in 1888. As he explains, the great expense of carpentry and lighting necessary to convert a parlour into a theatrical venue, necessarily coming out of pocket, could make such elaborate preparations impossible:

> If, however, the performances could be undertaken for the benefit of some benevolent object, the expenses might, by judicious and prudent management, not only be all defrayed without unnecessary burden to any individual, but a balance handed over in the cause of charity.[49]

This is, of course, a very good model, making one's hobby considerably less expensive, as Dickens discovered.

The use of public theatres made amateur theatricals vulnerable to public prejudices and censorship – elements of performance arguably side-stepped in private performance. For most of the century, for example, female amateurs did not appear on public stages for fear of being found unladylike.[50] Gentlemen amateurs hired professional actresses to fill the female roles. Dickens's production at Miss Kelly's theatre featured professional actresses whose performances go unacknowledged in public reviews. When the production of *The Frozen Deep* moved from Tavistock House to a charitable tour, Dickens's daughters were replaced by professional actresses. We know about these actresses now, of course, because of Dickens's relationship with Ellen Ternan.

Dickens undertook the production of *Every Man in His Humour* with no charitable goal, but a charitable need emerged. Explaining the initial scheme to George Cruikshank, he writes that the idea for the play was arranged 'quite offhand' at a country dinner; the play would seem to have been selected for the fun each amateur could have inhabiting Jonson's comic characters.[51] The week after the private performance at Miss Kelly's theatre, which took place on Saturday, 20 September, Dickens responded to a request for information about the next private performance of the play with this:

> If we should repeat *Every Man in his Humour* to a Private audience, I shall be happy to send you an Invitation. But we have no plan or idea of doing so, at this time, that I know of. And I should certainly, in my managerial capacity, have early knowledge of any such intention.[5]

Five days later, responding to a letter from Thomas Powell, who has presumably asked if another performance might be arranged to benefit the Southwood Smith Sanatorium, Dickens explains that requests for more performances have become a daily 'botheration', and suggests that 'a letter from Southwood Smith, or from some of the Committee addressed to me as Manager would be the best mode of bringing it before the Body of Amateurs, if you really desire that they should consider it in a business-like way'.[53] He writes to Southwood Smith on 9 October to say that he will be discussing the proposal with the group, but adds, 'Jerrold has a strong objection to playing to an audience who pay for their seats.'[54] By 26 October, he writes to Stanfield that Prince Albert, then serving as president of the Sanatorium Committee, has made it impossible to refuse:

> Here is the Devil to pay. Prince Albert has written to say that he dies to see the Amateur Performance on behalf of the Sanatorium, and can it be done on the

fifteenth! Lord and Lady Lansdowne and the 'Tarnal Smash knows who, have taken Boxes. And on the fifteenth (three weeks from yesterday) it must come off.[5]

He writes to Miss Kelly on 27 October to explain that they 'are obliged to go to the St James's Theatre' for the 'Sanatorium Representation', because 'Prince Albert is coming; and they have already exceeded your means of accommodation'.[56]

At some point, either as part of an original agreement with Kelly for the use of her theatre or after the amateurs agreed to perform for the Sanatorium benefit, Dickens promised to offer a private performance for her benefit. Dickens had been fairly terse with Kelly throughout negotiations for the use of her theatre, commenting on her anxieties about such an elite audience in her theatre to his friends. He writes to Forster on 10 August of a 'scene' he had with Kelly about their use of the theatre, relating the event as though he is testing it as a comic scene for a future novel:

> Heavens! Such a scene as I have had with Miss Kelly here, this morning! She wanted us put off until the theatre should be cleaned and brushed up a bit, and she would and she would not, for she is eager to have us and alarmed when she thinks of us. By the foot of Pharaoh, it was a great scene! Especially when she choked, and had the glass of water brought. She exaggerates the importance of our occupation, dreads the least prejudice against the establishment in the minds of any of our company, says the place already has quite ruined her, and with tears in her eyes protests that any jokes at her additional expense in print would drive her mad.[5]

The editors of Dickens's letters suggest that Kelly's anxiety resulted from the potential that the players of the company – so many being writers for *Punch* – might mock her humble establishment. Bush-Bailey adds much more detail to this explanation,[58] showing how these *Punch* men had already taken significant swipes at her theatre.[59]

The relationship between the amateur manager and the professional proprietor seems to have retained this hierarchy. The amateurs were doing her a favour by using her theatre, and they were directly alleviating her financial distress with the benefit in her honour, as evidenced in a letter dated 3 December:

> Yesterday was the first opportunity the Principals in our little Corps have had, of meeting together. We find from the nature of our various engagements, that it would be most unsafe and inexpedient to postpone the Play for your benefit until January. We could not do so, with any reasonable prospect of fulfilling our promise. And therefore we have decided to act on *Saturday the 27th of this month*. You may proceed accordingly, in the full confidence of that being the Night. In case you wish us to act in any Theatre but your own, it must not be larger than the Saint James's.
>
> We will communicate with you again, in a very few days, and tell you what Play and afterpiece we shall then have decided on, and what we shall ask you to act. But the Night is subject to no change or discussion.[6]

Important here is the way Dickens dictates how his 'little Corps' will fulfil their promise to Miss Kelly. He tells her the date (which *did* change, to 3 January), and will be telling her the plays that will be performed. This becomes an interesting intersection of

AMATEUR THEATRICALS

109

amateur performance and charity when one considers that he is managing the recipient of his benevolence. The announcement of the performance in *The Literary Gazette* elaborates on the reason for the benefit:

> It is, we believe, pretty generally known that, with all her talents, Miss Kelly, owing to unfortunate circumstances in the disposal of the money their exercise had acquired, did not retire from public life with that provision for the future she had so honourably earned; and therefore we cannot but hope that a bumper house will express the sympathy felt for her on the score of her own deserts.[6]

Bush-Bailey provides the context necessary to understand the dynamic between a well-connected amateur and the owner of a professional theatre. Most important, Bush-Bailey places Fanny Kelly's situation in the 1840s into the context of a challenging marketplace. What began as a private performance for invited friends in a rented public theatre led to a benefit performance in the service of a charitable cause, which just so happens to be the cash-strapped manager of that theatre.

It is important to understand how the very first performance of the play, which was intended to be very private, received such publicity and even culminated in a benefit performance. The most important thing to Dickens as a deliberate amateur – his reason for securing Miss Kelly's theatre – was to ensure a private performance. In explaining the scheme to Cruikshank, he emphasises several provisions for maintaining the privacy of the performance:

> We have Miss Kelly's little Theatre—which is strictly and perfectly private. We play on Saturday the 20th of next month—a month hence. We rehearse, on the stage, generally once a week; and the next Rehearsal is on Tuesday Evening at a quarter before Seven. [. . .] No names will be printed in our Bills, but the names of the characters. It will be done with every possible appliance in the way of arrangement, correct costume, and so forth. The admissions will be by a printed card of Invitation, addressed to the person invited by all concerned, as if it were a party. And no man can have any visitor (being obliged to make the names of his list known to the rest beforehand) to whom anyone else objects. [. . .] Every actor will have the privilege of inviting about five and thirty friends.[62]

One can interpret this as a provision against hecklers, but also as an attempt to recreate in a public theatre the select audience one was able to manage in a private residence.

Dickens reports in a letter to Madame de la Rue one week after the performance that 'on the night it was as much as we could do, with a strong body of Police, to keep the doors from being carried by force. It got into the Papers, notwithstanding all our precautions.'[63] In her note to the letter, Tillotson quotes *The Literary Gazette*'s report on 27 September that guests were admitted on the understanding that the evening was private:

> but it is not easy to keep from the press secrets entrusted to ten or fifteen score of confidants [. . .]. [W]e have been released from our implied pledge and may speak of the representation nearly as a public event.[64]

110   MARY ISBELL

Tillotson suggests that Forster sought out attention from the press, citing a letter from J. P. Collier of *The Morning Chronicle* apologising to Forster for not including mention of the performance and explaining that he had taken '"strictly private" quite literally'.[65]

This new understanding of Dickens's involvement with amateur theatricals can help us understand the mixed reviews of *Every Man in His Humour*. The amateurs' control over their audience shifted slightly when the performance occurred again for the Sanatorium. In early negotiations about the Sanatorium performance, Dickens writes, 'I have a great doubt whether the Company in general would like to play to that kind of audience; and I am not at all clear that I should like it myself.'[66] The announcement of the Sanatorium benefit performance in *The Morning Chronicle* explained that a special committee for issuing invitation cards had been formed, and one third of the announcement is devoted to listing their names.[67] Many of the members of the committee distributing invitations for the performance at St James's theatre had been present at the first performance, but their invitees were seeing it for the first time, and had little to no connection to the amateurs performing. While the public review was polite, Henry Greville recalls in his memoir that, between the acts, Lord Melbourne announced from his box, 'in a stentorian voice, heard across the pit, "I knew this play would be dull, but that it would be so damnably dull as this I did not suppose!"'[68] Had the amateurs a choice in their guest list – a privilege they had so carefully guarded for the first performance – such a spectator entering with a mind to criticise might not have been invited. We might assume Dickens refers to Lord Melbourne as a mover in the ''Tarnal Smash' he dreads in his initial letter to Stanfield about the repeat performance. In the frenzy of attention Dickens drew by publicising his efforts as a celebrated amateur for a private audience, Dickens slid a little closer to experiencing the life of an actor whose profession required the resolve to stand before a public audience and endure abuse if it should be hurled. It would seem he liked flirting with the line between actor and amateur, and he used charity as a useful shield as he continued to manage amateur productions in the years to come.

Notes

This chapter is expanded from my dissertation, with archival research funded by the American Society for Theatre Research, the UConn English department, the UConn Graduate School, the Society for Theatre Research and the UConn Humanities Institute.

1. Malcolm Morley, 'Theatre Royal, Montreal', *Dickensian* 45 (1949), 39–44.
2. 'To Madame de la Rue, 27 September 1845', *The Letters of Charles Dickens,* ed. by Madeline House, Graham Storey et al., Pilgrim/British Academy Edition, 12 vols (Oxford: Clarendon Press, 1965–2002). Subsequent citations: *PLets* followed by volume (year of publication), page. Here IV (1977), 388 n. 3.
3. James Shirley Hodson, *A History of the Printing Trade Charities* (London: Spottiswoode, 1883), 145.
4. Ibid., 93.
5. For the famous account of Dickens considering a career on the professional stage, see John Forster, *The Life of Charles Dickens*, ed. by J. W. T. Ley (London: Cecil Palmer, 1928), 380–1. Fred Kaplan, in *Dickens: A Biography*, rev. edn (Baltimore: Johns Hopkins University Press, 1998), finds it amazing that Dickens 'saw nothing incompatible in producing,

directing, and acting while writing [*Little Dorrit*] and editing *Household Words*' (352). In *Charles Dickens* (New Haven: Yale University Press, 2009), Michael Slater describes that same production as a 'continuation of his novel-writing by other means', noting Dickens's comment that the pleasure he derived from 'feigning to be somebody else' was 'akin to the pleasure of inventing' (qtd on 393). In Chapter 19 of *Charles Dickens: A Life* (London: Penguin, 2011), Claire Tomalin ascribes to *The Frozen Deep* a similar function, though she places less emphasis on Dickens's ability to multitask and more on the way the production provided an escape from his unhappy home life, particularly since it placed Dickens one step closer to the actress Ellen Ternan, who would take a part in the play when it was performed publicly.

6. Bratton's introduction to *Dickensian Dramas: Plays from Charles Dickens*, 2 vols (Oxford: Oxford University Press, 2017), I, offers the invaluable perspective of a theatre historian on Dickens's early involvement with the professional stage. In the history she reconstructs, we see the same fascination with the stage I recount here, along with the same prejudices that fuelled his deliberate amateurism. Bratton argues that the lack of enthusiasm in 1838 at Covent Garden for his play *The Lamplighter* prompted Dickens to decide 'that his rise to the top of his profession meant he must distance himself from the mob of jobbing, semi-anonymous writers whose markets included the popular stage' (xvii). The success of *Pickwick* and *Oliver Twist* 'made him suddenly aware that he had overcommitted and underpriced himself in a cut-throat marketplace, and that he urgently needed to put himself on a higher, more exclusive plane—that of the gentleman novelist' (xviii). Importantly, Bratton emphasises that Dickens's condescending assessments of his contemporaries are far from an objective portrayal of their work and value (xviii).

7. For example, see Sybil Rosenfeld, *Temples of Thespis: Some Private Theatres and Theatricals in England and Wales, 1700–1820* (London: Society for Theatre Research Press, 1978) and Karen J. Blair, *The Torchbearers: Women and their Amateur Arts Associations in America, 1890–1930* (Bloomington: Indiana University Press, 1994).

8. See Claire Cochrane, 'The Pervasiveness of the Commonplace: The Historian and Amateur Theatre', *Theatre Research International* 26.3 (2001), 233–42; David Mayer, 'Parlour and Platform Melodrama', *Melodrama: The Cultural Emergence of a Genre* (New York: Palgrave, 1996), 211–34; Emily Bryan, 'Nineteenth-Century Charade Dramas: Syllables of Gentility and Sociability', *Nineteenth Century Theatre and Film* 29 (2002), 32–48; and Heidi Weig, 'Amateur Theatricals and the Dramatic Marketplace: Lacy's and French's Acting Editions of Plays', *Nineteenth Century Theatre and Film* 44.2 (2017), 173–91.

9. *Le Grand Robert* finds it meaning 'personne qui aime, cultive, recherche (certain choses, certaines activites)' as early as 1504, but in 1762 it took on a second definition: 'Personne qui cultive un art, une science pour son seul plaisir (et non par profession)'.

10. See Magali Sarfatti Larson, *The Rise of Professionalism: A Sociological Analysis* (Berkeley: University of California Press, 1977); Penelope J. Corfield, *Power and the Professions in Britain, 1700–1850* (London: Routledge, 1995); and Jennifer Ruth, *Novel Professions: Interested Disinterest and the Making of the Professional in the Victorian Novel* (Columbus: Ohio State University Press, 2006).

11. See, for example, Marjorie Garber, *Academic Instincts* (Princeton: Princeton University Press, 2001) and Philippa Levine, *The Amateur and the Professional: Antiquarians, Historians, and Archaeologists in Victorian England, 1838–1886* (Cambridge: Cambridge University Press, 1986).

12. For more on this dynamic, see discussions of The Pic Nic Society, one of the earliest amateur dramatic societies: Rosenfeld, 12; Gillian Russell, *The Theatres of War: Performance, Politics, and Society, 1793–1815* (Oxford: Clarendon Press, 1995), 127; and Michael Dobson *Shakespeare and Amateur Performance: A Cultural History* (Cambridge: Cambridge University Press, 2011), 74.

13. Emily Eden, *Miss Eden's Letters* (London: Macmillan, 1919), 177.
14. Richard Cumberland, 'Remarks Upon the Present Taste for Acting Private Plays', *The European Magazine* (1788), 115–18.
15. Charles Dickens, 'Amusements of the People (I)', in *Dickens' Journalism*, ed. by Michael Slater and John Drew, 4 vols (London: J. M. Dent, 1994–2000), II (1997), 179–85, 181–2.
16. J. Ellen Gainor, 'The Provincetown Players' Experiments with Realism', *Realism and the American Dramatic Tradition* (Tuscaloosa: The University of Alabama Press, 1996), 61–2.
17. Jane Austen, *Mansfield Park: Authoritative Text, Contexts, Criticism* (New York: Norton, 1998), 118–19.
18. See Janine Marie Haugen, 'The Mimic Stage: Private Theatricals in Georgian Britain' (unpublished doctoral thesis, University of Colorado, 2014).
19. Christoph Bode has contributed considerably to our understanding of the reputation of this play by exploring Inchbald's modifications from the German in 'Unfit for an English Stage? Inchbald's *Lovers' Vows* and Kotzebue's *Das Kind der Liebe*', *European Romantic Review* 16.3 (2005), 297–309.
20. Marvin A. Carlson, *The Haunted Stage: The Theatre as Memory Machine* (Ann Arbor: University of Michigan Press, 2001).
21. Geoffrey Wansell, *The Garrick Club: A History* (London: Unicorn, 2004), 9.
22. Charles Dickens the Younger, 'Glimpses of Charles Dickens', *North American Review* 160.462 (1895), 535.
23. Slater, 413.
24. 'Private Theatricals at Tavistock House', *Illustrated London News* (17 January 1857), 51–2.
25. Charles Haywood, 'Charles Dickens and Shakespeare, or, the Irish Moor of Venice, *O'Thello*, with Music', *Dickensian* 73 (1977), 67–88, 68.
26. See W. G. Elliot, *Amateur Clubs and Actors* (London: Edward Arnold, 1898).
27. Dickens, qtd in Kaplan, 56.
28. 'To H. W. Kolle [?15 April 1833]', *PLets*, I (1965), 19.
29. K. Mattacks, 'Acts of Piracy: *Black Ey'd Susan*, Theatrical Publishing and the Victorian Stage', in *Pirates and Mutineers in Victorian Culture*, ed. by Grace Moore (Farnham: Ashgate, 2011), 136.
30. John Howard Payne, *Clari, or The Maid of Milan* (London: J. Cumberland, 1823).
31. John Howard Payne, *Home, Sweet Home* (New York: Charles T. Dillingham, c.1880).
32. Richard Brinsley Peake, *Amateurs and Actors* (London: J. Cumberland, 1827).
33. Helen E. M. Brooks, '"One Entire Nation of Actors and Actresses": Reconsidering the Relationship of Public and Private Theatricals', *Nineteenth Century Theatre and Film* 38.2 (2011), 1–22, 4.
34. Peake, 17.
35. Ibid., 6.
36. Ibid., 18.
37. Ibid., 20.
38. Ibid., 20.
39. *Examiner*, 14 June 1835. Qtd in Gilli Bush-Bailey, *Performing Herself: AutoBiography and Fanny Kelly's Dramatic Recollections* (Manchester: Manchester University Press, 2011), 19.
40. Bush-Bailey, 19; V&A theatre collection, Dean Street box. Qtd in Bush-Bailey, 68.
41. V&A theatre collection, Dean Street box. Qtd in Bush-Bailey, 68.
42. Bush-Bailey, 68.
43. Ibid., 70–7.
44. *The Times*, 16 May 1840. Qtd in Bush-Bailey, 74.
45. Bush-Bailey, 74.

46. 'Chit Chat', *Theatrical Journal; London* 1.21 (May 1840), 178–9.
47. 'To Miss Fanny Kelly, 11 August 1847' and 'To Miss Fanny Kelly, 12 November 1847' *PLets*, v, 146, 195. Cited in Bush-Bailey, 89.
48. See St Vincent Troubridge and the Society for Theatre Research, *The Benefit System in the British Theatre* (London: Society for Theatre Research, 1967).
49. James Shirley Hodson, *Private Theatricals: Being a Practical Guide for the Home Stage* (London: W. H. Allen, 1881), 31.
50. Eileen Curley, 'Tainted Money?: Nineteenth-Century Charity Theatricals', *Theatre Symposium* 15.1 (2012), 52–73.
51. 'To George Cruikshank, [?22 August 1845]', *PLets*, IV, 361–2.
52. 'To Dr J. A. Wilson, 24 September 1845', *PLets*, IV, 386.
53. 'To Thomas Powell, 29 September 1845', *PLets*, IV, 392.
54. 'To Dr Southwood Smith, 9 October 1845', *PLets*, IV, 402.
55. 'To Clarkson Stanfield, 26 October 1845', *PLets*, IV, 415.
56. 'To Miss Fanny Kelly, 27 October 1845', *PLets*, IV, 416.
57. 'To John Forster, [?10 August 1845]', *PLets*, IV, 351.
58. Bush-Bailey, 86.
59. *Punch* (January 1842), 111. Qtd in Bush-Bailey, 81. *Punch* (December 1842), 248. Qtd in Bush-Bailey, 81–2; *Punch* (20 April 1844). Qtd in Bush-Bailey, 83.
60. 'To Miss Fanny Kelly, 3 December 1845', *PLets*, IV, 445. Italics in the original.
61. 'Miss Kelly', *The Literary Gazette and Journal of the Belles Lettres* (3 January 1846), 14.
62. 'To George Cruikshank, [?22 August 1845]', *PLets*, IV, 361–2.
63. 'To Madame de la Rue, 27 September 1845', *PLets*, IV, 387–8.
64. 'Drama Extraordinary', *The Literary Gazette and Journal of the Belles Lettres* (27 September 1845), 644–5.
65. 'To Madame de la Rue, 27 September 1845', *PLets*, IV, 388 n. 3.
66. 'To Thomas Powell, 29 September 1845', *PLets*, IV, 392–3.
67. 'Performance in Aid of the Sanatorium', *Morning Chronicle* (3 November 1845), 5.
68. Charles Cavendish Fulke Greville, *The Greville Memoirs: A Journal of the Reign of Queen Victoria from 1837 to 1860* (New York: D. Appleton, 1885), 39 n. 1; 'To Benjamin Webster, 17 November 1845', *PLets*, IV, 435 n. 3.

Further Reading

Malcolm Andrews, *Charles Dickens and His Performing Selves: Dickens and the Public Readings* (Oxford: Oxford University Press, 2006)

Jacky Bratton and Jim Davis, eds, *Dickensian Dramas: Plays from Charles Dickens*, 2 vols (Oxford: Oxford University Press, 2017)

Malcolm Morley, 'Theatre Royal, Montreal', *Dickensian* 45 (1949), 39–44

Alan S. Watts, 'Amateur Theatricals of Dickens', in *Oxford Reader's Companion to Charles Dickens: Anniversary Edition*, ed. by Paul Schlicke (Oxford: Oxford University Press, 2011), 12–14

8

Nineteenth-Century Stage Adaptations

Jim Davis

Nineteenth-century stage adaptations of Dickens were not only a means of bringing Dickens's novels and stories to a wider public, but they were also a major influence on nineteenth-century theatre. They impacted on dramaturgy and acting, providing a series of outstanding character roles which not only enhanced the careers of many actors but also deepened and developed character acting on the British stage. Although George Bernard Shaw refers rather contemptuously to such performances as 'famous impersonations', there is plenty of evidence to suggest that Dickensian characterisations on stage were of far greater significance than Shaw allows.[1] John Glavin indicates why this was so when he writes that Dickens's characters tend to be drawn from the stage and that, however much they 'are caricatured on the page, generations of actors have found [them] matchlessly thrilling and rewarding to play'.[2] This perspective acknowledges the theatricality of Dickens's work, its origins in theatrical prototypes, and why adaptations for the stage remediate theatre back to theatre.

Dickens as an author was clearly influenced by the theatre and enjoyed participating in theatrical activities. Of his engagement in an amateur production of *The Frozen Deep* he wrote that, 'when it is made as good as my care can make it, I derive a strange feeling out of it, like writing a book in company'.[3] As Mary Isbell explores in this volume, there are many references to Dickens's painstaking oversight of the amateur performances he organised, as well as his skills as an actor. This suggests that he might have had a major impact on the professional theatre of his time if he had so wished. However, the low esteem in which the professional theatre and the profession of playwright were held in this period, particularly by those who believed the drama was in decline and threatened by the growth of more popular forms such as melodrama,[4] meant that a career as a novelist was both more lucrative and socially acceptable; it also enabled Dickens to maintain control over his work at a time when dramatic authorship was collaborative rather than autonomous. Dickens's reactions to theatrical adaptations of his work were sometimes negative, but in certain instances he also collaborated with theatrical managements and dramatists in staging versions of his novels.

While the theatre introduced Dickens to audience members unfamiliar with his work, the popularity of his novels ensured that other audience members brought a prior knowledge of the source material with them to the theatre. *The Era* (19 April 1868) considered that, 'Now that his books are within the reach of the great majority of his countrymen the urge to see his many lifelike characters embodied must be both strong and general.'[5] However, *The Times* (23 March 1877) warned against presuming this familiarity was true in every case and against the assumption that the intelligibility of any adaptation was therefore implicit.[6] Nevertheless, the representation of already familiar characters was important:

> The success of pieces of this kind, which purport chiefly to interest the public by the visible representation of characters already familiar through the medium of narrative, necessarily depends as much on the actors as on the dramatist. Indeed, the former stand in as immediate a relation to the novel as the latter, since it is from the novelist that every indication of individual peculiarity is derived, the work of the dramatist consisting of little more than arrangement, save when he goes out of his way to produce some marked 'effect', with which the display of character has little to do.[7]

In fact, successful adaptations of the novels depended on the dramaturgical skills of the dramatist rather than on a mere facility for 'arrangement' and sometimes, with the longer novels, on a process of selection which involved concentrating on one or two plots and subplots rather than the novel in its entirety.

Nevertheless, the success of Dickens's adaptations was regularly attributed to the actor rather than to the dramatist, as this chapter will demonstrate. Throughout the nineteenth century the actor is a crucial factor in the effective realisation of Dickens's work on stage. Robert and Mary Ann Keeley were among those who effectively represented Dickens's characters on stage in the earliest adaptations. Subsequently, actors and actresses such as Céline Céleste, Charles Fechter, J. L. Toole, Henry Irving, Jennie Lee and John Martin Harvey were to draw praise for their assumption of Dickensian characters. Dickens himself occasionally adapted (or was involved in the adaptation of) his own works, latterly for his highly performative public readings.

Early Adaptations: *The Pickwick Papers, Oliver Twist* and *Nicholas Nickleby*

In 1837 *The Pickwick Papers* (1836–7) was adapted for the stage long before its serialisation was completed, eight issues ahead of its completion in one instance, seven issues ahead in two others. (This tendency continued with adaptations of *Oliver Twist* (1837–9) and *Nicholas Nickleby* (1838–9), although the practice then declined.) W. Leman Rede adapted *The Pickwick Papers* for the Adelphi Theatre; Edward Stirling's version was performed at the City of London; and W. T. Moncrieff prepared a version for the Strand Theatre. The last of these enjoyed a considerable run; ironically, Moncrieff, together with Dickens, was on a shortlist of authors whom Chapman and Hall had considered approaching to write the text for a series of illustrations by Robert Seymour, which were to form the basis of this work.[8] Dickens referred to Moncrieff in a letter to John Forster stating that 'if the *Pickwick* has been the means of putting a few shillings in the vermin-eaten pockets of so miserable a creature and has saved him from the workhouse or a jail, let him empty out his little pot of filth and welcome'.[9] Moncrieff was actually a successful and popular playwright, best known perhaps for his dramatisation of Pierce Egan's *Tom and Jerry*. His dramatisation probably helped boost *Pickwick*'s popularity, as did his *Sam Weller, or, The Pickwickians*, written for actor-manager William James

Hammond. Hammond embodied Sam Weller for many spectators who had not read the original, bringing to life this cockney stereotype in London and the provinces.

As indicated above, *Oliver Twist* and *Nicholas Nickleby* were also adapted for the stage multiple times before the serial publication of each novel was completed. Dickens wrote to Frederick Yates, the manager of the Adelphi, offering to dramatise *Oliver Twist* for his theatre, but the offer was declined.[10] Dickens also attempted, unsuccessfully, to persuade Macready to let him adapt the novel for Covent Garden Theatre, but Macready declined on the grounds of 'the utter impracticability of *Oliver Twist* for any dramatic purpose'.[11] Nevertheless, *Oliver Twist* was widely adapted for the stage, not always to Dickens's liking. The Surrey Theatre's 1839 version, probably by George Almar, was visited by Dickens who, in the middle of the first scene, allegedly lay down on the floor in a corner of the box and did not rise until the final act-drop fell.[12] At least one dramatisation of *Nicholas Nickleby* drew a more positive response, even though Forster called it an 'indecent assault' upon the novel.[13] This was Edward Stirling's adaptation, performed at the Adelphi in 1838 under Yates's management. Yates also played Mantalini in what appears to have been an exceptionally well-cast production including Mary Ann Keeley as Smike. Dickens wrote to Yates explaining that his objection to adaptations of his works, especially those that were incomplete, was to those that vulgarised his characters and diminished ongoing interest in the novel. However, he had no such objections concerning this version and particularly praised the performances of Yates and Mrs Keeley, as well as O. Smith as Newman Noggs.[14] Edward Stirling was also responsible for the first London adaptation of *The Old Curiosity Shop* (1840–1) in 1840 at the Adelphi Theatre and for a version of *Barnaby Rudge* (1841) at the Strand in 1841. Up to this point, Dickens's response to dramatisations of his work was ambivalent. He was hostile to those he found ineffective, but happy to condone those he considered successful. In turn, the dramatisations certainly contributed to public awareness of this up-and-coming novelist.

Collaboration/Adaptation

Dickens's collaboration in theatrical representations of his works took several forms. His participation in amateur theatricals was ostensibly collaborative, although he clearly liked to be in control. He also collaborated with Wilkie Collins in the adaptation of their jointly written Christmas story *No Thoroughfare* (1867) (although this was largely Collins's work), later concocting his own dramatisation for performance in France. Thirdly, he collaborated with actors and dramatists in the professional theatre, advising on and helping to stage productions based on his work.

Mary Ann Keeley, whose Smike in Stirling's version of *Nicholas Nickleby* had been widely admired, was to play a significant role, together with her husband, Robert Keeley, in several adaptations involving the third type of collaboration with Dickens. It is quite possible that Dickens provided advice during *Nickleby* rehearsals, for Mary Ann Keeley recalls how 'the adapter had put into Smike's mouth a lot of stuff about "the little robins in the field". I shall never forget Dickens's face when he heard me repeating these lines. Turning to the prompter he said, "D – n the robins; cut them out."'[15] Dickens provides no evidence that he collaborated in this production, although his objection to these lines is recorded in a letter to Forster.[16] In 1844 the Keeleys took on the lease of the Lyceum Theatre and staged, with Dickens's permission, Edward Stirling's adaptation of *Martin Chuzzlewit*. Although Dickens was reluctant to provide a prologue for the play, he offered to work on the production itself: 'if you rehearse on Friday, I will gladly come down at any time you may appoint on that morning and go through it with you all.'[17] Keeley played Mrs Gamp; his wife Bailey, the boy servant. A prologue written by Albert Smith praised Dickens's propensity for his depiction of 'the powerful romance of common life'.[18]

Prior to this production Dickens had not only given Stirling exclusive permission to dramatise his 1843 Christmas book *A Christmas Carol* for the Adelphi Theatre, but had also assisted at rehearsals, according to Stirling.[19] The *Christmas Books* were to prove ideal material for stage adaptation, and subsequently Dickens contrived that publication of the stories would coincide with the presentation of adaptations in the West End.[20] Two versions of *The Chimes* opened in December 1844, both claiming Dickens's permission. The Adelphi version was by Gilbert Abbott à Beckett and Mark Lemon, to whom Dickens had sent advanced proof sheets; Stirling's Lyceum version featured Keeley as Trotty Veck. A year later *The Cricket on the Hearth*, which seems ready structured for theatrical adaptation, was widely staged.[21] Dickens authorised the version performed by the Keeleys, sending proof sheets in advance to Albert Smith who was responsible for the Lyceum adaptation. Mary Ann Keeley was highly praised as Dot, both for her 'busy, bustling, affectionate manner in the first "chirp"' and 'her anxiety in the last one'.[22] This was an extremely popular adaptation, although superseded by Dion Boucicault's more spectacular *Dot* in the 1860s. The following year Dickens sold the pre-publication rights of *The Battle of Life* (1846) to the Keeleys, coming back from Paris to assist at final rehearsals and reading the cast the complete story on the morning of the first night.[23] The Keeleys played a pair of servants: Clemency Newcome and Benjamin Britain. Mary Ann Keeley was widely praised for her Clemency, which *The Illustrated London News* (26 December 1846)[24] claimed was 'a most unqualified success', asserting that both author and dramatist [Albert Smith] were indebted to her performance – although Dickens may have been astute enough to create an outline that he knew Mary Ann Keeley would bring to life in performance. The actress was able to combine effectively both comedy and pathos and was particularly commended for her performance of the serious aspects of her character. Jacky Bratton writes, of one of her previous roles – Bailey in *The Chimes* – that she 'brought salt and scepticism – a kind of realism [. . .] – as her partial contribution to the Dickensian picture of common life'. She describes '[h]er comic ability to capture characters from the bottom rungs of the social scale and make them appear as living reflections of the new world, actual human beings not yet made over into art', adding that 'a slightly acerbic, unsentimental but delightfully moving common touch remained her contribution as an actress in the ensuing collaborations with Dickens'.[25] These are qualities that Mary Ann Keeley also contributed to her performance of Clemency, providing a partial basis perhaps for Bratton's subsequent claim that:

> *The Battle of Life* displays a kind of embodied and visual poeticism, an independence of plot, and attitude to character as psychological mirroring, that is and is not Realism: it suggests a kind of playwriting that was not to surface decisively for another fifty years, on the other side of the Naturalist revolution.[26]

Interestingly, as Bratton notes, a Russian adaptation of *The Battle of Life* became a part of the Moscow Art Theatre repertoire in 1924. The implicit modernism of the piece, to which Bratton refers, is also present in Mark Lemon's adaptation of *The Haunted Man* (Adelphi Theatre, 1848).

Dickens's close association with the Keeleys ended after *The Battle of Life*, but he continued to engage occasionally in preparing adaptations of his novels for the stage. After the publication of *A Tale of Two Cities* (1859), he had tried to interest his friend the French actor François Regnier in a Paris-based dramatisation, sending him proof sheets and asking him what he thought of it 'being dramatized for a French theatre'.[27] Regnier felt a Paris production would be politically unwise at the time, to which Dickens responded that, if it had been possible, then he 'wished to have the piece as well done as possible, and would even have proposed coming to Paris to see it rehearsed'.[28] Meanwhile he had agreed to a request by actor-manager Céline Céleste to stage a production based on the novel at the Lyceum Theatre, London. Although the dramatist Tom Taylor adapted the novel, Dickens seems to have strongly influenced both adaptation and production. His letters show that he intervened in the casting and the staging, suggesting to Taylor that he had 'a stage notion for the last Scene, that I could have made a great deal of, if I had done the piece with amateurs. It is very easy and frightfully suggestive!'[29] A few days later he sent Céleste his own conception for the Carmagnole, the revolutionary dance that had not been included in Taylor's original adaptation. On 19 January 1860 he wrote to Taylor:

> You may like to know that I have attended with the greatest care to the Rehearsals of the Piece, and that it is in very good train, and that the crowd (to which I have given particular attention) is on the whole good and fierce—and not quite conventional. Tomorrow nothing is done but the Carmagnole. It will be produced on Wednesday. If it should be at all inconvenient for you to attend the full rehearsal on Sunday, rely on me; I shall not fail to be there from first to last, and look to it closely.[30]

Dickens's involvement in the production process was publicly acknowledged. An advance notice in a playbill for 26 January 1860 declared that Dickens 'has in the kindest manner, not only sanctioned the adapting [of] the Tale for representation at this Theatre, but he will likewise aid the production of the Drama by giving to Madame CELESTE the benefit of his valuable suggestions during the progress of the rehearsals'.[31] On 23 January the production had been advertised as under Dickens's personal supervision, while the playbill for the first performance refers to his superintending the production. This version was very much a vehicle for Céleste's Madame Defarge, pronounced by Dickens's son to be 'one of the most effective and lifelike pictures from the Dickens dramatic gallery that I can recall'.[32] The action takes place entirely in Paris and Carton's execution takes place off-stage. His hypothetical speech at the end of the novel is spoken here at the conclusion of the penultimate scene as he leaves gaol, although in the final scene he is glimpsed from the window of Tellson's Bank passing on the tumbril en route to his execution.

Dickens was less fortunate when it came to the staging in 1867 of *No Thoroughfare*, an adaptation of a Christmas story he had written jointly with the novelist Wilkie Collins. His absence in North America meant that both the adaptation and the staging were left in Collins's hands.[33] Dickens had offered to collaborate in adapting and staging a version in New York, but he was thwarted both by the lax copyright laws in America and the lack of interest shown by New York theatre managers. He was critical of Collins's adaptation, largely on the grounds of length and Collins's tendency to overexplain everything. He claimed that if he had supervised the staging he would have cut an hour from the running time. Nevertheless, this version enjoyed a considerable run at the Adelphi Theatre, boosted by the outstanding performance of the Swiss actor Charles Fechter in the part of Obenreizer, in which:

> cunning, cruelty, and treachery, lurking beneath a suave and ingratiating exterior, were indicated with consummate art. The evil romantic glamour with which this super-scoundrel was invested raised the embodiment far beyond the level of the ordinary but effective melodramatic stuff by which it was surrounded. The tigerish stealth and ferocity [. . .] was terrifying.[34]

Dickens's frustration at not overseeing the London production was partially assuaged when he and Fechter supervised a production of Dickens's own adaptation of *No Thoroughfare*, entitled *L'Abîme*, in Paris, on 2 June 1868. Dickens felt that his involvement was essential, believing that many opportunities for striking stage-effects had been missed at the Adelphi. Of the Paris production, he wrote:

> I particularly wanted the drugging and attempted robbery in the Swiss inn to be done to the sound of a waterfall rising and falling with the wind. Although in the very opening of the scene they speak of the waterfall and listen to it, nobody thought of its mysterious music. I could make it, with a good stage-carpenter, in an hour.[35]

The Daily News (5 June 1868) noted 'a novel trick' in this production, leading the audience to fancy 'they hear the crunching of snow under the feet of the people on the stage'.[36] John Coleman, who saw this production, felt it handled the denouement more effectively than the Adelphi version.[37] In the latter, the attempted murder of George Vendale on the mountain provides a sensational climax to Act IV, and the plot is then resolved during a lengthy fifth act. Dickens's version sets the final scene on the mountain, avoids a long-winded fifth act resolution, and concludes the play with George's rescue.

Dickens's concern about the effective staging of his novels is also revealed in the advice he gave to Andrew Halliday (who authored some of the later 'Joe Whelks' theatre essays) over his adaptation of *David Copperfield* into *Little Em'ly*, performed at the Olympic Theatre in 1869.[38] The plot lines focus on Steerforth's seduction of Emily and Micawber's exposure of Uriah Heep, although Steerforth and Emily are involved in very little of the on-stage action. Dickens approved Halliday's preliminary notes, but felt that any additional scenes after the shipwreck might be anti-climactic.[39] His own public reading from *David Copperfield* had focused largely on Little Emily and concluded with the shipwreck and death of Steerforth.[40] As with his Parisian dramatisation of *No Thoroughfare*, Dickens preferred to finish with a strong dramatic climax. This is not generally a feature of his written fiction, but it does indicate his understanding of the need for economy and theatrical impact in live performance. Overall,

120   JIM DAVIS

although his involvement in dramatisations of his fiction was often selective and not always widely advertised, Dickens certainly influenced the staging of several adaptations of his work in his own lifetime. Such collaborative engagement is a significant, if often unrecognised, part of the history of Dickens adaptations on the nineteenth-century stage and evidence of his ability to distinguish between a literary text and performance text, as well as between the different techniques involved in their realisation.

Adaptations for Actors

Dickensian adaptations were significant in enhancing the reputation of many nineteenth-century actors. From Hammond as Sam Weller to the Keeleys in a succession of Dickensian roles, not to mention Fechter's Obenreizer and Céline Céleste's Madame Defarge, the characters created by Dickens achieved three-dimensional life through the skills of the actors who played them, while exposure to such characters further contributed to the range and development of the actors themselves. *The Daily Telegraph* (28 December 1867) implies the centrality of the actor in Dickens adaptations without perhaps acknowledging what Dickens was giving to the actors:

> We may be reminded of the success achieved at the Strand Theatre by Mr W. J. Hammond as Sam Weller, of the frequent dramatic renderings of Dickens by the Old Adelphi troupe, renderings which the Smike and Little Nell of Mrs Keeley, the Newman Noggs and Sikes of O. Smith, the Mantalini, Fagin and Quilp of Frederick Yates have endeared to the memory of many an old playgoer. At a later period, during the occupation of the Lyceum by Mr and Mrs Keeley, 'Martin Chuzzlwit' had a successful run, and the impersonation of Mrs Gamp and Bailey, jun, by the manager and his wife are prominent ever in their roll of triumphs. But in all these pieces the success has been the success of the artist, and not of the work—a fact well understood by that accomplished tactician Mr Dion Boucicault, when, in dramatizing the 'Cricket on the Hearth', he subordinated all the other characters, even the heroine Dot herself, to Caleb Plummer, who has by no means such an important position in the story.[41]

This is a potentially limiting view of the relationship between the actor and the original text and is countered by the following comment which praises Dickens for not creating stock or flat characters, thereby confounding a tendency to create theatrical stereotypes:

> Dickens's characters are too like nature for that. No individual is, in real life, always being funny or behaving wickedly, or eternally breathing forth sentimentality. The same persons have their time for being gay and for being sad; they have their times for being brilliant and their dull moments; and so have the life portraits which Dickens draws.[42]

This is not to dispute Dickens's debt to stage characterisation, but to recognise that his particular mode of writing enabled actors to be creative and imaginative in realising his characters. The challenge set by Dickens to actors and dramatists is implicit in Percy Fitzgerald's reference to the hints, associations, delicate touches and narrative factors beyond the characters themselves by which Dickens brings them to life.[43] Additionally, Dickens leaves space for the imagination of the actor (and reader):

> Mr Dickens's characters are sketched with a spirit and distinctness which rarely fail to convey immediately a clear impression of the person intended. They are, however, not complete and finished delineations, but rather outlines very clearly and sharply traced, which the reader may fill up for himself.[44]

This is an early appraisal of Dickens's approach to characterisation, but one that provides another key to understanding why his characters enhanced the creative skills of the actors who played them.

In *Dot*, Boucicault's adaptation of *The Cricket on the Hearth*, first staged in New York in 1859 and at the Adelphi, London, in 1862, the role of Caleb Plummer, invested by Boucicault with both comedy and pathos, was seminal for the careers of both Joseph Jefferson in New York and J. L. Toole in London. Toole feared he might not do the part justice, but eventually considered that he had got inside it: 'I know I felt for the sufferings of Caleb, and did my best to make the audience feel them.'[45] He continued to play Caleb for over forty years. Seymour Hicks remembered the tenderness of Toole's performance:

> Never did I see him make his first entrance in the little toymaker dressed in a sack with 'glass with care' stamped across it that tears did not come to my eyes; and to watch his tender deception as in his poverty he painted a picture of happy affluence to his blind child was as heart-breaking a thing as has ever been given to the theatre.[46]

Caleb Plummer, perhaps more than any other role he ever played, enabled Toole, the leading low comedian of the late Victorian era, to demonstrate that he could transcend the repertoire of farcical characters he usually played and achieve genuine pathos.

Toole played many Dickens characters including Bob Cratchit at the Adelphi Theatre in 1860, the Artful Dodger, Trotty Veck, Benjamin Britain and Serjeant Buzfuz. The Dodger was another role that stayed long in his repertory. He first played the Dodger at the Edinburgh Theatre in March 1854; in 1868 he played the role again at the Queen's Theatre in John Oxenford's version of *Oliver Twist* (with Henry Irving as Bill Sikes), meeting a mixed response. This may have been because Oxenford had overwritten the role and given it disproportionate emphasis in the adaptation or because Toole's 'slangy gaieties' did not strike a chord with the audience.[47] Nevertheless, *The Era* (19 April 1868) found Toole's Artful Dodger:

> intensely powerful in its way. As an elaborate study of character it must be pronounced almost unrivalled. Every look and every gesture is full of meaning, and beyond the mere external quaintness of the performance there is a depth of meaning indicative in the highest degree of Toole's real artistic capability.[48]

As with Caleb Plummer, Toole was still playing this role thirty years later. A further role, Serjeant Buzfuz in *Bardell v. Pickwick*, was also highly acclaimed. First performed at the Gaiety Theatre in 1871, this adaptation by John Hollingshead (the theatre's manager) was based on Dickens's reading copy of this episode from *The Pickwick Papers*. Toole knew Dickens, but there is no evidence as to whether his performance drew on Dickens's own public enactment of this character.

Among Victorian actors well served by Dickens was Henry Irving. Dickensian characters played early in his career, Bill Sikes apart, allegedly included David Copperfield, Jonas Chuzzlewit, Daniel Quilp, Montague Tigg, Mr Dombey, Wackford Squeers, Ralph Nickleby, James Steerforth, John Peerybingle, and Mantalini.[49] Edward Gordon Craig considered Dickens a major influence on Irving:

> all Dickens was especially wonderful to Irving, and when he is *Dubosc* he is Dickens, and when he is *Lesurques* he is Dickens. He is guided by Dickens in *Richard III* and in *Charles the First*, as well as in *Eugene Aram* and *Robert Landry*. Only in *The Bells* is he all Irving—though Dickens, Daumier, Boucicault, Kean (Edmund) may be hanging around somewhere in the wings.[50]

Craig implies another sort of adaptation here, indicating that in creating some of his most successful roles Irving embodied the energy and detail characteristic of Dickens's novels. Dickens also provided Irving with one of his most enduring roles: Jingle from *The Pickwick Papers*. Irving first played Jingle in James Albery's adaptation of *The Pickwick Papers* at the Lyceum Theatre in 1871. Although Irving won praise for his depiction of Jingle, the production was not highly regarded and the play was later reduced as a vehicle for Irving and turned into a one-act farce retitled *Jingle*. This in turn was further adapted, but remained in Irving's repertoire and was often performed as a double bill with *The Bells*. Austin Brereton references reviews praising Irving for:

> his grotesque, shabby-genteel appearance—the dignified serenity with which he performed his ulterior aims—his imperturbable impudence and unflinching confidence [. . .]. The facile hands were never quiet, the plotting eyes were always glinting, and the ready tongue was never at a loss.[51]

Elsewhere, *The Era* (14 July 1878) praised his assumption of:

> the jaunty air, the swaggering impudence, the cool assurance of the adventurer [. . .]. This Jingle borrowed a ten pound note or stole a watch with delightful *sangfroid*; and getting out of seedy habiliments into fine ones, he wore them as if he had been accustomed to them all his life.[52]

Irving's performance of Jingle brought back to life the comic style of those light comedians, including William Lewis, which had informed Dickens's conception of Jingle in the first place.

Both Toole and Irving achieved distinction in Dickens adaptations, although they are only representative examples of Dickens's innate ability through his novels to create characters for actors. There were a smaller number of strong female roles, although Miss Havisham (excluded by Gilbert from his 1871 dramatisation of *Great Expectations*), Rosa Dartle, Lady Dedlock, Hortense, Madame Defarge and Nancy were among those roles that offered strong acting opportunities to Victorian actresses. Gilbert's exclusion of Miss Havisham may have been based on the need for a tight adaptation and the assumption that audience familiarity with the novel (published ten years earlier) ensured her continued existence in the popular imagination anyway. The exclusion of Madame Defarge from John Martin Harvey's *The Only Way* nearly thirty years later is more easily explained on the likely grounds that Harvey did not want his own performance as Sydney Carton upstaged by a strong character actress in the role of Defarge.

One of the most successful roles played by an actress in a Dickens adaptation was that of Jo the crossing sweeper in J. P. Burnett's adaptation of *Bleak House*, staged in London in 1875. This spawned a whole series of further adaptations around the character of Jo, most notably George Lander's at the Pavilion Theatre, Whitechapel. This was infinitely better than *Lady Dedlock's Secret*, Palgrave Simpson's 1874 version, which had considerably altered the original. Jo in Burnett's version was played by his wife, Jennie Lee, also well known as a performer of travestie (cross-dressed or breeches) roles in burlesque.[53] Cross-dressed performances of Dickens's male characters, invariably children or young men, date back to some of the earlier adaptations. (Female impersonation was less common, although male actors occasionally played roles such as Mrs Gamp or Tilly Slowboy.) Mary Ann Keeley was a particularly successful Smike, but also played Oliver Twist, Barnaby Rudge and Master Bailey. On her first appearance as Smike in Stirling's dramatisation of *Nicholas Nickleby* the audience began to laugh:

> But, when the actress rose and walked totteringly to the footlights, where she remained still speechless and staring blankly at vacancy, the laughter gradually subsided, and long before Smike's opening lines were over, there was hardly a dry eye in the house.[54]

Many actresses played travestie versions of Dickensian characters, including the popular burlesque actress Nellie Farren, who was the original Sam Weller in *Bardell v. Pickwick*. According to the *Birmingham Daily Post* (30 January 1871):

> *Sam* is a difficult character for a male performer [. . .]. [I]t would be difficult to present him on the stage without a touch of vulgarity, and so the part was wisely given to Miss Farren. Her youthful, girlish face, her characteristic coolness and self-possession, and her voice, which lends itself naturally to Cockneyism and innocent slang, threw a certain poetry and refinement over the presentation. *Sam* was capitally made up, and came into Court with a piece of hay or straw in his mouth [. . .] to indicate his carelessness and *insouciance*. All the well-known points were brought out amid a running fire of laughter.[55]

Sam Weller was not usually played as a travestie role, and the casting of Nellie Farren on this occasion may have owed more to her popularity in male roles at the Gaiety Theatre, where the play was first staged, and to the fact this was a charity performance in aid of the Royal Dramatic College. This particular critic's comment about the vulgarity of the role in male hands is not typical.

Female-to-male cross-dressing was not just associated with burlesque; actresses also played younger male roles in comedy and farce. Thus, in W. S. Gilbert's adaptation of

Great Expectations both the younger and older Pip were played by female performers. As the *Academy* commented, when the production was revived at the Aquarium Theatre in 1877:

> [The older] Pip is played by Miss Maggie Brennan with no insistence whatever upon the fact that the youth is acted by a woman: not as a tour de force at all, but naturally and vigorously, so that the choice of the actress for the part is amply justified.[56]

The Morning Post (19 March 1877) considered that Brennan assumed 'the garb and bearing of the simulated sex with considerable success', even though 'young men who have been trained as blacksmiths are scarcely likely to scream when being seized by their enemies'.[57] It has been argued that such cross-gender casting served to emphasise masculine weakness and vulnerability as well as the constructed nature of gender stereotyping in the Victorian era.[58]

When Jennie Lee first played Jo the crossing sweeper in London, she elicited an initial response similar to that which greeted Mary Anne Keeley's Smike. The first-night audience, familiar with her travestie performances in pantomime and burlesque, took her catchphrase, 'He was werry good to me, he was', as a cue for laughter. However, they were soon won over, and her performance was widely praised for its truth, realism, detail and pathos. *The Daily News* stated that 'the good nature of the poor forlorn neglected lad, struggling through hopeless ignorance, and blunted sense of early and habitual privation and hard usage, are depicted by Miss Jennie Lee with a degree of truth of a rare kind'.[59] *The Athenaeum*, reviewing the first London performance, claimed that she acted the character of Jo with:

> a realism and pathos difficult to surpass. A more striking revelation of talent has seldom been made. In get-up and in acting the character was thoroughly realised; and the hoarse voice, the slouching, dejected gait, and the movement as of some hunted animal were admirably exhibited.[60]

Jennie Lee's career was subsequently built around Jo, a role she was still playing into her eighties. Contemporaries noted the mixture of artistry and social realism she brought to denoting Jo's pathos and vulnerability: the appeal was partly sentimental, but was also grounded in the credibility of the performance and a sense of social justice.

Dickens Adapting Dickens

In discussing nineteenth-century adaptations of Dickens's work, it is also appropriate to discuss Dickens's own adaptations of his stories and novels into various forms of public entertainment. The earliest instance was Dickens's short story 'The Great Wingleberry Duel', which was adapted in 1836 as a burletta, *The Strange Gentleman*, for the St James's Theatre, London, where it ran for sixty-four performances (indicative of a successful run for the period). Dickens's farcical story and the play itself turns on mistaken identity and a series of misunderstandings experienced by the strange gentleman (named Walker Trott in the dramatisation).[61] John Pritt Harley, a popular low comedian, played the title role. Dickens had almost certainly adapted the story with Harley in mind for the strange gentleman and embellished the part accordingly. Harley basically played Harley, according to one review, a tendency to which Dickens drew attention years later.[62] Although Harley's face and style expressed 'mirthfulness in activity', claimed Dickens, 'he was always full of his own humour, 'and showed it, as much as to say, "See how funny I am!"'.[63] In 1836 Harley had become a close friend of Dickens, who, in dedicating the published version of *The Village Coquettes* to Harley, wrote 'My dramatic bantlings are no sooner born than you father them. You have made my *Strange Gentleman* exclusively your own.'[64] Once again it is the actor who brings to life a Dickens story on stage: Dickens has created an effective vehicle for Harley while also capturing exactly the tone of so many of the short comedies and farces performed at the Olympic and St James's Theatres in the 1830s. Dickens himself later disowned his adaptation, saying that he undertook it as 'a sort of practical joke for Harley', without regard to reputation, and now wished it forgotten.[65] He maintained his friendship with Harley, the first professional actor whom he had got to know well, but this was later eclipsed by his close association with William Macready.

Although, as we have seen, Dickens was involved with subsequent dramatisations of his works, his public readings were to offer him greater scope and control over public representations of his work. Other authors had occasionally given public lectures or readings of their work, but there was an underlying assumption at the time that giving public readings for financial gain was ungentlemanly. And authors such as Thackeray or Collins certainly lacked Dickens's unique theatrical flair. He had first undertaken public readings for charity, but he commenced giving readings professionally in 1858. As Philip Collins notes:

> These were by no means mere readings-aloud of the text, but elaborate dramatic performances: and similarly what Dickens 'read' (in fact he recited, for he knew his scripts by heart, and often improvised, or improved upon his original version) was by no means the published text of his fictions, but a much amended, abbreviated and heightened revision of them.[66]

In other words, they were adaptations to be performed by a narrator rather than by actors. Given Dickens's skill as an actor and the theatrical quality of much of his work, there was certainly an actorly quality to the readings, as indicated by Thomas Carlyle's comment on them as 'a whole tragic, comic, heroic *theatre*, performing under one hat'.[67] Dickens shortened his originals, discarded superfluous characters and irrelevant subplots, and omitted physical details. Although he originally gave readings focused on just one tale, his later preference was for a two-hour reading consisting of two items. As with the earlier stage adaptations, the *Christmas Books* furnished useful material for his readings because of their length and *A Christmas Carol* remained one of the most popular. Selections from longer works were often made because of their comic potential (*The Trial from Pickwick*, *Mrs Gamp*), their sentimental appeal (*The Story of Little Dombey*) or their melodramatic content (*David Copperfield* with a focus on Little Emily and climaxing with the death of Steerforth in the storm, *Nicholas Nickleby at the Yorkshire School* and latterly *Sikes and Nancy*). In fact, Dickens's selection of specific narrative threads or self-contained episodes reflected exactly the approach that some contemporary dramatists took to adapting his work. Dickens's own prompt copies for his readings were adapted as performance scripts, according to Malcolm Andrews.[68] Indeed, Dickens's readings were enhanced by his ability to embody each of his characters both physically and mentally within a narrative framework, a type of imitation that Andrews compares to Charles Mathews the Elder's *At Homes*, which had strongly influenced the younger Dickens.[69] Mathews had been praised for his powers of observation, his delineation and his freedom from caricature. Dickens's readings were also allegedly free of caricature, a factor that enabled him to stress the credibility of the characters he had created.[70] This was exactly what the more successful actors of Dickensian characters also achieved.

Genre and Spectacle

Dickens proved easily adaptable to nineteenth-century genres, in part because he himself drew so strongly from the theatre for plotting and characterisation. While some Dickens adaptations sit comfortably within the genres of comedy and farce, melodrama is the form that is most predominant. This was sometimes to the detriment of the work adapted, especially when subtlety and complexity were lost for the sake of dramatic expediency. Reviewing W. S. Gilbert's version of *Great Expectations*, *The Pall Mall Gazette* (31 May 1871) considered that the novel had been 'mutilated' and 'tortured' into melodramatic form and was totally unsuited to the refined environment of the Court Theatre, where it was first staged. Of the actors playing the convicts, it added that, 'Gesticulation so vehement and shouting so obstreperous have been for some time rare in London theatres of any distinction.'[71] Melodramas were increasingly associated with spectacle and this also impacted upon Dickens adaptations. The on-stage representation of the shipwreck in Halliday's *Little Em'ly* has already been cited, but Halliday went even further in *Nell*, his adaptation of *The Old Curiosity Shop* for the Olympic Theatre in 1870. This included a vivid fairground scene in Act II, while Act III concluded with a spectacular scene in which Quilp falls from the roof of a burning building into the river, the building collapses and a mist then rises to reveal Quilp's body by moonlight among the reeds. The play concludes with an apotheosis, during which Nell, to a background of music and singing, is transported aloft by angels.[72] While Dickens's prose provides his readers with ample means to visualise the events he depicts, theatre is a visual medium that can enhance and even replace the need for description. Thus wordy adaptations such as *The Golden Dustman*, a version of *Our Mutual Friend*, performed at Sadler's Wells Theatre in 1866, seem far too reliant on dialogue in comparison to Halliday's scripts.

In 1899 John Martin Harvey's production of *The Only Way*, an adaptation of *A Tale of Two Cities*, at the Lyceum Theatre, combined melodrama, spectacle, a star performance and a carefully wrought adaptation to create a production that would live on into the twentieth century. Although the dramatisation was attributed to the Rev. Canon Langbridge and the Rev. Canon Freeman Wills, it was extensively developed by Martin Harvey and his wife. Madame Defarge and Jerry Cruncher were excised, while a new character, Mimi, was introduced, based on the seamstress who goes to the scaffold with Sydney Carton. This version closed with Carton about

NINETEENTH-CENTURY STAGE ADAPTATIONS 127

to die upon the scaffold. Harvey's lavish staging was said to owe something to the 'Irving school of picturesque melodrama'.[73] The Revolutionary Tribunal Scene, based on a picture by Pierre Bouillon, was particularly praised:

> [T]he mad crowd, the concentrated calmness of Carton, the helpless prisoner, the distracted Lucie, and the sorrowful Dr Manette all go to form a strong picture. But it is a picture of life and action [. . .]. It is a great scene where yelling, half-crazy men and women, thirsting for blood, give full vent to their animal desire.[74]

Harvey's Carton was an aestheticised, sensitive portrayal: in the view of American critic Alan Dale, his strength as a melodramatic actor was that he was mystical rather than attitudinising.[75]

The range and chronology of nineteenth-century adaptations of Dickens for the stage has been comprehensively documented by H. Philip Bolton.[76] In this chapter I have attempted not to demonstrate how the plays were adapted into dramatic texts but to argue how, through the remediation of his fiction into theatrical performance, not to mention his occasional participation in staging productions, Dickens adaptations made a substantial contribution to Victorian theatre and to Victorian acting. Actors such as the Keeleys, Toole and Jennie Lee were able to develop a deeper sense of characterisation, a possibility not always available to them in other roles, and promote a subtler mode of character acting, an influence that continues to this day. Dickens's contribution to the staging of adaptations of his work, particularly with the Keeleys and Céleste, indicates his innate understanding of the practice of performance and adds an additional dimension to our understanding of collaborative adaptation in this period. Consequently, the mediation of his stories and novels in the theatre, by some of the most talented performers of the time, was a crucial factor in keeping his work continually before the nineteenth-century public.

Notes

1. Bernard Shaw, *Our Theatre in the Nineties*, 2 vols (London: Constable, 1932), II, 134. Much has been written on theatrical adaptations of Dickens's work. Among early studies T. E Pemberton's *Dickens and the Stage* (London: Redway, 1888), S. J. Adair Fitzgerald, *Dickens and the Drama* (London: Chapman & Hall, 1910) and F. Dubrez Fawcett, *Dickens the Dramatist* (London: W. H. Allen, 1952) provide useful surveys of the territory. More recently, H. Philip Bolton, *Dickens Dramatized* (Boston, MA: G. K. Hall, 1987), has provided a major reference work on dramatisations of Dickens. Passing references are made to several Dickens adaptations in *Dramatic Dickens*, ed. by Carol H. MacKay (Basingstoke: Macmillan, 1989). Recent studies providing critical perspectives on adaptations of specific works include Richard Pearson, *Victorian Writers and the Stage: The Plays of Dickens, Browning, Collins and Tennyson* (Basingstoke: Palgrave Macmillan, 2015), Karen E. Laird, *The Art of Adapting Victorian Literature, 1848–1920: Dramatizing* Jane Eyre, David Copperfield *and* The Woman in White (Abingdon: Routledge, 2016) and, on *Oliver Twist*, Joanna Hofer-Robinson, *Dickens and Demolition: Literary Afterlives and Mid-Nineteenth Century Urban Development* (Edinburgh: Edinburgh University Press, 2018). The two-volume *Dickensian Dramas: Plays from Dickens*, ed. by Jacky Bratton and Jim Davis (Oxford: Oxford University Press, 2017) includes a cross-section of nineteenth-century adaptations of Dickens.

2. John Glavin, 'Introduction', in *Dickens Adapted*, ed. by John Glavin (Farnham: Ashgate, 2012), xv–xxiv, xx.
3. 'To Sir James Emerson Tennent, 9 January 1857', *The Letters of Charles Dickens*, ed. by Madeline House, Graham Storey et al., Pilgrim/British Academy Edition, 12 vols (Oxford: Clarendon Press, 1965–2002). Subsequent citations: *PLets* followed by volume (year of publication), page. Here, VIII (1995), 255–6.
4. For a fuller discussion of this issue, see Jacky Bratton, *New Readings in Theatre History* (Cambridge: Cambridge University Press, 2003), 17–19.
5. 'Queen's Theatre', *The Era* (19 April 1868), 14.
6. 'Theatres', *The Times* (23 March 1877), 4.
7. 'Court Theatre', *The Times* (2 June 1871), 5.
8. See Mary Teresa McGowan, 'Pickwick and the Pirates: A Study of Some Early Imitations, Dramatizations and Early Plagiarisms of *Pickwick Papers*', unpublished PhD thesis, University of London, 1974, 170, n. 2, quoting J. Grego, *Pictorial Pickwickiana*, 2 vols, (London: Chapman & Hall, 1899), II, 12, 20, 279.
9. John Forster, *The Life of Charles Dickens*, ed. by J. W. T. Ley (London: Cecil Palmer, 1928), 95.
10. Bolton, 113–14.
11. *The Journal of William Charles Macready, 1831–1851*, ed. by J. C. Trewin (London: Longmans, 1967), 126.
12. Forster, 125.
13. Ibid.
14. 'To Frederick Yates, [?29 November 1838]', *PLets*, I (1965), 463–4.
15. 'Literary News and Notes', *Westminster Gazette* (13 March 1889), 3.
16. 'To John Forster, 23 November 1838', *PLets*, I, 460, n. 1.
17. 'To Robert Keeley, 24 June 1844', *PLets*, IV (1977), 150.
18. Qtd in *Dickensian Dramas: Plays from Dickens*, I, 242.
19. Edward Stirling, *Old Drury Lane: Fifty Years' Recollections of Author, Actor and Manager*, 2 vols (London: Chatto & Windus, 1881), I, 187.
20. See Bratton, 'Introduction' to *Dickensian Dramas: Plays from Dickens*, I, xiii–xxxiv, xxix.
21. Dickens's story was also highly influential on early cinema through D. W. Griffith's silent film version in 1909, which was later celebrated in Eisenstein's essay 'Dickens, Griffith and the Film Today', in *Film Form: Essays in Film Theory*, ed. and trans. by Jay Leyda (New York: Harcourt, Brace & World, 1949), 195–255.
22. 'The Theatres: Lyceum', *Illustrated London News* (27 December 1845), 413.
23. 'To Catherine Dickens, 19 December 1848', *PLets*, IV, 680–1.
24. 'Lyceum Theatre', *Illustrated London News* (26 December 1846), 413.
25. Jacky Bratton, *The Making of the West End Stage: Marriage, Management and the Mapping of Gender in London, 1830–1870* (Cambridge: Cambridge University Press, 2011), 182.
26. Bratton, 'Introduction' to *Dickensian Dramas: Plays from Dickens*, I, xxxiii.
27. 'To François Regnier, 15 October 1859', *PLets*, IX (1997), 132.
28. 'To François Regnier, 16 November 1859', *PLets*, IX, 163.
29. 'To Tom Taylor, 1 January 1860', *PLets*, IX, 189.
30. 'To Tom Taylor, 19 January 1860', *PLets*, IX, 198.
31. Lyceum Theatre Playbill, 23 January 1869, Theatre Collection, Victoria & Albert Museum.
32. Charles Dickens the Younger, 'Introduction', *A Tale of Two Cities and The Mystery of Edwin Drood* (New York: Macmillan, 1896), xxix.
33. For a discussion of the fraught collaboration of Dickens and Collins on *The Frozen Deep*, see Lillian Nayder, *Unequal Partners: Charles Dickens, Wilkie Collins and Victorian Authorship* (Ithaca: Cornell University Press, 2002), 60–99.

NINETEENTH-CENTURY STAGE ADAPTATIONS

34. J. Rankin Towse, *Sixty Years of Theatre: An Old Critic's Memories* (New York: Funk & Wagnalls, 1916), 77–8.
35. 'To Mrs J. T. Fields, 25 May 1868', *PLets*, XII (2002), 120.
36. 'France', *Daily News* (5 June 1868), 5.
37. John Coleman, *Players & Playwrights I Have Known*, 2 vols (London: Chatto & Windus, 1888), II, 313.
38. See Andrew Halliday, *Town and Country Sketches* (London: Tinsley, 1866), 125–91 for reprints of Halliday's 'Joe Whelks' essays from *All the Year Round*.
39. Laird, 101.
40. *Charles Dickens: Sikes and Nancy and Other Public Readings*, ed. by Philip Collins (Oxford: Oxford University Press, 1983), 166.
41. 'Boxing Night at the Theatres: Adelphi', *Daily Telegraph* (27 December 1867), 2.
42. 'The "Cricket" at the Lyric', *The Almanack of the Month* (January 1846), 47–8, qtd in T. E. Pemberton, *Charles Dickens and the Stage* (London: Redway, 1888), 159.
43. Percy Fitzgerald, *Principles of Comedy and Dramatic Effect* (London: Tinsley, 1870), 52–3.
44. *Edinburgh Review* 68 (October 1838), 84, qtd in Deborah Vlock, *Dickens, Novel Reading and the Victorian Popular Theatre* (Cambridge: Cambridge University Press, 1998), 12.
45. Joseph Hatton, *Reminiscences of J. L. Toole* (London: Hurst and Blackett, 1889), 143–4.
46. Seymour Hicks, 'He Lived and Laughed: An Actor's Memoirs of J. L. Toole', *Evening Standard* (12 March 1932), 15.
47. Qtd in Austin Brereton, *The Life of Henry Irving*, 2 vols (London: Longmans, Green & Co., 1908), I, 92.
48. 'Queen's Theatre', *The Era* (19 April 1868), 14.
49. H. Chance Newton, *Cues and Curtain Calls* (London: Lane, 1927), 4.
50. Edward Gordon Craig, *Henry Irving* (London: Dent, 1930), 133–4.
51. Brereton, I, 111–12, quoting *The Standard* and *The Liverpool Porcupine*.
52. 'Henry Irving's Benefit', *The Era* (14 July 1878), 13.
53. See Laurence Senelick, *The Changing Room: Sex, Drag and Theatre* (London: Routledge, 2000) and Jacky Bratton, 'Mirroring Men', in *The Cambridge Companion to the Actress*, ed. by Maggie B. Gale and John Stokes (Cambridge: Cambridge University Press, 2007), 235–52.
54. Walter Goodman, *The Keeleys on the Stage and at Home* (London: Bentley, 1895), 30.
55. 'Private Correspondence', *Birmingham Daily Post* (30 January 1871), 5.
56. 'The Stage: Great Expectations', *The Academy* (24 March 1877), 260.
57. *Morning Post* (19 March 1877), 6.
58. See Carolyn Williams, *Gilbert and Sullivan: Gender, Genre, Parody* (New York: Columbia University Press, 2010), 205 and Bratton, 'Mirroring Men', 248.
59. *Daily News* (undated), quoted in the programme for the 1876 Globe production of *Jo*, Theatre Collection, Victoria & Albert Museum.
60. 'Drama', *Athenaeum* (26 February 1876), 307, qtd in S. J. Adair Fitzgerald, *Dickens and the Drama* (London: Chapman & Hall, 1910), 247.
61. See also Pearson, *Victorian Writers and the Stage: The Plays of Dickens, Collins, Browning and Tennyson*, 23–6, 34–43.
62. 'The Theatre', *Carlton Chronicle* (1 October 1836), 206.
63. Goodman, 157–8.
64. Charles Dickens, *The Village Coquettes* (London: Bentley, 1836), 3.
65. 'To R. H. Horne, 13 November 1843', *PLets*, III (1974), 598.
66. Collins, x.
67. J. A. Froude, *Thomas Carlyle: A History of His Life in London, 1843–1881*, 2 vols (London: Longmans, Green & Co., 1884), II, 270, quoted in Collins, vii.

68. Malcolm Andrews, *Charles Dickens and His Performing Selves: Dickens and the Public Readings* (Oxford: Oxford University Press, 2006), 79.
69. Andrews, 109–25. See also Jim Davis, *Comic Acting and Portraiture in Late-Georgian and Regency England* (Cambridge: Cambridge University Press, 2015), 195–246. Dickens's daughter described how Dickens himself theatrically embodied his characters in front of a mirror in the process of creating them. See Mamie Dickens, *My Father as I Recall Him* (London: Roxburgh, 1896), 47–8.
70. See Andrews, 242–9.
71. 'Great Expectations', *Pall Mall Gazette* (31 May 1871), 11.
72. 'Nell, or, The Old Curiosity Shop. A. Halliday.' November 1870. ADD. MSS. 53, 090 (A), ff. 90, British Library.
73. '"The Only Way" at the Prince of Wales's', *Observer* (2 April 1899), 6.
74. 'London Theatres: The Lyceum', *The Stage* (23 February 1899), 14.
75. Clipping, Martin Harvey Scrapbook, New York Public Library. For further discussion, see Jim Davis, '*The Only Way* and the Other Way: A Dickens Adaptation for the 1890s', in *British Theatre in the 1890s: Essays on Drama and the Stage*, ed. by Richard Foulkes (Cambridge: Cambridge University Press, 1992), 59–70.
76. See Bolton, *Dickens Dramatized*.

Further Reading

H. Philip Bolton, *Dickens Dramatized* (Boston, MA: G. K. Hall, 1987)
Jacky Bratton and Jim Davis, eds, *Dickensian Dramas: Plays from Dickens*, 2 vols (Oxford: Oxford University Press, 2017)

9

DICKENS AND DRAMA

Gillian Piggott

The Parameters of the Debate

Every good actor plays direct to every good author, and every writer of fiction, though he may not adopt the dramatic form, writes in effect for the stage.

–Charles Dickens, 'Speech to the Royal General Theatrical Fund', 29 March 1858[1]

In *Drama in Performance* (1954), Raymond Williams sets out how drama criticism must overcome the limitations of either confining itself to a literary study of the dramatic text, or, on the other hand, merely taking up criticism of a performance:

The relation between text and performance will be seen, in practice, to vary; but to bring them together, in analysis, seems to me a necessary emphasis. In much contemporary thinking, a separation between literature and theatre is constantly assumed; yet the drama is, or can be, both literature and theatre, not the one at the expense of the other, but each because of the other.[2]

This chapter examines one critically acclaimed adaptation of a Dickens novel, and, with the spirit of Williams's mapping of the terrain of drama criticism in mind, the aim is to give ample space to an examination of performance as well as to a discussion of literary and philosophical issues.

The adaptation to be considered is the Olivier and Tony award-winning *Life and Adventures of Nicholas Nickleby*: the 1980–1 Royal Shakespeare Company (RSC) production, adapted by David Edgar, and directed by Trevor Nunn and John Caird at the Aldwych Theatre.[3] The question addressed is, what kind of 'drama' does this twentieth-century adaptation draw out of the author? Central to the discussion is how a particular style of acting within the medium contributes to the kind of drama that is made from Dickens, and how this frames Dickens in the twentieth century.

In focusing upon an acting style as an important part of the analysis, the approach taken will rather be to understand the term 'drama' from a practitioner's perspective. The chapter concerns itself with an immanent analysis, or with the ontology of 'drama'. The approach is to perceive 'drama' as words or text in action – as acting and the effect acting has upon the audience. It is an attempt to utilise an understanding of acting, and of what goes into directing, and to interpret a performance with the interpretative tools of the drama critic. This approach continues to bear in mind, but is not hidebound by, the literary and philosophical categories with which traditional definitions of 'drama' deal.[4] Hence, in terms of the present task, one can view a stage adaptation as 'drama' without getting too mired in the complexities of what kind of drama it might amount to – to begin with. One can then tease out important and fruitful elements by which this adaptation is characterised, before finally going on to reintroduce considerations of what drama is today; to learn something of the kind of drama Dickens produces, why this might be the case, and what it says about our current cultural context.

In the case of the RSC *Nickleby*, classically trained stage actors perform in a lively 'cloth and stick' ensemble piece, as far as possible using Dickens's text.[5] The production was chosen deliberately for analysis because it is so arrestingly Dickensian, in ways that will be discussed. It is a product of an elite cultural institution (the RSC), a company at that time still operating within the influential legacy of Peter Hall's ideas on speaking Shakespearean verse.[6] Trevor Nunn, who co-directs *Nickleby* with John Caird, puts the text (Dickens's text, with material by David Edgar) at the centre of the production. It will be argued that this point – with respect to classical acting and approaching character through the text – is crucial to an understanding of why this production is uniquely successful, and unrepeatable.

Through a reading of this adaptation, it will become clearer what happens to the Dickens thoroughly rooted in Victorian and earlier forms of popular entertainment, whose aesthetic encompasses the rough, tough and even illegitimate modes of burlesque, grotesque and pantomime, as well as the emotions and gestics of melodrama. This will open up the discussion of why Dickens has become respectable in the twentieth and twenty-first centuries, and whether there is a taming of the 'dangerous' Dickens going on; that is, the Dickens seemingly so connected and committed to radicalism and the tradition of popular entertainment. And if there is, what is it about this historical context that needs to do this with adaptations of Dickens?

It is worth briefly rehearsing what it is about Dickens's works that make both his form and content so suitable for dramatisation. Dickens's 'intimate familiarity with the theatre of his day infuses his art at every level', as Paul Schlicke argues, resulting in wrought extremes of emotion, comic and sentimental scenes, and fast-moving action, drawn from the stage tradition of melodrama.[7] Dickens's novels (and his journalism) lend themselves to theatre by throwing a light on stark levels of poverty and inequality in society, offering affective, pathos-filled scenes for the director to create. Throwing a decidedly theatrical, brash light upon the dark lives he often depicted, Dickens drew flamboyantly large and often grotesque character types which are a gift to actors, who can execute a physically large character performance. There is also plenty of scope for comedy in such material. The political issues discussed by Dickens are often tied to moral language and emotional effects – which are also attractive to directors and actors, who are expert in representing a convincing moral argument or effecting an audience emotionally. Furthermore, Dickens wanted to entertain as well as inform, and his devotion to popular culture, particularly melodrama, lies in its ability to literally take the reader/audience out of themselves with tears, laughter and joy. This is manna for directors (and actors) who can shape a scene meticulously as to how intensely the effect of pathos/sadness and comedy is played upon an audience.[8] For example, performance, timing, lighting, music – in other words, technique – all determine how 'big' a laugh will be. Dickens demonstrated that the most serious, the most politically radical art could also be entertaining and popular. His ability to straddle the high/low cultural divide is well documented, and quality stage productions aim for a similar goal.[9]

This is a brief overview of what makes Dickens eminently adaptable, and it is interesting to bear in mind that institutions with enormous cultural capital today, such as the RSC, are prolifically adapting him. The task here is to see what sort of drama they create from Dickens, and what that might say about the society that creates such a version of the great author.

The RSC *Nickleby*

Joint directors Trevor Nunn and John Caird chose *Nicholas Nickleby* (1838–9) out of a possible selection that included *Our Mutual Friend* (1864–5) and *Hard Times* (1854). They thought the novel 'the best vehicle' for the range of acting talent they had in the Stratford company; they could see particular actors as particular characters.[10]

Nunn, a grandee of the school of directors who place the text at the centre of theatre production, was determined to adapt as much of the novel as he could and to retain Dickens's language wherever possible. This included the non-dramatic passages – 'the narrative episodes and moral digressions', as assistant director Leon Rubin put it – although the interpolated tales were excluded.[11] Nunn instructed actors to improvise in groups, using nothing but their bodies and voices to find innovative representations of whole narrative passages – a process of ensemble experimentation that lasted five weeks.

Playwright David Edgar, who had provided scripts for the initial devising phase, then wrote the full script, with some rewrites. As Edgar explains:

> we had a rule that we weren't going to cut a sub-plot, and we wanted to preserve the teeming richness of Dickens's narrative voice. Hence the adaptation ended up in two parts, adding up to eight and a half hours. Even then of course I had to edit hugely (if you read the novel out loud, it would take you 40 hours).[12]

The theatre practitioners' instinct here not to cut the text if possible is a canny insight into one of the most important properties of Dickens's works: his bountifulness and excess.

Ensemble Creativity

In an attempt to master all this excess, the usual hierarchy of actors gave way to the idea of collective work, multiple roles and ensemble creativity. After the initial period of collective research, the parts were cast. Again, it is apt that the RSC chose to work collectively as an effective way into Dickens. The reading of Dickens's serialised novels was itself a collective activity. As the readers awaited the next instalment, *Nicholas Nickleby* would be filtered through their engagement with the world – through their personal and public events and interactions, their anticipations and fantasies. Readers often consumed the serialised novel in groups, as they were read aloud and discussed. In this sense, *Nicholas Nickleby*, the novel, becomes a kind of 'transcendental text' or, as Paul Davis terms it, a 'culture-text', experienced in countless ways by the community.[13] Hence, it makes sense that the RSC *Nickleby* should capture that spirit by expressing the narrative in ensemble, collective form. As Nunn and Caird put it: 'the whole company possessed the whole story which they passed between them.'[14] Dickens's textual characters resemble a collection of actors, whom Dickens directs, like a company. The author, as we know, ventriloquised the voices of his characters ahead of writing material down.[15] Dickens's novels bear a similarity to a mechanism with many cogs and parts – voices, subplots, destinations, environments, streets and narrative complexities and positions – a rich collection of parts resembling some sort of cyberpunk computer station. The RSC actors 'became' the set, 'became' carriages, doors, objects, 'became' the London street, 'became' narrative voices. It could be argued that theatre-making, Dickens's novels and his political worldview are all about the collective: the idea of the whole community coming together as a collective device to solve life's problems. The RSC's ensemble approach captures the spirit of this.[16]

The *Nickleby* production shares with Dickens's novels a dynamic relationship to historical forms of popular entertainment.[17] Among approaches the RSC used in the initial research phase and final show version were mime, bodily gestures and physical theatre, grotesque humour, verbal comedy and comic timing, choric narration, music and song, direct addresses to the audience, and audience participation; with the effect of clamour and laughter in the audience. Improvisation, used by actors to arrive at the most effective forms of theatrical storytelling, was one of the central comic principles in *commedia dell'arte*.[18] The 'cloth and stick' approach the RSC took as a whole is itself a kind of tribute to pantomime's transformation scene – whereby something is magically conjured from nothing, and the audience witnesses in full view the mechanism of the transformation as part of the pleasure of the event.[19] These techniques – ensemble working, improvisation, cloth and stick theatre – would not be out of place in the pantomimes, melodramas, burlettas, circuses and taverns of London that Dickens loved and in which his aesthetic is so thoroughly steeped.

Rough, Tough Theatre

The RSC's aim was to deal in poor theatre – rough, tough 'real theatre' – the kind of theatre the Crummles were practised in. As storytellers, the actors physically became sets, crowded city streets, and, of course, grotesque and straight characters. No illusion is attempted; nothing is hidden from the audience, the mechanism is foregrounded. The actors performed on a bare stage with two movable trucks with ropes attached; they 'became' images and tableaux such as doors, carriages, shop windows, the London street, the London market, the poor and the rich, through ensemble physical theatre and mime.[20] Actors stood or sat watching and sometimes augmented the action with vocal sounds or physical movement, in view of the audience, in addition to working scene changes.[21]

The RSC approach captures Dickens's *theatrum mundi* notion – there is no separation between the audience and the actors/stage; all the world is theatre. Moreover, a rough style of theatre – with its wooden trucks, old clothes into which actors change, and the make-do-and-mend vibe of the actor's costumes, props and sets – reflects the sorts of environments Dickens visits in his novels, the material conditions within which many of his characters exist. The approach was also used because the RSC was in financial trouble and had received a drastic cut in its grant from the Arts Council in 1979.[22]

The foregrounding of the processes and materiality of theatre in the RSC production reproduces in theatrical terms the constructed-ness of Dickens's universe: Dickens's showmanship, in his text. Dickens's narrative voice, resembling a master of ceremonies lifting the curtain on a scene, often foregrounds itself. At times, it addresses directly not only the reader, but the characters themselves: 'Do you hear, Jo? [. . .] You are by no means to move off, Jo, for the great lights can't at all agree about that. Move on!'[23] The narrative voice, as William F. Axton argues, is a kind of 'apostrophe' directed at Jo, encouraging the reader to alter her position towards the narrative and to step within its framework, as if, as it were, to 'share a spectatorial position with the narrator that is [. . .] intimate and extra-fictional'.[24] Like a circus ringmaster, then, or, as Dickens himself puts it, a 'Stage-manager', Dickens coaxes the reader into his novel/theatre, but it is a theatre of which we are constantly made aware, and one in which seemingly limitless constituent characters and tendencies are competing for attention, clamouring for voice and are given full rein, not least among a variety of narrative voices.[25]

An Uncanny Multitude of Voices – Ventriloquism

Edgar ensured that he implemented the innovation of collective storytelling, of 'passing the story between actors', which included writing the recap at the beginning of part two of the play. The company narration of the text takes a number of forms: choric narration (the company speaks narrative lines together); ventriloquial narration (where an on-stage actor narrates the action and vocalises the speech of another character); in-character self-narration; and the narration of action.[26]

Using these approaches, *Nickleby* showcases the uncanniness in many of Dickens's texts, whereby characters can appear so strangely heightened and vividly wrought as to have a unique 'quiddity' about them. The RSC *Nickleby* foregrounds ventriloquism, opening with actors forming a tight group image as the lights go down; the opening shot is of a stylised tableau of the whole company, a block of faces facing out front. In this sense, each in turn narrates a sentence or clause of the opening of the novel, the family saga of the Nicklebys.[27] In the DVD version, each actor gets a mid shot, speaking directly to camera, with the camera aping the live experience of an audience member focusing on a speaking actor – though the camera cannot reproduce the shock effect on the live audience of the concatenation of voices coming from the group of actors. The disturbing effect is twofold. The shock effect of being confronted with multiple faces, brightly lit, smiling, looking out front and voicing the narrative – shiny-eyed faces pitted closely together – gives the uncanny feeling of the ventriloquist's dummy, with a slightly mechanical verve, as the script is recited. Secondly, the audience is not sure from where the next voice will emerge. The duping of an audience as to the source of a voice was a further popular theatre device – one used by ventriloquists, such as Charles Mathews (1776–1835), with whom Dickens had a particular obsession – and who in his voice-throwing 'Monopolylogues' act, ventriloquised six to eight characters on stage simultaneously.[28] The camera shot reverts back to whole company again, to reiterate the collective effect of the narration, and at one point, the whole company ritualistically speaks a line as a chorus,

'Mr Nickleby'. This too is disturbing. There is an intriguing moment of self-narration in this production, when Roger Rees narrates himself, Nicholas, into a piece of acting – a sigh, which he then performs as if in inverted commas, as it were.[29] Again, this has the uncanny resonance of the ventriloquist who is talking about, and to, himself, and then performs as the dummy.

Transforming the intensity of Dickens into a live performance of polyvocal ventriloquism is a great directorial choice; such a device showcases the slight artificiality within the context of the heightened forces and extreme rushes of energy of the novelist's universe. From the audience being attacked by Dickens's narrative, aurally and corporeally, through to the lively voices, high energy, choreographed movement and charismatic presence of actors in real time – this style of live performance captures the texture of Dickens's writing. It also captures a quality of comedy found in Dickens. A feeling of uncanniness, edginess and excess in the scenes easily transmutes or tips over into comedy, and especially, in heightened performances such as these, slapstick comedy or even violence. This, with examples, will be expanded upon below.

Classical Acting, Energy and Character in *Nickleby*

Nunn's work at the RSC was characterised by the centrality of the text and hence the creation of character occurred via the text. The actors Nunn worked with were classical actors. Classical actors conceive of a character who sometimes needs to speak in verse.[30] These performers are adept at creating realistic characters who speak in verse, trained, as they are, to perform the 'classical plays' of the past (such as Shakespeare, written in Elizabethan English), in which often highly formalised and carefully structured language is the predominant element. This is not to imply that 'classical' texts automatically rarify or limit the sort of language actors will be tackling. There will be a high degree of linguistic structure, or poetic or rhetorical device within such texts. Yet, in the case of Shakespeare, for instance, 'Shakespeare uses bawdry, filth, colloquial slang, courtly delicacy, lawyers' language, seaman's language, the rough speech of soldiers and the chop-logic of politicians.'[31]

Classical acting involves a particular honing of the voice and articulation, and an honouring of rhythm or structures within language, such that poetic meaning or the image can reverberate over and above any action. Such actors are less attached to finding psychological through-lines for their characters.[32] For Raymond Williams, the challenge for the actor in Shakespeare, for example, is not the representation of naturalistic behaviour, but the speaking of dramatic poetry.[33] Putting naturalism to one side, the classical performance invests huge amounts of energy into articulating language through the voice, and through the body, resulting in heightened stage performances. Hence, the classical actor puts the onus on accurately playing the form of language, or its rhythms, and through this attention to language's structure, his or her character starts to appear. An actor such as Roger Rees as Nicholas, for example, plays the words Dickens/Edgar has given for his character (which is prose that does at times seem to have something of a structured rhythm to it). As rehearsal goes on, Rees allows himself to inhabit those words, and develops a rich and complex colouration within the speaking of it, as well as within the costume and within the reality of the world on stage created in relation to other characters. Rees does not, it seems

DICKENS AND DRAMA

137

to me, play a generalised or overall judgement of his character; nor does he resort to an exploration of 'interiority'. Character is a series of active linguistic moments for the actor, an expression and inhabiting of a series of exploding performed actions. Rehearsal is a space where actor and director have the chance to decide on which colour (or way of playing) on a particular moment or beat should be played, to tell the clearest story in a scene.

In *Dickens' Villains*, Juliet John – talking about how Dickens creates characters in the novels, rather than about classical acting – argues that Dickens uses a complex 'melodramatic poetics', whereby the originary impulse behind creating a character is not to represent interiority directly or, implicitly, as the mainspring of character.[34] Nunn's insistence upon the classical approach to speaking Dickens (as well as to the speaking of Shakespearean verse) is similarly a claim that character comes about through the concentration upon externality, in this case language, the outward vocal and physical expression of it.[35] Hence there appears to be common ground between Dickens's approach to creating character in his novels (if we follow John's argument), and that approach taken by classical actors in the *Nickleby* production – the delineation of character evoked from an external viewpoint. This adds to the general picture of Dickens as fundamentally a writer for the theatre (as Dickens himself announces at the start of this chapter), and it adds weight to John's complex analysis of him as being steeped in the aesthetics of melodrama. It is also worth recalling that, wherever possible, the language the *Nickleby* production used was Dickens's own. Dickens's dialogue, as well as his narrative descriptions that typically delineate characters from the outside, then, fed directly into the mouths of the actors. Dickens's novels, in this sense, are a blueprint for a theatre production of the kind the RSC creates here. The success of this production, and its uncannily convincing characters, can be put down to the extensive use of Dickens's text and the heightened performance and huge energy drawn from the classical technique which sees the actors use Dickens's language to realise or release the character. The actors' bodies and voices come into play in the energising of the language. Seen in this light, Dickens emerges as far more a playwright for production than a novelist being adapted to the stage.

One could argue that this is due to an historical accident, wherein a certain company at a particular moment in historical time has specific skills at its disposal. This is more accident than choice because classical acting at the RSC and Nunn's approach to language were around at that particular moment (1980–1), something that for broadly historical and economic reasons is no longer found within elite institutions like the RSC in the twenty-first century.

The classical style of acting is not only non-naturalistic; it appears to assume a non-essentialist and fundamentally theatrical notion of character (such that character is a process or action brought about by the utterance of a series of words on a page), and, strangely, it has similarities to the way we experience other people in 'real life' – making it particularly convincing. We do not experience the whole of a person at each meeting (whatever that could mean), but just some aspect or aspects of them. The audience, external to the character, knits together the series of sides they see of Rees's Nicholas, for example, forming in reality less a 'rounded' or whole character than a montage of fragments of character.[36] In terms of time, character for an audience is a nebulous, retrospective collection of impressions, an exciting process whereby anything, including contradictory or unexpected directions, is possible of a character. Hence, here is non-naturalistic acting that is utterly convincing, and which, in a sense, has a relationship to 'the real'.

The 'High Culture' Version of 'Low Culture'?

The fascinating irony of this RSC production of *Nickleby* is that, in effect, a leading cultural organisation producing 'high cultural' Shakespeare for an educated, largely middle-class constituency in the 1980s, turned its attention to Dickens and his rootedness in popular theatrical traditions. The kind of performance and entertainment that ran through Dickens's veins, of course, was not that of the patented 'legitimate' theatre, which had permission to produce extensive passages of the spoken word on stage.[37] Dickens's influence, rather, came from the unlicensed minor theatres – from those theatrical forms shaped by practitioners and artists who found a way around the ban on spoken-word passages – in other words, through the uses of music, melodrama, ballet, song, pantomime, burlesque and clowning.

Classical acting, the non-naturalistic and highly energised approach to vocally and physically releasing character *through an extensive concentration upon language*, achieves the physicality and energy of character of those early forms of performance that evolved and thrived in spite of, and because of, the *bans upon the spoken word*. This is something of a fascinating paradox within the *Nickleby* production. Dickens's works too, so crammed with wonderful language and the influence of at times subversive popular entertainment, express this paradoxical marriage of language and the non-verbal. Further, classical actors, who train to recreate older or period forms and styles of performance through their voices and bodies, are in a good position to make that leap into remote performance styles handed down by the past.

The *Nickleby* cast brings a very specific quality to the production – a Shakespearean energy and bearing to the text. Members of the company were performing *Merry Wives of Windsor* and *Othello* in the evenings, after *Nickleby* rehearsals; speaking in verse and within a non-naturalistic context of performance and character was habitual territory. The actors, then, appear to approach Dickens's text – which is often archaic, formal or temporally remote – as if it is a classical text.

Heightened Performance and Comedy

Dickens is a comic writer. Comedy underpins his worldview and his love of eighteenth-century novels and satire; his engagement with popular theatre and entertainment is all part of that energetic drive to see the injustices of his world through the lens of humour and hope. From the acting point of view, Dickens includes characters with idiosyncratic voices, accents, lisps or colloquialisms for comedy purposes – as well as including comedy situations and events. The RSC production completely masters this ingredient.

In the texts, Dickens's characters are often physically portrayed, with an emphasis on bodily tics, specificities and gestures, rather than directly representing interiority. The heightened energy of classical acting naturally leads to physical comedy, and Bob Peck's John Browdie is a good example of this.[38] Peck, a huge man, wraps his voice and body round the language, foisting his expressive body upon the scene and fellow characters. His antics, his unmannerly, clumsy eating and loud Yorkshire garrulousness are matched by bodily gestures and movements that are so large and lively, they take up comically large amounts of stage space. But he can also turn to bullish anger on a sixpence. In this sense, his performance is on the cusp of tipping over into slapstick comedy or even slapstick violence. The power of this lies in the energy the classical actor gives to the language and the physical expression of it. Another performance worth considering is Alun Armstrong's Wackford Squeers, which demonstrates the scope Dickens can offer actors to create comic villainy, through the grotesque.[39] Differing from the kindly John Browdie, Squeers's villainy is in the form of physical aggression and violence of the clownish kind – the sort of anarchic, disruptive slapstick action Dickens found and loved in Joseph Grimaldi (1778–1837). Dickens introduces Squeers:

> Mr Squeers's appearance was not prepossessing. He had but one eye, and the popular prejudice runs in favour of two. The eye he had was unquestionably useful, but decidedly not ornamental [. . .]. The blank side of his face was much wrinkled and puckered up, which gave him a very sinister appearance, especially when he smiled, at which times his expression bordered closely on the villainous. (90, ch. 4)

In the RSC *Nickleby*, Armstrong's Wackford sits hidden behind a newspaper, while fellow actors, a barmaid, the tavern owner, narrate Dickens's description. The first two sentences are split between them, one feeding the line and the other landing the punchline, 'not prepossessing'. At that moment, Armstrong brings the newspaper down, revealing a hideous visage, a comic effect of timing. Armstrong uses make-up and rouge and manipulates his facial muscles, tightly closing one eye, to create a sneering, ghastly expression with a voice to match. He pours with sweat, has filthy greasy hair and teeth, and is physically brutal to the boys – physical brutality being the leitmotif of Dickens's villains. Armstrong physicalises the expression of Dickens's language seamlessly through his voice and through his body, both of which take on a huge and grotesque image.[40]

Melodrama and Sentimentality

As Carolyn Williams and Sharon Aronofsky Weltman explore in this volume, Dickens's famous 'streaky bacon' passage from *Oliver Twist* indicates his debt to melodrama. The *Nickleby* production features a number of scenes of high emotional conflict and melodrama. A fine example of this is the scene in Act II where Ralph Nickleby (played by John Woodvine) relates Nicholas's assault of Squeers to Kate and Mrs Nickleby (played by Emily Richard and Jane Downs respectively); Nicholas returns in the middle of the discussion, delivering the line: 'But what he says is still untrue!' After the general uproar that greets his surprise entrance, Mrs Nickleby pleads: 'Refute these accusations!' The scene continues in a series of melodramatic exchanges ending with a warning to Ralph Nickleby from Nicholas: 'This isn't over, you'll hear from me!'[41]

As artificial as this dialogue sounds on the page, the heightened degree of elaboration with which the actors pitch this (and all) their material, coupled with the actors' complete conviction and confidence in terms of delivering the language and character, bring a convincing patina to the scene. The apparent extravagance of the representations is understood by the audience to be connected to the intensity of the moral issues at stake and their representation, and the crisis is happening within what is still recognisable: an evenly pitched, though heightened, context. The classical acting approach means that a melodramatic passage in the text such as this is fully integrated into a heightened representation of language across the entire production and, hence, is more convincing.

Much of the successful execution of the melodramatic mode in this production lies in its bountiful use of music, which, it should be remembered, echoes what 'melodrama' was historically, words or passages of words and action accompanied by music or interspersed with song and orchestral music.[42] The *Nickleby* production makes extensive use of Stephen Oliver's music and songs, including leitmotifs for particular characters, music identifying good actions or suggesting the forces for good, and music to support the sentimental scenes – all techniques related to melodrama. An example of music suggesting a force for good is the arrival of a letter for Nicholas at Dotheboys at the most harrowing moment, from the 'good' Newman Noggs.[43]

There is certainly evidence of 'a side of streaky bacon' whereby harrowing, sad or sentimental scenes alternate with comic ones, and vice versa. The production is particularly adept at depicting sentimental scenes. The penultimate scene of Act I, Part ii sees Nicholas preventing Squeers from whipping Smike by beating him in turn; this elicits huge cheers, elation and applause from the audience as the villain gets his comeuppance. This elation is immediately followed by the meeting of Nicholas and Smike on the road to London.[44] David Threlfall magnifies Dickens's description of Smike as 'lame'; a painfully crippled body and gentle childlike visage are coupled with real gentleness, spirit and vulnerability. When they meet, Smike's leitmotif is heard; sweet single notes on a piano play to introduce him. Silence. He kneels before Nicholas, who asks, 'Why do you kneel to me?' Smike replies: 'Go anywhere, go everywhere to the world's end, to the churchyard or grave. You'll let me come away with you? You are my home.' His incomplete sentences, together with his lack of fluency and trusting nature, enhance the sentimentality. Rees's Nicholas is so moved, he hesitates. Smike, thinking this is a rejection of him, begins to weep. But, with the swelling orchestral version of the leitmotif behind them, Nicholas holds out his hand and raises Smike from his knees. They go off together, and that completes the act. This is a deliberate playing up of sentimentality and a celebration of emotion in theatre. It is done through a thoughtful playing of Dickens's language that expresses bravery, gentleness and vulnerability in character, the timing of moves, and the uses of music. This beautiful sadness comes hard on the heels of the recent elation of seeing the villainous Squeers punished, a switch from joy to tears and back again for the audience.

Nickleby: The Spirit of Dickens

The RSC *Nickleby* successfully captures the vibrant spirit of Dickens and adapts to the stage the important effects of his texts, including some of the more difficult or remote theatrical influences. Using Dickens's language where possible, the practitioners take an approach to character and comedy that replicates the theatrical vim, vigour and intensity of Dickens's world. The company's non-psychological approach to character works well with Dickens's externalised aesthetics, and the actors' physically heightened performances and tendency to energise through the lines and honour the text, create convincing characters (often with complexity and colouring built into the process) which fly in the face of the orthodox critical accusation aimed at Dickens that his characters have scant complexity or realism. The company also makes a success of representing crucial aesthetic elements in Dickens: the Gothic (the uncanny, ventriloquism), the melodramatic and sentimental scenes. Success is achieved through the company's evenness of performance, its heightened structure, an excess within control.

But what kind of drama is the RSC *Nickleby* production, and what does it tell us about the period in which it was mounted? The RSC's choice to adapt Dickens by taking inspiration from the performance traditions of the past meant that a number of revivified techniques of popular theatre and entertainment and unlicensed, subversive forms were made available to audiences in 1980. The company had to hand the skills of classical acting with which to rediscover those forms – an historically specific development in performance, then, helped determine a convincing account of historically remote and specific art forms. One of this country's great theatre companies, the RSC, renowned worldwide for producing serious 'drama' with a capital 'D', reproduced a direct, committed rendition of popular entertainment and theatre to evoke the spirit of Dickens.

If this proves anything, it demonstrates how the categories of 'serious drama' or 'high culture' (often applied to the RSC) or 'popular' or 'non-elite culture' (applied to 'illegitimate' performance forms in the past) are entirely unstable and subject to history. Over a century later, popular theatrical forms, developed mostly for working-class, poorer audiences and shaped by censorship and disapproval – with everything subversive and radical that that offered the audiences of that time – are being plundered by two of the country's leading directors and cultural leaders (Nunn/Caird) for a very different type of audience and for a very specific moment. Nunn and Caird were attempting to capture what that meant. The celebration of the collective and the diminution of the importance of the individual, right at the beginning of the Thatcher era of rampant individualism, is politically significant, particularly when put on by the flagship subsidised Shakespeare company. For David Edgar: 'The success of *Nicholas Nickleby* was partially attributable to its time; a year into Margaret Thatcher's government, as unemployment rocketed and swathes of industrial Britain collapsed, people wanted to hear that there was more to life than money.'[45]

If, as John argues, 'Dickens's political commitment [was] to externalized aesthetics and to a melodramatic, symbolic art of the visual which he associated with non-elite culture',[46] here was what one can only see as an elite cultural institution looking to non-elite, even subversive performance styles. It could be argued that the RSC was looking for the sort of danger and political cut-through that those forms generated from irreverence, raucousness and laughter, the effect of being historically marginalised and censored – and the sort of theatrical expression that would have its later incarnation in agitprop theatre and Brechtian *Verfremdungseffeckt*.[47] The RSC draws upon popular theatrical forms to capture the humorous, vibrant and life-affirming Dickens – and also to express his politics. The dangerous, radical and exciting side to Dickens is clear in, among other things, his critique of capitalist greed and power and his lampooning and punishment of the pompous and the powerful. Yet there is a tendency in Dickens to pull back from a full-scale unlicensed radicalism. Laughter at the unlicensed theatre for working and poorer classes was an opportunity to in a sense 'articulate popular opinion' about the world's injustices and to 'vicariously release subversive feeling' through that very laughter, as Jonathan Buckmaster puts it.[48] Laughter and kindness for Dickens are both an expression of radicalism and a tool of its suppression. One could argue that the RSC production manages to capture this Dickensian quality – this quality of not quite fully realising the possibilities of its own subversive nature. As eminently skilled and technically aware as the RSC practitioners are, this is an elite institution *recreating* traditional, popular cultural performance forms for an audience that is, for the most part, fairly well to do. Hence, when the RSC audience laughs at the antics of Squeers, and cheer when Nicholas bests Ralph Nickleby, what this is not is the revolutionary and explosive state of affairs where a working-class audience – experienced in the material deprivations being depicted on stage – is offered up something by the illegitimate theatre. Any possibility of radicalism and political subversion – which the directors and Edgar hoped audiences would enjoy and apply to their own lives in 1980 – must be viewed within this light. At some level this RSC version remains, ultimately, an excellent work offering an educated audience insight into traditional art forms and the material conditions of the past; political commentary remains an echo rather than a refrain.

Nickleby, the Past and the Future

While the RSC production is successful in providing a convincing rendition of Dickens's project, it is not one that is likely to be repeated again. The kind of actor and the kind of performance approach that evokes Dickens so extraordinarily well is waning in the industry. A whole set of broad historical and cultural factors have effected this, including the demise of the repertory system and the arrival of television.[49] Interestingly, it is at the moment when the conditions of the possibility of this sort of production (the RSC *Nickleby* production) are diminishing that the quality of the *Nickleby* production seems to take on a more poignant and significant status. This is not to say 'the past' is a settled given that determines the present, nor that history is a determined progress towards the future. How exactly 'the past' and 'the present' are understood is unstable; they are sites subject to ideological and material struggle. One could almost invoke (but perhaps without the theological resonances) a moment from Walter Benjamin's 'Theses on the Philosophy of History' (1940) in which he calls for a constant alertness to important moments from a past that, in conjunction with the present, gives one a glimpse of something that will quickly fade, like exposed photographic film.[50] The 'truths' that the RSC *Nickleby* appears to open up concern what has been already argued – that remote language, energised, externalised characterisation, the grotesque, the melodramatic, the comedic, the Dickensian life force grounded in unlicensed theatrical forms, forms an overall aesthetic that goes hugely to the heart of what Dickens has to offer as an artist. These forms are remote from us now; they may be puzzling, unrecognisable, unreadable even – but they disclose an important quality, an Otherness, representing, perhaps, the Otherness of the past, a past that Dickens both inhabited and transcended.

Notes

1. Charles Dickens, *Speeches of Charles Dickens: A Complete Edition*, ed. by K. J. Fielding (Hemel Hempstead: Harvester Wheatsheaf, 1988), 202.
2. Raymond Williams, *Drama in Performance* (Milton Keynes: Open University Press, 1991), 18.
3. *Nicholas Nickleby*, dir. Jim Goddard for the Royal Shakespeare Company, Richard Price Television Associates for Channel Four UK (1982); a two-part 8.5-hour recording, based on Trevor Nunn and John Caird's stage production. Although I saw the original two-part eight-hour stage production in 1981, my analysis is based upon this filmed stage performance. This was shot at the Old Vic (not the Aldwych Theatre), but apart from a walkway through the centre of the audience at the Old Vic it comes very close to being a record of the original stage production.
4. The history of philosophy is replete with extraordinary accounts of different types of drama and studies of its central importance to culture and metaphysics. Aristotle in his *Poetics* (c.335 BCE), introduces the famous concepts of 'the Unities' in tragedy, and the idea that tragedy involves catharsis (purging) of terror and pity; Nietzsche, in *The Birth of Tragedy* (1872), develops the notion of the Apollonian and the Dionysian tendencies in art, derived from a discussion of ancient Greek tragedy.
5. 'Cloth and stick' is a phrase used by theatre practitioners, which gestures back to approaches taken by travelling theatre companies. The phrase indicates the approach whereby there are no expensive sets or production values in a show, you just turn up at a place with nothing and perform. Barrie Rutter's Northern Broadsides is an example of a contemporary company that takes this approach. But this is a venerable tradition that goes back to the travelling troupes of Shakespeare's day or even earlier. It suggests a poor theatre, without funds.
6. See Peter Hall's *Shakespeare's Advice to the Players* (London: Oberon Books, 2003), where Hall outlines his approach to productions after fifty years of directing Shakespeare. For him, the formal properties of Shakespeare's texts (the iambic beat, playing the verse) are the guide for the actor's performance, and are central to an audience's understanding of the play: '[I]f an actor understands a speech and expresses its meaning through the form, the audience will understand also' (11). Trevor Nunn worked closely with Hall and was his 'ideal successor' (Michael Billington, Obituary, 'Peter Hall: A Titan of the Theatre and a vulnerable, sensitive man', *Guardian*, 13 September 2017).
7. Paul Schlicke, *Dickens and Popular Entertainment* (London: Routledge, 2016), 46.
8. Melodramatic or sentimental scenes are often treated very carefully in contemporary theatre productions. There are a number of possible theories as to why this might be the case, but huge intensities of emotion appear not to be part of a modern audience's palate. For a fascinating argument that tests this question, see Michael Stewart, 'The Enduring Reach of Melodrama in Contemporary Film and Culture', *Genre Trajectories: Identifying, Mapping, Projecting*, ed. by Garin Dowd and Natalia Rulyova (London: Palgrave Macmillan, 2015), 165–82.
9. See Juliet John, *Dickens and Mass Culture* (Oxford: Oxford University Press, 2010), 1–35 and passim.
10. Leon Rubin, *The Nicholas Nickleby Story: The Making of the Historic Royal Shakespeare Company Production* (London: Heinemann, 1981), 17.
11. Ibid., 32.
12. David Edgar, Private Correspondence with Gillian Piggott, 25 October 2017.
13. Paul Davis, *The Lives and Times of Ebenezer Scrooge* (New Haven: Yale University Press, 1990), 4.
14. David Edgar, Private Correspondence with Gillian Piggott, 30 October 2017.

15. As many biographers have noted, Dickens made faces in the mirror and voiced out loud his characters during the writing process. See Robert McParland, *Charles Dickens's American Audience* (New York: Lexington Books, 2010), 177.

16. The RSC's approach of sharing the narrative across a number of voices is interesting in view of research on the collaborative processes involved in Dickens's 'conducting' of his journals *Household Words* and *All the Year Round*; see Melisa Klimaszewski, *Collaborative Dickens: Authorship and Victorian Christmas Publications* (Ohio: Ohio University Press, 2019), which argues for viewing 'authorship' in a new light. Perhaps writing the novels for Dickens was a harnessing of many voices, an alchemical coalescence of the voices in the author's head. Forster's evocative description of Dickens's production adds ballast in this regard: 'The first conceiving of a new book was always a restless time [. . .]. [T]he characters that were growing in his mind would persistently intrude themselves into his night-wanderings.' *The Life of Charles Dickens*, ed. by J. W. T. Ley (London: Cecil Palmer, 1928), 388.

17. Much brilliant and enduring work has been written on Dickens's roots in Victorian popular culture, and the influences it exerted upon his imagination. In addition to Schlicke, see George Worth, *Dickensian Melodrama: A Reading of the Novels* (Lawrence: University of Kansas, 1978); Deborah Vlock, *Dickens, Novel Reading and Victorian Popular Theatre* (Cambridge: Cambridge University Press, 1998); Juliet John, *Dickens's Villains: Melodrama, Character, and Popular Culture* (Oxford: Oxford University Press, 2001); and Sally Ledger, '"Don't be so melodramatic!" Dickens and the Affective Mode', *19: Interdisciplinary Studies in the Long Nineteenth Century* 4 (2007), 1–14, 7 <http://doi.org/10.16995/ntn.456>.

18. Michael Hollington argues that *commedia dell'arte* had a lasting impact upon Dickens's imagination; the author would have been exposed to *commedia*-style acting during his trip to Naples in 1844–5 and may have seen Antonio Petito, famous for his Pulcinella performances. See 'Dickens and the Commedia dell'arte', in *Texts, Contexts and Intertextuality: Dickens as Reader*, ed. by Norbert Lennartz and Dieter Koch (Göttingen: V&R Unipress, 2014), 39–65, 44–5.

19. For a fascinating discussion of the pantomime, 'the transformation scene', and its connection to Dickens, see Jonathan Buckmaster, *Dickens's Clowns: Charles Dickens, Joseph Grimaldi and the Pantomime of Life* (Edinburgh: Edinburgh University Press, 2019).

20. For example, see *Nickleby* Disc 1, carriage sequence: horn blows (22:31) and carriage are created from table, trunks and bags (22:46–23:49); and the London street (3:56 onwards).

21. *Nickleby* Disc 1, actors watch action and provide a range of effects (3:44 onwards), including snow from buckets (28:52); and a door knock. At 10:57–11:03, Roger Rees as Nicholas enables a scene change by carrying a chair on stage.

22. See Sylvia Morris, 'The *Nicholas Nickleby* Phenomenon: A Royal Shakespeare Company Triumph Remembered', *The Shakespeare Blog*, 6 September 2011. <theshakespeareblog.com/2011/09/the-nicholas-nickleby-phenomenon-a-royal-shakespeare-company-triumph-remembered> [accessed 27 March 2020].

23. Charles Dickens, *Bleak House* (London: Penguin, 1983), 320, ch. 19.

24. William F. Axton, *Circle of Fire: Dickens's Vision and Style and the Popular Victorian Theater* (Lexington: University of Kentucky Press, 1966), 145.

25. Dickens's 'stage manager' announcement came at the conclusion of the tenth number of *Pickwick* in December 1836. Qtd by Schlicke, 43.

26. Choric narration: Disc 1, 3:00; in-character narration: Disc 2, 7:32–7:43.

27. Disc 1, 1:14–3:47.

28. Qtd in Simon Callow, *Charles Dickens and the Great Theatre of the World* (London: Harper Press, 2012), 37. Dickens learned Mathews's monopolylogues by heart and practised them over and over at home.

29. Disc 2, 7:32–7:43.
30. See Peter Hall's *Shakespeare's Advice to the Players*, which is a kind of instruction manual for, and a celebration of, the classical actor, specifically drawing upon the Shakespearean productions Hall pursued during his Memorial Theatre, Stratford and RSC days (1956–68) and his time at the National Theatre (1973–88), which put form, verse speaking and the text at the centre of creativity. Hall's 'The Wars of the Roses' cycle in the 1960s is often cited as one of the greatest Shakespearean events ever. The book lays out the ideas after they have already begun to wane, and at times, Hall seems to sense this.
31. Ibid., 159.
32. Classical acting is a British phenomenon dating from the eighteenth century. Most of the classical actors I have seen on stage trained in the 1950s or 1960s, many in repertory companies, such as the great Shakespearean Alan Howard (1937–2015), who literally played all of Shakespeare's eponymous kings during his incredible career at the RSC and elsewhere. Laurence Olivier (1907–89) trained at drama school, but he too learned his craft in rep in the 1920s. It may be that the demise of the rep system is connected to the demise of classical acting since apprentice actors learned how to attack the classics watching older actors or actor managers, like Donald Wolfit (1902–68) or Anew McMaster (1892–1962), on the job. In an interview with *The Guardian*, artistic director of the RSC Greg Doran gives credence to this view. He claims that the RSC now has a training system, 'a gym' as he terms it, where everybody 'has the iambic pentametre in their bloodstream [. . . and knows] how to look for the clues that Shakespeare writes in to the plays'. He continues: 'This is increasingly important [. . .] with the decline of the regional theatre rep system and the training of actors becoming more focused on preparing them for television and film [. . .] People coming out of drama school often have less experience of the classic texts. [. . .] We have to just be careful that the craft does not diminish or get lost so we keep on making sure that post-drama school, while they are here, we are a sort of training ground.' Mark Brown, 'I don't care who wrote Shakespeare, says RSC artistic director', *Guardian*, 4 February 2020. <https://www.theguardian.com/stage/2020/feb/04/i-dont-care-who-wrote-shakespeare-says-rsc-artistic-director> [accessed 15 March 2021].
33. Shakespearean actor Andrew Jarvis's paraphrase of Raymond Williams's point in *Drama in Performance*, 73. In his analysis of how actors might perform *Antony and Cleopatra* in Chapter 4, Williams argues: 'Shakespeare wrote his dramatic verse, not to decorate a situation but to [. . .] create [. . .] effects [. . .] The persons are not so much represented in behaviour, as created in performance, through the intensity of the dramatic rhythm, which the text exactly prescribes, and which the performance communicates, in a single embodiment of voice and movement.' This comes close to being a perfect definition of classical acting.
34. John's description of Dickens's aesthetics is convincingly and complexly built. See especially Chapter 4, 'Melodramatic Poetics and the Gothic Villain', in *Dickens's Villains*, 95–121. See also Timothy Clark, 'Dickens through Blanchot: The Nightmare Fascination of a World without Interiority', in *Dickens Refigured: Bodies, Desires, Other Histories*, ed. by John Schad (Manchester: Manchester University Press, 1996), 22–38.
35. This analysis of how character is produced in *Nickleby* is based upon my understanding of the way actors have worked with directors such as Nunn and Hall, where language is at the centre of the craft of acting. It is also based upon how characters appear in this production. It must be added that individual actors will have a variety of ways of working within such a system.
36. One could even suggest that character here is a sequence of pictures or tableaux. This position is worth comparing with an argument put forward by John in her analysis of Dickens's 'melodramatic narrative prose'. John describes Dickens's externalisation of the 'inner lives' of characters through narration as tantamount to a series of metonymic static

scenes, tableaux or images painted by Dickens. These knit together in the reader's mind to form a fluid as well as static and convincing account of a character's inner thoughts and feelings. John captures this process in a vivid image: 'Reading Dickens is (to quote Coleridge on Kean) like seeing by flashes of lightening.' *Dickens's Villains*, 107. It is also worth looking at the arguments set out in John Abraham Heraud's 'The Spirit of Fiction' in *All the Year Round* 431 (27 July 1867), XVIII, 118–20, where the issue of how we process character from external parts in real life is discussed.

37. For more on the Royal Patents and its effect upon culture going forward, see Judith Buchanan, *Shakespeare on Silent Film* (Cambridge: Cambridge University Press, 2009), 42.

38. *Nickleby* Disc 2, 8:55–15:36.

39. See Holllington, *Dickens and the Grotesque* (New York: Routledge Revivals, 2014), 67 onwards for an analysis of Squeers as a grotesque.

40. Significantly, Hollington traces the grotesque back to physicalised performance or mime: 'physiognomy is of ancient origin, resting as it does on that perception of formal similarities between human and animal features (and apportioning moral qualities according to an emblematic taxonomy of species) that also informed early caricature and mime' (*Dickens and the Grotesque*, 14). See Disc 1, 47:49–50:36 for Armstrong's performance.

41. Disc 3, 27:39–31:56.

42. The word 'melodrama' literally means 'music-drama' or 'song-drama' and derives from Greek, but reached Britain via the French *mélodrame*, first used in 1772. The 'father' of *mélodrame* was René-Charles Guilbert de Pixérécourt (1773–1844), who used the term to describe his pieces about the French Revolution: see Juliet John, 'Melodrama and Its Criticism: An Essay in Memory of Sally Ledger', *19: Interdisciplinary Studies in the Long Nineteenth Century* 8 (2009), 1–20, 2 <https://doi.org/10.16995/ntn.496>. Also see the 1960s–70s resurgence in critical interest in melodrama: Michael R. Booth, *Melodrama* (London: Herbert Jenkins, 1965); Peter Brooks, *The Melodramatic Imagination* (New Haven: Yale University Press, 1976); and Robert B. Heilman, *Tragedy and Melodrama* (Seattle: University of Washington Press, 1968).

43. Disc 1, 37:37.

44. Disc 2, 51:21 onwards.

45. David Edgar, Private Correspondence with Gillian Piggott, 25 October 2017.

46. John, *Dickens's Villains*, 107 and Chapter 4.

47. 'Agitprop' is a highly politicised form of theatre that originated in Europe in the 1920s, and some aspects of the *Nickleby* production could be seen, in terms of style, to have a relationship to it. Bertold Brecht's (1898–1956) work is part of that tradition, argues Richard Bodek in *Proletarian Performance in Weimar Berlin: Agitprop, Chorus, and Brecht* (1997). Brecht's alienation effect (in German *Verfremdungseffekt*) provides the sort of experience Brecht believed could help audiences to think about issues rather than getting emotionally swept along by them.

48. Buckmaster, 5.

49. The idea that the waning of classical acting may be due to the waning of the repertory system in the English regions was discussed above (n. 32). Acting styles appear to mutate and develop along with technology in drama productions, as well as with – of particular interest here – cultural tastes and political contexts. The arrival of television had a profound effect on what was required of actors, their preparation and their training. At first, experienced stage actors were recruited for TV drama, and heightened, theatrical performances persisted on the small screen. As film became more prevalent in the shooting of television shows, and with a growing interest in creating contemporary, gritty dramas, Hollywood film and other more tempered acting techniques had an influence; with less rehearsal built into television filming schedules, spontaneity became central, and behavioural, minimal or naturalistic acting has become more fashionable in television work.

Less recruitment of stage actors for TV; less knowledge of and interest in classical stage acting; and drama schools offering courses specifically for film and television careers, have tempered theatricality in television acting as well as on stage. For an in-depth discussion of television acting, see Tom Cantrell and Christopher Hogg, *Acting in British Television* (London: Palgrave, 2017).

50. See Walter Benjamin, 'Theses on the Philosophy of History, Thesis V', in *Illuminations*, trans. by Harry Zohn (New York: Schocken Books, 1968), 225.

Further Reading

Malcolm Andrews, *Dickens and His Performing Selves* (Oxford: Oxford University Press, 2006)

Peter Hall, *Shakespeare's Advice to the Players* (London: Oberon Books, 2003)

Juliet John, *Dickens's Villains: Melodrama, Character, Popular Culture* (Oxford: Oxford University Press, 2001)

Paul Schlicke, *Dickens and Popular Entertainment* (London: Routledge, [1985]; 2016)

Part III
Performing Arts

10

DANCE

Goldie Morgentaler

Broadly speaking there are two ways in which dance features in Dickens's fiction, both of them reflective of the dance's role in Victorian society: firstly, as a social activity, and secondly, as a professional one for dance masters and stage performers. While dance does not feature prominently in the fiction, it is still a notable presence, occurring most frequently within a broad symbolic framework that links the dance scenes to the larger thematic concerns of the novels.[1]

There are a number of reasons for Dickens's interest in dance, not least the fact that Dickens himself loved to dance. We have evidence of this from his daughter Mamie, among others. In her reminiscences about her father Mamie remembers that he asked his two daughters to teach him the polka – a dance that was wildly popular during the 1840s – which he was very intent on practising. He also asked her and her sister Katey to teach him the schottische, a partnered country dance that originated in Bohemia and was popular in Victorian ballrooms.[2] Mamie also recounts an anecdote from her parents' courting days when Dickens surprised his fiancée, Catherine, by jumping through a French window and dancing a hornpipe. Although Mamie thought that her father was not a particularly good dancer, he was obviously a very enthusiastic one and insisted that all his children be taught to dance.[3]

While personal predilection certainly accounts for some of Dickens's use of dance in his fiction, it does not explain his extraordinary ability to capture the rhythms and motions of dance in prose, for instance in this account of the shawl dance from the essay called 'The Dancing Academy' in *Sketches by Boz* (1836):

> As to the shawl-dance, it was the most exciting thing that ever was beheld: there was such a whisking and rustling, and fanning, and getting ladies into a tangle with artificial flowers; and then disengaging them again; and as to Mr Augustus Cooper's share in the quadrille, he got through it admirably. He was missing from his partner now and then certainly, and discovered on such occasions to be either dancing with laudable perseverance in another set, or sliding about in perspective, apparently without any definite object; but, generally speaking, they managed to shove him through the figure, until he turned up in the right place.[4]

Notice here the onomatopoeia conveyed by the verbs whisking, rustling and fanning, as if the sound of the language could mimic the sounds of the dance. Both the humour of the passage and the mimetic emphasis on sound and rhythm are hallmarks of Dickens's depictions of dance.

A similar example occurs in *American Notes*, which recounts Dickens's 1842 visit to the United States. He was taken to a dance hall called Almack's in the Five Points section of Lower Manhattan. Mindy Aloff writes that 'among the things that this part of Manhattan was known for in the nineteenth century was tap dancing—a hybrid kind of virtuosic stepping that evolved through competitions between African American buck-and-wing dancers and Irish clog dancers'.[5] The dancer being described in the following passage from Chapter 6 of *American Notes* is the legendary African American virtuoso Juba, who is often credited with being the originator of tap dance:

> Single shuffle, double shuffle, cut and cross-cut: snapping his fingers, rolling his eyes, turning in his knees, presenting the back of his legs in front, spinning about on his toes and heels like nothing but the man's fingers on the tambourine; dancing with two left legs, two right legs, two wooden legs, two wire legs, two spring legs—all sorts of legs and no legs—what is that to him? And in what walk of life, or dance of life, does man ever get such stimulating applause as thunders about him, when having danced his partner off her feet, and himself too, he finishes by leaping gloriously on the bar-counter and calling for something to drink [. . .].[6]

The passage not only demonstrates Dickens's sharp eye for movement, but also his exuberant use of hyperbole that moves from describing actual dance steps – single shuffle, double shuffle, cut and cross-cut – to suggesting impossible moves, such as dancing with two left legs, two wooden legs, two wire legs and two spring legs. The stylistic trick of incremental repetition, that is, of listing a number of similar things with only slight alterations – two left legs, two right legs – not only introduces a rhythmic pulse into the prose that mimics the beat of the dance, but also moves the description of the dance from the realm of the possible into the realm of the fantastic. In doing so, it conveys some of the quality of the dance that Dickens saw. Because of its recourse to the physically impossible, the passage conveys not merely the exuberance of the dance, but also its incredible physicality and virtuosity, the implication being that what Dickens observed in Juba's dance was so extraordinary that it might as well have been impossible.

The most famous of Dickens's literary descriptions of dance occurs in the Fezziwig's ball section of *A Christmas Carol*. Published in 1843 in time for Christmas, this little book was intended to provide a lesson to the complacent Victorian middle class about the need for compassion and charity, especially during the Christmas season.

A Christmas Carol describes the transformation through supernatural means of Ebenezer Scrooge from an uncharitable, mean-spirited miser into a kind and benevolent human being. One of the steps in Scrooge's conversion from misanthrope to philanthropist occurs when the Ghost of Christmas Past takes him back to his youth as an apprentice to Mr Fezziwig, just as the latter is getting ready for the annual Christmas ball. Symbolically, Dickens exploits the joyous spirit of good fellowship and harmony evoked by the dance to teach a lesson to Scrooge. He also exploits the rhythms of his own prose to mimic the rhythms of the dance, so that language and content seem to meld into one seamless whole that bridges the apparent gap between literature, music and movement. Dickens's hyperbolic style, with its emphasis on incremental repetition, is perfectly suited to conveying both the mimetic and the symbolic possibilities of the dance:

In came a fiddler with a music book [. . .]. In came Mrs Fezziwig, one vast substantial smile. In came the three Miss Fezziwigs, beaming and lovable. In came the six young followers whose hearts they broke. In came all the young men and women employed in the business. In came the housemaid, with her cousin the baker. In came the cook, with her brother's particular friend the milkman. In came the boy from over the way, trying to hide behind the girl from next door. In they all came one after another; some shyly, some boldly, some gracefully, some awkwardly, some pushing, some pulling; in they all came, anyhow and everyhow. Away they all went, twenty couples at once, hands half round and back again the other way; down the middle and up again; round and round in various stages of affectionate grouping; old top couple always turning up in the wrong place; new top couple starting off again as soon as they got there; all top couples at last and not a bottom one to help them [. . .].

And when old Fezziwig and Mrs Fezziwig had gone all through the dance; advance and retire, hold hands with your partner; bow and curtsey; corkscrew; thread-the-needle, and back again to your place; Fezziwig 'cut' – cut so deftly, that he appeared to wink with his legs and came upon his feet again without a stagger.[7]

It is remarkable how successful Dickens is here in conveying the exuberant joy of the dance – as well as its rhythm. The pulsating beat of this passage mimetically allows the language to evoke the movement of the dancers, thereby illustrating the positive aspect of dance, its joyous life-affirming qualities that are meant to stand as a rebuke to Scrooge's unhealthy, miserly, anti-life philosophy. Fezziwig's ball is a model of healthy exertion, led by a man, Mr Fezziwig, who is described as being both old and vigorous enough to be able to cut and return to the ground without a stagger – a 'cut' being a leap into the air while alternating the position of the legs. The ball is also a model of social equality, allowing all to join in and be top couples at the last. The ball erases social distinctions: apprentices, housemaids, bakers, milkmen, all dance on equal terms with their employer and patron, Mr Fezziwig, and with his family. The passage thus suggests that dance is good for the body politic in the same way as it is good for the individual body, that it promotes health and harmony through promoting pleasure and good-feeling towards one's fellow humans.

The dance here is the Sir Roger de Coverley, a fast reel that was the traditional culmination to an evening of English country dancing. The term 'country dancing' is misleading; these dances may have been performed in the country, but they were also the basis of all social dancing in Great Britain in both city and country, among the upper classes and the lower, until well into the nineteenth century. The designation 'country' in 'country dances' is a corruption of the French term, *contre-danse*, or *contradanse*, which refers to the two rows of men and women standing facing each other and thus forming a 'set'. The popularity of country dancing was supplanted in the early nineteenth century by dances imported from Europe, such as the waltz, the quadrille and Queen Victoria's favourite, the polka.[8] Dickens himself chronicles the eclipse of country dances in *The Old Curiosity Shop* (1840–1), when he has Dick Swiveller dance a quadrille, because, says the narrator, 'country-dances being low were utterly proscribed'.[9] By the time Dickens published *A Christmas Carol* in 1843, the Sir Roger de Coverley was almost the last of the country dances that still found favour in the ballroom. Since Fezziwig's ball, as conjured up by the Spirit of

Christmas Past, is based on Scrooge's memory of his youth, it is fitting and historically accurate that the dance Dickens describes should be a country dance. Yet here, in what is arguably one of the most successful descriptions of a country dance in literature, Dickens instils a caveat, because this egalitarian vision of Fezziwig's ball is not real; it is a fantasy designed by the Spirit to demonstrate the folly of Scrooge's ways. It has no more substance than the memory on which it is based and vanishes as soon as the Spirit vanishes.

Something similar occurs at the end of another Christmas book, *The Cricket on the Hearth* (1845), where the culminating dance that seems to resolve all the complications of the plot in good fellowship, gaiety and camaraderie is dismissed as insubstantial by the narrator, who informs us that Dot, the heroine, 'and the rest have vanished into air, and I am left alone. A Cricket sings on the Hearth; a broken child's-toy lies upon the ground; and nothing else remains.'[10]

By undercutting the reality of the dance in both *A Christmas Carol* and *The Cricket on the Hearth*, Dickens suggests the ephemeral quality of movement, that it can exist only in one moment of time and then is gone. While John Leech's famous drawing of Mr and Mrs Fezziwig in mid-caper seems to stop time and immortalise the dance, the reality is that movement is never fixed, nor immutable. One may repeat the same movement over and over again, but it will never be exactly the same every time. Through this suggestion of the dance's impermanence and insubstantiality, Dickens hints at one of the reasons that dance traditionally evokes both positive and negative associations.

An example of this duality occurs in another of the Christmas books, *The Battle of Life* (1846), which tells the story of two sisters, one of whom sacrifices herself for the other by renouncing the man she loves so that he may marry her sister. The opening paragraphs of the story describe an ancient battleground, now buried under the fertile fields that surround the prosperous town where the story takes place. The narrative lingers on the devastation caused by the ancient battle, and especially on its effects on nature: 'Many an insect deriving its delicate colour from harmless leaves and herbs, was stained anew that day by dying men [. . .]. The painted butterfly took blood into the air upon the edges of its wings.'[11] After this ghoulish introduction, the narration shifts to a description of how the buried bodies of men and horses have, over time, fertilised the fields and enriched the crops, even as the memory of the battle has been erased from the minds of the present-day inhabitants.

No sooner has the narrator finished describing the transformation from bloody war to bucolic peace than he moves to a scene of two girls dancing on top of the very ground that he has just so vividly depicted as a mass grave:

> It was charming to see how these girls danced. They had no spectators but the apple-pickers on the ladders [. . .]. They danced to please themselves [. . .]; and you could no more help admiring, than they could help dancing. How they did dance!
> [. . .] Their streaming hair and fluttering skirts, the elastic grass beneath their feet. The boughs that rustled in the morning air—the flashing leaves, their speckled shadows on the soft green ground—the balmy wind that swept along the landscape, glad to turn the distant windmill, cheerily—everything between the two girls and the man and team at plough upon the ridge of land [. . .] seemed dancing too. (140–1)

The two girls are literally dancing on the graves of young men killed in war in a story whose very title evokes a battle. Here again we see the Dickensian propensity to portray dance as a joyous activity, but a joy that is undercut by what is underfoot. The macabre juxtaposition of joy and horror in this passage suggests the symbolic duality of dance, its potential for suggesting the sinister in tandem with the life-affirming.

A more obvious example of the sinister qualities of dance occurs in *A Tale of Two Cities* (1859), where Dickens depicts the frenzy of the Carmagnole. The Carmagnole was a dance of the French Revolution performed to the singing of a popular song whose lyrics glorified the revolution and gloated over the downfall of the monarchy. A popular punishment for those who did not support the revolution was to humiliate them by making them sing and dance the Carmagnole. The dance was performed in a long line snaking around liberty trees and the guillotine. In Dickens's depiction, it is an instrument of a frenzied mob drunk on chaos and murder:

> There could not be fewer than five hundred people, and they were dancing like five thousand demons. There was no other music than their own singing. They danced to the popular Revolution song, keeping a ferocious time that was like a gnashing of teeth in unison. [. . .] At first, they were a mere storm of coarse red caps and coarse woollen rags; but, as they filled the place, and stopped to dance about Lucie, some ghastly apparition of a dance-figure gone raving mad arose among them. They advanced, retreated, struck at one another's hands, clutched at one another's heads, spun round alone, caught one another and spun round in pairs, until many of them dropped. While those were down, the rest linked hand in hand, and all spun round together: then the ring broke, and in separate rings of two and four they turned and turned until they all stopped at once, began again, struck, clutched, and tore, and then reversed the spin, and all spun round another way. Suddenly they stopped again, paused, struck out the time afresh, formed into lines the width of the public way, and, with their heads low down and their hands high up, swooped screaming off. No fight could have been half so terrible as this dance. It was so emphatically a fallen sport—a something, once innocent, delivered over to all devilry—a healthy pastime changed into a means of angering the blood, bewildering the senses, and steeling the heart. Such grace as was visible in it, made it the uglier, showing how warped and perverted all things good by nature were become.[12]

As the last three lines make clear, Dickens sees the Carmagnole as a perversion of all that is right and good about dancing. The dancers' repeated attempts at establishing order in their ranks are confounded by the impetuousness of their gestures, so that in the end the circles cannot hold and all spin alone or fall down or strike randomly at each other's hands and heads, the chaotic dance implying by extension the chaos that has gripped revolutionary France. The healthy joy and good feeling that Dickens depicted in Fezziwig's ball have been perverted here into a form of murderous madness that stands in for the revolution and leads directly to the guillotine.

Dance has always served to foster sexual attraction, so it is no surprise that one of the most important functions of society balls during the Victorian era was to facilitate courtship. Dickens's use of symbolism in the narrative of *The Battle of Life* makes the sexual implications clear, since the two young women who are supposed to be dancing alone, for their own pleasure, are not alone. They are being watched by apple pickers on ladders, an allusion to the biblical story of Adam and Eve. Since the plot of *The Battle of Life* revolves around love and marriage, the fact that these two young women are dancing on a field made fecund by the bodies of countless men and horses buried beneath their feet signals the young women's potential fertility, as well as the close symbolic association between reproduction and death. The dance introduces us to the story's main female characters, thereby also underlining the importance of dance to nineteenth-century assumptions about female desirability. In fact, Dickens here seems to be anticipating Ruskin's 1860 assertion from *Ethics of the Dust* that 'dancing is the first of girls' virtues'.[13]

As Ruskin's formulation suggests, dancing was vitally important to the marriage market of the Victorian era. It was also one of the few forms of physical recreation that was acceptable for middle- and upper-class girls and women. Ironically, because the dances of the time required strength and endurance, dancing was also the one activity for which the prevailing ideology of the fragile female body was set aside. Queen Victoria's dance master, Joseph Lowe, insisted that his charges do calisthenics to increase their endurance and even made them work with chest expanders. Victoria herself was known to be particularly fond of dancing the polka, a dance that required precision, speed and strength. And if the queen could sanction such a demanding dance, then other young women need have no fear of also indulging a fondness for dancing.[14]

Social dancing, especially at balls, not only provided exercise for young women and facilitated courtship, but was also important as a means of networking and as a manifestation of social hierarchy. Unlike the joyful egalitarian chaos that Dickens celebrated in Fezziwig's ball, in most organised society balls, it mattered vitally who led the dance and who danced with whom. The importance for both sexes of knowing how to dance can be seen in the prominence of dancing masters on the social scene. Dickens himself attached so much importance to knowing how to dance that he hired private dance instructors for his children. In fact, dancing schools were an integral part of the educational landscape, a *sine qua non* for the future careers of young men and the marriages of young women.

In *Bleak House* (1852–3), Dickens gives us a portrait of one such dancing school: Mr Turveydrop's Academy. The Academy is run by the elder Mr Turveydrop, a dance master who does not dance, and his son, Prince, who dances too much. Mr Turveydrop senior is the primary target of Dickens's satire, since he regards himself as a model of deportment, deportment being associated by the Victorians with learning to dance. Dickens's criticism of the senior Mr Turveydrop's deportment is really a criticism of the way in which Victorian society privileged the kind of education that instilled outmoded ideals of gentility, false values and snobbery. The obvious place to locate this kind of social criticism was in the dance schools, which claimed to teach deportment along with dance steps.

Deportment refers to good conduct, good manners, and the correct way of conducting oneself in society, implying a knowledge of social codes and proper behaviour. Deportment and dancing went hand in hand because they were public expressions of gentility. From the Middle Ages and well into the Victorian era, knowing how to dance well was a must for any young man hoping to get ahead in society and for this reason it was also gendered as primarily a male activity. In the seventeenth century

DANCE 157

John Locke had extolled the virtues of dance as an indispensable part of the education of a gentlemen: 'I think [children] should be taught to dance as soon as they are capable of learning it; for though it consists only in outward gracefulness of motion, yet, I know not how, it gives children manly thoughts and carriage more than anything.'[15]

Locke here defines children as male and dancing as a masculine activity. The passage is noteworthy for the parallel it draws between outward gracefulness and inner grace. Knowing how to move well in public space, Locke implies, benefits the formation of the inner man. The dance manuals of Victorian times echoed Locke's formulation. 'Dancing', one of them asserts, 'permeates the soul with grace' and gives rise to 'manly thoughts'.[16]

Despite his enthusiasm for learning to dance and his insistence that all his children take dancing lessons, Dickens would not entirely have concurred with Locke. His depiction of Mr Turveydrop the elder implies that whatever grace the old man may have is artificial and hollow. His is a false front that bespeaks a false essence. The first description we get of the elder Mr Turveydrop emphasises his artificiality:

A fat old gentleman with a false complexion, false teeth, false whiskers and a wig [. . .]. He was pinched in and swelled out and got up, and strapped down as much as he could possibly bear [. . .]. He had a cane, he had an eye-glass, he had a snuff-box, he had rings, he had a wristband, he had everything but any touch of nature [. . .]. He was like nothing in the world but a model of Deportment.[17]

Dickens's portrayal of Mr Turveydrop's put-upon son Prince, who is the actual dance master, is more sympathetic. In Prince Turveydrop, Dickens gives us a portrait of a dance master from the mid-Victorian era that emphasises the amount of work that was required in this profession. Prince works twelve-hour days teaching in the dancing school, a gruelling regime that eventually causes him to go lame:

Prince Turveydrop sometimes played the kit [fiddle], dancing; sometimes played the piano, standing; sometimes hummed the tune with what breath he could spare, while he set a pupil right; always conscientiously moved with the least proficient through every step and every part of the figure; and never rested for an instant. His distinguished father did nothing whatever, but stand before the fire a model of Deportment. (226, ch. 14).

As the last sentence makes clear, Dickens's interest here is less in criticising the profession of dance master per se than in portraying Mr Turveydrop as a bad parent. If deportment implies proper behaviour, then the parasitic way in which Mr Turveydrop senior lives off the labour of his son suggests the hollowness of the concept, as well as its hypocrisy. This is in keeping with one of Dickens's major themes in *Bleak House*, namely, the abuses that children suffer at the hands of inadequate parents.

It is worth noting here, however, that Prince's work schedule is in keeping with that of other dance masters of the period. Joseph Lowe was Queen Victoria's dance master during the 1850s, the decade which saw the publication of *Bleak House*. Lowe kept a journal, so we know that he gave approximately eighty dance lessons during an eighteen-day period. Lowe also accompanied eight general dancing sessions in which Queen Victoria and Prince Albert joined. Many of the household staff of the

Court engaged him for lessons, sometimes even taking two lessons in one day if the timetable permitted. Nor does this take into account the lessons that Lowe gave at his own academy in Edinburgh, the time required to travel form Edinburgh to Windsor, and the fact that Lowe also arranged the music for the court musicians who played at the royal balls, in addition to, occasionally, conducting their playing.[18] Yet Lowe still found time to go fishing and hunting with Prince Albert, the Queen's husband.

I emphasise the frenetic nature of Lowe's activities as a way of contrasting an actual dance master with Esther Summerson's description of Prince Turveydrop in *Bleak House*:

> A little blue-eyed fair man of youthful appearance, with flaxen hair parted in the middle and curling at the ends all round his head. He had a little fiddle [. . .] under his left arm, and its little bow in the same hand. His little dancing shoes were particularly diminutive, and he had a little innocent, feminine manner, which not only appealed to me in an amiable way, but made the singular effect upon me: that I received the impression that he was like his mother. (224, ch. 14)

Here is a feminised male character presented to us from the point of view of a female narrator. As if to underline the effeminacy of Prince, notice all the 'littles' in this passage, an adjective that Dickens always employs when indicating femininity. Dickens depicts all of Prince's students as being girls, thereby further associating him with the feminine, even though dance masters at this time would have been teaching both sexes, sometimes separately and sometimes together. Certainly Dickens's own earlier portrait of the dancing school from *Sketches by Boz* depicts the sexes as learning to dance with each other.

In insisting on the feminine aspects of dance, Dickens seems to be implying that being soft, feminine, conformable and eventually going lame is the price that Prince Turveydrop pays for the selfishness of his father. But in his gendering of dance as feminine Dickens is also reflecting a changing reality and predicting a cultural shift.

By the early 1850s, when Dickens published *Bleak House*, dance was moving from an activity primarily associated with young men to one primarily associated with girls and women. Until the mid-nineteenth century dance was considered a male activity. Dance manuals were consequently addressed to men and routinely carried quotations from classical writers such as Socrates and Plato and philosophers such as John Locke. Dance instruction was considered as essential to a young man's career as instruction in the classics and similar academic accomplishments, all of which, being educational, were the purview of men.

No surprise, then, that the vast majority of dance masters were male. In fact, being a dance master was an occupation often handed down from father to son, as with the Turveydrops. Joseph Lowe, Queen Victoria's dance instructor, came from a family of male dance instructors. His three brothers were all prominent in the field and his son Joseph Eager Lowe emigrated to New Zealand and founded a dance academy there. But Dickens changes this gender dynamic in *Bleak House*. The elder Mr Turveydrop may have his name on the doorplate of the dance academy, but the founder of the dance school was actually his wife, 'a meek little dancing mistress' (226, ch. 14), who worked herself to death in the service of Mr Turveydrop.

The introduction of this feminine element into the genealogy of the Turveydrop Dancing Academy is significant. Not only does it suggest that the academy owes its existence to a woman – which would have been unusual enough – but also that dancing itself is a feminine occupation, even when conducted by a man. The feminisation of the Turveydrop Academy is thus significant in reflecting a change in attitude towards dance, especially in terms of its centrality to education. Because dance was more and more considered an activity appropriate to girls and women, it was also coming to be viewed as more marginal to the education of young men. This sex-change had a variety of reasons, not least the enormous popularity of the ballet in England in the 1840s, a popularity enhanced by the cult of the ballerina. Male audiences preferred to see female dancers on stage and were far less interested in seeing male dancers.

We can see this shift to the feminisation of dance in a later Dickens novel that features a female professional dancer, Fanny Dorrit of *Little Dorrit* (1855–7). Dickens had earlier included female stage dancers in his work, albeit briefly. Most notable, perhaps, is his wonderfully comic description of the overblown dancing and miming of the Infant Phenomenon in Chapter 23 of *Nicholas Nickleby* (1838–9), a dancer whose main selling point appears to be her youth. The Phenomenon's father boasts that she is only ten years old, but it soon emerges that she has been ten years old for the past five years and has a 'comparatively aged countenance'.[19] Her short, child-like stature is ascribed to 'an unlimited allowance of gin-and-water from infancy, to prevent her growing tall' (365, ch. 23). Thus the artificiality of the performance she gives is mirrored by the artificial existence of the performer herself and in the cruel regime that fosters the illusion that she is younger than she is.

There are other fleeting references to professional female dancers in Dickens's work, notably the brief mention of female circus performers in *Hard Times* (1854). But, in *Little Dorrit*, Dickens gives a more extended portrayal of a professional dancer in the person of Fanny Dorrit. *Little Dorrit*, Dickens's great novel about prisons, bureaucracy and bankruptcy, not only features a professional dancer as one of its main characters, but it implicates her in the financial crisis that is at the heart of the novel's second part. Fanny Dorrit is the elder sister of Amy, who is the Little Dorrit of the title. Fanny and Amy have grown up in the Marshalsea, London's debtors' prison, because their father was declared insolvent and has been imprisoned for debt for nearly twenty-five years when the novel opens. Fanny Dorrit learns her trade as dancer in prison, where she takes lessons from a dancing master who has also been incarcerated for debt. Thus, from the beginning, Dickens ties the art of stage dancing to economics and to economic hardship.

Fanny's subsequent career will follow a trajectory of economic bust, boom and bust, as well as tapping into well-worn stereotypes about dancers as materialistic gold-diggers, sexually and morally suspect. Fanny begins her professional career as a member of the corps de ballet at one of the music halls in the West End, where she catches the eye of a wealthy young man named Edmund Sparkler, whom she later marries. She then lives a life of wealth and privilege until the bankruptcy at the centre of the novel brings financial ruin to both her husband and her family.

Despite the fact that Fanny's career is dependent on being a stage dancer, we never actually see her dancing, a curious omission for a novelist who has elsewhere written extraordinary descriptions of dancers in motion. But Dickens is more interested in Fanny's materialism and social climbing than he is in depicting her as a stage performer.

There is, after all, an element of artistry involved in dancing, and Dickens would rather not distract readers from the theme of endemic societal corruption that lies at the heart of his novel. He makes Fanny a dancer, I believe, because that is one of the few ways in which he can portray a working-class girl on the rise without unduly besmirching her reputation. Stage dancing as a career for young women in the Victorian era inhabited the grey zone between the morally suspect and the impoverished genteel. And while Dickens endows Fanny with a certain arch charm, the overall portrait is of a self-centred, mean-spirited, snobbish gold-digger, who marries a wealthy man despite the fact that she thinks he is an imbecile.

Dickens is in general not kind to female performers in his novels, witness the Infant Phenomenon mentioned above. The Phenomenon's stunted growth is depicted as a deceit foisted on a credulous public rather than as a cause for pity. The female circus performers in *Hard Times* come in for kinder treatment, even though they do show their legs, and certainly the circus child Sissy in that novel is a sympathetic character. But this is for ideological reasons in a novel that has a point to make about the importance of fancy. For all of his vaunted sympathy for the poor and disenfranchised, Dickens is often unsympathetic to women who need to earn a living and choose to do so in non-traditional ways.

Nevertheless, Dickens's portrayal of Fanny is consistent with attitudes typical of the time towards female dancers. Part of the problem had to do with the dual place held by female dancers in the imagination of the Victorians. During the 1830s and 1840s ballet was the most popular of all the performing arts in England and prima ballerinas like Marie Taglioni, Carlotta Grisi, Fanny Cerrito and Fanny Elssler were the objects of a cult of celebrity. Nineteenth-century ballets required female dancers to portray ethereal creatures, such as fairies, sylphs, angels and supernatural spirits of various sorts – visions of an idealised and otherworldly femininity that wafted across the stage on tiptoe apparently removed from the corporeal, physical and economic constraints of daily life. Paradoxically the dancer's means of communicating this transcendent quality was through the movements of her body, thus eroticising femininity even in the process of presenting it as a sexless ideal. The costumes of female dancers were made of light diaphanous material, uncorseted and flowing. While the material itself was not see-through, the fact that it allowed the body greater freedom of movement gave the illusion of its being transparent. The looseness of the costume seemed to imply the looseness of the body inside it and hence its sexual availability.

This double vision of the ethereal and the sexual with regard to the bodies of female dancers hid the mundane difficulties of their lives from public view. Off-stage, the day-to-day reality of dancers' lives was decidedly unglamorous. Ballet girls were apprenticed to ballet masters, which not only meant attending regular dance classes, but also performing such menial tasks as fetching the beer and peeling potatoes. Rehearsals began at ten or eleven o'clock in the morning on the bare stage, often ending late at night. Corps de ballet dancers were poorly paid and were required to pay for their stage costumes, including tights, shoes and muslin dresses. They were fined if they were late for rehearsals. Many of them lived just on the edge of poverty, supplementing their income with piecework and other menial jobs. Added to the economic hardships, ballet and music hall girls were continually subjected to workplace hazards, not least, in the days before electric lighting, the risk of having their costumes catch fire while on stage. This danger was so common that in 1868

The Lancet published an article called 'The Holocaust of Ballet-Girls', which deplored the danger to dancers. The introduction of gas lighting in theatres in the early nineteenth century enabled great progress in the creation of stage effects, but it also added to the dangers which dancers faced as they moved rapidly about the stage, sometimes too near the open flames of gas jets, which easily set muslin skirts ablaze.[20]

In other words, professional female dancers belonged to the underpaid labouring classes, their pay and working conditions not much different from those of female factory hands. But they had one important advantage over other lower-class female labourers, and that was that they were exposed to a large pool of eligible, upper-class men who frequented the theatres in order to view the dancers. This constant exposure to young male admirers whose interest in the ballet was primarily voyeuristic contributed to the dubious sexual reputation of the ballet girl. And it is this aspect of the stage dancer's life, rather than her dancing, that interests Dickens in his portrayal of Fanny.

We learn nothing about the hardships of dancers' lives in Dickens's portrayal of Fanny. The closest we come to a suggestion of what their lives were like is the description of the theatre in Chapter 20 of the novel when Amy Dorrit goes in search of her sister Fanny. Dickens conveys the sleaziness of the dancers' existence by his description of their environment:

> When [Amy] was directed to a furtive sort of door, with a curious up-all-night air about it, that appeared to be ashamed of itself and to be hiding in an alley, she hesitated to approach it; being further deterred by the sight of some half-dozen close-shaved gentlemen with their hats very strangely on, who were lounging about the door [. . .]. On her applying to them [. . .] for a direction to Miss Dorrit, they made way for her to enter a dark hall—it was more like a great grim lamp gone out than anything else—where she could hear the distant playing of music and the sound of dancing feet. A man so much in want of airing that he had a blue mould upon him, sat watching this dark place from a hole in a corner, like a spider; and he told her that he would send a message up to Miss Dorrit by the first lady or gentleman who went through.[21]

For young women like Fanny, stage dancing, despite its low pay, could represent an open door to female independence. The fact that some dancers became celebrities, worshipped by their fans and handsomely rewarded for their labours made dance an attractive option for lower-class girls like Fanny. And here I believe lies the real problem for Dickens in his portrayal of Fanny, namely, that dancing – a profession that involved the public exposure of female bodies – nevertheless allowed for upward female mobility, tied to a possibility of financial independence that was considered unseemly in women altogether. With financial independence comes the potential for sexual independence, a possibility that the Victorian public found threatening. One way of diffusing this threat was to keep women in their place by assailing their morality, so that the sexuality that seemed so threatening in young women could be policed and restrained, or made subservient to the requirements of male lust. No wonder Dickens punishes Fanny by having her marry a husband who is a simpleton and then having them both lose all their money in the failed Ponzi scheme.

In all the examples I have given above, Dickens's complex attitude towards the constraints of class is closely tied to the way he presents dance, veering as it does from the exuberant carnivalesque portrayal of a country dance in Fezziwig's ball to the more jaundiced portrayal of Fanny Dorrit in *Little Dorrit*. His keen eye recorded the dynamics of the dance while his literary sensibility enhanced and broadened his presentation to connect the ephemeral art of dancing to the more concrete requirements of literature.

Notes

1. Very few critical texts have addressed the issue of dance in Dickens's writing, and I am not aware of any book-length study of this topic. Among the critical essays that do focus on dance in Dickens's work are Rodney Stenning Edgecombe's long essay on 'Theatrical Dance in Dickens' in *Dickens Studies Annual* 41 (2010), 1–23; and my own 'Dickens and Dance in the 1840s', in *Partial Answers: Journal of Literature and the History of Ideas* 9.2 (June 2011), 253–66. There are a number of essays on the motif of the dance of death in Dickens's fiction, for instance Michael Hollington's 'The Dance of Death in Charles Dickens's *Dombey and Son*', in *Tanz und Tod in Kunst und Literatur* (Berlin: Duncker & Humblot, 1993), 201–11, but these essays focus more on the theme of the macabre in Dickens's writing rather than on his thematic use of dance. Two important monographs on literature and dance in the nineteenth century appeared in 2009: Cheryl A. Wilson's *Literature and Dance in Nineteenth-Century Britain: Jane Austen to the New Woman* (Cambridge: Cambridge University Press); and Molly Engelhardt's *Dancing Out of Line: Ballrooms, Ballet and Mobility in Victorian Fiction and Culture* (Athens: Ohio University Press). But neither of these studies focuses on Dickens's writing. Sections of this chapter have appeared in expanded form in my essay 'Dickens and Dance in the 1840s', cited above.
2. Mamie Dickens, *My Father as I Recall Him* (Amsterdam: Fredonia Books, 2005), 27.
3. Ibid., 24.
4. Charles Dickens, 'The Dancing Academy', in *Sketches by Boz*, ed. by Dennis Walder (London: Penguin, 1995), 296–303, 302.
5. Mindy Aloff, *Dance Anecdotes: Stories from the Worlds of Ballet, Broadway, the Ballroom and Modern Dance* (Oxford: Oxford University Press, 2006), 134.
6. Charles Dickens, *American Notes*, ed. by Patricia Ingham (London: Penguin, 2002), 102.
7. Charles Dickens, *A Christmas Carol*, in *The Christmas Books*, ed. by Michael Slater, 2 vols (Harmondsworth: Penguin, 1975), I, 76–7.
8. Frances Rust, *Dance in Society* (London: Routledge and Kegan Paul, 1969), 66. Rust dates the decline in popularity of the country dance to the 1850s, but I believe it starts at least a decade earlier given that Dickens's is already noting its demise in 1840, when he publishes *The Old Curiosity Shop*.
9. Charles Dickens, *The Old Curiosity Shop* (Harmondsworth: Penguin, 1985), 113, ch. 8.
10. Charles Dickens, *The Cricket on the Hearth*, in *The Christmas Books*, II, 120.
11. Charles Dickens, *The Battle of Life*, in *The Christmas Books*, II, 136. Further references appear in the text.
12. Charles Dickens, *A Tale of Two Cities* (London: Penguin, 1985), 307, bk 3, ch. 5.
13. Qtd in Sharon Aronofsky Weltman, *Performing the Victorian: John Ruskin and Identity in Theatre, Science and Education* (Columbus: Ohio State University Press, 2007), 31.
14. Engelhardt, 143. See also, *A Most Excellent Dancing Master: The Journal of Joseph Lowe's Visits to Balmoral and Windsor (1852–1860) to Teach Dance to the Family of Queen Victoria*, ed. by Allan Thomas (New York: Pendragon Press, 1992). In the entry for 29 October 1852, Lowe writes that the doctor Sir James Clark was present for the dance lesson to ensure that the Princess Royal and Princess Alice came to no harm from using the chest expanders.

15. Qtd in Engelhardt, 35.
16. Ibid., 36.
17. Charles Dickens, *Bleak House*, ed. by Nicola Bradbury (Harmondsworth: Penguin, 1996), 225, ch. 14. Further references appear in the text.
18. Lowe, 7.
19. Charles Dickens, *Nicholas Nickleby*, ed. by Michael Slater (London: Penguin, 1978), 365, ch. 23.
20. Ivor Guest, *Victorian Ballet-Girl: The Tragic Story of Clara Webster* (New York: Da Capo Press, 1980), 2.
21. Charles Dickens, *Little Dorrit*, ed. by John Holloway (Harmondsworth: Penguin, 1985), 278, bk 1, ch. 20.

Further Reading

Alexandra Carter, *Dance and Dancers in the Victorian and Edwardian Music Hall Ballet* (Aldershot: Ashgate, 2005)

Molly Engelhardt, *Dancing Out of Line: Ballrooms, Ballet and Mobility in Victorian Fiction and Culture* (Athens: Ohio University Press, 2009)

Ivor Guest, *Victorian Ballet-Girl: The Tragic Story of Clara Webster* (New York: Da Capo Press, 1980)

Cheryl A. Wilson, *Literature and Dance in Nineteenth-Century Britain: Jane Austen to the New Woman* (Cambridge: Cambridge University Press, 2009)

11

MUSIC

Matthew Ingleby

IN HIS THOUGHTS ABOUT *NICHOLAS NICKLEBY* (1838–9), published in 1911, G. K. Chesterton casts Dickens in a curious musical role, heroically marshalling the collective spirit of a host of 'unsuccessful' men in a kind of 'wonderful chorus':

> There are vast prospects and splendid songs in the point of view of the typically unsuccessful man; if all the used-up actors and spoilt journalists and broken clerks could give a chorus, it would be a wonderful chorus in praise of the world. But these unsuccessful men commonly cannot even speak. Dickens is the voice of them, and a very ringing voice.[1]

Dickens, who cast himself as the 'Conductor' of his periodical *Household Words* (1850-9), is not here given to direct this notional performance from a podium, however. The men of his chorus – their careers suggesting failed alternative versions of Dickens – are so 'broken' they cannot 'speak', let alone sing. Rather, it is the 'very ringing voice' of Dickens that serves as a substitute for the unmusical masses, enunciating the song they would have sung, in an act of choral advocacy.[2]

As a way into thinking about the politics of Dickens's writing, Chesterton's 'chorus' metaphor is both highly suggestive and problematically slippery; as such it says more about his own early twentieth-century concerns than it does about Dickens's. The 'one for all' chorus analogy, in which a single dictatorially 'ringing' voice drowns out weaker voices in exchange for elevating symbolically the corporate *polis* into which these voices have been subsumed, seems to conjure a populist authoritarianism of an early twentieth-century variety; Chesterton explicitly flirted with fascism when he fell for Mussolini in the 1920s, retracting only with the rise of Hitler. That sole reference to *men* – without women – moreover, betrays Chesterton's contemporaneous opposition to female participants in the British political sphere, suffrage campaigners. But what if we turn Chesterton's 'choral Dickens' metaphor upside down, and think less about its 'tenor' (the demotic or populist or democratic quality of Dickens's writing) and more about its 'vehicle', that is, amateur music-making? What sort of musical practice does Chesterton think of when he thinks of Dickens, and why? Indeed, which 'wonderful chorus', in particular, might be at the back of his mind?

The 'Hallelujah' chorus, from George Frederick Handel's *Messiah* (1741), is one strong possibility. Handel's 'Hallelujah', which uses the adjective 'wonderful' repeatedly, was a cornerstone of Victorian amateur choral society repertoire, helping to mobilise a mass musicianship in which tens of thousands of relatively 'unsuccessful'

MUSIC 165

men and women participated, with or without notably 'ringing' voices.[3] Along with one of Dickens's favourite living composers, the German émigré Felix Mendelssohn, the eighteenth-century naturalised German Handel satiated nineteenth-century British culture's 'appetite for momentous performances of [non-staged, religiously themed] oratorios with highly-populated choruses'.[4] Handel is the composer Dickens favours most explicitly in his writing. A number of his novels reference the composer of *Messiah*, most famously *Great Expectations* (1860–1), in which Herbert Pocket displays his affection for the protagonist Pip by giving him an extra pet name, Handel, after that composer's famous keyboard work, 'The Harmonious Blacksmith' (1720), wringing out the pun rather literally for his uncultivated friend: 'We are so harmonious, and you have been a blacksmith.'[5] Handel is here associated with social as much as musical harmony, the social harmony of friends enjoying each other's company, which was as big a part of the draw of the Handelian chorus for Victorian oratorio singers as the religious content of the lyrics or the sublimity of the music. Handel is granted a similar association with benevolent sociability in Dickens's final, uncompleted sensation novel, *The Mystery of Edwin Drood* (1870), in which the composer is the musical hero of the Rev. Mr Crisparkle ('early-riser, musical, classical, cheerful, kind, good-natured, social, contented, and boy-like') and the subject of a portrait over a closet in his dining-room.[6] A keen amateur choral singer, Crisparkle is a member of Cloisterham's 'Alternate Musical Wednesdays' Society, and sits up long into the evening to practise his own parts in 'concerted vocal music' (60, ch. 8).

Chesterton's choral metaphor picks up on this important though neglected aspect of Dickens's imagination: his writing's strong affiliation with a vernacular culture of amateur music-making that is exemplified by the Handelian, Crisparklian, chorus. There are multiple references throughout Dickens's fiction to music made approximately or inexpertly, by non-professionals, often with the intention (if not the result) of producing 'social harmony'. Dickensian musical happenings are sometimes so 'amateur' (in the sense of 'unskilled'), they almost fail to register to readers as musical performances at all.[7] But it is precisely in the self-effacing nature of the sociable and therefore often bathetic kind of music he chooses to focus on that its interest lies. This essay explores the general affiliation in Dickens's writing for amateur music-making over elite or professional musicianship, especially, the opera. It then unpacks such an affiliation as it is articulated in one particularly musical novel, *Little Dorrit* (1855–7), arguing that music plays a role in the story's moral economy that is far from ornamental. The final section or coda briefly considers Dickens's rather underwhelming operatic afterlife and speculates upon the reasons behind the comparative failure of his famously adaptable novels to translate into opera, that *other* great narrative form of the nineteenth century.

Amateur versus Professional

Dickens was himself a talented amateur musician and possessed a tenor voice of sufficient quality for his maternal uncle John Barrow to commend it to the staff of *The Morning Chronicle*. In 1833, when he wrote to them on behalf of his underemployed nephew, he stated that, in addition to Charles being a fine journalist, he was also a 'good singer of a comic song'.[8] As Michael Slater suggests, in convivial surroundings Dickens could sometimes seem a bit like a human jukebox, able to bring out on demand all the popular songs from the period in amusing parodies, like his character Dick Swiveller does in *The Old Curiosity Shop* (1840–1).[9] While Dickens enjoyed and contributed to amateur music-making, he knew too the distinct value of trained, professional musicianship, as one account of being 'quite overcome' by the beauty of the performance of Charles Gounod's *Faust* (1859) when he heard it in Paris indicates.[10] Victorian bourgeois culture was more musically literate than our own, so we should be wary of exaggerating Dickens's musical appreciation in relation to his peers.[11] Nonetheless, from the various references to listening experiences scattered throughout his letters, the novelist appears to have been an enthusiastic and fairly knowledgeable follower of the art music of his day, prizing in particular the melodious and light-textured forms of Mendelssohn's *Lieder* (art songs for voice with a piano accompaniment) or Chopin's solo piano music, while also being a great lover of earlier classical figures, like Mozart. His musical ear is perhaps unsurprising, given that he came from a musical family, his older sister Fanny being a professional singer, who trained and then taught at London's leading conservatory, the Royal Academy of Music.[12]

Despite his musical appreciation, there are few references in Dickens's novels to professional performances of art music, and no episodes in which characters encounter a technically honed beauty as overpoweringly effective as that which the novelist found one night, for example, in *Faust*. There is nothing, moreover, like the moment in Gustave Flaubert's *Madame Bovary* (1857), in which Emma is lifted out of her petty 'denigrating impulse[s]' when she hears the sextet from Gaetano Donizetti's *Lucia di Lammermoor* (1835) at the Paris Opera, realises all she has been missing in her humdrum provincial life, and even imagines an alternative fate for herself in which she becomes the lover of the tenor, the hero of the opera, Edgar.[13] Nor, relatedly, does any novel by Dickens make use of the *topos* of exceptional professional musicianship to signal absolute, autonomous genius. There is no equivalent of the figure of Julius Klesmer in George Eliot's *Daniel Deronda* (1876), who provides such a contrast to Gwendolen Harleth, and spells out to readers that social butterflies like her do not have what it takes, musically or morally, to be a serious, professional singer.[14]

While Dickens was himself an appreciative opera goer, his writings are often sceptical about or satirical upon operatic culture. In an article entitled 'The Amusements of the People', published in *Household Words* in 1850, he draws attention to the substantial dramaturgical (if not musical) overlap between two forms of theatre, cheap melodrama and Italian opera, and thereby calls into question the social divide that positioned these cultural forms poles apart:

> When the situations [in a melodrama] were very strong indeed, they were very like what some favourite situations in the Italian Opera would be to a profoundly deaf spectator. The despair and madness at the end of the first act, the business of the long hair, and the struggle in the bridal chamber, were as like the conventional passion of the Italian singers, as the orchestra was unlike the opera band, or its 'hurries' unlike the music of the great composers. So do extremes meet; and so is there some hopeful congeniality between what will excite MR WHELKS, and what will rouse a Duchess.[15]

In *Our Mutual Friend* (1864–5), a pair of references satirise the social exclusivity of the preferred form of musical entertainment of said duchesses. In one scene, the

MUSIC 167

avaricious Lammles borrow the 'sparkle and glitter' associated with the opera in their wicked attempt to mismatch Georgiana Podsnap to the odious Fledgby.[16] In another, the poor doll's dressmaker Jenny Wren gains fashion inspiration from the great ladies getting in and out of their carriages in the vicinity of the entrance to the Italian Opera, at Covent Garden, an institution to which she has no hope of access. These two episodes serve as parallels to one another, like many other parallels set up in this novel which put one or other activity into perspective from alternate sides of the class divide in order to highlight the extent of inequality in modern London. In *Bleak House* (1852–3), opera is shown explicitly to function within the fashion system, that ever-fluctuating hierarchy which 'bore[s Lady Dedlock] to death', despite her whims being its raison d'être.[17] The Italian Opera is represented in this novel as one obeisant satellite among many, all of which encircle Lady Dedlock and vie for this enervated woman's attention, trying to anticipate her sense of what might be new, and therefore temporarily, of value:

> Yet every dim little star revolving about her, from her maid to the manager of the Italian Opera, knows her weaknesses, prejudices, follies, haughtinesses, and caprices and lives upon as accurate a calculation and as nice a measure of her moral nature as her dressmaker takes of her physical proportions. Is a new dress, a new custom, a new singer, a new dancer, a new form of jewellery, a new dwarf or giant, a new chapel, a new anything, to be set up? (12, ch. 2)

In her superficial, uncommitted interest in opera, Lady Dedlock shares traits with another character from this novel, who lives only for the moment, Skimpole, who '[is] a composer—[or rather] had composed half an opera once, but got tired of it' (73, ch. 6).

That idea of the opera as a cipher for extravagant yet unfulfilled promises crops up too in *Nicholas Nickleby*, in a scene in which a carriage overturns in a snowdrift. The passengers are compelled to wait together for another carriage in a local public house, and someone proposes 'sing[ing] a song to lighten the time', arguing that 'where people who are strangers to each other are thrown unexpectedly together, they should endeavour to render themselves as pleasant, for the joint sake of the little community, as possible'. As for repertoire, he suggests 'Some little Italian thing out of the last opera brought out in town', though, as it happens, no musical performance transpires, because nobody is able to 'remember the words of anything without the book'.[18] The complicity of professional operatic culture in an endlessly disruptive fashion system impedes the party's amateur musical communion just as the snowdrift impedes their journey. Music here fails to happen because fashion-driven operatic culture has implicitly overproduced and therefore reified its musical commodities beyond the mnemonic musical mainstream of everyday life.

The closest we get to description of exceptional professional musical performance in Dickens is not in any opera scene, but in *The Mystery of Edwin Drood*, in the liturgical singing of the cathedral lay clerk John Jasper, whose 'beautiful voice [. . .] quite astonishes his fellows by [its] melodious power': 'He has never sung difficult music with such skill and harmony, as in this day's Anthem. His nervous temperament is occasionally prone to take difficult music a little too quickly; to-day, his time is perfect' (128, ch. 14). Jasper's musical perfection is the reverse side (and therefore a part) of his villainy: the duplicitous singer by day is an opium addict by night, and probably much worse. Tellingly, the beautiful music Jasper performs in church services as part of his job does not so much constitute one part of the dichotomy within his character as hold in tension the attractive and the very ugly. To Edwin, Jasper's voice is simply 'celestial', but to the musician's own ears, his singing 'often sounds [. . .] quite devilish': 'The echoes of my own voice among the arches seem to mock me with my daily drudging round' (11, ch. 2). Here, Dickens seems to associate the demonic in Jasper's music with the fact that it is paid work, his 'daily drudging round' appearing to the musical worker's own ears an alienating closed circuit of repetition, like other forms of labour, rather than something glorious in its simplicity, like a *round*, a polyphonic choral work in which the interweaving vocal lines are perfect imitations of one another. When the amateur Crisparkle practises his isolated musical part alone late into the evening, he is inspired by the harmonious whole of the 'concerted music' into which his part will be inserted, but the only harmony Jasper intuits is the dissonance of his own voice thrown back at him in a parodic echo by the very arches of the building in which he sings.[19]

While Dickens's novels can be allergic to professional music-making, they are often implicitly generous about the messy compromises and approximations that constitute the musical performances of people of limited abilities or none. The amateur musician frequently features as a figure of inclusion, using music to build or maintain the social fabric, as in Captain Cuttle's celebration of the young love of Walter and Florence, which manifests itself in the very exuberant rendition of a song:

> [it] excited him so much, that on very festive occasions, as birthdays and a few other non-Dominical holidays, he would roar through the whole song in the little back parlour; making an amazing shake on the word Pe-e-eg, with which every verse concluded, in compliment to the heroine of the piece.[20]

Dickens's novels are replete with similar episodes of robust, unfastidious music-making, in which semi-musical characters prioritise the social realm above the aesthetic, another example being when *Bleak House*'s Mr Bucket, who played the fife in his youth – 'Not in a scientific way' – enjoins the young Bagnet boy to play an old military 'tune to warm an Englishman up!'

> Nothing could be more acceptable to the little circle than this call upon young Woolwich, who immediately fetches his fife and performs the stirring melody, during which performance Mr Bucket, much enlivened, beats time and never fails to come in sharp with the burden, 'British Gra-a-anadeers!' In short, he shows so much musical taste that Mr Bagnet actually takes his pipe from his lips to express his conviction that he is a singer. Mr Bucket receives the harmonious impeachment so modestly, confessing how that he did once chaunt a little, for the expression of the feelings of his own bosom, and with no presumptuous idea of entertaining his friends, that he is asked to sing. (675, ch. 49)

At other times, aesthetic edification is the amateur musicians' intention, but is not, alas, within their technical grasp, as in the chaotic performance of a Beethoven concert overture narrated in 'Mrs Joseph Porter' from *Sketches by Boz* (1836):

MUSIC   169

Ting, ting, ting! went the prompter's bell at eight o'clock precisely, and dash went
the orchestra into the overture to 'The Men of Prometheus.' The pianoforte player
hammered away with laudable perseverance; and the violoncello, which struck in
at intervals, 'sounded very well, considering.' The unfortunate individual, however, who had undertaken to play the flute accompaniment 'at sight,' found, from
fatal experience, the perfect truth of the old adage, 'ought of sight, out of mind;'
for being very near-sighted, and being placed at a considerable distance from his
music-book, all he had an opportunity of doing was to play a bar now and then
in the wrong place, and put the other performers out. It is, however, but justice
to Mr Brown to say that he did this to admiration. The overture, in fact, was not
unlike a race between the different instruments; the piano came in first by several
bars, and the violoncello next, quite distancing the poor flute; for the deaf gentleman too-too'd away, quite unconscious that he was at all wrong, until apprised,
by the applause of the audience, that the overture was concluded. A considerable
bustle and shuffling of feet was then heard upon the stage, accompanied by whispers of 'Here's a pretty go!—what's to be done?' &c. The audience applauded
again, by way of raising the spirits of the performers; and then Mr Sempronius
desired the prompter, in a very audible voice, to 'clear the stage, and ring up.'[21]

Here, ambitions towards the musical sublime are swiftly dashed by a sharp veer
towards the farcical. The parts become unstuck from one another, and what might
have been a rousing testament to the Promethean possibilities of collective musicianship resembles a risible 'race' between 'unfortunate individuals', all of whom cannot
help but put each other off in their attempts to stay in the game. Ironically, the musical paratext of the prompter's bell, which serves as the starting gun for this raggedy
scramble, is the only element that is timed precisely in this orchestral curtain raiser for
the amateur theatrical production of a scene from *Othello* that follows. Importantly,
however, the bathos produced by imagining Beethoven in suburbia (we are in 'Rose
Villa, Clapham Rise') is not snobbish or exclusionary, but affectionate. Plenty of virtues are on display and are noted as such by the narrator – not only the 'laudable perseverance' of the contestants in the 'race' but also the 'admiration' of the listeners for
those taking part. Out of musical dissonance, indeed, there appears to emerge a kind
of social harmony, because the traditional hierarchy between passive audience and
active performers is levelled when the former applauds repeatedly, expressly to raise
the spirits of the performers, rather than the other way around. That specific house
address, after all, does not serve only to socially index the hosts, but also smuggles in
a pun, 'Clapham', containing within it the imperative 'Clap 'em!' Give the applause
this risky failure of an occasion needs, if not deserves, Dickens ventures.

Dickens understands that objectively 'bad' amateur musical performances have
potential value because of the moments of social sympathy they engender between
performers and listeners. In *Little Dorrit*, this idea is elaborated through the example
of Old Nandy, whose 'weak' performances of an 'out of date' repertoire Mrs Plornish
elevates:

Mrs Plornish was as proud of her father's talents as she could possibly have been
if they had made him Lord Chancellor. She had as firm a belief in the sweetness
and propriety of his manners as she could possibly have had if he had been Lord

Chamberlain. The poor little old man knew some pale and vapid little songs, long out of date, about Chloe, and Phyllis, and Strephon being wounded by the son of Venus; and for Mrs Plornish there was no such music at the Opera as the small internal flutterings and chirpings wherein he would discharge himself of these ditties, like a weak, little, broken barrel-organ, ground by a baby. On his 'days out,' those flecks of light in his flat vista of pollard old men, it was at once Mrs Plornish's delight and sorrow, when he was strong with meat, and had taken his full halfpenny-worth of porter, to say, 'Sing us a song, Father.' Then he would give them Chloe, and if he were in pretty good spirits, Phyllis also—Strephon he had hardly been up to since he went into retirement—and then would Mrs Plornish declare she did believe there never was such a singer as Father, and wipe her eyes.[22]

At first glance, 'weak' amateur performance here serves humorously to show how strong bonds of affection can blur objectivity, but Dickens's use of music can also be read more subversively. Old Nandy's song – and Mrs Plornish's generous reception of it – can be seen as a form of resistance to the marginalisation the singer has suffered since his enforced 'retirement' from productive labour and his committal to the workhouse, one disciplinary institution within a whole network of them mapped by this novel. The tearful catharsis achieved in the performance signals a kind of emotional communion between performer and listener that heroically survives the atomising ravages of nineteenth-century political economy. Old Nandy may resemble to some ears a 'broken barrel-organ', but he is a human being too, still capable of exciting powerful feelings in others. His 'small internal flutterings and chirpings' make a claim for his intrinsic equality with such personages as the Lord Chamberlain, an official who, as censor of theatrical performances, exemplifies not only the upper class in general, but also the alarming power of that class to dominate (and regulate) artistic production.[23]

Little Dorrit and Musical Mobilities

When Mrs Plornish compares her father's performance favourably with opera, she contributes to *Little Dorrit*'s wider scepticism about the social function within London's high society of this most exclusively fashionable musicianship. In this novel, snobs like the Barnacles go to the opera in order to be seen conspicuously consuming the fashion system's latest commodity, which could alternately be 'the Nile, Old Rome, the new singer, or Jerusalem' (401, bk 1, ch. 34). The opera is where wealthy young men such as Mr Sparkler go to ogle beautiful working girls like Fanny Dorrit, when, in the first half of the novel, she is a dancer at the opera house. It is, moreover, where wealthy, young women – as Fanny has become by the second half of the novel – go to enhance their social capital, as she does when she plays zero attention to the performance and courts instead the fascination of the audience, to Mr Sparkler's chagrin. The narrator, by contrast, likens Old Nandy's voice to the most degraded and denounced form of mid-Victorian music-making, barrel organ grinding, which was regarded by many commentators as mere noise pollution, being not only a mechanised and unskilled form of music-making, but also peripatetic and unsolicited, like begging.[24] Despite the obvious differences between opera singing in the grandest of London's theatres and a literally manual class of musical street-work, each of these forms of commercial music-making was heavily associated with Italians in this period, and therefore with Italy, the space, after London, that is represented most in *Little Dorrit*.[25]

Music-making is a central thread running throughout *Little Dorrit*, helping delineate the moral disposition of its characters and distribute information between them to further the plot. The novel draws together different strands of the attitude to music Dickens displays elsewhere in his writing, including his celebration of everyday amateur musicianship's capacity to bring about social harmony, and his related concerns about the extent to which professional musicianship is exploitative to those who produce it and ill-appreciated by those who can afford to pay for it. Dickens interweaves these musical concerns with the novel's complex and much more discussed interest in geography, deploying his musical theme within the parallel he draws between two inverse spatial practices, poor Italian migration to London and rich British tourism in Italy. The instinctively musical John Baptist Cavalletto, an Italian migrant, might be expected to become yet another commercial barrel organ grinder on London's streets, when this was the classic form of employment for poor Italians in the British capital, but is found lodgings with the Plornishes and given another less alienating or precarious job to do. Meanwhile, Frederick Dorrit, a British professional clarinettist, is pressured into giving up playing his embarrassingly low-status instrument when he embarks with his family on their Grand Tour to Italy, a silencing that seems to crush his spirits, shutting down a means of self-expression amid the delusory sham that is Dorrit family life. Dickens thus makes musicianship a way of probing the reifying constraints of social identities as the novel's musical characters move within and between London and Italy.

In the first chapter of *Little Dorrit*, music characterises the Italian Cavalletto as one of the novel's minor heroes, showing him to possess noble feelings that belie his status as a prisoner. When the turnkey comes to bring food for his cellmate, the villain Rigaud, he brings with him his little girl, who sings 'Compagnons de la Marjolaine', a seventeenth-century French children's song Cavalletto knows. Despite being incarcerated, the Italian feels it 'a point of honour to reply at the grate, and in good time and tune, though a little hoarsely' the refrain of the song (8, bk 1, ch. 1). Their call-and-answer duet establishes a link of sympathy between prisoner and child, which reflects well on the former, and differentiates his basic goodness from the psychopathy of his higher-class cellmate. The song slips through the prison bars and, in so doing, acts as one of many symbolic forms of resistance to the novel's much discussed carceral structures. Later on, towards the end of the novel, the song assumes a more material potency, when it is heard by Cavalletto again, but this time on the streets of London, hummed as it is by Arthur Clennam, who has picked up this 'ear worm' of a tune from a mysterious foreign gentleman he has encountered at his mother's house. The tune enables Cavalletto to unmask this figure as his old cellmate Rigaud, who has escaped prison and his death sentence, and is living under the name of Blandois.

Vicky Greenaway has framed the politics of Cavalletto's heroic opposition to Rigaud in relation to the Italian Risorgimento, reading the former character as a kind of Italian nationalist who throws off the foreign yoke by 'perform[ing] an instrumental act of "identification" of the cosmopolitan criminal [. . .] which brings about his fall'.[26] In the opening scene, Cavalletto draws a map of the Italian peninsula on the prison wall, which seems to affiliate him with the great nationalist project of his day, the unification of Italy, a project of which Dickens was himself by this time very supportive. But the *musical* aspect of Cavalletto's Italian identity has been hitherto underappreciated. The spontaneous, humane musical participation of this ebullient, affable figure, to begin with, completes a national stereotype, which was very much in circulation in London at the time of the novel's publication, a city which disproportionately relied on Italians for the commercial production of its music. Due in no small measure to the political instability Italy experienced from the 1830s to the 1860s, London was subject to waves of Italian immigration, and many of these Italian migrants, political or economic, found work on the streets as entertainers of one kind or another, and most classically, as barrel organ players. By the later 1850s, when *Little Dorrit* appeared, London's periodicals published a number of articles about the modern phenomenon of 'street minstrelsy', which stressed the Italian nationality of barrel organ grinders.[27] Contemporary readers might therefore have expected Cavalletto to have become an itinerant musician on the streets of London, given the way the novel's opening chapter associates him with music. Cavalletto is rescued from the streets and this alternative career as a street musician by the grace of novelistic coincidence, when he is run over by a mail coach and attended to by a passing Good Samaritan in the form of Arthur Clennam. Through this providential collision with a well-travelled British national, the Italian is found much better employment in the Doyce factory and is allowed to assimilate into the 'native' working-class culture of Bleeding Heart Yard. It is surely no coincidence Dickens chooses this actual address in Clerkenwell to house his Italian migrant, as the neighbourhood was known in the mid-nineteenth century as 'little Italy', and was the metropolitan centre of Italian street musicianship.[28]

The ghost of Cavalletto's alternative career as a street musician haunts the novel. When Mr Meagles bungles the Italian's name, he tellingly links it with music: 'Cavallooro (I stick at his very name to start with, and it sounds like the chorus to a comic song)' (511, bk 2, ch. 9). The stereotypical Italian migrant's source of income, the barrel organ, meanwhile, is used repeatedly as a metaphor for the characters closest to the Italian. The rent collector Pancks employs it to express his distaste for the degrading work he has to perform, to the benefit of his boss, Mr Casby. '"Here's the Stop," said Pancks, "that sets the tune to be ground. And there is but one tune, and its name is Grind, Grind, Grind!"' (778, bk 2, ch. 32). The barrel organ's machinic repetition, whose single tune grinds down and irritates all listeners, allows Pancks to articulate his resistance to his own labour, while, for Arthur Clennam, it indicates the mindless grooves of bureaucratic circumlocution he is forced to engage, when he chases up an enquiry on Mr Doyce's behalf:

> 'I want to know,' said Arthur Clennam,—and again stated his case in the same barrel-organ way. As number one referred him to number two, and as number two referred him to number three, he had occasion to state it three times before they all referred him to number four, to whom he stated it again. (110, bk 1, ch. 10)

The anomalous case of Cavalletto as the poor Italian in London who finds a career beyond street entertainment intersects with the equally anomalous case of Frederick Dorrit, an Englishman and amateur musician who turns professional when his material circumstances suffer, before being forced, because of social prejudice, to renounce music-making entirely when his prosperity returns. In a backstory disclosed near the end of the novel, readers learn that Frederick was in his 'prosperous' youth a patron of the arts, who implicitly turned to music only to make a living when the Dorrit family debt led to their imprisonment. In the first half of *Little Dorrit*, set in the Marshalsea, we witness snatches of him practising his instrument in preparation for the theatre pit, where he appears to fellow workers an eccentric, risible figure:

> The carpenters had a joke to the effect that he was dead without being aware of it; and the frequenters of the pit supposed him to pass his whole life, night and day, and Sunday and all, in the orchestra. They had tried him a few times with pinches of snuff offered over the rails, and he had always responded to this attention with a momentary waking up of manner that had the pale phantom of a gentleman in it: beyond this he never, on any occasion, had any other part in what was going on than the part written out for the clarionet; in private life, where there was no part for the clarionet, he had no part at all. (231, bk 1, ch. 20)

These jokey speculations that the clarinettist's life extends only so far as the orchestral parts written for his instrument amount to a kind of dystopian fantasy of professional musicianship as a totally alienated labour, which leaves the labourer a dead shell in his leisure hours only to revive him on cue for the next performance. At the same time, those cruel moments when 'pinches of snuff' are deployed to conjure the 'pale phantom of a gentleman', with some claims to a 'private life', out of this musical zombie, hint at the Dorrits' past, in which music was for Frederick an amateur pursuit, among others such as philanthropy.

In the second half of the novel, which narrates the Dorrit family's reacquaintance with prosperity, Frederick relinquishes the musical part he had been playing hitherto. When he embarks on the Grand Tour through France to Italy, he is convinced by his snobbish relatives to renounce the clarinet, on the basis that it is too 'low' an instrument, the object bearing, like Amy's treasured old dress, traces of the life of penury and hard work the Dorrits had endured before their reversal of fortunes. For Frederick to play again for pleasure the tunes he recently performed as labour might inadvertently cast the 'shadow of the Marshalsea wall' (257, bk 1, ch. 21) upon the company, who go abroad expressly to enact a life of leisure and thus to exorcise any trace of previous poverty. Importantly, when Frederick goes to Italy, his clarinet is 'confiscated' (474, bk 2, ch. 5), that word linking the clarinettist to the figure of the smuggler, and therefore to Cavalletto, our working-class musical Italian, who migrates to London, like so many Italians during the Risorgimento, as Greenaway has suggestively explored. To put the reading in its strongest form, the unconscious reason Frederick is expected to give up his 'low' instrument when on holiday may be because, in music-making, he might too closely resemble a working Italian and thus fail to distinguish himself completely as that ostensibly different order of human, the spectacularly unproductive British tourist abroad.[29]

The backstory in which we learn of Frederick Dorrit's previous amateur music-making tends to be better remembered for the way it yields the novel's main secret: that Arthur's biological mother was other than the forbidding Mrs Clennam. The musicality of Arthur's biological mother is rarely recalled, despite the fact that Mrs Clennam holds musical culture partly responsible for her moral fall:

> 'If [Frederick Dorrit] had not been a player of music, and had not kept, in those days of his youth and prosperity, an idle house where singers, and players, and such-like children of Evil turned their backs on the Light and their faces to the Darkness, she might have remained in her lowly station, and might not have been raised out of it to be cast down. But, no. Satan entered into that Frederick Dorrit, and counselled him that he was a man of innocent and laudable tastes who did kind actions, and that here was a poor girl with a voice for singing music with. Then he is to have her taught. Then Arthur's father, who has all along been secretly pining in the ways of virtuous ruggedness for those accursed snares which are called the Arts, becomes acquainted with her. And so, a graceless orphan, training to be a singing girl, carries it, by that Frederick Dorrit's agency, against me, and I am humbled and deceived!' (757, bk 2, ch. 30)

A stern proponent of ultra-conservative Calvinism, a branch of Christian theology particularly suspicious of music, Mrs Clennam associates singing not only with sensuality but also with a naive disposition towards 'kind actions', which she believes facilitates moral dissolution. She herself attempts to maintain an anti-musical, antisocial silence, which becomes only more extreme at the very end of her life, after her brief moment of disclosure, when she is also temporarily released from paralysis: 'the rigid silence she had so long held was evermore enforced upon her, and except that she could move her eyes and faintly express a negative and affirmative with her head, she lived and died a statue' (772, bk 2, ch. 31).

If we take the musicality of Arthur's biological mother as seriously as his antimusical maternal guardian does ('Satan entered'), it would not be overstating it to recognise music as a structuring element in this novel's moral economy. In this light, Arthur Clennam's initial choice to take lodgings in Covent Garden, home of London's Italian Opera, rather than live with his mother at the gloomy Clennam family residence, hints proleptically at the backstory's secret, Clennam showing an instinctual affiliation with music and, thus, with his biological mother, who had been training to be a singer when she met his father.[30] In associating Arthur with music, his residential choice unconsciously affiliates him likewise with the virtues shared by the other musical characters in the novel he will in due course meet: that is, generosity, bravery, love of freedom, love.

Dickens's Minor Operatic Afterlife

In Christine Edzard's 1987 film of *Little Dorrit*, the soundtrack consists of music by one composer alone, that great contemporary of Dickens, Giuseppe Verdi, whose first opera, *Oberto*, came out in 1839, just a few years after the start of the novelist's career. Cavalletto, the novel's own Italian, fails to be included in the screenplay, falling foul of the extensive cuts to the literary source material for which this six-hour cinematographic adaptation has been much criticised, but his character might be seen to be ghosted throughout via the ubiquitous auditory presence of Verdi, whose music has become the sonic emblem of Risorgimento Italy.[31] If Cavalletto had been included in Edzard's film, one could very easily imagine him cheerfully whistling the tune to 'Va Pensiero', the chorus from *Nabucco* (1841) that came popularly to serve as the Risorgimento's anthem, and which would be another plausible candidate for that chorus at the back of Chesterton's mind, when he was analogising Dickens's populism.[32] As it is, Verdi's operatic orchestral music features in this film both extradiegetic ally, to establish mood, and intradiegetically, when Frederick Dorrit is shown practising his instrument in the Marshalsea. At one point, this intradiegetic music is allowed to continue over from one scene into the next, becoming a different location's extradiegetic soundtrack, one of several ways in which this film destabilises its realism with surely intentional nuance, and not, as Grahame Smith sees it, out of mere ineptitude. The Verdi soundtrack is, I suggest, a masterful choice, hinting proleptically at the Dorrits' future (as wealthy tourists in Italy), but also, analeptically, pointing to Frederick Dorrit's past, as a musical philanthropist with an interest in a young singer.

Though Verdi wrote a number of operas based on Shakespeare, including, in Dickens's lifetime, *Macbeth* (1847), neither he nor any other contemporaneous composer of an enduring international reputation wrote a Dickens opera. While Bulwer Lytton's novel *Rienzi* (1835) was turned, in 1840, into an opera by Wagner, and Donizetti used Scott for his *Lucia di Lammermoor* (1835), none of Dickens's much translated and frequently theatrically adapted stories were transmediated with sufficient success to make it into opera's global canon. Despite the enormous popularity of many of Dickens's novels in Europe, when European composers did write Dickens operas, they generally confined themselves to the *Christmas Books*, and most frequently to *The Cricket on the Hearth* (1845), as David Haldane Lawrence, in a helpful 2011 article about the wider topic of Dickens and opera, has explored.[33]

Early Dickens texts were favoured on the rare occasions when composers from Britain, not in the nineteenth century known for its homegrown opera industry, penned their own Dickens operas. *The Pickwick Papers* (1836–7) inspired an operetta by Edward Solomon and F. C. Burnand (1889) (and later a 1936 light opera by Albert Coates), while the *Christmas Books* resulted in Sir Alexander Mackenzie's *The Cricket on the Hearth* (written in the late nineteenth century but only performed in 1914). Throughout the Victorian era the tendency of Britain to import its serious opera from Italy and other continental European countries can explain the poor faring of Dickensian opera. But from the 1920s on, when figures from the 'English Musical Renaissance' such as Ralph Vaughan Williams, Frederick Delius and Gustav Holst had started to build up a serious national vernacular operatic repertoire, the continuing dearth of operatic adaptation of the nation's greatest novelist begs more questions. None of the major British composers of the mid-twentieth century, when Britain was establishing itself as an operatic nation, contributed a Dickens opera. Benjamin Britten – the finest of all modern British opera composers, and the first to achieve international success since Purcell – did, in the 1930s, seriously consider adapting one of Dickens's novels for the operatic stage, although this, of course, never transpired, and we are only left with the tantalisingly unrealised concept of a 'phantom adaptation' to chew on.[34] The most substantial Dickens opera to be actualised from the mid-twentieth-century moment was *A Tale of Two Cities* (1950), composed by Arthur Benjamin, who is probably best known these days for having taught Britten the piano at the Royal College of Music. This piece, which was commissioned for and premiered at the Festival of Britain, received positive reviews at the time, but has received no modern revival or been recorded.

Why this general dearth of Dickens opera, both here and abroad? Why should no operatic version of any of Dickens's work have managed to capture an enduring spot on the UK's opera stages, let alone in the international opera canon, despite the author's centrality to not only the nation's literary imagination but to world literature, too?

These questions, if answered with due sense of their complexity, would require another chapter at least as long as this one. One by no means exhaustive reason suggests itself in the textual evidence presented in the first part of this chapter, however. The explicit anti-operatic currents and the related preference for musical amateurism displayed in the novels themselves, especially the later ones, may have put serious operatic composers off attempting a Dickens opera. Dickens's delight in unskilled musical participation and wariness about the opera was precisely what an ambitious, aspirational British musical culture of the twentieth century was trying to exorcise; trappings such as these must have seemed of a comparatively stagnant and philistine British Victorian musical culture. Though Dickens's critics seem to have neglected the broad attitudes towards music displayed in his novels, his professional musician, composer readers are unlikely to have missed them.

Notes

1. G. K. Chesterton, *Appreciations and Criticisms of the Works of Charles Dickens* (London: J. M. Dent, 1911), 36–7.
2. The topic of Dickens and music is a complex one, which raises a number of important critical questions, most of which are yet to be tackled substantively by scholars, despite an entertaining, gazetteer-style monograph devoted to such matters having appeared as early as 1912, James Lightwood's *Charles Dickens and Music* (London: Charles H. Kelly, 1912). A couple of recent monographs suggest the topic is starting to receive the attention it deserves, namely Robert Terrell Bledsoe's *Dickens, Journalism, Music:* Household Words *and* All the Year Round (London: Continuum, 2012), which traces Dickens's changing attitudes to music through his role in editing (or 'conducting') periodicals in the 1850s and 1860s, and James Lyon's *Charles Dickens. La Musique et la vie artistique à Londres à l'époque Victorienne* (Paris: Beauchesne, 2015), which explores Dickens's musical tastes and affiliations in relation to the complex historical context of Victorian musical culture.
3. Fiona M. Palmer, 'The Large-Scale Oratorio Chorus in Nineteenth-Century England: Choral Power and the Role of Handel's *Messiah*', in *Choral Societies and Nationalism in Europe*, ed. by Krisztina Lajosi and Andreas Stynen (Leiden: Brill, 2015), 99–110.
4. Ibid., 100.
5. Charles Dickens, *Great Expectations*, ed. by Margaret Cardwell (Oxford: Oxford University Press, 1993), 177, ch. 22.
6. Charles Dickens, *The Mystery of Edwin Drood*, ed. by Margaret Cardwell (Oxford: Oxford University Press, 1972), 6, ch. 2. Subsequent references are inserted parenthetically in the text.
7. For twenty-first century readers, the basic assumption that musical skill has an objective and not only a subjective or relative referent might seem over-essentialising and elitist, but Dickens, despite his concerns about the socially exclusive nature of opera or his interest in the social aspects of amateur music-making, does not appear to find the distinction

MUSIC   177

between the musical success or otherwise of performances problematic in itself. For the mid-Victorians, steeped as they were in a culture that was suffused with live music, both amateur and professional, it was possible to recognise – and mischievously have fun with – the incorrect intonation or timing of under-skilled musicians, yet still identify with a progressive cultural politics. The idea that good and bad musicianship is only a social construct, which drives our present scepticism about musical quality, is not a Victorian one, emerging, probably, in the 1960s, as part of wider radical anti-hierarchical movements within art and society.

8. Michael Slater, *Charles Dickens* (New Haven: Yale University Press, 2009), 39.

9. Ibid.

10. Lightwood, 2.

11. See Delia da Sousa Correa, *George Eliot, Music and Victorian Culture* (Houndmills, Basingstoke: Palgrave Macmillan, 2003), which qualifies the importance of music within Eliot's fictional imagination by sagely acknowledging that 'Music occupied a place of far greater significance in Victorian culture' (3) than we afford it today; 'music [. . .] was central to her [and, by extension, Dickens's] culture as a whole' (6).

12. Slater, 16.

13. 'His [Edgar's] love, Emma felt, must be infinite, if he could pour it forth so lavishly over the audience. Every denigrating impulse evaporated as the poetic power of the role gripped her and, drawn to the real man by the mirage of the fictional character, she tried to imagine his life, that dazzling, extraordinary, sumptuous life, a life she might have lived had fate so decreed. They might have met, they might have loved one another!' Gustave Flaubert, *Madame Bovary*, trans. by Margaret Mauldon (Oxford: Oxford University Press, 2004), 200.

14. George Eliot's *Daniel Deronda* might be seen to rewrite the musical part of the plot of *Little Dorrit*, in that the later novel has the singing biological mother of the titular character survive, as a professional musician, in Italy, rather than die, as Arthur Clennam's biological mother does in the earlier novel, by Dickens.

15. Charles Dickens, 'The Amusements of the People (II)', 13 April 1850, in *Dickens' Journalism*, ed. by Michael Slater and John Drew, 4 vols (London: J. M. Dent, 1994–2000), II (1997), 193–201, 201. In drawing attention to the way the opera-loving Duchess is entertained by theatrical tropes that, when components of popular melodrama, would be considered base and cheap, Dickens is clearly making a subversive satire upon reifying social hierarchies operating in nineteenth-century culture. It is worth noting, however, that the satire does not extend to the purely musical aspect of the two forms he compares, as it is only a 'profoundly deaf spectator' that would fail to notice the difference between the hurriedly written music for the melodrama and the work of the 'great' composers one might encounter, as Dickens did, on the operatic stage. Maintaining simultaneously an overt anti-hierarchical agenda in relation to the class politics of culture and an implicit acceptance of objective standards of musical quality might now seem a contradiction, but this does not seem to have been the case in Dickens's day.

16. Charles Dickens, *Our Mutual Friend* (Oxford: Oxford University Press, 1957), 283, bk 2, ch. 4.

17. Charles Dickens, *Bleak House* (Oxford: Oxford University Press, 1948), 153, ch. 2. Subsequent references are inserted parenthetically in the text.

18. Charles Dickens, *Nicholas Nickleby* (Oxford: Oxford University Press, 1950), 56, ch. 6.

19. A telling contrast can be drawn between the professional John Jasper and another amateur church musician from a different novel, Tom Pinch, 'the volunteer who plays the organ in the church, and practises on summer evenings in the dark', and thus demonstrates again his trusting and trustworthy character. Charles Dickens, *Martin Chuzzlewit*, ed. by Margaret Cardwell (Oxford: Oxford University Press, 1984), 22, ch. 2.

20. Charles Dickens, *Dombey and Son*, ed. by Alan Horsman (Oxford: Oxford University Press, 1974), 112, ch. 9.
21. Charles Dickens, *Sketches by Boz* (Oxford: Oxford University Press, 1957), 426–7.
22. Charles Dickens, *Little Dorrit*, ed. by Harvey Peter Sucksmith (Oxford: Oxford University Press, 1979), 357–8, bk 1, ch. 31. Subsequent references are inserted parenthetically in the text.
23. See John Russell Stephens, *The Censorship of English Drama* (Cambridge: Cambridge University Press, 1980).
24. See James Winter, *London's Teeming Streets, 1830–1914* (London: Routledge, 1993), 72–9.
25. Dickens was one of a number of cultural celebrities who put their pen to a petition in 1864 to regulate the street music trade at a time when it was heavily associated with Italian migrants. The conservative press made the connection with racist vigour, calling these street musicians 'filthy Italian refugees', who have left 'the Abruzzi for Saffron Hill for the musical instruction of our foggy land' (Winter, 74). Interestingly, the two Italian musical professions, opera and organ grinding, were linked not only by the nationality of the players but by their shared Italian repertoire, melodically catchy opera tunes from the latest shows being some of those most commonly played by mid-Victorian barrel organs.
26. Vicky Greenaway, 'The Italian, the Risorgimento, and Romanticism in *Little Dorrit* and *The Woman in White*', *Browning Society Notes* 33 (2008), 40–57, 49–50. The political nuances of the 'ear worm' as plot device in *Little Dorrit* have yet to be explored, and they deserve much more scholarly consideration than I have been able to afford them here, given the novel's explicit nod to that most famously contagious of revolutionary melodies, 'La Marseillaise'. As Meagles says to Clennam: 'we know what Marseilles is. It sent the most insurrectionary tune into the world that was ever composed' (15, bk 1, ch. 2).
27. See, for instance, [Eliza Lynn Linton and William Henry Wills], 'Street Minstrelsy', *Household Words* 478 (21 May 1859), XIX, 577–80.
28. Bleeding Heart Yard is only a stone's throw from Laystall Street, where one can now find the blue plaque to Risorgimento exile Giuseppe Mazzini.
29. See John Urry, *The Tourist Gaze* (London: Sage, 1990), for an account of the various kinds of social production performed in the particular kind of conspicuous consumption known as tourism, including the central importance to the tourist of being seen *not to work*. See also Catherine Waters, 'Commodifying Culture: Continental Travel and Tourism in *Household Words*', in *Imagining Italy: Victorian Writers and Travellers*, ed. by Catherine Waters, Michael Hollington, and John O. Jordan (Newcastle upon Tyne: Cambridge Scholars, 2010), 35–52, for a helpful contextualisation of the tourism scenes in *Little Dorrit* amid the mid-century democratisation of continental tourism.
30. The Opera House in Covent Garden, known at the time as the Royal Italian Opera, burned down in 1856, in the middle of the writing of *Little Dorrit*.
31. Grahame Smith, in a generally highly negative account of Edzard's adaptation, notes the good fit between Verdi and Dickens's narrative, though he does not spot the (surely intentional) connection with the Italian theme of the novel: 'The aural world counts for little, unfortunately, apart from the intelligent choice of Verdi for the musical soundtrack, although even here the appropriately melodramatic musical overtones are contradicted by the flatly realistic visual surface.' Grahame Smith, *Charles Dickens and the Dream of Cinema* (Manchester: Manchester University Press, 2003), 43.
32. The myth of Verdi's catchy, rousing melody becoming the musical bearer of the spirit of Italian nationalism in the period of the Risorgimento is a popular one, and it would have been known well by Chesterton, who would have imbibed it with the newspaper reports of Verdi's mass-attended funeral in 1901. This myth has been much qualified of late by revisionist scholars. Roger Parker insists that the chorus, literally about the Israelites in

Babylonian exile, did not possess a clear political meaning when *Nabucco* premiered at La Scala in Milan in 1842 and had not accumulated such a meaning until possibly as late as 1860, while its mythological canonisation as the hymn of the Risorgimento by its patriot composer laureate was really completed only in the latter decades of the nineteenth century.

33. David Haldane Lawrence, 'Charles Dickens and the World of Opera', *Dickensian* 107.1 (Spring 2011), 5–21. The preference of opera composers for the *Christmas Books* probably derives in part from the musicality of the festive season from which they emerged, and, of course, the resonances of the stories and their titles, whose 'chimes' and 'carols' announce their strong interest in the world of sound and music.

34. 'Charles Osborne: An Interview [with Benjamin Britten]', *London Magazine* 3 (1963), 91–6. As Britten's biographer Paul Kildea claims, it seems very probable that the novel in question was *David Copperfield* (1849–50), which the composer read repeatedly throughout the period in question, and which features, through its Yarmouth scenes, the East Anglian coast, which Britten famously made his own when he settled in Aldeburgh. Paul Kildea, *Benjamin Britten: A Life in the Twentieth Century* (London: Penguin, 2013), 182. Scholars of Britten's most famous opera, *Peter Grimes*, have pointed out that the first production's rendering of Grimes's boat-cum-house borrowed directly from Phiz's original illustrations for Peggotty's beached abode in Dickens's autobiographical novel. Gilles Couderc, 'Les opéras de Benjamin Britten: un art du témoignage', *Cercles* 24 (2012), 86–102.

Further Reading

Robert Terrell Bledsoe, *Dickens, Journalism, Music:* Household Words *and* All the Year Round (London: Continuum, 2012)

David Haldane Lawrence, 'Charles Dickens and the World of Opera', *Dickensian* 107.1 (Spring 2011), 5–21

James Lightwood, *Charles Dickens and Music* (London: Charles H. Kelly, 1912)

James Winter, *London's Teeming Streets, 1830–1914* (London: Routledge, 1993)

12

MUSICAL THEATRE

Sharon Aronofsky Weltman

'MAY THE GOOD DICKENS FORGIVE US,' said Lionel Bart, when he stood on stage for the twenty-third curtain call at the premiere of *Oliver!*[1] Bart wrote the music, lyrics and book (everything that is not music and lyrics) for the now classic 1960 musical adapted from Dickens's second novel, *Oliver Twist* (1837–9). Referring to the liberties he and his creative team took, Bart's comment acknowledges that for many an adaptation's faithfulness to its source text matters. While much of contemporary adaptation theory pushes back against the sanctification of fidelity, Bart's statement hints that musical theatre audiences already understand this and indicates how useful musicals can be in theorising adaptation.[2] Elevating Dickens to godlike status (the phrase is usually 'May the good Lord forgive us') pokes gentle fun at the great author's canonicity – no one standing on a West End stage for the twenty-third curtain call on opening night is focusing on negative judgement about adherence to conventions of dramatisation. While we have all heard someone say of a film adaptation that the book is better, such a comment makes little sense in relation to musical theatre. So much of the entertainment and artistry occurs through song and dance that no one expects a direct comparison to a novel as source text to hold.

Rupert Holmes, who wrote the music, lyrics and book of the 1985 hit musical *The Mystery of Edwin Drood*, foregrounds the pressure that genre places on fidelity in adapting novels to musical theatre in two complementary ways. On the one hand, he uses the same title as its source, highlighting its contiguity. On the other, he writes on the libretto title page that the musical is 'suggested' by Dickens's unfinished 1870 novel, underscoring its divergence.[3] By framing Dickens's story as a play within a play performed in a Victorian music hall, Holmes uses the music hall convention of the Chairman to teach the playgoers (who are simultaneously the 'music hall' audience and *The Mystery of Edwin Drood* audience) about the conventions of Victorian melodrama and pantomime, including cross-dressing and audience participation. Such broad licence to innovate on the musical stage goes back to the earliest stage adaptations of Dickens, which were in fact to musical theatre genres (such as burletta and melodrama). In other words, as this essay will prove, the history of Dickens and theatre has always been the history of Dickens and musical theatre.

Dickens has a long performance history. In *Dickens Dramatized* (1987), H. Philip Bolton lists around three thousand dramatisations of all kinds, including musicals, straight plays, operas, films, radio and television. Part of the reason Dickens is so often dramatised is that he writes theatrically: his daughter Mamie describes performance as part of his writing technique; he would compose in front of a mirror, acting out the different parts.[4] But another part of Dickens's adaptability is surely, as

Jacky Bratton argues, that Dickens wrote his books with an eye to their stage adaptation; she cites his own articulation of this point when, in an address to the General Theatrical Fund annual dinner in 1858, he stated: 'Every writer of fiction, though he may not adopt the dramatic form, writes in effect for the stage.'[5] Despite Dickens's sometimes vexed relationship with adaptors, he shared his proofs with handpicked playwrights such as Albert Smith, who in 1846 adapted Dickens's *A Cricket on the Hearth* (1845) in collaboration with the author.[6] I argue that, if Dickens was writing for stage performance, then he was surely also writing for musical stage performance.

Dickens makes this clear in the oft-quoted opening paragraphs of Chapter 17 in *Oliver Twist*, which present his aesthetic as rooted in melodrama:

> It is the custom on the stage: in all good, murderous melodramas: to present the tragic and comic scenes, in as regular alternation, as the layers of red and white in a side of streaky, well-cured bacon. The hero sinks upon his straw bed, weighed down by fetters and misfortunes; and, in the next scene, his faithful but unconscious squire regales the audience with a comic song. We behold, with throbbing bosoms, the heroine in the grasp of a proud and ruthless baron: her virtue and her life alike in danger; drawing forth her dagger to preserve the one at the cost of the other; and, just as our expectations are wrought up to the highest pitch, a whistle is heard: and we are straightway transported to the great hall of the castle: where a grey-headed seneschal sings a funny chorus with a funnier body of vassals [. . .].
>
> Such changes appear absurd; but they are not so unnatural as they would seem at first sight. The transitions in real life from well-spread boards to death-beds, and from mourning weeds to holiday garments, are not a whit less startling.[7]

The passage is frequently cited to illustrate Dickens's consciousness of writing in the melodramatic mode, and his understanding of that choice as realism.[8] Sally Ledger explores 'Dickens's propensity to shift through the affective gears from pathos to laughter and back again', noting that these 'rapid reversals' are important to take seriously because 'the effect of such sharp affective juxtapositions is to throw into relief the moments of pathos and enable, by the force of the contrast, the reader to "re-see", or perceive anew, such affects'.[9] I agree, but there is even more to this passage than critics typically consider. In addition to emphasising melodrama's realism and its affective alternation between tragedy and comedy, Dickens pointedly includes scenes of musical theatre entertainment (the squire's 'comic song' and the 'grey-headed seneschal' who 'sings a funny chorus with a funnier body of vassals') as crucial to the experience of melodrama – and hence to his technique in fiction-writing. Dickens's artistry in narrative prose is achieved through a musical theatrical writing practice.

Many, perhaps most, Victorian dramatisations of Dickens were melodrama (once called melody-drama), which were fundamentally dependent on musical underscoring and song. The earliest adaptations of Dickens's work are burlettas, also a musical theatre genre. But in addition to melodrama and burletta, most other adaptations in the 150 years that Bolton documents are also in some way musical, such as silent films (which were accompanied by music) and sound film (which continues to include musical underscoring as part of the sound track), in addition to modern musical theatre productions such as *Oliver!* and *The Mystery of Edwin Drood*. Although I do not have room to discuss all the musical theatre adaptations of Dickens here, I will suggest the plenitude of musical theatrical adaptations by providing a selective chronicle showing how, from the very beginning, *The Pickwick Papers* (1836–7) was transformed for the musical stage. Examining musical adaptations helps us to recognise that the novel burgeons with scenes that beg for musicalisation. After a longitudinal look at the musical theatre progeny of *The Pickwick Papers*, I shift to other shows of note, including a few significant failures, primarily Al Kasha and Joel Hirschhorn's *Copperfield* (1981). Although adapted from the 1849–50 novel *David Copperfield*, it owes much to *Oliver!* Such bald imitation of a prior landmark musical foregrounds fidelity in another way, highlighting how *Oliver!* has influenced Broadway's vision of Dickens forever afterward. Finally, I turn to the two best-known and most acclaimed modern stage musicals based on Dickens: *Oliver!* and *The Mystery of Edwin Drood*. Great successes with audiences and critics, both amply demonstrate the musical theatricality of Dickens's fiction. They emphasise his rich use of musical metaphor and highlight the many depictions of song, dance and spectacle in his narratives.

The Pickwick Papers from burletta to Broadway

The Pickwick Papers is full of songs and dances.[10] Composers have set the in-text poems, such as 'The Ivy Green' and 'The Christmas Carol', to music many times.[11] At least two illustrations depict performances ('The Election at Eatanswill' and 'Christmas Eve at Wardles'), and many others present hilariously inventive movement before spectators, such as Pickwick's signature hand under coat-tails movement shown in 'Mr Pickwick Addresses the Club' and his precarious near-split in 'Mr Pickwick Slides'. Such moments of music, dance and gesture make the work irresistible for adaptation to musical theatre. These passages and images are often staged, as in the electioneering scene in the 1963 West End musical *Pickwick*. Martin Meisel has taught us about the pleasure Victorian audiences took (that we still take) in recognising a familiar image realised on stage as the actors assemble to replicate it, holding still for a tableau. Added to that is the pleasure of seeing actors freeze in a living facsimile of the image and move in realisation of the activity evoked by Robert Seymour's and Hablot K. Browne's lively illustrations.

Bolton lists over 212 dramatisations of *The Pickwick Papers* for stage, screen or radio between 1837 and 1985, many musical.[12] Theatrical adaptation of Dickens's novels to the stage typically began before their serial publication was even complete. For example, *The Pickwick Papers* prompted its first staging just twelve monthly instalments into the twenty-part novel: Edward Stirling's *Pickwick Papers; or, The Age We Live In* at the City of London Theatre (27 March 1837) with music by T. H. Tully.[13] Just a week later came William Leman Rede's *The Peregrinations of Pickwick; or, Boz-i-a-na* at the Adelphi (4 April 1837).[14] Dramatisations often involve odd choices – even more so early in a novel's serialisation. This production interpolated 'Jump Jim Crow', the wildly popular signature song of the American blackface comedian Thomas Dartmouth 'Daddy' Rice. The role in the show was unrelated to Dickens's plot.[15] However, Rede had written a star vehicle for Rice that he performed at the Adelphi in July 1836, *A Flight to America, or Ten Hours in New York*, and so he was reprising the bit in a new show.[16] A later production of Rede's *The Peregrinations of Pickwick* included four Irish airs to be sung by a Mrs Fitzwilliam, for whom the character of an Irish maid was inserted into the plot instead.[17] Just two months after Rede's *Peregrinations* premiered, *Sam Weller!; or, The Pickwickians* by W. T. Moncrieff with music by Mr Collins opened at the Strand (5 June 1837).[18] *Pickwick*'s concluding number was still four months away.[19]

All three of these earliest adaptations of *The Pickwick Papers* are listed by Nicoll and Bolton as burlettas. The definition of 'burletta' shifts over time because the rules regarding what made a burletta a burletta varied by law or custom during the nineteenth century. Always a brief operatic comedy (that is, always a musical genre), it was sometimes required to parody the music of other musical entertainments, though at other times this was forbidden; sometimes the dialogue had to be in verse and other times was allowed to employ prose; it had to use recitative or might include spoken dialogue; it had to have a minimum of five songs overall or some minimum number of songs per act, preferably relevant to the plot but often not so in practice.[20] In all these permutations, the burletta incorporated numerous songs and instrumental accompaniment.[21] But even before the *Pickwick Papers*, a few of Dickens's *Sketches by Boz* (collected into volume form in 1836) made it to the boards. The earliest theatrical adaptation of Dickens that Bolton chronicles – J. B. Buckstone's *The Bloomsbury Christening* (13 October 1834) at the Adelphi, based on the short story of the same name first published in *The Monthly Magazine* (April 1834) – is also a one-act burletta.[22] And so, from the very inception of Dickens's dramatisation, adapting Dickens to the stage has meant adapting him to the musical stage.

Prior to 1843, any non-patent theatre mounting an adaptation of Dickens's novels (or any theatrical entertainment of any kind) would have needed to include enough music so that it would not be considered spoken drama, according to the Licensing Act 1737. Only the royally patented, or 'major', houses (in London, Drury Lane, Covent Garden, and – in the summer – the Haymarket) were licensed to produce plays. A non-patent, or so-called 'minor theatre' (no matter how opulent, fashionable or successful, non-patent theatres are called 'minor'), would be fined for performing any purely spoken drama, which was known as 'legitimate' drama. The Adelphi and all the theatres dramatising *The Pickwick Papers* mentioned above were minor or 'illegitimate' theatres, so their choice to musicalise their plays was a legal necessity. Dickens knew that any play based on his work produced at minor theatres (the vast majority of playhouses) up to 1843 would by law be an adaptation largely set to music.

By the end of 1838, twenty-six productions of *Pickwick* had appeared, mostly designated as musical genres by Bolton, often with the composer noted, as in *Pickwick or the Sayings and Doings of Sam Weller* by F. C. Nantz and with music by Pindar, including the 'Pickwickian Quadrilles'.[23] By 1900, long after any legal requirement to include music had dropped, over sixty productions of *The Pickwick Papers* entertained audiences in Britain or the United States; Bolton reports that many included 'a great deal of music' and 'some of these songs were in fact published'.[24] All of Dickens's novels inspired composers to create and often publish an abundance of quadrilles, waltzes, tarantellas and polkas, such as the 'Pickwick' Waltz by William Willing (1876).[25] Many were written for theatrical adaptations; polkas and waltzes originating on stage – either as musical accompaniment or as incidental music – were particularly marketable.[26] One such composer is Edward Solomon, best known for his sparkling operetta compositions (and for his bigamous marriage to Lillian Russell). With words by Francis Cowley Burnand (who worked with Sullivan as his librettist before Gilbert), *Pickwick, a Dramatic Cantata* premiered at the Comedy Theatre in 1889 and was revived in 1894.[27] This comic operetta may remind modern listeners of Gilbert and Sullivan since Solomon wrote music for the D'Oyly Carte Company.[28] At least two other operettas based on *The Pickwick Papers* appeared before the turn of the twentieth century: *Gabriel Grub*, a Cantata Seria Buffa with music by George E. Fox, in 1879 and 1881, and *The Great Pickwick Case*, a comic operetta with lyrics by Robert Pollitt and music by Thomas Rawson, in 1884.[29]

The first twentieth-century musical version, *Mr. Pickwick*, ran for thirty-two performances (respectable at the time) at the Herald Square Theater in New York, opening on 19 January 1903, with music by Manuel Klein, book by Charles Klein, and lyrics by Grant Stewart. This was followed by productions in Newark and Denver the same year and in Pittsburgh in 1912.[30] Early films – like Victorian stage melodrama – would always have been screened with live musical accompaniment, but most of the stage, radio and television adaptations from this point on are not musical. With cinema replacing theatre as a prime entertainment of the working class, the stage increasingly became a highbrow genre. The shrinking number of live theatres offered more 'legitimate' dramas and comedies to distinguish themselves both from the Victorian illegitimate theatre of the previous century and from film, the main inheritor of Victorian illegitimate theatre's melodramatic techniques. Although grand opera is also a musical theatre genre, nothing could be more highbrow with its highly trained voices, full orchestral accompaniment, swanky patrons and elaborate opera houses. The next notable musical dramatisation is, surprisingly, a full-scale opera: Albert Coates composed *Pickwick* (1936), directed by Vladimir Rosing for the British Music Drama Opera Company and performed at Covent Garden. *The Musical Times* praised its fluency, liveliness and originality. But the review finds it lacking in musical Englishness, smacking too much of 'xylophone and glockenspiel', with echoes of Russians and Germans such as Rimsky-Korsakov, Mussorgsky, Stravinsky and Wagner instead of British composers like Purcell, Sullivan and Elgar.[31] Its great claim to fame – and the feature that brings Dickens even in operatic form appropriately to the widest audience possible – is that it was the first-ever televised opera. This came very early in TV history: after being on the air for just eleven days, the BBC broadcast several specially prepared scenes of Coates's *Pickwick* for twenty-five minutes on 13 November 1936, just prior to its opening at Covent Garden on 20 November.[32]

Also named *Pickwick*, an unequivocally English-sounding West End musical, with hints of both Sullivan and Gilbert, opened at the Saville Theatre on 4 July 1963. It was a big show with book by Wolf Mankowitz, music by Cyril Ornadel and lyrics by Leslie Bricusse. Coming just two years after *Oliver!* (which was still playing at the New Theatre), *Pickwick* ran for 695 performances until 27 February 1965. The hit show was directed by Peter Coe, who had also directed *Oliver!*, and the set was designed by Sean Kenney, the designer of *Oliver!*'s innovative scenery. With both *Oliver!* and *Pickwick* succeeding simultaneously in West End productions, Dickens's fiction in the early 1960s must have seemed a musical theatre cornucopia. *Pickwick* followed *Oliver!* in transferring to Broadway on 4 October 1965 (46th Street Theatre), with Coe again directing and Kenney designing. But even with this creative team, David Merrick (who had brought *Oliver!* to Broadway) as the producer, and the acclaimed Harry Secombe reprising his West End role as Mr Pickwick, the Broadway *Pickwick* closed after just fifty-six performances.[33]

MUSICAL THEATRE

185

The show's biggest hit was the anthem 'If I Ruled the World', recorded not only by Secombe, but also by Tony Bennett, The Supremes, Sammy Davis Jr and Celine Dion. After bumbling his political speech when running for office, the kindly Mr Pickwick sings of his remarkably democratic worldview: 'Every man would be as free as a bird / Every voice would be a voice to be heard'. During the long introductory section of the song (not included in the popular artists' recordings) that bridges the electioneering dialogue with the anthem that promotes joy for 'every heart', trumpets flourish with a militaristic air. They recall Lerner and Lowe's title song in *Camelot* (1960), which depicts Britain as a monarchy founded in democratic processes. This section of 'If I Ruled the World' demonstrates (and ironises) a Pickwickian worldview – warm-hearted and inclusive, certainly, but also a bit jingoistic, imperialist and sexist – the song promotes individual and electoral freedom *and* world domination, with lines exhorting the gathered crowd to vote for 'Men who want a world that's fine and free / Men like Nelson, Wellington, and Drake, and me'. In 1969 the BBC produced an abbreviated *Pickwick* starring Secombe; ABC aired it for an American audience in 1973. Whereas the *New York Times* considered the 1965 Broadway production a 'misfire [. . .] a bit precious and distinctly British', it lauded the cosiness of the teleplay, 'very much at home on the home screen', particularly praising Secombe as 'the kindly, rotund Mr. Pickwick', loveable as 'an ideal Dickens hero'.[34] Its domesticated Englishness was no longer read as twee, but instead as comfortably joyous as a Victorian family singing around the home parlour piano.

Beyond *Pickwick*

Pickwick is just one of many modern musicals based on Dickens. *Great Expectations* (1860–1861), Dickens's third-most adapted novel, has inspired at least four, though none transferred to Broadway.[35] The best known was composed by Cyril Ornadel, who wrote the music for *Pickwick*, with book and lyrics by Hal Shaper. It toured the UK in 1975 and, like *Pickwick*, won the Ivor Novello Award for Best British Musical, but it never made it to the West End. Dickens's most adapted work, *A Christmas Carol* (1843), has inspired modern stage musicals that are mounted in dozens of cities for annual Christmas runs; an excellent example is Barbara Field's 1975 adaptation for the Guthrie Theater in Minneapolis, produced for thirty-five years.[36] Community theatres often rely on their annual *Christmas Carol* productions to finance the rest of the year's theatrical season, just as ballet companies depend on *The Nutcracker* to keep afloat. Madison Square Garden hosted *A Christmas Carol: The Musical* for ten years, from 1994 to 2003, with music by Alan Menken, lyrics by Lynn Ahrens, and book by Mike Ockrent and Lynn Ahrens. A different well-known star led the cast as Scrooge almost every season, including Frank Langella and F. Murray Abraham.

It is a fun, campy, light-hearted holiday family entertainment, chiefly emphasising effects, with snow that falls on the audience during the finale. The best-known song is 'Link by Link', Marley's catchy, pun-filled exhortation to reform; it fully exploits the sonic and percussive potential in clinking chains. One of the most spectacular dance numbers depicts Fezziwig's Ball, with Mr and Mrs Fezziwig stepping out of John Leech's original illustrations, demonstrating how they explode with movement. Bits of other novels by Dickens find their way into this play: Scrooge's father goes to debtor's prison as in *Little Dorrit*; a twelve-year-old Scrooge works at a shoe factory job

– represented by steampunk cogs and wheels in the Broadway set – an addition that seems to come out of *David Copperfield* or Dickens's own biography; and there is even a beadle imported from *Oliver Twist* (or, more proximately, *Oliver!*). Scrooge's initial hard-heartedness is exaggerated: rather than merely refusing to give to charity and insisting Bob Cratchit work on Christmas Eve, he evicts families falling behind as if he is playing a role in a rent-day melodrama and even insists on hard terms in extending a loan to good Mr Fezziwig, suddenly and inexplicably in debt. Paradoxically, making Scrooge a cartoonish villain reduces the novella's social critique because he actively harms others rather than scrimping on comforts, withholding charity and avoiding fellowship – traits that readers or audiences might recognise in themselves. Rather than striking a 'sledge-hammer' blow against social injustice, the show packages all of Dickens as a Christmas treat.[37] Nevertheless, the annual *Christmas Carol*s contribute to the novella's status as what Paul Davis calls a 'culture-text', one that everyone knows without ever having read the original.[38]

Not all musical versions of *A Christmas Carol* are designed as seasonal. *Comin' Uptown* (1979), set in Harlem and starring Gregory Hines as a dancing slumlord Scrooge who is about to foreclose properties, began with an open-ended run. Hines explains in an interview with *Jet* magazine, 'The intention was to run as long as possible. We approached it not as a Christmas story, but as a man getting together. It could have taken place during Halloween.'[39] With book by Philip Rose, book and lyrics by Peter Udell, and music by Garry Sherman, *Comin' Uptown* opened on 20 December 1979 at Broadway's Winter Garden Theater and closed on 27 January after just forty-five performances – a flop, but about right for a Christmas entertainment.[40] Although the *New York Times* praised Hines's extraordinary dancing, it disparages virtually every other aspect of the production.[41] Nevertheless, the show had some fun touches besides Hines's Tony-nominated performance; for example, instead of buying a Christmas turkey for the Cratchits, this New Yorker Scrooge picks up a takeout feast of Jewish Deli and Chinese. Because *A Christmas Carol* is so often adapted, with new versions appearing every year not only in musical theatre but also in virtually every medium imaginable, it is a model for Linda Hutcheon's point that the pleasure in adaptation comes from 'repetition with variation'.[42]

Keep Calm and *Carrie* on: Dickensian Disasters

Sometimes the theme and variation that Hutcheon alludes to varies insufficiently from preceding adaptations. Anyone who has read *The New York Times*, *Time Out* or *The New Yorker* in the past thirty-five years has surely seen the phrase 'Not since *Carrie*', used relentlessly to describe the most recent Broadway musical fiasco, with the proclamation that 'not since Carrie' has Broadway seen such a catastrophe.[43] Yet there were many crushing defeats on Broadway long before the abysmal *Carrie* (based on Stephen King's horror novel) in 1988, when it lost over seven million dollars in its three-day run. Ken Mandelbaum wrote a whole book about this subcategory of musical theatre calamity, *Not Since Carrie: Forty Years of Broadway Musical Flops* (1991), which chronicles Broadway musical bombs from 1950 to 1990. Among them is only one musical based on a novel by Charles Dickens, the 1981 *Copperfield*, so derivative of *Oliver!* that, as Mandelbaum says, it is surprising that the name does not end with an exclamation point.[44]

With book, music and lyrics by Al Kasha and Joel Hirschhorn, *Copperfield* won some praise for George S. Irving as Micawber, for Carmen Matthews in the final Broadway show of her long and distinguished career, and for the scenery by Tony Straiges and costumes by John David Ridge – but little else.[45] At the time, Kasha and Hirschhorn were best known for writing theme songs for disaster movies such as *Towering Inferno* and *The Poseidon Adventure*.[46] *Copperfield* lasted only thirteen performances. Critics panned it as clunky, dull and suitable only for out-of-town children. They reasoned that even elementary school New Yorkers would know better because they would have already seen the far superior *Annie*, which had opened in 1977 and would keep going strong till 1983. *Copperfield* was so imitative that Frank Rich's review in *The New York Times* famously declared 'This is the kind of musical that sends you out of the theater humming every score other than the one you've just heard.'[47]

Rex Reed in the New York *Daily News* concurred, commenting that 'everything they say or sing seems to be borrowed from other shows'.[48] In particular, Reed seizes on 'Mama, Don't Get Married', sung by David and Peggotty, which sounds 'suspiciously like "If Mama Gets Married" from *Gypsy*'.[49] The copying goes beyond the music: Rich points out that *Copperfield*'s Uriah Heep strangely resembles *Annie*'s Miss Hannigan, and Reed notes the use of a device reminiscent of one used in *The Rothschilds* (1970) to show time passing in song.[50] In *Copperfield*, this device occurs in 'Here's a Book' during which the boy David disappears 'behind a tableful of books', and 'the handsome young man David smilingly rises from behind them'.[51] But the most egregious rip-off (so close that Rich calls it 'embarrassing') is little David Copperfield's song 'Is there Anyone?', a straightforward reworking of Oliver Twist's 'Where is Love?' from *Oliver!*.[52] Kasha and Hirschhorn include 'at least three songs in "Copperfield" that are built around the same concepts (and even placed in roughly the same positions)' as *Oliver!*, rather than working organically from the novel.[53] Critics repeatedly noticed the show's debt to Bart's hit, with the *Christian Science Monitor* contending that the collaborators 'have sought to do for "David Copperfield" what Lionel Bart's "Oliver!" did for "Oliver Twist"'.[54]

Copperfield came towards the start of a decade teeming with adaptations of Dickens to stage and screen. Three examples stand out as particularly innovative. As Gillian Piggott discusses in this volume, the Royal Shakespeare Company produced a critically acclaimed eight-and-a-half-hour *Nicholas Nickleby* in 1980, which transferred to Broadway in 1981. Even before it arrived, *Nickleby* provided Clive Barnes a rich counter-example for critical complaint about *Copperfield*.[55] Coming halfway through the decade, Holmes developed *The Mystery of Edwin Drood* for Joseph Papp's highly regarded The Public Theater, solving the problem posed by Dickens's dying halfway through writing the book by having the audience vote every night on the solution to the mystery of who killed Drood. Christine Edzard's experiment in parallel narrative in filmmaking, *Little Dorrit* (1987), comprised two three-hour movies, each from different point of view, one Arthur Clennam's and the other Amy Dorrit's. Why did the 1980s bring so many adaptations of Dickens to film and the stage, including two Broadway musicals? Neil Sinyard argues that the Royal Shakespeare *Nicholas Nickleby* and Edzard's *Little Dorrit* prove Dickens to be 'the most relevant and trenchant of social commentators in a Thatcher era that openly espoused the virtues of self-interest and so-called "Victorian values"'.[56] In contrast,

Dianne F. Sadoff critiques heritage film and television in the 1980s and 1990s as romanticising upper-class privilege for middle-class audiences who find themselves 'applauding private ownership of stately mansions' as compensation for their own dearth of capital.[57] For some critics, the lavish sets and costuming of *Copperfield* are the point: the *St. Louis Post-Dispatch* gushed, 'If Lady Diana is lucky, she will find a wedding dress half as charming as the one lovely Mary Mastrantonio gets to wear here' in her role as Dora.[58]

Copperfield's set design consolidates its status as a costume drama. The director-choreographer Rob Iscove explains, 'it should have the feeling that it is a book come to life'.[59] Though Victor Gluck praises just this 'brilliant visual look of period illustrations that come to life on the stage of the ANTA Theatre', the technique seems not to have worked quite as Iscove and Straiges hoped.[60] Most critics saw instead 'a somewhat stilted greeting card picture' of Victorian life; 'what is gutsy vigor in Dickens' writings is cutesy and quaint affection in this inept stage effort'.[61] At best, the set's 'colorful settings' come across as an 'illustrated children's story'.[62] The set as well as the costumes lay bare Sadoff's point that much costume drama subsists on a conservative ideology that largely fails in adapting Dickens, whose social critique undermines a purely heritage approach, just as the derivativeness of *Copperfield*'s songs misses the point of Dickens by relying too heavily on adapting merely the form of the prior adaptations instead of reappropriating the source.

Perhaps Kasha and Hirschhorn took the advice of the many critics who said the show was best suited to children. *Copperfield* went on to a strange afterlife as a much abbreviated 1993 made-for-TV cartoon video for the Christmas market (David is born at Christmas time), in which a star-studded cast (including Julian Lennon, Michael York, Sheena Easton and Howie Mandel) voiced the characters, now represented as a variety of anthropomorphic animals. It was entitled, remarkably, in what must have been a burst of irony, *Charles Dickens's David Copperfield*. Including the name of the canonical source text's author in the title of mainstream-but-arty feature film adaptations was all the rage in the 1990s. Sadoff argues that as Peter Kosminsky's *Emily Brontë's Wuthering Heights* (1992) 'brands his film as genuine', the same authorisation is true for Francis Ford Coppola's *Bram Stoker's Dracula* (1992) and Kenneth Branagh's *Mary Shelley's Frankenstein* (1994).[63] In a *Back Stage* feature article before the Broadway *Copperfield*'s opening, the musical's creative team told Victor Gluck that they did 'a great deal of research' to make the show authentic. Iscove described spending 'hours at the Library of the Performing Arts at Lincoln Center' studying waltzes and polkas for the two big production numbers, plus 'schottishes, reels and rounds'. Kasha states, 'We listened to a lot of Sir Edward Elgar of that period and to Benjamin Britten of this world but sort of both worlds'; Hirshhorn adds that 'It is really flavoring [. . .] You want an overtone of flavoring.'[64] Yet no one could watch Kasha and Hirshhorn's musical cartoon *Copperfield* and think they were experiencing any kind of authentic Dickens let alone the autobiographical *David Copperfield*: David the fox pup labours in Murdstone's cheese factory, makes friends with the Duke's daughter Agnes, escapes with her to the forest and fights off boars, traps the villainous Murdstone in a thick layer of cheese, and finally opens a nice orphanage for his formerly enslaved workmates. Several of the Broadway show's songs appear in the animated entertainment in some form, including 'Is There Anyone?', though due to the synthetic pop sound none retains any Victorian 'flavour'.

No such cartoon transformation has met *A Tale of Two Cities* (2008) by Jill Santoriello, a pop musical neo-melodrama that reminded critics of *Les Misérables* (1985), 'another, better musical about another, lesser French revolution'.[65] It lasted only sixty performances but has subsequently appeared satisfactorily on regional, university and international stages. There have been at least three musicals based on this novel before Santoriello's (the only one to play on Broadway), most notably *Two Cities*, which opened on 27 February 1969 at London's Palace Theatre, with music by Jeff Wayne, lyrics by his son Jerry Wayne, and book by Constance Cox, who had just written several respected BBC serial adaptations for television. But it ran for only forty-four performances. A musical that opened on 6 June 2000 at London's Haymarket to mixed reviews and lasting a lacklustre ninety-five performances is *Hard Times: The Musical* by Christopher Tookey and Hugh Thomas. With more than one nod to *Drood* (as Holmes's musical is often called), it sets the tale inside a circus performance, incorporating elements from music hall and British pantomime.

Success tells only part of the story of Dickensian musicals. Including failures results in a fuller history of how contemporary culture uses Dickens, marking the limits of what audiences will accept as Dickensian. Little scholarly criticism exists on these large-scale collaborative efforts that succeeded modestly or flopped outright. Yet they have much to teach us about Dickens and musical theatre. For one thing, if Dickens is adapted with too much attention to costumes and too little to social criticism the result seems cartoonish. In musical theatre adaptation, when music and dance are too derivative, we see confirmation that to make theme and variation work requires variation not only from the source but also from prior variations, proving again that each adaptation always has, as Thomas Leitch explains, 'more than one text to be faithful to'.[66] Whereas musicals such as *Oliver!*, *Pickwick* and *Drood* reveal moments of musical theatricality in Dickens's texts, *Copperfield* squanders such scenes by eliminating most of the characters that provide songs in the novel, such as Mr Peggotty and Steerforth, placing the music and dance instead formulaically according to prior musical theatre successes. Whether flop or hit, it is clear that all Dickens musicals since 1960 are in dialogue with *Oliver!*

Oliver! and *Drood*

The musical against which all others based on Dickens are compared is the smash hit *Oliver!*, which ran for 2,618 performances on the West End, the longest-running musical in London until Andrew Lloyd Webber's *Jesus Christ Superstar* (1972). It moved to Broadway in 1963 and ran for 744 performances, the record for British musicals until Webber's *Evita* stormed New York in 1979.[67] Like *A Christmas Carol*, Dickens's *Oliver Twist* is a culture-text, and its musical theatre legacy contributes to this phenomenon. As Julie Sanders points out, adaptations keep source texts alive in the cultural imagination.[68] Joseph Litvak argues that Oliver's asking 'Please sir, I want some more' is the most famous scene in the novel, crediting its ubiquity 'to Lionel Bart's musical version'.[69] One element that makes this moment so theatrical is that the narrative embeds spectators for Oliver in his request, not only his interlocutor but also the workhouse children anxious to see the outcome. As we saw with *The Pickwick Papers*, what ripens such scenes for musical dramatisation is that movement creates a necessary part of the spectacle.

A perfect example in *Oliver Twist* comes when the boys practise picking Fagin's pockets as the old man dexterously moves to evade them, 'slapping all his pockets in turn, to see that he hadn't lost anything, in such a very funny and natural manner, that Oliver laughed till the tears ran down his face'.[70] Despite the scantiness of the source material (a short paragraph with no dialogue), every significant adaptation since George Almar's burletta in 1838, first performed before the serial run of the novel completed, has realised this passage as an elaborate sequence on stage.[71] In *Oliver!*, it becomes the rollicking song-and-dance number 'You've Got to Pick a Pocket or Two', a vehicle for the physical comedy of whoever plays Fagin. When we look back to the novel from the vantage point of the adaptation, the creation of a big musical number here seems inevitable.

This song-and-dance number is also a vehicle for recuperating Fagin, beginning his transformation from the damaging anti-Semitic stereotype of the novel to Bart's lovable rogue.[72] In the musical, as in the novel, the boys eagerly learn their trade, now repeating in a piping treble Fagin's lyrics as they practise their art of pulling wallets and watches from Fagin's back pockets: 'Have no fear, attack the rear | Get in and pick-a-pocket or two'. While part of the song's humour is the incongruity of angelic voices rehearsing their criminal catechism, it also works to focus our attention on the novel's moments of Fagin's fun that help readers find a way into a novel that might be too painful to approach otherwise.

Like *Oliver!*, Holmes's *The Mystery of Edwin Drood* also succeeded popularly and critically on Broadway (where it ran for 608 performances) and the West End (1987), with multiple revivals in both New York and London. In 1870 Dickens died without completing *The Mystery of Edwin Drood*, so that theatrical adapters immediately (and ever since) have created their own solutions to the mystery. Holmes (best known before *Drood* for his 1979 chart-topper 'Escape', otherwise known as 'the Piña Colada song') manages this innovatively in *Drood* by offering multiple endings and allowing the audience to vote on which they prefer. This central gambit garners the most critical attention, but another feature of the show – as with *Pickwick* and *Oliver!* – is that it helps us to recognise that the novel is full of musical theatrical moments and incidents. Like *Pickwick*, this novel is replete with songs and music, which is unsurprising given that the villain, John Jasper, is the cathedral organist and the ingénue Rosa Bud's voice teacher.[73] But almost everyone else in the novel sings and/or plays an instrument, too. An old adage in musical theatre is that when emotion becomes too strong for characters to speak, they sing; and when it becomes too strong for song, they dance. This is abundantly the case in Dickens's *The Mystery of Edwin Drood*.

The clearest instance is the scene when Jasper plays the piano while Rosa sings for a drawing-room audience. Luke Fildes's illustration 'At the Piano' (Figure 12.1) makes clear the power dynamic between accompanist and soloist and all those assembled in the room, whose performance or reaction to the music reveals how much they love, hate or are indifferent to one another. Jasper stares fixedly at his pupil's beautiful lips while she performs. Her best friend, Helena Landless, glares at Jasper, whose lust and villainy she has discovered. Helena's brother, Neville, gazes adoringly at Rosa, establishing his rivalry with Jasper and Edwin, who has been Rosa's intended since they were both babies. The Reverend Crisparkle contemplates Helena, in love. And Edwin plays with a fan, bored by it all. When Rosa can no longer bear the intensity

Figure 12.1 Luke Fildes, 'At the Piano', an illustration for Charles Dickens's *The Mystery of Edwin Drood* (1870). Courtesy of the Charles Dickens Museum, London [F2806].

of Jasper's fierce attention, she breaks off her song, cries out and conveys her distress nonverbally, by covering her eyes with her hands. Helena gestures to the company that which she also says aloud, 'Don't speak to her for a moment', forbidding further verbalisation.[74] The novel tells us that musical performance conveys what language cannot, and that when music breaks down, movement takes over. The scene insists we understand it through the conventions of musical theatre.

It is no surprise that even ostensibly non-musical dramatisations (such as the 1935 Universal Studios movie and the 2012 BBC television production) stage a song at this juncture. The first British play adapted from *The Mystery of Edwin Drood*, Walter Stephens's melodrama *Lost* (1871) interpolates the old song 'When the Stars are in the Quiet Skies'. In all cases, the selection is a love song that allows Jasper to put the words he wants to hear into the mouth of the unwilling woman whom he desires. The musical *Drood*'s song for this moment is 'Moonfall', a haunting art song that has become popular as a solo recital and audition piece. Holmes's lyrics emphasise the sexual threat Jasper poses; by writing this song for her, he forces her to sing 'betwixt our hearts, let nothing intervene' and in the moonlight 'I'll give myself to you', lines that denote fleshly as well as sentimental intentions. Yet the power struggle is genuinely a struggle and Jasper's control is tenuous. Because of the technical difficulty of this song in which the soprano playing the role of Rosa dominates the orchestra (Jasper's onstage piano accompaniment is merely and obviously acted since strings swell to drown out the keyboard), the balance of power shifts to the point that, by the second act, the student is ready to murder her music master.[75]

Dickens is a mainstay of musical theatre entertainment and has been since the very first dramatisation of any of his works. As surely as Dickens knew that his fiction would be adapted to the stage, he knew that it would be adapted first to the musical stage and more frequently than to any other dramatic format. Despite our current expectations that legitimate drama dominates as a literary form in the theatre, non-musical theatrical adaptations of Dickens and other nineteenth-century novelists are more outliers historically than musical ones. Recognising this fact changes how we understand cultural consumption of Dickens and of Victorian fiction generally. However, Dickens in particular – because he thought and wrote theatrically to begin with – created literature that is inherently musical theatrical, with characters that sing and dance popping up everywhere, just as he has described of 'all good, murderous melodramas'. While there are many reasons for a current musical adaptation to fail on Broadway or the West End, one factor would be to miss the opportunity to stage aspects of the source text that are ready-made for musical theatrical realisation and instead to rely on formulaic imitation of prior hits. Flops or triumphs, modern musicals based on Dickens carry on a tradition that helps us to see the ways in which he wrote not only theatrically but also musical theatrically.

Notes

1. Samantha Ellis, 'Lionel Bart's *Oliver!*, June 1960', *Guardian*, 18 June 2003 <www.theguardian.com/stage/2003/jun/18/theatre.samanthaellis> [accessed 26 March 2011].
2. On the importance of not judging an adaptation according to its accuracy in rendering its source material, see Linda Hutcheon, *A Theory of Adaptation* (New York: Routledge, 2006); Thomas Leitch, *Film Adaptation and Its Discontents* (Baltimore: Johns Hopkins University Press, 2007); and Julie Sanders, *Adaptation and Appropriation* (London: Routledge, 2005).
3. Rupert Holmes, *The Mystery of Edwin Drood* (Garden City, NY: Nelson Doubleday, 1986).
4. Mamie Dickens, *My Father as I Recall Him* (New York: E. P. Dutton, 1898), 49–50.
5. Jacky Bratton 'Introduction', in *Dickensian Dramas: Plays from Charles Dickens*, ed. by Jacky Bratton and Jim Davis, 2 vols (Oxford: Oxford University Press, 2017), I, xiii–xxxiv, xvi.
6. Allardyce Nicoll, *A History of English Drama, 1660–1900*, 6 vols (Cambridge: Cambridge University Press, 1952–9), IV, 98.
7. Charles Dickens, *Oliver Twist*, ed. by Fred Kaplan (New York: Norton, 1993), 117–18, ch. 17.
8. Elaine Hadley, *Melodramatic Tactics: Theatricalized Dissent in the English Marketplace, 1800–1885* (Stanford: Stanford University Press, 1995), 117–19.
9. Sally Ledger, '"Don't be so melodramatic!" Dickens and the Affective Mode', *19: Interdisciplinary Studies in the Long Nineteenth Century*, 4 (2007), 1–14, 7 <http://doi.org/10.16995/ntn.456>.
10. In *Pickwick* song or dance (even a band) features in chapters 6, 7, 8, 11, 13, 15, 19 and 28; also chapters 16, 29, 32, 33, 35, 36, 37, 41, 43, 49 and 54 incorporate musical elements or mention music in a way that is not merely metaphorical.
11. See Percy Fitzgerald, 'Dickens and Music', *Dickensian* 4 (1908), 173–7, 174.
12. H. Philip Bolton, *Dickens Dramatized* (London: Mansell, 1987), 75–103.
13. Phillip V. Allingham, 'Dramatic Adaptations of Dickens's Novels', *The Victorian Web* <www.victorianweb.org/authors/dickens/pva/pva228.html> [accessed 11 December 2017].
14. Nicoll, IV, 390.

MUSICAL THEATRE 193

15. Bolton, 78.
16. Nicoll, IV, 390. For more on Rice and his performances in London, see W. T. Lhamon, *Raising Cain: Blackface Performance from Jim Crow to Hip Hop* (Cambridge, MA: Harvard University Press, 1998), 213.
17. Percy Fitzgerald, *The History of Pickwick: An Account of Its Characters, Localities, Allusions, and Illustrations* (London: Chapman & Hall, 1891), 326.
18. Nicoll, IV, 360. For more on this play and its extensive use of traditional airs in the English Ballad tradition (in addition to the music composed by Collins), see Mark Napolitano, 'Making Music with the Pickwickians: Form and Function in Musical Adaptations of *The Pickwick Papers*', *Dickens Studies Annual* 42 (2011), 33–53.
19. Bolton, 78.
20. Nicholas Temperley, 'Burletta', *Grove Music Online* <https://doi.org/10.1093/gmo/9781561592630.article.04385>.
21. Nicoll, IV, 135–41.
22. Bolton, 68.
23. Ibid., 81.
24. Ibid., 75.
25. C. Edgar Thomas, 'The Music and Musicians of Dickens', *Musical Times* 61.930 (1920), 532–5, 534.
26. Michael Pisani, *Music for the Melodramatic Theatre in Nineteenth-Century London and New York* (Iowa City: University of Iowa Press, 2014), 115.
27. Robert Ignatius Letellier, *Operetta: A Sourcebook*, 2 vols (Cambridge: Cambridge Scholars Publishing, 2015), II, 946.
28. Edward Solomon and F. C. Burnand, *Pickwick, a Dramatic Cantata*, Retrospect Opera, 2016.
29. Fitzgerald, 220.
30. Bolton, 89, 91.
31. McN, 'British Music Drama Opera Company', *Musical Times* 77.1126 (1936), 1132.
32. Michael Kennedy, 'Albert Coates', *Grove Music Online*, <https://doi.org/10.1093/gmo/9781561592630.article.05999>.
33. Ken Mandelbaum, 'Obscure Videos: Two British Musicals', *Broadway Buzz*, 4 November 2005 <www.broadway.com/buzz/10892/obscure-videos-two-british-musicals> [accessed 10 December 2017]. Mandelbaum points out that because it had already recouped its financial outlay in its successful pre-Broadway production in San Francisco, it did not lose money.
34. Howard Thompson, 'TV Review', *New York Times* (17 December 1973), 75 <www.nytimes.com/1973/12/17/archives/tv-review-pickwick-people-pay-musical-visit-at-7.html> [accessed 16 December 2017].
35. Mary Hammond, *Charles Dickens's* Great Expectations: *A Cultural Life, 1860–2012* (Farnham: Ashgate, 2015), 146.
36. Fred Guida, *A Christmas Carol and Its Adaptations: A Critical Examination of Dickens's Story and Its Productions on Screen and Television* (Jefferson, NC: McFarland, 2000), 210. Rohan Preston, 'Barbara Field, a "queen of adaptations" and champion of playwrights, dies at 87', *Star Tribune* (23 February 2021). <https://www.startribune.com/barbara-field-a-queen-of-adaptations-and-champion-of-playwrights-dies-at-87/600026656/?refresh=true> [accessed 13 January 2024].
37. Guida, 29.
38. Paul Davis, *The Lives and Times of Ebenezer Scrooge* (New Haven: Yale University Press, 1990), 4.
39. 'Broadway Actor Hines High Steps It To Top', *Jet* (6 March 1980), 60.
40. Thomas Hischak, *Broadway Plays and Musicals: Essential Facts of More than 14,000 Shows through 2007* (Jefferson, NC: McFarland, 2012), 89.

41. Walter Kerr, 'Scrooge Struts in "Comm"', *New York Times* (21 December 1979), 5.
42. Hutcheon, 4.
43. Michael Shulman, 'Is "Carrie" the Worst Musical of All Time?', *New Yorker*, 27 January 2012 <www.newyorker.com/culture/culture-desk/is-carrie-the-worst-musical-of-all-time> [accessed 11 November 2017].
44. Ken Mandelbaum, *Not Since Carrie: 40 Years of Broadway Musical Flops* (New York: St Martin's Press, 1991), 208.
45. Victor Gluck, 'Copperfield', *Back Stage* (1 May 1981), 50. *Variety* provides a roundup of the critic's responses from the previous week, reporting that *Copperfield* opened to 'one favorable notice, [. . .] two mixed, [. . .] and six pans'. 'Copperfield', *Variety* (29 April 1981), 92.
46. Harry Haun, 'Dickensian Delight', *New York Sunday News*, Leisure (12 April 1981), 3.
47. Frank Rich, 'Dickens Sings Again in "Copperfield"', *New York Times* (17 April 1981), C3.
48. Rex Reed, '"Copperfield" Leaden', New York *Daily News* (17 March 1981), 5–16, 5.
49. Ibid., 16.
50. Ibid.
51. Douglass Watt, 'Musical "Copperfield" a Computerized Cartoon', *Daily News* Friday Section (17 April 1981), 3.
52. Rich, C3.
53. Ibid.
54. John Beaufort, 'Charles Dickens to Music—or half of him at least', *Christian Science Monitor* (21 April 1981), 18.
55. Clive Barnes, '"Copperfield" doesn't shine', *New York Post* (17 April 1981), 29.
56. Neil Sinyard, 'Dickens on Television', *BFI Screen Online* <www.screenonline.org.uk/tv/id/1420996> [accessed 16 September 2018].
57. Dianne Sadoff, *Victorian Vogue: British Novels on Screen* (Minneapolis: University of Minnesota Press, 2009), xvii.
58. Judy J. Newmark, '"Copperfield" Debuts at American', *St. Louis Post-Dispatch* (6 March 1981), 4D.
59. Victor Gluck, 'What Makes "David" Run? The Making of a Musical', *Back Stage* (27 March 1981), 66, 70, 80, 66.
60. Victor Gluck, 'Copperfield', *Back Stage* (May 1981), 50.
61. Hobe Morrison, 'Copperfield', *Variety* (22 April 1981), 192.
62. Ernest Leogrande, 'Kids Make Convincing Critics', New York *Daily News* (21 April 1981), 37.
63. Sadoff, 81.
64. Gluck, 70.
65. Ben Brantley, 'Revolution (and Love) on Their Minds', *New York Times*, 19 September 2008 <www.nytimes.com/2008/09/19/theater/reviews/19tale.html> [accessed 29 December 2017].
66. Leitch, 201.
67. Stanley Green, *Broadway Musicals: Show by Show* (London: Faber & Faber, 1985), 201.
68. Sanders, 8.
69. Joseph Litvak, *Caught in the Act: Theatricality in the Nineteenth-Century Novel* (Berkeley: University of California Press, 1992), 33. But, of course, the scene is staged and filmed much earlier, as Juliet John points out in *Dickens and Mass Culture* (Oxford: Oxford University Press, 2010), 215–16. For more on the genealogy of adaptation of *Oliver Twist* from Victorian melodrama through early film to *Oliver!*, see my chapter on 'Adopting and Adapting Dickens since 1870: Stage, Film, Radio, Television', in *The*

Oxford Handbook of Charles Dickens, ed. by Robert L. Patten, John O. Jordan and Catherine Waters (Oxford: Oxford University Press, 2018), 738–55.

70. Dickens, *Oliver Twist*, 69–70, ch. 9.
71. George Almar, *Oliver Twist: A Serio-Comic Burletta, in Four Acts*, French's Standard Drama No. 228 (New York: Samuel French, 1864?), 11–12.
72. For further discussion, see my '"Can a Fellow Be a Villain All His Life?": *Oliver!*, Fagin, and Performing Jewishness', *Nineteenth-Century Contexts* 33.4 (2011), 371–88. See also Sharon Aronofsky Weltman, 'Melodrama and the Modern Musical', in *Cambridge Companion to English Melodrama*, ed. by Carolyn Williams (Cambridge: Cambridge University Press, 2018), 262–76.
73. For example, songs and music occur in chs 1, 2, 5, 8, 12, 18, 20 and 22, often multiple times.
74. Charles Dickens, *The Mystery of Edwin Drood* (London: Penguin, 1974), 92–3, ch. 7.
75. For more on these arguments regarding the musicals *Oliver!* and *The Mystery of Edwin Drood*, see my *Victorians on Broadway: Literature, Adaptation, and the Modern American Musical* (Charlottesville: University of Virginia Press, 2020).

Further Reading

Robert Gordon and Olaf Jubin, eds, *The Oxford Handbook of the British Musical* (Oxford: Oxford University Press, 2016)

Marc Napolitano, *Oliver!: A Dickensian Musical* (Oxford: Oxford University Press, 2014)

Streaky Bacon: A Guide to Victorian Adaptations. <www.streakybacon.net>

Tony Williams, 'Modern Stage Adaptations', in *Charles Dickens in Context*, ed. by Sally Ledger and Holly Furneaux (Cambridge: Cambridge University Press, 2011), 59–66

13

RAP MUSIC

Melisa Klimaszewski

MANY READERS, SCHOLARS, MUSIC FANS AND culture critics tend to regard the words 'Dickens' and 'rap' as incongruous. Yet artists as varied as A Tribe Called Quest, Kanye West, Sage Francis, OutKast and Method Man have included references to Dickens or his characters in their music, and not all of the artists employ Dickens in the same way. Dickens does use words like 'botheration', which sounds like it could forecast a Mary J. Blige song, but those Dickens-isms are not the ones that rappers tend to sample most. Rather, they use his name itself and refer to specific characters.[1] Jay-Z and Ludacris embed extended references to *Oliver Twist* (1837–9) into songs while the Beastie Boys namecheck Dickens.[2] Criticism and responses to rap and hip-hop culture have matured over the past two decades, fostering a more widespread understanding of rap as a poetic musical and literary form that draws upon complex cultural histories. President Barack Obama's 'membership in hip-hop's foundational generation', friendship with rappers, and comfort inviting performers like Chance the Rapper and De La Soul to the White House also elevated rap's status on the global stage and even spawned an Oxford collection titled *The Hip Hop & Obama Reader*.[3] That many observers call Obama the first hip-hop president and that such a title is widely regarded as a compliment constitutes a fusion of politics, power and hip-hop that continues to impress those who recall the days when gathering around a boom box to listen to the Sugarhill Gang rap about macaroni was subversive.[4]

Now, instead of all rap – especially gangsta rap – being dismissed as harmful music that will corrupt youth (which was never an accurate supposition and routinely ignored early progressive rappers such as Queen Latifah), a broader perceived gap divides glitzy, commercial performers from more intellectually identified rappers. Of course, artists themselves have always blurred such lines, yet many discussions of rap cling to the notion that, if it is a literary form or a form that mixes poetic talent with musical performance, it must not be gangsta rap. Although specialists in hip-hop and rap culture, critical race studies and musicology often have more nuanced views of the form, even in academic circles, the most common first response I receive to delivering a paper about rappers who mention Dickens is one of surprise or amusement.[5] Such a distinction is riddled with problems, and my approach aims to show that, even in songs that might be characterised initially as unserious pop music, references to Dickens constitute a complex and strategic use of a dominant figure from the Western literary canon.

Focusing on a small set of examples from Jay-Z, Ludacris and Clipse featuring Ab-Liva, I suggest that some rappers' references to Dickens appropriate the white icon and his characters in an interrogatory manner as they resist histories of cultural appropriation and negotiate a redefinition of Black masculinity in relation to wealth. Having noticed far more nods to Dickens in rap and hip-hop than there is space to analyse here, my analysis of a few uses of *Oliver Twist* acts as a starting point for broader understandings of how such allusions operate in rap music. Invoking Dickens as part of a performance of masculinity moves well past riffs and puns that take advantage of the parallel between Dickens's surname and sexual slang.[6] Alongside the various literacies that scholars like Miles White bring into astute analyses of hip-hop culture, including 'a literacy of music and rhetoric' and 'a literacy of the body and the visual', one must not forget the most straightforward, literary literacy: knowledge of and facility with the written word, past and present.[7] Literary allusions are an important way that rappers construct identity, and when the namechecks or riffs point to an author like Dickens, they challenge some of the most persistent and racist images of Black masculinity that critics like White wish to highlight.

Building upon the work of many scholars who have advocated for recognition of rap music as a valuable form of art that emerged from African American culture and merits respect, I am confident in saying that references to Dickens in rap are not mistakes or meaningless accidents. Tricia Rose's foundational work emphasises that rap's contradictions and tensions, rather than disqualifying the form from serious intellectual consideration, should instead motivate scholars to understand its counter-hegemonic discourses more deeply. Rose's argument in *Black Noise* remains persuasive, as does her insistence that critics must be tasked with revealing and contesting rap's own hidden politics in order to interrogate the form productively. Rose's points are anchored in a recognition of rap as an art form rooted in African American cultural politics, and Henry Louis Gates Jr has situated rap in a history of signifying that has roots in African rhetorical tradition.[8] In a discussion of rappers using Black slang and 'black cultural figures', Rose explains: 'For rap's language wizards, all images, sounds, ideas, and icons are ripe for re-contextualization, pun, mockery, and celebration.'[9] Oversimplified analyses and straight-up dismissals of rap's literary attributes have not paid enough attention to the complexity of the 're-contextualization' Rose describes. In the case of Dickens references, whether they are 'pun, mockery' or something altogether different merits further investigation, as it is not only language and tradition from specifically African American–identified histories that these rappers invoke.

Scholarship on hip-hop and rap appeared first in the fields of cultural studies and sociology, but rap's poetic qualities have increasingly contributed to an uptick in literary studies of the form. Alexs Pate argues that, in order to properly appreciate and understand rap as a form of poetry, one must decrease focus on the beat. Pate urges listeners to stop hearing the music and to privilege narrative and poetic aspects in order to make a case for rap as a purposeful literary form.[10] He acknowledges the social commentary present in rap music but lessens the emphasis that critics such as Rose have placed on rap as a form of resistance to disenfranchisement, violent living conditions and other crises. My approach rejects a dichotomy between these two forms of analysis. Fully appreciating rap as an art form that often emphasises oppositional and resistant social commentary demands that the musical and the literary remain wed. Rhyming, invoking, repeating, sampling, alluding – in rap songs

198   MELISA KLIMASZEWSKI

that mention Dickens, one cannot understand the significance of the gesture if the elements are completely separated. As Imani Perry explains:

> Rap music is a mixed medium. As an art form, it combines poetry, prose, song, music, and theater. It may come in the form of narrative, autobiography, science fiction, or debate. The diversity of media poses a challenge for the critic because she or he is called to evaluate the artistic production from a variety of disciplinary perspectives.[11]

My argument analyses lyrics and thematics more deeply than musical or rhythmic detail, but I include consideration of musical elements as much as possible and hope that further musicological scholarship will bring attention to the convergence of literary references, poetics and rhythmic strategies in rap.

Jay-Z and Ludacris are two of the most commercially successful rappers in the history of the genre. For a period in the early 2000s Ludacris contributing a verse to any song seemed to guarantee hit status, and he has won three Grammy Awards. Jay-Z, also a multiple Grammy winner, was a founder of Roc-A-Fella Records and CEO of Def Jam Records for four years.[12] The songs I focus on most extensively here are Jay-Z's 'Anything', a guest track on Beanie Sigel's *The Truth* (2000), and Ludacris's 'Large Amounts' from 2004's *The Red Light District*, a record that received critical praise and sold over two million copies.[13] These artists and songs are not at all obscure, and for their choruses each samples a different piece of Lionel Bart's 1968 Academy Award–winning musical *Oliver!*[14] Weaving complicated patterns between Dickens, his characters, Bart and the rappers, each song interacts with multiple hypotexts to create dense layers of sonic and literary meaning.

A seemingly straightforward avowal of commitment, the song 'Anything' in Bart's musical begins as a declaration of love for Nancy. The Artful Dodger teaches Oliver the words as they declare that they would climb hills and wear daffodils for Nancy, who then joins in teaching Oliver more verses. The number lightly gestures towards more serious themes when Nancy asks Dodger, 'Even fight my Bill?', which foreshadows her own murder. Fagin only enters at the end of the episode, shifting the focus of the loyalty from Nancy to himself by directly asking if the boys would 'rob a shop' at the risk of death by hanging, which he describes rather explicitly given the peppy rhythms of the song. He asks, 'Would you risk the "drop"? Tho' your eyes go, "pop". When you come down "plop?"', with each phrase answered by a hearty 'Anything!' from the boys, who then swear 'Hang ev'rything! We'd risk life and limb to keep you in the swim'. Critics hold differing opinions on the ultimate effect of this number. Does the serious content of the lyrics manage to cut through the cheery music to maintain some sense of the gravity of the situation presented in the novel? Or is the upbeat song (and its dance routine) so saccharine that it trivialises the violence and child exploitation at the heart of the novel's story? Regardless of one's appraisal of the musical's interpretive choices, it is crucial to note two points relevant to Jay-Z's use of the song: first, the direction of the allegiance here is from the boys to Nancy and then Fagin and second, when Fagin deftly shifts the boys' loyalty from a maternal figure to himself, nothing in the performance of the song sends up irony flags or suggests that the value of that loyalty changes when it is sworn to Fagin. The chorus, 'I'd risk everything | for one kiss everything | Yes, I'd do anything, anything for you', is the piece Jay-Z uses for his 'Anything'.

Within 'Anything', Jay-Z takes the sentiment in the chorus and occupies different subject positions in the relationship. Jay-Z's invocation of the chorus in the first verse seems to wholeheartedly endorse the original power dynamic, but by the song's conclusion he has shifted the premise upon which the loyalty rests and redefined it. Before analysing the verses closely, I want to take a moment to consider the musical structure and character of the song. For this track, the sampling is not choppy or pastiche in style. The high-pitched, bouncy backbeat that forms the base of the song is slightly slowed down and remixed, of course, from the musical, where it mimics the sound of horseshoes hitting the street in the imagined carriage that Dodger uses to pretend he takes Nancy to 'the palace' as they imitate aristocrats. The other boys in the gang act the role of horses, and the high backbeat both represents the sound of and emphasises the rhythm of their feet hitting the ground. To make that element of the musical's song the grounding backbeat of Jay-Z's song immediately injects fantasies of economic and social advancement into the track. Envisioning the solidarity and family bonds of street life through the highly unlikely scenario of a visit to the royal palace unites the two historical moments in the realms of performance and play. The song begins with Jay-Z calling for his DJ to 'Bring the chorus in', and the lines from Bart's musical precede the first verse. As the beat stays steady and keeps heads bobbing, a single piano key plays some but not all of the notes from the melody. The same piano line runs through the chorus and the verse, and that piano line is so central that it causes the listener to hear a constant conversation (or duet) between the chorus and Jay-Z. When Dodger's voice takes the place of Jay-Z's in the chorus, the piano key continues to play the same single notes from the melody. The presence of the consistent piano line through Dodger's singing links Dodger's and Jay-Z's voices, each in a similar relationship to the piano line and to each other. Significantly, at the end of the chorus, those piano notes are aligned rhythmically with Dodger's voice. Because Dodger's voice in the chorus appears before Jay-Z's first verse, and at the end of that chorus Dodger's voice is in alignment with the piano line, the through-line immediately brings Jay's voice in the verses together with Dodger's. In this way, the song's sonic structure enhances the commentary of the lyrical conversation between Jay-Z and Dickens's characters.

In the song's first verse, Jay-Z addresses another adult male – a peer in same age cohort who has grown up in the hood with him. Reminiscing about their exploits together as kids, Jay declares that he will sacrifice anything for his friend in terms noticeably similar to those used by Fagin in the musical: Jay would 'Do a bid' or 'lose a rib' for his brother and 'exchange my life for yours'. He espouses something akin to gang loyalty, and his devotion to his peer is deep. As they progress from 'thuggin' to being successful rap moguls, the devotion does not diminish. Jay next offers to act as a substitute father: 'when you ain't around | I'll spank ya son | keep him in line. | If you should die | I'll keep him like mine'. At face value, one might read this shift as Jay moving from the peer role – a character like Dodger having Oliver's back – to the leader role of Fagin as he adopts figurative sons and welcomes them to a community in the absence of parents. This section resonates differently, however, once one hears the rest of the song.

The second verse honours Jay-Z's single mother. He thanks her for what she provided, acknowledging that 'the streets' often took him from the safe home she tried to establish. Now that he is successful, his mother deserves to share his wealth, which is why he will do 'anything' for her. Thinking back to *Oliver!* the musical, Jay is now back in the role of the boys swearing love to Nancy as their maternal figure. This is one point in the song where the boys singing the chorus and Jay-Z are in nearly exact alignment, but the third verse shifts Jay completely out of the child role. It begins, 'Dear nephews | I'm writin' this with no pen or a pad | And I'm signin' it | ya uncle, ya best friend, and ya dad'. Linking back to the first verse, Jay repeats that he will be a second father not only if a boy's father dies but also if they just part ways, 'if it comes a time | when you ain't feelin' your real dad | put my face on his body'. At this point, rapping primarily about solidarity among men in the ghetto, addressing his 'nephews' and explicitly envisioning himself as a father figure for those who have been literally or practically orphaned, it would again be easy to read Jay-Z as a version of Fagin. He says that the boys should call him 'when it's code red'; he is obviously their leader when they're in trouble, perhaps with the law. But by the end of this verse, the song is in some ways resisting the message of its own Dickensian chorus.

As the substitute father, Jay tells his 'nephews' to do the reverse of what the chorus says. He tells them: 'don't follow', 'Stand on your own two' and 'Don't listen to your crew'. Commanding 'Bite your tongue for no one', he also advises that they 'stand back' from tense situations to gain perspective. These declarations are the opposite of blind gang loyalty. Thinking back to the first verse when Jay tells his friend, 'If you should die | I'll keep him like mine', he no longer looks like a creepy version of Fagin, gathering orphaned boys for any number of exploitative purposes. Rather, with the emphasis on independent thinking and ignoring 'your crew', Jay is more similar to Mr Brownlow. He has taken the sentiment of the boys' chorus and corrected it, shifting its foundation. At its core and in the centre of the song as the middle verse, Jay's position parallels that of his single mother (and perhaps Nancy) who warns against the lure of an ill-advised street life. One effect of Jay-Z's use of Bart and Dickens here is that Jay's message is ultimately more in line with that of the novel than the musical. The song does not endorse the musical's cloying conclusion that shows Fagin and Dodger skipping off into the sunset. Rather, it has engaged with the musical by using the chorus of 'Anything' to make a point more in accordance with the novel's emphasis on abandoning gang loyalty in favour of domestic stability. Charley Bates finds happiness once he has 'turned his back upon the scenes of the past' to become a grazier; the novel rewards him (in contrast to Nancy) for showing a willingness to split from the gang.[15] Jay-Z's adaptation does not naively suggest that young men entirely avoid suspicious substitute parental figures (Brownlow is odd in his own way, and Jay-Z's rapper persona is not flawless). Rather, it guides the listener through a process of determining which options offer the safer route out of a dangerous criminal scene. Jay-Z's rapper persona, as the deliverer of this message, also occupies the position of Charles Dickens, appropriating the canonical author in a manner that at once respects and displaces him.

Drawing upon Bakhtinian literary criticism, George Lipsitz notes that music must be included in the list of genres for which a dialogic approach is appropriate. Although Lipsitz's focus is on rock and roll, his argument applies to rap and hip-hop:

Popular music is nothing if not dialogic, the product of an ongoing historical conversation in which no one has the first or the last word. The traces of the past that pervade the popular music of the present amount to more than mere chance: they are not simply juxtapositions of incompatible realities. They reflect a dialogic process, one embedded in collective history and nurtured by the ingenuity of artists interested in fashioning icons of opposition.[1]

The conversation that artists like Jay-Z create with Lionel Bart and Dickens shows that dialogue happens not just across decades but also across literary forms and genres. The radical nature of Lipsitz's claim that 'no one has the first or last word' in such conversations merits emphasis. Disrupting linear time, Jay-Z at once responds to Dickens and displaces both him and Bart as the author, or 'first word' maker, of the song's message.[17] Far from having a 'last word', Jay-Z leaves listeners of 'Anything' with a cross-cultural, cross-generic and looping conversation.

One of Ludacris's uses of Dickens exemplifies a similar type of engagement with the musical adaptation of *Oliver Twist*. The song 'Large Amounts' opens with the very first lines of 'You've Got to Pick a Pocket or Two' from Bart's musical. The lines 'In this life | One thing counts | In the bank | Large amounts' serve as Ludacris's chorus. In the musical, Fagin and his gang are teaching Oliver how to pick pockets, and the song endorses criminality as the best way of making money. Ludacris's song, like Jay-Z's, seems to value Fagin's teaching but is ultimately conflicted about at least some of the values the chorus suggests. Ludacris does not begin the track with a call for the chorus; the song simply begins in Fagin's voice as listeners, for the only time, hear the chorus unimpeded. Just as the Jay-Z track uses a piano line to link the verses and chorus, the Ludacris track uses the repetition of a guitar line (single string plucks in place of single piano key strikes) to create sonic coherence. In contrast to the smooth conversation between Jay-Z, Bart and Dickens, Ludacris creates a more confrontational soundscape. Following each verse, the song shifts into the chorus with Ludacris saying 'Because . . .', but then he speaks behind or over the chorus. He does not rap to the beat, as he does in the verses. Rather, he speaks or yells over Fagin's singing, and his statements are exhortations that confirm what he says in the verses, calling people to agree with him and emphasising that he is right.

'Large Amounts' is a song of complaint in which Ludacris enters the familiar territory of rich people complaining about being rich because everyone now asks them for money. He likes his wealth, but managing it is difficult: 'bein' rich is such a beautiful thing | But mo' money, mo' problems'. Ludacris also predictably complains about women who want their men to have money, and although there is a sideways admission of responsibility in the line 'So we splurge, even though our lives ain't in the right place yet', he still refers to such women as gold-digging 'whores' and promises to raise his daughter with better values. Even though cash should not change him, it has done, as he is 'guilty of splurgin'. The chorus from *Oliver!* keeps repeating the fact that the one thing that counts in life is large amounts of money in the bank. And each time Ludacris speaks over the chorus, Clive Revill's voice and Ludacris's voice are heard at the same time. Revill is singing and Ludacris talks over him, or to him, essentially taking Fagin to task. Ludacris's complaints are all about people who believe that money is the only thing one should 'count'. He wants his family, and women, to 'count' things besides money. He also reminds people to pay taxes – something Fagin discourages in a later verse in the musical's song. During the chorus, then, he is talking back to the source text, disagreeing with it.

Why use Dickens and the *Oliver!* musical to make this commentary? Frustration over people wanting one to share wealth is not a particularly original theme to explore in a rap song, so invoking Dickens to make that point clues one into the fact that more is at stake. Using Dickens establishes that there is a parallel between rising out of an African American ghetto scene and what has been presented as a white British ghetto scene. I am not convinced that any community presented as 'pure white' in a British context is actually as 'pure' as it claims to be, but my point is that both the Ludacris and Jay-Z songs place themselves in a tradition, claiming the *Oliver Twist* history as one to which their stories are connected. That move works against a view of rap and hip-hop as being culturally shallow, illiterate or as belonging strictly to an African American context. I agree with critics who emphasise that rap and hip-hop emerge from specifically African American artistic forms and linguistic traditions, and I also think that, as the form stands now, it has drawn upon those traditions without being limited to them. Speaking about the relationship between space and identity in hip-hop, Craig Wilkins explains that 'sonically constructed communities are linked to time through an interactive, reciprocal conversation with history that shapes the socially defined public arena in which music is produced, reproduced, and received'.[18] That 'interactive, reciprocal conversation with history' is one that Jay-Z and Ludacris expand to include not only Victorian London but also the way it has been continually re-envisioned in American culture.

In moving past the socio-political to include the literary and historical conversations taking place in this music, I build on Imani Perry's warning to hip-hop critics to avoid oversimplifying all rap and hip-hop as angry diatribes about ghetto life. Perry cautions, 'It is quite dangerous for the critic or listener to interpret it purely as a reflection of social and political conditions, without thought to the presence of artistic choice in every narrative and composition.'[19] The difficult living conditions, physical danger and child exploitation of some modern, poverty-stricken urban landscapes are not always very different from Fagin's Den or the unforgiving streets Jo wanders in *Bleak House*. But, following Perry, I argue that critics must also see that there is an aesthetic sophistication and critical cleverness to the way these rap artists are invoking Dickens. Furthermore, the conversation with Dickens (and with adaptations of Dickens) does not simply echo his social commentary; rather, the conversation builds upon, challenges and reworks Dickens's narratives. If Ludacris is telling Fagin that he is wrong, or if Jay-Z is telling Lionel Bart that he does not get Dickens quite right, then we must retune our ears to listen for a conversation across genres, cultures and centuries.

To conclude, let us consider yet another *Oliver Twist* appearance that engages directly with Dickens, not via a second-layer adaptation. Clipse's song 'Ride Around Shining' is, unsurprisingly, all about riding around in a fancy car with shiny accessories. To understand the context for this sudden literary reference, one must know that HREs are expensive rims and a Modena is a Ferrari model.[20] The artists behind this song, brothers Terrence 'Pusha-T' Thornton and Gene 'Malice' Thornton (later 'No Malice'), form Clipse (sometimes called 'The Clipse'), and Dickens emerges in a verse featuring a guest rapper, Ab-Liva:

V12 on a Modena you can see the pistons
HRE's on it, Mommy see it glisten
When I make Oliver Twist like Dickens
It's feelin' like parts is missin'
Tops don't push soul
Got it drive it like pole positions 'til my soul's risen

The density of consumer culture references alongside intense rhythms, references to death, and rhymes (to which Dickens is central) makes these lines difficult to unpack, highlighting just how confusing sudden uses of Dickens can be. 'Oliver' here is a verbal/aural pun meaning 'all of her', which feminises both the character of Oliver and the novel as a whole. Given Oliver's extreme passivity in the novel, proclivity for heroine-esque fainting spells at crucial moments of the plot's action, and the existence of prostitution within Fagin's crime ring, it is not an interpretive stretch to feminise Oliver as a character. Given, however, that he is a child, it is rather odd for Ab-Liva to claim (with pride) to take a sexually dominant position over that particular character.[21] Ab-Liva also states that Dickens specifically is the one who makes Oliver Twist, aligning himself as the twister of 'all of her' with the canonical author. He further draws a clear parallel between the twisting of a hangman's rope, the constant underlying threat of Oliver's surname, and the presumably pleasurable twisting of sexual intercourse. The verse's concluding focus on death (the rising of the rapper's soul), then, emerges somewhat logically out of the Twist reference, although there is no resolution of the somewhat jarring juxtaposition of sexual boasting, materialistic displays of wealth, and death.

Again, the question arises: why use Dickens to make such a boast about one's riches and prowess? Jay-Z offers helpful reminders and some guidance in his book *Decoded* when he explains:

> even when a rapper is just rapping about how dope he is, there's something a little bit deeper going on. It's like a sonnet [. . .] Sonnets have a set structure, but also a limited subject matter. They are mostly about love. Taking on such a familiar subject and writing about it in a set structure forced sonnet writers to find every nook and cranny in the subject and challenged them to invent new language for saying old things. It's the same with braggadacio [*sic*] in rap. When we take the most familiar subject in the history of rap—why I'm dope—and frame it within the sixteen-bar structure of a rap verse, synced to the specific rhythm and feel of the track, more than anything it's a test of creativity and wit [. . .]. And there are always deeper layers of meaning buried in the simplest verses.[22]

Ab-Liva occupying the same space as Dickens in his boast, then, operates as a strong example of the 'deeper layers of meaning' that Jay-Z explains. The 'creativity and wit' for which rappers are known – the talent that encompasses all manner of punning, riffing and signifying – have literary qualities that challenge listeners to pay rappers a more comprehensive respect. At the very least, references to Dickens, his works and his characters include knowledge of a particular canon in the boasts, which adds intellectual dexterity to the list of rappers' talents. In the instances I have analysed above, Jay-Z, Ludacris and Ab-Liva via Clipse demonstrate far more than basic knowledge of Dickens by reworking thematics and redirecting the power of his legacy.

To use Dickens in this way is to challenge a long history of white cultural producers using Black art forms for the benefit and profit of white producers and audiences. As Russell Potter reminds us, 'For every musical form that black culture has produced has been appropriated and commodified by white culture in the name of a very particular kind of *spectacle*, whether it be a minstrel show, a big band concert, or a rock-n-roll extravaganza.'[23] Miles White further points out:

> Minstrelsy represents the first sustained cultural project in which the agency of the black male body and black subjectivity are usurped by white actors as fetishized commodity. The effects of this particular racial counterfeit have been critical in the construction of black masculinity in the white imagination up to the present day.[24]

Building on the work of scholars like Potter and White, we can envision performers like Jay-Z, Ludacris and Ab-Liva/Clipse pushing back against that history by appropriating Dickens's legacy, name and imagined body in a way that commodifies and objectifies the white literary body in order to enhance the Black. It is impossible to reverse the power dynamics of the exploitation, as white canonical figures and white people in the present day obviously do not exist in the oppressed spaces of Black people from previous centuries (which is why terms like 'reverse racism' are nonsensical). Yet it is very possible to reverse the direction of objectification, as well as the agency of the objectifier, and to enhance the power of the Black rapping voice with strategic use of white-identified canonical history. As hip-hop culture has developed and grown, the question of whether the profits have flowed back to enough Black Americans to justify the form's often troubling objectification of Blackness and both male and female sexuality, for instance, remains a subject of debate. What I want to emphasise is that references to literary giants like Dickens not only continue to create the ruptures in linear time that are central to hip-hop but also, in a small way, constitute a layer of resistance that challenges the direction of cultural appropriation.

This type of possession of Dickens may help explain the discomfort some Dickens readers, fans and scholars experience when they learn that people are rapping about Dickens. Such discomfort often exceeds the more typical hostile responses that traditionalists have to adaptations that vary from standard interpretations of canonical works. The underlying yet usually unspoken presumption of such comments is that Dickens is not 'theirs' (rappers') to play with and that rappers, especially Black or brown ones, do not have the right to talk back to him. An even more offensive reaction is, surprisingly, one that people usually feel comfortable articulating: that the rappers must be referencing Dickens by accident or must not know what they are talking about when they make such references. Such reactions boldly assume that rappers are not intelligent enough to actually know much about Dickens and scoff at the idea that a rapper would have read a Dickens novel or developed a sophisticated analysis of a Dickens adaptation. Ideally, Dickens scholars and hip-hop fans alike will begin to respond to news of Dickens in rap not with the question 'Really?', but rather with a more affirmative 'Of course'.[25] Dickens and his works (himself as a literary icon as well as some of his characters) resonate consistently in the phenomenally popular art form of rap, an art form based in African American tradition with worldwide appeal. It is imperative for Dickens scholars of the present and future to engage with this cultural form. Studying the work of rap artists who invoke Dickens not only enhances our understanding of the many ways to read Dickens and his relationship to the arts but also brings important attention to one of his most exciting and complex afterlives. Rappers are already having multiple conversations with Dickens, and all readers of Dickens will benefit from, and perhaps even be entertained by, giving those conversations a listen.

Notes

Thanks to Erin Mercurio for her work as my research assistant during the formulation of this essay.

1. 'The botheration of that No. has been prodigious', Dickens writes to Wilkie Collins on 12 December 1855, referring to *The Holly-Tree Inn*, which was a collaboratively written Christmas issue of Dickens's journal *Household Words*. See *The Letters of Charles Dickens*, ed. by Madeline House, Graham Storey et al., Pilgrim/British Academy Edition, 12 vols (Oxford: Clarendon Press, 1965–2002), vii (1993), 762. Mary J. Blige's song 'Family Affair' includes the lyric 'Don't need no hateration' (written by Blige, Andre Young, Bruce Miller, Camara Kambon and Michael Elizondo for *No More Drama*, MCA Records, 2001).
2. When 'Anything' was released, Jay-Z consistently spelled his name with a hyphen, and I retain the hyphen here. Later, Jay officially removed the hyphen from his name, although it regularly appears in both forms (see Sean Michaels, 'Jay-Z to become Jay Z in massively disrespectful move against hyphens', *Guardian*, 19 July 2013 <https://www.theguardian.com/music/2013/jul/19/jay-z-drops-hyphen-from-name> [accessed 27 June 2018]). Beastie Boys, 'Shadrach' (written by Michael Diamond, Adam Horovitz, Adam Yauch, Mike Dike, John King and Michael Simpson for *Paul's Boutique*, Capitol Records, 1989).
3. Ta-Nehisi Coates, 'My President was Black', *The Atlantic* 319 (January/February 2017), 46–66, 49; *The Hip Hop & Obama Reader*, ed. by Travis L. Gosa and Erik Nielson (Oxford: Oxford University Press, 2015).
4. The Sugarhill Gang, 'Rapper's Delight' (1979). See *The Anthology of Rap*, ed. by Adam Bradley and Andrew Dubois (New Haven: Yale University Press, 2010), 96–106.
5. Some scholars have resisted the general dichotomy I describe. Rosen and Marks, for instance, not only contextualise gangsta rap within African American poetic traditions but also consider 'its remarkable affinities with a historically unrelated tradition, namely the genres of poetic satire and mockery in Greco-Roman classical antiquity'. See Ralph M. Rosen and Donald R. Marks, 'Comedies of Transgression in Gangsta Rap and Ancient Classical Poetry', *New Literary History: A Journal of Theory and Interpretation* 30.4 (1999), 897–928, 899. See also Adam Bradley, *Book of Rhymes: The Poetics of Hip Hop* (New York: BasicCivitas, 2009).
6. Rappers' use of Dickens in sexual slang is my focus in another essay in progress, 'Makin' All of Her Twist: Rappers and Their Dickens'. For more on Dickens's legacy and afterlives, see '*Oliver Twist* on Screen', in Juliet John's *Dickens and Mass Culture* (Oxford: Oxford University Press, 2010) and *Contemporary Dickens*, ed. by Deirdre David and Eileen Gillooly (Columbus: Ohio State University Press, 2009).
7. Miles White, *From Jim Crow to Jay-Z: Race, Rap, and the Performance of Masculinity* (Urbana: University of Illinois Press, 2011), 33.

8. Henry Louis Gates, Jr, *The Signifying Monkey* (New York: Oxford University Press, 1988). Gates applies his theory directly to rap in subsequent pieces, including the foreword to *The Anthology of Rap*, xxii–xxvii.

9. Tricia Rose, *Black Noise: Rap Music and Black Culture in Contemporary America* (Hanover, NH: Wesleyan University Press, 1994), 3.

10. Alexs Pate, *In the Heart of the Beat: The Poetry of Rap* (Lanham: Scarecrow Press, 2010), 3.

11. Imani Perry, *Prophets of the Hood: Politics and Poetics in Hip Hop* (Durham, NC: Duke University Press, 2004), 38.

12. For more on Jay-Z's business success, see White, 81–2. On the founding of Roc-A-Fella Records, see Greenburg, *Empire State of Mind* (New York: Portfolio/Penguin, 2015), 31–49. It is worth noting that the song that propelled Jay-Z's career into superstardom was 'Hard Knock Life (Ghetto Anthem)', which features a hook from Mark 'The 45 King' Howard James that samples *Annie*. Jay-Z describes the relationship between Annie's narrative and his own as 'different dimensions of the same reality' (*Decoded* (New York: Spiegel & Grau, 2010), 240). His later use of the *Oliver!* sample shows continued comfort with the use of songs from musicals and a more complicated (though perhaps no less politically radical) conversation between his own lyric and the source text.

13. 'Anything' (written by Shawn Carter and Lionel Bart on Beanie Sigel's *The Truth*, Roc-A-Fella Records, 2000) and 'Large Amounts' (written by Christopher Bridges, Matthew McAllister and Lionel Bart on *The Red Light District*, Def Jam Recordings and Disturbing tha Peace, 2004). The *Red Light District*'s double platinum certification from the Recording Industry Association of America indicates that sales figures reached at least two million units. <www.riaa.com/gold-platinum/about-awards> [accessed 27 June 2018]. Ludacris, in establishing his own recording label Disturbing tha Peace, also heads 'a minor media empire that *Forbes* magazines estimated to be worth tens of millions of dollars' (*Anthology of Rap*, 678).

14. *Oliver!*, dir. by Carol Reed, music and lyrics by Lionel Bart (Columbia Pictures, 1968).

15. Charles Dickens, *Oliver Twist* (London: Penguin, 2003), 452, ch. 53.

16. George Lipsitz, *Time Passages: Collective Memory and American Popular Culture* (Minneapolis: University of Minnesota Press, 1990), 99.

17. For more on African American art and resistance to dominant models of time, see Russell A. Potter, *Spectacular Vernaculars: Hip-Hop and the Politics of Postmodernism* (Albany: State University of New York, 1995), 3–4.

18. Craig L. Wilkins, '(W)rapped Space: The Architecture of Hip Hop', *Journal of Architectural Education* 54.1 (2000), 7–19, 8.

19. Perry, 39.

20. *Hell Hath No Fury*, Arista Records, 2006.

21. In addition to Nancy's prostitution, the boys in the crime ring may be exploited sexually. See Larry Wolff, '"The Boys are Pickpockets, and the Girl is a Prostitute": Gender and Juvenile Criminality in Early Victorian England from *Oliver Twist* to *London Labour*', *New Literary History* 27.2 (1996), 227–49.

22. Jay-Z, 26.

23. Potter, 8.

24. White, 14.

25. Here, I echo Matt Kohl's point in his blog post for Oxford Dictionaries, '"The Dickens, reminiscent of Charles": Boz and the Language of Hip-Hop', 16 February 2012 <blog.oxforddictionaries.com/2012/02/16/boz-and-the-language-of-hip-hop> [accessed 27 June 2018]. I became aware of Kohl's work after having collected approximately fifteen rap references to Dickens and have benefited from correspondence with Kohl. To my knowledge, Kohl is the only other scholar to date who has tracked references to Dickens in rap and hip-hop.

14

PUPPETS

David Ellison

HOUSEHOLD WORDS CONTRIBUTORS DUDLEY COSTELLO AND W. H. Wills begin their brief historical survey of the puppet arts, 'The Pedigree of Puppets' (1852), by airily dispensing with the need to cover their 'tedious' origins in the ancient world.[1] Anyone attempting a related survey of Dickens and puppets would be unwise to emulate this selective approach. Puppets are simply too rarely encountered in Dickens's work to leave anything out. There are a clutch of specific references across both major and minor works, as well as two better-known and more substantial engagements in *The Old Curiosity Shop* (1840–1) and the 'Genoa' chapter of *Pictures from Italy* (1846). And yet, arguably, 'Dickens and puppets' does not suggest a paltry category of inquiry. We tend to invariably bundle the Punch puppets and assorted marionettes with their more abundant cognates (the toys, dolls, waxworks, automata, prostheses and even, on occasion, corpses) that cumulatively vouchsafe our sense of Dickens's fascination with all things human-shaped and of uncertain animation.[2] Locating the puppet within this broader field of the puppet-like has proved a fruitful point of entry into Dickens's work, but there is also something to be said for, and about, puppets as puppets – as the sometimes obdurate and sometimes yielding objects Dickens chose to write about. As we shall see, Dickens's critics viewed his relationship to puppets somewhat censoriously, but this external view differs markedly from Dickens's own account, which is more searching and unresolved.

That there might be an especially noteworthy connection between Dickens and puppets was observed during his lifetime. It registers, for example, in 'A Modern Frankenstein' (1869), an anonymously authored story in *All the Year Round* about a self-described 'foolish man' so beguiled by an itinerant Punch performance that he purchases the puppet and returns home.[3] As Punch is laid out on the parlour table, the narrator, like his namesake, hopes for some animating force, although the object here is domestic diversion. This is a Promethean allegory emptied of metaphysical ambition, where a convenient knock at the door heralds an 'uncouth person with unkempt hair' who provides an elixir that stirs Punch to desired life and inevitable fury.[4] In short order, Punch lives up to his reputation as both noun and verb, attacking the narrator and smashing his possessions before being wrestled into the consuming hearth.

A prosaic coda reveals the elixir-deliverer was, in fact, a beer-boy collecting bottles drained by the narrator who, in all likelihood, has drunkenly destroyed his own parlour. The point here is not really to promote temperance, but rather to divide the story into disparate parts. On one side, the puppet occasions an intense encounter that carries the burden of the story's (admittedly, scarcely realised) literary pleasures; on the other, the bathetic, mystery-dispelling concluding paragraph returns the reader to the grimmer realities of urban and domestic tedium. The writer of 'A Modern Frankenstein' underscores the Dickensian aspect of the fantastical, puppet-entertaining portion of the story. He is haltingly present in the tone of enforced drollery that might, unfairly, be termed Dickens-y; more directly, he appears in the narrator's explanation for his actions that find their origins in childhood privation, echoing *Great Expectations* (1860–1). Principally, though, Dickens looms over this story in the way it treats Punch as more than simply an object of beguiling and uncertain properties. As the coda reveals, it is Punch that retrospectively makes eventful narrative out of otherwise mundane incoherence. That is, the puppet figures in an admittedly crude, but obliquely sympathetic, model of the writerly imagination finding form.

Without recourse to parody, 'A Modern Frankenstein' makes a small, intuitive stab at the importance of puppets for Dickens and his writing. In that regard, it is inadvertently party to an oddly belligerent critical tradition. An unsigned review of *Hard Times* (1854) in the *Westminster Review*, for example, contrasts Thackeray's plausible characterisations with Dickens's shallow tendency to furnish his characters:

> with some peculiarity, which, like the weight of a Dutch clock, is their ever-gravitating principle of action. The consequence is, they have, most of them, the appearance of puppets which Mr Dickens has constructed expressly for his present purpose.[5]

Towards the end of Dickens's life George Stott made a related complaint in *Contemporary Review*, acknowledging the author's puppets as accomplished, but only when restricted to their proper domain of farce. Dickens's puppets become a problem, Stott suggests, when his ambitions push towards 'loftier aims'.[6] Hamley's 'Remonstrance with Dickens' also treats puppets symptomatically, aligning their emergence with the waning of Dickens's creative powers from their Pickwickian heights:

> [The more recent novels] which, besides being destitute of a well-considered plot [. . .] can scarcely be a great picture of life; indeed, the number of puppets, dummies, and unnatural creations that grimace and jerk their way along the scenes, forbid it to be so considered. 'All the world's a stage,' says Shakespeare, 'and all the men and women merely players.'—'All the world's a puppet-show,' says Dickens, 'and all the men and women fantoccini [. . .]. Observe now, when I pull the strings (and I don't mind letting you see me pull the strings all through the exhibition – no deception, ladies and gentlemen, none), how natural the action! how effective the character!'[7]

If Shakespeare's is an art of limitless expansion, Dickens's is one of crass constriction, so the argument goes; he is novelist-as-puppeteer or, worse still, in a mean-spirited poke at the author's tireless capacity for self-promotion, the novelist-as-barker. It is bad enough that Dickens is seen to pull his characters' strings, but so much worse, it seems, for him to boast that his genius for string-pulling transcends the deficiencies of the form. Such criticisms look to liberally mix Dickens's apparent faults as a writer with his fabled weakness for popular culture or, tendentiously, with his moral failings as a man.[8]

G. H. Lewes's remarkably sour posthumous assessment similarly relies on the figure of the puppet, but extends the criticism outwards from Dickens to reproach the sympathetic and collaborative weaknesses of his readers. For Lewes, this amounts to a cultural crisis, Dickens's irresistible toys opening a pathway that can only end in puppet mastery over the readers themselves:

> Just as the wooden horse is brought within the range of the child's emotions, and dramatizing tendencies, when he can handle and draw it, so Dickens's figures are brought within the range of the reader's interests, and receive from those interests a sudden illumination, when they are the puppets of a drama every incident of which appeals to the sympathies.[9]

Hostile critics name the puppet as a key to Dickens's gift because it is both potent and infantile, formative yet inconsequential – an object that he and we, his readers, should have left behind. Given the dizzying breadth of Dickens's work, it is surprising that Lewes, among others, would emphasise the puppet and the puppeteer as such revelatory metaphors, over, say, his treatment of hats, kettles, chairs or anything else in the object-dense field of his fiction. Surveying these passing references to puppets in Dickens's writing demonstrates how meagre the resources providing sustenance to this particular line of critical thought are. There is little evidence to show that Dickens conceived of writing in terms drawn from puppetry (again, unlike Thackeray's showman in the 1847–8 *Vanity Fair*), or that he was an uncritical champion of the form. Indeed, one of Dickens's earliest references to puppets relies on a commonplace understanding of the art's halting capacity for realism:

> The unfortunate grey mare [. . .] floundered along at her own will and pleasure until the Maypole was no longer visible, and then, contracting her legs into what in a puppet would have been looked upon as a clumsy and awkward imitation of a canter, mended her pace all at once, and did it of her own accord.[10]

When Dickens chooses to dwell upon the significance of puppets, or the puppet-like, it is by locating them, even isolating them, within the narrower gauge of recalling his best Christmases.

Dickens's 'A Christmas Tree' (1850) is a memory exercise that constructs a compound tree out of a host of seasonal experiences. Moreover, the tree is the occasion to consider the heady effects of childhood objects the narrator does 'not care to resist'.[11] Dickens places his earliest Christmas at the top of the tree where he finds a Tumbler:

> with his hands in his pockets, who wouldn't lie down, but whenever he was put upon the floor, persisted in rolling his fat body about, until he rolled himself still, and brought those lobster eyes of his to bear upon me—when I affected to laugh very much, but in my heart of hearts was extremely doubtful of him.[12]

Such finely observed childhood anxiety provides the comic charge, but it is the details that are telling: the Tumbler's refusal to submit to the conventions of motion and rest, the painted eyes that nevertheless cast a look, and, importantly, the child's dutiful laugh delivered in recognition that the toy both demands it and is mollified by it – effectively forcing the young Dickens to warily simulate delight. Moving further down the tree, other intractable toys (the demoniacal Counsellor, the large cardboard man, and the unnerving mask prefiguring the rigour of death) come into view as things that similarly refuse, as Jane Bennett has it, 'to dissolve completely into the milieu of human knowledge'.[13] Further down still, the focus shifts to dolls, their houses and then to Dickens's beloved toy theatre and a miniature production of Isaac Pocock's *The Miller and His Men*:

> In spite of a few besetting accidents and failures (particularly an unreasonable disposition in the respectable Kelmar, and some others, to become faint in the legs, and double up, at exciting points of the drama) a teeming world of fancies so suggestive and all-embracing, that far below it on my Christmas Tree, I see dark, dirty, real Theatres in the day-time, adorned with these associations as with the freshest garlands of the rarest flowers, and charming me yet.[14]

Here, Romantic certainties about the formative effects of child's play on adult experience are subjected to sharper ironies; those early fantasies not only persist, but, of necessity, must compensate for the tawdry realities of Victorian theatre. As for the toy stage itself, Kelmar and his castmates' predictable unsteadiness on their feet is both a technical incapacity (yet another instance of the puppet's unreliable hold on realism) and an example of the paper actor communicating too much of the manipulator's affect (in this case, excitement) while also resisting the imposition and expression of the manipulator's purpose or, to use a somewhat grander term, their will. When Costello and Wills come to discuss the English origins of the puppet, they note the way that the 'ancient fondness for these little actors leaves its trace in the terms of endearment applied to children'.[15] Such bygone sentimentality contrasts with the more 'humorous and satirical enjoyment of Marionnettes [*sic*]' that lives on in the modern form of puppet, 'when we apply it to some representatives in Parliament, or other person who is said to be the mere instrument of another's will'.[16] This problem of the will and who exerts it on whom in the puppet–manipulator relationship, much less between human actors, forms a speculative thread that ties these oddly resistant childhood toys to the marionettes Dickens witnessed in Italy and to the Punch troupe that Nell and her grandfather stumble on in a graveyard in *The Old Curiosity Shop*.

Puppet Life in *The Old Curiosity Shop*

When first encountered in Chapter 16 of *The Old Curiosity Shop*, Punch is both instantly recognisable and yet also barely formed:

> his nose and chin as hooked and his face as beaming as usual. Perhaps his imperturbable character was never more strikingly developed, for he preserved his usual equable smile notwithstanding that his body was dangling in a most uncomfortable position, all loose and limp and shapeless, while his long peaked cap, unequally balanced against his exceedingly slight legs, threatened every instant to bring him toppling down.[17]

PUPPETS 211

Punch's imperturbability speaks directly to his time-honoured indifference to the violence he visits on others and that is, in turn, visited on himself. But, it also notes
an absence of perturbation, which, for the puppet, equates to the dramatic liveliness conferred by the manipulator's hand. That is, the manifest difference between
Punch in his characteristically untroubled but active mode (doling out and receiving
hits) and the drooping, motionless thing that is clearly unlike Punch, or not yet fully
Punch, collapses as both versions resist (moral or physical) influence. In a letter to
Mary Tayler, Dickens elaborated on the threat to pleasure posed by the prospect of
an improved and responsive Punch – one who was morally instructive and physically
affected by circumstance:

> In my opinion the Street Punch is one of those extravagant reliefs from the reali-
> ties of life which would lose its hold upon the people if it were made moral and
> instructive. I regard it as quite harmless in its influence, and as an outrageous joke
> which no one in existence would think of regarding as an incentive to any kind
> of action, or as a model for any kind of conduct. It is possible, I think, that one
> secret source of the pleasure very generally derived from this performance [. . .] is
> the satisfaction the spectator feels in the circumstance that likenesses of men and
> women can be so knocked about, without any pain or suffering.[18]

Dickens fends off the all-too-familiar objections raised in the face of violent popular
culture (that it corrupts and incites) to argue instead that the source of Punch's liberating joy and enduring interest lies precisely in his unfeeling response to the blows
he delivers and receives. In *The Old Curiosity Shop*, Dickens expands on Punch's
refusal to be moved by having Nell discover him among graves that harbour things
that prove similarly resistant to influence of any kind and yet, again, much like the
puppet, continue to exert an outsized sway over the imagination. Although Codlin
explains they have retreated to the privacy of the cemetery to preserve their commercial advantage of novelty, the entire enterprise brims with death:

> In part scattered upon the ground at the feet of the two men [. . .] were the other
> persons of the Drama. The hero's wife and one child, the hobby-horse, the doctor,
> the foreign gentleman [. . .], the radical neighbour who will by no means admit
> that a tin bell is an organ, the executioner, and the devil, were all here. Their
> owners had evidently come to that spot to make some needful repairs in the stage
> arrangements, for one of them was engaged in binding together a small gallows
> with thread, while the other was intent upon fixing a new black wig, with the aid
> of a small hammer and some tacks, upon the head of the radical neighbour, who
> had been beaten bald. (176–8, ch. 18)

Considering the puppet, or the puppet-like, in light of the buried dead in their variously feared and mourned aspects (a pathway Dickens firmly etched in 'A Christmas
Tree') complicates Punch and his cohort, making them figures to reckon with beyond
their familiar comic remit. For critics like Paul Schlicke, Punch's mortal aspect in *The
Old Curiosity Shop* foreshadows the impending collapse of popular entertainments
like puppetry itself.[19] Or, if not puppetry's outright demise, then at least some recognition that it is a decaying thing that may only be recalled nostalgically, which is

also a kind of death.[20] Claire Wood cannily locates the Punch play within a series of commercially staged 'death-based narratives' that are shadowed by, and eventually overlap with, sentimentalising spiritual narratives finding their apotheosis in Nell's death. Conventionally, the Punch play unfolds as a series of seven murders including those of Punch's wife and child, while the earthly and divine punishments are dodged in the death of his hangman and then the Devil himself.[21] While the deaths that radiate outwards from the traditional Punch gesture towards Nell's inevitable demise, albeit in a different register, the puppet also suggests continuities with Nell's deeply eccentric tormenter, Quilp.

Like Punch, Quilp is not bound by human constraints of fatigue or hunger. He is possessed of ferocious and virtually inorganic energies, fuelled by an impossible diet of unshelled eggs, gnawed cutlery, boiling liquors and foul pipes (106, ch. 5). Not only does his body borrow from the range of puppet motions comprising dips, jerks and sudden plunges, but his frantic abuse of the wooden effigy is Punch-like in its ferocity. Quilp's uncanny affinity with Punch has nourished critical speculation around his degree of autonomy. Is he a self-directed human, free in his choices, or, like the automaton (another instance of the puppet-like), bound to an inflexible script that may only simulate the appearance of free choice?[22] The puppet's capacity to provoke such philosophical speculation originates in Dickens's reversal of the representational order: conventionally, the puppet stands in (comically deficient) place of the human, whereas Quilp, Codlin and Short all exhibit puppet attributes under their skin. Short is described as someone who 'seemed to have unconsciously imbibed something of his hero's character', while Codlin is 'perhaps inseparable from his occupation as well' (177, ch. 16). Such a transfer of properties from puppet to human is also at odds with Nell's first encounter in the graveyard, where Punch offered nothing beyond the likelihood of his wonted performance on stage. In other words, when this obdurate and imperturbable thing appears in *The Old Curiosity Shop* as an influence, an abstraction or a source of imitable characteristics, we may see Dickens exploring the puppet less in terms of its seemingly ungraspable ontology and more by way of its affordances. Rather than engaging with what it is, he closely and rather coldly observes what can be done to and with it, as well as what it may be said to enable: the spontaneous formation of social audiences, the cultivation of nervous fixations, and the animating effects on the puppeteers obliged to furnish puppet liveliness. In this regard, the puppet's very detachment may not lend itself to the novelist's assumed ends. That is to say that Punch's inorganic life proves resistant to vitalised characterisation until it finds a double in the marginally organic Quilp. This is unsurprising, as the (admittedly grudging) realism of *The Old Curiosity Shop* militates against a more engaged puppet encounter and with it the burden of taking a fuller measure of puppet life. Oddly, Dickens's writing is freer and more roomily speculative in his non-fictional accounts of puppet life, specifically in experiences recounted in *Pictures from Italy*.

Political Puppets

Dickens arrived in Italy in the summer of 1844, settling first in Genoa where, among such activities as boating and disparaging the 'trash and tinsel' of the local church, he visited the Carlo Felice Opera House.[23] There he was struck by the 'uncommonly hard and cruel character' (67) of the audience, which he sought to understand in terms of their habitually censored energies finding a marginally permissible expressive outlet: 'as there is nothing else of a political nature at which they are allowed to express the least disapprobation, perhaps they are resolved to make the most of this opportunity' (67). He also noted the menacing behaviour of the Piedmontese officers who were granted free seats as a governor-mandated privilege. He observed they were 'lofty critics in consequence, and infinitely more exacting than if they made the unhappy manager's fortune' (67). And of the performances staged at the day theatre, Dickens reported that, beyond an occasional Goldoni comedy, most of what he saw was French because 'anything like nationality is dangerous to despotic governments, and Jesuit-beleaguered kings' (68). Cumulatively, these observations reveal that, for Dickens, some of the dizzying political complexity of Genoa under the then-reactionary House of Savoy was grasped through the total experience of theatre – from the vagaries of the ticketing policy to the choice of repertoire and the shifting line dividing permissible from impermissible forms of reception. And it is from within such a situated understanding that Dickens paid several visits to the marionette theatre where he saw 'a famous company from Milan' presenting what he called 'the drollest exhibition I ever beheld in my life' (68).

Dickens carefully distinguished his response to the marionette programme, comprising a ballet and a comedy, from that of the appreciative local audience, 'mainly composed of the common people' (68), by fixing on its idiosyncrasies. He was particularly struck by the scalar instabilities of the marionette stage:

[The marionettes] look between four and five feet high, but are really much smaller; for when a musician in the orchestra happens to put his hat on the stage, it becomes alarmingly gigantic, and almost blots out an actor. (68)

Before the hat farcically disrupts proceedings, Dickens's impression that the marionettes approach life size draws attention to one of the apparent peculiarities of puppets, namely, that their self-evident artificiality is suppressed in performance. The Swiss theatre reformer Adolphe Appia attributed this to the way puppets resolved or neutralised the contrast between flesh and blood actors and painted scenery flats.[24] Unlike an actor, the wooden and paste marionette inhabits a stage that affirms the appearance of lifelikeness, until Dickens seizes upon the moment of disjuncture.

The ballet is similarly received as something so riddled with absurdity that it is principally enjoyed as a thing archly retold. Where the comedy disturbed Dickens at the level of scale, the chief defect of the ballet resides in the marionettes' excess of motion issuing from a wavering observance of gravity:

a procession of musicians enter; one creature playing a drum, and knocking himself off his legs at every blow. These failing to delight [the kidnapped bride], dancers appear. Four first; then two; *the* two; the flesh-coloured two. The way in which they dance; the height to which they spring; the impossible and inhuman extent to which they pirouette; the revelation of their preposterous legs; the coming down with a pause, on the very tips of their toes, when the music requires it [. . .] the final passion of a pas-de-deux; and the going off with a bound! (69)

Although clearly hyperbolic, Dickens concludes that he 'shall never see a real ballet, with a composed countenance again' (69). This does more than distance him from the routine pleasures of the audience; it purports to find something so corrosively ludicrous in the performance that it threatens to permanently and ruinously dissolve the differences between marionette and dancer. Such estranging effects observed of the ballet and comedy are thrown into even sharper relief when Dickens turns to his main theme: the performance of 'St. Helena, or the Death of Napoleon', which, in his telling, is notably anti-English. These puppets play out a strange drama for Dickens. His efforts to take their cultural measure reveals uneasiness about their political potency within the Italian moment, and, perhaps, a troubling capacity to stir other, more personal associations.

The play begins 'by the disclosure of Napoleon, with an immense head, seated on a sofa in his chamber at St. Helena' (69). He is joined by his gaoler, Sir Hudson Lowe, whose brutality towards his captive is prefigured in the marionette's physical build. Dwarfing Napoleon, Lowe is described as 'a perfect mammoth of a man', 'hideously ugly; with a monstrously disproportionate face, and a great clump for the lower jaw, to express his tyrannical and obdurate nature' (69–70). Although briefly sketched, it is clear Lowe's role is to humiliate the fallen emperor:

> [Lowe] began his system of persecution, by calling his prisoner 'General Buon-aparte;' to which the latter replied, with the deepest tragedy, 'Sir Yew ud se on Low, call me not thus. Repeat that phrase and leave me! I am Napoleon, Emperor of France!' (70)

Such an emphasis on title-recognition suggests the play's origins in the work of Emmanuel de Las Cases's *Mémorial de Sainte-Hélène* (1823), which is especially attentive to the adverse effects of Lowe's refusal to pay the emperor his due. Towards the end of this passage, Dickens turns away from the stage action and towards the audience's enthusiastic reception of the emperor's hostility towards the English:

> Throughout the piece, Napoleon [. . .] was very bitter on 'these English officers,' and 'these English soldiers;' to the great satisfaction of the audience, who were perfectly delighted to have Low bullied; and who [. . .] quite execrated him. It would be hard to say why; for Italians have little cause to sympathise with Napoleon, Heaven knows. (70)

Given the awareness of Italian politics evinced elsewhere in *Pictures from Italy*, including remarks about the Genoese theatre, Dickens's blind-spot for the possibility, much less the reality, of pro-Napoleonic nostalgia is surprising.

Even the question he poses about audience sympathies is not the one the passage logically prompts: why hate the English? Dickens's aggrieved response does more than affirm his distance from the audience's pleasures – he disavows the marionette play's content. He denies, for example, there is a plot:

> There was no plot at all, except that a French officer, disguised as an Englishman, came to propound a plan of escape; and being discovered, but not before Napoleon had magnanimously refused to steal his freedom, was immediately ordered

off by Low to be hanged. In two very long speeches, which Low made memorable, by winding up with 'Yas!'—to show that he was English—which brought down thunders of applause. Napoleon was so affected by this catastrophe, that he fainted away on the spot, and was carried out by two other puppets. Judging from what followed, it would appear that he never recovered the shock. (70–1)

Putting aside the question of whether a foiled escape amounts to a plot (it clearly does), Dickens's amused account grudgingly acknowledges the play's concern with questions of liberty, specifically Napoleon's refusal to 'steal' his freedom – a choice that leads to his deathbed. In other words, the question of individual liberty is resolved, transcendently, in the emperor's sacrificial death. In this respect, the play takes its cues from Las Cases, but it also cleaves to the general shape of the *retour des cendres* (the return of ashes) – Louis Philippe's attempt to buoy his declining stocks by attaching himself to Napoleon's resurgent popularity. The *retour* made a grand pageant of the repatriation and reinternment of Napoleon's remains at Les Invalides within a broader context of reassessment and, importantly, rehabilitation of his political legacies. In death, Napoleon emerged cleansed of imperial excess – a forerunner of modern liberalism and sacred to the memory of the French state.[25] Although Dickens cannot or, perhaps, will not see a plot for the marionettes, much less the play's ties to Napoleon's posthumous continental emplotments, he is prepared (as he was at the comedy and the ballet) to attend very closely to the outlandishness of puppet motion:

It was unspeakably ludicrous. Buonaparte's boots were so wonderfully beyond control, and did such marvellous things of their own accord: doubling themselves up, and getting under tables, and dangling in the air, and sometimes skating away with him, out of all human knowledge, when he was in full speech – mischances which were not rendered the less absurd, by a settled melancholy depicted in his face. (71)

Here, for Dickens at least, the marionette's contortions cancel out the play's manifest efforts to stir tragic, political emotions, although it is worth pausing over his impression of Napoleon's 'settled melancholy'. Generally speaking, marionettes were incapable of the facial mobility that would permit anything to 'settle' on the face. Their fixed expressions typically conveyed neutral or broad emotional states corresponding to recognisable character types. Writing of the Victorian marionette theatre, John McCormick describes how compensatory shorthand gestures, such as head and body posture, were used to convey feelings the face could not express. A raised head might indicate pride, for example, while a lowered one, depression.[26] This may be what Dickens construed as the outward sign of Napoleon's melancholy, but his impression of the event lingers on the unlikely, even supernatural, mobility of that face. Much as he reads 'St. Helena, or the Death of Napoleon' against the grain of its political intention, the marionette too is misconstrued, its dramatic range narrowed and fixed as a wildly kinetic thing. If the prospect of such anti-English, pro-Napoleonic feeling left Dickens perplexed or even anxious, his response (this strange act of partial witness) revives a much older practice of warily eyeing the emperor, one that was similarly drawn to his antic postures and spectacular volatility in both movement and scale.

DAVID ELLISON

In Britain, as fears of French invasion sharpened towards the close of the eighteenth century, caricatures of a fantastically mobile Napoleon emerged. In some of these illustrations, he was depicted as gigantic, either marching across a dwarfed globe or leaping impossible spans between continents.[27] Napoleon's lean, sprung legs galvanised these images, condensing all manner of dread regarding the ambition and scope of the French armies. Making his first appearance in Gillray's inspired 'Little Boney' of 1803, Napoleon proved utterly helpless in the face of a colossal George IV who alternately threatened to eat his tiny rival, to blithely inspect him as a curiosity, or to simply snuff him out. Fellow illustrators followed suit, pitting the cowed emperor against, among others, a vast Britannia or the towering spirit of British commerce itself.[28] In these caricatures, Georgians registered their insecurities, as well as finding reassuring, if intermittent, evidence of their superiority as Napoleon's ductile form rendered the impossibly menacing as hearteningly trivial. This composite and narrowly Georgian Napoleon resembles the wildly kinetic figure Dickens encountered on the marionette stage: a figure of fun whose clownish gestures obscured the more potent political symbol capable of stirring audience sympathies.

Several years after the publication of *Pictures from Italy*, Dickens was provided with an opportunity to reflect on such Georgian satire. In 1848 John Forster asked Dickens for an essay on the occasion of a newly published collection of his friend John Leech's prints from *Punch*. Dickens contrasted his appreciation of Leech's work with a waspish dismissal of his Georgian precursors. Compared with Leech's much-admired drawings (comprising gentle pokes at the charmed lives of middle-class children), Georgian satire was seen to be obsessively mired in the brute disfigurement of the world:

> If we turn back to a collection of the works of Rowlandson or Gilray [*sic*], we shall find, in spite of the great humour displayed in many of them, that they are rendered wearisome and unpleasant by a vast amount of personal ugliness. Now, besides that it is a poor device to represent what is satirized as being necessarily ugly, which is but the resource of an angry child or a jealous woman, it serves no purpose but to produce a disagreeable result.[29]

Dickens does not speak directly to Gillray's and Rowlandson's depictions of Napoleon as a demonic imp, a ravenous spider devouring Spanish and Austrian flies, or a Corsican crocodile, but these would, presumably, have attracted the same criticism; the emperor, or for that matter his supporters and his opponents, are rendered comically repulsive. This sweeping rejection of Georgian satire turns on the recognition that its apparently irresistible impulse (satirical disfigurement) was the resource, first of the angry child. Such a finding on Dickens's part arrives doubly framed by his fabled fascination with the grotesque, on the one hand, and the author-forging effects of his anger in the face of childhood neglect, on the other.[30] It is also worth observing that the national anxieties Gillray and Rowlandson spoke to in their satires found a different and more practical shape in towns like Chatham, where John Dickens, Royal Naval Pay Office clerk, moved his family in 1816, not long after Napoleon was imprisoned on St Helena. The young Charles lived amid sailors and soldiers from the local regiments and was taken to see military exercises along the Chatham Lines, which were a complex network of clearances and fortifications primed for the arrival of invading French forces.[31] There is no way of knowing which of these elements, if any, combined to inform Dickens's rejection of Georgian satire, but they do contribute to a useful, albeit overdetermined, context for his evasive response to 'Napoleon's Death on St Helena', a work that, like Rowlandson and Gillray's satire, appears to have produced in Dickens 'a disagreeable result'. That result may register in his disavowal of the play's meanings, but his descriptive response to the work (his scrupulous attention to marionette absurdity) draws the puppet within the ambit of palliative farce, which is a method for mitigating some harsher realities while restoring a measure of control over its effects.

Dickens identifies the moment of peak farce as the 'unspeakably ludicrous' spectacle of Napoleon frogmarched across the stage by his own boots. Napoleon's struggle for control plays out in terms of his boots' ungovernability or rather their indifference to the sovereignty of the will. In 'The Pedigree of Puppets', Costello and Wills similarly align the idiosyncratic nature of puppet motion with the question of a controlling agency:

> there is a certain hovering indecision when [the puppets] make their first appearance—a spasmodic twitching which accompanies their actions, and a something between sailing and staggering in their departures, which suggests that they are not altogether voluntary agents. But this is part of the humour and drollery of such performances.[32]

Costello and Wills's point goes to the likelihood of amusement in the face of the hamstrung manqué, whereas Dickens's account of marionette movement recalls nothing so much as a familiarly encountered feature of his work. His novels teem with characters who find themselves similarly overshadowed by the perverse force of their parts: Wegg, Trotty Veck and Cousin Feenix's fiercely independent limbs, Carker's teeth, Jagger's hands, Bagstock's tumescent flesh, Mrs Merdle's bosom and Marley's head, among others. Rather than observing the unsettling spectacle of Napoleon's melancholy heroism, Dickens finds the too lively part – those risible, self-marching boots – rejects and draws his energies away from the intolerable threat of his continental resurgence. Re-troping Napoleon along such Dickensian lines is the last of Dickens's actions against the general.

Although the Napoleon puppet is recast as comically eccentric, his powers remain unchallenged in the sense he is unnervingly, even supernaturally, self-propelled. At no point does Dickens choose to trace those frantic and farcical limb movements through the wire to the manipulator's technique. Indeed, all of the puppets Dickens describes in Genoa are effectively string-less, disconnected from the point of origin that might allow further enquiry. By excluding the manipulator, Dickens returns to the ambivalent figures found on or about his Christmas tree, specifically the dubious Tumbler whose comic tendency towards autonomous movement is received within a context of anxiety-concealing amusement.

Dickens returned to the Italian marionette theatre once more on his visit to Rome in 1853. There, according to Forster, he avidly sought out and 'eagerly enjoyed' a 'theatre of the smallest pretension'.[33] His visit was prompted by a memory of a recommendation heard in Genoa that the 'finest Marionetti' were to be seen there.[34] Dickens soon discovers the theatre to be nothing more than a sort of stable 'attached

218 DAVID ELLISON

to a decaying palace'.[35] Where this might be read as an elegiac sign of puppetry's declining fortunes, the description that follows suggests a vibrant art:

> It was a wet night, and there was no audience but a party of French officers and ourselves. We all sat together. I never saw anything more amazing than the performance—altogether only an hour long, but managed by as many as ten people, for we saw them all go behind, at the ringing of a bell. The saving of a young lady by a good fairy from the machinations of an enchanter, coupled with the comic business of her servant Pulcinella (the Roman Punch) formed the plot of the first piece. A scolding old peasant woman, who always leaned forward to scold and put her hands in the pockets of her apron, was incredibly natural. Pulcinella, so airy, so merry, so life-like, so graceful, he was irresistible. To see him carrying an umbrella over his mistress's head in a storm, talking to a prodigious giant whom he met in the forest, and going to bed with a pony, were things never to be forgotten. And so delicate are the hands of the people who move them, that every puppet was an Italian, and did exactly what an Italian does. If he pointed at any object, if he saluted anybody, if he laughed, if he cried, he did it as never Englishman did it since Britain first at Heaven's command arose—arose—arose, &c. There was a ballet afterwards, on the same scale, and we really came away quite enchanted with the delicate drollery of the thing. French officers more than ditto.[36]

The doubly noticed presence of the French officers in attendance serves only to affirm a shared appreciation of the play and not to speak to the army's raison d'être: shielding Rome and the Papal States from Italian unification. In other words, Dickens elects to suppress the political meaning of the French audience members and, by extension, the performance itself, which appears only as an exemplary instance of drollery and enchantment. The details he chooses to record are significant in that they systematically reverse or cancel out the disturbing elements encountered in 'The Death of Napoleon'. This time the marionettes do not confuse, alienate or reject his sympathies. Their grace and merriment restore the conditions for pleasurable identification that permitted Dickens to imagine himself, in other settings, as wholly Italian.[37] Unlike their seemingly self-propelled and convulsive Genoese counterparts, the Roman marionettes exhibit an 'incredibly natural' acting style that is, this time, attributed to the 'delicate hands' of the puppeteers. Moreover, their gift to perform things 'never to be forgotten' lay down superlative, if passive, memories, unlike the apparently permanently ruinous experience of the comic ballet witnessed in Genoa. The Roman performance is restorative, integrative and even therapeutic. His appreciative act of witness converts the marionette theatre from a place of local (Genoese) political consequence to one expressive of a tempered folk aesthetic. Dickens returns the marionette and, by extension, the puppet to the quieter and less disruptive category of the mundane, which it to say that they receive the hyperbolic treatment he lavishes upon things he likes.

Notes

1. [Dudley Costello and W. H. Wills], 'The Pedigree of Puppets', *Household Words* 97 (31 January 1852), IV, 438–43, 438.

PUPPETS 219

2. This critical truism is endorsed by Michael Slater, among others. See Slater, *Charles Dickens* (New Haven: Yale University Press, 2009), 3. Also Barbara Hardy, *Dickens and Creativity* (London: Continuum, 2008), 40; John Carey, *The Violent Effigy: A Study of Dickens' Imagination* (London: Faber & Faber, 2011); Katherine Inglis, 'Becoming Automatous: Automata in *The Old Curiosity Shop* and *Our Mutual Friend*', *19: Interdisciplinary Studies in the Long Nineteenth Century* 6 (2008), 1–39 <http://doi.org/10.16995/ntn.471>; Timothy Clark, 'Dickens through Blanchot: The Nightmare Fascination of a World without Interiority', in *Dickens Refigured: Bodies, Desires, and Other Histories*, ed. by John Schad (Manchester: Manchester University Press, 1996), 22–38; and Herbert Sussman and Gerhard Joseph, 'Prefiguring the Posthuman: Dickens and Prosthesis', *Victorian Literature and Culture* 32 (2004), 617–28.

3. 'A Modern Frankenstein', *All the Year Round* New Series 9 (30 January 1869), 1, 200–4, 200. On the itinerant Punch show, see Rosalind Crone's chapter 'About Town with Mr Punch' in *Violent Victorians: Popular Entertainment in Nineteenth-Century London* (Manchester: Manchester University Press, 2012), 39–74.

4. 'A Modern Frankenstein', 201.

5. *Westminster Review*, October 1854, qtd in *Dickens: The Critical Heritage*, ed. by Philip Collins (London: Routledge & Kegan Paul, 1971), 305–8, 307.

6. George Stott, 'Charles Dickens', *Contemporary Review*, January 1869, qtd in Collins, 492–501, 495.

7. [E. B. Hamley], 'Remonstrance with Dickens', *Blackwood's Magazine*, April 1857, qtd in Collins, 358–62, 360.

8. Of course, later critics would rightly celebrate Dickens's attraction to popular culture as one of the strengths of his art. See Juliet John, *Dickens and Mass Culture* (Oxford: Oxford University Press, 2010), and Paul Schlicke, *Dickens and Popular Entertainment*, 2nd edn (London: Routledge, 2016).

9. G. H. Lewes, *Fortnightly Review*, February 1872, qtd in Collins, 569–77, 572–3.

10. Charles Dickens, *Barnaby Rudge* (Philadelphia: Lea & Blanchard, 1842), 63, ch. 13.

11. [Charles Dickens], 'A Christmas Tree', *Household Words* 39 (21 December 1850), II, 289–95, 289.

12. Ibid.

13. Jane Bennett, *Vibrant Matter: A Political Ecology of Things* (Durham, NC: Duke University Press, 2010), 3.

14. Ibid., 292.

15. [Costello and Wills], 441.

16. Ibid.

17. Charles Dickens, *The Old Curiosity Shop* (London: Chapman and Hall, 1841), 176, ch. 16. Subsequent references are inserted parenthetically in the text.

18. 'To Miss M. E. Tayler, 6 November 1849', *The Letters of Charles Dickens*, ed. by Madeline House, Graham Storey et al., Pilgrim/British Academy Edition, 12 vols (Oxford: Clarendon Press, 1965–2002), V (1981), 640.

19. Schlicke, 120.

20. Ibid., 127.

21. Claire Wood, *Dickens and the Business of Death* (Cambridge: Cambridge University Press, 2015), 82.

22. This question of Quilp's autonomy is discussed in Inglis, 14–19; S. J. Newman, *Dickens at Play* (London: Macmillan, 1981), 67, 77–8; and Schlicke, 102.

23. Charles Dickens, *Pictures from Italy* (London: Bradbury & Evans, 1846), 64. Subsequent references are inserted parenthetically in the text.

24. John McCormick, *The Victorian Marionette Theatre* (Iowa City: University of Iowa Press, 2004), 4.

25. Sudhir Hazareesingh, *The Legend of Napoleon* (London: Granta Books, 2004), 122.
26. McCormick, 74.
27. Robert L. Patten, 'Conventions of Georgian Caricature', *Art Journal* 43 (1983), 331–8, 335; Stuart Semmel, *Napoleon and the British* (New Haven: Yale University Press, 2004), 50.
28. See Alexandra Franklin, 'John Bull in a Dream: Fear and Fantasy in the Visual Satires of 1803', in *Resisting Napoleon: The British Response to the Threat of Invasion, 1797–1815*, ed. by Mark Philp (London: Routledge, 2016), 125–40; also Patten.
29. Dickens, qtd by John Forster, *The Life of Charles Dickens*, ed. by J. W. T. Ley (London: Cecil Palmer, 1928), 492.
30. Forster initiates this long critical tradition of observing the effects of Dickens's fascination, calling it the 'profound attraction of repulsion', 11. See also Michael Hollington, *Dickens and the Grotesque* (London: Routledge, 2014) and Steven Marcus, 'Who is Fagin?', in *Dickens: From Pickwick to Dombey* (New York: Basic Books, 1965), 358–78.
31. Slater, 7.
32. Costello and Wills, 443.
33. Forster, 584.
34. Ibid.
35. Ibid.
36. Dickens, qtd by Forster, 584.
37. On Dickens's identification as an Italian, see Michael Hollington and Francesca Orestano, *Dickens and Italy:* Little Dorrit *and* Pictures from Italy (Cambridge: Cambridge Scholars Publishing, 2009), xvi.

Further Reading

Kenneth Gross, *Puppet: An Essay on Uncanny Life* (Chicago: University of Chicago Press, 2011)

John McCormick, Clodagh McCormick and John Phillips, *The Victorian Marionette Theatre* (Iowa City: University of Iowa Press, 2004)

Dassia N. Posner, Claudia Orenstein, and John Bell, eds, *The Routledge Companion to Puppetry and Material Performance* (London: Routledge, 2014)

Part IV

Visual Arts

15

ILLUSTRATION

Julia Thomas

Reading Dickens's Illustrations

'IN THE MATTER OF PICTORIAL EMBELLISHMENT, the writings of Charles Dickens may be regarded as occupying a unique position.'[1] So begins the first major study of Dickens and his illustrators, written by Frederic George Kitton and published in 1899. Kitton was himself an accomplished illustrator, having been apprenticed as a wood engraver on the *Graphic* and later contributing to *The Illustrated London News* and *The English Illustrated Magazine*.[2] There is some authority, then, in Kitton's assertion that the illustrations that accompanied Dickens's writings 'are representative of nearly every branch of the art of the book-illustrator'.[3] Certainly, the illustrations that appeared in Dickens's novels incorporated a variety of material and aesthetic characteristics: they were published in different formats (monthly parts, periodicals, books); they were reproduced using different methods (steel etching, wood engraving); and they were designed by different artists with their own signature styles, from the caricaturist tendencies of George Cruikshank and Hablot K. Browne (Phiz), to the more realist, and even painterly, style of Marcus Stone, the illustrator of *Our Mutual Friend* (1864–5). The publication of Dickens's novels, beginning with *The Pickwick Papers* (1836–7) and ending with the unfinished *The Mystery of Edwin Drood* (1870), coincides with a defining moment in the history of illustration that saw the burgeoning of illustrated fiction, the exponential growth of illustrated magazines, and the birth of illustrated newspapers.[4]

There is a sense, however, in which the images that appear in Dickens's texts are not merely 'representative', to use Kitton's phrase, but play a more participatory role in the history of illustration. Jane R. Cohen, for instance, regards the publication of *The Pickwick Papers* in illustrated monthly parts as leading to a situation where 'Illustrations, once a luxury, now became commonplace'.[5] Dickens also overturned what was a familiar working relationship between author and artist, in which authors provided the letterpress to accompany pictures. This was the genesis of *The Pickwick Papers*, with Dickens commissioned to 'write up' to the pictures of the well-known comic artist Robert Seymour.[6] Seymour's suicide after the second monthly instalment resulted in Dickens assuming control of the narrative; the illustrators who followed Seymour also 'followed' the author's text. Dickens's illustrators do not meekly conform to a model of textual and authorial supremacy, though. Debates still ensue as to whether Seymour was really the creator of *The Pickwick Papers*, with Stephen Jarvis fictionalising this controversy in *Death and Mr Pickwick* (2014).[7] The artist George Cruikshank also famously claimed that he was the originator of *Oliver Twist* and that Dickens penned his novel after seeing some of Cruikshank's pictures.[8]

Seymour's and Cruikshank's claims may or may not be true, but they have shaped critical discussions of Dickens's illustrations, which have focused, almost obsessively, on the relationship between Dickens and 'his' artists. Anecdotes about Dickens correcting and expunging plates, and of the explicit and implicit resistance of his illustrators, have dominated illustration studies, from Kitton's early analysis to Cohen's *Charles Dickens and His Original Illustrators*, published almost a century later, which adopts Kitton's biographical agenda. Accounts by John Harvey and Michael Steig have similarly emphasised the creative relationship between Dickens and Browne.[9]

But there is another, albeit anonymous, partner in this illustrative relationship: the Victorian reader. By focusing on the creative battle between Dickens and his artists, scholarly accounts have marginalised the role of the reader in creating the meanings of these illustrations. Where Victorian readers are mentioned, they are usually figured as passive, even ignorant, observers, who are unable to 'decode' the wealth of information in the images. Steig goes as far as to assert that the details of the illustrations are so rich and their viewing requires so much knowledge that we are 'better readers' than Dickens's own contemporaries.[10] Underpinning such comments is an assumption about authorial and artistic intentions: the idea that the conscious meanings of the author/illustrator are made manifest in the words and pictures, which the reader then absorbs, or is meant to absorb. As Steig puts it, 'Even if not a single Victorian reader recognized the complexities of the illustrations, they are there, like the complexities of the texts; they are at once an expression of Dickens' intentions and Browne's interpretations.'[11]

But the meanings generated by readers are also *there* in Dickens's illustrated novels. The complexities of illustrations lie as much in the reading of these novels as in the (largely unknown) intentions of the author and artists. The question that is central to this analysis, then, is to what extent, and how, were Dickens's novels read as specifically illustrated works? It is a question that has not been addressed, despite its significance for understanding how readers engaged with this bi-medial (verbal–visual) form, and for the broader issue of the cultural status of illustration and its conceptualisation as an 'art'. Even those critics who discuss the Victorian reading of Dickens's novels are noticeably silent on how the illustrations figured in this reading.[12] Yet the fact that Dickens's novels were illustrated was integral to their interpretation, with only two of the novels published in their original form without pictures.[13] As one Victorian commentator put it, Dickens's words and illustrations 'meet the public eye together'.[14]

The silence of scholars around the reading of Dickens's illustrated novels is mirrored by Victorian readers themselves. The few clues that exist about how these novels were read are scattered across different sources, such as diaries, letters, auto/ biographies and reviews, each of which has its own contextual imperatives. This silence, however, is itself revealing, suggesting the extent to which illustrations were taken for granted, regarded as inferior to the text and not worthy of comment, or were difficult to describe in words. Indeed, I would place the reading of Dickens's illustrated novels at the centre of an emerging vocabulary of illustration, as the catalyst for articulating the meanings and definitions of this hybrid genre, and as a direct intervention in the making of the novels and the discourses that surround them.

In what follows, I shall analyse what it meant to read Dickens's illustrated novels in their original contexts. Of course, there is no single method or type of 'reading', and this plurality is intensified in the diverse formats in which the novels appeared as well as in the fact that this reading is also a viewing. These novels challenge the very definition of what it means to 'read' by transgressing the boundaries and temporality of this activity: the illustrations are viewed in their conjunction with Dickens's words, but they also exist as prior to, and distinct from, the text, and they linger on after the text has been laid aside.

Beyond Words

Beginning to read Dickens's illustrated novels is less of a beginning, a fixed starting point, than an activity that happens beyond the words, or before the words are read. The model of illustrative antecedence is one that characterises the Victorian reading of Dickens's novels where the pictures came before the words. Many readers would have been introduced to Dickens's novels through the illustrations displayed in the windows of booksellers' shops and on outdoor stalls. The rise of the illustrated novel in this period presented new opportunities for advertising books in terms of their illustrations, with booksellers mimicking the popular displays of print sellers' shops. Book openings that showed only text were less likely to attract the attention of passers-by: the print might be small and time was needed to read the words, but illustrated page openings could attract even the most fleeting glances. Readers of Dickens often stayed for longer at the bookseller's window. The publisher Henry Vizetelly recounts how '"Pickwick" was then appearing in its green monthly covers, and no sooner was a new number published than needy admirers flattened their noses against the booksellers' windows, eager to secure a good look at the etchings'.[15] As Vizetelly's observation suggests, the reading of the illustrated novel was part of the urban landscape, a mobile, public activity that privileged the visuality of the images.

When the monthly parts were removed from the window and purchased by the consumer, the illustrations still assumed priority. The 'green' cover to which Vizetelly refers was the highly recognisable wrapping that encased Dickens's monthly instalments. The wrapper was a heavily illustrated title page that included visual motifs, emblems, characters and scenes from the novel, presenting the story in a condensed graphic form before it was read. The cover, as one Victorian reviewer remarked, presented a 'pictorial foreshadowing of the story'.[16] The effect of 'foreshadowing' extended to the plates themselves, which in the monthly parts appeared after an advertising section (itself illustrated) and before the text. This model of the prior illustration was retained in *Oliver Twist* (1837–9), which was serialised in the periodical *Bentley's Miscellany* rather than in separate monthly parts. In this novel, the steel etching by Cruikshank was positioned on the page facing the beginning of the instalment and thus showed an event from later in the text.

The placement of these illustrations before the words meant that they often acted as 'spoilers'. The final number of *Little Dorrit* (1855–7) began with an illustration of the heroine signing the marriage register, leading one critic to comment that 'the illustration at the beginning [. . .] sufficiently indicate[s] to the reader the principal event in the *dénouement*'.[17] There are instances where this prior positioning of the illustrations is exploited in their pictorial content. The image of Little Dorrit's

Figure 15.1 Hablot K. Browne ('Phiz'), 'Our Pew at Church', an illustration for Charles Dickens's *David Copperfield* (1849–50). Courtesy of the Charles Dickens Museum, London [F2994].

nuptials might have promised readers a happy ending, but there is a more troubling air hanging over the presence of an unidentified man with prominent sideburns, who stares at David Copperfield's mother in the first monthly illustration for the novel (1849–50) (Figure 15.1). The man, standing in the pew in the left foreground, is not mentioned in the textual episode relating to this picture. It is only by returning to this image after reading the rest of the instalment, or by recognising the figure from a later illustration, that the reader would be able to identify him as Mr Murdstone, David's future stepfather.[18]

This illustrative 'before-ness', characteristic of the first incarnations of Dickens's novels, was partly a consequence of the technical processes by which the images were reproduced. As steel etching was an intaglio method, the images could not be printed on the same page as the 'relief' letterpress, whereas the woodcut illustrations for *The Old Curiosity Shop* (1840–1) and *Barnaby Rudge* (1841), serialised in the weekly periodical *Master Humphrey's Clock*, could be interspersed with the words. When the monthly parts appeared as volumes, the green wrapper was disposed of and the plates were bound in proximity to the textual moment depicted. However, it is likely that, even when the images were placed near the relevant text, they were still viewed before the words, with the readers' eyes drawn to the pictures and their fingers flicking through the pages to seek them out. The actor William Macready sees the death of Little Nell before he reads it. On opening the November number of

Master Humphrey's Clock, he 'saw one print in it of the dear dead child that gave a dead chill to my blood'. The prior viewing of the image here both repels him and compels him to read on: 'I dread to read it, but I must get it over.'[19]

The fact that the pictures came first is crucial for an understanding of how contemporary readers interpreted Dickens's novels. The illustrations precipitate the movement and flow of the reading process. They are propulsive, driving the reader forwards (from the prior images to the text) and backwards (from the text to the images at the beginning of the instalment). In this way, illustrations can be seen to participate in what narrative theorists have termed the 'dynamics' of a text, the progression through time by which readers make sense of a story.[20] Peter Brooks describes the reading of plot as 'a form of desire that carries us forward, onward, through the text'.[21] While they enact this narrative drive, however, illustrations also complicate it in significant ways. The reader's desire for meaning, which is aroused by the textual plot in unillustrated novels, might have different stimuli and motivations in novels with illustrations. The appearance of the pictures before the words is a promissory note, a teaser of what is to come, whether this is the textual 'explanation' of what the image shows ('Our Pew at Church') or its realisation and repetition (the marriage of Little Dorrit or the death of Little Nell). The illustrations, in other words, elicit a desire *for* the text.

It is a desire, moreover, that does not necessarily keep time with the words. The organising structure of the plot and the movement of a narrative from beginning to end are subverted in those illustrations that appear before the text begins and that point forward to events in the textual future. The presence of these illustrations instigates a different narrative dynamics to reading a text without illustrations because the pictures influence and shape how the words themselves are read. As one Victorian reader of Dickens remarked, 'The artist's Pickwick dictates from the first the reader's notion of the Pickwick of the text.'[22] It is easy to envisage how the comic figure of Pickwick represented here with his companion, Sam Weller, became embedded in the reader's imagination (Figure 15.2). Appearing in the final (double) monthly part, this image draws together those aspects of Pickwick made familiar to readers over the course of the novel's publication. Indeed, although it was published at the end of the novel's run, this illustration was also placed at its beginning, serving as the frontispiece for the novel when it was bound together in book form.

In their position of anteriority, illustrations 'dictated' how readers interpreted the text. They also determined how readers filled textual gaps. This had some bearing for the iconic figure of Pickwick himself, for at no point does Dickens specify that he is rotund. This textual omission, 'rectified' by the illustrations, was picked up by Victorian reviewers: 'only a faint notion could be formed of the outward man of the great Pickwick himself from the scattered hints afforded in the letter-press,' wrote a critic in *The Quarterly Review*, 'namely, that he wore *tights*, gaiters, and spectacles. It is the pencil, not the pen, which completes the vivid conception we undoubtedly possess of his personal appearance.'[23] In this account, the details of the illustrations supplement and take precedence over the 'scattered hints' of the words.

Although the conjunction of text and image is an important aspect of how these illustrated novels were read (and I will turn to this later), the positioning of the illustrations, their sense of 'before-ness', and the shaping of the words by the pictures suggest the relative autonomy of the illustrations. This autonomy is intensified in the way

Figure 15.2 Hablot K. Browne ('Phiz'), Frontispiece for the final 'double' number of Charles Dickens's *The Pickwick Papers* (1836–7). Courtesy of the Charles Dickens Museum, London [F538].

that these illustrations were interpreted in terms of their distinct iconographic features and traditions. Scholars have pointed out the indebtedness of Dickens's illustrations to other art forms, most notably satirical prints and paintings (note, for instance, the allusion to William Hogarth's print *The Sleeping Congregation* (1736) in Phiz's 'Our Pew at Church' for *David Copperfield*). However, illustrations were also viewed in relation to other illustrations, as part of a complex network of illustrative allusions and references that I have called 'affillustration'.[24] The affiliative interplay between illustrations is generated when readers turn from one illustration to another, or when they generate their own semantic groupings of illustrations. One contemporary reader singled out the illustrations of Captain Cuttle in *Dombey and Son* (1846–8), reading across them to identify the illustrations where his hook swapped hand.[25] 'Our Pew at Church' generates affiliative links with Phiz's other church scenes, including 'I Am Married' (*David Copperfield*, June 1850), which, in its composition and pictorial details, explicitly references the first illustration in the novel.

Affillustration raises the possibility that, when Victorian readers read Dickens, the meanings of the texts were informed by a relation between illustrations that was, to a certain extent, constituted 'outside' the words.[26] Such affiliative networks were highly familiar in the illustrated publications that framed Dickens's novels. 'Recapitulations' or 'gatherings' of illustrations by artists like Seymour, Cruikshank and John Leech (the illustrator of *A Christmas Carol* in 1843) appeared in the 1830s on the front page of issues of the popular journal *Bell's Life in London* and in the publication of its annual broadsides.[27] These recapitulations presented multiple illustrations together and, in so doing, placed them in dialogue with each other. Likewise, in the middle decades of the century, collections of illustrations from disparate works and by different artists were gathered together in popular gift books such as *The Cornhill Gallery* (1864) and the poetry anthology *A Round of Days* (1866). The advertisement for *A Round of Days* describes how the material was 'promiscuously inserted – scenes of various, and, perhaps, of opposite kinds following close together'.[28] This 'promiscuity' was also evident in extra-illustrated (or grangerised) editions of Dickens's works, with illustrations sold in batches for readers to create their own illustrated copies.

The reading of multiple illustrations side by side and across Dickens's work had the effect of creating a 'Dickensian' style of illustration. One reviewer describes his reading of *Bleak House* (1852–3) in precisely these terms: 'Another light-green shilling book, having a most suggestive title page by "Phiz," opens with two engravings, which one recognises at once as illustrating the text of Dickens.'[29] Illustrations might instantly be recognisable as 'illustrating the text of Dickens', but affillustration also means that the illustrations were read in a way that was not necessarily determined by the text. Victorian readers coming to a novel illustrated by Cruikshank would have viewed those illustrations in the context of Cruikshank's illustrations for other texts, a mode of reading that is implied, and even encouraged, in reviews where illustrations by specific artists are seen (and critiqued) together. Cruikshank's women, for example, were collectively described as 'vulgar', while Phiz was lambasted for endlessly repeating his 'tall Copperfield young man and young lady with flowing skirts'.[30] Illustrations were also frequently brought together in exhibitions, with the acclaimed Cruikshank exhibition, held in Exeter Hall in 1863, showing some of the artist's illustrations for Dickens.

This reading of illustration as a body of work that crosses textual boundaries is suggested in Henry James's recollection of his boyhood reading of *Oliver Twist*, where he questions if his enjoyment of the novel stemmed mainly from George Cruikshank's 'splendid' images:

> It [*Oliver Twist*] perhaps even seemed to me more Cruikshank's than Dickens's; it was a thing of such vividly terrible images, and all marked with that peculiarity of Cruikshank that the offered flowers or goodnesses, the scenes and figures intended to comfort and cheer, present themselves under his hand as but more subtly sinister, or more suggestively queer, than the frank badnesses and horrors. The nice people and the happy moments, in the plates, frightened me almost as much as the low and the awkward [. . .].[31]

For James, it is Cruikshank's distinct illustrative style, his 'peculiarity', that determines how he reads the novel. Moreover, this reading is detached from Dickens's words, and even from the intention of Cruikshank himself. As James asserts, 'the scenes and figures *intended* to comfort and cheer, present themselves under his hand

230 JULIA THOMAS

as but more subtly sinister, or more suggestively queer, than the frank badnesses and horrors.' What James makes clear is that reading Dickens's illustrated novels is not solely an interaction with the words, but also lies in the connections that the reader makes between and across illustrations.

Between the Lines

The reading of Dickens's illustrated novels, then, takes place beyond the words: in the viewing of prior illustrations and in an affiliative interplay of images that transgresses the confines of the book. But this reading is also bound up in the conjunction of word and image, in the space between the etched or engraved lines of the illustration and the written lines of the letterpress. Notions of how the pictures and the words were read together can be gleaned from contemporary reviews. It is important, of course, to distinguish between professional reviewers, who were writing for particular audiences, and 'common readers'. As Richard D. Altick argues, 'it must be borne in mind that *vox critici* is by no means *vox populi*': reviewers are 'exceptional readers', who do not speak for the majority.[32] Nevertheless, the comments of reviewers are of some significance in the context of Dickens's illustrated novels. Spanning a period that can only be described as an illustrative revolution, the reviews of Dickens's novels actively construct ways of reading illustrated texts, creating a new discourse for illustration and effectively teaching 'common readers' how to read this bi-medial form. It is a critical reading, moreover, that is enmeshed in ideological and evaluative assumptions about the status and role of illustration as an art and its relation to the text.

In some reviews, there is a reticence to notice the illustrations at all, with critics either ignoring the images or banishing them to the end of the discussion, a position that effectively reverses their position at the beginning of Dickens's instalments. Here, they receive only scant attention: '"Phiz" has furnished, as usual, two good illustrative sketches of the principal scenes described'; or, 'The two illustrations by Phiz are very indifferent.'[33] Other reviews, though, attempt to read the novels as a unified form in which the words and images are interpreted together. As a reviewer of *Bleak House* comments, 'For a picture of these characters, and of the scenes of joy and sadness in which they played their part, we refer our readers to the chapters and illustrations.'[34] The use of the word 'picture' is telling here, referring as it does both to the words and the images, the 'chapters and illustrations'. The text and the illustration signify together, and this togetherness is embedded in the act of reading: the readers (both the critic and the imagined readers constructed in the review) are invited to interpret the words and the illustrations in their mutual relationship. Such commentary moves beyond individual responses to the novels to suggest the ways in which illustrated texts can be read.

These endorsements of illustration, however, went hand in hand with criticisms of the genre, which became more pronounced as the novelty of *The Pickwick Papers* wore off and the number of illustrated texts in circulation began to grow. As one reviewer of Dickens's novels remarked:

the vast popularity of these works may, perhaps, in some degree be owing to the indolence of the reading public, and [. . .] the very clever 'illustrations' which accompany them all, may have contributed greatly to their success. No reader need ever task his mind's eye to form a picture corresponding to the full description; he has but to turn the page, and there stands the Pickwick, Pecksniff, or Tom Pinch, embodied to his hand, and kindly saving him the labour of thought.[35]

The reading of Dickens's illustrated novels is defined here as a lazy form of reading that thwarts the imaginative engagement with the words and appeals to an indolent public or what another critic calls '*idle* readers'.[36] This was a judgement both of a certain type (or class) of reader and of the illustrated novel more broadly. The cultural status of the illustrated novel in the period was far from secure. As a genre, illustration was not inherently regarded as an 'art', with all the values that entailed. Rather, its classification as art depended on the cultural status of the text, the author and the artist, factors that were often separate from the actual qualities and characteristics of the image. The status of the reader was also integral to these value judgements. In this review, it is the type of reader ('indolent') along with the sheer number of readers (illustrated works have a 'vast popularity') that suggest that the illustrated novel is removed from the ideals of fine art. Illustrations are mass-produced and consumed. Their 'cleverness' does not lie in their aesthetic value but in the way they manipulate the reader and the text, disabling the 'mind's eye' and draining the artistic effects of the words. Indeed, the repeated assertion that illustrations 'dumb down' the text is bound up in an evaluative judgement about the novels themselves, with the suggestion that those works that rely on illustration are inadequate and inferior: 'The more perfect the letterpress, the less it needs graphic aid.'[37]

So where does this leave Dickens's letterpress? As less than 'perfect'? The criticism of illustration threatened to devalue Dickens's words. There was an increasing awareness, for example, that illustration played its own part in influencing Dickens's writing, and not always for the better:

> The writer's '*mind's* eye' becomes thus obedient, insensibly, to the eye of his body; and the result is, a perpetual and unconscious straining after situations and attitudes which will admit of being similarly illustrated. Thus the writer follows the caricaturist, instead of the caricaturist following the writer; and *principal* and *accessory* change places.[38]

In a culture dominated by illustrations it was becoming increasingly difficult to determine whether the artist or the author came first. *The Pickwick Papers* might have privileged the author of the illustrated novel by making Dickens the creative lead, but, as this review suggests, the situation is rather more complex. Illustrations are so prevalent that authors begin to 'see' in terms of illustrations, 'straining' to write scenes that can be presented in pictures. The 'proper' aesthetic order, therefore, is challenged, even though it is an order that this particular reviewer is keen to reinstate (note, for instance, the derogatory use of the word 'caricaturist' instead of the more respectable 'artist' and the labelling of the writer as 'principal' and the illustrator as 'accessory').

If the hierarchical relation between the author and illustrator is unfixed, then so are the activities that define them. The blurring of the roles of the writer and the illustrator is a familiar trope in critical readings of the novels where Dickens is described in terms of his visual and 'artistic faculty'.[39] *The Spectator* went as far as to describe

232   JULIA THOMAS

Dickens as 'the Cruikshank of writers'.[40] This slippage was potentially problematic because, if Dickens was 'the Cruikshank of writers', then he was also a caricaturist, and it was this aspect of his writing that was frequently criticised.[41] When the merging of the text and illustrations went too far, however, they could always be torn asunder. Reviewers defended Dickens by censuring the illustrations: Dickens never caricatures, it was argued; the illustrations just make readers imagine he does.[42] Such comments, of course, are themselves testament to the extent to which illustrations impacted on the reading of the novels.

In fact, it was Dickens's elevation above the illustrations that helped to secure his reputation. Assertions about the superiority of the text to the illustrations are exemplified in this popular account of his career from 1865:

> When, some thirty years ago, Messrs Chapman & Hall began to look for a clever young man to write comic letterpress to the late Mr Seymour's etchings, and found at last their clever young man up two stairs in Furnival's Inn, in the person of an energetic reporter to a daily newspaper, they desired less a great master in letters – whose fame was destined to be world-wide, and who was to hold for more than a quarter of a century almost undivided sway over the readers of books wherever the English language is spoken or understood – than a facile and accommodating hack. But the clever young man very speedily threw the illustrator into the background. For a long time the spiteful and stupid, amazed and envious at a success so rapid and so unprecedented, were fond of asserting that at least half the merit of his works consisted in the illustrations. Yet poor Seymour was succeeded by Hablot Browne, and George Cruikshank, and Cattermole, and Marcus Stone; while at intervals there appeared work from Mr Dickens' pen without any illustrations at all; and the clever young man kept on his way, ripened into maturity, and grew every year in excellence and in power. George Cruikshank's 'Fagan [sic] in the Condemned Cell,' and 'Sykes Attempting to Destroy the Dogs [sic],' were no doubt marvellous etchings. The spectacles and gaiters of Mr Pickwick, the shirt-collar and eye-glass of Mr Pecksniff, are graphic creations which will ever be associated with the name of 'Phiz;' but 'Oliver Twist' would have been a triumphant success without Cruikshank's etchings; and the 'Pickwick Papers' and 'Martin Chuzzlewit,' in their latest and cheapest form, bereft of any pictorial embellishments, are as absorbing as ever. The truth simply amounts to this, that the young newspaper reporter, in the words of one of his earliest and one of his most ardent admirers, William Makepeace Thackeray, 'came calmly among us and took his place at the head of English Literature.' His genius and his perseverance have enabled him to keep his place ever since.[43]

This description of the rise of the 'clever young man' to the status of towering 'genius' in some ways speaks to the growing cultural capital of the author as opposed to the illustrator. But the illustrators listed here were all celebrated and prominent figures. There is a tension throughout between the construction of the superiority of the author and an uncomfortable awareness of those aspects of his novels that are 'graphic' rather than textual creations. Paradoxically, it is the very success of the illustrations on which Dickens's heroic status depends. His position at 'the head of English Literature' is constituted by his ability to 'throw off' the illustrations, however 'marvellous' (although, interestingly, it is the publishers of the cheap editions who are doing most of the discarding here by stripping away the illustrations).

Dickens himself seems to have recognised a need for distance from the illustrations. His public readings of the novels sometimes disappointed members of the audience because of their failure to impersonate the illustrations. In the words of one disgruntled critic:

> There are few people among those who have heard DICKENS read who were not surprised and even disappointed at his impersonation of the immortal PICKWICK, whose tight gaiters, broad-brimmed hat, and glasses are, through the medium of PHIZ and SEYMOUR's pictures, so familiar to all of us.[44]

Dickens's public performances might have disappointed, but they form part of a tradition of reciting these novels aloud, which is attested to by numerous Victorian readers. In what is a strikingly familiar picture, the architect Charles H. Reilly remembers Saturday evenings round the fire listening to his father read Dickens.[45] Likewise, Rose Macaulay remembers her father reading Dickens to the family, while Algernon Swinburne developed a fondness for reading Dickens's novels aloud in his later years.[46] This reading aloud seems to have crossed class divides. The father of the trade unionist Alice Foley was a drunk and violent factory worker in Bolton, but 'when in sober mood, he read aloud to the family the novels of Dickens'.[47]

One might assume that the activity of reading Dickens aloud was one in which the illustrations did not figure, but this was not necessarily the case. There is often the suggestion of a prior private reading in which the images could have influenced the subsequent recitation. The playwright Herman Merivale tells of his grandfather preparing to read *The Pickwick Papers* to his large family: 'He always studied them himself for an hour or two, in order to be able to read them aloud with decent gravity.'[48] The performative nature of these readings might have retained more than a trace of the illustrations. William Henry Hudson, who grew up on a ranch in Argentina, records that his tutor would read to the household for two hours every evening:

> Dickens was then the most popular writer in the world, and he usually read Dickens, to the delight of his listeners. Here he could display his histrionic qualities to the full. He impersonated every character in the book, endowing him with voice, gestures, manner, and expression that fitted him perfectly. It was more like a play than a reading.[49]

It is tempting to think that the tutor's 'impersonations' were of the pictures as well as the words. Indeed, if the readings were like plays, the plays themselves were like the illustrations. It is well documented that stage versions of Dickens's novels drew explicitly on the illustrations, using scenery that realised these images, costumes that replicated them, and tableaux that recreated them.[50]

The domestic and private readings of Dickens, of course, remained largely that. Those readings that are easier to find evidence of are the public and communal ones. 'Penny Readings' held in town halls, schools and mechanics' institutes were a popular form of entertainment, with Dickens featuring as one of the most prominent authors.[51] It is likely that the illustrations played a part in how these performances

234   JULIA THOMAS

were received by the audience (thus the 'disappointment' when some spectators saw Dickens). Even those spectators who were illiterate would have seen the illustrations on display and in public circulation. Revealingly, the anthologies for these Penny Readings were frequently illustrated, suggesting that the pictures had a specific role in informing how the texts were read aloud. *Cassell's Penny Readings*, originally issued in weekly parts between 1866 and 1868, contained numerous illustrations to accompany excerpts from Dickens's work, including those by Cruikshank and Phiz. As the editor, Tom Hood, states, *Cassell's Penny Readings* were intended as 'a hand-book for public readings' and were published serially on the basis that, 'in the absence of a Public Reading, some member of your family may give you a Home Reading'.[52] The illustrations here govern the reading of the words: 'The drawings will, by the direct appeal they make to the eye, assist materially in impressing on your memories the recollection of the passages placed before you.'[53] Illustrations, therefore, influence how the words are read aloud as well as how they are listened to.

Etched in the Memory

The address to the reader in *Cassell's Penny Readings* draws attention to an enigmatic and intangible quality of illustrations: their ability to leave a lasting 'impression'. The reading of Dickens's illustrated novels, which begins before the reading of the text, extends beyond a material and physical engagement with the words. The author and illustrator George du Maurier commented that illustrations 'may continue to haunt the memory when the letterpress they illustrate is forgotten'.[54] Du Maurier's comments raise the intriguing possibility that illustrations are remembered even when the book has been closed and the textual lines have faded away. This possibility is suggested in the modern findings of neuroscience and psychology where the so-called 'picture superiority effect' indicates that images are more likely to be remembered than words, possibly because they are encoded twice in the brain in the form of visual and verbal codes whereas words are encoded only once.[55] Of course, many Victorian readers would have actively memorised and successfully recalled quotations from Dickens's novels. The point, however, is that, once seen, illustrations are never quite forgotten.

Contemporary readers of Dickens comment on this after-effect of the illustrations: 'it is difficult to say, on laying down the book [*Oliver Twist*], how much of the powerful impression we are conscious of may be due, not to the pen, but to the pencil.'[56] The use of the term 'impression' to describe this illustrative effect implies that the images are printed on the brain, or (a more common phrase) on the 'mind's eye', just as they are printed onto paper. This characteristic of illustration is also described by Henry James in his account of his boyhood reading of Dickens, a reading that is framed by the immediacy of the illustrations (they are 'vividly terrible' and 'frighten' him), and the fact that they persist as memories that influence his recollection of real people: Dr Parkhurst, a respectable but feared dentist, 'extremely resembles, to my mind's eye, certain figures in Phiz's illustrations to Dickens'; while Mr Dolmidge, the writing master, 'was to remain with me a picture of somebody in Dickens, one of the Phiz if not the Cruikshank pictures'.[57]

In a sense, the Victorian reading of Dickens's illustrated novels always depends on the fact that the images endure as memories, whether it is the memory of the illustrations seen in the booksellers' windows, the memory of the illustrations that appear at the beginning of the monthly parts, the memory of other illustrations in other publications, or the memory of illustrations that are recollected when the text is read aloud. In 'Our Pew at Church', memories and the act of remembering are part of the content of the image itself. *David Copperfield*, described by its first-person narrator as a 'written memory', is presented in Phiz's illustration as a specifically pictorial memory that presents a different viewpoint from the words.[58] In place of the textual perspective of the child (who sees the church as a potential playground), the image, with its dozing parishioners and dusty, cobwebbed artefacts, is the stuff of grown-up, adult satire, as its allusion to Hogarth's *The Sleeping Congregation* implies. There are other anachronistic elements in this image: in the right foreground, staring directly at the bewhiskered Mr Murdstone, is yet another unidentified male figure. A reader familiar with the novel's later illustrations might notice the resemblance between this figure and illustrations of David Copperfield as an older man.[59] The inclusion of the older David in this scene of his childhood (his younger self sits in the pew in the back right) emphasises the gap between the textual and visual memory. As he stares at Murdstone, the figure is caught in the act of looking back and remembering, an act that characterises the reading of Dickens's illustrated novels. Indeed, the Victorian viewer might also have recalled a similarity in features between this figure and the numerous portraits of Dickens that were in circulation, including the engraving of Daniel Maclise's portrait of Dickens that had appeared in the last number of *Nicholas Nickleby* (1838–9) and was placed as the frontispiece to the first book edition. The prominent side parting with the tuft of hair over the ear was a feature not only of David Copperfield, but of Dickens himself. Phiz's church, packed full of memorials, stands as a memorial to Dickens, with the ambiguous figure in the foreground evoking both the work and its author.

The reading of Dickens's illustrated novels, then, is inherently paradoxical: illustration is seen to inhibit the imaginative interaction with the words, but it can also function as a mechanism for remembering the text. Indeed, a testament to the success of illustration as a memorial tool can be seen in more recent commemorations of Dickens. Between 1992 and 2003 an illustration of the cricket match between Dingley Dell and All Muggleton from *The Pickwick Papers* featured on the £10 note alongside a portrait of Dickens. At times of memorialisation, the illustrations stand in a metonymic relation to the novels as a substitute for the text. On the centenary of Dickens's death in 1970 the Royal Mail issued stamps showing illustrations from Dickens's novels, a practice that was repeated for the bicentenary of Dickens's birth in 2012. One of the highlights of the bicentenary was a film installation at the Museum of London that used Robert William Buss's memorial painting *Dickens's Dream* (1875) as a backdrop for animated versions of the illustrations, including Cruikshank's Oliver, who hobbles up to the workhouse master, bowl and spoon in hand, to ask for more. When the incensed master throws the spoon behind him, it promptly boomerangs back and hits him on the head.[60] Buss was himself one of Dickens's illustrators, having stepped in to replace Seymour for the third monthly instalment of *The Pickwick Papers* (Buss was the illustrator responsible for the cricket match used on the £10 note). He was subsequently dismissed in favour of Phiz. His painting of *Dickens's Dream*, which shows Dickens's characters swarming around the author as he relaxes in his chair, might be an act of wish fulfilment (Buss creates the illustrations here that he was never destined to produce for the published work), but it also emphasises the way that illustration is

236 JULIA THOMAS

implicated in the making of memories and memorials. The 'clever young man' discovered in Furnival's Inn has morphed into a godlike creative force, but he has done so through the vibrancy of his *visual* imagination. Dickens dreams in illustrations.

Perhaps the Victorian reader also dreamed in illustrations. The reading of Dickens's novels created a new language and vocabulary for illustration, a way of understanding and articulating the meanings and parameters of the genre at a time when it was rapidly expanding. These parameters were often fluid, with illustrations undermining their temporal limitations, seen before the words, and remaining long after the text was laid aside. An awareness of this complex and multifaceted process leads to a stark realisation: that the experience of reading Dickens's novels *with* the illustrations is fundamentally different from the experience of reading those same novels *without* the illustrations.[61] This difference is embedded in every aspect of this reading: in the engagement with the materiality of the illustrated text, in the multiple modes of interpretation that the illustrated novel enables, and in the ways that these illustrated texts are remembered. It is a realisation that should inform our own reading of Dickens's novels. An unillustrated reading is not so much a misreading of the novels, but it is a missed reading, a lost opportunity to analyse the interplay of text and image that defined Dickens's novels in their original form, and a forgetting that this reading was also a viewing.

Notes

1. Frederic G. Kitton, *Dickens and His Illustrators* (London: Redway, 1899), vii.
2. See Simon Houfe, *The Dictionary of Nineteenth-Century British Book Illustrators and Caricaturists* (Suffolk: Antique Collectors' Club, 1998), 200.
3. Kitton, vii.
4. Richard Maxwell has argued that this burgeoning of illustration came about because of innovations in book production and publishing, the rise of British literature as an institution, and a desire for visual stimulation among the public. See *The Victorian Illustrated Book*, ed. by Richard Maxwell (Charlottesville: University of Virginia Press, 2002), xxiii–xxvi. The growth of illustration was also precipitated by changes in printing technologies that brought these images to a mass market. See Geoffrey Wakeman, *Victorian Book Illustration: The Technical Revolution* (Detroit: Gale Research, 1973).
5. Jane R. Cohen, *Charles Dickens and His Original Illustrators* (Columbus: Ohio State University Press, 1980), 4.
6. Brian Maidment's essay in this volume discusses Robert Seymour's varied output in more detail, including his interest in graphic narrative.
7. Stephen Jarvis, *Death and Mr Pickwick* (London: Vintage, 2014).
8. This claim was made public in R. Shelton Mackenzie, *Life of Charles Dickens* (Philadelphia: T. B. Peterson, 1870), 164–5.
9. Michael Steig, *Dickens and Phiz* (Bloomington: Indiana University Press, 1978); John Harvey, *Victorian Novelists and Their Illustrators* (New York: New York University Press, 1971).
10. Michael Steig, 'The Critic and the Illustrated Novel: Mr. Turveydrop from Gillroy [*sic*] to *Bleak House*', *Huntington Library Quarterly* 36.1 (November 1972), 55–67, 57–8.
11. Ibid., 5.
12. See, for example, Amy Cruse's classic account of Victorian readers, which does not mention Dickens's illustrations: *The Victorians and Their Books* (London: Allen & Unwin, 1935). George H. Ford is also silent on illustrations in *Dickens and His Readers* (New York: Norton, 1965). Richard D. Altick gestures towards the issue of how illustrations

ILLUSTRATION 237

were read, but concludes that we simply do not know, in 'Varieties of Readers' Response: The Case of *Dombey and Son*', *The Yearbook of English Studies* 10, Special Number (1980), 70–94, 92–4. More recently, Sarah Winter describes the memory formed by 'interconnected verbal and visual elements' in her discussion of Dickens's mass audience, but illustrations are not central to this discussion. Sarah Winter, *The Pleasures of Memory: Learning to Read with Charles Dickens* (New York: Fordham University Press, 2011), 16.

13. These were *Hard Times* (1854) and *Great Expectations* (1860–1), which were illustrated in subsequent book editions. The lack of illustrations did not escape censure. Reviewing *Great Expectations*, one critic commented that 'We want the old serial, in the old green cover, with the old, charmingly perplexing emblematic frontispiece, and the old etchings by Phiz'. 'Literature and Art', *Illustrated London News* (20 July 1861), 53.

14. 'Illustrated Literature', *The Reader* 2.50 (12 December 1863), 687–8, 688.

15. Henry Vizetelly, *Glances Back through Seventy Years: Autobiographical and Other Reminiscences*, 2 vols (London: Kegan Paul, Trench, Trübner, 1893), i, 123.

16. 'Mr. Dickens's New Story', *London Review* (30 April 1864), 473.

17. 'Literature', *John Bull and Britannia* (29 June 1857), 410.

18. The other illustration in which Murdstone appears is 'The Momentous Interview' (September 1849).

19. *The Journal of William Charles Macready 1832–1851*, ed. by J. C. Trewin (London: Longmans, 1967), 169.

20. See James Phelan, 'Narrative Progression', in *Narrative Dynamics: Essays on Time, Plot, Closure, and Frames*, ed. by Brian Richardson (Columbus: Ohio State University Press, 2002), 211–16.

21. Peter Brooks, *Reading for the Plot: Design and Intention in Narrative* (Cambridge, MA: Harvard University Press, 1984), 37.

22. 'Illustrated Literature', 688.

23. *Quarterly Review* 59.118 (October 1837), 497.

24. For a discussion of 'affillustration', see Julia Thomas, *Nineteenth-Century Illustration and the Digital: Studies in Word and Image* (New York: Palgrave Macmillan, 2017), 96–102.

25. 'Our Illustrations', *Graphic* (11 April 1874), 335.

26. By 'outside the words', I am referring to a distinct relationship between illustrations that is not determined by the texts illustrated. J. Hillis Miller points to the repeated motifs and structures in Cruikshank's illustrations (what I would call 'affillustration') to argue against the notion that the illustrations are simply mimetic and represent a real world 'outside' the text. See 'The Fiction of Realism: *Sketches by Boz*, *Oliver Twist*, and Cruikshank's Illustrations', in *Dickens Centennial Essays*, ed. by Ada Nisbet and Blake Nevius (Berkeley: University of California Press, 1971), 85–153.

27. See Brian Maidment, 'The Draughtsman's Contacts: Robert Seymour and the Humorous Periodical Press in the 1830s', *Journal of European Periodical Studies* 1.1 (Summer 2016), 37–52, 40.

28. Advertisement by the Brothers Dalziel, *A Round of Days* (London: Routledge, 1866).

29. 'Literature', *Era* (14 March 1852), 10.

30. 'The Illustrating Artists of Great Britain', *Fine Arts' Journal* 1.20 (20 March 1847), 312; 'The Arts', *Critic* 14.331 (15 January 1855), 39.

31. Henry James, 'A Small Boy and Others', in *Henry James: Autobiography*, ed. by Frederick W. Dupee (London: Allen, 1956), 69.

32. Altick, 75.

33. 'Literature', *Caledonian Mercury* (10 September 1838), 4; 'Reviews on Literature', *Musical World* 21.41 (10 October 1846), 500.

34. '*Bleak House*. By Charles Dickens', *Eclectic Review* 6 (December 1853), 665–79, 670.

35. [Thomas Cleghorn], 'Writings of Charles Dickens', *North British Review* 3.5 (May 1845), 65–87, 79.

36. [Thomas Henry Lister], 'Dickens's *Tales*', *Edinburgh Review* (October 1838), 75–97, 76.
37. Charles T. Congdon, 'Over-Illustration', *North American Review* 139.336 (November 1884), 480–91, 484.
38. [Samuel Warren], 'Dickens's *American Notes for General Circulation*', *Blackwood's Edinburgh Magazine* 52.326 (December 1842), 783–801, 785. Italics in original.
39. '*Pendennis* and *Copperfield*: Thackeray and Dickens', *North British Review* 15.29 (May 1851), 57–89, 70.
40. 'Second Series of *Sketches by Boz*', *The Spectator*, 26 December 1836, 1234.
41. See, for example, 'Reviews on Literature', *Musical World*, 10 October 1846, 500. This review accuses Dickens of caricaturing 'to excess'.
42. See, for example, *A New Spirit of the Age*, ed. by R. H. Horne, 2 vols (London: Smith, Elder & Co., 1844), I, 25.
43. This version is from 'Charles Dickens', *Aberdeen Press and Journal*, 1 November 1865. The article also appeared in *The Glasgow Herald*, 27 October 1865, the *Dundee Courier and Argus*, 30 October 1865, and the *Maidstone Telegraph*, 25 November 1865. The original source is credited as *The Daily Telegraph*.
44. 'Phiz', *Judy, or the London Serio-Comic Journal*, 14 July 1869, 117.
45. Philip Waller, *Writers, Readers, and Reputations: Literary Life in Britain, 1870–1918* (Oxford: Oxford University Press, 2006), 21.
46. These examples of reading Dickens can be found on the *Reading Experience Database (RED), 1450–1945* <www.open.ac.uk/Arts/RED/> [accessed 15 July 2018].
47. Kate Flint, *The Woman Reader, 1837–1914* (Oxford: Oxford University Press, 1993), 231.
48. Percy Fitzgerald, *The History of Pickwick: An Account of Its Characters, Localities, Allusions, and Illustrations* (London: Chapman & Hall, 1891), 26.
49. William Henry Hudson, *Far Away and Long Ago: A History of My Early Life* (London: Dent, 1918), 29.
50. Martin Meisel discusses this in *Realizations: Narrative, Pictorial, and Theatrical Arts in Nineteenth-Century England* (Princeton: Princeton University Press, 1983), 247–65.
51. For a discussion of Dickens and Penny Readings, see Malcolm Andrews, *Charles Dickens and His Performing Selves: Dickens and the Public Readings* (Oxford: Oxford University Press, 2006), 51–9.
52. Tom Hood, 'Cassell's Illustrated Readings Conducted by Tom Hood', *Cassell's Penny Readings*, ed. by Tom Hood, 2 vols (London: Cassell, Petter & Galpin, 1866), I, 1.
53. Ibid.
54. George du Maurier, 'The Illustrating of Books from the Serious Artist's Point of View. – I', *Magazine of Art* (January 1890), 349–53, 350.
55. See Allan Paivio, *Imagery and Verbal Processes* (New York: Holt, Rinehart & Winston, 1971).
56. [Richard Ford], '*Oliver Twist*', *Quarterly Review* 64.127 (June 1839), 83–102, 101–2.
57. James, 'A Small Boy and Others', 39; 117.
58. Charles Dickens, *The Personal History of David Copperfield* (London: Bradbury & Evans, 1850), 580.
59. See, for example, David's receding hairline and side parting in 'A Stranger Calls to See Me' (November 1850).
60. *Dickens's Dream*, dir. Laurie Hill (2012). Available at <www.annexfilms.co.uk/portfolio/dickens-dream> [accessed 15 July 2018].
61. While more research needs to be conducted on this difference in neurological terms, the notion that reading books with pictures is a different experience to reading books without pictures has long been central to the psychology of reading children's illustrated books. See, for example, *The Psychology of Illustration. Volume 2: Instructional Issues*, ed. by Harvey A. Houghton and Dale M. Willows (New York: Springer, 1987).

16

CARICATURE

Brian Maidment

THIS ESSAY, WHICH IS CENTRED ON Dickens's cultural experience in the 1830s, has two main purposes. The first comprises a consideration of the ways in which an essentially visual medium – the caricature – can usefully be connected with the textual forms that Dickens uses early in his career: the sketch and the novel. In what ways do the graphic and the verbal intersect? And to what extent were the representational codes and graphic tropes associated with caricature embedded in Dickens's literary method? The second is concerned with the dialogue between two key elements which emerge within caricature and comic art in the 1830s – the growing status of hasty and even random graphic social observation and the evolution of new narrative forms within comic print making at that time.

The dominant critical modes for approaching these issues have followed two methods of investigation. One line of analysis is literal and has sought to find precise visual sources within contemporary caricature for aspects of Dickens's work. Such an approach can perhaps be simply demonstrated by the hunt for the physiognomy, body and social presence of Mr Pickwick from *The Pickwick Papers* (1836–7). The search for the graphic origins of Samuel Pickwick have largely been focused on those publications by *Pickwick*'s first illustrator, Robert Seymour, which pre-dated the novel's first publication and which might have prefigured Samuel Pickwick, either knowingly or unknowingly, in Dickens's observational stock and literary memory.[1] As the tumultuous output of comic prints, caricatures and illustrated humorous literature from the 1830s (newly accessible through digitisation) is further explored, it will doubtless become possible to find many images that seem to have specific verbal counterparts in Dickens's work. The range of newly available images will also make available a more sophisticated awareness of the visual tropes that circulated freely during his childhood, youth and early career. Sally Ledger has, for instance, connected the combined efforts of Dickens and Cruikshank in establishing the image of Mr Bumble in *Oliver Twist* (1837–9) with a minor but significant figure in Robert Seymour's large print 'Heaven and Hell', which was published in 1830.[2] Ledger was confident in presenting a graphic image as a direct source for a textual reinvention. She stated firmly that the etching 'prominently features an overweight, pompous figure of a parish beadle immediately recognisable as a Bumble prototype'.[3]

As a serendipitous outcome of my own trawl through the graphic culture of the 1830s, various images have appeared that might be reassessed as 'sources' for Dickens's early work. Figure 16.1, for example, shows an extremely Pickwickian male gathering taken from George and Robert Cruikshank's three-volume *Universal Songster*.[4]

Figure 16.1 George Cruikshank, 'The Nightingale Club', a wood-engraved illustration from *The Universal Songster* 1 (London: Jones, 1825). Courtesy of Brian Maidment.

The frequently reprinted *Universal Songster* formed a huge gathering of texts and provided a publication that was centrally concerned with extracting songs from their performance base in the homosocial sites of London supper clubs, song rooms and theatres, and presenting them in a format that might foster their reperformance in the genteel drawing room. Cruikshank's image can be usefully compared with one of Seymour's *Humorous Sketches*, 'The Club', first published by Richard Carlile in February 1835 (Figure 16.2). Both images attest to the availability of a stock of established comic graphic tropes that could be repeatedly drawn upon by artists.

Despite the feverish efforts of successive generations of scholars and enthusiasts, it might even be possible to find new graphic sources for Samuel Pickwick himself. Here is an entirely Dickensian image, a caricature trope of a carriage leaving the Belle Sauvage Inn en route from London to Cheltenham (Plate 1). Such a scene formed a staple topic for print makers throughout the late eighteenth and early nineteenth century. It was drawn by John Orlando Parry, a significant acquaintance of Dickens. Parry was one of a number of his friends who, among their many talents, were highly competent comic artists.[5] It is dated 1835 and exists as both a drawing and an etched plate. The reference to a page number suggests it was intended as an illustration for a novel, although I have not been able to find out if it was ever published. The point here is not so much to claim a new graphic source for Pickwick but rather to suggest the mass of visual material available to Dickens to be found in print-shop windows,

Figure 16.2 Robert Seymour, 'The Club', an engraving from *Sketches by Seymour* 5.4 (London: Carlile, March 1835). Courtesy of Brian Maidment.

in drawing-room portfolios, on the walls of chop houses, taverns and theatres, and on the streets.

The critical issue remains, however, discovering ways of connecting this mass of graphic comedy to Dickens's fiction in ways that step beyond the identification of precise visual sources for characters and scenes in his novels, and which acknowledge a broader sweep of influence than that of such doubtlessly significant but by now well-understood figures as William Hogarth and George Cruikshank. Thus a second possible mode of analysis is more amorphous and seeks to find a generalised caricatural sensibility at work in Dickens's publications, a mode of observational and satirical humour that is shared with, in particular, the graphic art produced by William Hogarth, James Gillray, Thomas Rowlandson and George Cruikshank. A number of traditional caricatural ways of thinking and seeing are immediately apparent in Dickens's work. He frequently evoked the grotesque and was especially interested in the ways in which social behaviour and the human form become warped into travesties of the ideal or the normal.[6] He revelled in exaggeration, and especially the way in which the minutiae of bodily features and everyday conduct become peculiarities through endless repetition, and thus become ways of actualising the whole person through magnified minor characteristics. He understood the particular complexity of the caricaturist's point of view in which the artist implicates viewers in sharing his or her mockery of human folly while unknowingly laughing at themselves. The reformist trajectory of caricature was also useful to Dickens – if caricature appeared purposive then its comic vision transcended the merely entertaining or the cruelly mocking.[7]

Stressing such aspects of Dickens's observational methods and writing practices locates him as the inheritor of a satirical tradition that elides generic and formal differences into a shared worldview. It informs, for example, John Dixon Hunt's exploration of Dickens's comic visual imagination. Dixon Hunt notes, however, that 'this kind of analysis [that is to say locating Dickens's work within a satirical tradition] can only stress parallels between Dickens's imagination and that of the graphic artists rather than exact sources', but goes on to consider ways in which 'the writer's presentation of material was shaped by his acquaintance with graphic art' so that Dickens 'will see what his eye has learnt to look for rather than paint "what he sees"'.[8] Such a shared modal relationship, concentrating on ways of seeing as much as on the content of what is seen, between Dickens and the best known British satirical artists establishes Dickens as part of a 'great tradition' of comic and satirical art.

Richard Vogler addressed similar issues in his essay '*Oliver Twist:* Dickens's Pictorial Prototypes'.[9] Vogler offered a close analysis of Cruikshank's illustrations in order to assess the extent to which they stepped beyond a precise visual equivalence to Dickens's text. He acknowledged the extent to which George Cruikshank's work was extensively dependent on repeated stock figures and visual tropes that had become central to his vast published output of images, but was also concerned to show the extent to which Cruikshank both responded to and remained independent from Dickens's emerging text. Such an analytical mode inevitably raised questions about the authorship of Dickens's text. As Vogler notes:

> Once it is established that most of the major characters as portrayed in the illustrations did exist in Cruikshank's pictorial repertoire prior to the writing of *Oliver Twist,* the question of the degree of author–artist collaboration and possible mutual influence becomes something more than speculation.[10]

The subsequent analysis of the interrelationship of Cruikshank's work and Dickens's novel is a dense and useful exploration of both the nature and extent to which visual sources might inform a text. Yet there are important limitations to Vogler's mode of analysis. He acknowledges that 'some basic art-historical problems are not dealt with in this study' including the 'question of how Cruikshank came by his stock figures or how many of them were original with the artist himself'.[11] Nor is he willing to resolve the tension between the extent to which caricaturists drew from life as well as from an inherited repertoire of graphic tropes and stereotypes.

Without wanting to diminish the value of the kinds of detailed analysis of the relationship between Dickens's texts and their illustrations carried out by Vogler and Dixon Hunt, this essay seeks to connect Dickens to caricature in the 1830s in broader and less explicitly evidential ways. Aligning Dickens with the leading figures of the British tradition of comic and satirical art, especially Hogarth and Cruikshank, of course serves to acknowledge Dickens's genius in transforming visual observation into text, but it also detaches Dickens from the wider context of graphic humour in the 1820s and 1830s.[12] Such a reading also serves to reduce Cruikshank's art to 'prototypes' for Dickens's greater artistic achievement. While Dixon Hunt acknowledged that 'Dickens drew upon and was conditioned by the same graphic traditions that gave him his illustrators', his discussion does not venture far beyond the established figures of Hogarth, Gillray and Cruikshank in looking for the location of Dickens's imagination within the context of contemporary comic art. Dixon Hunt asserted that Dickens invoked in *Pickwick* a range of 'motifs [. . .] amazingly similar to the current graphic scene' and touched a range of 'familiar graphic themes', but there is little sense in his analysis of the wider burgeoning and inventive circumambient array of humorous prints.[13] Even Vogler, more open than Dixon Hunt in acknowledging the limits of his detailed analysis, argues that focusing solely on Cruikshank's work is the most productive way of proceeding:

> Although many of Cruikshank's pictorial types may be related to similar images created or used by any number of predecessors, the tracing of such remote possibilities in unimportant in this context [. . .] Since George Cruikshank was the most original comic illustrator in England at the time he worked with Dickens, it seems to serve little purpose to look for Cruikshank's stock figures as they appear in the work of his less original contemporaries.[14]

The stress here on the authority of authorship and on creative achievement foregrounds a 'great tradition' of originality at the expense of a broader understanding of the comic graphic world in which Dickens came to consciousness.

As we have already seen, and as Ledger has noted, it may be Seymour's beadle and not Cruikshank's that found its way into *Oliver Twist*. Ledger has been more willing than any other Dickens critic to push analysis on beyond the best-known satirical artists available to the young Dickens to consider 'a whole host of satirical and melodramatic illustrations from the 1830s and 1840s that would importantly shape – and subsequently be influenced by – Dickens's response to the New Poor Law in *Oliver Twist*'.[15] In looking for sources for the novel, she describes the close friendship between William Hone and Cruikshank and their collaboration on a melodrama titled *Confession of Thomas Bedworth* (1815).[16] She also considers R. B. Peake's melodrama *The Climbing Boy*,[17] first performed in 1832 at London's Olympic Theatre, and analyses a wide range of satirical graphic depictions of the effects of the Poor Law drawn by Robert Seymour, Cruikshank and C. J. Grant. She connects these sources to the novel through modal similarities (the Manichaean structures of melodrama) and through a shared analysis of the disastrous human consequences of the Poor Law.[18] Beadles can be widely found in such sources. Ledger's willingness to extend the range of graphic influences that were likely to have borne on Dickens's early visual experiences to lesser-known caricatures and satirical images serves as a prompt for what follows here.

Accordingly, the rest of this essay seeks to connect Dickens more broadly to the rapidly expanding mass of humorous and satirical prints produced in the 1830s and to the newly formulated ways in which they were being published. In particular, it is interested in a widely visible organisation of images into gatherings and sequences published between 1820 and 1840 which, both in terms of the formulation of the individual page and in the use of serial and volume publications, prefigure graphic narrative. In Britain, unlike France, for example, the drive towards visual narrative never evolved in the early nineteenth century towards foregrounding the comic strip as a popular and significant graphic form. But the possibility of a narrative comprised almost exclusively of graphic images largely independent of text hung in the air in the 1830s, and it forms an important backdrop to Dickens's early work, especially when associated with Robert Seymour, described by Ledger as 'the most important single popular influence on *The Pickwick Papers*'.[19]

The early 1830s in particular formed a moment of massive change in the forms, readerships and modes of publication of comic images driven on by a frantic entrepreneurial energy and opportunism. Dickens grew up at a time when the production, distribution and modality of comic art was being transformed. Single-plate caricature, while still widespread, was nonetheless giving way in the 1820s and 1830s to other modes and forms of relatively cheap comic print making. The central characteristics of single-plate graphic satire – topicality, dense allusiveness, wit, a continuing interest in the grotesque (and especially the grotesque body and human physiognomy), and the graphic interplay between word and image – were edging towards a different humorous modality centrally concerned with the comedy of manners being acted out on the streets and within domestic interiors through the chance encounters occasioned by the dense contiguity of urban life. While informed by a lingering deference to the grotesque, a new generation of comic artists, led by George Cruikshank but also including now lesser-known figures such as Henry Heath, William Heath, Charles Jameson Grant, Joe Lisle, J. L. Marks, Henry Alken and, most significant of all, Robert Seymour, were publishing their work in a variety of new formats. These prolific artists were rapidly joined in the 1830s by Thomas Onwhyn, Kenny Meadows, the short-lived Thomas Sibson, Thomas Hood and Albert Forrester ('Crowquill'). Several of these artists produced significant series of extra illustrations for Dickens's work, and such graphic re-enactments of Dickens's narratives were often bound up alongside the original illustrations.[20] Recent scholarship, building on the riches to be found in Grego's *Pictorial Pickwickiana*, has begun to take a more detailed interest in the ways in which extra illustration comments on, or even re-enacts, Dickens's texts.[21]

The two key changes in the making, publishing and distributing of comic images in the late 1820s and early 1830s, which occurred alongside a continuing and expanding production of cheap, vulgar and aesthetically unambitious single-plate caricatures of social subjects mainly produced using lithography, can be summarised as follows. First, the increasingly widespread use of the vignette wood-engraved image as a medium for illustrating a range of print forms including songbooks, small-scale political pamphlets, comic annuals and reprints of short classic humorous texts known as 'facetiae' or 'jeux d'esprit' led to a miniaturisation of the comic image. Implicitly a small-scale form because of the dimensions of the box wood blocks used in its making, the wood engraving was rapidly adapted to the pocket-sized formats which were emerging as the best way to formulate comic publications for a rapidly broadening marketplace. The relative cheapness and rapidity of production belonging to the wood engraving was a further inducement away from more traditional etched or metal engraved forms of visual comedy.

Second, those caricaturists who felt that their traditional association with single-plate caricature had run its course began to draw on the potential of the minia-turised image increasingly used by wood engraving in order to build up multi-image plates assembled from a plenitude of small-scale sketches, one-off visual/verbal jokes, sketchbook doodles and other material drawn from notebooks or incomplete larger-scale work. Such plates, almost invariably using the landscape format and size of the traditional single-plate caricature, combined an exuberant and energetic expression of the artist's visual energy along with a new focus on contemporary manners and social interaction. Such images were frequently gathered together to form a short series of etched or engraved plates – six, eight or ten were the most usual numbers – with a mass of small images assembled on each sheet. Series of this kind could be bought as separate prints or gathered together in paper covers ready for rebinding. They were expensive publications especially when the costs of binding were added in to the purchase price.

Most of these series were concerned with the comedy to be found in contemporary social interaction and manners. In the first instance, series of this kind were unashamed of their miscellaneous and relatively trivial content. Cruikshank's several series of *Scraps and Sketches* provides an obvious example of the kinds of commercial opportunism that underlay the publication of assorted or random notebook doodling.[22] Other popular artists, such as Alken, offered their least ambitious work in the form of a series of plates devoted to 'Scraps', thus opening another line of market appeal to those customers interested in structuring their own graphic universe.[23] Henry Heath, a prolific draughtsman who worked extensively in this mode, republished all his short series of plates as a volume modestly called the *Caricaturist's Scrapbook*, thus making sure that their full commercial value could be realised.[24] One element assembled in the *Caricaturist's Scrapbook* was called 'Omnium Gatherium', an accurate summary of its miscellaneous nature.

But comic artists quickly began to recognise the need to offer something beyond random moments of humorous or satirical observation. Accordingly, however hasty and opportunistic their work might still have been, artists like Heath, Alken and Lisle began to shape and focus their output into themed series of plates which offered a sustained examination of a comic idea. Many of these sequences worked out from interactions between verbal or print forms and unexpected visual equivalents. The six plates of Heath's 'The Nautical Dictionary', for example, reprinted in the *Caricaturist's Scrapbook*, illustrated seafaring phrases with punning depictions of everyday experiences – 'fitting-out' shows a seaman watching his wife replenish her gaudy wardrobe in a dressmaker's shop, 'Prize – a vessel taken from the enemy' shows a fishwife crowing over an enfeebled-looking dustman (a prize indeed!) who has been inveigled away from his current *innamorata*, and 'By the board – over the ships side' depicts a row of overdressed and very seasick passengers. 'Fly-boat – a large flat bottomed Vessel it is distinguished by a very broad stern' offers a rear view of a sailor smoking and exhibiting a truly astonishing 'very broad stern', thus bringing together caricature tropes of the outlandish or grotesque human body with an interest in visual/verbal play. The title ascribed to these plates, 'The Nautical Dictionary', also deals in disparities by rendering the ponderous print form of a dictionary into a frivolous and disrespectful set of small-scale caricatures. Such plates, despite their commercial origins and seemingly trivial content, offered a new kind of formal potential to comic art. A range of quickly observed incidents could be organised on to the page in ways that retained a sense of immediacy and simultaneity and yet allowed for separately rendered details to be shaped into something approaching coherence through the exploration of a shared single humorous idea.

246 BRIAN MAIDMENT

Something of this profusion of miscellaneous observation informs Dickens's early work. As Luisa Calè has noted:

> for Walter Bagehot the writing of Dickens still had the feel of 'graphic scraps; his best books are compilations of them'. The memory of the incomplete, disconnected form of the monthly publication, a vehicle for prints and accompanying letterpress, still associated Dickens's writing with a culture of scrapbooks and extra-illustrations.[25]

In some of the *Sketches by Boz* (1836), even the typography furthers this sense of accumulated moments of observation laid out on the page as simultaneous comic experiences. Here is his description of a closely observed parade of tea garden promenaders:

> What a dust and noise! Men and women – boys and girls, – sweethearts and married people – babies in arms, and children in chaises – pipes and shrimps – cigars and periwinkles – tea and tobacco. Gentlemen, in alarming waistcoats, and steel watch-guards, promenading about, three abreast, with surprising dignity (or as the gentleman in the next box facetiously observes, 'cutting it uncommon fat')[26]

The passage continues on through 'ladies', 'husbands', 'boys' and 'gentlemen in pink shirts and blue waistcoats', all ascribed to a particularly visualised – and verbalised – comic moment of presence within the writer's attention. The sequence of dashes here provides the miscellaneity and multifariousness of the assembled observations with a verbal structure that translates the immediacy and variety of the presence of multiple images on the caricaturist's page into literary terms. Calè goes on to suggest that Dickens's increasing use of the volume format allowed him to stabilise his later novels and dissipate the memory of the 'culture of scrapbooks and extra-illustrations' that had haunted his early works.[27]

It is important to acknowledge the importance of miscellaneous comic observations as an aspect of Dickens's early work. But an understanding of the 'incomplete' and 'disconnected' aspects of contemporary visual culture that can be seen reflected in Dickens's ways of seeing and understanding needs to be aligned with different, perhaps seemingly contradictory, strands within the print-cultural production of graphic humour in the 1830s. The first was a burgeoning interest in narrative as a potential means of organising, controlling and publishing comic images. Such an interest is closely tied to the recognition by publishers and artists that single free-floating prints, while they did have some economic value, needed to be framed and presented in different ways to exploit their full commercial potential. The management of the available mass of images centrally involved ways of translating profusion into forms that stepped beyond the miscellaneous and the trivial and connected images into coherence either by content or by form. The second concerns a recognition of the potential offered by sustained seriality as a mechanism for the imagining, creating and producing humorous images. The 1820s had seen a number of high-selling serialised collaborations between a picaresque text and comic illustrations, most obviously Pierce Egan's *Life in London* from 1823, along with its attendant train of rapidly produced imitations and the various Dr Syntax books written by William Combe and illustrated by Thomas Rowlandson. But the early 1830s saw seriality extensively applied to the production of graphic comedy without recourse to a textual counterpoint. The most ambitious of Robert Seymour's extended graphic series, *Humorous Sketches* (1834–6) and *New Readings of Old Authors* (1832–4), to a large extent resisted the idea of 'illustration' by relegating printed text to brief captions largely present to sustain or underline the comic disparities to be found between what people say and how they act. Seymour, the artist most closely involved in Dickens's reinvention of *Pickwick* as a commodity text, worked in ways that sought to resist the kind of 'textualising', or subordination of the visual to the verbal, represented by *The Pickwick Papers*, by beginning to develop structures through which comic images might be amassed into proto-narrative sequences.[28] While the success of *Pickwick* subsequently caused *Humorous Sketches* to be 'novelised' and re-presented to mid-Victorian readers as an extended work of illustrated fiction, it was conceived, and originally understood, as a comic graphic serial with the presence of a few words as expository prompts. Only in retrospect was *Humorous Sketches*, a work preoccupied with the rural adventuring of rather naive urban travellers, reinvented as an inevitable, and inferior, prefiguring of *Pickwick*, a disjointed graphic 'text' waiting to find the words that would give it substance, form and depth.

Robert Seymour was a central figure in the development of graphic narrative forms, not just in *Humorous Sketches* but also in the work he produced in the short sequences of large-scale prints described above. A consideration of his work thus forms a useful and informative way of suggesting some of the developments in the marketplace for print that enabled Dickens to formulate his version of illustrated narrative. Seymour's work remains relatively little known beyond the unfortunate celebrity brought upon him by *Pickwick* and his suicide. He is generally summarised by the not entirely approbatory term of 'sporting artist' and by Simon Houfe's judgement that he was 'a somewhat inadequate draughtsman', a phrase that has been unthinkingly repeated by subsequent writers.[29] But Seymour, as a widely published but not widely celebrated jobbing comic artist, is a figure that offered in the early 1830s a much more varied account of Dixon Hunt's 'familiar graphic themes' ('from coaching to skating, hunting to courtship, theatres to law courts').[30] Indeed, more so than his contemporary George Cruikshank who had, by this time, turned largely to book illustration rather than the varied modes of publication that Seymour was forced to use.

Dickensian scholars have shown surprisingly little interest in bringing Seymour's extremely varied and complicated career to bear substantially on an understanding of Dickens's cultural milieu. Jane R. Cohen wrote in 1980 that 'a lack of reliable information about the reclusive artist further complicates the issue' of the origins of *Pickwick*.[31] She cites a comment from *The Athenaeum* in 1887 that suggests 'it is astonishing that so little should be known of him in our time', and adds, 'nearly a century later we know little more.'[32] Over forty years later Robert L. Patten acknowledges that Seymour's connections with Dickens remain unexplored – 'It is useful to have a fuller account of Seymour's career. Among other payoffs, [such] discussion renews one's sense that there was more of the artist's material in the opening chapters of *The Pickwick Papers* than Dickens or posterity has granted.'[33] While it cannot be shown that Dickens had any detailed knowledge of the artist's work, their careers begin to elide as early as 1834 when Seymour supplied a small wood-engraved vignette to *The Monthly Magazine* perhaps without knowing that the article he was illustrating had been written by Dickens.[34] Yet, while it is not possible to know how much of the artist's work Dickens knew, Seymour's career offers a useful and significant way of tracing the drive towards narrative and seriality within comic graphic visual culture that pre-dated, and was perhaps largely disrupted by, the publication of *Pickwick* in 1836–7.

Despite his varied, even hyperactive, output, Seymour has usually been characterised as a 'sporting artist'. Sporting art was widely popular throughout the first four decades of the nineteenth century, with its manifestations ranging from ambitious oil paintings through large-scale coloured furniture prints to humorous graphic commentary on the 'cockney' adventures of amateur townees as they sought to master the rural pursuits of hunting, fishing and shooting. Alken, who produced a mass of illustrations and series of prints celebrating rural sports, was also the best-known commentator on the comic failings and ludicrous ambitions of sporting aspirants. But Seymour also worked across the full range of sporting prints. He drew a number of portraits for *The New Sporting Magazine* which were reprinted in 'Wildrake's' 1841 *Cracks of the Day*.[35] He designed elaborate decorative furniture prints of angling subjects. *R. Seymour's Fishing Subjects* (n.d. ?1837), for example, consisted of large lithographs published by Ackermann as part of a posthumous series which drew on both the sublime and idyllic pastoral for inspiration.[36] In a completely different idiom Seymour produced *Waltonising or – Green-land Fishermen*, a large etched caricature published by Thomas McLean, which suggests how inexperienced urban sportsmen were subject to all kinds of calamity as a result of their 'greenness'.[37] Different again were images of cats grotesquely kitted out as sportsmen and women that featured in other single-plate caricatures. Seymour also provided twelve small lithographs for Richard Penn's *Maxims and Hints for an Angler; and Miseries of Fishing* (1833).[38]

The *Humorous Sketches*, with their extended interest in Cockney sportsmen on their out-of-town sporting adventures, offers the most direct playing out of the tropes that coalesce into a proto-Pickwickian narrative. As Ledger notes, 'it is in the *Humorous Sketches* published between 1834 and 1836 that Seymour's influence on early Dickens is initially in evidence.'[39] And it is in the *Humorous Sketches* that Seymour began to think through ideas of how to construct a graphic narrative in an extended serial form. The book has an extremely complex publishing history and the two 'novelisations' in the 1840s fundamentally changed its nature.[40] In these heavily annotated and textualised versions, *Sketches by Seymour* remained popular throughout the nineteenth century. These later reissues added in a variety of textual elements and reduced the number of plates considerably. They also strengthened Seymour's reputation as a 'sporting artist' by eliminating most of the urban scenes from the run of original plates and turning the remaining prints into a narrative of sporting mishap. The titles of various editions of R. B. Peake's reworking of Seymour's original project are revealing – resultant publications, apparently both issued in 1846, were called *Snobson's Seasons, Being Annuals of Cockney Sport* (London: M. A. Nattali, n.d.) and *An Evening's Amusement or the Adventures of a Cockney Sportsman, by R. B. Peake, Esq., Illustrated with Ninety Two Plates by Seymour* (no publisher given). Such reissues were obviously a retrospective attempt to cash in on the popularity of *The Pickwick Papers* by insisting on the Pickwickian content of the *Humorous Sketches*. They also provide a very interesting commentary on how not to turn a sequence of comic images into a novel.

The original *Humorous Sketches*, published by Carlile between March 1834 and April 1836, comprised five 'volumes' of thirty-six images along with seventeen additional 'Popular Sketches', 179 images in all.[41] The sequence contained around 120 images of sporting subjects but also over sixty plates devoted to urban incident. Along with Seymour's other major project serialised under his own name, the 260 small lithographs that made up *New Readings of Old Authors* (1832–5),[42] the *Humorous Sketches* offers a major source of closely observed urban commentary produced in a manner that retains something of the carnivalesque grotesquery of late eighteenth-century caricature as well as the more whimsical narrative of cockney sporting adventures. The central dynamic of Seymour's sequence was, of course, an extended narrative of the comic cultural misunderstandings caused by the attempts of gauche town dwellers to engage with the unfamiliar and transgressive pleasures of the countryside, and it is this narrative that also underlies the structure of *The Pickwick Papers*. For Seymour, an avid fisherman, the countryside nonetheless proved to be a place in which accident, nuisance and misadventure ruled. Such an imagined place was constructed out of the tropes of late eighteenth-century and early nineteenth-century farcical comedy, and provided a model for the narrative of misapprehension and embarrassment that informs *Pickwick*. Underlying this narrative are broader issues to do not just with topography and out-of-placeness but with also class and cultural difference. Seymour's London emerges as a mass of immediate scattered vision moments – a teeming world of street collisions and urban presences – scavengers, dustmen, sweeps, draymen and the like – largely rendered through grotesque caricature modes. A dialogue between the urban grotesque and a gentler comedy of reversal, out-of-placeness and mutual incomprehension between the city and the country is thus set in motion by the *Humorous Sketches*.

As well as this framing narrative, the *Humorous Sketches* also acknowledges the extent to which single images can be packed with narrative content. In one early plate a beautifully elegant drawing shows a fisherman dozing against a tree (Figure 16.3). The caption runs:

> Walked twenty miles overnight – up before peep o'day again: got a capital place – fell fast asleep – tide rose up to my knees – my hat was changed, my pockets pick't and a fish run away with my hook – dreamt of being on a polar expedition and having my toes frozen.[43]

Here, the image compresses an entire narrative into a graphic trope inherited from the accumulated presence of contemporary comic sporting art. The text here served to illustrate and annotate the immediate impact of the image. The words offer an extended but compressed dramatisation of the scene through adopting the conversational voice of the fisherman turning his day out into an anecdote to be shared with friends. Seymour here reimagines his image as a verbal anecdote offering an alternative means of expressing his comic purpose.

Seymour's lesser-known works also show him exploring the narrative potential of a series of comic images in ways that relate significantly to the development of the novel form to be found in Dickens's work. Seymour produced a number of these kinds of short series of multi-image plates organised round a shared idea or theme.[44] *The Heiress – A Farce in Six Plates* (Thomas McLean, 1830) began to explore the narrative

Figure 16.3 Robert Seymour, 'Fisherman Dozing Against a Tree', in *Sketches by Seymour* 1.9 (Tregear, ?1834). Courtesy of Brian Maidment.

potential both of this particular graphic form and of the image sequence more generally (Figure 16.4). The six plates that comprise *The Heiress* form an exemplary narrative – a poor girl being brought up by her uncle and aunt unexpectedly inherits wealth, undergoes transformation into a society belle, willingly enough, is wooed by a feckless and impecunious major, and runs off to Gretna Green to marry him, pursued as he is by debt collectors. Each plate, in a landscape format rather than the usual oblong folio used by contemporary caricaturists, has a large central image that carries the dominant narrative, and offers the occasion for lightly satirical depictions of society events, manners and fashions. These central images are surrounded by smaller vignettes satirising the hangers-on, opportunists and pseudo-helpful people who swarm round the heiress to usher her into society, and, of course, to take her money. The overall effect is remarkably novelistic, with the smaller images acting as subplots or picturesque 'character studies' to the central narrative. There is also a sense in which this is a lighter-hearted version of the Hogarthian moral narrative translated into the medium of the multi-image sequences of plates widely available in the late 1820s and 1830s. The graphic structure of *The Heiress* thus offered a creative dialogue between a sustained Hogarthian narrative and the idea of the miscellany as a graphic mode.

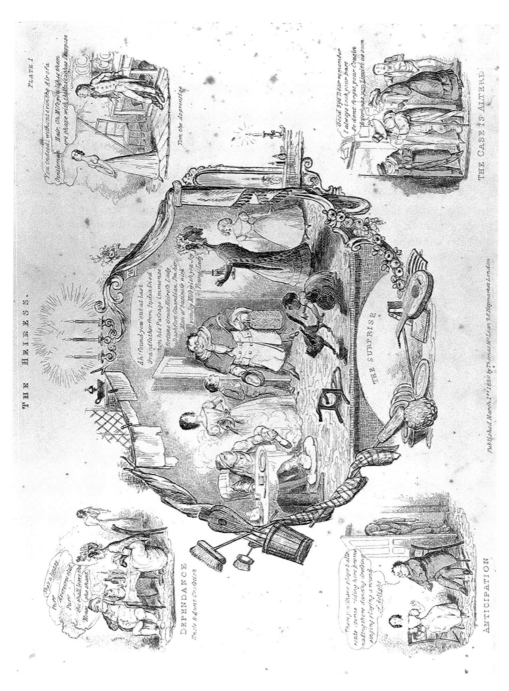

Figure 16.4 Robert Seymour, *The Heiress – A Farce in Six Plates*, plate 1 (McLean, 1830). Courtesy of Brian Maidment.

The use of the landscape format and the deployment of images in the plates for *The Heiress* also suggests the kind of title pages used by the issue parts of the early Victorian serialised novel, where a complex central image is embedded, often by elaborate framing, within a circle of smaller depictions that offer some sense of the narrative events in the novel. While there are several precedents for this structure derived from earlier novels like Pierce Egan's *Life in London* (1823), the emblematic elements used in Egan's work were frequently slackened in part-issue novels published in the 1840s and 1850s, and turned into more descriptive versions of narrative incidents. Dickens frequently used these kinds of multi-image issue title pages to brand his books and give a kind of visual summary of his text – Plate 2 shows the issue title page for *Our Mutual Friend* (1864–5), which, despite the elaborate framing, is extremely reminiscent of *The Heiress*.

From a very early stage of his career, Seymour had a particular specialism in the production of elaborate multi-image title pages, and was brought in to provide them even when he had not contributed more widely to the volume. He had, for example, drawn the complex title page for *The Terrific Register*, a compendium of melodramatic tales published in 1825.[45] He was also brought in to provide the volume title page for *Pierce Egan's Book of Sports and Mirror of Life*, which had been serialised in twenty-five parts, each devoted to a particular sporting activity (Figure 16.5).[46]

Figure 16.5 Robert Seymour, title page for *Pierce Egan's Book of Sports and Mirror of Life* (London: Tegg, n.d.). Chronicle/Alamy Stock Photo.

Figure 16.6 Pierce Egan, engraved title page to *Pilgrims of the Thames* (London: Strange, 1838). Courtesy of Brian Maidment.

Attempts to render precis of extended fictional narratives in these condensed graphic terms were an important feature of the early Victorian novel and suggest the ways in which such fictions organised and combined the local intensity of observed incident with a broader narrative drive. The title page to Pierce Egan's *Pilgrims of the Thames* (1838), for example, was drawn as a crowded frame of faces and views that serve to fill out the garlanded roundel devoted to the central protagonists of the novel located at the centre of the page (Figure 16.6).

It was Seymour, of course, who drew the graphic frame of sporting paraphernalia and active sportsmen which enclosed the typeset elements of the part issues of *The Pickwick Papers*. More work needs to be done on the morphology of the multi-image title page as a narrative form, but such visual constructions undoubtedly derived from a growing interest in graphic narrative to be found in late Regency caricature.

The Schoolmaster Abroad (1834), while comprising a short sequence of oblong folio plates in the established format of the time, is a very different work.[47] Offering nine coloured lithographed plates, *The Schoolmaster Abroad* combined images and a substantial text by providing an extended commentary printed on a separate page opposite each plate (Plate 3). The publication forms an extended political satire on Lord Brougham's activities in promoting mass education through the Society for the Diffusion of Useful Knowledge and its ground-breaking publication, *The Penny Magazine*. Brougham's fervent pursuit of the 'march of intellect' had been widely mocked by caricaturists, and Seymour had repeatedly returned to the subject.[48]

The Schoolmaster Abroad provides a particularly upmarket and glossy reworking of this recurrent theme, but its originality lies in figuring Brougham's project in narrative terms. *The Schoolmaster Abroad* forms a pastiche version of the Dr Syntax narratives, which formed the most popular model for the picturesque literary journey.[49] However, here the 'picturesque' is replaced with something much more culturally and politically contentious: the Whig educational policy. The title is immediately provocative. Brougham was ascribed the sarcastic title of 'schoolmaster' as a result of a notorious 1828 speech in which he laid out his belief in the profound significance of popular education as a socially progressive force and declared that 'the schoolmaster is abroad'.[50]

Brougham's tour, then, was not 'picturesque' but rather a polemical or indeed an ideological journey in which Brougham was forced to engage with the actualities of cultural values and their expression across a wide spectrum of social and geographical locations and confront the likely outcomes of Whig policy. Seymour's visually dense and allusive plates, which take on the shape of a picaresque fictional journey, take him through a country that offers him a nightmare travesty of his educational policy – a landscape of rioting and ignorant peasantry, socially pretentious gatherings such as 'The Brummagen Conversazione', unscientific science, and narrowly sectarian bigotry. By the time he returns home, he is forced to reassess his reformist project. Seated in melancholy solitude in a room that resembles a Hogarthian scholarly retreat, he throws manuscripts he has prepared for *The Penny Magazine* on to the fire. Such a complex use of a picaresque journey through the English provinces that combined image and text in dialogue form suggest the increasingly available options that were becoming visible just at the time Dickens was beginning to write.

Rather than pursuing the established lines of research that have related Dickens's early work to specific sources within contemporary caricature, this essay has sought rather to offer some account of formal, modal, and structural changes in the conceptualisation and production of comic art in the late 1820s and 1830s that construct something of the visual environment that would have been familiar to the young writer. Dickens's debts to caricature have been, and will continue, to be extensively explored. The search for precise visual referents from within contemporary caricature for Dickens's texts, aided by the availability of new digital resources, will continue to foster discussion of ways in which these form sources for, prototypes of, or equivalents to their textual counterpart, thus informing further debates about the relationship between text and image. The understanding of Dickens's use of the close observation of human foibles characteristic of caricature in order to construct the comic grotesque will be further recognised. The moral energy underlying the use of repeated behavioural tropes drawn from caricature to construct individual identity in novelistic form will also be more extensively acknowledged. Beyond these characteristics derived from caricature that exhibit themselves textually in the novels, a broader study that will reconnect Dickens with the mass of ephemeral graphic production that surrounded him in London is also required. Such a study will address the historical and critical processes that have separated out a 'great tradition' of satirical utterance from the vast production of visual comedy and the continuing affirmation of Dickens as the most significant inheritor of this tradition. As Luisa Calè has argued, the 'canonization of Dickens has separated his works as "literature" from the "ephemera"' with which they flourished [. . .]. In the wake of

Dickens's rise as an author, literary practice has divorced his works from their material culture.'[51]

This essay has suggested that there are two particular aspects of the 'material culture' of 1830s caricature that need further exploration in order to understand Dickens's brilliant assimilation of ideas inhering in contemporary print culture into his novelistic and commercial practices. The first, widely visible in the 1830s as a new potentiality for the publication of caricature, concerns seriality as both a creative formal possibility and, equally important, a commercial opportunity. Seymour was a key figure in exploring the potentiality of serialisation as a mechanism for constructing graphic forms that would engage the reader in the long-term consumption of visual pleasure. The second was a burgeoning interest among humorous artists in shaping isolated comic insights into narrative form. Dickens was astute enough to translate the visual potentialities envisioned in this way into those verbal forms that increasingly rendered scattered picaresque moments as 'the novel'.

In this way, two countervailing practices were being brought together within the graphic production of comic artists in the 1830s. The first, suggested by the title of one of Seymour's major works, was the 'humorous sketch', the rapidly observed, seemingly random moment suggestive of the conduct of everyday events. The second, equally visible in the *Humorous Sketches*, but also found elsewhere in Seymour's work, was an interest in graphic storytelling, a mode of narration that never fully entered into British popular culture in the comic strip forms to be found widely in France, Belgium and the United States.[52] *The Pickwick Papers*, among its many significances in the history of print as a new form of commodity text, may well represent the moment when the momentum towards a sustained graphic narrative with a subordinated text was diverted from fulfilling its full potential by the arrival of the illustrated novel.

Notes

1. The usually cited prototypes for the figure of Samuel Pickwick in Seymour's work are plate 2 in Richard Penn's *Maxims and Hints for an Angler* (London: Murray, 1833) and 'The Silent System', an image to be found in *The Squib Annual* (London: Chapman and Hall, 1836), 29.
2. Sally Ledger, *Dickens and the Popular Radical Imagination* (Cambridge: Cambridge University Press, 2007), 78–9.
3. Ibid., 79.
4. *The Universal Songster*, 3 vols (London: Jones, 1825, 1826, 1827).
5. See Janet Snowman, 'John Orlando Parry and Charles Dickens: Some Connections', *Dickensian* 110.492 (2014), 5–23.
6. On the grotesque, see Michael Hollington's *Dickens and the Grotesque* (London: Croom Helm, 1984).
7. For a further account of Dickens's use of caricature, see Michael Steig, *Dickens and Phiz* (Bloomington: Indiana University Press, 1978), especially Chapter 2 on 'The Beginnings of "Phiz": *Pickwick*, *Nickleby* and the Emergence from Caricature' (24–50). See also Alfie Bown, 'Caricature in Dickens and Thackeray', *Comedy Studies* 3.1 (May 2012), 75–82.
8. John Dixon Hunt, 'Dickens and the Tradition of Graphic Satire', in *Encounters: Essays on Literature and the Visual Arts*, ed. by John Dixon Hunt (London: Studio Vista, 1971), 124–40, 126.

9. Richard A. Vogler, '*Oliver Twist* – Cruikshank's Pictorial Prototypes', in *Dickens Studies Annual 2*, ed. by R. B. Partlow (Carbondale: Southern Illinois University Press, 1972), 98–118.
10. Ibid., 99–100.
11. Ibid., 98.
12. For an overview of comic art in the late Regency and early Victorian period, see Brian Maidment, *Comedy, Caricature and the Social Order, 1820–1850* (Manchester: Manchester University Press, 2013).
13. Dixon Hunt, 'Tradition', 124.
14. Vogler, 99.
15. Ledger, 79.
16. The full title for this play is *The Power of Conscience Exemplified in the Genuine and Extraordinary Confession of Thomas Bedworth* (London: Hone, 1815).
17. Peake was commissioned to 'narrativise' Seymour's sequence of *Humorous Sketches* into something approaching an illustrated novel a few years after *Pickwick* was published. *Seymour's Humorous Sketches Comprising Ninety Two Caricature Etchings Illustrated in Prose* by R. B. Peake was published by George Routledge in 1846. This version of the *Sketches* also appeared as *An Evening's Amusement of the Adventures of a Cockney Sportsman, by R. B. Peake, Esq.* (no publisher, 1846) and as *Snobson's Seasons, Being Annuals of Cockney Sports* (M. A. Nattali, n.d.).
18. Ledger, 79–92.
19. Ibid., 75.
20. *Pictorial Pickwickiana: Charles Dickens and his Illustrators*, ed. by Joseph Grego, 2 vols (London: Chapman & Hall, 1899).
21. See, for example, Adam Abraham, 'Plagiarising Pickwick', *Dickens Quarterly* 32.1 (March 2015), 5–20; Luisa Calè, 'Dickens Extra-Illustrated: The Case of *Nicholas Nickleby*', *Yearbook of English Studies* 40 (July 2010), 8–32; and Chris Louttit, 'Boz without Phiz: Reading Dickens with Different Illustrations', in *Reading Dickens Differently*, ed. by Leon Litvak and Nathalie Vanfasse (Chichester: Wiley Blackwell, 2019) 149–64.
22. Cruikshank's *Scraps and Sketches* was published in four parts between 1828 and 1832, and frequently reissued.
23. Henry Alken's *Scraps from the Sketchbook of Henry Alken* was published by Thomas McLean in 1821.
24. See Brian Maidment, 'Henry Heath's "The Caricaturist's Scrapbook" (1840)' *Victorian Review* 38.2 (Fall 2012), 13–18.
25. Calè, 9.
26. Charles Dickens, 'London Recreations', in *Sketches by Boz* (London: Chapman & Hall Collected edn, 1839), 103.
27. Calè, 9.
28. For a broader discussion of the relationship between the verbal and visual in early Victorian culture, see Brian Maidment, 'The Explicated Image – Graphic "Texts" in Early Victorian Print Culture', in *Drawing on the Victorians: The Palimpsest of Victorian and Neo-Victorian Texts*, ed. by Anna Maria Jones and Rebecca N. Mitchell (Athens: Ohio State University Press, 2016), 39–66.
29. Simon Houfe, *The Dictionary of British Book Illustrators and Caricaturists, 1800–1914*, rev. edn (Woodbridge: Antique Collectors Club, 1981), 446.
30. Dixon Hunt, 'Tradition', 129.
31. Jane R. Cohen, *Charles Dickens and his Original Illustrators* (Columbus: Ohio State University Press 1980), 39.
32. Ibid.
33. Robert L. Patten, review of Maidment *Comedy, Caricature and the Social Order*, in *Victorian Studies* 57.4 (Summer 2015), 722.

Plate 1 John Orlando Parry, unpublished and unsigned pen drawing, 'Starting for Cheltenham' (c.1835). Courtesy of Brian Maidment.

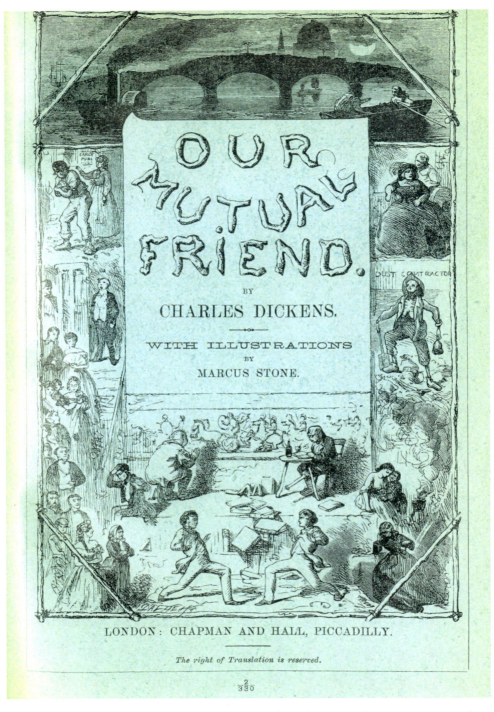

Plate 2 Marcus Stone, part issue title page for Charles Dickens's *Our Mutual Friend* (1864–5). Courtesy of the Charles Dickens Museum, London.

Plate 3 Robert Seymour, 'Repentance!!!', lithographed plate 9 for *The Schoolmaster Abroad* (London: McLean, 1834). Courtesy of Brian Maidment.

Plate 4 Day and Martin's Blacking Bottle. Courtesy of the Charles Dickens Museum, London [DH534_R3].

Plate 5 Hablot K. Browne ('Phiz'), 'Damocles', an illustration for Charles Dickens's *Little Dorrit* (1855–7). Courtesy of the Charles Dickens Museum, London.

CARICATURE   257

34. Cohen, 41.
35. Wildrake (George Tattersall), *Cracks of the Day* (London: Ackermann 1841).
36. David Beazley, *Images of Angling: Three Centuries of British Angling Prints* (Haslemere: Creel Press, 2010), 164.
37. Ibid., 65.
38. Richard Penn, *Maxims and Hints for an Angler; and Miseries of Fishing* (London: Murray, 1833).
39. Ledger, 75.
40. See Brian Maidment, 'A Draft List of Published Book and Periodical Contributions by Robert Seymour', published in the Digital Annex to *Victorians Institute Journal* 38 (2010), hosted by *NINES: Nineteenth-Century Electronic Scholarship Online* <www.nines.org/exhibits/robert_seymour> [accessed 4 June 2018].
41. The Carlile edition began with seventeen 'Popular Sketches' published in 1832 before the subsequent serial issue of the extended sequence of *Humorous Sketches*.
42. Originally published by Effingham Wilson, and issued as monthly parts each comprising ten plates, the series was taken over by Charles Tilt, and reissued by Tilt and Bogue in 1841–2. The publication never seems to have enjoyed the success of the *Humorous Sketches*.
43. Beazley, 222.
44. See, for example, *The Omnibus* (McLean, 1830), which comprised six oblong folio coloured etchings issued in printed paper covers. The subtitle printed on the paper covers runs – 'What sort of company go in the omnibus?' 'O! All sorts'. Thus the title is used to suggest both the miscellaneous gathering up of disparate elements in one common place but also the 'democracy' or Clapham omnibus ordinariness of the images.
45. *The Terrific Register; or, Record of Crimes, Judgments, Providences and Calamities* (London: Sherwood, Jones, 1825).
46. Pierce Egan, *Pierce Egan's Book of Sports and Mirror of Life* (London: Tegg, 1832).
47. Robert Seymour, *The Schoolmaster Abroad* (London: McLean, 1834).
48. Brian Maidment, 'The "March of Intellect" and Graphic Satire, 1820–1840', in *Shaping Belief: Culture, Politics, and Religion in Nineteenth-Century Writing*, ed. by Victoria Morgan and Clare Williams (Liverpool: Liverpool University Press, 2008), 149–71.
49. For an account of the Dr Syntax books, see Harlan W. Hamilton, *Doctor Syntax: A Silhouette of William Combe, Esq.* (London: Chatto & Windus, 1969).
50. The phrase 'the schoolmaster is abroad' was drawn from a January 1828 speech made by Lord Brougham. The phrase was endlessly invoked by those who opposed the Whig programme of educating the mass of the population through the medium of print. Brougham's precise words were: 'Let the soldier be abroad, if he will; he can do nothing in this age. There is another personage abroad [. . .]. The schoolmaster is abroad; and I trust to him, armed with his primer, against the soldier in full military array.'
51. Calè, 11, 31.
52. See David Kunzle, *The History of the Comic Strip: The Nineteenth Century* (Berkeley: University of California Press, 1990).

Further Reading

Jane R. Cohen, *Charles Dickens and His Original Illustrators* (Columbus: Ohio State University Press, 1980)

Catherine J. Golden, *Serials to Graphic Novels: The Evolution of the Victorian Illustrated Book* (Gainesville: University Press of Florida, 2017)

Ian Haywood, *The Rise of Victorian Caricature* (Cham: Palgrave Macmillan, 2020)

J. Hillis Miller, *Illustration* (London: Reaktion Books, 1992)

17

LANDSCAPE

Malcolm Andrews

The fact is, my love, I'm tired of the country; green fields, and blooming hedges, and feathered songsters, are fine things to talk about and read about and write about; but I candidly confess that I prefer paved streets, area railings and dustman's bells, after all.

–Charles Dickens, *Is She His Wife?*[1]

DICKENS IS FAMOUSLY THE NOVELIST OF the city, the first great writer of the modern metropolis. It is often remarked that correspondingly he has little poetic feel for country scenery or sublime landscapes. The character in his comic burletta *Is She His Wife?* (1837) who voices his weariness with country life has his prejudices built into his name – Alfred Lovetown. He casts the components of country scenery in stale, generalised eighteenth-century descriptive language (those 'feathered songsters'), whereas their urban counterparts ('railings' preferred to 'hedges') are precisely detailed. It is almost as though the countryside itself is already, and inescapably, an array of visual clichés. This discrepancy in the quality of descriptive language is noticeable more broadly in Dickens's fiction, especially in the early novels: city scenes are sharply focused and vividly energised with quirky detail, whereas his country scenery is distinctly hackneyed (at Dingley Dell, at the idealised country retreat where Oliver recuperates, at Little Nell's ancient country village). Ruskin complained of *The Old Curiosity Shop* (1840–1): 'It is evident the man is a thorough cockney, from his way of talking about hedgerows, and honeysuckles, and village spires [. . .] that turn for the picturesque which leads him into perpetual mannerism.'[2] We shall explore Dickens's handling of landscape in his fiction as well as the way he responds to different landscapes in his own life, particularly in his letters and travel books. Let us start with the latter, and in particular his deployment of that vogue term invoked by Ruskin – 'the picturesque'.

Picturesque Tourism

Dickens began his writing career at a time when British landscape scenery had become one of the principal motives for summer tourism. Roads were rapidly improving for the touring carriages of the middle and upper classes, and by the middle of the century the railways were bringing hundreds of sightseers from all classes into the remoter regions of the country to enjoy spectacular landscapes. Wordsworth was

LANDSCAPE 259

outraged by the planned intrusion of the railway into the heart of the Lake District: 'Is then no nook of English ground secure | From rash assault?'[3] That famous cry of horror in 1844 was echoed ironically two years later by Dickens, in *Dombey and Son* (1846–8), when the inhabitants of Staggs's Gardens (based on London's Camden Town district), who regarded their neighbourhood as 'a sacred grove not to be withered by railroads', lamented: 'Oh woe the day! when "not a rood of English ground" – laid out in Staggs's Gardens – is secure!'[4]

Dickens by and large welcomed the new. He affectionately caricatured the sentimentalised pastoralism of the Staggs's Gardeners, in much the same spirit as he portrayed old Tony Weller's abuse of the railway train that was making the stage coach an endangered species: 'a nasty, wheezin', creaking, gasping, puffin, bustin' monster [. . .] like a unpleasant beetle in that 'ere gas magnifier'.[5] No wonder Ruskin characterised Dickens as 'a pure modernist—a leader of the steam-whistle party *par excellence*'.[6]

I would guess Dickens felt about Wordsworth's reaction to the railway invasion into Lakeland's natural beauty much as he felt about Macaulay's comments, in his *History of England*, when he (Macaulay) wrote of the 'gazers and stretchers' swarming into the Scottish Highlands, and the 'thousands of clerks and milliners who are now thrown into raptures by the sight of Loch Katrine and Loch Lomond'. In his *Household Words* essay 'Insularities', Dickens reads this passage as contemptuous of the lower classes:

> The accomplished Mr Macaulay, in the third volume of his brilliant History, writes loftily about 'the thousands of clerks and milliners who are thrown into raptures [. . .]'. No such responsible gentleman, in France or Germany, writing history – writing anything – would think it fine to sneer at any inoffensive and useful class of his fellow subjects. If the clerks and milliners – who pair off arm in arm, by thousands, for Loch Katrine and Loch Lomond, to celebrate the Early Closing Movement, we presume – will only imagine their presence poisoning those waters to the majestic historian as he roves along the banks, looking for Whig Members of Parliament to sympathise with him in admiration for the beauties of Nature, we think they will be amply avenged in the absurdity of the picture.[7]

Dickens is perhaps oversensitive to the tone of Macaulay's remarks: it is not at all certain, in the larger context, that 'the majestic historian' is sneering. However, there is much in these remarks that reveals Dickens's broader attitudes towards landscape tourism: he was himself sceptical about the fashionable vogue for the picturesque, and the sentimental devotion to 'the beauties of Nature'. That is where it will be useful to start discussion.

The Pickwick Papers (1836–7) began life as a comic take on tourism, with a group of naive but earnest adventurers running into all sorts of mishaps on their tour. It followed a tradition that included William Combe and Thomas Rowlandson's highly popular *The Tour of Doctor Syntax in Search of the Picturesque* (1813), where the naive pedant Syntax is hilariously accident-prone as he visits the prime picturesque sites in Britain. The Pickwickians travel in search of social and natural interests, and

260 MALCOLM ANDREWS

these include landscape and antiquities. Soon after reaching Rochester, Mr Pickwick is rewarded with a classic picturesque view of 'a rich and varied landscape', as he stands on Rochester Bridge:

> On the left of the spectator lay the ruined wall, broken in many places, and in some, overhanging the narrow beach below in rude and heavy masses. Huge knots of sea-weed hung upon the jagged and pointed stones, trembling in every breath of wind; and the green ivy clung mournfully round the dark, and ruined battlements. Behind it rose the ancient castle, its towers roofless, and its massive walls crumbling away, but telling us proudly of its old might and strength, as when, seven hundred years ago, it rang with the clash of arms, or resounded with the noise of feasting and revelry. On either side, the banks of the Medway, covered with cornfields and pastures, with here and there a windmill, or a distant church, stretched away as far as the eye could see, presenting a rich and varied landscape, rendered more beautiful by the changing shadows which passed swiftly across it as the thin and half-formed clouds skimmed away in the light of the morning sun. The river, reflecting the clear blue of the sky, glistened and sparkled as it flowed noiselessly on; and the oars of the fishermen dipped into the water with a clear and liquid sound, as their heavy but picturesque boats glided slowly down the stream.[8]

Conventional picturesque aesthetics required the spectator to shape the landscape scene into a framed view, with a foreground, a middle-ground and a distant background, and the whole bordered by 'side-screens' of trees or cliff-face or riverbanks which would nudge the eye into exploring the centre ground and its interestingly romantic ruins. This is the format observed in Dickens's description, which might have come straight from a picturesque guidebook to Rochester. The banks are sketched in and particular attention given to the ruined castle, then we move into the central, broader landscape as it stretches back to the horizon, from which we return to the middle- and foreground activity on the sparkling river. It is a complete picturesque view. That word 'picturesque' is introduced at the end, to describe the boats. What does it mean? It doesn't give any detailed information about the shapes or colours, but just assures the reader that they are aesthetically keyed into the larger picture. Dickens does, however, indicate elsewhere that he knows well the more specifically denotative value of the term. In 1841 he and Catherine undertook a tour of the Highlands of Scotland, by then a very popular picturesque destination, enhanced by associations with Walter Scott's poetry and novels. They arrive at Loch Katrine – 'a glorious scene' Dickens reported to John Forster – and the rain was relentless. 'We conveyed Kate up a rocky pass to go and see the island of the Lady of the Lake, but she gave in after the first five minutes, and we left her, very picturesque and uncomfortable, with Tom holding an umbrella over her head, while we climbed on.'[9] 'Picturesque' comes to mean somewhat dishevelled (roughness and variety had become signature definers of the picturesque according to its chief theorists, William Gilpin and Uvedale Price). When in his *Household Words* essay on 'Our Watering Place' (i.e. Broadstairs) he comes to describe the pier, he has this to say about it: 'a queer old wooden pier, fortunately without the slightest pretensions to architecture, and very picturesque in consequence'.[10] Here he associates the picturesque with eccentricity, with a conspicuous lack of planned elegance and modernity. Picturesque comes to

LANDSCAPE 261

designate a shabby old-world charm, a congeries of superannuated qualities lost in the modern world of sophisticated technological progress.

Bit by bit the term acquired an ethically disreputable connotation by the way it was associated with the squalid and the down-and-out. It tended to aestheticise scenes of poverty as pictorially romantic. Thus, when Dickens was touring Italy's landscapes and townscapes, he arrived in Naples (in 1845) and was confronted by abject beggary. He was shocked by the beggary, but also disgusted by the way such scenes had become absorbed into the tourist experience: 'The condition of the common people here is abject and shocking. I am afraid the conventional idea of the picturesque is associated with such misery and degradation that a new picturesque will have to be established as the world goes onward.'[11]

Just the year before, in the Third Quarter of his Christmas Book *The Chimes* (1844), Dickens had taken the opportunity to castigate the taste for picturesque rustic poverty when the labourer Will Fern tells the 'Gentlefolks' about the place where he has lived for many years:

> 'You may see the cottage from the sunk fence over yonder. I've seen the ladies draw it in their books, a hundred times. It looks well in a picter, I've heerd say; but there an't weather in picters, and may be 'tis fitter for that, than for a place to live in.'[12]

The reproach to the aestheticising gentry is sharply made. The 'sunk fence' refers to the landscaped garden's ha-ha, which separated the formal gardens of the great house from the relatively uncultivated parkland. It prevented grazing deer or cattle from encroaching on the elegant lawns and parterres, but it gave the illusion of uninterrupted landscape vistas for those interested in pictorialising the 'natural' views; and within this pictorialising the occasional decaying old cottage could form a picturesque feature.

From Will Fern's sour remarks to Mrs General's affected aestheticism in *Little Dorrit* (1855–7) is but a short step. In middle and later Dickens, those who practice picturesque connoisseurship are subjects for satire and indignation. Mrs Skewton, for instance, in *Dombey and Son*, shrilly rhapsodises about the charming bygone days as so picturesque, and, in *Bleak House* (1852–3), the Dandy clique at Chesney Wold includes those who would make the vulgar very picturesque by cancelling a few hundred years of history. No wonder Dickens called for 'a new picturesque', one that would be more appropriate to an age with raised concerns about the condition of England and its poor and dispossessed.

While Dickens wished to dissociate himself from the conventional connoisseur's picturesque in his appreciation and description of landscape, he did evidently have some appetite for crafting a picturesque of his own. In July 1851 he wrote to his *Household Words* subeditor W. H. Wills about a project that had apparently been in his mind in the late 1830s. The 'Horne' he mentions here is the writer Richard Henry (or Hengist) Horne, a prolific contributor to *Household Words* and author of *A New Spirit of the Age*, which contained his long analytical essay on Dickens:

> The notion I think of trying with Horne, is a kind of adaptation of an old idea I once had (when I was making my name) of a fanciful and picturesque 'beauties

of England and Wales'. For I never look at the grimgriffinhoof 'Beauties' without thinking what might be done [. . .]. Don't you think a series of Places, *well* chosen, and described *well*, with their peculiarities and popularities thoroughly seized, would be a very promising series?—And one that people would be particularly likely to identify with me?—[13]

The 'Beauties' he mentions refers (according to the Pilgrim Editors) to *The Beauties of England and Wales*, a twenty-six-volume topographical guide, published between 1801 and 1816, which described scenic spots and incorporated picturesque engravings. Such publications – a blend of lavish plates and letterpress – were legion in the early decades of the nineteenth century. Dickens acquired a full set of the *Beauties* in 1839, when he probably had in mind a similar series of descriptions of places and people for his new project *Master Humphrey's Clock* (1840–1). His letter to Wills emphasises the importance of the quality of the descriptive writing, that it would concentrate on the 'fanciful and picturesque', and that it would be distinctively 'Dickensian' (*avant la lettre*). What was the outcome of this proposal? The first move was for Dickens and Horne to go down to Chatham and 'take certain bits of the Dockyard & fortifications', as Dickens suggested.[14] Horne, in his later memoirs, recalled that Dickens would undertake description of the fortifications and country scenery there, and Horne the dockyard itself. The published result was 'One Man in a Dockyard', which appeared in *Household Words* on 6 September 1851.[15] Dickens most likely contributed the opening seven paragraphs, where, in the persona of John Strongitharm, he saunters around Rochester and Chatham observing the castle, Watts Charity Almshouses and the Chatham Lines high above the town and dockyard, where as a boy Dickens had watched the spectacular military drill parades and mock battle manoeuvres.

Dickens's observations on the scenery are determinedly connected with its human associations, rather than prompting reflections on any formal landscape aesthetics of the picturesque kind. Ruined Rochester Castle, for instance, he animates by vividly describing 'the great holes where the rafters of floors were once – bare as toothless gums now – or [. . .] glimpses of the Medway through dreary apertures like eye-sockets without eyes'.[16] This decaying corpse of a building, together with the old houses below in the cathedral precincts, the fragments of city gates and the old trees, serve only to remind John Strongitharm of his own youth and insignificance, not to stimulate ideas of scenic beauty or sublimity. Later, up on the Chatham Lines, it is the same story as he 'mused among the fortifications' which now lie quiet.[17] The landscape is little more than a memento of lost human activity.

This, we might think, typifies Dickens's general handling of descriptive material that in other hands would have stimulated verbal landscape painting of a picturesque kind – even when he sets out with the explicit intention of producing 'a fanciful and picturesque "beauties of England and Wales"'. Even though he travelled to famous beauty spots – such as the Lake District with Wilkie Collins in 1857 (for the *Lazy Tour of Two Idle Apprentices*), the West Country in 1842 with Forster and two painters, Maclise and Stanfield, and, of course, his tours in Italy and North America – his appetite for purely landscape pleasures pales beside his impulse to convey the human scene or places where he can evoke pungent human associations. He seems at a loss when this cannot happen, especially when the landscape seems to him to have virtually no individual distinctive features and little movement at all in its contours. Such a challenge was posed by his sight of the American Prairies, as he describes in *American Notes* (1842):

> Looking towards the setting sun, there lay, stretched out before my view, a vast expanse of level ground; unbroken, save by one thin line of trees, which scarcely amounted to a scratch upon the great blank; [. . .]. There it lay, a tranquil sea or lake without water, if such a simile be admissible [. . .]. Great as the picture was, its very flatness and extent, which left nothing to the imagination, tamed it down and cramped its interest. I felt little of that sense of freedom and exhilaration which a Scottish heath inspires, or even our English downs awaken. It was lonely and wild, but oppressive in its barren monotony.[18]

The emptiness and lack of any animating variety depressed Dickens's imagination. What was meant to be a great landscape experience (and he had travelled a long way to see this spectacle of the Looking-Glass Prairie) simply left him missing the feelings inspired by familiar British equivalents to such huge expanses of nearly empty, open countryside. In his letters home (on which he based much of the *American Notes*), he remarked: 'I felt no such emotions as I do in crossing Salisbury plain [. . .] Marlborough downs, or any of the broad, high, open lands near the sea [. . .] are fully as impressive [as the prairie]; and Salisbury plain is *decidedly* more so.'[19] Dickens is very consciously assessing his aesthetic reactions here. In fact, he recalls that 'I retired from the rest of the party, to understand my own feelings the better.'[20] Every tourist to sites that are already famous faces this challenge: 'What do I think of this? Is it as great as it is supposed to be? If not, am I missing something here?' And in the assessing of one's own reactions, the natural reflex is to make comparisons with similar scenery that is more familiar to one. The whole exercise of the picturesque is, by definition, one of comparison: this landscape is 'like a picture', its individual features and/or its general composition resemble a distinctive landscape painting, and it thereby acquires by association an artistic value to add to any other kind of sensory value it might afford.

The other great aesthetic challenge for the touring Dickens, in landscape terms, was Niagara Falls. He reached here later in the same month, April 1842, and stayed for over a week. This time his imagination was galvanised by the spectacle. At the same time, he is assessing the experience in quite a methodical way, as he writes to his American friend Charles Sumner:

> I had a vague sense of the greatness of the scene, as we crossed; but it was not until I got upon Table Rock, that I was able to comprehend it—for I was in a kind of whirl up to that time, and should have been rather at a loss if I had been suddenly called upon to state what part of me I regarded as my head, and what as my heels. But when I had looked at the Great Horse Shoe Fall for a few minutes, from this point, I comprehended the whole scene. [. . .] From the first, the impression on my mind was one of Beauty, unmixed with any sense of Terror.[21]

'Beauty' and 'Terror', the capitalised sensations, were routinely attributed to the primary effects of grand scenery. The popularity of those terms in the tourists' vocabulary stemmed from Burke's famous arguments over distinctions between the Beautiful and the Sublime (Terror being the key component in the Sublime), and much debate was generated in the writings of the picturesque theorists and others about the appropriate response-label to apply to particular landscape experiences. Dickens is decisive here about which of the two was paramount in his experience of the Niagara Falls. We notice also that he is concerned to 'comprehend' the scene, to exchange 'a vague sense' of its greatness for a full understanding of its totality. This is an exercise of control. The Sublime is typically the experience of loss of control, when the mind is overwhelmed and disoriented by the thrilling spectacle and cannot gather its faculties. But Beauty is experienced with the recovery of control, with 'comprehension'. And, in line with this sensation of Beauty, the 'train of thought' always prompted in Dickens (so he tells Sumner) by the Falls was 'Peaceful Eternity; without the least admixture of trouble or commotion'.[22]

Dickens, in spite of his frequent pillorying of the clichés of picturesque connoisseurship, showed himself to be touched by some of its influence and terminology. He is also a reflective tourist when confronted with the great landscape experiences of Europe and North America. How much of these mixed responses find their way into his fiction and help to shape its narrative? That is the next question to explore.

The Living Landscape

Oh! the glory of the sudden burst of light; the freshness of the fields and woods, stretching away on every side and meeting the bright blue sky; the cattle grazing in the pasturage; the smoke, that, coming from among the trees, seemed to rise upward from the green earth; the children yet at their gambols down below—all, everything, so beautiful and happy. It was like passing from death to life; it was drawing nearer Heaven.

–Charles Dickens, *The Old Curiosity Shop*[23]

Who can describe the pleasure and delight, the peace of mind and soft tranquillity, which the sickly boy felt in the balmy air, and among the green hills and rich woods of an inland village! Who can tell how scenes of peace and quietude sink into the minds of pain-worn dwellers in close and noisy places [. . .] and [who], carried far from the scenes of their old pains and pleasures, have seemed to pass at once into a new state of being, and crawling forth from day to day to some green sunny spot, have had such memories wakened up within them by the mere sight of sky, and hill, and plain, and glistening water, that a foretaste of Heaven itself has soothed their quick decline [. . .]. The memories which peaceful country scenes call up, are not of this world, nor of its thoughts and hopes.

–Charles Dickens, *Oliver Twist*[24]

Ruskin's contempt for Dickens's 'cockney' visions of the countryside was based on the early novels, where indeed the passages of description of natural landscape often have a sentimentalised, soft-focus conventionality, as in these examples from *Oliver Twist* (1837–9) and *The Old Curiosity Shop*. But one needs to ask in these cases what function the description is serving. In both passages Dickens is not interested in topographical detailing or particularised depiction of the natural scene's flora and fauna. This country scenery is deliberately idealised so as to play its part in the near-allegorical mode of the novel. It is to serve as an image of heaven on earth, deliberately generalised as a site of peace and freshness, beauty and happiness. Ruskin's caustic remarks seem not to allow for that. The passage from *Oliver Twist* has often been associated with Wordsworth's 'Ode: Intimations of Immortality from Recollections of Early Childhood' (which Dickens knew) in its representation of nature's beauty as an intimation of the heavenly world from which the child has come and to which the grown man can be assured he will return. Both Oliver and Nell find the countryside a paradisal asylum from the threats that have beset them in the city.

But for all its proclaimed freshness and its capacity to restore the vitality of the jaded or 'pain-worn' city dweller, this countryside in Dickens's description seems decidedly lacking in energy and animation. It is *so* reassuringly and insistently peaceful as to induce atrophy. It is like being at rest in death, in the imagined life hereafter. Nell's ancient country village has stopped living, in the sense that it seems now impervious to change and development: 'even change was old in that old place', as the narrator puts it.[25] This is ideal for the exhausted Nell. When the kind schoolmaster asks her, 'A peaceful place to live in, don't you think so?' Nell replies: 'Oh yes [. . .]. A quiet, happy place—a place to live and learn to die in!'[26] As a welcome refuge from the dizzying and disorienting changefulness of the city, the countryside in early Dickens (and it is much the same in that earlier rural sanctuary, *Pickwick*'s Dingley Dell) is constructed as the reassuring image of relative changelessness. Sharp, lively rural detail would disturb that role.

Elizabeth Bowen prescribed the novelist's use of scene or setting in succinct terms: 'Scene is only justified in the novel where it can be shown, or at least felt, to act upon action or character. In fact, where it has dramatic use. Where not intended for dramatic use, scene is a sheer slower-down. Its staticness is a dead weight.'[27] Dickens's much maligned bland pastoral landscapes in the early novels are there for the allegorical purposes I suggested, but they also serve to slow the narrative down just where he wants it to be slowed – during the periods of convalescence for Oliver and Nell after their furious flights from the torments of the city. This is consistent with Dickens's commitment in his early novels to a pattern of highlighted contrasts.

'Scene' is justified 'where it has dramatic use.' As Dickens's writing matures so he assimilates his landscapes into the novel's action so that they become dramatic auxiliaries rather than picturesque backdrops. Ruskin, who had been so dismissive of Dickens's early landscape description, lavished praise on some of the middle-period writing, claiming that 'His powers of description have never been enough esteemed.'[28] He instanced the storm in *David Copperfield* (1849–50), Carker's journey through the French countryside near the end of *Dombey*, and this striking landscape scene in *Martin Chuzzlewit* (1843-44), when Jonas is on the brink of murdering Tigg Montague in a lonely wood.

The last rays of the sun were shining in, aslant, making a path of golden light along the stems and branches in its range, which, even as he looked, began to die away: yielding gently to the twilight that came creeping on. It was so very quiet that the soft and stealthy moss about the trunks of some old trees, seemed to have grown out of the silence, and to be its proper offspring. Those other trees which were subdued by blasts of wind in winter time, had not quite tumbled down, but being caught by others, lay all bare and scathed across their leafy arms, as if unwilling to disturb the general repose by the crash of their fall. Vistas of silence opened everywhere, into the heart and innermost recesses of the wood; beginning with the likeness of an aisle, a cloister, or a ruin open to the sky; then tangling off into a deep green rustling mystery, through which gnarled trunks, and twisted boughs, and ivy-covered stems, and trembling leaves, and bark-stripped bodies of old trees stretched out at length, were faintly seen in beautiful confusion.[29]

In what respects does this beguiling and quite protracted natural description 'act upon action or character'? At first sight it seems like just a quiet interlude in a tense narrative in which we have been following Jonas as he travels towards the place where he is to kill Montague. At the end of this passage he will disappear into the wood where his prey lurks. Minutes later (or longer? – though it is only a short paragraph afterwards) he will burst from that wood and run for the road that leads back to London. We do not see the murder.

The scene is a mixture of radiant beauty, as the setting sun gilds the wood's edge, and of stillness. But within this refulgent silence light takes on a subtle mobile quality, and then a vegetable quality, as it seems to spawn the soft moss around the trees. In fact, Dickens is weaving a synaesthetic spell in this description. Sound and sight coalesce in '[v]istas of silence', and in the 'deep green rustling mystery' in the recesses of the wood. That is one kind of expressive effect. Another is the way in which the beauty and calm of the evening is counterpointed by the spectacle of terrible violence – the ruined trees, blasted by storms and flayed of their bark. In its own way the natural description is highly active in reinforcing the narrative tension by the ominous stillness and the scenes of brutal wreckage amid beauty. When it is compared with the set-piece, picturesque description of the Medway from Rochester Bridge in *Pickwick*, this passage resonates with the 'dramatic use' stipulated by Bowen for justifying 'scene' in a novel.

Dickens's signature animism, which turns buildings into characters, fog into some tentacular creature, and furniture into human bodies, acts also in his landscape scenes in the more mature novels. He sheds the formality of the stilted picturesque representation in favour of a much more dynamic and expressive – even expressionist – mode. To this end he will sometimes establish a keynote, as he does explicitly in introducing Coketown in *Hard Times* (1854). The physical features of the town as well as its dominant 'triumph of fact' ethos (the latter infusing the character of the former throughout) are ushered in by this sentence: 'Let us strike the key-note, Coketown, before pursuing our tune.'[30] It can be the same in his landscape representation. One might exchange the musical term 'keynote' for the more painterly one, 'master tone', for these descriptions. The various, heterogeneous components of the landscape are coordinated and harmonised by this compositional principle.

A keynote is established in the second chapter of *Bleak House*, where we have been transported from London and its plague-like fog up to Lincolnshire and the ancestral estate of Sir Leicester Dedlock at Chesney Wold. The geographical shift is a big one, but metaphorically we are in the same 'Condition of England' state. Like the world of Chancery, Chesney Wold 'is a deadened world, and its growth is sometimes unhealthy for want of air'. The view of the parkland is therefore one of stagnation:

The waters are out in Lincolnshire. An arch of the bridge in the park has been sapped and sopped away. The adjacent low-lying ground, for half a mile in breadth, is a stagnant river, with melancholy trees for islands in it, and a surface punctured all over, all day long, with falling rain. My Lady Dedlock's 'place' has been extremely dreary. The weather, for many a day and night, has been so wet that the trees seem wet through, and the soft loppings and prunings of the wood-man's axe can make no crash or crackle as they fall. The deer, looking soaked, leave quagmires where they pass. The shot of a rifle loses its sharpness in the moist air, and its smoke moves in a tardy little cloud towards the green rise, coppice-topped, that makes a background for the falling rain. The view from my Lady Dedlock's own windows is alternately a lead-coloured view and a view in Indian ink. The vases on the stone terrace in the foreground catch the rain all day; and the heavy drops fall, drip, drip, drip, upon the broad flagged pavement, called, from old time, the Ghost's Walk, all night. On Sundays, the little church in the park is mouldy; the oaken pulpit breaks out into a cold sweat; and there is a general smell and taste as of the ancient Dedlocks in their graves. My Lady Dedlock (who is childless), looking out in the early twilight from her boudoir at a keeper's lodge, and seeing the light of a fire upon the latticed panes, and smoke rising from the chimney, and a child, chased by a woman, running out into the rain to meet the shining figure of a wrapped-up man coming through the gate, has been put quite out of temper. My Lady Dedlock says she has been 'bored to death.'[31]

Sir Leicester Dedlock grants that, on the whole, Nature is 'a good idea', but thinks it 'a little low, perhaps, when not enclosed with a park-fence'.[32] Where it has been emparked by the Dedlocks, the vulgar natural world's vital energies have been suppressed. The same applies to the larger condition of England. It is as if the suffocating fog of the first chapter, emanating from the great patrician-dominated public institutions, has been cleared of its metropolitan pollutants and has now become condensed to swamp the Dedlock acres and spread its stagnating influence. Normally crisp sounds – a rifle shot or axe stroke on timber – are fatally muffled. Colour is washed away too: the whole picture is a landscape grisaille.

One small detail flares briefly in the gloom as Lady Dedlock (who suffocated passion long ago) catches sight of the keeper's lodge: light, fire, people running, a man shining – sudden vitality lights up the landscape. Then it is quenched. In fact, it has been partially suffocated anyway by being carried within the long sentence of Lady Dedlock's dulling gaze. This glimpse of life is almost anathema to one who insists she is being bored to death. We know why, of course. The vibrant sight of a child with loving parents must be too sharp a pain for one (*not* 'childless') who forsook her own child long ago; so the brief experience must be smothered. She is a type of the England that has abandoned its poor children. Her blighting act has stained the landscape she surveys.

The Victorian period was particularly rich in virtuoso mood landscapes in poetry and fiction (Tennyson and Emily and Charlotte Brontë inter alia). Ruskin was initially critical of the practice of transferring private moods so that they stain the representation of the external world: 'All violent feelings have the same effect. They produce in us a falseness in all our impressions of external things, which I would generally characterize as the "pathetic fallacy".'[33] But he came to recognise that, while this practice in landscape literature and painting distorted the objective truth, it gave instead a different kind of account of the natural world – an emotional truth that reflected the vital perceptual relationship between the human and the natural world. In the case of Turner's landscapes, for instance, where a photograph or even the human eye would give some grandeur of height to an Alpine crag, the painter rears it even higher and correspondingly dwarfs the village at its foot, in order to convey the sublime impact of the scene on the mind.

Dickens practises this too, when he wants to raise the level of intensity of certain scenic effects. One example comes in the first chapter of *Little Dorrit*. The narrator presents a Provencal landscape in August, where the ferocious heat virtually knocks out all forms of life:

> Strangers were stared out of countenance by staring white houses, staring white walls, staring white streets, staring tracts of arid road, staring hills from which verdure was burnt away. The only things to be seen not fixedly staring and glaring were the vines drooping under their load of grapes. These did occasionally wink a little, as the hot air barely moved their faint leaves. [. . .] The universal stare made the eyes ache. Towards the distant line of Italian coast, indeed, it was a little relieved by light clouds of mist, slowly rising from the evaporation of the sea; but it softened nowhere else. Far away the staring roads, deep in dust, stared from the hill-side, stared from the hollow, stared from the interminable plain. Far away the dusty vines overhanging wayside cottages, and the monotonous wayside avenues of parched trees without shade, drooped beneath the stare of earth and sky. [. . .] Everything that lived or grew, was oppressed by the glare; except the lizard, passing swiftly over rough stone walls, and the cicala, chirping his dry hot chirp, like a rattle. The very dust was scorched brown, and something quivered in the atmosphere as if the air itself were panting.
>
> Blinds, shutters, curtains, awnings, were all closed and drawn to keep out the stare. Grant it but a chink or keyhole, and it shot in like a white-hot arrow. The churches were the freest from it. To come out of the twilight of pillars and arches – dreamily dotted with winking lamps, dreamily peopled with ugly old shadows piously dozing, spitting, and begging – was to plunge into a fiery river, and swim for life to the nearest strip of shade. So, with people lounging and lying wherever shade was, with but little hum of tongues or barking of dogs, with occasional jangling of discordant church bells and rattling of vicious drums, Marseilles, a fact to be strongly smelt and tasted, lay broiling in the sun one day.[34]

This is just about as oppressive as the grey, sodden English landscape at Chesney Wold. The keynote controlling this wide-roaming landscape is the reiterated 'staring' effect of the fierce light and heat. Everything is staring and there seems to be no escape from the stare if one is anywhere outside. Exposure to this heat and glare is intolerable. The relentless, oppressive, blinding light of the sun and its ferocious heat is there not to be just catalogued and painted (like the *Pickwick* view from Rochester Bridge), but worked into the feel of the prose itself. Dickens reaches for extravagant and powerful metaphors for this searing light and air-quivering heat – 'a white-hot arrow', 'a fiery river'.

Altogether, this landscape 'fact', as he terms it, is 'to be strongly smelt and tasted'; it must be enacted as a multisensory assault on the reader, much as the fog in *Bleak House*'s opening was to have a virtual impact on the congested lungs of the reader as it accumulates ('at compound interest') through those repetitive paragraphs. This is a

LANDSCAPE   269

key difference from that *Pickwick* landscape view. It is like the difference between the
early topographical Turner with his limpid wash-drawn records of the Lake District
or North Wales scenery, and the later Turner with his tempestuous evocations of sea
storms and avalanches, or of Italy shimmering in a blaze of golden light and purple
hills. The contours of the landscape have become submerged or melted by the atmospheric conditions, and one is principally aware of the onslaught of light and colour
and heat emanating from the representation – of sheer energy.

When Dickens was staying in Switzerland in 1846 he experienced great difficulty in composition (writing *Dombey* at the time) because of 'the absence of streets
and numbers of figures'.[35] He could write vigorously for a week or two in a retired
place, like Broadstairs, but then would need a day in London to revitalise his creative
energy: 'the toil and labour of writing, day after day, without that magic lantern, is
IMMENSE!!'[36] The magic lantern is not a landscape viewer's Claude glass: instead
of one steadily held mirror view of a scene, the lantern offers a succession of images,
a moving sequence. And it is this mobility of scenes and figures that Dickens craves.
He expresses this in a forthright way in his *Household Words* essay 'Out of Town':

> Sitting, on a bright September morning, among my books and papers at my open
> window on the cliff overhanging the sea-beach, I have the sky and ocean framed
> before me like a beautiful picture. A beautiful picture, but with such movement
> in it, such changes of light upon the sails of ships and wake of steamboats, such
> dazzling gleams of silver far out at sea, such fresh touches on the crisp wave-tops
> as they break and roll towards me – a picture with such music in the billowy rush
> upon the shingle, the blowing of morning wind through the corn-sheaves where
> the farmers' waggons are busy, the singing of the larks, and the distant voices of
> children at play – such charms of sight and sound as all the galleries on earth can
> but poorly suggest.[37]

He writes this in Folkestone where he was staying with his family in a house over-
looking the sea. The window provides a frame for the landscape view, and that makes
it a 'picture'. The key word in this unfolding composition is 'but': 'A beautiful picture, but with such movement in it.' He could have written 'beautiful picture, and
with such movement', and we would have thought little more about it. That 'but'
ushers in a long anaphoric sentence, a hymn to *movement*. The initial beautiful landscape 'picture' in its frame is static, and as such inadequate. What is missing from the
framed landscape picture is the changing light as it glances off the ocean, the roll and
break of the sea and the sound of its surf, the wind through the cornfield, birdsong
and the cries of playing children.

Dickens was passionate about the presence of natural energies in motion, and any
landscape experience that defaulted in that respect left him cold. For him, static quickly
threatened stagnation ('*My* figures seem disposed to stagnate without crowds about
them', he discovered, in that same letter where he longed for the magic lantern of city
streets). The dream of a broad and deep landscape view with all the natural kinetic
energy that could be desired came true when he was given his Swiss Chalet at Gad's Hill:

> I have put five mirrors in the Swiss châlet (where I write) and they reflect and
> refract in all kinds of ways the leaves that are quivering at the windows, and the

great fields of waving corn, and the sail-dotted river. My room is up among the branches of the trees; and the birds and the butterflies fly in and out, and the green branches shoot in, at the open windows, and the lights and shadows of the clouds come and go with the rest of the company. The scent of the flowers, and indeed of everything that is growing for miles and miles, is most delicious.[38]

The picture of the natural world is no longer a framed landscape: it invades his room, where the changing light and the birds and butterflies are multiplied by the mirrors, and where the profusion of countryside scents play around him as he sits, quill in hand. That landscape experience is assimilated and then finds its way into his writing, not just in the letters where he rhapsodises about the Chalet views. On the afternoon of 8 June 1870 he was up in that mirror room writing his monthly instalment of *The Mystery of Edwin Drood* (1870), just hours before his fatal stroke. That view from the Chalet found its way onto the very last page he wrote: it was a summertime view of old Cloisterham (Rochester), its surrounding landscape and indeed the whole country:

A brilliant morning shines on the old city. Its antiquities and ruins are surpassingly beautiful, with a lusty ivy gleaming in the sun, and the rich trees waving in the balmy air. Changes of glorious light from moving boughs, songs of birds, scents from gardens, woods, and fields – or, rather, from the one great garden of the whole cultivated island in its yielding time – penetrate into the Cathedral, subdue its earthy odour, and preach the Resurrection and the Life. The cold stone tombs of centuries ago grow warm; and flecks of brightness dart into the sternest marble corners of the building, fluttering there like wings.[39]

The summer sunshine animates the land, its flora and fauna. It awakens the scents of the natural world that are powerful enough to overcome all that emanates from the dead past. It is a moving landscape, in every sense. The sun's warming flecks of brightness (temperate versions of those Provencal 'white-hot arrows') bring light and energy into the cold dark recesses of that solemn, formal place. It is an apt emblem of Dickens's own invasive, radiant and revivifying work.

Notes

1. Charles Dickens, *Is She His Wife? Or Something Singular* (Boston: Osgood, 1877), 8.
2. John Ruskin, in a letter to W. H. Harrison, 6 June 1841, qtd in *Charles Dickens: The Critical Heritage*, ed. by Philip Collins (London: Routledge, 1971), 100.
3. William Wordsworth, 'Sonnet on the Projected Kendal and Windermere Railway', in William Wordsworth, *Guide to the Lakes*, ed. by Ernest de Selincourt (Oxford: Oxford University Press, 1977), 146.
4. Charles Dickens, *Dombey and Son*, ed. by Andrew Sanders (London: Penguin, 2002), 80, ch. 6; 246, ch. 15.
5. Charles Dickens, *Master Humphrey's Clock*, 2 vols (London: Chapman & Hall, 1840), I, 72.
6. John Ruskin, in a letter to Charles Eliot Norton, 19 June 1870, qtd in Collins, 443.
7. Charles Dickens, 'Insularities', *Household Words* (19 January 1856), in *Dickens' Journalism*, ed. by Michael Slater and John Drew, 4 vols (London: Dent, 1994–2000), III (1998), 338–46, 344.

LANDSCAPE

271

8. Charles Dickens, *The Pickwick Papers*, ed. by James Kinsley (Oxford: Oxford University Press, 2008), 52, ch. 5.

9. 'To John Forster, [5 July 1841]', *The Letters of Charles Dickens*, ed. by Madeline House, Graham Storey et al., Pilgrim/British Academy Edition, 12 vols (Oxford: Clarendon Press, 1965–2002). Subsequent citations: *PLets* followed by volume (year of publication), page. Here II (1969), 322.

10. Charles Dickens, 'Our Watering Place', *Household Words* (2 August 1851), in *Dickens' Journalism*, III, 9–18, 14.

11. 'To John Forster, [11 February 1845]', *PLets* IV (1977), 266.

12. Charles Dickens, *The Chimes*, in *A Christmas Carol and Other Christmas Books*, ed. by Robert Douglas-Fairhurst (Oxford: Oxford University Press, 2006), 136–7.

13. 'To W. H. Wills, 30 July 1851', *PLets* VI (1988), 451.

14. Ibid.

15. Harry Stone, *The Uncollected Writings of Charles Dickens:* Household Words, *1850–1859* (London: Penguin, 1969), I, 331–42.

16. Ibid., 333.

17. Ibid., 335.

18. Charles Dickens, *American Notes*, ed. by Patricia Ingham (London: Penguin, 2004), 201–2.

19. 'To John Forster, 16 April 1842', *PLets* III (1974), 201.

20. Ibid.

21. 'To Charles Sumner, 16 May 1842', *PLets* III, 239.

22. Ibid.

23. Charles Dickens, *The Old Curiosity Shop*, ed. by Elizabeth M. Brennan (Oxford: Oxford University Press, 1999), 401, ch. 53.

24. Charles Dickens, *Oliver Twist*, ed. by Philip Horne (London: Penguin, 2003), 261–2, bk 2, ch. 9.

25. *Curiosity Shop*, 388, ch. 52.

26. Ibid., 389, ch. 52.

27. Elizabeth Bowen, 'Notes on Writing a Novel', in *The Mulberry Tree: Writings of Elizabeth Bowen*, ed. by Hermione Lee (London: Vintage Classics, 2015).

28. John Ruskin, in a letter to his father, 18 January 1863, qtd in Collins, 443.

29. Charles Dickens, *Martin Chuzzlewit*, ed. by Patricia Ingham (London: Penguin, 2004), 679, ch. 47.

30. Charles Dickens, *Hard Times*, ed. by Kate Flint (London: Penguin, 2003), 27, bk 1, ch. 5.

31. Charles Dickens, *Bleak House*, ed. by Nicola Bradbury (London: Penguin, 2003), 20–1, ch. 2.

32. Ibid., 21, ch. 2.

33. John Ruskin, *Modern Painters* (London: Allen, 1901) III, 165, ch. 12.

34. Charles Dickens, *Little Dorrit*, ed. by Stephen Wall and Helen Small (London: Penguin, 2003), 16, bk 1, ch. 1.

35. 'To John Forster, [30 August 1846]', *PLets* IV, 612–13.

36. Ibid.

37. Charles Dickens, 'Out of Town', *Household Words* (29 September 1855), in *Dickens' Journalism*, III, 324–30, 325.

38. 'To Mrs J. T. Fields, 25 May 1868', *PLets* XII (2002), 119.

39. Charles Dickens, *The Mystery of Edwin Drood*, ed. by David Paroissien (London: Penguin, 2002), 270, ch. 23.

18

PHOTOGRAPHY

Daniel A. Novak

I walked from Durham to Sunderland, and made a little fanciful photograph in
my mind of Pit-Country [. . .]. I couldn't help looking upon my mind as I was
doing it, as a sort of capitally prepared and highly sensitive plate.
                –Charles Dickens, 'Letter to W. H. Wills', 24 September 1858[1]

THE INVENTION OF PHOTOGRAPHY IN THE late 1830s marked a seismic shift not
only in the visual arts, media history and global communication, but also in all
other forms of representation including literary fiction.[2] For the first time, people were
confronted with an image ostensibly drawn by what photographic inventor Henry
Fox Talbot termed 'The Pencil of Nature', or, as Susan Sontag later put it, a 'thin slice
of space as well as time' – a piece of the real world, rather than a representation of
it.[3] Photography could provide easily accessible and trustworthy information – what
Lady Elizabeth Eastlake called 'cheap, prompt, and correct facts [. . .] the purveyor
of such knowledge to the world [. . .] the sworn witness of everything presented to
her view'.[4] As a 'mirror with a memory' in Oliver Wendell Holmes's famous phrase,
photography could also picture our personal and collective present and record the
personal and collective past.[5] In his *All the Year Round* essay 'The Philosophy of
Yourself' (1863), George Augustus Sala argues for using photography as a vehicle for
an 'intimate self-acquaintance'. He suggests having:

> his carte de visite taken at least once a month – with a life-sized photograph once
> a year. He should keep the collection, not for public exhibition, but for private
> contemplation. He should muse over his multiplied effigies [. . .]. Let there be no
> touching up, no smoothing away of furrows, no darkening of hair and whiskers.
> Let him insist on having the real, raw, untampered with, photographs.[6]

The wide availability and circulation of cheap *cartes de visite* (paper photographs
mounted on a small, stiff card the size of a visiting card) made such 'intimate' contact
with oneself possible – an intimacy that would extend to one's friends, celebrities
and even strangers as 'cartomania' (the craze for collecting card photographs) took
hold.[7] In turn, photography would also provide a record of and connection to both a
changing nation and an expanding British Empire with its sphere of influence.[8] If we
lament today's culture of the 'selfie' and the ubiquity of images on screens, the abid-
ing desire to capture and record our lives and ourselves in photographs is an enduring
tie to our Victorian past.

While he was not particularly fond of sitting for his photograph and frequently declined the opportunity to have his 'counterfeit presentment' taken, Charles Dickens understood the importance and utility of allowing his readers the tactile intimacy of holding the 'inimitable' in their hands.[9] As Leon Litvack points out, 'over two hundred images of the novelist circulated in his lifetime', and Dickens both sought out photographers and managed which images would see the light of day.[10] Dickens's career as a writer overlapped with some of the most important developments in photographic history, from the invention and rapid popularisation of the daguerreotype to the industrialisation, mass reproduction and distribution of images on paper.

In the pages of the journals that Dickens edited, writers explored a broad array of technologies and formats. Various articles also explored photographic culture more broadly, ranging from essays on the stereoscope and opportunities for women to work in photographic studios, to humorous pieces on forays into the 'dark chambers' of photographers and stories of predatory celebrity photographers.[11] In turn, photographers looked to Dickens's novels as inspiration, whether in art photography or photographic magic lantern shows.[12] Oscar Rejlander's *Hard Times* (1860) is loosely based on the novel and combines multiple scenes in a single image using double exposure, while his 'Poor Jo' (1860) or 'Night in Town' was seen as so effective – despite the boy's transparently fake 'rags' – that the philanthropic Shaftesbury Society used it in its campaigns through the 1980s.[13]

Yet Dickens's novels feature only a handful of direct references to photography, none of which shows much interest in, or engagement with, specific technologies or devices. Perhaps the most memorable of these is the opening of *Great Expectations* (1860–1) in which Pip has to imagine what his parents looked like from their headstones, since 'their days were long before the days of photographs'; or *Oliver Twist* (1837–9), with its too honest 'machine for taking likenesses'.[14] Instead, just as Dickens uses photography as a metaphor for his memory and imagination in the epigraph to this essay, critics have routinely turned to photography as an analogue for his style and realism since the 1840s to the present. As Daniel Brown argues, until the later nineteenth century, what constituted literary 'realism' was very much a matter of debate, and 'those who first tried to understand realism did so primarily through analogy and exemplification, by referencing new movements in the visual arts'.[15] In turning to photography, both Dickens and his critics appeal more broadly to the photographic imaginary – the desire to freeze, record and preserve time in a reproducible and 'objective' image – and to the discourse of photographic realism rather than to specific references to the new technology.

But, as I and others have argued elsewhere, there was neither a single photographic technology in the nineteenth century nor a single 'photographic imaginary'.[16] Photography was figured as both an objective 'mirror with a memory' and a form of visual illusion; as both the 'Pencil of Nature' and highly mediated; as a piece of the real and a trick from the theatre. Associating Dickens with photography, then, was hardly a straightforward proposition. For some, the 'sensitive plate' of Dickens's mind yielded a rich landscape of realistic detail. For others, the plate was *too* 'sensitive', indiscriminately capturing details (whether meaningful or not), and yielding a photograph that was more 'fanciful' than accurate. At the same time, photography served to capture the complexity of Dickens's hybrid realism – his 'fusion of realist and anti-realist tendencies'.[17] When Dickens insists on the accuracy of his representation of poverty and criminality, while also lingering on the 'romantic side of familiar things', he is equally engaged with the discourse and culture of photography in the nineteenth century.[18] In the first part of this essay, I will focus on the often contradictory ways in which photography was used as an analogy for Dickens's style. The second section explores photography's association with theatrical illusion (the forms are linked from the moment of photography's invention), as well as the relationship between the frozen temporality of photography and both theatrical and narrative forms of stasis. Photography, I suggest, foregrounds a complicated relationship (or potential disconnect) between descriptive snapshot and narrative time, so crucial to understanding Victorian fiction. The final section argues that in *Oliver Twist*, both identity and narrative closure ironically depend on a form of photographic 'still-life' – on bodies frozen in time, on reproducibility and on temporal suspension.

Dickens and Photography as Analogy

The multiple ways photography was deployed as an analogy for Dickens's style might appear incoherent; yet that diversity is a symptom of how photography itself was understood in radically different ways.[19] Moreover, reviewers used photography to understand different aspects of Dickensian realism – the precise but mechanical nature of its detail, the representation of social hierarchy and characterisation. For example, a review of *Martin Chuzzlewit* (1843–4) notes that 'the frequent recurrence of such ludicrous minuteness in the trivial details induces us to compare Mr Dickens' style of delineation to a photographic landscape. There, everything within the field of view is copied with unfailing but mechanical fidelity.'[20] A review of *Bleak House* (1852–3) deploys the comparison in a more favourable light, suggesting that:

> as usual, Mr Dickens has, in this book, given to his readers many intellectual daguerreotypes to carry away. These are at once called up by the mere names of the characters; and with those names they will be identified for evermore. [. . .] Now, however, a word bears the significance of half a dozen hours' delineations.[21]

Here, rather than simply record a landscape or 'trivial details', Dickens's 'intellectual daguerreotypes' have a curious power to compress time, space and meaning. A representational unit as seemingly slim and flat as a character's name or a photograph conjures an image that both captures a single moment in time and conveys the depth and significance of 'half a dozen hours' of description and reading. Even Dickens's characters were associated with their creator's power of vision: Esther in *Bleak House* is read as having been granted 'the immediate power of the daguerreotype in noting at once the minutest singularities of so many exceptional people'.[22]

The reviewer's analogy between Esther's vision and the 'daguerreotype' appears close to nonsensical: Esther's point of view is explicitly differentiated from the parallel omniscient narration. Instead, the reviewer seems to connect photography to Dickens's political and social realism. Esther's ability to capture not only 'many exceptional people', but also the *un*exceptional and overlooked people and details (however 'ludicrous', poor or criminal) enables her to act as the medium through which Dickens establishes and defines the 'connexion' (as he puts it in Chapter 16 of

Bleak House) between the upper and lower classes. Photography's reputation for a wide and democratic range of representation – from Queen Victoria to the crossing sweep – seemed to act as a visual embodiment of Dickens's project. As Sala notes in 'The Philosophy of Yourself', 'from the cartes de visite, we learn that kings and queens are in dress and features precisely like other people [. . . M]any of them look like very coarse and vulgar mortals too. They have the same number of arms and legs as us plebeians.'[23] Elsewhere, Andrew Wynter directly ties photography to social levelling: 'here, on the contrary, social equality is carried to its utmost limit, and Tom Sayers is to be found cheek-by-jowl with Lord Derby'.[24]

This association between photography and a flattened social hierarchy was particularly salient for those who felt Dickens's 'unfailing but mechanical fidelity' failed to discriminate high and low, important and insignificant details. For example, in response to *Bleak House*, a reviewer complains precisely about these kinds of cross-class 'connexions' in photographic terms:

> So crowded is the canvas which Mr. Dickens has stretched, and so casual the connexion that gives to his composition whatever unity it has, that a daguerreotype of Fleet Street at noon-day would be the aptest symbol to be found for it; though the daguerreotype would have the advantage in accuracy of representation.[25]

If, as Nancy Armstrong, John Tagg and others have argued, nineteenth-century photography was used to categorise people and fix hierarchies of difference, in this case, we can see how photography was simultaneously seen as lacking a unifying or meaningful perspective.[26] For the reviewer, Dickens embodies photography's failure to differentiate between objects, bodies and classes, while also falling short of its presumed 'accuracy'. Like the review of *Chuzzlewit* from which I quoted earlier, another reviewer grants him a photographic 'accuracy', but complains that such indiscriminate and mechanical attention to detail is democratic to a fault:

> But, then, the imitating agent takes exactly the same pains with the dunghill and the gutter, as with the palace and the forest tree [. . .]. Mr Dickens' pencil is often as faithful and not more discriminating. He lavishes as much attention on what is trivial or useless as on the more important part of the picture, as if he could not help painting everything with equal exactness. [. . .] There is no judicious perspective, and withdrawing from view of disagreeable particulars.[27]

This is what G. H. Lewes would later denigrate as 'detailism, which calls itself Realism [. . .] it confounds truth with familiarity, and predominance of unessential details'.[28] For George Eliot, Dickens's true gift is his 'power of rending the external traits of our town population' – a power she compares to photography. But, precisely for that reason, its 'artistic truthfulness' is insufficient. In her famous backhanded compliment in 'The Natural History of German Life' (1856), she argues that Dickens mechanically records surfaces and 'external traits' with the 'delicate accuracy of a sun picture' while becoming 'transcendent in his unreality' when he turns to emotion and psychology.[29] If, for one reviewer, a Dickensian 'photographic' character has the 'depth of half a dozen hours' delineations', for Eliot, character delineated with the 'accuracy of a sun picture' is as flat as the surface of a photograph.[30]

276   DANIEL A. NOVAK

As Eliot's comment suggests, even reviewers who linked Dickensian detail to photography understood his characterisation as anything but accurate or realistic. Even photographers felt this way. When *The Photographic News* mused about the possibility of producing photographic illustrations for Dickens's novels, they noted that such a 'realistic author' should be 'connected with real life', yet added (in a perhaps dubious distinction) that such a connection ought to stick to locations and landscapes, since 'Dickens exaggerated many of his personages, but his localities were very true to nature'.[31] Just as critics linked Dickens's style to photography, they compared his characterisation to visual and theatrical forms that would seem to be the obverse of photographic realism, like caricature or melodrama.[32] As John Ruskin famously argued of the novelist's 'wit and insight' in his use of caricature, Dickens 'chooses to speak in a circle of stage fire'.[33] Dickens was not only linked to theatre and performance by his contemporaries, but was drawn to theatricality in his roles as a playwright, actor and public reader.[34] More broadly, as Juliet John has argued, Dickens draws on melodramatic aesthetics both in his prose and characterisation as a counter to Romantic models of individualism, interiority and ethics, and as part of a broader critique of 'cultural elitism'.[35]

Critics such as Juliet John, Joss Marsh and Grahame Smith have linked Dickens's attraction to Victorian popular entertainment to film.[36] But if, as Smith has argued, Dickens 'dreamed' of a future cinema, he lived with and through photography, and it is on the relationship between photography, theatre and Dickensian realism that the remainder of this essay will focus. As much as photography was associated with forms of objectivity and documentary realism – whether visual or social, whether sufficient or insufficient – it was also associated with illusion, deception and performance. Jordan Bear has most recently argued that Victorian audiences were 'primed not to receive photography as unquestionably objective' and saw it as part of a 'cornucopia of visual illusion', as well as being fully aware of 'photography's fundamentally mediated status'.[37] If the reviews I quoted from suggested (at least) two different theories of photography, it was because photography was simultaneously understood in radically different ways. Dickens's 'unfailing but mechanical fidelity' could give readers what Wemmick from *Great Expectations* might call the 'portable property' of 'intellectual daguerreotypes' that serve as touchstones for beloved characters and the experience of reading itself.[38] And yet, for others, that very attention to detail serves to distort reality rather than reflect it. In what follows, I focus on the intersection of photography and theatre specifically through the register of temporality, as a way of thinking about the relationship between characterisation and narrative temporality in a short reading of *Oliver Twist*.

'Still Life'

Reading Dickens through the conjunction of theatre and photography reframes two key critical questions that have been revived in recent Dickens criticism and criticism on the novel form: first, both nineteenth-century and contemporary critiques of Dickens's theatrical, 'stereotypical' or 'flat' characterisation; and, second, the relationship between visual stasis and narrative temporality. If the frozen temporality of photography seems incompatible with Dickensian narrative (or narrative itself), critics have increasingly been arguing for the importance of immobility in realist

PHOTOGRAPHY 277

narratives and have turned to theatrical forms like the melodramatic tableaux as a way of understanding the relationship between forms of stillness and narrative motion in the novel.[39]

While theatrical performance may seem the antithesis of photography, they were linked from photography's invention. Louis Daguerre, the first to successfully popularise the invention in 1839, ran a diorama theatre. The typical studio is patterned on the proscenium theatre and was a site for performance in costumes or in front of elaborately painted backgrounds. Victorian periodicals routinely mocked these backgrounds and props for their transparent unreality and clunky theatricality. 'The Carte de Visite' (1862), published in *All the Year Round*, notes the 'bewildering' array of props intended to indicate the various professions of potential sitters, as well as the 'wretched painted scene'.[40] Other essays in Dickens's journals represent the work of photography itself as a kind of theatrical picture-making and photographers as former photographic models playing roles in such pictures. As the bankrupt former 'bill-discounter' turned photographer of James Payn's 'Photographees' argues:

> before a man can become a first-rate photographer I hold it necessary that he should have had some experience as a photographee [. . .] I was that hussar whom you know so well in the stereoscopic pictures, who is making love to the young lady in ball costume [. . .] I was the groom who is biting the puppy's tail off with an expression of enjoyment (price six shillings and sixpence, and cheap at the price, besides the hire of the puppy).[41]

While actors and actresses also made use of photographs to publicise plays and boost their own fame and notoriety, even 'normal' photographs appear theatrical both to nineteenth-century and contemporary audiences, partly because slow exposure times (before the development of 'snapshot' photography) required sitters to hold poses and expressions for an uncomfortable amount of time. For example, reading a group photograph of Dickens with family and friends at Gad's Hill, Litvack concludes that 'it resembles a *tableau vivant*'.[42]

In turn, photography became a subject for Victorian theatre.[43] A few plays depict photography as a vehicle for representing an objective and unquestionable truth beyond the world of the theatre, most famously in Dion Boucicault's *Octoroon* (1859, Winter Garden Theatre, New York; 1861, Adelphi Theatre). In the play's climactic scene, a photograph inadvertently taken in the aftermath of a murder of a slave serves as irrefutable evidence that exonerates the accused Native American and condemns the scheming villain. Yet, the majority of plays about photography were farces and comedies that undermined the new technology's claims to accurately record anything, let alone the kind of minute and mechanical detail that the reviewers I quoted above invoke. This is not merely an effect of infusing photography with theatricality by putting it on stage. Instead, as I have argued elsewhere, more often than not, theatrical performance emerges as the more trustworthy form, while the ostensibly objective photomechanical reproduction was associated with illusion, fraud and even violence.[44] Edmund Yates, Dickens's close friend and sometime employee, wrote (along with N. H. Harrington) one of the earliest plays featuring photography on stage, *Your Likeness – One Shilling* (appearing at the Strand Theatre on 22 April 1858). The play features a swindling tailor turned fraudulent photographer, a sitter who fears that the camera is a kind of gun, and a conclusion that likens theatre to the processes and products of photography:

> your approbation is the quicksilver that will speedily develop me; so if you approve, here I stop. You'll find me a liberal fellow; to everyone who pays me a visit, I'll present a likeness of himself in a neat frame, *with a hook* – patronize me, then – here are my cards. (*throws them into the House.*) You'll find no other shop where you'll get a correct likeness for a shilling.[45]

Addressing the audience, the photographer figures himself as a photograph ('developed' by the applause of the crowd), the audience as patrons who have had their 'likeness' made, and the play itself as the sitting. The idea of representing a person as a photographic negative whose development is arrested at a particular moment ('here I stop') echoes Dickens's depiction of his own mind as a 'sensitive plate'.

Nineteenth-century critics themselves drew connections between Dickens, photography and theatre. In his review of *Little Dorrit* (1855–7) in *Fraser's Magazine*, William Forsyth suggests a number of the associations between photography and Dickensian style that we have already seen: its simultaneous 'fidelity' of detail and 'minute description', its 'exaggeration' or 'caricature', and its wide visual scope and incoherence. However, here these aspects are yoked to Victorian melodrama:

> His tone is *melodramatic* throughout [. . .]; Mr Dickens delights in the sayings and doings of strange, grotesque, out-of-the-way people, of whom we hardly ever meet the prototypes in flesh and blood; and in every one of his tales he fastens some distinctive oddities upon two or three of his characters, and never allows them to speak without bringing out the peculiarity in the most marked and prominent manner. His portraits are in fact *caricatures*. He *daguerreotypes*, so to speak, a particular grimace, and presents it every time that the features come into view.

Forsyth's association of 'caricature' and 'daguerreotypes' is symptomatic of the dynamic I have been exploring at the heart of responses to both Dickens's style and photography more generally. Dickens himself makes this connection in one of the rare references to photography in his fiction; in *Our Mutual Friend* (1864–5), a character suggests that a photograph is 'so like as to be almost a caricature'.[46]

But I am more interested here in the relationship Forsyth draws between the experience of seeing and the experience of reading:

> His characters are all exaggerations. We doubt if there is one which, as he has drawn it, occurs in real life [. . .] nature disowns the resemblance [. . .]. He has also a marvellous talent for minute description. No Dutch painter ever depicted an interior with more servile fidelity than Mr Dickens draws still life with his pen. [. . .] But while we admire the painter we are apt to grow weary of the writer. The eye of the spectator can take in the whole of a picture at a glance, but the mind of the reader must go through the successive points of a description until it becomes fatigued by the multiplicity of details.[47]

On the one hand, he seems to invoke a distinction familiar from Lessing's *Laocoön* (1766), between the visual and the verbal as a distinction between the spatial and temporal: 'signs arranged side by side [in painting] can represent only objects existing side by side, or whose parts so exist, while consecutive signs [in poetry] can express only objects which succeed each other, or whose parts succeed each other, in time.'[48] On the other hand, while Dickensian 'melodrama' aspires to the immobility of a 'still life' or a 'daguerreotype', it excessively 'fatigue[s]' the reader who 'must go through the successive points of a description', disrupting both narrative movement and ekphrastic description. In Forsyth's description, Dickens's 'servile' attention to detail fails as literary 'still life' *and* as plot; it is experienced sequentially, but neither represents the movement or passage of time, nor successfully conjures a static image through text. For Forsyth, a (misguided) drive towards a 'daguerreotype'-style realism (or, as Lewes would have it, 'detailism') both produces 'melodramatic' effects and threatens the function of narrative itself.

Along these lines, I want to linger on the phrase 'still life' in three interconnected senses: as a register of temporality, as a mode of characterisation, and as a marker of Dickensian visuality. Recent work on the novel has been interested in structures of discontinuity and temporal stasis. In her book *Still Life: Suspended Development in the Victorian Novel* (2016), Elisha Cohn explores the 'lyrical narrative pauses' that (temporarily) suspend agency, but also character development and self-knowledge:

> Suspension contains a paradoxically static intensity – still life, vibrant in its absorptive movelessness. Arresting the ordinary conditions of consciousness, suspension creates a subtle disturbance in received categories of thinking, knowing, and doing that organise development – but only for a moment.[49]

Others have argued that these non-narrative elements are more central to novelistic realism than we have thought. Amanpal Garcha's *From Sketch to Novel* (2009) reminds us how much consists of 'purely descriptive prose, of extraneous and episodic narrative fragments, and of essayistic discursiveness' rather than narrative or elements of plot.[50] Focusing on these elements not only returns us to one overlooked origin of the novel (the 'sketch' genre with which Dickens and other authors began their careers), but also to Victorian modes of reading that attended to 'static elements' of description and style.[51] More broadly, in *Antinomies of Realism*, Fredric Jameson has argued that 'realism is the consequence of a tension' between linear narrative time ('récit') and an 'eternal present' he connects with a temporality of 'affect'.[52]

If, as Jameson would have it, realism is made possible by a tension or oscillation between stillness and motion (lyric and narrative, affect and 'récit'), it also brings realism closer to elements of both Victorian theatre and photography. In Victorian theatre this tension is most vividly embodied in the melodramatic tableau – the freezing of actors in a dramatic pose usually at the end of a scene.[53] As Carolyn Williams argues, the melodramatic tableau 'establishes a moment of hieratic silence and stillness within the ongoing action of the play', but one that is necessarily temporary: 'The stillness of the stage picture, then, is paradoxically moving. And in fact, soon the picture literally *will* move again.'[54] For Williams, the realist novel (in particular George Eliot) incorporates a number of melodramatic technologies, including the tableau.[55] John has also argued that the 'fluidity' of Dickensian prose is in fact like a series of static 'pictures' or tableaux, but that this stasis is 'illusory [. . .] stasis can never be other than metamorphosis'.[56]

Recent re-evaluations of realism have also worked to question the distinction between realist and melodramatic modes of characterisation. As Williams argues, both melodrama and the realist novel traffic in types; 'it is the form of typification alone that differs'.[57] Photography (in both its form and deployment) was also used to picture and understand types and collectivities, both professional and theatrical (as in the stereotyped props and costumes of the studio). Armstrong sees this play between individual and type in photography as central to the work of realism: 'It is the mission of literary realism, I believe, to authorize a rather primitive classification system of visual types while endowing certain exemplary members of the dominant group with uniquely complex identities.'[58] As Bear has argued, for Victorian viewers, the mass production of studio images associated photography less with the capture of a singular and unique moment or individual, and more with the 'irrelevance of uniqueness' and '[t]he negation of the singularity of the moment'.[59] In this context, the photograph records a form of identity, but one that is tied neither to the individual nor to a specific time or place. The photographed body is outside of time not because it is forever trapped in a unique moment but because, like the melodramatic stock character, the type precedes and exceeds the figure who embodies it. As I will argue, *Oliver Twist* articulates a theory of character that privileges both a form of temporal stasis and bodily reproducibility that I have traced in Victorian photography and theatre.

'There was its Living Copy'

As Elaine Hadley points out, like other anti–Poor Law texts, *Oliver Twist* participated in a broader 'melodramatic response to the new law' that borrowed tactics from stage melodrama.[60] If, as Hadley states in relation to the representations of suffering in these melodramatic texts, Dickens's novel was 'factually inaccurate', his defence of his realism and his defence of melodrama are remarkably similar: both, he argues, may *appear* absurd but are 'true'.[61] As he puts it in the 'Author's Introduction to the Third Edition' of *Oliver Twist* in 1841,

> there are people of so refined and delicate a nature, that they cannot bear the contemplation of these horrors. Not that they turn instinctively from crime; but that criminal characters, to suit them, must be, like their meat in delicate disguise [. . .]. Now, as the stern and plain truth, even in the dress of this – in novels – much exalted race, was a part of the purpose of this book, I will not, for these readers, abate one hole in the Dodger's coat, or one scrap of curl-paper in the girl's dishevelled hair [. . .]. It is useless to discuss whether the conduct and character of the girl seems natural or unnatural, probable or improbable, right or wrong, IT IS TRUE. (458–60).

John argues that this preface and Dickens's claim is 'propagandist', and that 'the "realism" of the novel (in the sense of its photographic truth-to-life) is largely irrelevant to Dickens's ideological and moral scheme in *Oliver Twist*'.[62] Dickens appeals to one aspect of the photographic imaginary by explicitly linking 'part of the purpose of this book' to his determination to record every minute (and often unappealing and unessential) detail, 'even in the dress' of prostitutes and thieves. Moreover, he appropriates the same transcendent objectivity some reserved for photography, linking the faithful recording of detail to a 'truth' outside of questions of 'improbability'. As the photographer of Boucicault's *Octoroon* says, the image is made by 'eye of the Eternal', and 'the apparatus can't lie'.[63] But Dickens's claim also demonstrates his awareness of the complex dynamic I have been tracing in responses to his 'mechanical fidelity', in ways that make the preface relevant to Dickens's style beyond the novel and beyond the 'local critical debate' of the Newgate controversy.[64] That is, he is aware that his effort to represent the 'stern and plain truth' may produce something which appears 'unnatural' or 'improbable'. As I discuss below, Mrs Bedwin's joke that the 'machine for taking likenesses' was 'a deal too honest' neatly encapsulates the paradox of a 'photographic' Dickensian realism; photographic 'honesty' yields a 'truth' that may appear exaggerated, caricatured and even grotesque (90, bk 1, ch. 12). For G. H. Lewes, Dickens's belief in the unquestionable 'truth' of even 'fantastic' images could be contagious: 'He, seeing it thus vividly, made us also see it; and believing in its reality however fantastic, he communicated something of his belief to us. He presented it in such relief that we ceased to think of it as a picture.'[65] Even for someone as critical of the 'unreal[ity]' of Dickens's style, the most 'fantastic' of Dickens's 'pictures' (at least temporarily) efface their own status as representations.

It is in *Oliver Twist*, of course, that Dickens compares the structure of his narrative (favourably) to 'murderous melodrama' in the famous 'streaky, well-cured bacon' passage (134, bk 1, ch. 17), as Carolyn Williams and Sharon Aronofsky Weltman discuss in this volume. Dickens defends the 'absurd' 'sudden shiftings of the scene' as more realistic than one would imagine: 'Such changes appear absurd; but they are by no means unnatural' (135, bk 1, ch. 17). As John points out, 'what at first appears to be a straightforward comparison of the novel to stage melodrama is in part a defence of the realism of melodrama.'[66] Even some of Dickens's descriptions self-consciously foreground this logic by which the seemingly 'unnatural' is also unquestionably naturalistic: 'her face, distorted into a mumbling leer, resembled the grotesque shaping of some wild pencil than the work of Nature's hand' (192, bk 2, ch. 2). The Dickensian grotesque and 'improbable' body, one might say, is drawn by the 'Pencil of Nature'.[67]

Armstrong singles out *Oliver Twist* as a novel that resists a reduction to images, arguing that character and class in the novel are less dependent on the visual than on speech and other sources of information. However, the novel's theory of identity, inheritance and narrative time adheres to the logic of the photographic and melodramatic type.[68] In the opening scene of the novel, when Oliver is born, the narrator suggests that his body bears no signs of his class status or origins: 'he might have been the child of a nobleman or a beggar' before he is 'badged and ticketed', marked as the 'orphan of a workhouse' (5, bk 1, ch. 1). Yet, apart from these opening pages, in the rest of the novel Oliver's 'nature or inheritance' (7, bk 1, ch. 2), temporarily obscured by the 'power of dress' (5, bk 1, ch. 1), continues to assert itself in visual terms, whether in George Cruikshank's illustrations (in which Oliver is distinguished from the grotesque faces around him) or in the consequential similarity between Oliver's face and the portrait of his mother, Agnes. In response to Oliver's question about the portrait, Mrs Bedwin turns to early (or proto-)photographic technology to explain the beauty of the painting by distinguishing it from the 'too honest' 'machine for taking likenesses': 'painters always make ladies out prettier than they are, or they wouldn't get any custom, child' (90, bk 1, ch. 12). And yet, as a shocked Mr Brownlow looks at Oliver and the portrait, the narrator describes Oliver as 'its living copy' in photographic terms: 'the eyes, the head, the mouth; every feature was the same. The expression was for the instant so precisely alike, that the minutest line seemed copied with an accuracy which was perfectly unearthly' (93, bk 1, ch. 12). Biological inheritance is figured as a form of mechanical reproduction; the 'minutest line' of the dead parent is 'copied' in the form of a living body, which serves as a kind of 'unearthly' animated photograph. But Oliver is also a reproduction of an *image* of that parent – a copy of an expression captured, seen and shared across time in an 'instant'. Much depends, of course, on this resemblance. By the end of the novel, after Monks throws Agnes's locket in the Thames, there is no tangible proof left except these parallel images to prove his familial origins and his right to his inheritance. That inheritance, moreover, is contingent on Oliver's retention of the 'gentle heart and noble nature' inherited from his mother, and on not 'stain[ing] his name with any public act of dishonour' (433, bk 3, ch. 13). In other words, in Oliver's case, 'uniqueness' is not simply 'irrelevant' but injurious. Moreover, the 'living copy' is also crucially a form of temporal 'still life'. By definition, to change would render Oliver no longer a 'copy', no longer embodied proof of his parentage, and no longer a representative of Agnes's 'noble nature'. Fagin and Monks's plot to convert Oliver into a thief fails because, in an important sense, Oliver is more image than person, a copy not an original, a collective type rather than an individual.

More broadly, *Oliver Twist* imagines an efficient visual economy in which such types are immediately recognisable. When an injured and sick Oliver is apprehended at the Maylie household, the sage Doctor Losberne condescendingly explains to a naive Rose Maylie that 'Vice [. . .] takes up her abode in many temples, and who can say that a fair outside shall not enshrine her?' (239, bk 2, ch. 7). Even as Rose imagines circumstances that lessen Oliver's culpability, ultimately it is his 'delica[cy]' that renders the idea of his criminality 'impossible' (241, bk 2, ch. 7). When Doctor Losberne intimidates the eyewitnesses into doubting their own account, he disingenuously insists that '[i]t's a simple question of identity' (243, bk 2, ch. 7). Identity both is and is not 'simple' in the novel. The search for Oliver's familial ties drive the novel from his birth in the workhouse to the end of the novel. At the same time, for the most part, the visual logic of the novel is very much on Rose's side: 'identity' is 'simple' because it is barely hiding in plain sight in a 'fair outside' that is not subject to change.

Or, rather, more frequently, identity resides in the less than fair outsides of Jews, criminals and prostitutes whose bodies and characters are fixed in time and type. Our first introduction to Sikes includes a description of his legs 'which in costume always look in an unfinished and incomplete state without a set of fetters to garnish them' (98, bk 1, ch. 13). Fagin complains that with all other boys, 'their looks convict 'em' (160, bk 1, ch. 19), while he hopes to exploit Oliver's innocent face; his 'mug is a fortin' to him' (177, bk 1, ch. 22). Fagin, of course, has himself long been read as an embodiment of anti-Semitic stereotypes, many of which are drawn from the theatrical 'stage-Jew'.[69] In this way, Fagin is also a composite identity – what one might call (borrowing from Alex Woloch's *One vs. the Many*) a 'many' in the 'one'.[70] This takes an even more literal form when, after an Old Clothes Man collects Oliver's rags at Mr Brownlow's, Fagin ends up returning them to Oliver after

PHOTOGRAPHY   283

his abduction, suggesting either that the Old Clothes Man was Fagin in disguise or that Fagin knows all the Old Clothes Men.[71]

If Sikes and Fagin are immediately recognisable as theatrical and visual types, others have any individual or even group features effaced through forms of social and physical violence. Describing the prostitutes at the Three Cripples, the narrator pictures the women as neither women nor individuals any longer:

> Cunning, ferocity, and drunkenness in all its stages were there in their strongest aspects; and women – some with the last lingering tinge of their early freshness almost fading as you looked, and others with every mark and stamp of their sex utterly beaten out, and presenting but one loathsome blank of profligacy and crime; some mere girls, others but young women, and none part of the prime of life, – formed the darker and saddest portion of this dreary picture (207, bk 2, ch. 4).

If these women have their 'sex utterly beaten out' into a 'loathsome blank' and 'dreary picture', it is significant that Nancy – one of the characters who becomes the mouthpiece for a discourse of development and change – is literally 'beaten' to a pulp and turned into a haunting image, a 'ghastly figure following at his heels' (402, bk 3, ch. 10). Pleading for her life, Nancy implores Sikes: 'let us both leave this dreadful place, and far apart lead better lives [. . .]. It is never too late to repent. They told me so – I feel it now – but we must have time – a little, little time' (396, bk 3, ch. 9). But time is precisely what Nancy does not have, not just in terms of her imminent death, but also in the way the novel as a whole rules out the kind of time she needs: time for repentance and change. Nancy herself is about to be turned into a form of 'still life', as her body is fixed by the sun's 'equal ray': 'It lighted up the room where the murdered woman lay. It did. He tried to shut it out, but it would stream in.' Sikes himself is immobilised: 'He had not moved: he had been afraid to stir' (397, bk 3, ch. 10). Both Sikes and Nancy are frozen in a grim tableau that remains still for too long; this uncomfortably extended moment of stasis is made visible and made into a still image by the action of light – a light that reveals an image that blurs the difference between life and death, person and picture. Both this image and the image of Nancy that follows Sikes ('a corpse endowed with the mere machinery of life' (402, bk 3, ch. 10)) have the uncanny effect of a post-mortem photograph. As Roland Barthes notes, 'the corpse is alive, *as* corpse: it is the living image of a dead thing.'[72] Rather than 'blur[ring] the line between stasis and movement' as in film, the scene as a whole brings together the brutal punishment of a desire for movement, change and development, with both the process of being turned into a still image and being unable to escape it.[73]

Ultimately, it is Oliver's unchanged and unchanging 'fair outside' that offers an initial clue to his familial identity as Brownlow notes his resemblance to Agnes, even before he measures him against the portrait, musing 'there is something in that boy's face' (80, bk 1, ch. 11). Oliver's imperviousness to Fagin's criminal 'school', the failure of Bildung or the action of time to effect 'nature or inheritance' (7, bk 1, ch. 2), the refusal of the parish boy to 'progress', all ensure both the proper transmission of inheritance and an ironic form of narrative closure – one that requires a return to and recognition of origins and identities that have been visible from the beginning. Oliver's status as a 'living copy' of the painting – a painting that operates more like a photograph – elevates reproducibility and sameness above individual difference and development over time. Both in the case of minor and major characters, identity in the novel is not tied to the *telos* of narrative, but is bound up in and expressed through the spectacle of bodies frozen in time – whether in the 'pictures' and tableaux of Victorian melodrama, in the trans-temporal stock type, or in the confines of the photographic image.[74]

The often contradictory ways in which photography was understood in the nineteenth century can help us better picture the paradox of a Dickensian style that can simultaneously produce 'intellectual daguerreotypes' whose fidelity is 'marvelous' and a 'melodrama' whose 'characters are all exaggerations'. What I have suggested here is that Dickens's realism functions through forms that appear antithetical to the realist imaginary or even to the operations of narrative itself. In other words, rather than think of either photography or Dickens's fiction as violating Victorian or contemporary standards for 'realism', both forms ask us to complicate and reframe what both novelistic and photographic realism looked like. The photographic imaginary served, and still serves, as an important basis on which to debate what place Dickens would have in the critical narrative about literary realism.

Notes

1. *The Letters of Charles Dickens*, ed. by Madeline House, Graham Storey et al., Pilgrim/ British Academy Edition, 12 vols (Oxford: Clarendon Press, 1965–2002), VIII (1995), 669.
2. Experiments in fixing the image made by a camera obscura were carried out as early as the end of the eighteenth century by Thomas Wedgwood and Sir Humphry Davy. Nicéphore Niépce is credited with producing the first photograph (or heliograph) in 1827, although 'his letters leave no doubt that he had succeeded in fixing the camera's image a decade earlier'. Louis-Jacques-Mandé Daguerre and Henry Fox Talbot officially announced their inventions (using different processes) in 1839. L Beaumont Newhall, *The History of Photograph from 1839 to the Present* (New York: The Museum of Modern Art, 1982), 13.
3. Susan Sontag, *On Photography* (New York: Farrar, Straus and Giroux, 1977), 22; 4.
4. Lady Elizabeth Eastlake, 'Photography', in *Classic Essays on Photography*, ed. by Alan Trachtenberg (New Haven: Leete's Island Books, 1980), 39–68, 65.
5. Oliver Wendell Holmes, 'The Stereoscope and the Stereograph', in *Classic Essays*, 71–82, 74.
6. [George Augustus Sala], 'The Philosophy of Yourself', *All The Year Round* 217 (20 June 1863), IX, 391–4, 392.
7. William C. Darrah, *Cartes de Visite in Nineteenth Century Photography* (Gettysburg: Darrah, 1981), 4.
8. Francis Frith's images of the 1850s and 1860s exposed viewers to Egypt and Palestine for the first time. Towards the end of the century, the survey and record movement would record a rapidly disappearing British national past. See Elizabeth Edwards, *The Camera as Historian: Amateur Photographers and Historical Imagination, 1885–1918* (Durham, NC: Duke University Press, 2012).
9. Qtd in Susan Cook, 'Season of Light and Darkness: *A Tale of Two Cities* and the Daguerrean Imagination', *Dickens Studies Annual* 42 (2011), 237–60, 243. Leon Litvack discusses how the size of card photographs helped to foster intimacy between authors and readers in 'Dickens Posing for Posterity: The Photographs of Herbert Watkins', *Dickens Quarterly* 34.2 (2017), 96–158, 141.

10. See Leon Litvack, 'Dickens in the Eye of the Beholder: The Photographs of Robert Hindry Mason', *Dickens Studies Annual* 47 (2016), 165–99, 185–6. See also Gerard Curtis, *Visual Words: Art and the Material Book in Victorian England* (Burlington: Ashgate, 2002).

11. See [Henry Morley and W. H. Wills], 'Photography', *Household Words* 156 (19 March 1853), VII, 54–61; [John Hollingshead], 'A Counterfeit Presentment', *Household Words* 432 (3 July 1858), XVIII, 71–2; and [Rev. James White], 'Your Life or Your Likeness', *Household Words* 383 (25 July 1857), XVI, 73–5.

12. *The Old Curiosity Shop* and an excerpt from *A Christmas Carol* entitled 'Marley's Ghost' were popular lantern slide subjects. See William Main, 'Charles Dickens and the Magic Lantern', *History of Photography* 8.1 (1984), 62–72.

13. Stephanie Spencer, 'O. G. Rejlander's Photographs of Street Urchins', *Oxford Art Journal* 7.2 (1984), 17–24.

14. Charles Dickens, *Great Expectations*, ed. by Edgar Rosenberg (New York: Norton, 1999), 9, ch. 1; Charles Dickens, *Oliver Twist*, ed. by Philip Horne (London: Penguin, 2003), 90, bk 1, ch. 12. Subsequent references are inserted parenthetically in the text.

15. Daniel Brown, *Representing Realists in Victorian Literature and Criticism* (Houndmills, Basingstoke: Palgrave Macmillan, 2016), 2.

16. See Owen Clayton, who addresses the way writers self-consciously engaged with specific photographic technologies in *Literature and Photography in Transition, 1850–1915* (Houndmills, Basingstoke: Palgrave Macmillan, 2015).

17. Juliet John, *Dickens and Mass Culture* (Oxford: Oxford University Press, 2010), 196. On critical tendencies to separate these two aspects of Dickens's style, see John, *Dickens's Villains: Melodrama, Character, Popular Culture* (Oxford: Oxford University Press, 2001) 1–20.

18. Charles Dickens, *Bleak House*, ed. by Nicola Bradbury (New York: Penguin, 1996), 7.

19. For a reading of photography *as* analogy (rather than index, referent, or copy), see Kaja Silverman, *The Miracle of Analogy: Or The History of Photography, Part 1* (Stanford: Stanford University Press, 2015).

20. [Thomas Cleghorn?], 'Writings of Charles Dickens', *North British Review*, May 1845, qtd in *Dickens: The Critical Heritage*, ed. by Philip Collins (London: Routledge and Kegan Paul, 1971), 186–91, 190.

21. [Unsigned review], *Illustrated London News*, 24 September 1853, qtd in Collins, 280–2, 282.

22. [Henry Fothergill Chorley], *Athenaeum*, 17 September 1853, qtd in Collins 276–9, 277.

23. Sala, 393.

24. Andrew Wynter, 'Cartes de Visite', *Once a Week* 6.135 (25 January 1862), 134–7, 135. For more on the juxtaposition of classes and photography, see Rachel Teukolsky, 'Cartomania: Sensation, Celebrity, and the Democratized Portrait', *Victorian Studies* 57.3 (2015), 462–75.

25. [George Brimley], *Spectator*, 24 September 1853, qtd in Collins, 283–6, 284.

26. Nancy Armstrong, *Fiction in the Age of Photography: The Legacy of British Realism* (Cambridge, MA: Harvard University Press, 1999), 156. On photography's role in policing the criminal type, see John Tagg, *The Burden of Representation: Essays on Photographies and Histories* (Minneapolis: University of Minnesota Press, 1993); Alan Sekula, 'The Body and the Archive', *October* 39 (1986), 3–64; and Jennifer Green-Lewis, *Framing the Victorians* (Ithaca: Cornell University Press, 1996).

27. [Cleghorn?], 'Writings', qtd in Collins, 190. See also David Trotter, 'Household Clearances in Victorian Fiction', *19: Interdisciplinary Studies in the Long Nineteenth Century*, 6 (2008), 1–19, <doi: 10.16995/ntn.472>: '[T]he description – itself a levelling down – of objects levelled down to matter or stuff. Such descriptions are a description of the world

as it will be like when we are no longer here to see it (when for us there is no longer any narrative desire to be frustrated)' (9).

28. *Principles of Success in Literature*, ed. by W. M. Dallam Armes (Berkeley: University of California Students' Co-Operative Association, 1901), 100. The book originally appeared as a series of essays in *The Fortnightly Review* in 1865.

29. George Eliot, 'The Natural History of German Life', in *Selected Essays, Poems and Other Writings*, ed. by A. S. Byatt and Nicholas Warren (London: Penguin, 1990), 107–39, 111.

30. See Daniel Stout's reading of E. M. Forster on Dickens's 'flat' characters. Forster notes that, even as Dickens's characters are 'no thicker than a gramophone', Dickens, through a 'conjuring trick', makes them appear to have substance and depth. *Corporate Romanticism: Liberalism, Justice, and the Novel* (New York: Fordham University Press, 2017), 121.

31. 'Notes', *Photographic News* 26.1241, 16 June 1882, 345. The article laments the failure of a photographically illustrated edition of *Edwin Drood* and suggests taking photographs of the 'localities' featured in the novels, many of which were fast disappearing.

32. Comments on Dickens's use of exaggeration and caricature extend from his nineteenth-century reviewers through the twentieth century. For a summary of these critical discussions, see Daniel A. Novak, *Realism, Photography, and Nineteenth-Century Fiction* (Cambridge: Cambridge University Press, 2008), 174.

33. John Ruskin, *Unto This Last* (New York: Penguin, 1985), 171.

34. See Deborah Vlock, *Dickens, Novel Reading, and the Victorian Popular Theatre* (Cambridge: Cambridge University Press, 1998) and Edwin M. Eigner, *The Dickens Pantomime* (Berkeley: University of California Press, 1989).

35. John, *Dickens's Villains*, 16; 20. Her reading of Dickens's 'melodramatic poetics' (104) also suggests that the distinction made by the *Photographic News* between 'localities' and 'characters' is a questionable one.

36. John, *Dickens and Mass Culture*, 187–206; Grahame Smith, *Dickens and the Dream of Cinema* (Manchester: Manchester University Press, 2003); and Joss Marsh, 'Dickens and Film', in *Cambridge Companion to Charles Dickens*, ed. by John O. Jordan (Cambridge: Cambridge University Press, 2001), 204–23. See also John Plunkett on Dickens and the magic lantern in 'Optical Recreation and Victorian Literature', in *Literature and the Visual Media*, ed. by David Seed (Gateshead: Athenaeum, 2005), 1–28.

37. Jordan Bear, *Disillusioned: Victorian Photography and the Discerning Subject* (University Park: Penn State University Press, 2015), 5; 27; 33.

38. See John Plotz, *Portable Property: Victorian Culture on the Move* (Princeton: Princeton University Press, 2008), xv.

39. For more on the relationship between realism and melodrama, see Frederic Jameson, *Antinomies of Realism* (New York: Verso, 2015), 139–40; 155–6; 183.

40. 'The Carte de Visite', *All The Year Round* 157 (26 April 1862), vii, 165–8, 167.

41. [James Payn], 'Photographees', *Household Words* 394 (10 October 1857), xvi, 352–4, 352. See also [Henry Fothergill Chorley], 'An Area Sneak', *All the Year Round* 312 (15 April 1865), xiii, 282–4.

42. Litvack, 'Eye of the Beholder', 171.

43. For work linking photography to theatricality, see Joel Anderson, *Theatre and Photography* (New York: Palgrave, 2015); Daniel A. Novak, '"Caught in the Act": Photography on the Victorian Stage', *Victorian Studies* 59.1 (2016), 35–64; and Bear.

44. See Novak, 'Caught in the Act'.

45. N. H. Harrington and Edmund Yates, *Your Likeness – One Shilling: A Comic Sketch in One Act*, *Lacy's Acting Edition of Plays, Dramas, Farces and Extravaganzas*, v.36. 1858, 2–14, 14.

46. Charles Dickens, *Our Mutual Friend*, ed. by Adrian Poole (London: Penguin, 1997), 409, bk 2, ch. 16.

PHOTOGRAPHY 287

47. [William Forsyth], 'Literary Style', *Fraser's Magazine*, March 1857, qtd in Collins, 350–2, 350–1.
48. Gotthold Ephraim Lessing, *Laocoön: An Essay upon the Limits of Poetry and Painting*, (1766), trans. by Ellen Frothingham (1873; reprinted, New York: Noonday, 1965), 91.
49. Elisha Cohn, *Still Life: Suspended Development in the Victorian Novel* (Oxford: Oxford University Press, 2015), 5.
50. Amanpal Garcha, *From Sketch to Novel* (Cambridge: Cambridge University Press, 2009), 42.
51. Garcha, 19. See also Helena Michie, 'Victorian(ist) "Whiles" and the Tenses of Historicism', *Narrative* 17.3 (2009), 274–90, and Caroline Levine and Mario Ortiz-Robles's edited collection, *Narrative Middles: Navigating the Nineteenth-Century British Novel* (Columbus: Ohio State University Press, 2011).
52. Jameson, 26–7.
53. See Martin Meisel, *Realizations: Narrative, Pictorial, and Theatrical Arts in Nineteenth-Century England* (Princeton: Princeton University Press, 1983). As Meisel explains, 'the fullest expression of a pictorial dramaturgy is the tableau, where the actors strike an expressive stance in a legible symbolic configuration that crystallizes a stage of the narrative as a situation, or summarizes and punctuates it' (43).
54. Carolyn Williams, 'Moving Pictures: George Eliot and Melodrama', *Compassion: The Culture and Politics of an Emotion*, ed. by Lauren Berlant (New York: Routledge, 2004), 105–44; 109–10, 113.
55. On reading the novel through theatrical form, see also David Kurnick, *Empty Houses: Theatrical Failure and the Novel* (Princeton: Princeton University Press, 2011).
56. In *Dickens's Villains*, John draws an analogy to the film-making process, with its 'photographic stills shown in rapid succession', although she argues that Dickens's novels 'ultimately refuse the illusory naturalism of film' (107).
57. Williams, 116.
58. Armstrong, 156.
59. Bear, 70; 76.
60. Elaine Hadley, *Melodramatic Tactics: Theatricalized Dissent in the English Marketplace, 1800–1885* (Stanford: Stanford University Press, 1995), 116.
61. Ibid., 107. See also the preface to *Martin Chuzzlewit* (both the preface to the First Edition and the preface to the 'Charles Dickens Edition').
62. John, *Dickens's Villains*, 129.
63. Dion Boucicault, *The Octoroon* (Peterborough: Broadview Press, 2014), 65.
64. John, *Dickens's Villains*, 125. For more on *Oliver Twist* and the Newgate controversy, see 122–40.
65. G. H. Lewes, 'Dickens in Relation to Criticism', *Fortnightly Review* 11.62 (February 1872), 141–54, 146.
66. John, *Dickens and Mass Culture*, 203.
67. Writers continued to link photography, Dickens and melodrama into the twentieth century. Sergei Eisenstein points to this appeal to melodrama as itself emblematic of Dickens's cinematic style, reading the digression as 'Dickens's own "treatise" on the principles of this montage construction of the story'. Sergei Eisenstein, *Film Form and the Film Sense*, trans. by Jay Leyda (New York: Harcourt Brace, Jovanovich, 1977), 195–255; 223. See also Jeremy Tambling, 'Dangerous Crossings: Dickens, Digression, and Montage', *The Yearbook of English Studies* 26 (1996), 43–53, and John, *Dickens and Mass Culture*, 189–206.
68. Elsewhere, focusing on *Bleak House*, Armstrong argues that the substitution for and layering of Esther's image on her mother's produces a sense of 'thickness' of character, 'something that passes for the substantiality of flesh' (158–9). See also Michal Peled

Ginsburg, 'Truth and Persuasion: The Language of Realism and of Ideology in "Oliver Twist"', *NOVEL: A Forum on Fiction* 20.3 (Spring 1987), 220–36.

69. See Harry Stone, 'Dickens and the Jews', *Victorian Studies* 2.3 (1950), 223–53; Ellen Schiff, *From Stereotype to Metaphor: The Jew in Contemporary Drama* (Albany: SUNY Press, 1982); Edgar Rosenberg, *From Shylock to Svengali: Jewish Stereotypes in English Fiction* (Stanford: Stanford University Press, 1960); and John, *Dickens's Villains*, 129. John offers a good overview of the scholarship on Dickens and anti-Semitism in *Dickens and Mass Culture*, 211–12.

70. Alex Woloch, *The One vs. the Many: Minor Characters and the Space of the Protagonist in the Novel* (Princeton: Princeton University Press, 2003).

71. In similar ways, Fagin is connected to all of the Jews in the novel, such as Barney at the Three Cripples, or even the members of the community he rejects as he waits in jail towards the end.

72. Roland Barthes, *Camera Lucida: Reflections on Photography*, trans. by Richard Howard (New York: Hill, 1981), 79.

73. John, *Dickens and Mass Culture*, 199. John argues that in other texts Dickens 'fuse[s] photographic thought with what he called "moving pictures"' (198).

74. Decades ago, Joseph Sawicki offered a different context for this distinction: '[A]nother logic – that Oliver's goodness is based on his origin – takes over, as the narrator sets out the machinery that results in the unraveling of the secret of Oliver's birth. Jonathan Culler's distinction between "story" and "discourse" can be helpful in assessing this shift.' 'Oliver (Un)Twisted: Narrative Strategies in *Oliver Twist*', *Victorian Newsletter* 73 (Spring 1988), 23–7, 24.

Further Reading

Nancy Armstrong, *Fiction in the Age of Photography: The Legacy of British Realism* (Cambridge, MA: Harvard University Press, 1999)

Jordan Bear, *Disillusioned: Victorian Photography and the Discerning Subject* (University Park: Penn State University Press, 2015)

Alexander Bove, *Spectral Dickens: The Uncanny Forms of Novelistic Characterization* (Manchester: Manchester University Press, 2021)

Owen Clayton, *Literature and Photography in Transition, 1850–1915* (Houndmills, Basingstoke: Palgrave Macmillan, 2015)

Susan Cook, 'Season of Light and Darkness: *A Tale of Two Cities* and the Daguerrean Imagination', *Dickens Studies Annual* 42 (2011), 237–60

Juliet John, *Dickens and Mass Culture* (Oxford: Oxford University Press, 2010)

Leon Litvack, 'Dickens in the Eye of the Beholder: The Photographs of Robert Hindry Mason', *Dickens Studies Annual* 47 (2016), 96–158

Grahame Smith, *Dickens and the Dream of Cinema* (Manchester: Manchester University Press, 2003)

Ronald Thomas, *Detective Fiction and the Rise of Forensic Science* (Cambridge: Cambridge University Press, 2000)

19

HIGH ART

Jeremy Tambling

DICKENS'S RELATIONSHIP TO PAINTING, SCULPTURE AND — after its invention in 1839 – photography, is, like his relationship to music, less easy than, for example, his knowledge of theatre, which he discusses confidently, as he does literature, where it is becoming obvious that he knew more than was allowed for by G. H. Lewes, or even John Forster, or comparatively recent critical thinking. The visual image is essential for the title *Sketches by Boz* (1836), and for Dickens's interest in political caricature – Thomas Rowlandson (1756–1827), James Gillray (1756–1815) and George Cruikshank (1792–1878). It is implicit, too, in his choice of good illustrators: Cruikshank, Phiz (1815–82), John Leech (1817–64), Luke Fildes (1843–1927) and George Cattermole (1800–68), antiquarian of the Gothic and pupil of the architectural antiquarian John Britton, whose *Beauties of England and Wales* (26 volumes) Dickens bought in 1839.[1] His awareness of art showed, too, in conversational ease with friends who were artists: Daniel Maclise (1806–70), Edwin Landseer (1802–73), C. R. Leslie (1794–1859), Clarkson Stanfield (1793–1867), the marine and landscape painter Frank Stone (1800–59) and his son Marcus (1840–1921), and David Wilkie (1785–1841).[2] There was further association with the artists for *Punch*.

Yet Dickens does not often discuss art at length: an exception being Benjamin Robert Haydon (1786–1846), whom he called 'unquestionably a very bad painter' while obviously holding a deep admiration and knowledge of him. He had read Haydon's *Diary* and *Lectures on Painting and Design* (1844–6), and attended his exhibition at the Egyptian Hall in Piccadilly.[3] Haydon's exceptional interest as connected with Romanticism (as how he writes on Henry Fuseli as the artist of terror) would have aroused Dickens's interest, but this comment on Haydon is a comparatively rare instance of what he could do. As with all Dickens's comments, on art, literature or politics, the critique is found in the concentrated imagination of the novels, less in stated pronouncements or in discursive prose. Perhaps he felt diffident: he tells Alfred D'Orsay that 'High Art' is 'out of my reach'.[4] The *Oxford English Dictionary* cites 1794, and Sir Joshua Reynolds, and the Royal Academy, to define the scope of 'High Art'. I discuss it here through what is known of Dickens's approaches to art, and then, in what he said on contemporary English art; here, much has been said already in good critical accounts.[5] Finally, I give a theory about Dickens as a baroque artist himself.

Dickens's Knowledge of Art

Where does Dickens discuss paintings? Obviously, in *Pictures from Italy* (1846), itself given four illustrations by Samuel Palmer. Also in the letters accompanying his

Italian visit (2 July 1844 to 30 November 1844 and 20 December 1844 to 3 July 1845), his base being the Palazzo Pallavicino delle Peschiere in Genoa (23 September to 6 November 1844; 20 December 1844 to 19 January 1845; 9 April to 9 June 1845). The palazzo, written about enthusiastically, had frescoes and painted ceilings throughout; its architect was Galeazzo Alessi (1560); its painted rooms by the brothers Andrea and Ottavio Semini; from it Dickens could see 'the wide expanse of the Mediterranean, as blue, at this moment, as the most pure and vivid prussian blue on Mac[clise]'s palette when it is newly set'.[6] That journey included travelling in Paris; just as from 31 May 1846 through to 28 February 1847, he was in the Rhineland travelling to Geneva, and returning via Paris for a lengthy stay, and visiting the Louvre. He was in Europe many times subsequently, including a two-month stay in Switzerland and Italy, with Wilkie Collins (an artist's son) and Augustus Egg (10 October to 11 December 1853), but we should also note his Paris visits (12 to 20 February 1855, with Wilkie Collins), and, alternating with London, between 15 October 1855 and 29 April 1856. In these visits he would have seen far more than was possible in the National Gallery, even under the improvements made by its aggressive acquisitions keeper (after 1843), Charles Eastlake.

Before his American tour, where he saw Benjamin West's work (Philadelphia), and much other American art elsewhere, his familiarity with William Hogarth is signalled from 'The Boarding House' (1834); is emphasised in his 1841 'Author's Introduction to the Third Edition' of *Oliver Twist*, and made the subject of a discussion which includes Charles Lamb on *Gin Lane*, while reviewing, in *The Examiner* (8 July 1848), George Cruikshank's moralising pictures in *The Drunkard's Children*.[7] That Dickens followed Hogarth was an early commonplace in criticism of *The Pickwick Papers* (1836–7); it relates to perceptions of Dickens's debts to Henry Fielding, another Hogarth admirer. In 'The Boarding House', Mr Tomkins, 'a clerk in a wine-house', was 'a connoisseur of paintings and had a wonderful eye for the picturesque'.[8] In 'Horatio Sparkins', the 'master of ceremonies' in a downmarket linen-draper's shop, 'in his large white neckcloth and formal tie looked like a bad "portrait of a gentleman" in the Somerset-house exhibition'.[9] Annual exhibitions of the Royal Academy, founded 1769, were held there from 1780 until 1837, when it moved to the National Gallery in Trafalgar Square (founded 1824, opened 1838).[10] Modelling legs for the Royal Academy is mocked in Chapter 2 of *Nicholas Nickleby* (1838–9); the subject of artists' models recurs frequently, as with 'The Ghost of Art'.[11] In *The Pickwick Papers*, Mr Pickwick, in retirement, in the last chapter, visits the Dulwich Gallery: England's oldest public gallery (1817). I have argued elsewhere that baroque pictures of street urchins in Seville by Bartolomé Estaban Murillo (1617–82) ('Invitation to the Game of Pelota' and 'Three Boys'), admired by William Hazlitt, disliked by John Ruskin, influenced the creation of Fagin's gangs of boys in *Oliver Twist*, though Dickens could make his own observation of these.[12] I will revisit these paintings, and Ruskin.

There was otherwise little publicly accessible art except in churches, such as Westminster Abbey, or St Paul's. Dickens had access to Samuel Rogers's private collection after 1839, while Chapter 27 of *Dombey and Son* (1846–8) shows his knowledge of Warwick Castle's art collection.[13] Access to the National Gallery in the 1840s created the generation who became the Pre-Raphaelites at the end of that decade. But Dickens knew art, even before Italy. How else did he get that image of the excited Scrooge trying to get dressed, 'making a perfect Laocoön of himself with his stockings'?[14] It is as witty as the exhausted Mr Pocket dropping on the sofa 'in the attitude of the Dying Gladiator' (from the Capitoline Museum, Rome).[15] Or as pointed as the reference to Thomas Stothard's picture of Chaucer's Canterbury pilgrims, hanging at the Veneerings' house in *Our Mutual Friend* (1864–5).[16]

The Italian tour brought Dickens into contact with Baroque (sometimes Spanish) painters; many from the earlier Renaissance; and Leonardo (Milan), Raphael (Rome) and Michelangelo (Rome and Florence). Dickens in Venice admires Tintoretto, but if we compare his reaction to art with Blake or Ruskin, painters and art critics, we see how different it is. He does not visit Italy for its paintings, nor try to bring it to consciousness, unlike Ruskin. He neither makes a fetish of the work of art (making fun of those who would, based on the sterility of guidebook knowledge, especially when this is classically formed), nor does he isolate painting from its setting. He has gone to see Italy: the art is part of that. Nor, as with Blake, who barely left London, and knew art through reproduced prints, is there a sense of making paintings and sculpture his way to articulate a criticism of life (admiring line over colour and Gothic art). Nor does he periodise art, nor think in terms of art history. Nor could he have gained a history of art from galleries: Manchester was the first to hang pictures, in chronological order, in its 1857 exhibition. He refuses to think of painting as comprising 'high art', just as, when artists appear in his work, as with Miss La Creevy in *Nicholas Nickleby*, they are working for their own subsistence: the artist he hates is Henry Gowan in *Little Dorrit* (1855–7), the gentleman-amateur (like *Bleak House*'s Harold Skimpole) who declines to be 'professional': a sufficient condemnation.

Those fictional artists remind us that the dominant subject of art for bourgeois homes was portraiture, a point which associates with the development of photography.[17] Even going to prison required sitting for one's portrait (see Chapter 40 of *Pickwick Papers*). Portraiture associates for Dickens with hypocrisy, as with that of the profiteering landlord Christopher Casby, whose picture shows him as a boy:

> though disguised with a haymaking rake, for which he had had, at any time, as much taste or use for as a diving-bell; and sitting (on one of his own legs) upon a bank of violets, moved to precocious contemplation by the spire of a village church. [. . .] Nevertheless, in the Seraphic creature with the haymaking rake, were clearly to be discerned the rudiments of the Patriarch with the list shoes.[18]

Obviously, mock-pastoral has an ideological function in concealing character. This extract is typical of a hermeneutics of suspicion present throughout Dickens's response to art and artists. Yet artists and their work are increasingly referenced. In his most sophisticated, most cosmopolitan novel, *Little Dorrit*, old pictures of the plagues of Egypt are part of the decoration at Mrs Clennam's house (bk 1, ch. 3). Portrait painter and Royal Academy President Sir Thomas Lawrence is mentioned disparagingly (bk 1, ch. 10). Chapters 16 and 17 of Book 1, in dealing with fakes for the art market, mention Guercino, Sebastiano del Piombo, Titian, Claude and Aelbert Cuyp. Chapter 18, Book 2, adds in Charles Le Brun, and there is a strong visual sense throughout the Italian scenes, exceeding *Pictures from Italy*, and indeed implicitly taking issue with its judgements. Hampton Court, which had been opened to the public in 1839, is often mentioned (Dickens knew its considerable art collection). Yet there is not the use of pictures as cultural references as there is in, say, Thackeray's

JEREMY TAMBLING

The Newcomes (1854–5), which draws out how much of Thackeray is concerned with knowledge of art.[19] But Thackeray was more at home with alliances between art, art collecting, property-dealing and social cachet than Dickens (who used Thackerayan traits for Henry Gowan). He notes connections between unreality and the commodity status of art, as in *Bleak House* (1852–3), when Sir Leicester Dedlock, possessing a gallery full of portraits at Chesney Wold, relaxes at his London house:

> He has his pictures, ancient and modern. Some, of the Fancy Ball School, in which Art occasionally condescends to become a master, which would be best catalogued like the miscellaneous articles in a sale. As, 'Three high-backed chairs, a table and cover, long-necked bottle (containing wine), one flask, one Spanish female's costume, three-quarter face portrait of Miss Jogg, the model, and a suit of armour containing Don Quixote'. Or, 'One stone terrace (cracked), one gondola in distance, one Venetian senator's dress complete, richly embroidered white satin costume with profile portrait of Miss Jogg the model, one scimitar superbly mounted in gold with jewelled handle, elaborate Moorish dress (very rare), and Othello.[20]

The chapter follows 'The Ironmaster', where Sir Leicester has had to confront industrial modernity, now safely ignored. This art is for the market, selling itself and its subjects. Don Quixote and Othello are diminished by association with the exotic and the commodity. Paintings are assemblages of clichés, satisfying only the desire not to look at anything new; Dickens demands something higher. The novel includes critique of 'that truly national work, The Divinities of Albion, or Galaxy Gallery of British Beauty, representing ladies of title and fashion in every variety of smirk that art, combined with capital, is capable of producing' (330, ch. 20).[21] 'Smirk' recalls Miss La Creevy, on portrait painting: 'it must be either serious or smirking'.[22] 'Serious' means 'religious'; a smirk comes from having 'capital'. Pictures from these adorn Mr Weevle/Jobling's room at Mr Krook's, the room where Nemo died. 'As the Gallery of British Beauty wears every variety of fancy dress, plays every variety of musical instruments, fondles every variety of dog, ogles every variety of prospect, and is backed up by every variety of flowerpot and balustrade, the result is imposing' (330–1, ch. 20). The way that Dickens makes 'variety' mean 'sameness' – just altering the standard accompaniments – is typical. Later, Weevle hangs a representation of Lady Dedlock culled from one of these collections (510, ch. 32). Dickens combines satire against portraiture, as in: 'she is represented on a terrace with a pedestal upon the terrace, and a vase upon the pedestal' (510, ch. 32), adding dramatic irony (the portrait of a lady replaces Nemo's dead body), and social comment (the 'celebrity', in fashion, is about to be brought down by the scandal-loving mores of the *petite bourgeoisie*). We can note Harold Skimpole's accurate wit, describing the Chesney Wold art collection: 'Sir Somebody Dedlock, with a battle, a sprung-mine, volumes of smoke, flashes of lightning, a town on fire and a stormed fort, all in full action between the horse's two hind legs' (604, ch. 37). Dickens is ambivalent about Skimpole, who recalls – negatively – the bohemian of S. L. Blanchard's article in *Household Words*, who puts 'art before all' in the spirit of 'art for art's sake', and – positively – the spirit opposing convention, 'duty' and business. His will for Ada's path to be 'strewn with roses', to 'lie through bowers' in 'perpetual summer', recalls the rococo art of François Boucher

HIGH ART

293

(1703–70) and Jean-Honoré Fragonard (1732–1805), distantly inspiring the artistry of the 'Divinities of Albion'; but Skimpole also represents the artist as marginal to bourgeois society.[23]

Dickens and the Pre-Raphaelites

Bleak House follows Dickens's disparagement of *Christ in the House of His Parents* (Royal Academy exhibition in 1850) by John Everett Millais (1829–96). The novel becomes Dickens showing that he has a sense of what pictorial art can do, in several innovatory features.[24] Its anti-Pre-Raphaelitism shows in scorning 'Young England', and Mrs Pardiggle's Anglo-Catholicism (a form of art for art's sake), and critique of dandyism. His dislike of an ascetic tendency in medieval Catholicism had already showed in the Keatsian 'Eve of St Agnes' inspired story of the 'Five Sisters' in *Nicholas Nickleby* (ch. 6). His anti-Millais article has won little praise, beginning with Humphry House in 1941.[25] It is time that House's view was questioned. In 'Old Lamps for New Ones' (1850) in *Household Words*, Dickens tells the readers that they must abandon all 'elevated thoughts' about the Holy Family for 'the lowest depths of what is mean, odious, repulsive, and revolting':

> You behold the interior of a carpenter's shop. In the foreground [. . .] is a hideous, wry-necked, blubbering, red-headed boy, in a bed-gown; who appears to have received a poke in the hand from the stick of another boy with whom he has been playing in an adjacent gutter, and to be holding it up for the contemplation of a kneeling woman, so horrible in her ugliness, that [. . .] she would stand out from the rest of the company as a Monster, in the vilest cabaret in France, or the lowest gin-shop in England. Two almost naked carpenters, master and journeyman, worthy companions of this agreeable female, are working at their trade; a boy, with some small flavour of humanity in him, is entering with a vessel of water; and nobody is paying any attention to a snuffy old woman who seems to have mistaken that shop for the tobacconist's next door, and to be hopelessly waiting at the counter to be served with half an ounce of her favourite mixture. Wherever it is possible to express ugliness of feature, limb, or attitude, you have it here expressed. Such men as the carpenters might be undressed in any hospital where dirty drunkards, in a high state of varicose veins, are received. Their very toes have walked out of Saint Giles's.[26]

The article is sarcastic about desiring to be Pre-Raphaelite, 'cancelling all the advances of nearly four hundred years' (248); it critiques a medievalism, identified with Pugin (247); it finds no satisfaction that 'the shavings which are strewn on the carpenter's floor are admirably painted' (246). The painting has High Church, or Tractarian sympathies, and it is interesting to compare Ruskin's hostility to it, and to 'Romanist' tendencies in the PRB.[27] Here it is relevant to note that William Holman Hunt had little use for J. M. W. Turner.[28] Pre-Raphaelite compositions – the subject is centred, colours flat and clear, the perspective shallow, and the lighting of the picture evenly distributed – do not relate to Turner, the most distinguished, and modern, nineteenth-century artist. Hunt contrasts with Dickens who seems to have understood what Turner wants in landscape (Dickens's renderings of landscape in

American Notes (1842) and *Martin Chuzzlewit* (1843–4), for instance, are subtle and extensive).[29] There is an incongruity in Millais between the religious sentiment and the desire for realism, yet 'art requires something more than the faithful portraiture of shavings' (246).[30] Dickens resists the realism receiving accreditation in the 1850s, against which *Bleak House, Hard Times* (1854) and *Little Dorrit* work. George Eliot's review of Ruskin's *Modern Painters* (1856) finds that the 'truth' that Ruskin teaches 'is *realism* – the doctrine that all truth and beauty are to be attained by a humble and faithful study of nature, and not by substituting vague forms, bred by imagination on the mists of feeling, in place of definite substantial reality' (Ruskin's word is 'realisation').[31] Her 'The Natural History of German Life' (also 1856), which criticises *Little Dorrit* and Dickens, accusing him of 'melodrama' (Dickens 'scarcely ever passes from the humorous and external to the emotional and tragic without becoming as transcendent in his unreality as he was a moment before in his artistic truthfulness'), reviews two studies of peasant life by the German sociologist Wilhelm Heinrich Riehl.[32] She notes 'how little the real characteristics of the working classes are known to those who are outside them, how little their natural history has been studied'.[33] *Adam Bede* (1859), consequently, praises the 'truthfulness' in seventeenth-century Dutch paintings.[34] Realism must associate with pastoral, with the small town at most, and with the traditional. Eliot asks: 'what English artist ever attempts to rival in truthfulness such studies of popular life as the pictures of Teniers or the ragged boys of Murillo?'[35] That is complex: implicitly making Eliot side with Dickens, noting the 'Victorianism' in nineteenth-century art, including the PRB, where pictorial realism becomes a matter of overbright colours, picturing reality by holding it at a nostalgic, historical distance, so 'containing' what is seen. For the 'Fine Arts' 'must array themselves in the milliners' and tailors' patterns of past generations, and be particularly careful not to be in earnest, or to receive any impress from the moving age' (*Bleak House* 189, ch. 12).

Millais's picture was untitled, but carried the inscription, 'And who shall say unto him, What are these wounds in thine hands? Then he shall answer, Those with which I was wounded in the house of my friends' (Zechariah 13.6). Dickens could have noted that such an apocalyptic, melodramatic statement demands more than the tameness and sentimentality of the boy's wounded hand, alongside the picture's symbolism (for example, the sheep representing the faithful in the back of the picture). But his satire is withering enough, coming from his own art less timid about melodrama, or even about the extreme potentialities in the biblical statement. Dickens's rejection of Millais's everyday realism, as feeding religious sentimentalism, making the realism fail in objectivity, means that he is ready for G. H. Lewes contending against the realism of spontaneous combustion in Chapter 32 of *Bleak House*; the apocalypticism here being desire for revolution, in an anger which implicitly (not openly) pre-judges 'realism' as conformist to existing political arrangements as these emerged after 1848 and the triumphalism of the Great Exhibition (1851). A commissioner for the latter was Henry Cole (1808–82), General Superintendent of the Department of Practical Art (1852). *Hard Times* caricatures him as the bureaucratic government officer in Gradgrind's school; a literalist in the industrial arts, deriding imagination and declaring that people (especially working-class people) must use 'combinations and modifications (in primary colours) of mathematical figures which are susceptible of proof and demonstration', eliminating 'Fancy'; equating taste with fact.[36]

We can align Dickens's reaction against fact, realism and practicality with his art criticism. He may lack a vocabulary of art criticism and affect an empiricism about Hunt's picture (not assuming that he knows what is going on in it), but his target is bourgeois conventionalism. From Paris, November 1855, he writes to Forster about British art at the Exposition Universelle in Paris. He criticises William Mulready, and Clarkson Frederick Stanfield ('too much like a set-scene' – that is, too theatrical, perhaps melodramatic), and Charles Robert Leslie's picture of Sancho Panza which 'wants go'; finding in all 'a horrible respectability [. . .] a little, finite, systematic routine in them, strangely expressive to me of the state of England itself'. The best there are by William Frith, E. M. Ward and Augustus Egg. In contrast, with the French (for example, Eugène Delacroix), he notes 'the fearlessness [. . .] the bold drawing, the dashing conception; the passion and action'. The Belgian display is 'full of merit. It has the best landscape in it, the best portrait, and the best scene of homely life, to be found in the building.' But:

> mere form and conventionalities usurp, in English art, as in English government and social relations, the place of living force and truth. I tried to resist the impression yesterday, and went to the English gallery first, and praised and admired with great diligence, but it was of no use. I could not make anything better of it than what I tell you. Of course, this is between ourselves. Friendship is better than criticism and I shall steadily hold my tongue. Discussion is worse than usefulness when you cannot agree about what you are going to discuss.[37]

He ends despairingly, recalling discussion with one interlocutor: 'they seem to me to have got a fixed idea that there is no natural manner but the English manner.'[38]

It is apparent that Dickens's likings, friendships and opinions in letters may not reliably indicate his opinion; that he knows that art and politics are inseparable, and that if a country has conventional politics that will show: Mr Podsnap's view of art (see *Our Mutual Friend*, bk 1, ch. 11) is relevant. He values art more than for realism and feels at odds with his contemporaries – even with Forster, if it is true that Podsnap has Forsterian traits. Dickens's absence of nationalism, especially post-1848, is refreshing. While it is unnecessary to argue that the terms of Dickens's art criticism are those of a sophisticated art critic, we may ponder how much the artists he knew could teach him. And it seems that he does not admit the hegemony of art-critical terms: there is not even an agreement as to what is being discussed. This seems to have been the case with his Millais critique.

Dickens, Allegory and the Baroque

Aversion to portraiture is accompanied by a feel for landscape, apparent in the few, but interesting, comments Dickens makes on Turner; in the sense of perspective, and its tricks, and in his sense of colour, which takes in shadow and dimness and night, whereas such an artist as Frith paints with homogeneity and a sense of uniform colour.[39] Bright colours, in *Little Dorrit*, for example, are often a sign of alienation, as in the description of Marseilles, its staring and its blueness. Dickens in Italy disliked Bernini's Baroque work in Rome and, equally, that of the Mannerist Giulio Romano (Shakespeare's only named painter) in the Mantua Palazzo Te.[40] This slighting of

296 JEREMY TAMBLING

Baroque is unfortunate, considering the term's critical currency in modernism and beyond, but, equally, educated Americans of the nineteenth century found Baroque antipathetic, until Heinrich Wölfflin's *Principles of Art History* (1915), which defined it as anti-objectivist (so anti-classical) and open to contradictions and tensions between disparate elements in architecture, sculpture or painting.[41] These Americans did no better than Dickens. Ruskin, too, never mentions 'baroque', though *The Stones of Venice* (1851–3), sometimes against his own grain, approves of 'the grotesque renaissance'.[42] And here we reach Dickens's own art and likings.

'Grotesque', a word used more in *Pictures in Italy* than anywhere else in Dickens, as if everything in Italy tended to the grotesque, applies to what he says of the Palazzo Te, 'standing in a swamp'; 'desolate and neglected'; Giulio Romano frescoes 'unaccountable nightmares'; with 'a leering Giant over a certain chimney-piece', while, in another room, the giant Titans warring against Jove are so 'inconceivably ugly and grotesque that it is marvellous how any man could have imagined such creatures', having 'every distortion of look and limb'; 'exaggerated to the utmost pitch of uncouthness' (375–6). The sense of deformity belongs, of course, to an anti-classical baroque aesthetic. It may seem strange that Dickens should be so bemused since he works throughout with the grotesque. Walter Benjamin, quoting Karl Borinski, finds the grotesque as baroque, associating the grotesque's 'enigmatically mysterious character' with:

> its subterraneanly mysterious origin in buried ruins and catacombs. The word is not derived from *grotto* in the literal sense, but from the 'burial' – in the sense of concealment – which the cave or grotto expresses. [. . .] The enigmatic was therefore part of its effect from the very beginning.[43]

Concealment, or repression, gives the grotesque psychoanalytic interest; Dickens's account of giants 'staggering under the weight of falling buildings, and being overwhelmed in the ruins; upheaving masses of rock, and burying themselves beneath; vainly striving to sustain the pillars of heavy roofs that topple down upon their heads; and in a word, undergoing and doing every kind of mad and demoniacal destruction' (*Pictures*, 376) responds to an ambiguity in the words 'undergoing' (passive) and 'doing' (active): these giants create ruins which they pull down on themselves. They are baroque in their excess, fascination with death and their death-drive; they are enigmatic, and there is a kinship between enigma with allegory; further, the grotesque is allegorical, that being a key to the Baroque.[44]

Dickens responded to a violence in the Palazzo Te not present in the PRB. Other writers were squeamish over the filth in Millais's picture, showing that in English nineteenth-century painting, realism, carried over into ideal subjects (that is, those which are religious, or spiritual), had, necessarily, to consort, contradictorily, with another episteme present in medieval art, which made reality anagogical and symbolic. The realism (including 'deformity') may be baroque, especially if a comparison is made with those Murillo paintings which disturbed Ruskin, for example, calling the boys' dirty feet, pointed towards the viewer in a deliberate torsion, 'a mere delight in foulness'.[45] The feet indicate sensuousness, which perhaps Ruskin noticed unconsciously and drew back from, but they also evoke death; the soles are dusty, a naturalistic detail both de-idealising and allegorical, inscribing the pictures as double:

life and death together. Ruskin contrasted Murillo unfavourably with Holman Hunt, whose paintings of beggars and peasant boys he called 'picturesque'. Ruskin was distinctive, but not exceptional, in disliking a realism inclusive of dirt. The contradiction, present in the PRB (for example, Millais's wood shavings), shows a divided intention, to be realist and idealist at once, which also characterised the baroque art which Dickens saw in Italy. But where baroque emphasises the disparity, becoming grotesque, nineteenth-century art cannot. Hence Dickens was fascinated by Giulio Romano's giants, but could only become baroque in his novels.

A baroque in Dickens is hinted at with Paul Dombey's perceptions of the wallpaper at Doctor Blimber's, where he 'found out miniature tigers and lions running up the bedroom walls, and squinting faces leering in the squares and diamonds of the floorcloth. The solitary child lived on, surrounded by this arabesque work of his musing fancy.'[46] 'Arabesque', perhaps from Poe (for example, 'Ligeia', 1838), with the play of line which perhaps recalls Daniel Maclise's strangely Blakean frontispiece for *The Chimes* (1844), combines the grotesque and the Gothic with the fantasy world of *The Arabian Nights* in baroque form. Lack of classical decorum in the arabesque compares with the baroque ceiling above Mr Tulkinghorn's head, 'where Allegory, in Roman helmet and celestial linen, sprawls among balustrades and pillars, flowers, clouds, and big-legged boys, and makes the head ache – as would seem to be Allegory's object always, more or less' (*Bleak House* 158, ch. 10). It seems to 'swoop upon him' (259, ch. 16), unnoticed by the realist Tulkinghorn. Allegory moves in a different world from that of 'a staring old Dedlock in a panel, as large as life and as dull, [who] looks as if he didn't know what to make of it' (185, ch. 12); life without imagination. Allegory points as if towards the window (259, ch. 16), but also towards Tulkinghorn (669, ch. 42) and the floor when Tulkinghorn has been shot (750–2, ch. 48). This last becomes the subject of one of Phiz's ten 'dark plates' for the novel, that new development in Phiz and Dickens, imposing Caravaggio-like baroque darkness on the text, and in six cases completely abstracting people from it. Use of allegory blends with the emblematic details of pictures which Dickens would have learned from Hogarth, but Allegory's ambiguous pointing is part of a trompe l'oeil – which way is he pointing? When Dickens critiqued the shallow perspectives of Pre-Raphaelitism, he noted Hogarth's 'idea of a man on a mountain several miles off, lighting his pipe at the upper window of a house in the foreground' – *not* the version of Hogarth Dickens is usually associated with, but evidence that it was not enough for Dickens that early criticism connected him with Hogarth: he made a study of him himself.[47] Such deployment of perspective as serving illusion is baroque; a fine example of Dickens playing with the concept, and with the traditional artistic 'prospect' of the English cathedral, appears in the hallucinatory tricks of the first paragraph of *The Mystery of Edwin Drood* (1870). Allegory is baroque, unlike symbolism, which, centring the subject by imposing unity between signifier and signified, is classical or romantic. Allegory, sensuously 'sprawling', not centred, de-centres and defers access to full meaning: why is Allegory pointing? Phiz makes him indicate an empty chair and a 'stain' before it as a metonymy for the absent body, showing the power of nothingness, and something which remains incongruous, challenging legibility, like dirt, showing what the Tulkinghorn world has excluded, repressed, like Giulio Romano's giants.

'Allegory' resembles the mirror above Charles Darnay's head when he is on trial: not a picture, it speaks of absence, – the mirror cannot give back its reflections

298   JEREMY TAMBLING

of past prisoners – and it doubles Darnay with the power of illusion, as Sydney Carton doubles him.[48] Allegory's presence in *Bleak House* prompts the expectation of emblematic details, as when Esther sees Vholes and Richard riding off: 'the gaunt pale horse with his ears pricked up [. . .] driving away at speed to Jarndyce and Jarndyce' (608, ch. 37). Behind the Apocalyptic reference (Revelation 6.8), which may also recall Albrecht Dürer's woodcut series *The Revelation of St John*, lies Hans Holbein's *Dance of Death* sequence (1523–6), as an essential emblematic motif, of a skeletal death in a series of plates dancing with various victims, from different social groupings, and different professions, which Dickens knew and of which he possessed an edition.[49] So Traddles draws skeletons in *David Copperfield* (1849–50). Dickens could not have endorsed the Pre-Raphaelite sense of piety incarnated in medieval artists whom the Pre-Raphaelites claimed to be looking back to. His imagery is full of death claiming life in the midst of its activities, as when Mrs Skewton is struck by Paralysis (allegorised, by the capitalisation: *Dombey* 574, ch. 37). The Dance of Death constructs *A Christmas Carol* (1843), when Jacob Marley comes to claim the miser, Scrooge, or later, when the Ghost of Christmas Yet to Come escorts him to his own gravestone (Dickens's sense of the visual often turns him to the decorated form of epitaphs). Yet even before Marley appears in Scrooge's room, having first been seen in the transmuted baroque doorknocker, Scrooge appears to be possessed:

> The fireplace was an old one, built by some Dutch merchant long ago, and paved all round with quaint Dutch tiles, designed to illustrate the Scriptures. There were Cains and Abels, Pharaoh's daughters, Queens of Sheba, Angelic messengers descending through the air on clouds like feather-beds, Abrahams, Belshazzars, Apostles putting off to sea in butter-boats, hundreds of figures to attract his thoughts; and yet that face of Marley, seven years dead, came like the ancient Prophet's rod, and swallowed up the whole. If each smooth tile had been a blank at first, with power to shape some picture on its surface from the disjointed fragments of his thoughts, there would have been a copy of old Marley's head on every one. (56)

The abolition of this comfortable Protestant art, wittily noted and described, in secular manner (the angelic messengers anticipate the Roman Allegory of *Bleak House*) happens through Scrooge's anxious awareness of Marley as *not* 'dead as a doornail'. The biblical allusion to Exodus 7.12, where Aaron's rod becomes the figure of death, with power to annihilate all reality, gives a baroque sensibility, where the religious force of good is ambiguous: this dance of snakes is enigmatic, unknowable in the voracious force which uncannily consumes the known instruments of judgement and power. For one 'meaning' of the Dance of Death is that the self is always paired with the unknown, and unknowable: there is no full knowledge of the self; knowledge, ceasing to be whole, fragments, like Scrooge's thinking.

   Dickens's insight is more knowing, aware of the uncanny, more complexly religious than any Pre-Raphaelite picture. It aligns him with three disparate but related artistic moments: first, the late medieval, where Death is a grotesque, and partly a figure of comedy; second, the Baroque, where allegory and darkness point to the 'nothing' which pervades uncannily, and which suggests the power of illusion (*engaño* in the Spanish Baroque: there illusion holds such a figure as Don Quixote, with the power of madness); and third with eighteenth-century 'graveyard' texts such as Robert Blair's *The Grave* (1743 – did Dickens know Blake's engravings (1808) for this?) and Thomas Gray's *Elegy Written in a Country Churchyard* (1751). There is evidence of his knowledge of Piranesi's *Carceri d'invenzione* in *Bleak House*, informing the imagery within Esther's delirium (555, ch. 35).[50] Liking Smollett and Sterne, he criticises Enlightenment reason; that places him in a tradition associated with Francesco Goya (1746–1828), an artist influenced by Gillray, and certainly known to Thackeray.[51] Dickens's writing, and feeling for art is anti-Enlightenment, anti-classical: in a word, baroque. Carnivalesque motifs in the Dance of Death contrast exactly with the morbid asceticism in the PRB.

The Dance of Death becomes bitter carnival when Miss Wade's 'History of a Self-Tormentor' explains her relation to Henry Gowan, where the 'dance' is sexual (sexuality as death):

> He was like the dressed-up Death in the Dutch [i.e. Deutsch] series; whatever figure he took upon his arm, whether it was youth or age, beauty or ugliness, whether he danced with it, sang with it, played with it, or prayed with it, he made it ghastly. (*Little Dorrit* 700, bk 2, ch. 21)

Holbein's traditional motif is turned to another purpose: portraying an artist whose fashionable triviality and nihilism equals the contamination of death. Dickens would almost certainly have concurred with Benjamin, quoting Leopardi, on Fashion as 'Madam Death'.[52] John Harvey speculates that Bruegel ghosts the reference in *Nicholas Nickleby* to the hero entering fashionable London, where Life and Death flit by 'in motley dance like the fantastic groups of the old Dutch painter, and with the same stern moral for the unheeding restless crowd' (391–2, ch. 32).[53] The visual imagination which sees the city must read allegorically, undoing empirical realism. Mental images present themselves in visual exterior form. At the Paris Morgue, New Year's Eve, 1846, a dead body looked like 'an impersonation of the wintry eighteen hundred and forty-six'.[54] Nell in *The Old Curiosity Shop* exists 'in a kind of allegory' because everything around her becomes an image.[55] Richard Maxwell connects this with Dürer's *Melencolia I* (1513), making comparison with the 43rd print from Goya's *Caprichos* (*The Sleep of Reason Produces Monsters*).[56] Perhaps Holbein's *Dance of Death* series is a master-key to Dickens, making him write in the third person:

> imagining Master Humphrey in his chimney-corner, resuming night after night, the narrative – say, of the Old Curiosity Shop [. . .] he [Dickens] has insensibly fallen into the belief that [the spirits of the characters] are present to his readers as they are to him, and has forgotten that like one whose vision is disordered he may be conjuring up bright figures where there is nothing but empty space.[57]

Unsurprisingly, the novels associated with Master Humphrey produced some of the most baroque or rococo, Gothic, arabesque-like figures for Dickens's own work; as if Dickens's awareness of art was more extensive before the Italian visit than has been allowed. Or, as if no art that he ever saw could ever do more than supplement the phantasmagoric visions, real to him, which worked within him, far exceeding ordered perception.

We should be more ambitious in thinking of Dickens and high art: the hint about Goya suggests one direction for research.[58] He needs comparing not with 'the lamentable Pre-Raphaelites' (Michael Fried's phrase, comparing them with Adolph Meisel (1815–1905), urban artist of Berlin),[59] but with Gustave Courbet, and the Impressionists he anticipates (who borrowed from the Turner Dickens admired). Or criticism could begin by comparing Charles Baudelaire on caricature, or on art (as in 'The Painter of Modern Life'), with Dickens, who needs bringing into the European contexts to which we have seen he himself felt an affinity: here we shall find resources that far exceed the limitations of English nineteenth-century art.[60]

Notes

1. See Jane R. Cohen, *Charles Dickens and His Original Illustrators* (Columbus: Ohio State University Press, 1980).
2. See the speech to the Royal Academy, 30 April 1870, after Maclise's death, in *The Speeches of Charles Dickens*, ed. by K. J. Fielding (Oxford: Clarendon Press, 1960), 419–22. Dickens addressed the Royal Academy earlier, in 1853 and 1858 (163–4, 264–5), both times with Sir Charles Eastlake chairing (see also 154). For a tribute to Wilkie, see 13–14.
3. 'To Thomas Chapman, 3 July 1846', *The Letters of Charles Dickens*, ed. by Madeline House, Graham Storey et al., Pilgrim/British Academy Edition, 12 vols (Oxford: Clarendon Press, 1965–2002). Subsequent citations: *PLets* followed by volume (year of publication), page. Here IV (1977), 576.
4. 'To Count Alfred D'Orsay, 18 March 1845', *PLets*, IV, 283.
5. For an account of Dickens and painting, see Richard Lettis, *The Dickens Aesthetic* (New York: AMS Press, 1989), 19–87. Leonée Ormond wrote pioneering essays, 'Dickens and Painting: The Old Masters' and 'Dickens and Painting: Contemporary Art', *Dickensian* 79 (1983), 131–51, and 80 (1984), 2–24. See also *Dickens and the Artists*, ed. by Mark Bills (New Haven: Yale University Press, 2012).
6. 'To John Forster, [? April 1845]', *PLets*, IV, 298–9; compare his letter to Maclise, 22 July 1844, *PLets*, IV, 158–62.
7. Charles Dickens, 'Review: *The Drunkard's Children*', in *The Dent Uniform Edition of Dickens' Journalism*, ed. by Michael Slater and John Drew, 4 vols (London: Dent, 1994–2000), II (1996), 102–7. See my *Dickens's Novels as Poetry: Allegory and the Literature of the City* (London: Routledge, 2014), 48–50.
8. Charles Dickens, *Sketches by Boz*, ed. by Dennis Walder (London: Penguin, 1995), 346. On the 'picturesque', see 'To John Forster, [11 February 1845]', *PLets*, IV, 266.
9. Dickens, *Sketches*, 425.
10. Richard D. Altick, *The Shows of London* (Cambridge, MA: Harvard University Press, 1978), 416.
11. Charles Dickens, 'The Ghost of Art' (*Household Words*, 20 July 1850), in *Dickens' Journalism*, II, 257–64.
12. Jeremy Tambling, 'The Workhouse World of *Oliver Twist*: Mother, Orphan, Foundling', in *Liminal Dickens: Rites of Passage in his Work*, ed. by Valerie Kennedy and Katerina Kitsi-Mitakon (Newcastle upon Tyne: Cambridge Scholars, 2016), 111–14.
13. See 'To Mrs Charles Dickens, 1 November 1838', *PLets*, I (1965), 447.
14. Charles Dickens, *The Christmas Books vol. 1: A Christmas Carol and The Chimes*, ed. by Michael Slater (London: Penguin, 1971), 127. Subsequent references are inserted parenthetically in the text.
15. Charles Dickens, *Great Expectations*, ed. by Angus Calder (London: Penguin, 1965), 219, ch. 23.

HIGH ART   301

16. Charles Dickens, *Our Mutual Friend*, ed. by Adrian Poole (London: Penguin, 1997), 27, bk 1, ch. 3. See on this my 'Dickens and Chaucer', *English* 64 (2015), 4–64.

17. See Regina B. Oost, '"More Like than Life": Painting, Photography, and Dickens's *Bleak House*', *Dickens Studies Annual* 30 (2001), 141–58.

18. Charles Dickens, *Little Dorrit*, ed. by Stephen Wall (London: Penguin, 2003), 160, bk 1, ch. 13.

19. Richard D. Altick, *The Presence of the Present: Topics of the Day in the Victorian Novel* (Columbus: Ohio State University Press, 1991), 480–92.

20. Charles Dickens, *Bleak House*, ed. by Nicola Bradbury (London: Penguin, 2003), 458–9, ch. 29. Subsequent references are inserted parenthetically in the text.

21. See Maria Ioannou, 'A "Pretty" Ending: Female Beauty, Agency and Identity in *Bleak House*', *Dickensian* 115 (2019), 155–68.

22. Charles Dickens, *Nicholas Nickleby*, ed. by Mark Ford (London: Penguin, 2003), 121, ch. 10.

23. See Robyn Cooper, 'The Relationship between the Pre-Raphaelite Brotherhood and Painters before Raphael in English Criticism of the Late 1840s and 1850s', *Victorian Studies* 24 (1981), 405–38. Blanchard's article is 'The True Bohemians of Paris', *Household Words* 86 (22 November 1851), IV, 190–2.

24. Donald H. Ericksen, '*Bleak House* and Victorian Art and Illustration: Charles Dickens's Visual Narrative Style', *Journal of Narrative Technique* 13 (1983), 31–46.

25. Humphry House, *The Dickens World* (Oxford: Oxford University Press, 1941, repr. 1950), 126–30.

26. Charles Dickens, 'Old Lamps for New Ones' (*Household Words*, 15 June 1850) in *Dickens' Journalism*, II, 242–8, 245; 246. Subsequent references are inserted parenthetically in the text.

27. Ruskin, *The Library Edition of the Works of John Ruskin*, ed. by E. T. Cook and Alexander Wedderburn, 39 vols (London: Allen, 1903–12), XII, 320. For Ruskin on the Pre-Raphaelites, see XII, 319–93.

28. *Ruskin, Turner, and the Pre-Raphaelites*, ed. by Robert Hewison (London: Tate Gallery, 2000), cat. no. 5 and cat. no. 201.

29. See my 'Wreckage and Ruin: Turner, Dickens, Ruskin', in *Reading Dickens Differently*, ed. by Leon Litvack and Nathalie Vanfasse (Chichester: Wiley, 2019), 125–47, and Nanako Konoshima, 'Storm and Sunset: Turnerian Landscapes in *David Copperfield*', *Dickensian* 113 (2017), 150–9.

30. Dickens and Millais are discussed in J. B. Bullen, *The Pre-Raphaelites Body: Fear and Desire in Painting, Poetry, and Criticism* (Oxford: Clarendon Press, 1998), 6–48.

31. George Eliot, *Selected Essays, Poems, and Other Writings*, ed. by Nicholas Warren (Harmondsworth: Penguin, 1990), 368. See also John Murdoch, 'English Realism: George Eliot and the Pre-Raphaelites', *Journal of the Warburg and Courtauld Institutes* 37 (1974), 313–29.

32. Eliot, *Selected Essays*, 111.

33. Ibid., 108.

34. George Eliot, *Adam Bede*, ed. by Stephen Gill (Harmondsworth: Penguin, 1980), 179.

35. Eliot, *Selected Essays*, 108.

36. Dickens, *Hard Times*, ed. by David Craig (London: Penguin, 1969), 51–2, (bk 1, ch. 2); see K. J. Fielding, 'Charles Dickens and the Department of Practical Art', *Modern Language Review* 48 (1953), 270–7.

37. 'To John Forster, [?11–12 November 1855]', *PLets*, VII (1993), 742–3.

38. Ibid., VII, 744.

39. See my 'Modern Painters: Dickens and Cézanne', *E-rea: Revue électronique d'études sur le monde anglophone* 13.2 (2016) <10.4000/erea.4903>.

40. Dickens, *American Notes and Pictures from Italy*, ed. by F. S. Schwarbach and Leonée Ormond (London: Everyman, 1997), 422–44 and 375. Subsequent references are inserted parenthetically in the text.
41. See William L. Vance, 'The Sidelong Glance: Victorian Americans and Baroque Rome', *The New England Quarterly* 58 (1985), 501–32.
42. Ruskin, XI, 135–95.
43. Walter Benjamin, *The Origin of German Tragic Drama*, trans. by John Osborne (London: New Left Books, 1977), 171.
44. On allegory and enigma, see Angus Fletcher, *Allegory: The Theory of a Symbolic Mode* (Ithaca: Cornell University Press, 1964), 73; see also my *Allegory* (London: Routledge, 2010).
45. Ruskin, *The Stones of Venice* in X, 228–9.
46. Dickens, *Dombey and Son*, ed. by Andrew Sanders (London: Penguin, 2002), 190, ch. 12. Sanders notes a later reference to Rembrandt's 'Hundred Guilder Print' (218 n.8, 971). Subsequent references are inserted parenthetically in the text.
47. 'Old Lamps', *Dickens' Journalism*, II, 247. On Hogarth's 'Satire on False Perspective' (1754), see *Hogarth's Graphic Works*, ed. by Ronald Paulson (London: British Museum, 1989), cat. 232.
48. Dickens, *A Tale of Two Cities*, ed. by Richard Maxwell (London: Penguin, 2000), 66, bk 2, ch. 2.
49. Michael Hollington, 'Dickens and the Dance of Death', *Dickensian* 74 (1978), 67–85. See Claire Wood, *Dickens and the Business of Death* (Cambridge: Cambridge University Press, 2015), 38, and Jeremy Tambling, *Dickens,* Nicholas Nickleby *and the Dance of Death* (London: Routledge, 2019).
50. See my *Dickens, Violence, and the Modern State* (London: Macmillan, 1995), 88–93.
51. See Dominique Peyrache-Leborgne, '*L'Histoire du roi de Bohême* and *Oliver Twist* under Cruikshank's Patronage: The Dynamics of Text and Image at the Core of the Grotesque in the Novel of the 1830s', in *The Grotesque in the Fiction of Charles Dickens and Other 19th-Century European Novelists*, ed. by Isabelle Hervouet-Farrar and Max Vega-Ritter (Newcastle upon Tyne: Cambridge Scholars, 2014), 12–26, 21–3. There, Michael Hollington, 'Giants and Grotesques: The Dickensian Grotesque and the Return from Italy' (51–62), finds *Pictures from Italy* using 'grotesque' the most in Dickens (51).
52. Walter Benjamin, *The Arcades Project*, trans. by Howard Eiland and Kevin McLaughlin (Cambridge, MA: Harvard University Press, 1999), 8.
53. J. R. Harvey, *Victorian Novelists and their Illustrators* (London: Sidgwick & Jackson, 1970), 71–4.
54. 'To John Forster, [early January 1847]', *PLets*, V (1981), 3.
55. Dickens, *The Old Curiosity Shop*, ed. by Norman Page (London: Penguin, 2000), 22.
56. Richard Maxwell, 'Crowds and Creativity in *The Old Curiosity Shop*', *Journal of English and Germanic Philology* 78 (1979), 49–71.
57. Dickens, *Master Humphrey's Clock and Other Stories*, ed. by Peter Mudford (London: Everyman, 1997), 23–5.
58. See *The Discovery of Spain: British Artists and Collectors, Goya to Picasso*, ed. by Christopher Baker (Edinburgh: National Galleries of Scotland, 2009): William Stirling's *Annals of the Artists of Spain* (1848) was the first significant account of Spanish art in Britain, including Goya (21).
59. Michael Fried, *Menzel's Realism: Art and Embodiment in Nineteenth-Century Berlin* (New Haven: Yale University Press, 2002), 154.
60. See Michele Hanoosh, *Baudelaire and Caricature: From the Comic to an Art of Modernity* (University Park: Pennsylvania University Press, 1992).

20

ARCHITECTURE

Ben Moore

IN CHAPTER 27 OF *GREAT EXPECTATIONS* (1860–1), Pip asks Joe Gargery, who is newly arrived in London, whether he has seen anything of the city yet. He receives the following response:

> Why, yes, Sir, [. . .] me and Wopsle went off straight to look at the Blacking Ware'us. But we didn't find that it come up to its likeness in the red bills at the shop doors; which I meantersay, [. . .] as it is there drawd too architectooralooral.[1]

As Charlotte Mitchell notes in the Penguin edition, both Day and Martin's and Warren's were blacking companies that illustrated their bottles with pictures of the warehouses where they had been manufactured (497–8, n. 6). Although Warren's had a particular resonance for Dickens given his traumatic childhood experience connected to it, Day and Martin's used red labels and posters, and had the more impressive frontage, so this is likely to have been Joe's destination.

As shown in Plate 4, Day and Martin's ink bottles carried an image of their premises on 97 High Holborn, built in a grand classical style that seemed to elevate the company beyond its prosaic business practices. A *Penny Magazine* article from 1842 describes a visit to Day and Martin's, remarking that 'the blacking-makers are more important personages now than they ever were; they surprise us with magnificent buildings – more like mansions than factories', as evident in the 'elegant exterior' of the Holborn establishment.[2] There is, of course, a comic naivety in Joe's selection of a blacking warehouse as the most important sight in London. But his choice also points to how commodities such as boot polish could act as emissaries for the capital city and its architecture, disseminating an image of London's grandeur that, for Joe at least, is more significant than its monuments to Church, State or Empire.

As Bill Brown and Elaine Freedgood have shown, unconscious or 'fugitive' meanings of commodities frequently function as counter-narratives within nineteenth-century fiction.[3] Clare Pettitt's discussion of Peggotty's work-box from *David Copperfield* (1849–50), illustrated with a view of St Paul's Cathedral, provides a resonant example. Although St Paul's was a common motif for commemorative objects, Pettitt argues that the apparently inconsequential work-box becomes a reminder that '"things" take on an extra burden of significance in a world of semi-literacy', signalling the importance of St Paul's as a tourist attraction for 'ordinary country people' like Peggotty, while also complicating the distinction between subjects and objects.[4] Though the work-box is more conventional in its choice of architecture than the bill Joe sees, both testify to the role of mechanical reproducibility in reducing grand buildings to the level of the commodity, multiplying and replicating them so that they became part of the fabric of everyday life. Such reproductions seem to detract from the architectural qualities of the buildings they depict, tarnishing what Walter Benjamin would call their 'aura'.[5] For Joe, the image on the shop bill is more impressive, more authentically architectural, than the building itself. Similarly, when Peggotty finally visits St Paul's, it has 'from her long attachment to her work-box' become 'a rival of the picture on the lid, and was, in some particulars, vanquished, she considered, by that work of art'.[6] Beyond simply the loss of aura, these instances register aura's displacement, its movement from the building to the image of the building. In such cases architecture turns against itself; signifier detaches from signified, copy from reality, yet what is detached seems to contain the essence of the architecture it leaves behind. In Jean Baudrillard's terms, this is the second order of the simulacral. In the simulacral, associated with 'hyperreality', signs of the real are substituted for the real itself, and 'simulation threatens the difference between the "true" and the "false"'.[7] In *Symbolic Exchange and Death* (1976), Baudrillard identifies three orders of this process, moving from the Renaissance to contemporary modernity. In the second order, dominated by industrial production, the relation between identical objects 'is no longer one of an original and its counterfeit, analogy or reflection, but is instead one of equivalence and indifference', beginning a decay of uniqueness that accelerates through the twentieth century.[8]

Partly inspired by these failures of architecture to match up with its image, this chapter suggests we take Joe's term 'architectooralooral' as the starting point to explore a counter-current of what can be called 'anti-architecture' within Dickens's writing.[9] By this I mean that Dickens's architecture does not secure the social world he portrays, a world where all groups, classes and places are to some extent interlinked. Such interconnection is evident in *Bleak House* (1852–3), where the 'world of fashion' is 'not so unlike the Court of Chancery, but that we pass from the one scene to the other, as the crow flies', and where Mr Bucket can 'mount a high tower in his mind' to command a panoptical perspective, like that of the author himself.[10] Nor does architecture merely act as a background to this world. Rather, it contributes to a network of shifting and uncertain signification in which social space reciprocally forms and is formed by the characters who move through it, lending architecture an ambiguity that manifests itself in a variety of ways. Julian Wolfreys's neologism 'Dickensian architextures' captures some of this shifting ambiguity, expressing what he calls Dickens's 'desire to shake the solidity of the monumental', and to '[speak] of architecture without speaking it. Privileging the narrative over the monumental, movement over the static, and informing us through the possible homology of structural resemblances between architecture and narrative, form and content.'[11] The way architecture is narrativised, and the way narrative can disrupt architecture, are also explored by Anthony Vidler, who describes 'the architectural uncanny', a feature of both houses and cities:

> In both cases, of course, the 'uncanny' is not a property of the space itself nor can it be provoked by any particular spatial conformation; it is, in its aesthetic dimension, a representation of a mental state of projection that precisely elides the boundaries of the real and the unreal in order to provide a disturbing ambiguity, a slippage between waking and dreaming.[12]

ARCHITECTURE 305

This perceptual uncanniness, which resembles the strange, in-between moment of awakening Walter Benjamin associates with nineteenth-century Paris, is a recurring feature of Dickens's architecture, and helps to explain why architecture and language frequently struggle to contain one another in his work.[13] Taking this uncanniness that lies on the border between real and unreal as a starting point, the rest of this chapter proposes a reading of Dickensian architecture that makes it oppositional to monumental order and structure. Yet Dickens's anti-architectural tendencies do not mean his writing is isolated from the architectural preoccupations of its time, so this chapter also considers how contemporary debates are registered and rearticulated in his work, most notably the long-running contest between Classical and Gothic style.

Ornamentality

While it is easy to read Joe's disappointment with the warehouse as inflected by Dickens's childhood experience of working in a blacking factory, it is perhaps more productive to focus on how Joe expresses his criticism: his claim that the image on the poster is 'drawd too architectooralooral'.[14] In response, Pip remarks: 'I really believe Joe would have prolonged this word (mightily expressive to my mind of some architecture that I know) into a perfect Chorus, but for his attention being providentially attracted by his hat, which was toppling' (222, ch. 27). The term 'architectooralooral' spirals out of control, turning architecture into an uncontrollable excess whose unnecessary ornamentation causes it to circle back on itself, like the curling capitals of the Corinthian columns on the façade of Day and Martin's (Plate 4). This ornamentation is signalled in the word's appearance on the page, where the column-like 'l's are accompanied by repeated 'o's that themselves become ornamental. As Pip implies in his sardonic reference to 'some architecture that I know', Victorian design had a tendency towards ornament for the sake of ornament. This is evident in both Gothic, as with George Gilbert Scott's Midland Grand Hotel (built 1868–74), and Classical design, as with Day and Martin's. These two traditions were the protagonists in what by the 1850s became known as the 'battle of the styles' – a contest in which St Pancras railway station, like the rebuilding of the Houses of Parliament after the 1834 fire, marked a victory for Gothic in an urban context.[15] The Victorian predilection for ornamentation – what might be called architectooraloooralism – was critiqued by John Ruskin, who warned against 'servile ornament', meaning ornament simplified and regularised to 'a standard which every workman could reach'. At the same time, Ruskin praised 'true' imaginative ornamentation as central to architecture's capacity for beauty and moral force.[16] In this respect, although he differs from them in much else, Ruskin anticipates the more extreme rejection of ornament by modernist architects in the early twentieth century, famously expressed in Alfred Loos's 1908 essay 'Ornament and Crime', which pronounces that 'ornament is wasted labour power and hence wasted wealth'.[17]

Ornament can be a term of criticism for Dickens, as in the opening of *Bleak House*, where Temple Bar is an 'appropriate ornament for the threshold of a leaden-headed old corporation' (14, ch. 1). Temple Bar is associated with the High Court of Chancery, located at the 'very heart of the fog' that obscures London, making it both an ornament of the law and an ornament of crime, since Chancery has become rotten (14, ch. 1). Temple Bar itself was a grand gate into the old City, rebuilt by

306   BEN MOORE

Christopher Wren after the Great Fire of London to include statues of James I, Queen
Anne, Charles I and Charles II.[18] As Jeremy Tambling points out, Temple Bar simultaneously marks the entrance into Holborn, Chancery and *Bleak House* itself, making
it a piece of threshold architecture.[19] As such, it instantiates the kind of cut between
radically different places or states that Walter Benjamin claimed was found in modern life only in cities and dreams.[20]

Pip's feeling that Joe's word 'architectooralooral' might become 'a perfect
Chorus' puts ornamentality into language as well as architecture. It implies the
multi-vocality of a choir, so that architecture becomes dialogic in the Bakhtinian
sense. His comment also recalls the choruses of popular songs, such as the one
mentioned in Chapter 15 of *Great Expectations*, whose refrain 'too rul loo rul'
echoes the end of the word 'architectooralooral', and causes Pip to reflect, 'I
thought (as I still do) the amount of Too rul somewhat in excess of the poetry' (109,
ch. 15).[21] This moment in turn recalls the Artful Dodger's reply in *Oliver Twist*
(1837–9) to Charley Bates's question of what Fagin will say when he finds out Oliver
has been caught: 'Toor rul lol loo, gammon and spinnage, the frog he wouldn't, and
high cockolorum'.[22] Gammon and spinach, and the frog, refer to the nursery rhyme
'A Frog He Would a-Wooing Go', so that the Dodger's 'toor rul lol loo' lies somewhere
between nonsense and a child's song.[23] In each case, Dickens catches language as it
breaks down, presenting another side to its apparently ordered rationality, just as
Joe presents us with architecture's other side, where grand monumentality turns
into a preoccupation with warehouses, and perambulating movement results in an
increasing instability signalled by Joe's hat toppling off his head.

Domestic Architecture and the Picturesque

Anti-architecture also features in Dickens's personal life. On 7 July 1858 he wrote to
William de Cerjat about his house at Gad's Hill in Kent:

> My little place is a grave red brick house (time of George the First, I suppose),
> which I have added to and stuck bits upon in all manner of ways, so that it is
> as pleasantly irregular, and as violently opposed to all architectural ideas, as the
> most hopeful man could possibly desire.[24]

Dickens puts himself on the side of the haphazard and irregular, in opposition to
'architectural ideas', which stand for any unified or restricted style. The alterations
he refers to were superintended by his brother-in-law Henry Austin, an architect
and civil engineer who also led renovation works when Dickens moved to Tavistock
House, Bloomsbury, in 1851.[25] Dickens seems to have tried to take charge of these
alterations himself, however, writing to Austin in a self-consciously manic letter of 7
September 1851:

> Going over the house again, I have materially altered the plans – abandoned con-
> servatory and front balcony – decided to make Stone's [i.e. Frank Stone, father
> of the illustrator Marcus Stone, who had the lease before Dickens] painting-
> room the drawing-room (it is nearly six inches higher than the room below), to
> carry the entrance passage right through the house to a back door leading to the

ARCHITECTURE   307

garden, and to reduce the once-intended drawing-room – now school-room – to a manageable size.[26]

Dickens's plans had raced ahead of reality, and his letter complains (three times, and in capital letters) that there are still 'NO WORKMEN ON THE PREMISES!'[27] Fiction put fewer limitations on his architectural ambitions, and the kind of 'pleasantly irregular' house he aimed to create at Gad's Hill recurs throughout his writing. Among the most prominent examples are Sol Gills's naval instrument shop in *Dombey and Son* (1846–8), Wemmick's house, which Pip calls 'the smallest house I ever saw; with the queerest Gothic windows (by far the greater part of them sham)' (206, ch. 25) and John Jarndyce's home, called Bleak House. Jarndyce's Bleak House is:

> one of those delightfully irregular houses where you go up and down steps out of one room into another, and where you come upon more rooms when you think you have seen all there are, and where there is a bountiful provision of little halls and passages, and where you find still older cottage-rooms in unexpected places with lattice windows and green growth pressing through them. (85, ch. 6)

This house promotes wandering, opening up into unexpected vistas in a manner reminiscent of the picturesque. In 1792 William Gilpin had defined the 'picturesque' as the breaking down of Edmund Burke's conception of the beautiful:

> A piece of Palladian architecture may be elegant in the last degree. [. . .] But if we introduce it in a picture, it immediately becomes a formal object, and ceases to please. Should we wish to give it picturesque beauty, we must use the mallet instead of the chisel: we must beat down one half of it, deface the other, and throw the mutilated members around in heaps. In short, from a *smooth* building we must turn it into a *rough* ruin.[28]

While Bleak House is not itself a ruin, its roughness is signalled by the 'crooked steps' that branch off unexpectedly from Esther's room, the 'uneven stones' outside the stable, and its eclectic 'old-fashioned' furniture, all of which combine to make it what John Jarndyce calls, in an echo of Dickens's letter to de Cerjat, a 'comfortable little place' (86, 87, ch. 6).

Nonetheless, it turns out two chapters later that Bleak House *has* been a ruin, when it was owned by Tom Jarndyce, whose obsession with the Court of Chancery led to the destruction of both man and building. John Jarndyce relates how:

> The place became dilapidated, the wind whistled through the cracked walls, the rain fell through the broken roof, the weeds choked the passage to the rotting door. When I brought what remained of him home here, the brains seemed to me to have been blown out of the house too; it was so shattered and ruined. (119, ch. 8)

Through this image of a head blown apart, the house becomes grotesque and obscene rather than picturesque, although Gilpin had already hinted at such a possibility by referring to the picturesque ruin's 'mutilated members'. Yet as the novel shows in Jarndyce's restoration of the original Bleak House and his creation of a second Bleak House, inhabited by Esther and Mr Woodcourt (959–72, ch. 64), what is ruined can sometimes be recovered. A similar transition from ruin to repair occurs in *Our Mutual Friend* (1864–5), when the Boffins move into Harmony Jail, symbolically renamed by Mrs Boffin as 'Boffin's Bower'.[29] However, Boffin's Bower can be reinvented as a comfortable home only by splitting it apart, between Mrs Boffin's side, with its 'flowery carpet' and 'hollow ornamentation' of 'stuffed birds' and 'waxen fruits', and Mr Boffin's side, with its floor of 'sand and sawdust' (63, bk 1, ch. 5). Through this splitting, the disjunctive thresholds of the modern city, as exemplified by Temple Bar, are replicated within the walls of the domestic home.

Although Bleak House is in the countryside, near St Albans, many of Dickens's ruined buildings are urban rather than rural, marking a difference from Gilpin's picturesque. As with Tom Jarndyce and Bleak House, bodies and buildings in the city are often doubles of one another, such as the house of the Veneerings in *Our Mutual Friend*, where 'all things were in a state of high varnish and polish', having no more depth than the couple that owns it (17, bk 1, ch. 2). Similarly, in *Little Dorrit* (1855–7), the familial relationship between the Marshalsea Prison and William and Amy Dorrit, its 'father' and 'child' respectively, replaces a personal relationship with an architectural one. In such symbiotic relationships, buildings can fall into ruin along with their inhabitants, perhaps most famously in the case of Miss Havisham. Pip remarks that when he and Estella visited Miss Havisham, 'we found her in the room where I had first beheld her, and it is needless to add that there was no change in Satis House' (302, ch. 38). The house and its inhabitant have become a single entity, so that to speak of one is to speak of the other, and it becomes impossible to say which haunts which. This chapter in fact begins with another architectural haunting: Pip's haunting of the 'staid old house near the Green at Richmond' where Estella lives, echoing Dickens's haunting of Maria Beadnell as a young man. Pip finds himself split apart by this process: 'Let my body be where it would, my spirit was always wandering, wandering, wandering, about that house' (300, ch. 38). The physical Pip is left a mere ruin, while his spirit wanders endlessly, in an unsettling inversion of the placid perambulations produced by Bleak House.

Five years before Miss Havisham, Dickens had created Mrs Clennam in *Little Dorrit*, whose house collapses when she leaves it after a dozen years spent in one room, an event that prompts a paralysis from which she never 'moved so much as a finger again, or had the power to speak one word'.[30] The accompanying illustration by Hablot K. Browne, titled 'Damocles', shows the building beginning to fall, with Blandois at its window (Plate 5). The classical outlines of the entranceway and pediment evoke a gravestone or entrance to a tomb, so that the house foreshadows and invites death.

If the house can be read as a kind of tomb even before it collapses, Mrs Clennam's voluntary imprisonment is a form of death, and leaving it is a resurrection (an idea Dickens returned to many times, especially in *A Tale of Two Cities* (1859) and *Our Mutual Friend*). If this is a resurrection, though, it is one that immediately fails, and the three years Mrs Clennam lives as a 'statue' (827, bk 2, ch. 31) – a kind of architectural monument herself – are a grotesque parody of the forty days spent on earth by Jesus between his resurrection and ascension (Acts 1.3).

Martin Chuzzlewit and Morality

For Dickens's most direct engagement with architecture, we need to turn to *Martin Chuzzlewit* (1843–4) and Mr Pecksniff, the self-aggrandising designer of churches. Pecksniff is defined by hypocrisy, since his pupils do all his work for him. Yet while he avoids material labour, he creates the impression of having a mastery of the profession: 'Of his architectural doings, nothing was clearly known, except that he had never built or designed anything; but it was generally understood that his knowledge of the science was almost awful in its profundity.'[31] This is parodic, the point being that Pecksniff is a teacher of architecture who never builds anything. However, it is also appropriate to the 1830s and 1840s, when architecture was becoming established as a profession in its own right, distinct from the practical concerns of engineering.[32] The formation of the Royal Institute of British Architects in 1834 marks a key moment in this process, which the architectural historian Sigfried Giedion calls a 'schism' between architects and engineers.[33] In this sense Pecksniff stands for the newly liberated 'idea' or 'essence' of architecture, which, as with Joe's poster, has become separated from a material architecture towards which it is becoming increasingly indifferent.

As Tambling observes, Pecksniff's hypocritical attitude towards language is significant here. Pecksniff never means anything he says, and so 'caricatures the language of morality in architecture, finding a moral in everything but with the saving proviso that "there is nothing personal in morality"'. In his language, 'everything is ornament, though not in the sense that anything is being adorned'. Instead it puts in question the difference between inner truth and outer appearance, so that the very concept of hypocrisy begins to fall away, having no centre to cling to. Through Pecksniff's satirising of architecture – his becoming its ornament, or making it ornamental – he is, as Tambling puts it, 'the saving of the text and helps make it anti-architecture'.[34]

Pecksniff must also be seen in the light of A. W. N. Pugin's influential book *Contrasts* (1836), which advocated a return to medieval designs, not only for aesthetic reasons but because they promoted a healthier, more cohesive and more Christian society. Medieval Gothic emanates from '*faith itself* ', expressing the 'self-denying, charitable, devout and faithful habits of the ages of faith', as opposed to 'the luxurious, corrupt, irreverent, and infidel system of the present time'.[35] In helping to establish a place for architecture at the heart of social concerns, Pugin lays the groundwork for both Pecksniff's subversion of this moral principle and the Gothic Revival that was gathering pace in the 1830s.

The ubiquity of Gothic architectural history is evident in the background of George Cattermole, one of Dickens's illustrators for *The Old Curiosity Shop* (1840–1). Cattermole trained as an architectural draughtsman under John Britton, for whom he illustrated *The Architectural Antiquities of Great Britain* (1821–3), a book devoted mainly to Gothic churches, abbeys and castles. This experience informs many of Cattermole's pieces for Dickens, including Little Nell sleeping in her grandfather's shop, surrounded by items including a medieval suit of armour, a Gothic chair and two Corinthian columns (Figure 20.1).

The same influence is evident in this picture's counterpart, Nell's deathbed, where Nell seems already entombed in the church where she has spent her final weeks (Figure 20.2). Her bed is backed by an elaborate Gothic headrest with a tableau

Figure 20.1 Samuel Williams, after George Cattermole, 'The Child in her Gentle Slumber', an illustration for Charles Dickens's *The Old Curiosity Shop* (1840–1). Courtesy of the Charles Dickens Museum, London.

Figure 20.2 George Cattermole, 'At Rest', an illustration for Charles Dickens's *The Old Curiosity Shop* (1840–1). Courtesy of the Charles Dickens Museum, London [F513].

ARCHITECTURE   311

of the Madonna and Child, emphasising Nell's own saintliness. It is perhaps no coincidence that the latter chapters of *The Old Curiosity Shop* find Dickens at his closest to Pugin and Gilpin, describing the church as 'an ancient ghostly place' that 'had been built many hundreds of years ago, and had once had a convent or monastery attached'.[36] Although Dickens is critical of Catholicism elsewhere, there is a hint of mourning for the pre-Reformation past in the schoolmaster's house, with its 'chamber once nobly ornamented by cunning architects, and still retaining, in its beautiful groined roof and rich stone tracery, choice remnants of its ancient splendour' (388, ch. 52).[37]

As the relative success of Pecksniff's business implies, *Martin Chuzzlewit* was published at a time of increasing construction, driven not only by economic growth but also by the Church Building Society, founded in 1818 in response to a perceived need to protect the spiritual wellbeing of an expanding urban population.[38] Against this background, the novel reveals the hypocritical money motive behind the building boom. Ultimately, Pecksniff would rather make money than make houses, and is easily seduced by Jonas's promise, under pressure from the conman Montague Tigg, that 'if I knew how you meant to leave your money, I could put you in the way of doubling it, in no time' (580, ch. 44). This English version of speculative avarice is, as Elizabeth Bridgham notes, rearticulated in a more utopian and forward-looking mode by the imaginary American town of Eden, which only ever exists on paper, dreamed up to profit from the fantasies of settlers and investors.[39]

Running counter to such transatlantic speculation was the Puginian idea that architecture had a moral role in society, often linked to a belief that architecture expressed national character. This was a topic pursued by John Ruskin, who wrote in 'Obedience', the seventh of his 'Lamps of Architecture', that 'The architecture of a nation is great only when it is as universal and as established as a language'.[40] Pecksniff, humorously but tellingly, is woven into the fabric of Britain by the 'gentleman of a literary turn' at Todgers's guesthouse, who produces a song 'of a classical nature' which shows 'that the Miss Pecksniffs were nearly related to Rule Britannia' and closes with the verse:

> All hail to the vessel of Pecksniff the sire!
> And favouring breezes to fan;
> While Tritons flock round it, and proudly admire
> The architect, artist, and man! (162, ch. 11)

This vision of nationalistic bombast built around Pecksniffian architecture is one Dickens opposes, not only when it takes the form of conservative Gothic churches, but also in the case of the Crystal Palace, whose modern, globally oriented, iron-and-glass construction is about as far away from Pecksniff as could be. In a letter of 1854, Dickens wrote that the Crystal Palace was 'a very remarkable thing in itself; but where so very large a building [is] continually crammed down one's throat, and to find it a new page in the whole Duty of Man to go there, is a little more than even I (and you know how amiable I am!) can endure'.[41] In his mocking phrase, a 'new page in the whole Duty of Man' (referring to both Ecclesiastes 12.13 and a popular devotional book of 1658 by Richard Allestree), Dickens recognises and condemns the attempt to establish the Crystal Palace as part of a Ruskinian national

312   BEN MOORE

moral language, refusing to allow architecture to be instrumentalised in the service
of ideology.

Yet Dickens was not immune from the pervasive link between architecture and
morality, particularly when it took the form of the pleasantly irregular domesticity he
advocated. Writing in *Household Words* in 1853 about Urania Cottage, the 'Home
for the reclamation and emigration of women' he ran for Angela Burdett-Coutts
between 1846 and 1862, Dickens commented: 'The house was never designed for any
such purpose, and is only adapted to it, in being retired and not immediately overlooked.'[42] Dickens's system imbued the house with new moral significance, so that,
'The garden gate is always kept locked; but the girls take it in turn to act as porteress,
overlooked by the second superintendent.'[43] Such modifications of the house's original purpose appealed to Dickens's liking for the offbeat and peculiar, even while its
quiet domesticity supported the ultimately conservative project of 'recovering' fallen
women through activities designed to instil a 'pride in good housewifery, and a [. . .]
sense of shame in the reverse'.[44]

Dream Architecture: Dickens, Ruskin and Venice

One of Ruskin's favourite cities was Venice, explored most extensively in *The Stones
of Venice* (1851–3), which praises the city's Byzantine and Gothic heritage. Ruskin's
approach to Venice bears comparison with Dickens's near-contemporary account in
Pictures from Italy (1846), since Dickens shares Ruskin's interest in Venice's capacity
for flux and its openness to a *flâneur*-like 'watchful wandering', while differing from
him in his lack of interest in the details of the city's construction and a refusal to see
London as Venice's opposite.[45] Venice also provides a route into interpreting the persistent association between buildings and dreams that is central to the uncanniness
of Dickens's architecture.

Writing from Italy to Douglas Jerrold in November 1844, Dickens summed up
Venice by saying: 'It is *the* wonder of the world. Dreamy, beautiful, inconsistent,
impossible, wicked, shadowy, d___able old place.'[46] A few days earlier he had written to John Forster that 'The gorgeous and wonderful reality of Venice is beyond
the fancy of the wildest dreamer. Opium couldn't build such a place, and enchantment couldn't shadow it forth in a vision.'[47] Dickens developed this characterisation further in *Pictures from Italy*, where the chapter 'An Italian Dream' pursues
an extended oneiric metaphor, beginning with him drifting towards Venice from
the mainland at night in a boat that moves on 'a dreamy kind of track, marked
out upon the sea by posts and piles', before going past a 'burial-place', then finding himself 'gliding up a street – a phantom street; the houses rising on both sides,
from the water'.[48] Houses and water turn into one another, failing to respect each
other's boundaries, in a manner reminiscent of dreams. This slippage, which typifies
Vidler's architectural uncanny, recurs throughout Venice, including in Dickens's tour
of San Marco Cathedral:

> I thought I entered the Cathedral, and went in and out among its many arches:
> traversing its whole extent. A grand and dreamy structure, of immense propor-
> tions; golden with old mosaics; redolent of perfumes; dim with the smoke of
> incense; costly in treasure of precious stones and metals, glittering through iron

ARCHITECTURE 313

bars; holy with the bodies of deceased saints; rainbow-hued with windows of stained glass; dark with carved woods and coloured marbles; obscure in its vast heights, and lengthened distances; shining with silver lamps and winking lights; unreal, fantastic, solemn, inconceivable throughout. (80)

The cathedral, with its mystifying incense and ornamentation, reinforces the dream experience of the walker, who floats through it as if still upon the boat that carried him to the city. There is an echo of this experience in the construction of the railway in *Dombey and Son*, the novel which followed Dickens's trip to Italy, where 'a hundred thousand shapes and substances of incompleteness' are 'wildly mingled out of their places [. . .] and unintelligible as any dream' (68, ch. 6). The 'inconceivable' cathedral and the 'unintelligible' building site are both dreams, hinting that the modernity of the railway is for Dickens only the other side of the ancient and immense cathedral. As Freud would later observe, dreams undo opposites, showing a 'particular preference for combining contraries into a unity or for representing them as one and the same thing'.[49] This blurring widens the scope of what should be considered architecture in Dickens, so that not only grand buildings, or even blacking warehouses, but also railways, rivers and building sites insert themselves into the conversation. If the railway and the cathedral are in any sense opposites in Dickens's writing, therefore, they can only be so dialectically, as different moments in what Benjamin calls the 'dream world' of nineteenth-century modernity.[50]

In a passage which shares much with Dickens, Ruskin also describes San Marco as a dream (though unlike Dickens he prefaces this moment with a detailed discussion of its history and architectural features):

Through the heavy door whose bronze network closes the place of his rest, let us enter the church itself. [. . .] Round the domes of its roof the light enters only through narrow apertures like large stars; and here and there a ray or two from some far away casement wanders into the darkness, and casts a narrow phosphoric stream upon the waves of marble that heave and fall in a thousand colors along the floor. [. . .] [T]he glories round the heads of the sculptured saints flash out upon us as we pass them, and sink again into the gloom. Under foot and over head, a continual succession of crowded imagery, one picture passing into another, as in a dream; forms beautiful and terrible mixed together; dragons and serpents, and ravening beasts of prey, and graceful birds that in the midst of them drink from running fountains and feed from vases of crystal; the passions and the pleasures of human life symbolized together, and the mystery of its redemption; for the mazes of interwoven lines and changeful pictures lead always at last to the Cross.[51]

Fantastical forms mix together here, while the marble itself seems to 'heave and fall' in 'waves' like the sea from which the city rises. Lights rise and flash and are lost again, as layers of symbolism pile upon one another like an illuminated manuscript. Unlike Dickens's briefer description, Ruskin allows for this confusion of light and shape to be unified under a Christian purpose, so that the 'changeful pictures lead always at last to the Cross'. The cathedral's flux and changeability is also integrated, as Ruskin later shows, by the principle of '*incrustation*', specifically 'the incrustation of brick with more precious materials', which provides a logic to its otherwise haphazard ornamentation.[52]

In the same chapter, Ruskin describes San Marco as a book, specifically a 'great Book of Common Prayer, a vast illuminated missal, bound with alabaster instead of parchment'.[53] This comparison is probably influenced, as Kite argues, by Victor Hugo's *Notre-Dame de Paris* (1831), a novel Ruskin claimed to find 'disgusting'.[54] Hugo's influential chapter 'This will Kill That' reflects on the transition from the Gothic cathedral to the printed book during the European Renaissance. Before Gutenberg, 'anyone who was born a poet became an architect', and 'architecture was the main, the universal form of writing', whereas afterwards the solidity of stone was replaced with something both more ephemeral and more lasting:

> In the form of printing, thought is more imperishable than ever; it is volatile, elusive, indestructible. It blends with the air. In the time of architecture it became a mountain and took forceful possession of an age and a space. Now it becomes a flock of birds, scatters to the four winds and simultaneously occupies every point of air and space.[55]

In this sense, Dickens as well as Ruskin reads San Marco as a book, since both see it as architecture become volatile and elusive, impossible to pin down, belatedly capturing the moment of transition Hugo describes. Indeed, Richard Maxwell suggests in a classic article that the view from Todgers's guesthouse in *Martin Chuzzlewit*, with its 'host of objects [that] seemed to thicken and expand a hundredfold', is either directly or indirectly influenced by Hugo's novel.[56] In Maxwell's reading, the perceptual fragmentation of London in this moment echoes Hugo's description of printing, so that the whole city takes on the character of a book.

For Ruskin, the connection between books and buildings runs both ways. *The Stones of Venice* imagines its reader constructing a building out of the materials he finds there, with Ruskin as a guiding architectural figure:

> I shall give him stones, and bricks, and straw, chisels, and trowels, and the ground, and then ask him to build; only helping him, as I can, if I find him puzzled. And when he has built his house or church, I shall ask him to ornament it, and leave it to him to choose the ornaments as I did to find out the construction.[57]

The apparent solidity of this architectural metaphor reverses again in the chapter 'The Nature of Gothic', where Ruskin compares the problem of describing 'Gothicness' with that of explaining 'the nature of Redness, without any actual red thing to point to'.[58] It is even more difficult to 'make the abstraction of the Gothic character intelligible, because that character itself is made up of many mingled ideas, and can consist only in their union'.[59] He later suggests that the greatness of Gothic is the 'restlessness of the dreaming mind, that wanders hither and thither among the niches', so that the 'mingled ideas' of Gothic are a dream whose essence Ruskin seeks to abstract.[60] This repeats in another mode the process Dickens satirises in Joe Gargery's poster, Peggotty's workbox and Pecksniff's hypocrisy, where the idea and materiality of architecture have become fundamentally separated. For Dickens, unlike Ruskin, the idea of bringing unity to these elements must be regarded with suspicion.

ARCHITECTURE 315

Dickens returned to Venice in *Little Dorrit*, where Amy's entrance to the city is preceded by an inability to separate past and present, memory and reality, so that she 'would wake from a dream of her birth-place into a whole day's dream', finding herself in 'a humbled state-chamber in a dilapidated palace' (489, bk 2, ch. 3). Venice is 'the crowning unreality, where all the streets were paved with water', and where Amy spends her evenings 'leaning on the broad-cushioned ledge' of her balcony, a threshold between house and city, thinking of another threshold: the 'old gate' of the Marshalsea Prison in London (489, bk 2, ch. 3). The walls of the city seem to become 'transparent' as Amy watches the water, which becomes a mirror of her mind, intimating a kind of spatial unconscious where she imagines her old life can still be found, so that the canal 'might run dry, and show her the prison again, and herself, and the old room, and the old inmates, and the old visitors' (491, bk 2, ch. 3). The point is not that Venice is real and London is a fantasy, or vice versa, but rather that Venice and London are two sides of the same coin. For Ruskin, at the end of Volume 1 of *Stones of Venice*, London exemplifies a city whose architecture removes us from nature, with its 'grim railings and dark casements, and wasteful finery of shops, and feeble coxcombry of club-houses', whereas noble architecture like Venice's 'has life, and truth, and joy in it'.[61] For Dickens, by contrast, there are always human resonances in London's architecture, even and perhaps especially when it is most alienating, as with the house of the Veneerings, Dombey's bourgeois townhouse, or the Marshalsea Prison. If Ruskin sees Venetian Gothic as dreamlike, it is Dickens who recognises that this dream cannot be contained within one architectural style or location, and it instead spills out across his writing.

Cities and Cathedrals

Ruskin defends a kind of Romantic unity in architecture, despite the variety inherent in Gothic, identifying a human preference for a 'guiding clue or connecting plan' in ornamentation.[62] Dickens, by contrast, sees that dreams are anti-architectural and that they do not respect boundaries. Nowhere is this clearer than in the opening to *The Mystery of Edwin Drood* (1870), focalised through John Jasper, who lies in an opium-induced stupor:

> An ancient English Cathedral Tower? How can the ancient English Cathedral tower be here! The well-known massive grey square tower of its old Cathedral? How can that be here! There is no spike of rusty iron in the air, between the eye and it, from any point of the real prospect. What is the spike that intervenes, and who has set it up? Maybe it is set up by the Sultan's orders for the impaling of a horde of Turkish robbers, one by one.[63]

This is an impossible vision of Cloisterham Cathedral in a London drug-den, which then becomes an oriental fantasy. The cathedral refuses to stay in its proper place, intruding where it is not wanted, precisely when Jasper is trying to escape its influence. But the cathedral is itself intruded upon by a 'rusty iron' spike, which turns out to be part of a bedstead. This spike, which pierces the pleasant prospect of ecclesiastical architecture, suggests an iron railing, which for Ruskin in 'The Work of Iron' (1858) represents the worst aspects of the modern city: it can 'shelter nothing, and support nothing', acting as 'an uneducated monster; a sombre seneschal, incapable of any words, except his perpetual "Keep Out!" and "Away with you!"'.[64] The railing, which polices borders, becomes in Jasper's dream that which undoes borders. It is a symptom of the paranoid and ugly city that symbolically cuts through the medieval cathedral, the archetypal symbol of Victorian architectural beauty. One answer to Jasper's question 'who has set it up?' is, of course, Dickens himself, who has orchestrated this scene, which simultaneously punctures the cathedral, makes it dreamlike, and acknowledges its centrality to the cultural imaginary of the nineteenth century.

This opening chapter of *Edwin Drood* again connects language and architecture, since the dream-vision of Jasper is complemented by the 'mutterings' of an intoxicated woman and 'incoherent jargon' of a drug-smoking 'Chinaman', both called 'unintelligible' by Jasper (10). Architecture becomes infected by nonsense, showing, as does Joe's word 'architectooraloorl', that for Dickens architecture cannot be a universal language. If it is a language at all, it can only be an idiosyncratic, faltering, ambiguous one.

I began by suggesting that city architecture is destabilised in Dickens's writing, but it is now clear that so too is the cathedral, European architecture's most iconic form. Yet while the cathedral becomes illusory in Venice and Jasper's opium den, and is reduced to the status of a commodity by Peggotty's work-box, at the very point of its expulsion it uncannily returns. If Joe Gargery's choice to visit a blacking warehouse is an implicit rejection of St Paul's Cathedral and Westminster Abbey, it is also the instantiation of a new kind of cathedral. The *Penny Magazine* observes that, if the sides of the filling rooms in Day and Martin's warehouse were thrown open, 'the whole would bear some resemblance to the form of a church: there would be a nave, or middle aisle, two side aisles, and two galleries over the latter'.[65] Joe's visit subtly registers that the location of the modern cathedral has shifted, moving away from grand religious structures towards prosaic spaces of commerce, which become invested with a phantasmagoric surplus of meaning beyond what use-value alone dictates. Joe therefore recognises implicitly what Sue Bridehead in *Jude the Obscure* (1895) states explicitly: 'The Cathedral has had its day!'[66] Such iconoclasm cuts two ways, since, as this chapter has endeavoured to show, Dickens's writing not only punctures the bombastic claims of nationalist, moral and monumental architecture, but finds ways to open up everyday buildings to new and unexpected possibilities for meaning.

Notes

1. Charles Dickens, *Great Expectations*, ed. by Charlotte Mitchell (London: Penguin, 1996), 222, ch. 27. Subsequent references are inserted parenthetically in the text.
2. 'A Day at "Day and Martin's"', *Penny Magazine*, December 1842, XI, 509–16, 510.
3. See Bill Brown, *A Sense of Things: The Object Matter of American Literature* (Chicago: University of Chicago Press, 2003) and Elaine Freedgood, *The Ideas in Things: Fugitive Meaning in the Victorian Novel* (Chicago: University of Chicago Press, 2006).
4. Clare Pettitt, 'Peggotty's Work-Box: Victorian Souvenirs and Material Memory', *Romanticism and Victorianism on the Net* 53 (2009) <http://dx.doi.org/10.7202/029896ar>.
5. See Walter Benjamin, 'The Work of Art in the Age of Its Mechanical Reproducibility: Second Version', in *Selected Writings: Volume 3, 1935–1938*, ed. by Howard Eiland and Michael Jennings (Cambridge, MA: Belknap Press, 2002), 101–33.

ARCHITECTURE   317

6. Charles Dickens, *David Copperfield*, ed. by Nina Burgis (Oxford: Oxford University Press, 1997), 462, ch. 33.
7. Jean Baudrillard, *Simulacra and Simulation*, trans. by Sheila Glaser (Ann Arbor: University of Michigan Press, 1995), 3.
8. Jean Baudrillard, *Symbolic Exchange and Death*, trans. by Iain Hamilton Grant (London: Sage, 1993), 55.
9. I draw here on Jeremy Tambling, '*Martin Chuzzlewit*: Dickens and Architecture', *English* 48 (1999), 147–68, 155 and Steven Connor, 'Babel Unbuilding: The Anti-archi-rhetoric of *Martin Chuzzlewit*', in *Dickens Refigured: Bodies, Desires and Other Histories*, ed. by John Schad (Manchester: Manchester University Press, 1996), 178–99. See also Denis Hollier, *Against Architecture: The Writings of Georges Bataille*, trans. by Betsy Wing (Cambridge, MA: MIT Press, 1990).
10. Charles Dickens, *Bleak House*, ed. by Nicola Bradbury (London: Penguin, 2003), 20, ch. 2; 864, ch. 56. Subsequent references are inserted parenthetically in the text.
11. Julian Wolfreys, *Writing London: The Trace of the Urban Text from Blake to Dickens* (New York: Macmillan, 1998), 148; 149.
12. Anthony Vidler, *The Architectural Uncanny: Essays in the Modern Unhomely* (Cambridge, MA: MIT Press, 1992), 11.
13. For instance: 'The situation of consciousness as patterned and chequered by sleep and waking need only be transferred from the individual to the collective' [K1,5]; 'The first tremors of awakening serve to deepen sleep' [K1a,9]. Walter Benjamin, *The Arcades Project*, trans. by Howard Eiland and Kevin McLaughlin (Cambridge, MA: Belknap Press, 1999), 389; 391.
14. On Dickens and Warren's Blacking Factory, see John Forster, *The Life of Charles Dickens*, ed. by J. W. T. Ley (London: Cecil Palmer, 1928), 23–37; Michael Allen, 'A Sketch of the Life' and Nicola Bradbury, 'Dickens's Use of the Autobiographical Fragment', in *A Companion to Charles Dickens*, ed. by David Paroissien (Malden, MA: Blackwell, 2008), 3–17, 5–6 and 18–32; and Michael Allen, *Charles Dickens's Childhood* (Houndmills, Basingstoke: Macmillan, 1988), 71–95.
15. See Barry Bergdoll, *European Architecture, 1750–1890* (Oxford: Oxford University Press, 2000), 200–3.
16. John Ruskin, *The Stones of Venice*, 3 vols (Boston, MA: Estes and Lauriat, 1911 [1851–53]). Subsequent citations: *SV* followed by volume, page. Here I, 159.
17. Alfred Loos, 'Ornament and Crime', in *Programs and Manifestoes of 20th-Century Architecture*, ed. by Ulrich Conrad, trans. by Michael Bullock (Cambridge, MA: MIT Press, 1971), 19–4, 22.
18. John Christopher, *Wren's City of London Churches* (Stroud: Amberley, 2012), 91.
19. Jeremy Tambling, *Going Astray: Dickens and London* (Harlow: Pearson, 2009), 149.
20. See, for instance, Benjamin, *Arcades*, 88 [c3,3].
21. Tambling also mentions this connection in 'Dickens and Architecture', 147.
22. Charles Dickens, *Oliver Twist*, ed. by Philip Horne (London: Penguin, 2002), 96, bk 1, ch. 13.
23. Ibid., 500, n. 2.
24. 'To William de Cerjat, 7 July 1858'. *The Letters of Charles Dickens*, ed. by Madeline House, Graham Storey et al., Pilgrim/British Academy Edition, 12 vols (Oxford: Clarendon Press, 1965–2002). Subsequent citations: *PLets* followed by volume (year of publication), page. Here VIII (1995), 597.
25. On Dickens as house manager, see Rosemarie Bodenheimer, *Knowing Dickens* (Ithaca: Cornell University Press, 2007), 126–69.
26. 'To Henry Austin, 7 September 1851'. *PLets*, VI (1988), 478–9.
27. Ibid.

28. William Gilpin, *Three Essays: On Picturesque Beauty; on Picturesque Travel; and on Sketching Landscape: To which is added a Poem, on Landscape Painting* (London: Blamire, 1792), 7–8. Emphasis in original text.

29. See Charles Dickens, *Our Mutual Friend*, ed. by Adrian Poole (London: Penguin, 1997), 60, bk 1, ch. 5. Subsequent references are inserted parenthetically in the text.

30. Charles Dickens, *Little Dorrit*, ed. by Stephen Wall and Helen Small (London: Penguin, 2003), 49, bk 1, ch. 3. Subsequent references are inserted parenthetically in the text.

31. Charles Dickens, *Martin Chuzzlewit*, ed. by Margaret Cardwell (Oxford: Oxford University Press, 1984), 11, ch. 2. Subsequent references are inserted parenthetically in the text.

32. See, for instance, Michael Brooks, *John Ruskin and Victorian Architecture* (London: Thames and Hudson, 1989): 'in the 1830s and 1840s [. . .] Ruskin's education cut him off from the Profession, as it was beginning to call itself' (1).

33. Sigfried Giedion, *Space, Time and Architecture: The Growth of a New Tradition*, 5th edn (Cambridge, MA: Harvard University Press, 1967), 182.

34. Tambling, 'Dickens and Architecture', 154; 155; 154.

35. A. W. N. Pugin, *Contrasts: or, a Parallel between the Noble Edifices of the Middle Ages, and Corresponding Buildings of the Present Day; shewing the Present Decay of Taste* (Edinburgh: Grant, 1898), 19.

36. Charles Dickens, *The Old Curiosity Shop*, ed. by Elizabeth Brennan (Oxford: Oxford University Press, 1998), 352, ch. 46. Subsequent references are inserted parenthetically in the text.

37. On Dickens's anti-Catholicism, see Mark Eslick, 'Architectural Anxieties: Dickens's *Pictures from Italy*', *English* 61.235 (2012), 354–64 and Dennis Walder, *Dickens and Religion* (London: George, Allen and Unwin, 1981). Conversely, one early twentieth-century critic, Marie-Elisabeth Belpaire, argued for Dickens's '"unconscious" Catholicism'. See Walter Verschueren, 'Dickens's Reception in Flanders', in *The Reception of Charles Dickens in Europe*, ed. by Michael Hollington, 2 vols (London: Bloomsbury, 2013), I, 298.

38. Hervé Picton, *A Short History of the Church of England* (Newcastle upon Tyne: Cambridge Scholars, 2015), 82.

39. Elizabeth Bridgham, *Spaces of the Sacred and Profane: Dickens, Trollope, and the Victorian Cathedral Town* (New York: Routledge, 2008), 8.

40. John Ruskin, *The Seven Lamps of Architecture* (Orpington: Allen, 1889), 202. Qtd in Tambling, 'Dickens and Architecture', 150.

41. 'To Mrs Watson, 1 November 1854'. *PLets*, VII (1993), 453–4.

42. [Charles Dickens], 'Home for Homeless Women', *Household Words* 161 (23 April 1853), VII, 161–75, 161.

43. Ibid., 172.

44. Ibid., 170.

45. See Stephen Kite, *Building Ruskin's Italy: Watching Architecture* (Farnham: Ashgate, 2012), 110. Kite puts Ruskin in a tradition of wandering that begins with the 'Classical Athenian student' and proceeds via the Baudelairean *flâneur* to the Situationist *dérive*.

46. 'To Douglas Jerrold, 16 November 1844'. *PLets*, IV (1977), 219–20.

47. 'To John Forster, 12 November 1844'. *PLets*, IV, 217.

48. Charles Dickens, *Pictures from Italy*, ed. by Kate Flint (London: Penguin, 1998), 78. Subsequent references are inserted parenthetically in the text.

49. Sigmund Freud, *The Interpretation of Dreams*, trans. by James Strachey (London: Penguin, 1976), 429.

50. Benjamin, *Arcades*, 13.

51. *SV* II, 74–5.

52. Ibid., 79.

53. Ibid., 96.

54. Kite, 10.
55. Victor Hugo, *Notre-Dame de Paris*, trans. by Alban Krailsheimer (Oxford: Oxford University Press, 1993), 197; 198.
56. Richard Maxwell, 'City Life and the Novel: Hugo, Ainsworth, Dickens', *Comparative Literature* 30 (1978), 157–71.
57. *SV* I, 58.
58 *SV* II, 153.
59. Ibid., 153.
60. Ibid., 181.
61. *SV* I, 346.
62. *SV* II, 138.
63. Charles Dickens, *The Mystery of Edwin Drood*, ed. by David Paroissien (London: Penguin, 2002), 7, ch. 1. Subsequent references are inserted parenthetically in the text.
64. John Ruskin, 'The Work of Iron', in *Unto this Last and Other Writings*, ed. by Clive Wilmer (London: Penguin, 1985), 115–39, 126.
65. *Penny Magazine*, 511.
66. Thomas Hardy, *Jude the Obscure*, ed. by Patricia Ingham (Oxford: Oxford University Press, 2002), 128.

Further Reading

Ellen Eve Frank, *Literary Architecture: Essays Toward a Tradition* (Berkeley: University of California Press, 1979)

Angeliki Sioli and Yoonchun Jung, eds, *Reading Architecture: Literary Imagination and Architectural Experience* (New York: Routledge, 2018)

David Spurr, *Architecture and Modern Literature* (Ann Arbor: University of Michigan Press, 2012)

Jeremy Tambling, ed., *Dickens and the City* (New York: Routledge, 2017)

Part V

Screen

21

SILENT DICKENS

Joss Marsh

DICKENS FILMS HAVE BEEN MADE FOR almost as long as films have been made: only two years separate the 'birth' of cinema – in fifty-second-long 'actualités' by the Lumière Brothers, in 1895 – from the Mutoscope Company's production of *The Death of Nancy Sykes* [*sic*]. Dickens films were made in all the phases of the silent era: from the 'primitive' years, 1895–1906, when pioneers and artisan film-makers explored the possibilities of the new invention; through the period of the early commercial cinema, 1906–14, when directors like D. W. Griffith articulated the 'grammar' of film and produced the first multi-reel fiction films; through the years 1914–18, when the feature film came to dominance, in tandem with vertically integrated companies (controlling production, exhibition, and distribution); to the heyday of the silent film as an achieved and distinctive art, and an international industry, 1918–28.[1]

It is therefore impossible to characterise, as a single group, *all* the hundred-odd silent Dickens films that are known to have been made before the transition to sound.[2] This is especially so since only just over one-third have survived the ravages of nitrate film decomposition, occasional fiery explosion, neglect (in the times before films were regarded as worthy of archival care) and hard-headed commercial thinking (which valued the silver in pre-1952 nitrate film stock more than the content of the films – hence the near-demise of the fine 1922 *Oliver Twist*). Of those silent Dickens films that survive, none are cinema masterworks, though the Hollywood pair by Frank Lloyd (which included that 1922 *Twist*) is notable.[3] The quartet by A. W. Sandberg of Denmark's Nordisk Films also come close, and the full hand of Dickensian productions by the British company Hepworth has great cultural interest.

This essay will therefore make no sweeping characterisations. Instead, it will suggest some modest propositions. Some of them apply to silent film generally. But it is only to silent films of Dickens's work that *all* apply, making them a special case for film history. The films also constitute a special inheritance of Dickens readings and remediations. To test its propositions, the essay concludes by examining three fascinating and very different silent versions of *David Copperfield* (1849–50).

Criticism That Sees Silent Film as Insufficient Cannot Comprehend Silent Dickens Films

We will not understand the silent Dickens films of 1897–1928 by applying to them outmoded assumptions about 'adaptation' and 'faithfulness'.[4] Some reviewers

324   JOSS MARSH

recoiled from any omission or change – especially in Britain, and directly in proportion to their claims to scholarly knowledge. *The Dickensian*'s reviewer, in 1914, for example, found *The Mystery of Edwin Drood* (Blaché, USA; dir. Tom Terriss):

> wrong all through [. . .]. Wrong period to start with. Coaching instead of early railway. Wrong dresses. Wrong scenes, or right scenes mixed up wrong. Wrong numbers, wrong vaults, wrong weirs, wrong hags, wrong Grewgious, [. . .] wrong people marry wrong people, wrong, wrong, wrong, every road.[5]

Others pragmatically accepted major omissions: thus the 1912 Hepworth *Oliver Twist* was 'one of the most accurately correct "animated novels" yet done', despite eliminating Charley Bates and Noah Claypole.[6]

Nor will we understand silent Dickens films by holding them to inappropriate or anachronistic standards. Short silent films, even of one reel (approximately 12–15 minutes), and what at first were called simply 'long films' are as different as lyric poems and novels. Sound film, meanwhile, communicates not only through images, but through spoken words, engaging the analytical and rational brain, while silent film appealed to audiences through the more purely emotional channels of image and music alone (supplemented by intertitles: narration or dialogue supplied by title cards, cut into the flow of images). As a result, melodrama was silent film's natural territory. It is often, also, melodrama stripped of its Victorian function of social criticism, either eliminated for reasons of length, or because time and change had rendered it less compelling: only one of the nine silent *Carol*s allows a glimpse of Ignorance and Want.

It *is* a lack specific to silent films of Dickens that we cannot hear the distinctive voices through which Dickens the novelist created character. Hence compensatory gestures in reviews and advertising are made to fill this gap: 'Toor rul lol loo, gammon and spinnage', wrote one, of the 1912 Hepworth *Oliver Twist*; 'as the "Artful Dodger", Mr. West is quite inimitable [. . .] – one can almost hear him'.[7] Hence also attempts by publicists and distributors to engage the absent voices: 'Mrs. Gummidge says: "I am a lone lorn creetur; [. . .] and I feel the cold more than other people." Bring out all the "lone lorn creetur's" [*sic*] to see David Copperfield, Mr. Exhibitor, and neither you nor the creetur's will feel the cold [. . .] – no need for radiators'.[8] Hence, too, unthinking blanket dismissals of 'silent Dickens' like Alistair Cooke's – 'as much of a contradiction as a talkative statue'.[9]

Silent Dickens films instead need to be understood in terms of how the filmmakers and audiences of their times received and enjoyed them. The use of intertitles is a case in point. Over-lengthy intertitles are often now seen as evidence of a failure to translate verbal into visual 'language'. But reviewers of the time criticised them, generally, only when they were used to paper over gaps in construction (some of them inherited from the novels), or when they were truly inordinately long (since the familiarity of the texts and the fertility of their language were a standing invitation to overindulge). It is entirely possible that what now seem bloated Dickensian intertitles sometimes gave silent-film audiences the positive pleasure of recognition.[10]

One thing is certain: silent Dickens was very popular. More than twice the number of Dickens films were made in the silent era than in the first half century of the sound film.[11] At first glance, this seems a paradox: surely the coming of sound precipitated a rush for Dickens, the man of many voices? But that transition, a great watershed in film history, in fact proved a watershed for the screen popularity of Dickens, as for many other Victorian authors. In the USA, where new immigrants were now a huge proportion of the population, the gap between the language(s) of Dickens and the language(s) of modern audiences instantly widened, while, in the UK, resistance stiffened to American adaptations – which was, very often, a resistance to American English. But while language played a role, it was more that – though the film industry remained so avid for filmable (and free) material that adaptations continued busily for some years – the end of the 'long' Victorian century precipitated by World War I, and the shift in social structures that ensued, suddenly made Dickensian material 'historical': less directly and emotionally understandable.

Silent-Film Dickens Was the Child of Magic-Lantern Dickens

Silent films based on Dickens's works were part of a media continuum. The first 'screen' versions of Dickens's novels and stories actually pre-date cinema, because they were made for the medium that pre-dated (and arguably gave birth to) cinema as a means of storytelling through projected images. An 'optical' version of *Gabriel Grub* (the inset Christmas tale from *Pickwick*), with moving slides and magnificent 'dissolving views' (which seemed to enable travel through time as well as space), was staged at the Royal Polytechnic Institution in 1875.[12] *A Christmas Carol* (1843) was inspired by the 'dissolving views' of Dickens's childhood.[13] Unsurprisingly, it proved attractive to lanternists. The story's lantern legacy is evident in the British pioneer R. W. Paul's technically sophisticated 1901 film *Scrooge, Or, Marley's Ghost* (the title of several lantern-slide sets), which opens with a lantern 'effect' (the dissolving of Scrooge's door knocker into Marley's face), and settles in for a regular lantern-show, as Scrooge draws a convenient screen-like curtain on to which his life can (in all senses) be 'projected'.[14]

The other Christmas tales, with their mix of realism and fantasy, and stories familiar from the public readings, inspired first lantern, then film, versions, like the Trial from *The Pickwick Papers* (1836–7), filmed by Edison in 1912. Stories that could be handled in one or two reels were at a premium in these years just before the heyday of the film serial, and the new medium was ravenous for out-of-copyright Victorian material. Vitagraph, America's other major Dickens investor in the silent years (Edison and Vitagraph both put out nine silent Dickens films), brought three of the racier *Pickwick* episodes to the screen in 1913.[15] The 1893 York & Son lantern-slide version of *Dotheboys Hall* appears to have inspired the short Gaumont UK film by the same title of 1903. Lantern versions of *Dombey and Son* (1846–8) followed Dickens's public reading in their restriction to little Paul's death; the novel was not filmed until the notable British director Maurice Elvey made a full-length, modern-dress version in 1917, which was roundly vilified by 'Dickens lovers'.[16]

The Works of Dickens Supported the Making of Different Types of Films in All Different Phases of the Silent Era

As that last example suggests, silent-film Dickens began to distinguish itself from lantern-slide Dickens as films pushed towards feature length. First, the shorter texts were adapted: the *Carol*, *A Tale of Two Cities* (1859), *Oliver Twist* (1837–9). Then, even *Bleak House* (1852–3) was tackled, in a 1920 version tightly focused on Lady Dedlock's story, by the offending Elvey. Atmospheric two-hour-plus versions of *Our Mutual Friend* (1864–5) and *Little Dorrit* (1855–7) appeared in 1921 and 1924. In terms of length, these films cannot be compared, say, to R. W. Paul's four-minute *Mr Pecksniff Fetches the Doctor* (1904). Dickens is unusual, in that his works supported the production both of short films in the pioneer period (rather like variety turns, at a time when films often still appeared as part of variety programmes) and feature-length films: Dickensian material could stretch or contract at will, because it was so varied and so familiar, and because it reached the cinema screen by way of so many other and varying media influences.

Silent-Film Dickens was Re-Viewed through and as Illustration

Silent film's second major inheritance was from the earlier visualisations of Dickens's texts provided by illustration: through familiar 'Dickensian' images, the films authenticated themselves, compensating for the absence of words. Indeed, in the 1910s, Dickensian cinema was regularly regarded as a superior form of illustration, as 'living pictures', and Dickens films were seen as constituting new 'editions' of the novels.[17] Thus, 'Dickens never had an abler illustrator than Mr. Bentley' (see below), 'who has the additional advantage of working in a living medium'.[18] The original illustrations by Phiz and Cruikshank provided inspiration and a guidebook to innumerable screen adaptations of both the silent and the sound era, as they had been to stage adaptations. To the UK trade magazine *The Bioscope*, for example, Willie West's Artful Dodger of 1912 seemed 'a Cruikshank brought to life' and the whole film 'a collected animation of Cruikshank's drawings'.[19]

However, what has eluded understanding of silent-film Dickens to date is that some of the illustrations that most inspired early filmmakers were *not* those of Phiz, Cruikshank and their contemporaries, but those familiar to the generation of Dickens readers who grew up after 1870. This generation often read Dickens in the posthumous 'Household Edition' of 1871–9, published in Britain by Chapman and Hall, with Frederick Barnard as lead illustrator.[20] His hundreds of illustrations – centred always on individual characters, or 'two-handed' scenes (like Dick Swiveller and the Marchioness) – circulated also in folio 'Souvenirs', and as prints, postcards and lantern slides, achieving significant cultural penetration. Harry Royston's characterisation of Sikes, in the British Hepworth *Oliver Twist* of 1912, was patterned, to the last detail of costume, gesture and posture (like the way Sikes's hands, in repose, form themselves unconsciously into fists) on Barnard's brutal image of a squat sitting Sikes, threatening his cringing dog.

Silent-Film Dickens Descends Directly from Stage Dickens, Which Valued Character over Plot

Not surprisingly, Barnard's illustrations also influenced the staging of Dickens (as did those of Cruikshank and Phiz), most productively in Sir John Martin-Harvey's *The Only Way* [*A Tale of Two Cities*] (1899). This illegitimate concoction by two underemployed Church of England clergymen was founded on Barnard's memorable image of Sydney Carton on the steps of the guillotine. Martin-Harvey toured and conquered the provinces with it until 1939: every actor-manager, after all, reshaped Dickens texts around himself and his company. His *Only Way*, and Barnard's illustration, cast a long creative shadow over *all* film adaptations, silent and sound. All are myopically Carton-centred: the influential 1911 Vitagraph production, starring Maurice Costello, produced by J. Stuart Blackton, one of the company's 1897 founders, and the director of its 1908 *Oliver Twist*;[21] the 1917 Fox film by Dickens enthusiast Frank Lloyd, the only version ever to have cast one star as both Carton and Darnay, in a production that marries split-second split-screen filming to historical spectacle;[22] and the almost-great 1925 British film of *The Only Way*, in which Martin-Harvey reprised his role for the camera, with extraordinary restraint for a stage actor. All of the silent films, like all of the major sound films (1935, starring Ronald Colman; 1958, starring Dirk Bogarde), climax with the same Barnard pose on the steps of the guillotine, an image which dominated publicity.

The 1905 Beerbohm Tree stage production of *Oliver Twist* inspired not one but *two* silent film versions in 1912: a first venture into Dickensland by the British Hepworth Company, and a much-publicised US version, released by General Films, starring the famous Nat C. Goodwin, fresh from playing Tree's role as Fagin, on the New York stage.[23] The *Carol* is the most filmed of all Dickens texts: it is an open invitation to special effects, and a mythic 'culture-text' that demands continual revisiting.[24] But *Twist*, the text most frequently adapted for the Victorian stage, follows hard on its heels: its sexual frissons, physical action and inside look at the criminal world appealed equally to melodramatic theatre and popular film. (The story was not a lantern favourite, probably because of its violence and lower-class subject matter.) Other UK and US versions were released in 1908, 1909, 1910, 1911 and 1916, the last with the fragile, white-faced Marie Doro starring as Oliver, following the stage convention of casting women as boys, which persisted on film through the 1910s. The book also inspired silent-film parodies and modern-dress versions.

Nineteenth- and early twentieth-century stage adaptations were not only star vehicles. Stock companies needed the kind of meaty character parts that Dickens provided, and later Victorian commentators talked of 'Dickensian' as well as 'Shakespearean' acting. The clergymen authors of *The Only Way* thus also concocted a second-string role for Martin-Harvey's wife as 'Mimi', Carton's servant, a waif he rescued from the streets. Similarly, when Edison made *Martin Chuzzlewit* (1843–4) in 1912, as Biograph did again in 1914, it was because it had parts for almost everyone on the payroll. Even as cinema's star system took hold, in the mid-teens, highly individuated Dickens roles remained prized character parts. Intertitles sometimes stopped the narrative to introduce them, one by one, with actors' names given below the characters' (a practice common in silent features of the late teens).

The Stage Tradition Inherited by Silent-Film Dickens Included Music Hall, in Which Character Ruled Supreme

'Dickens is just full of pitfalls for the film maker,' opined *The Moving Picture World*, in a review of a 1912 American *Nicholas Nickleby* (1838–9): 'The desire to bring in all that appeals to a lover of Dickens is fatal, for it begets confusion and bewilderment.'[25] After which warning, the reviewer strewed fulsome praise on every character presented on the screen by 'The Dickens wizards of New Rochelle' (Thanhouser, New York). Silent films of Dickens often sacrifice narrative coherence to give room to well-loved characters (though this film does not). That is, they were giving their audiences what they wanted – Dickens viewed through the lens of character. Reviewers endorsed them, even for audiences who did not read Dickens (and thus could get more 'confused'). Thus the 1921 *Old Curiosity Shop* (1840–1) deserved 'grateful thanks' for 're-creating the immortals who pass through the author's pages' for an entirely 'new public'.[26]

Character-centred Dickens was the Dickens of the music hall. When we noted that short Dickens films of the pioneer period resembled variety turns, we were noticing their inheritance from the strong music-hall tradition of Dickensian 'impersonation' (a term applied in the period to acting: 'becoming' the character).[27] The 1897 film *The Death of Nancy Sykes* was 'a record of the thrilling dramatic sketch that was given by Charles Ross and Mabel Fenton in vaudeville and burlesque houses'.[28] Longer films sometimes resembled a succession of character 'turns'.

The star Dickens turn of the music-hall stage was Bransby Williams, who graduated from 'taking off' leading actors and performers like Beerbohm Tree and Dan Leno to an all-Dickens act around 1897. (Climactically, he tackled almost the entire cast of *Barnaby Rudge*.) The vogue for his act took off at the same time as that for the quick-change artiste and the lightning-sketch artist: all were acts centred on character, and (crucially) on character recognition. Indeed, at the very beginning of his career, Williams worked as a lightning-sketch artist. This was also the time when caricaturists and cartoonists, such as 'Kyd' (Joseph Clayton Clarke), issued portraits of Dickens characters, shorn of scenery.[29]

Silent-Film Dickens was a National, Transatlantic and International Venture

Britain claimed Dickens as an exclusive inheritance: new silent Dickens films were repeatedly hailed in the press as 'Britain's greatest film' and 'A British masterpiece'.[30] Indeed, a new Dickens film has been the answer to every crisis in the beleaguered British film industry ever since. America hit back with a Dickens acceptable to Americans: thus, Biograph's 1914 *Martin Chuzzlewit* passes over the American episodes in a single intertitle. Often, however, American films were directed or produced by British-born filmmakers, as if Dickens were both a birth right and a trump calling card: most notably, W. Stuart Blackton (see above) and Frank Lloyd, who was born in Glasgow, began his acting career in London, and emigrated from there to Canada and the West Coast. But crucially, the competition for silent-screen Dickens also went beyond English-speaking nations.

The novels of Dickens were translated, within his lifetime, into all the major European languages.[31] It was therefore inevitable that they would become an international film inheritance, especially during an era when films did not speak. One of the six silent versions of *The Cricket on the Hearth* (1845), for example, was made in Russia (Сверчок на печи (Cricket on the Stove), 1915), and another was made in France

(*Le Grillon du foyer* (The House Cricket), 1922), where the only sound version was made in 1933; one of the lost silent versions of the *Carol* is the important Rome-based Cines Company's 1911 *Il sogno del vecchio usario* (The Old Usurer's Dream). One of the greatest revelations of the 2012 retrospective of silent Dickens at the Pordenone Silent Film Festival was a 1919 Hungarian *Oliver Twist*, which employs an 'unusually sophisticated' structure 'based on multiple flashbacks'.[32] (Only four of six reels survive.) A version of *Little Dorrit*, made in Berlin in 1917, was set in Holland, to avoid antagonising its audience in the middle of World War I.

The Legacy of Silent-Film Dickens Descends from Childhood Reading

The international silent-film Dickens inheritance was a specific reading inheritance. 'All of us read him in childhood,' wrote the great Soviet director Sergei Eisenstein (born 1898), in 1944, 'gulped him down greedily.'[33] The creative impact of Dickens on the first decades of cinema was as powerful as it is, because every child of the 1880s through the 1910s, who could read, and read fiction, read Dickens.[34] While some children read for the pleasure of language, nearly all read for character, situation, myth. For example, Little Eisenstein modelled himself on Dickens's 'favourite child':

Delicate,
thin,
short,
defenceless,
and very timid.[35]

The works of the 'David Copperfield from Riga' are full of suffering and martyred children, in a Dickensian vein, as in the Odessa Steps sequence of *The Battleship Potemkin* (1925).[36] From such child-fantasy also sprang the greatest essay on the origins and development of the feature film, Eisenstein's 'Dickens, Griffith, and the Film Today' (1944) – a work so convincing that it has encouraged us to look for Dickens's impact on film too exclusively in terms of editing and narration.

The Silent (and Later) Cinema Inheritance from Dickens Often Had Nothing to Do with Adapting Dickens

Childhood reading of Dickens did not necessarily result in the desire to make films of Dickens. Instead, Dickens infused the deep structure of the filmmaking mind. His influence is perhaps most powerfully felt where he is not directly adapted.

Griffith made one short Dickens film, *The Cricket on the Hearth* (1909). But he is Dickensian through and through. His development in the short films of 1908 to 1913 of parallel editing – cross-cutting from one line of narrative to another, and back again – may very well have been suggested by his reading of Dickens: so Griffith claimed in the press (somewhat defensively), and so Eisenstein demonstrates, in his bravura reading of proto-cinematic narration in *Oliver Twist* (cross-cutting, close-ups, montage, etc.), in that 1944 essay.[37] What has not received much attention is the indebtedness to Dickens of major Griffith films. *True Heart Susie* (1919), for example, reworks the David–Dora marriage from *David Copperfield* (with an emphasis on the bad cookery). *Orphans of the Storm* (1921) transposes the action of the 1874 play *The Two Orphans* (*Les Deux Orphelines*), to the period of the French Revolution, grafting on sequences from *A Tale of Two Cities*. Most importantly, the orchestration of sexualised violence (a central element in many Griffith films, and one that spurred his creativity) in the 1919 masterwork, *Broken Blossoms*, derives from the rape-like murder of Nancy: including the loving victim's last prayer for mercy, the phallic butt of the weapon used as bludgeon, and the craving for light when the deed is done.

Hitchcock never made a Dickens adaptation and steered clear of well-known writers as source material: all credit, in a Hitchcock film, was to go to Hitchcock. But his obsessive early reading of *Bleak House* surfaces in his career-long fascination with female guilt and the female double, as in *Vertigo* (1958). A striking visual memento of that novel appears at the beginning of *Blackmail* (1929), in which an artist attempts to seduce, then to rape, the heroine, Alice, who stabs and kills him with a household knife: as she leaves his studio, she slashes a life-size painting of a laughing clown, whose finger seems to point at her – a detail reminiscent of the 'Pointing Roman' that adorns the ceiling of the lawyer Tulkinghorn's room. Facing the technical challenge of this, his first sound film – which began life as a silent – Hitchcock also recapitulated the most hallucinatory sequence in 'The Flight of Sikes', from *Oliver Twist*: just as Sikes is startled into guilt by the repetition of the word 'stain!' in the patter of an itinerant peddler, in a Hatfield pub, so Alice is startled to frenzy, at the family breakfast table, when a nosy neighbour delivers an account of the news, in which the word 'knife!' slowly becomes the only recognisable word, in a marvellous early use of subjective sound.

Chaplin turned to Dickens at the major crux of his career, making his first feature-length film comedy: *The Kid* (1921) is a version of his favourite novel, *Oliver Twist*, by way of his idol Beerbohm Tree's landmark 1905 stage production, with himself as a benign version of Fagin, and the Kid, Charlie's miniature, played by Jackie Coogan, as an impish combination of Oliver and Dodger. Frank Lloyd's 1922 *Oliver Twist*, starring Coogan, is a back-formation that leads us to *The Kid*'s source, which had helped workhouse-child Charlie explain himself to himself.[38]

Silent-Film Dickens was Commemorative Dickens

Dickens's first centenary year, 1912, coincided almost exactly with the worldwide push from one- or two-reelers to feature-length films: hence, the duelling British and American *Twists* of that year. More importantly, it is a reason why Dickens figures prominently in the development of the feature film. No fewer than twenty Dickens films were released in 1912 and 1913, with half a dozen also released in each of the years 1910 and 1911, and eight in 1914. Some films, under pressure, fell short of perfection: 'We are not going to try to cram *Oliver Twist* into two reels or three reels,' wrote the enterprising young producer H. A. Spanuth, a German immigrant, of the 1912 US *Oliver Twist*; 'If it requires five reels, five reels it shall be. Or six, or seven [. . .]. We do not intend to allow this picture to look as if it had come out of a sausage machine, as some recent Dickens productions have given the idea.'[39] The prediction of *Motion Picture World* nearly came true, that 'within this centennial year we will add a complete cinematographic set of Dickens to the Library of Motion Pictures'.[40]

SILENT DICKENS

Silent-Film Dickens was a Solid Career Opportunity and Corporate Move

The centenary was a business opportunity. 'The time is ripe', opined the US *Moving Picture News*, in January 1912, for 'enterprising film producer[s]' to open new and 'undeveloped' Dickens 'gold mine[s] of humor and drama' like *Pickwick Papers* and *Sketches by Boz*: 'Now go to it! [. . .]. Only the surface of Dickens has been touched.'[41]

Once a studio made an investment in Dickens, it tended to make more Dickens: like Edison, Vitagraph or Pathé's subsidiary Britannia Films. That is, the studio staked out a Dickens 'brand'. In the 1910s, it was good financial strategy to utilise prime screen material that was free of copyright, could support feature-length production, and would attract a guaranteed audience, since 'There is no town in ENGLAND', as one UK distributor's publicity put it in 1914 (he might have added, 'indeed, half the world') 'that is not Filled with lovers of DICKENS.'[42] The Dickens 'brand' conferred literary prestige, respectability and educational value: thus, it was a handy riposte to the conservative social forces who still disapproved of the new medium: 'Book *Barnaby Rudge*', British exhibitors were urged in 1915, 'Because [. . .] You will secure as patrons "the people who don't go to cinemas".'[43] As early as 1911, American exhibitors were offered 'free sample copies of DAVID COPPERFIELD four-page illustrated [educational] Herald'.[44]

Similarly, once a filmmaker made an investment in Dickens, she or he tended to come back again. A prime example is British import Frank Lloyd; we will meet others shortly.

Silent-Film Dickens was a Screen Version of 'Dickensland'

Vitagraph's investment in Dickens was an investment in 'Dickensland'. The three *Pickwick* episodes the company brought to the screen as two-reel films in 1913 were 'Photographed on the Original Scenes in England' – The Bull coaching inn, the grounds of Rochester Castle, the picturesque streets and roads of Kent and London – by their British subsidiary, and starred their top comedian, John Bunny ('the most readily recognizable man on the screen'), who was shipped to England for the purpose.[45] This was 'a step in the right direction', declared *Moving Picture News*.[46] Settings, preferably 'exact location[s]' – the landscape of the 'Dickens world' – were almost as important to silent cinema of the 1910s and 1920s as the 'inimitable' (and much-imitated) characters.

Every Silent-Film Adaptation of Dickens, Like Every Other Adaptation, is an Act of Interpretation

These last propositions bring us to the three silent versions of *David Copperfield*: the 1911 Thanhouser Company's early feature, which was the first known film version of the novel and one of four Dickens films made by this small independent American producer between 1911 and 1913; Hepworth's 1913 British feature, one of five Dickens films made by the company; and the Nordisk Films production, the third of its four Dickens films, made in Denmark in 1922. The films have similarities. All three, for example, cast actors used in the companies' other Dickens films. Harry Royston of 'The Hepworth Stock Company', the brutal Sikes of its 1912 *Oliver Twist*, for example, 'makes the very utmost of his every minute on the screen as the bullying schoolmaster, Creakle'.[47] Top Hepworth players averaged three of five Hepworth Dickens films each. But the three *Copperfield*s are also very different films – each an act of interpretation, and each a vivid demonstration of the propositions put forward by this essay.

The Thanhouser *Copperfield* was released on the cusp of the shift to feature production, in three successive weeks in October 1911 – not as a single long film (running about 40 minutes), but as three separate stand-alone short films, *The Early Life of David Copperfield*, *Little Em'ly and David Copperfield* (from Em'ly's seduction to the shipwreck and the death of Ham) and *The Loves of David Copperfield*.[48] Besides (in the cheerfully frank film industry term) 'exploiting' the short films individually, exhibitors were encouraged later to run all three back-to-back at a later time, as part of a grand 'David Copperfield Night'.[49]

The film is distinctly American – astutely so, in its reading of un-American class relationships: Peggotty's expulsion for the 'crime' of loving her mistress and young David, for example. It has its flaws and oddities. Micawber leaps onto the screen, for example, as 'an eccentric friend' of the grown-up David (intertitle), inexplicably employed by Heep. In another move to save screen time, Agnes and Dora are turned into sisters, Wickfield's daughters: a condensation that turns the screw of Dickensian sentiment. Less successfully, thirteen-year-old Flora Foster is let loose with too much abandon and too much eye make-up as little David. However, nine-year-old Marie Eline, 'The Thanhouser Kid' (Thanhouser's very small Little Nell of 1911, who would play Wackford Squeers in 1912), is a sensitive and natural Little Em'ly. The scene in which she runs impulsively towards the all-endangering sea – which is consistently thematised by the film's beautiful cinematography – at least in part justifies the claim in a 1912 *Photoplay* article that she was 'one of the greatest child actresses on the screen or the legitimate stage'.[50]

The Thanhouser *Copperfield* is an emotionally direct and compelling film for its period, which excels most where it most departs from 'faithfulness'. Above all, it brings the story of Little Em'ly out of the shadows. Florence La Badie, Thanhouser's major female player of the years 1911–17, has the physical presence to make Em'ly's awakening to desire palpable and understandable; her yearning for children and for her own childhood are fleshed out in touching invented sequences of her life among Italian fisherfolk; and the film refuses point-blank to send her to Australia. Dickens it is not – but a compelling version of Little Em'ly's story it is: Thanhouser films regularly advocated women's rights.

Hepworth Company's 1913 *David Copperfield*, like its 1912 *Twist*, was the first four-reel, and only the second feature film, made in Britain. Like its *Twist*, it was directed not by Hepworth but by Thomas Bentley. He is one of film history's oddest and least-known figures, the record-holder for Dickens obsession, making (in a prolific career) no fewer than five silent Dickens films with Hepworth (*Twist*, *Copperfield*, *Old Curiosity Shop*, *The Chimes* and *Barnaby Rudge*), three more with other UK producers (including a second silent *Curiosity Shop* in 1921), and several Dickens sound films (including another version of *Shop*).[51] Hepworth Dickens films, under his guidance, became 'the standard pictorial Dickens edition'.[52]

Bentley introduced himself to Hepworth in 1912 as a 'great Dickens character "impersonator" and scholar'.[53] This was on the strength of nine years playing Dickens on the music-hall stage, and a performance of 'some of my character studies before the camera for Pathé Frères' (that is, Britannia Films), in the 1912 *Leaves from the Books of Charles Dickens*.[54] Hepworth thought Bentley 'a rum chap', but evidently considered Dickensian 'impersonation' an acceptable qualification for a film director – as, indeed it was, in an age that craved the 'incarnation' on film of Dickens characters. Above all, there was his overwhelming enthusiasm for the 'Master', to which Hepworth 'naturally warmed': both of them were 'saturated in Dickens'.[55] Following the success of their *Twist*, and pitching itself squarely at the national desire to reclaim Dickens for British filmmaking, their eight-reel *Copperfield* ran 1 hour and 47 minutes, 'the finest cinematograph film ever made by a British producer'.[56]

The film trumpeted its credentials in the opening credits: 'DAVID COPPERFIELD, Arranged by Thomas Bentley (THE DICKENSIAN CHARACTER ACTOR) / On the actual scenes immortalised by Charles Dickens'. Travel-guide intertitles are paired with topographical photo-opportunities: thus 'I pass through Canterbury on my way' (to Dover and Aunt Betsey's) is coupled with a shot of little David pausing by a medieval gateway. Like his *Twist*, Bentley's *Copperfield* was received by English reviewers in the same belief that 'the setting of the play [. . .] demands imperatively just that English touch about its scenery which is quite unprocurable outside our island'.[57]

Other effects of Bentley's Dickens passion were unfortunate, in cinema terms. He came back from a day's shooting in Dover and Broadstairs to announce to Hepworth, with 'joyful glee', that he 'had managed to secure *in the picture*' a distinct view of the plaque that confirmed one location was indeed 'the House immortalised by Dickens as the Home of Miss Betsey Trotwood'. 'I do not think he ever understood', Hepworth commented drily, 'why I received this news with so little enthusiasm.'[58] The imaginary-world-creating, filmic reality-effect was not to be secured by such Dickens-industry stamps of approval (though Hepworth Company – or, at least, its distributors – were glad to have their *Copperfield* endorsed by the Dickens Fellowship).[59]

But Bentley understood through and through that *silent-film Dickens was a screen version of 'Dickensland'*. (Indeed, *Leaves from the Books of Charles Dickens* had been shot on authentic sites from the novels, probably with his help.) Virtual tourism was indeed a key to the national Dickens project.

No one better understood this than Cecil Hepworth. Hepworth pictures were known for their pictorial beauty and showcasing of the English countryside, and Hepworth had made a success, in 1900, by shooting scenic *Phantom Rides* (filmic virtual journeys) from the front of a Great Western Railway train. Dickens had provided the soil in which his topographical fancies took root: his father was the eminent lantern-slide lecturer T. C. Hepworth, whose 'most successful lecture' was a topographical extravaganza called *The Footprints of Charles Dickens*, in which the future filmmaker 'gloried' as a child and 'heard over and over again'.[60]

Bentley's Dickens obsession offered an exact parallel to T. C. Hepworth's. His location choices made extended use of his 'unique collection' of photographs of '[the] places all over the kingdom mentioned in [Dickens's] books', '[m]any [. . .] taken by Mr. Bentley himself'. His 'signal facility, both technical and artistic', enthused *The Bioscope*'s interviewer, 'accounts for the phenomenal ease with which he transferred his activities to the making of films'.[61] The other credential Hepworth had recognised in Bentley was his grasp of the 'real' spaces of Dickens's fiction. Thus the psychology of Dickens fandom invaded and helped shape the feature film.

'There is no need to ransack the country for suitable localities,' declared a review of Bentley's *Copperfield*, because the 'Master' 'has arranged everything beforehand'.[62] And if one could not find the 'real' and 'original' location, one could build an 'exact replica': this has been the essence of film production design, ever since. For his fifth Hepworth Dickens film, 1915's *Barnaby Rudge* (now lost), his 'colossal' master-work, Britain's answer to *The Birth of a Nation*, Bentley raised 'an exact copy of an old London street' (150 yards long, complete with cobbles and link-holders) in a field near Hepworth's studio in Walton-on-Thames.[63] 'It [was] difficult', *The Star* newspaper enthused, 'to believe we are not witnessing the actual [. . .] scenes as described by Charles Dickens.'[64] Thus began that slippage by which films of Dickens's fiction came to masquerade (like Griffith's *The Birth of a Nation*) as historical reconstructions.

A few months later, Thomas Bentley became the first British director to be head-hunted by Hollywood, offered '[t]he boundless resources of the wonderful moving picture city which the Universal Company have created in California, U.S.A.', with a record salary, the man most 'worthy [. . .] to represent the art of the British film maker in America'.[65] Alas for poor Bentley – who thus realised, on the shoulders of Dickens, his 'greatest ambition' – World War I intervened. Hence his 1915 production for Universal's British subsidiary, Trans-Atlantic, of *Hard Times* – or, as one interviewer sympathised, 'Hard Lines'.[66]

For many years, Dickens was a dirty word in Denmark, where A. W. Sandberg almost bankrupted Nordisk Films, founded 1906, the world's oldest still-operational film company. Nordisk was one of the greatest producers of the silent era, at the head of a highly developed national cinema, which dominated not only Scandinavia but Russia and Germany, and competed strongly in other international markets. Born in 1887, Sandberg entered films in 1908 and became head of production at Nordisk in 1914 – able to indulge his passion for Dickens in four prestige productions: *Our Mutual Friend* (released 1921, possibly filmed in 1919/20: a *recherché* first choice of a text rarely filmed); *Great Expectations* (released 1922, probably filmed 1921: Miss Havisham's fiery death scene was 'partly achieved by painting flames on the individual prints of the film'); *David Copperfield* (1922); and *Little Dorrit* (1924).[67] His persistence smacks of 'greedy' childhood reading – and in particular editions, as we shall see. His *Copperfield* is also shaped by intimate familiarity with biographical sources, which we may speculate stemmed from 'editorial supervision' by B. W. Matz, editor of *The Dickensian*. The reading that follows is based on an American release copy of the film held at the Library of Congress: its special 'art [inter]titles' by 'Paleologue' feature emblematic motifs and character portraits, like a waif-like figure of the child David with St Paul's behind, almost as if to reinforce the idea of illustration as a positive value in cinema.

The film begins with a childhood idyll already under threat. Little David sits on the sun-dappled grass, reading with Peggotty. (He is played by Martin Herzberg, renamed 'Buddy' Martin for the American market, by analogy with 'Jackie' Coogan. Herzberg also played young Pip in *Great Expectations*.) Then we see his mother and Mr Murdstone, strolling arm-in-arm to the gate of the thatched, half-timbered cottage. As she introduces David, Murdstone (in medium close-up) takes Clara's timidly offered hand – at which the boy insinuates his own, figuratively competing for

SILENT DICKENS   335

her hand, in a brilliant piece of cinematic compression. The whipping scene which inexorably follows has painful intensity: Murdstone's tight-lipped threat; the misremembered lesson, expressed in uncomfortable close-ups of the panicking child, his anxious mother, Murdstone waiting his cue, and his sister implacably sewing; the violent and prolonged beating, while mother 'hears' the blows downstairs (shots that recall the harrowing scene in which Coogan's 'Kid' is abducted by the authorities, in Chaplin's 1920 film); the visceral bite, seen in explicit extreme close-up; and the final shot, from Murdstone's point of view, of the boy's slight body crumpled on the floor. The sequence has a deeply Dickensian understanding of the cycle of child abuse.

Next, the introduction of Micawber – Frederik Jensen (William Dorrit, in 1924), who betters even W. C. Fields's 1935 performance in the role, stealing every scene in which he appears. He eyes David with his monocle, while the degraded child wipes his hands on his apron, against a background of Dickensian clutter at Murdstone and Grinby's: a well-worn tall desk and stool; an interior window to the warehouse, for spying on the workers; a timekeeper's clock on the wall; judgement scales hanging next to the desk; sample jars on the shelves, feather pens and a litter of office papers. For Sandberg, as for Christine Edzard in her 1987 *Little Dorrit*, there is no such thing as 'background', only 'detail at a distance'.[68] His sense of the palpable life of the things that share the film with its characters makes him, of course, more 'Dickensian'.

The full title of Sandberg's film was *The Love Story of David Copperfield*, and that title tells us how Sandberg 'read' the book. Yarmouth, Little Em'ly and her competing story, which in 1911 and even 1913 pushed David to the edge of the frame, are eliminated in this version. Yet, Sandberg's Scandinavian *Copperfield* is still also a 'woman's film', not only in its emphasis on personal relationships, but in its capacity to open a first-person male narrative to female perspectives: those of David's mother (above), Dora and Agnes.

Taking his cue from Agnes's line in Chapter 62, 'I have loved you all my life', Sandberg makes a transposition purists may abhor, in giving us, as Em'ly's replacement, a child Agnes. This is made clear in a moving sequence, which animates Aunt Betsey's judgement on David, in Chapter 35, as 'blind, blind, blind!' in his infatuation with Dora: the young adult David and '"Sweet" Agnes' (intertitle) wander into the Wickfield stable, and a flashback shows the little Agnes of years ago, in the same dusty stable, delicately removing a speck from David's eye with her handkerchief, to be rewarded by a childish kiss. A wooden character, granted kinetic screen presence, can come to life in unexpected ways.

Ethereal and delicate, always crowned or associated with flowers, Dora meets David in her aunt's mangling room. (She is played by Sandberg's wife, Karina Bell; Bentley, perhaps more sage, married his Agnes, Edna Fineberg). She looks up at him in wonder: 'Now we are engaged – Isn't it wonderful!' An embrace fades into a summarising intertitle: 'Sweethearts living in a dream.' Now, in an iris shot (in which a black circle opens out to reveal the scene), we see David encircled by blossoms, reaching to pick a spray for Dora. She surprises and embraces him, and an intertitle takes us back ('dreamily') to her suspended sentence: 'and then we will marry as soon as we can.' The location for this imagined idyll, which must summarise so much text, was not dictated by opportunism or mere cliché: it is (again) rooted in Dickensian metaphor, in this case, Aunt Betsey's unwittingly foreboding nickname for Dora, 'Little Blossom'.[69] Sandberg remembers it in the time-lapse sequence that follow Dora's death: as chestnut trees bud, blossom and put out full leaf, so David returns to life. The time-travelling film medium enables what cost Dickens a rhetorical effort of 'pretty' writing to achieve.[70]

There was another spur to Sandberg's choice of blossom-time location. Some very particular illustrations are 'animated' by this film: Sandberg's idyll was surely based on a romantic image of Dora and David in a spring orchard by the watercolourist and *Punch* cartoonist Frank Reynolds, in the plush edition he illustrated in 1911. (It circulated widely in Europe: in some countries this was the cover image.) Reynolds's illustrations, like Barnard's, were either scenes of two characters in interaction, or portraits of individual characters – Micawber (fastidiously pulling on his gloves), Agnes (in sober dress and lace collar) and Clara (fiddling with her uselessly small parasol): images which were clearly models for Sandberg's actors. They were among the first in-book, full-colour illustrations to Dickens novels, and colour brought a newly nostalgic and sensuous dimension to Dickens illustration.

But let us return to Dora's line: 'Now we are engaged – Isn't it wonderful!' It concludes: 'Exactly as in your novel!' The readers of the 'Household Edition' of Dickens, 1871–9, ended their odyssey with the story of Dickens himself, since Forster's biography was the final volume in the set and printed, for the first time, the suppressed autobiographical fragment which Dickens transposed into the fiction of *David Copperfield*. Partly as a result, the makers of silent Dickens films, a generation that discovered Dickens in that and later editions, invested largely in Dickens the man and the sufferings of his childhood. In making 'An authentic version dedicated in reverence to the memory of the world-loved author' (opening title), Sandberg and his scenarist, Laurid Skands, recognised the identification of DC (David Copperfield) with CD (Charles Dickens), and grafted onto their *Copperfield* the subsequent story of Dickens's celebrity that Forster also tells. This becomes the motive for Dora's attraction to David: 'Is it really you who wrote that lovely story?' Then: 'I think your book is wonderful [. . .] I – I – am so excited about y—, about your charming story.' Inauthentic, yes, but a suggestive reading of the attractions of fame.

In the last shots of the film, David and Agnes wander again through the stable, and the yard, finding the relief of their declarations in mundane surroundings that contrast deliberately with the Dora blossom-time idyll. Then:

> Fifteen years later
> we find a famous
> author in the happiest
> period of his life. He
> calls himself . . .
> . . . David Copperfield . . .

In tranquil long shot, we now see David and his family (Agnes, a child, Peggotty and Aunt Betsey) in a large garden or park: he is reading aloud from a book. A kite floats up in the distance, where two more children play with Mr Dick. And we read:

> . . . But his real name is . . .
> CHARLES DICKENS . . .

Then, in close-up, we see the actor we can now only identify as 'CHARLES DICK-ENS'. For several seconds, the image is as still as if it were a photograph: immobilised, dead. Then, for a split second, he blinks – and the film medium (the *cinematograph*: 'animated' and 'living' pictures) fulfils its promise to bring the dead back to life, and Dickens to a new generation of 'Dickens lovers', as the credits roll:[71]

The Romance
of David Copperfield.
THE END.

Notes

1. The best evocation of the aesthetics and production practices of the silent era in Hollywood remains Kevin Brownlow's *The Parade's Gone By* (New York: Knopf, 1968); the best survey, which is also helpfully informed by literary-critical understanding, is William K. Everson's *American Silent Film* (New York: Oxford University Press, 1978). For British silent film, see Rachael Low's *The History of the British Film*, 4 vols (London: Allen & Unwin, 1948–50). A good short summary of the silent era, with an international perspective, is given in David A. Cook's *A History of Narrative Film*, 5th edn (New York: Norton, 2016).
2. For the most complete listing of silent Dickens films, extant or not, see Michael Pointer, *Charles Dickens on the Screen* (Lanham: Scarecrow Press, 1996), 117–33. The most important readily available resource is the British Film Institute DVD *Dickens before Sound*; other extant films are available to screen only at archives around the world.
3. See Graham Petrie, Catalogue for Pordenone Silent Film Festival (*Giornate del cinema muto*) 2012, 41. See also the catalogue's 'Charles Dickens, il padre della sceneggiatura / Father of the Screenplay' section, ed. by Petrie, Michael Eaton and David Mayer, 31–62 <http://www.cinetecadelfriuli.org/gcm/ed_precedenti/edizione2012/GCM12_Catalogo_Web_2p.pdf> [accessed 10 January 2018].
4. Adaptation studies have developed dramatically in the past decade. See, for example, Linda Hutcheon and Siobhan O'Flynn, *A Theory of Adaptation*, 2nd edn (London: Routledge, 2013) and the *Oxford Handbook of Adaptation Studies*, ed. by Thomas Leitch (Oxford: Oxford University Press, 2017).
5. Qtd in Pointer, 38.
6. *Bioscope*, 25 July 1912, 279.
7. Ibid., 281.
8. Advertisement for the 1911 Thanhouser *David Copperfield* (USA) in *Moving Picture World*, 7 October 1911, 2. Micawber featured in an advertisement of 30 September 1911, 930.
9. From his 1982 *Masterpieces*; qtd in Pointer, 23.
10. See Kamilla Elliott, 'Cinematic Dickens and Uncinematic Words', in *Dickens on Screen*, ed. by John Glavin (Cambridge: Cambridge University Press, 2003), 113–21.
11. Pointer lists ninety-nine silent films and forty-one sound films to 1993. See 117–44.
12. See 'Gabriel Grub', Disc 1, *Dickens before Sound*.
13. See Joss Marsh, 'Dickensian "Dissolving Views"', in *Cinematicity in Media History*, ed. by Karin Littau and Jeffrey Geiger (Edinburgh: Edinburgh University Press, 2013), 21–34.
14. Paul's film is also based on the 1901 play by J. C. Buckstone, which actor-manager Seymour Hicks made his career: a full scenario, published in *The Era*, is given in Pointer, 8–13.

15. One of these, 'The Pickwick Papers – The Honourable Event', dir. Larry Trimble, 1913, is found on Disc 1, *Dickens before Sound.*
16. This in turn inspired a USA-set, modern-dress, early sound film, *Rich Man's Folly* (1931).
17. Review of the Hepworth *Old Curiosity Shop*, *Bioscope*, 15 January 1914, 217.
18. Ibid.
19. *Bioscope*, 25 July 1912, 279.
20. Chris Louttit explores the widespread influence of this edition in '"A Favour on the Million": The Household Edition, the Cheap Reprint, and the Posthumous Illustration and Reception of Charles Dickens', *Book History* 17 (2014): 321–64.
21. Vitagraph's *Two Cities* had 'a far-reaching effect' on Rex Ingram (Pointer, 27), director of the landmark 1921 World War I drama *The Four Horsemen of the Apocalypse.*
22. Frank Lloyd (1886–1960) carved out a niche in costume- and swash-buckling melodramas 1922–31; later films included *Mutiny on the Bounty* (1935). On his *Tale of Two Cities*, see Judith Buchanan, with Alex Newhouse, 'Sanguine Mirages, Cinematic Dreams', in *Charles Dickens, A Tale of Two Cities and the French Revolution*, ed. by Colin Jones, Josephine McDonagh and Jon Mee (Basingstoke: Palgrave Macmillan, 2009), 126–45.
23. Goodwin reported to the Crystal Studio on 6 May 1912, 'together with his dog, who repeated its [stage] role' (Pointer, 29).
24. See Paul Davis, *The Lives and Times of Ebenezer Scrooge* (New Haven: Yale University Press, 1990), 4.
25. *Moving Picture World*, 9 March 1912, 858.
26. Review in *The Times*, qtd in Pointer, 45; no date given. The idea that Dickens characters had an independent existence is a constant theme in reviews. On character-centred Victorian 'continuations', see Carrie Sickmann, 'Pickwick's Other Papers: Continually Reading Dickens', *Victorian Literature and Culture* 44.1 (2016), 19–41.
27. See, for example, *The Times* (20 December 1873) review of the Keeleys' stage versions of *David Copperfield* and *Dombey and Son*, in which Samuel Emery played Dan'l Peggotty and Captain Cuttle: 'A more perfect specimen of impersonation can scarcely be conceived. [. . .] [H]e does not merely act, but he becomes the person he represents' (qtd in H. Philip Bolton, *Dickens Dramatized* (London: Mansell, 1987), 58).
28. Pointer, 7.
29. Kyd's Dickens portraits appeared first in *Fleet Street Magazine*, then in collections (1889, 1892). Five sets of 'Kyd' Dickens postcards appeared, as well as cigarette cards.
30. See, for example, *Bioscope*'s review of the 1913 Hepworth *David Copperfield*, 21 August 1913, 607–9.
31. The 'Timeline of the European Reception of Charles Dickens, 1833–2013', by Anthony Cummings and Michael Hollington (xxv–xliii), in *The Reception of Charles Dickens in Europe*, ed. by Michael Hollington, 2 vols (London: Bloomsbury, 2013), reveals that translations of novels by Dickens appeared before 1840 in German, Dutch, French, Danish, Czech, Italian and Polish. Hungarian, Norwegian, Rumanian, Russian and Spanish were added in the 1840s; Greek and Bulgarian in the 1850s; Icelandic, Portuguese, Croatian and Finnish in the 1860s. Between 1870 and 1900, translations also appeared in Estonian, Georgian, Catalan, Slovak, Latvian and Lithuanian.
32. Petrie, Catalogue, 39–40.
33. Sergei Eisenstein, 'Dickens, Griffith, and the Film Today', in *Film Form*, ed. and trans. by Jay Leyda (New York: Harcourt, 1949), 195–255, 201.
34. See Ellen Handler Spitz, *Inside Picture Books* (Bacova, VA: Windy Hill, 1999).
35. *Beyond the Stars: The Memoirs of Sergei Eisenstein*, ed. by Richard Taylor, trans. by William Powell (London: BFI, 1995), 18.
36. Ibid., 21. Taylor finds other Dickensian child-martyrs in Eisenstein's *Strike* (1925) and *Bezhin Meadow* (1937).

SILENT DICKENS

339

37. On this, see Grahame Smith, *Dickens and the Dream of Cinema* (Manchester: Manchester University Press, 2003), 119–28.
38. See Joss Marsh, 'The Tramp, the Kid, and the Jew', in *Charles Chaplin*, ed. by Michael Hammond, special issue of *Early Popular Visual Culture* 8.3 (2010), 315–35.
39. Qtd in Pointer, 29.
40. *Motion Picture World*, 9 March 1912, 858.
41. *Moving Picture News*, 20 January 1912, 18.
42. *Bioscope*, 19 November 1914, 800.
43. *Bioscope* supplement, 31 December 1914, viii.
44. Advertisement in *Moving Picture Word*, 11 November 1911, 2.
45. *Moving Picture News*, 26 July 1913, 21.
46. *Moving Picture News*, 15 February 1913, 10.
47. *Bioscope*, 21 August 1913, 609.
48. Vitagraph also released their 1911 *Tale of Two Cities* in three parts.
49. See the entry for *David Copperfield* in Q. David Bowers, *Thanhouser Films: An Encyclopedia and History*, 2012 <https://www.thanhouser.org/TCOCD/> [accessed 4 August 2020].
50. *Photoplay Magazine*, November 1912, qtd in Bowers.
51. Very few are extant. A digital transfer from two educational gauge 28mm copies of *Oliver Twist* was made by LOC in 2012; a section of *Copperfield*, which is held by the BFI, is available on the DVD *Dickens before Sound*.
52. *Bioscope*, 27 August 1914, 801, and 15 January 1914, 216.
53. Hepworth, *Came the Dawn* (London: Phoenix House, 1951), 111. In Bentley's version, it was Hepworth who approached him (*Pictures and the Picturegoer*, 13 January 1917, 336).
54. *Bioscope*, 18 March 1915, 995. Bentley (1880–1950) earlier worked as an engineer and a journalist. Between *Twist* and *Copperfield*, in 1912–13, he made a music-hall tour of Australia, where he founded the Sydney branch of the Dickens Fellowship.
55. Hepworth, 125; 111.
56. *Bioscope*, 21 August 1913, 607.
57. *Bioscope*, 25 July 1912, 279.
58. Hepworth, 125; my emphasis.
59. See the illustrated eight-page brochure circulated to exhibitors by the Award Film Service, distributers (Salisbury: Weymouth Press, n.d. [1913]).
60. Hepworth, 111. T. C. Hepworth's slides are not known to survive.
61. *Bioscope*, 18 March 1915, 994.
62. *Bioscope*, 21 August 1913, 607.
63. *Bioscope*, 6 August 1914, 529, and 24 September 1914, 1161.
64. Review of 15 January 1915, reprinted in the 'very remarkable souvenir' of *Barnaby Rudge* (*Bioscope*, 18 February 1915, 588) issued by the Kinematograph Trading Company.
65. *Bioscope*, 13 May 1915, 624.
66. *Pictures and the Picturegoer*, 13 January 1917, 336.
67. Pointer, 43. A digital copy of *Great Expectations* can be viewed at the Danish Film Institute.
68. Adam Mars-Jones, 'Victorian Principles', *Independent*, 10 December 1987, 16.
69. Sandberg was, of course, not the first to showcase the nickname: the popular song 'Good Night, Little Blossom' was first published in Boston, Massachusetts, in 1867. For production stills, see: <www.dfi.dk/en/viden-om-film/filmdatabasen/film/david-copperfield> [accessed 31 July 2018].
70. 'Pretty' writing is a phrase from Dickens's letter to Forster on 1 July 1861, explaining how he had 'put in as pretty a little piece of writing as I could' to cover his dramatic

340   JOSS MARSH

alteration of the original ending of *Great Expectations*, at the urging of Bulwer Lytton. *The Letters of Charles Dickens*, ed. by Madeline House, Graham Storey et al., Pilgrim/British Academy Edition, 12 vols (Oxford: Clarendon Press, 1965–2002), ix (1997), 433.

71. This final sequence improves on a lantern 'effect', whereby the magic of the 'dissolving view' replaced Dickens in 'The Empty Chair' of Luke Fildes's famous illustration.

Further Reading

F. [Frank] Dubrez-Fawcett, *Dickens the Dramatist: On Stage, Screen and Radio* (London: Allen, 1952)

Juliet John, *Dickens and Mass Culture* (Oxford: Oxford University Press, 2010)

Karen E. Laird, *The Art of Adapting Victorian Literature, 1848–1920: Dramatizing* Jane Eyre, David Copperfield, *and* The Woman in White (London: Routledge, 2015)

Graham Petrie, 'Silent Film Adaptations of Dickens', parts 1–3, *Dickensian* 97 (2001), 7–21, 101–15 and 197–213

22

TWENTY-FIRST CENTURY TELEVISION

Christine Geraghty

THE BBC/WGBH BOSTON ADAPTATION OF *Bleak House* in 2005 has been widely recognised as a 'significant turning-point in both the history of screen Dickens and in costume drama as a genre'.[1] It represented a shift in emphasis from adaptation to a new kind of 'edgy, modern drama' and was praised for its 'visual and aural density'.[2] Much of the publicity for *Bleak House* emphasised that the BBC was presenting a classic adaptation as a soap. In this essay, I argue that BBC Dickens adaptations since this seminal work have also been heavily connected with soap opera and will look at *Oliver Twist* (2007), *Little Dorrit* (2008) and *Great Expectations* (2011) with the aim of identifying more precisely what the key markers of that relationship might be. The essay concludes with a discussion of the issue of diversity and integrated casting – a distinctive feature of these post-2005 adaptations – and offers an analysis of *The Mystery of Edwin Drood* (2012), an adaptation which eschewed the soap opera influence but which subversively challenged the all-white landscape of the classic adaptation. My analysis does not provide a comparison between these adaptations and their source texts but instead looks at how they work, in their own right, as examples of popular television drama. Robert Giddings and Keith Selby, in their survey of the classic serial, demonstrated that 'For generations, classic serial production in Britain was dominated by Dickens'; this discussion seeks to demonstrate that adaptations of (at least some of) his work still have an appeal to audiences even in a rapidly changing television landscape.[3]

The period after 2005 was a turbulent one for classic adaptations on television. Much publicity was given to the BBC's announcement early in 2009 of a move away from the 'bonnet drama' represented by adaptations of nineteenth-century novels, a decision widely attributed to the declining UK audience figures for *Little Dorrit* in November/December 2008. But *Little Dorrit*'s achievement in winning seven Emmy awards reinforced it as a success for co-producer WGBH, and *Masterpiece*, the BBC's other partner, continued to value what veteran US co-producer, Rebecca Eaton, called 'interpretive adaptations' of the classics.[4] A change of heart at the BBC was prompted by the bicentenary of Dickens's birth in 2012. Though the organisers of 'Dickens 2012' were concerned that the BBC 'was going to avoid Dickens drama during the bicentennial year', its response in the end resulted in new adaptations of *Great Expectations* and *The Mystery of Edwin Drood*, as well as a host of Dickens-related programmes.[5]

In commenting on why she accepted the role of Miss Havisham in *Great Expectations*, Gillian Anderson indicated that 'The bottom line was knowing that the BBC would do a spectacular production.'[6] As Helen Wheatley demonstrates, 'spectacular television' was indeed a priority for television drama from the early 2000s in order to show off changes in television technology that were becoming standard; the BBC's use of *Bleak House* to promote HD as 'the next big adventure' is an indication that classic adaptations were to be an important part of this trend.[7] The richness and depth of the HD image combined with the dazzling speed of digital editing contributed to a visual style for *Bleak House* that emphasised spectacle. In a US context, West and Laird used it as an example of how 'visual style' in *Masterpiece* classic co-productions 'no longer plays second fiddle to dialogue nor does it function mainly to infuse adaptations with pictorial nostalgia'.[8] While this shift to visual richness is associated with prestige productions, it also had an impact on more routine drama including soaps; the BBC's *EastEnders* (1985–) was first broadcast in HD on Christmas Day in 2010. Multi-camera shooting was made more manageable by speedier digital editing and audiences began to associate soaps with a better picture and a wider repertoire of visual effects.

Melodrama and Soap Opera

Spectacular visuals fitted well with a further change in UK television drama which had been occurring over a longer period of time: an increasing recourse to melodrama as the basis for telling and resolving stories. British television drama has strong roots in realism, offering space to working-class characters and using identifiable social issues as the basis for social drama. That persists, and Lez Cooke's survey identified in a series like *Clocking Off* (2000–2003) a successful attempt to offer 'a new form of social realism for the twenty-first century'.[9] Nevertheless, Kristyn Gorton has pointed to 'an affective turn' in which 'the place of emotion in the public sphere', traditionally the site of realism, is now the subject of 'a debate on how feelings work towards the social good'.[10] As I have argued elsewhere, this emphasis on emotion has engendered a shift to melodramatic tropes; in the early 2000s, the BBC's lead soap, *EastEnders*, was adopting 'melodramatic tropes more consistently and boldly', in ways that seemed 'to express a darker vision of the world' in which the resources of family and community felt less secure.[11] Michael Stewart argues that this is not just a question of subject matter but of the overall framework in which stories are mapped out: 'melodrama is not "about" the family and the individual. These, rather, are means towards its end: psychic realism and moral legibility.'[12] Television drama of the early twenty-first century takes the stuff of realism – contemporary social issues and ordinary lives – but uses them to produce stories of 'moral conflict en route to moral legibility'.[13] It thus offers stories which are more clearly polarised morally in terms of good and evil and in which the emphasis is placed on what it *feels* like to be a character caught up in stories of betrayal, loss and abuse. This (partial) shift in mode has consequences for the aesthetic means used to tell these stories. Kay Mellor, a successful writer for British television who emphasises the importance of emotion in her writing, has identified formal devices, all features of melodramatic aesthetics, which she uses to generate an emotional connection with the viewer: 'Full face [close-up], writing, music [. . .]. Silence [. . .] and casting [. . .]. You need actors who can understand the kind of emotional depth you're trying to bring across.'[14] More broadly, a greater emphasis is placed on symbols, settings, camera work and lighting which help to express inner emotion.

The embedding of the melodramatic mode in Dickens's novels does not necessarily get carried over into their adaptations. Richards felt that there had been a tendency from 1958 onwards 'to de-melodramatize the work'.[15] The 1990s had seen an emphasis on a 'darker, more realist Dickens' with versions of *Our Mutual Friend* (1998) and *Great Expectations* (1999) which offered 'a bleaker, more naturalistic representation of the [Victorian] period'.[16] In the 2000s, though, classic adaptations participated in the more general shift towards melodrama, a move reinforced when one of the BBC's co-production partners, *Masterpiece*, relaunched in 2008 and began 'purposefully reviv[ing] the nineteenth-century tropes of melodrama in their twenty-first century adaptations'.[17] Such tropes could include plots which involve the acting out of and commentary on moral tests; characterisation which supports the construction of a polarised world view by identifying characters as good and evil; stories which tend to portray women and children as victims; and settings which take on a symbolic function in expressing the isolation of characters rather than their engagement with the community. These signs of melodrama will be familiar to those who have read and studied Dickens and are fully explored by Juliet John in her invaluable accounts of Dickens and popular culture.[18] But I dwell on them here because of their importance in any account of how recent Dickens adaptations relate to soap opera. Much of the publicity about *Bleak House* (2005) related to the decision to screen it immediately after *EastEnders* and to schedule it like a soap opera in short episodes ending with a cliffhanger – an approach which was compared to Dickens's practice of serialisation, and which was repeated with *Oliver Twist* in 2007 and *Little Dorrit* a year later.[19] But any assessment of the impact of soap opera on contemporary classic adaptations needs to engage with a fuller account of soap opera's melodramatic practices beyond those of serialisation.

The analysis that follows suggests that these twenty-first century Dickens adaptations not only work within a melodramatic mode but require an audience familiar with how melodrama works in television drama. In discussing adaptations, a distinction is often made between the knowing audience which has read the source text or knows previous versions of the adaptation, and the unknowing audience which is experiencing the story for the first time. Ann Heilmann and Mark Llewellyn offer a stark example of this kind of thinking in discussing two kinds of readers (and viewers) of neo-Victorian fiction: there are 'readers who know relatively little of the Victorian texts/authors being played with, and another type of reader who is aware of the "original" text (often an academic) and who can therefore engage on a more sophisticated level with the nature of the pleasures within the adaptation itself'.[20] This model emphasises literary knowledge and practices of reading but ignores the competencies of the television viewer and the specific understandings brought to an adaptation from the viewer's experience of how soap opera deploys the melodramatic mode to engage the viewer in a complex, unfolding narrative.

First, in terms of moral legibility, the work of the narrative is to distinguish between good and evil, to align characters in terms of their moral qualities, and to enable good to confront – and possibly overcome – evil. Soaps set out clear moral dilemmas, but solutions are not always clear. Although characters are generally clearly positioned in terms of good and evil traits, they are continuously rejudged, over the long narrative time of soap stories, in terms of how they handle moral dilemmas and deal with secrets and deceptions. Second, soap's emphasis on emotional legibility is not just a matter of valuing transparency but of recognising that feeling is integral to the moral dilemmas of the characters. It is crucial therefore that characters' emotions are presented directly to the audience through clear dialogue and visual signs. Finally, British soaps have a long history of developing stories which deal with contemporary social issues in terms of ethnicity, sexuality and gender and ask popular audiences for an empathetic approach to the decisions and judgements such stories involve. The distinctiveness of melodramatic expression in relation to soaps' handling of such issues lies in their refusal to make moral judgements a matter of critical distance and their lack of embarrassment at making feeling central to their practice.

The changes in television technology and the increasing recourse to melodrama can work together to spectacular effect. Digital camera work and editing enables a change in narrative pace which Andrew Davies refers to when he comments on audiences 'being able to guess things and wanting to cut out a scene sooner because they've already got a sense of what's coming next'.[21] In terms of visual organisation, the picture is not only clearer and wider but more overtly expressive with camera work, colour and lighting used to signify the moral dilemmas the characters are facing. Greater emphasis on the visual does not mean that words are less important. Dialogue is frequently highly charged and the rhythm of a scene, sequence or episode marked by emotional explosions which heighten the tension or unexpectedly redirect the story.

This essay discusses the impact of these factors on contemporary adaptations with examples from three classic serials. All were co-productions, *Oliver Twist* and *Little Dorrit* with WGBH Boston and *Great Expectations* with *Masterpiece*, and all were screened on BBC One. The choice of *Oliver Twist* and *Great Expectations* was unsurprising given that they have been regularly adapted and are among Dickens's best known stories; *Little Dorrit* is much less well known but it is a favourite of writer Andrew Davies and its story of financial crises and speculation had a contemporary resonance, given the global financial crisis in 2008.[22] *Oliver Twist* was shown just before Christmas 2007 in five episodes spread over the week. *Little Dorrit*, in November/December 2008, consisted of a sixty-minute opening episode, followed by twelve half-hour episodes and a sixty-minute finale. *Great Expectations* was screened in three fifty-minute episodes immediately after Christmas 2011. *Oliver Twist* and *Great Expectations* were written by Sarah Phelps with Andrew Davies responsible for *Little Dorrit*. The appearance of Phelps as an adaptor as well as the dominant Davies is significant given that Phelps began her career by writing soap opera for the BBC World Service before, in 2002, starting a successful period as a core writer on *EastEnders*. That Phelps should alternate with Davies, the most prolific adaptor on British television, underlines the impact of soaps on the Dickens adaptations I am discussing.[23] *Oliver Twist* was directed by Coky Giedroyc and produced by Sarah Brown; for *Little Dorrit*, Lisa Osborne was the producer with episodes directed by Adam Smith (6), Dearbhla Walsh (5) and Diarmuid Lawrence (3); while *Great Expectations* was directed by Brian Kirk and produced by George Ormond.

Moral Legibility

Phelps's *Oliver Twist* provides a clear account of a 'moral conflict en route to moral legibility'.[24] While Phelps was keen to toughen up Oliver (William Miller) and make him less of 'a portrait of what a Victorian audience would feel a deserving pauper

TWENTY-FIRST CENTURY TELEVISION 345

child was', he nevertheless remains the innocent test case for how other characters relate to good and evil. [25] Although Nancy is responsible for Oliver's recapture from the Brownlows at the end of episode one, by the middle of episode two she is taking up the role of his protector in Fagin's den. Despite their different class positions, she makes an alliance with Rose (Morven Christie) to rescue Oliver and the intuitive sympathy between them which arises from their concern for Oliver is made clear when Nancy marvels that Rose respectfully calls her 'Miss' like Oliver does. The two take on different roles. Nancy attempts to protect and care for Oliver when he is at risk in Fagin's den, reassuring him that his mother can still see him – 'she's a star in the sky, darling' – and advising him on how to treat Sikes (Tom Hardy). She nurses the boy when he falls sick, protecting him by literally crouching over him on the bed. Rose's determination to find Oliver provides clarity in terms of the plot. She takes to the streets to prove her belief that he is not a thief and realises well before her guardian, Mr Brownlow (Edward Fox), that not only is her sister Agnes dead but that Oliver is her lost child. Rose also broadens the moral theme of the plot. In a passionate speech, in episode three, she tells Brownlow that Oliver had been 'thrashed and beaten' and reminds him, and the audience, that 'this and worse happens to children every day [. . .] and we just sit here'. In her white dress with her face pale against a dark background she embodies the voice of innocence speaking truth to patriarchal power.

The men consistently fail to act morally towards Oliver and the two women who seek to save him. Fagin (Timothy Spall) uses Nancy to 'keep a leash on Bill' and seeks to sell Oliver for his own advantage. Mr Brownlow places his faith in his grandson, Edward/Monks (Julian Rhind-Tutt), and tetchily doubts the goodness of Oliver and Nancy. Sikes takes Oliver on a burglary and uses him as a shield so that he is wounded in the shooting that transpires. Nancy and Rose are positioned in a sympathetic, parallel relationship so far as the most evil male characters are concerned. Nancy cajoles Bill, drinks with him and dodges his threats until the nature of the abusive relationship is fully revealed in the violence of the murder. In a parallel storyline, Monks flirts with, spies on and seeks to control Rose while she resists his increasingly violent pressure to become his wife. Towards the end of episode three, the two threats are brought together. Monks bullies Rose, who is trying to stop him touching her, by warning her, as he tucks in a curl of hair on her neck, that 'Someone in your position must learn to endure anything'; a few minutes later Sikes, seizing Nancy round the neck, tells her directly, 'If you do anything to betray me, anything, then I swear I'll kill you.'

The final episode lays out the moral order that has been reconfigured, though it is not an entirely hopeful one. Motherhood is reinstated as Oliver is restored to Rose's care. Her place as his substitute mother is signified by the locket she wears; the two pieces she and Agnes had split between them are back in place, and she and Oliver light candles to indicate that his birth mother is also restored to her place in their memories. Fagin is hanged, though his evil is somewhat ameliorated by making clear the anti-Semitic prejudice which has pursued him. Dodger (Adam Arnold), who has lost his position within Fagin's family of boys, strides out of the adaptation with Sikes's dog, shouting aggressively to spectators, as Sikes had done, 'What you looking at? I'll have your eyes.' The moral logic of retribution is clearest in the handling of Sikes's death. The murderer of Nancy is not pursued by the mob in this version nor does he die in public. Instead, he dies alone in the sewers; it is made clear that it

346 CHRISTINE GERAGHTY

is the very visible ghost of Nancy – 'I won't ever leave you, Bill' – which has driven him to this death.

Great Expectations also sets up clear moral poles but there is greater emphasis on how Pip (Douglas Booth) as the central figure has to choose between them. Significantly, this adaptation retains the character of Orlick (Jack Roth). Brian McFarlane argues that Orlick can be omitted 'without obscuring [the narrative of] Pip's main line of development'.[26] However, retaining him provides a melodramatically evil figure in Pip's home environment to be set against the unfailing virtues of Joe (Shaun Dooley). Similarly, in London, the evil Bentley Drummle (Tom Burke) provides the opposite moral pole to the innocently good-hearted Herbert Pocket (Harry Lloyd). As in Phelps's *Oliver Twist*, violence against women is a clear sign of evil, and the invention of the scene in which Drummle takes Pip to a brothel may have arisen from the need to strongly underline his treatment of women as indicative of the evil pole which Drummle represents.

Such clarity is needed, it could be argued, since for a modern audience Pip's assumption that he deserves to have great expectations might not seem so unreasonable. This production emphasises how characters are shaped by events in their lives and, with characters who oscillate between good and evil, the soap practice of having judgements frequently subject to revision is at play here. Miss Havisham's plot to use Pip for her revenge is malevolent, but there is sympathy for her distress at having her letters returned by Estella (Vanessa Kirby) after her marriage. Similarly, Estella's cruelty to Pip is evident, but so too is her despair at the upbringing that has shaped her: 'I am what you designed,' she tells Miss Havisham, 'You cannot now complain, if you feel the blade.' The addition of a short scene in which Estella makes clear her reluctance to marry seems designed to make the audience sympathise with her at the moment when she is moving furthest from Pip. In the carriage bearing her to her wedding to Drummle she removes her veil, protesting, 'No, I can't. I don't want to,' but her companion restores the veil and significantly tells her to 'compose yourself', to restore herself to the creation Miss Havisham has made.

Emotional Legibility

The frequency with which Estella articulates her position in Phelps's adaptation seems to run counter to one of Davies's rules of adaptation: 'Never use a line of dialogue if you can achieve the effect with a look.'[27] But characters in soap operas consistently use dialogue not only to share knowledge and make judgements about moral behaviour, but also to reveal their own emotional state. This emphasis on dialogue as a means of accessing the emotional state of characters is an important characteristic of these adaptations. Dialogue is used flexibly, however, and its use is related to character and narrative situation.

Direct communication of emotion is associated with the melodramatic trope in which the innocent woman finally speaks clearly about how she feels. Rose in *Oliver Twist* offers examples of this which are the more powerful for the feminist resonances which Phelps consistently brings to these moments of defiance. In episode three, when quizzed at dinner about what she has been doing, Rose resists her guardian's attempt to prevent her searching for Oliver. When Mr Brownlow protests that her vehemence will make her ill, she leaves the table, explaining her true emotional state: 'I am not ill, I am angry.' In the final episode, as Monks tries to destroy the evidence of Oliver's birth, Rose rescues the documents from the fire and attacks Monks as a liar. This is dialogue which offers clarity between characters as well as to the audience.

But there are examples when the communication between the characters is not so clear but the meaning is evident to the audience. An example of this can be found early in *Great Expectations* when the young Pip (Oscar Kennedy) is taken to be inspected by Miss Havisham. He is standing in the hall, as she descends the stairs, her decaying finery trailing, her paleness exaggerated against the dark wood and diffused by the dusty light from the half-covered window. Pip addresses her as 'Madam', a title she rejects by telling him, 'I am not married.' Pip obeys but responds with a seeming non sequitur – 'Are your feet not cold, Miss?' – to which she replies, 'All of me is cold.' Pip is in awe and respectful, but confused about the status of this woman. Because of his small stature, her feet are coming closer to him as she moves down the stairs and his enquiry focuses in a childish way on something that seems striking but irrelevant. But like his assessment that the escaped convict was hungry and needed food so his childish concern for Miss Havisham's cold feet is an expression of Pip's capacity for human sympathy, a concern which will come close to being lost in London. Miss Havisham, however, turns Pip's practical observation into an existential one about the nature of her existence. The two speak directly, though they do not understand each other.

Phelps's use of language in such exchanges is strikingly uncomplicated and scarcely draws on the play of language which is a feature of Dickens's writing. Nor, following a trend since the 1980s, are these post-2005 adaptations noted for their use of the comic elements with which Dickens larded his melodrama. *Oliver Twist*, however, provides a comic duo in the form of Mrs Corney (Sarah Lancashire) and Mr Bumble (Gregor Fisher). While their cruelty towards Oliver and his mother is made clear, the pair provides a comic subplot in the manner of soaps in which Mrs Corney inveigles Mr Bumble into a state of sexual excitement which leads to a proposal and marriage. The actors here, particularly Sarah Lancashire as Mrs Corney, do not overplay Dickens's comic characters by exaggerating their vocal tics. Instead, the dialogue is spoken quickly, flowing, like the gin they consume, almost without emphasis but full of grandiose phrasing and comic innuendo. Part of Mrs Corney's villainy is her double-dealing in relation to her emotions; she conceals her desires in order to fulfil them. For example, when Mrs Corney invites the gentleman into her room she goes to some lengths to draw attention to the favours she is offering while all the while protesting at her own actions: 'I'm most unsuitably attired to confide in a gentleman [. . .]. And if the Board should hear that I received a gentleman in the intimacy of my rooms.' She uses language to give Mr Bumble a sense of the husband's power, sexual and otherwise, which he is then actually denied. In the last appearance of the pair in episode five, Mrs Bumble advises her husband to 'Stoke up the fire' while kicking his arse when he does so; the scene offers a concise insight into the nature of this marriage and a humorous puncturing of patriarchal aspirations to power.

I am arguing that the influence of soap opera on these adaptations can be seen in their use of language to communicate emotion and to make feelings, as well as morality, legible. In *Little Dorrit* (2008), this is something the heroine has to learn. In episode one, she is shy when Arthur Clennam (Matthew Macfadyen) comes to the Marshalsea Prison, and painfully embarrassed when her father (Tom Courtenay) explains to him the pecuniary recognition visitors make to the Father of the Marshalsea. When Arthur seeks permission to visit again, Amy (Claire Foy) replies in frustration that she cannot stop him speaking to her. By the end, Amy has not only learned to speak directly to Arthur about her love but insists on speaking first. With passion she declares, 'I won't let you send me away, ever again.' As the serial moves to its resolution, Amy is shown to be as capable as Rose in terms of speaking directly about the true situation.

But Kay Mellor also cited silence as a tool for engaging audiences emotionally and Davies's script uses such silence. Amy's reticence is not always caused by embarrassment or shyness. She has a gift for communicating to the audience, if not always to other characters, by not speaking, and Foy's performance exploits this by using her eyes and face to give access to her thoughts and feelings. Richard Butt, in considering the melodramatic qualities of this adaptation, cites how Amy proves her virtue by refusing to 'fight back against [. . .] the manifest injustice of her treatment by her father'.[28] This is demonstrated in the scene in episode four when she returns to her father after refusing a proposal of marriage and tends to him silently as he complains about how her rejection will affect his status in the prison. She does not speak back to defend her own position, but the camera dwells on her face, giving the audience access to a series of looks as she tries to comfort him while weeping over his self-centred boasting. Only a murmur comes from her: 'I know, Father, I know.'

Contemporary Issues

I have indicated that, in these adaptations, the stories of Rose, Nancy and Estella are strongly driven by the abusive relationships they are involved in. Viewers who are competent soap readers will recognise these situations even when they are only sketched in, and generally, in soaps, broader social issues can be recognised in individual storylines and inferred in backstories without being fully elaborated. I want to explore this more fully by looking at how issues of race and ethnicity arise from the use of Black actors, Sophie Okonedo and Freema Agyeman, in the roles of Nancy and Tattycoram. Both seem to be examples of integrated casting on merit, a practice which 'implicitly asks the audience not to attribute any specific meaning to the perceived racial identity of individual performers'.[29] As Agyeman put it, 'I was [. . .] delighted because Tattycoram is not written as a black part', but the complication of the issue is revealed when she goes on to suggest that her casting would render it so: 'She's an orphan, and in the 1820s there was a general prejudice against anyone who wasn't from an upper-class background. So the idea transposed well to a black character.'[30]

Rachel Carroll's excellent article on integrated casting in these productions analyses the issues at stake here. On one hand, Okonedo and Agyeman 'are cast in roles which are not racially marked within the dramatic action of the adapted screenplay'; neither they nor other characters ascribe a racial identity to their characters and the production arguably 'invites the viewing audience to follow their lead' (26). But Carroll argues that the casting of Okonedo and Agyeman as 'figures on the margins of legitimate society [. . .] dependent on paternalist charity or the criminal economy' undermines the intentions of integrated casting and 'could inadvertently confirm an impression that the origins of black British subjects must in some way be questionable, if not implicated in transgression or shame' (26). Carroll thus seems to argue that, despite the attempt at integrated casting, the invitation to understand these characters without taking race or ethnicity into account is at odds with the way race seems to offer an explanation for the characters' marginal positions and sometimes problematic behaviour. For Tattycoram, race might seem to explain her origins as an abandoned child and her seemingly irrational rage at her treatment by the philanthropic family which takes her in. For Nancy, a much more developed character, race might offer an explanation for her illegitimate origins, her recourse to prostitution, and her relationship with Sikes.

Carroll concludes that 'It is as if this casting strategy produces the very question which it attempts to pre-empt: the question of the legitimacy of a black presence in nineteenth-century England and, moreover, of a black presence in the period drama genre' (26). She is, however, approaching this question in the context of a genre, the classic adaptation, which rarely uses 'non-white actors' and creates a past which is 'exclusively populated by white men and women' (26, 27). But looking at these adaptations through the framework of soap opera can lead to a different conclusion. British soap audiences of the 2000s are used to seeing Black, Asian and ethnic minority actors on screen in long-running serials and series such as *EastEnders*, *Casualty* (1986–) and *Holby City* (1999–2022). Some of their stories centre on issues arising from their ethnicity while in others these issues are not specifically raised as the Black and ethnic minority characters take on the usual soap stories centring on work and family. While race and ethnicity are part of any character's ongoing identity, even when not offered as narratively significant, the soap opera genre offers a different approach to the question of how the roles of Nancy and Tattycoram, as played by Black actors, might be understood by audiences.

In *Oliver Twist*, Nancy's very marginality supports the central position she occupies in this adaptation because it draws attention to how the strengths which soaps value are being tested in her difficult situation. Her moral clarity in relation to Oliver is backed up by her bravery, and even beyond death she fulfils the role of the innocent heroine in speaking truth to the man who claims power over her. At the same time, her response to Oliver's needs reveals how emotionally open she is and the complexity of her relationship with Sikes shows how she maintains her own sense of purpose even in an abusive relationship. While, as Carroll suggests, race offers audiences a backstory for Nancy, the betrayal and violence she suffers also calls on the tropes of domestic abuse stories in soaps, inviting empathy rather than judgements about transgression. The values of the classic serial are overturned in favour of those operating in soap stories about social issues. The Brownlow household comes close to hypocrisy; luxury and formality hide threats, lies and snobbery. Rose's white privileges are underlined and, while she is clearly a sympathetic character, it is Nancy's marginality which allows Okonedo to fully occupy the mode of the melodramatic heroine.

The issue of race and casting affects Agyeman in *Little Dorrit* rather differently. Tattycoram is a smaller and more limited role, and her characterisation is dominated by her anger at the way she is treated by the family who have 'adopted' her. The audience is invited to observe how the kindly but patronising Mr and Mrs Meagles continually privilege their own daughter, Pet, and get Tattycoram to run errands for her. Tattycoram's resentment at continually being asked to carry Pet's shawl could be understood as ingratitude, but her angry response can be made more nuanced when framed in terms of the way that issues of racial identity are played out in soaps. The

350   CHRISTINE GERAGHTY

actions of the white characters are put under scrutiny, and Tattycoram's anger can
be understood as morally legitimate and emotionally legible. This is, however, complicated by the way the lesbian relationship between Tattycoram and her mysterious rescuer, Miss Wade (Maxine Peake), is handled. This storyline gets rather stuck,
bound up in the complicated mystery about Miss Wade's actions and limited by Tattycoram's monotonous characterisation as resentful and confused. The soap opera
framework does not offer an entry into this relationship which, in the end, remains
an enigma, a problem when it is emotional legibility which is being valued. Tattycoram's actions which help to resolve the plot are handled rather perfunctorily as she
returns to the fold, appearing briefly in the happy crowd celebrating the wedding.[31]

Diversity and *The Mystery of Edwin Drood* (2012)

The three dramas I have discussed so far were all shown on BBC One, the BBC's
most popular channel.[32] *The Mystery of Edwin Drood*, another co-production with
Masterpiece, was made for BBC Two and screened in the UK in two fifty-minute episodes on consecutive evenings in January 2012. It was written by Gwyneth Hughes
who specialises in crime drama/thrillers, directed by Diarmuid Lawrence and produced by Lisa Osborne, both of whom had also worked on *Little Dorrit*. The adaptation shares some of the soap features discussed above. These centre strongly on
the treatment of the two young women: Rosa (Tamzin Merchant), who is initially
engaged to Edwin Drood (Freddie Fox), and Helena Landless (Amber Rose Revah),
who arrives from Ceylon (Sri Lanka) with her brother, Neville (Sacha Dhawan). In
terms of moral legibility, Rosa appears to be established as the innocent heroine who
is caught between a callow but good man (Edwin Drood) and an evil one (his uncle,
John Jasper (Matthew Rhys)). Helena is her support and helper; from their first meeting there is an affinity between the two women based on the candour and direct
speaking associated with emotional legibility. At various points the untangling of the
plot depends on this; Edwin praises Rosa for 'your courage, your clarity of thought',
and Helena bravely confronts Jasper, demanding that he 'look at the real Rosa, not
the one of your dreams'.

However, all is not what it seems, and the young couple are not destined for a
happy ending. Edwin describes his fiancée as 'all thorn and no petals' and, rather
more seriously, is himself quickly exposed as arrogant and spoilt. Significantly, the
idealisation of the couple involves a misconstruction by Jasper; Rosa and Edwin
appear at their most blond and angelic at the beginning of the serial in an image that
turns out to be a vision from one of Jasper's opium-addled dreams. Even when he is
awake, Jasper's view of the happy couple's engagement is a misreading of the scene
which he observes from afar in which they actually agree not to marry.

This indicates a major difference between this adaptation and the conventions at
work in soap opera because it is an example of how *Edwin Drood* frequently puts
the viewer into the viewpoint of a character – something that almost never happens in
British soaps. The adaptation makes visual Jasper's delusions and positions the audience inside them. The first images of the drama are of Jasper's dreams of strangling
Edwin, dreams which are repeated throughout the two episodes in different contexts
and indeed with different victims; 'I remembered it all wrong,' he mutters at the end,
and the viewer has shared that false memory. We share Jasper's other visions when,

for example, the ghost of the apparently dead Edwin appears to him in the doorways of a London courtyard. And we see in close-up the drops of sweat which Jasper sees on Rosa's neck as she sings to his accompaniment, a sign of his obsession and her unease. Although Jasper's immoral behaviour towards Rosa and indeed Neville and Helena is never in doubt, the different approach of this adaptation is indicated by the fact that the final speech of justification and accusation is given not by one of the women (as with Rose in *Oliver Twist* or Amy in *Little Dorrit*) but by Jasper. In the ending which Hughes devised so as to put the unfinished novel on screen, Jasper admits to Reverend Crisparkle (Rory Kinnear) that he had previously killed Edwin Drood Sr, who was his own father (and not his brother-in-law as previously thought). Jasper explains that he was an unloved and rejected child; 'the wicked man' he became 'was a bastard boy of seven [. . .] sent away to learn of his sin while a little fat fair baby [the younger Edwin Drood [. . .] sucked up all the love in the house so there was none left'.

Edwin Drood's second major difference from the soap modes of adaptation is in the treatment of Neville and Helena Landless as Brown actors. Dickens scholars have discussed the possible multiracial origins of the twins and emphasised the ambiguity of their representation; 'their possible mixed race embodies their foreignness and lack of belonging,' comments Laura Peters; 'the hybridity of the Landless twins leaves them in an ambivalent position [. . .] with a claim to British subject status yet profoundly alienated within the British community.'[33] But Hughes is decisive in her portrayal of the twins' ethnicity and origins:

> Helena Landless and her fiery brother Neville presented a visual challenge. These young orphan twins are from Ceylon, but have English names. I inspected the original illustrations closely. Were those crisscrossing lines on their faces meant to suggest brown skin? How exciting! I decided, on no textual evidence, that they had a British father and a Tamil mother.

Hughes perhaps exaggerates the lack of textual evidence, but her excitement clearly arises from the impact she thinks the characters would make in a television period drama on television: 'With great enthusiasm, the production team put two young British Asian actors into starring roles in a costume drama for the first time.'[34] The writer's relishing of this situation is striking, and the treatment of the pair indicates something different from the indifference of integrated casting or the soap opera impulse to embrace marginality as heroic. Instead, this adaptation produces a version of the discomfort which Carroll suggests is caused by 'a black presence in the period drama genre' (26) but re-presents it to the audience as a source of interest and pleasure.

At one level, these characters are used to demonstrate the hostility and fear of white characters. Neville recalls how his white stepfather had accused him of having the 'touch of the tiger in his blood', and this racial attitude pervades a number of exchanges in the first episode. Edwin resents Neville's interest in Rosa, and his patronising attitude quickly turns to insults as he drunkenly drawls out, 'I find I tire very quickly of the Wisdom of the East [. . .] You are no judge of white men.' Jasper insults Neville's mother by calling her a 'native concubine'. And even the gentle Crisparkle nevertheless sees, in Helena's acute observation that Jasper is 'devouring

352   CHRISTINE GERAGHTY

Rosa with his looks', an improper knowledge of sensuous feeling which is implicitly associated with her race.

This emphasis on the racism of the white characters and the use of racist behaviour to inspect the moral claims of characters as different as Edwin and Mrs Crisparkle (Julia McKenzie) seems to reflect a sensitivity to debates about the lack of diversity in British drama and the need to confront racism. As such it could fall into the trap of presenting race and ethnicity as an issue only when Black and ethnic minority actors appear on screen while preserving whiteness as the norm. I would argue, though, that this adaptation places the whiteness of the classic adaptation under pressure. The presence of Asian characters/actors turns the production back on itself and makes strange some of the conventional pleasures of the genre. While the adaptation draws attention to the incongruity of these characters/actors in a costume drama, the effect is to emphasise the oddness of some of the staple scenes of classic adaptations. An establishing shot of the small cathedral town introduces the scene in which the newcomers emerge from the stagecoach they have travelled in. Their appearance is only gradually revealed, allowing the audience to see the visible surprise of Reverend Crisparkle and his mother at these characters who do not fit their (or our) expectations. Later, the familiar comfortableness of tea in an English garden is disrupted as Helena and Neville sit stiff-backed, politely drinking tea and responding to questions which are just slightly off the mark; 'It's like talking to a pair of brick walls,' Mrs Crisparkle giggles when out of earshot, though her own behaviour has been seen to be just as forced and with less reason. Reverend Crisparkle is surprised again when he finds the brother and sister walking the marshes, and the audience is invited to share his surprise when a long shot places the two in the green and beautiful scenery typically associated with classic adaptations. But Helena demonstrates her openness to new experiences by explaining that this 'restorative walk' is a 'new pleasure for us. We do not come from a walking country.' Something similar occurs when Neville voices appreciation of Gothic architecture in the darkened cathedral: 'such beauty frozen into stone'. What seem natural elements in many an adaptation – cottage gardens, country walks, appreciation of ancient buildings – are exposed as specifically English habits, which are being used to exclude others rather than to welcome them.

A further element in the handling of ethnicity is the way that the language of colour runs as a persistent thread through the discussions of evil in a way that is unusual in classic adaptations. The Mayor talks of the case having 'a generally dark look to me' as Jasper accuses Neville of murder. Rosa tells Jasper that his nephew 'never knew that his [uncle's] [. . .] heart was black as coal'. Later Helena, in protecting Rosa from Jasper, repeats the metaphor and tells him to examine his own actions, to 'look into your own black heart'. Spoken passionately by white-skinned Rosa to the man who is abusing her, the words are dramatic and forceful. But repeated by dark-skinned Helena with calm conviction, the clichéd association of blackness with evil is foregrounded and the melodramatic binaries of good and evil, light and darkness, are briefly available for scrutiny.

Edwin Drood's difference from the other adaptations discussed here is distilled in its final scene which plays with the conventionally happy endings of marriage and family reunions. An engagement is agreed, but, unconventionally, Helena moves to the centre of the marriage plot when she accepts a proposal from the shy Reverend Crisparkle which he has not actually articulated: 'I said "yes" anyway,' she says, kissing his hand. Rosa, the central heroine, is not paired off, and her future remains unclear. Her former lover, Edwin, is going into business in Egypt with his former rival and new partner, Neville: 'They will bring home exotic brides and cause consternation,' Helena whispers to Rosa, who responds with an amused, 'I do hope so.' Certainly, this adaptation, while not causing 'consternation', provided a sly dig at the conventions of the all-white, classic serial while also demonstrating that the shift towards soap opera is not the only approach to adapting Dickens in the twenty-first century.

The BBC's battle to retain its status as a public service broadcaster and justify the universal licence fee has taken on a new urgency in the twenty-first century. That helps to explain why the BBC was so keen to exploit elements of soap opera as a way of appealing to viewers who are adept at handling issues, characters and themes across complex storylines. For many critics, this approach can be tainted by its appeal to mass audiences. Heilmann and Llewellyn, for instance, seem to have little sympathy for contemporary adaptations when they comment that Phelps's *Oliver Twist* tries 'to relate the nineteenth-century popular text to our contemporary attraction to the narrative techniques of soap opera; *EastEnders* meets *Oliver!* in a culturally hybrid mode that seems to do little to enhance the reputation of either.'[35] The contempt of this attitude contrasts with Sarah Phelps's more democratic wish that new audiences might come to claim these stories for themselves and her advice to new writers that an adaptation is 'your passionate response to that text'.[36] Adaptations are always culturally hybrid. The soap-influenced adaptations I have discussed here are most powerful when they work with the grain of melodrama and the competencies of their viewers to re-present Dickens's stories, characters and themes with the clarity, directness and empathy which mark the best of soap opera.

Notes

1. Rebecca Arwen White, 'The Classic-Novel Adaptation from 1995 to 2009' (unpublished doctoral thesis, Durham University, 2010), 233. <etheses.dur.ac.uk/443/> [accessed 1 August 2018].
2. Iris Kleinecke-Bates, 'Historicizing the Classic Novel Adaptation: *Bleak House* (2005) and British Television Contexts', in *Adaptation in Contemporary Culture: Textual Infidelities*, ed. by Rachel Carroll (London: Continuum, 2009), 111–22, 113; John Caughie, 'Television and Serial Fictions', in *The Cambridge Companion to Popular Fiction*, ed. by David Glover and Scott McCracken (Cambridge: Cambridge University Press, 2012), 50–67, 63.
3. Robert Giddings and Keith Selby, *The Classic Serial on Television and Radio* (Basingstoke: Palgrave, 2001), 203. The book provides a comprehensive account of the development of the classic serial on British television up to 2000. See also Jeffrey Richards, 'Dickens, Our Contemporary', in *Films and British Identity: from Dickens to Dad's Army* (Manchester: Manchester University Press, 1997), 326–50 for an influential account.
4. Nancy West and Karen E. Laird, 'Prequels, Sequels, and Pop Stars: "Masterpiece" and the New Culture of Classic Adaptation', *Literature/Film Quarterly* 39.4 (2011), 306–26, 315.
5. Florian Schweizer, 'Afterword: The 2012 Bicentenary', in *Dickens and Modernity*, ed. by Juliet John (Cambridge: D. S. Brewer, 2012), 209–22, 217. BBC Radio 4 also offered *A Tale of Two Cities* over five afternoons from 26 to 30 December 2011 and a reworking of *Martin Chuzzlewit* in a three-part dramatisation by Ayeesha Menon as *The Mumbai Chuzzlewits* from 1 January 2012.

6. Gillian Anderson, 'Great Expectations: Falling in Love with Miss Havisham', *BBC Love TV Blog*, 27 December 2011, <www.bbc.co.uk/blogs/tv/entries/9f7e1026-fe98-3947-988b-9c2343e4f871/> [accessed 23 August 2017].
7. Helen Wheatley, *Spectacular Television: Exploring Televisual Pleasure* (London: I. B. Taurus, 2016), 124.
8. West and Laird, 314.
9. Lez Cooke, *British Television Drama: A History* (London: BFI, 2003), 3.
10. Kristyn Gorton, *Media Audiences: Television, Meaning and Emotion* (Edinburgh: Edinburgh University Press, 2009), 56.
11. Christine Geraghty, 'Discussing Quality: Critical Vocabularies and Popular Television Drama', in *Media and Cultural Theory*, ed. by James Curran and David Morley (Oxford: Routledge, 2006), 221–32, 228.
12. Michael Stewart, 'Introduction', in *Melodrama in Contemporary Film and Television*, ed. by Michael Stewart (Basingstoke: Palgrave Macmillan, 2014), 1–21, 3.
13. Ibid.
14. Qtd in Gorton, 93.
15. Richards, 344.
16. Iris Kleinecke-Bates, 'Historicizing the Classic Novel Adaptation', 118.
17. West and Laird, 319.
18. See Juliet John, *Dickens and Mass Culture* (Oxford: Oxford University Press, 2010) and *Dickens's Villains: Melodrama, Character, Popular Culture* (Oxford: Oxford University Press, 2003), as well as Carolyn Williams's essay in this volume.
19. See Christine Geraghty, *Bleak House* (Basingstoke: Palgrave Macmillan, 2010), 14–31 for a discussion of how far the comparisons between soap opera conventions and Dickens's practice of serialisation can be taken.
20. Ann Heilmann and Mark Llewellyn, *Neo-Victorianism: The Victorians in the Twenty-First Century, 1999–2009* (Basingstoke: Palgrave Macmillan, 2010), 228.
21. Deborah Cartmell and Imelda Whelehan, 'A Practical Understanding of Literature on Screen: Two Conversations with Andrew Davies', in *The Cambridge Companion to Literature on Screen*, ed. by Deborah Cartmell and Imelda Whelehan (Cambridge: Cambridge University Press, 2007), 239–51, 250.
22. See 'Little Dorrit: Life and Debt', *Telegraph*, 18 October 2008 <https://www.telegraph.co.uk/culture/tvandradio/3562235/Little-Dorrit-Life-and-debt.html> [accessed 27 April 2020]. For discussion of different adaptations of *Oliver Twist*, see Chapter 7 of John, *Dickens and Mass Culture*, and Chapter 1 of Christine Geraghty, *Now a Major Motion Picture: Film Adaptations of Literature and Drama* (Lanham: Rowman & Littlefield, 2008). Mary Hammond provides information on adaptations of *Great Expectations* in *Charles Dickens's* Great Expectations: *A Cultural Life, 1860–2012* (Farnham: Ashgate, 2015).
23. Phelps was later a writer for the twenty-episode *Dickensian* (BBC Television/Red Planet Pictures, 2015–16), an imaginative mash-up of Dickens's characters brought together from a number of his books. Producer and writer Tony Jordan met Phelps through *EastEnders* where he had a lengthy spell as writer and advisor before setting up Red Planet Productions. The series is sympathetically reviewed in Valerie Purton, 'Dickensian', *Journal of Victorian Culture* 21.2 (2016), 242–6.
24. Stewart, 3.
25. Serena Davies, 'An Oliver for our Times', *Telegraph*, 15 December 2007 <https://www.telegraph.co.uk/culture/tvandradio/3669961/An-Oliver-for-our-times.html> [accessed 27 August 2017].
26. Brian McFarlane, *Charles Dickens'* Great Expectations: *The Relationship between Text and Film* (London: Methuen Drama, 2008), 149.

27. Andrew Davies, 'Andrew Davies on How to Adapt Literary Classics for TV', *Telegraph*, 18 February 2011 < https://www.telegraph.co.uk/culture/tvandradio/8328055/Andrew-Davies-on-how-to-adapt-literary-classics-for-TV.html> [accessed 27 August 2017].
28. Richard Butt, 'Melodrama and the Classic Television Serial', in *Melodrama in Contemporary Film and Television*, ed. by Michael Stewart, 27–41, 33.
29. Rachel Carroll, 'Black Britain and the Classic Adaptation: Integrated Casting in Television Adaptations of *Oliver Twist* and *Little Dorrit*', *Adaptation* 8.1 (2014), 16–30, 20. Subsequent page references are provided within the text.
30. BBC Press Pack, 'Freema Agyeman Plays Tattycoram', *BBC Press Office*, 13 October 2008 <http://www.bbc.co.uk/pressoffice/pressreleases/stories/2008/10_october/13/dorrit11.shtml> [accessed 22 August 2017].
31. For a fuller discussion of this aspect of Andrew Davies's screenplay in relation to the source text, see Kim Edwards Keates, '"Wow. She's a Lesbian. Got to Be": Re-reading and Re-viewing Dickens and Neo-Victorianism on the BBC', in *Dickens and Modernity*, ed. by Juliet John, 170–92.
32. The BBC's Annual Report for 2017/18 reported that BBC One reached 68.9 per cent of 'the UK population who use the service each week' (63).
33. Laura Peters, *Orphan Texts: Victorian Orphans, Culture and Empire* (Manchester: Manchester University Press, 2001), 136.
34. Gwyneth Hughes, '*The Mystery of Edwin Drood*: A Dickens of a Whodunnit', *Guardian*, 4 January 2012 <https://www.theguardian.com/books/2012/jan/04/mystery-edwin-drood-dickens-bbc/> [accessed 24 August 2017].
35. Heilmann and Llewellyn, 216.
36. BBC College of Production podcast, with Hazel Marshall, ft. Sarah Phelps and Stewart Harcourt, 'Great Adaptations', *BBC Academy*, 16 February 2012 <http://www.bbc.co.uk/academy/production/ideas-and-research/storytelling/article/art20130702112135556> [accessed 29 August 2017].

Further Reading

Will Stanford Abbiss, 'Dickens Adaptations Beyond the Bicentenary', in *Post-heritage Perspectives on British Period Drama Television* (Abingdon: Routledge, 2023)

Rachel Carroll, ed., *Adaptation in Contemporary Culture: Textual Infidelities* (London: Continuum, 2009)

Iris Kleinecke-Bates, *Victorians on Screen: The Nineteenth Century on British Television, 1994–2005* (Basingstoke: Palgrave, 2014)

Imelda Whelehan, 'Neo-Victorian Adaptations', in *A Companion to Literature, Film, and Adaptation*, ed. by Deborah Cartmell (Chichester: Wiley-Blackwell, 2012), 272–91

23

Hollywood and British Cinema

Barry Langford

OPENING TITLES UNFOLD TO A SOUNDTRACK medley of Christmas carols and other seasonal tunes. Bordering the cast and crew credits, a densely crowded frieze of small illustrated figures, adults and children, in Victorian garb. Once the credits conclude, a further card briefly postpones the start of the action, to winsome strings, reproducing Charles Dickens's declaration (from his 'Preface' to the 1867 edition) that 'like many fond parents, I have in my heart of hearts, a favourite child. And his name is DAVID COPPERFIELD'. Dickens's signature is appended beneath. We then dissolve to the opening page of *Copperfield* itself – 'I Am Born' and David's famous opening meditation on whether he will prove to be 'the hero of my own life' – and finally fade in to a shot of wind-tossed trees on a tempestuous evening, tilting down to take in a brisk-looking middle-aged woman striding determinedly through the near-gale towards the front door of a quaint country cottage.

Thus begins MGM's celebrated 1935 adaptation, produced by David O. Selznick and directed by George Cukor, tremendously successful on its original release and – notwithstanding the radical surgery required to cram the principal action into a 120-minute feature – still among the best-regarded screen versions of any Dickens novel. A 'prestige' production promoted by Selznick in the face of front-office resistance, its enduring reputation owes much to the vivid impersonations by MGM contract players of *Copperfield*'s rich roster of supporting characters, including Edna Mae Oliver's Aunt Betsey, Roland Young's Uriah Heep and, above all, W. C. Fields's Wilkins Micawber. But what do the ways in which the film announces itself to – and, in so doing, situates – its audience tell us about Selznick and Cukor's approach to adapting Dickens? And are there broader implications for understanding Dickens's long and ongoing journey through mainstream commercial narrative cinema?

Selznick took pains establishing his film's Dickensian credentials, undertaking a highly publicised English research trip incorporating a consultation with the Dickens Fellowship. Hugh Walpole's recruitment to co-author the screenplay also lent the production a suitably 'English' literary imprimatur.[1] *Copperfield* can be understood as a high-profile example of studio-era Hollywood's intermittent mission to bridge mass and high culture, and, not least (especially in the febrile period following the belated enforcement of the Production Code in 1934), its own cultural respectability. As an author who himself combined literary prestige with continuing popularity and accessibility, Dickens was – and arguably remains – especially well suited to this task.[2]

But how was this generalised cultural currency converted into the picture that premiered in New York on 18 January 1935? What 'version', not only of *Copperfield* but of Dickens himself, informs and is articulated by Cukor's film? Take that Yuletide musical accompaniment to the opening titles: seemingly misplaced, given that neither novel nor adaptation include extended Christmas scenes, but equally perfectly conventional, even predictable, given the baked-in association of Dickens and 'Christmas spirit', not least via the popularity of *A Christmas Carol* (1843) on both sides of the Atlantic during the interwar period.[3] In the absence of Christmas itself onscreen, moreover, the seasonal music conveys a generalised sense of generosity, good cheer, charity and conviviality – all attributes of the generically 'Dickensian'. While the busy little figures in the title's frieze cannot readily be distinguished as characters from the novel, and only the eagle-eyed and textually informed could spot details (a tombstone, a country cottage) that foreshadow the impending narrative, collectively the design – evoking Phiz's swarming frontispieces for *Martin Chuzzlewit* (1843–4), *Dombey and Son* (1846–8) and so on – suggests an idea of active, harmonious community: not least, perhaps, national community, an idea important and relevant both to Dickens's original readership and to the film's Depression-era audience.[4]

Compared to the prevailing conventions of classic literary adaptations in the 1930s, which often sought to authenticate their relationship to source texts by imaging leather-bound volumes, turning pages and so forth, as tokens of a venerable literary heritage, the film's slightly atypical direct citation of Dickens's own authorial voice (*Copperfield* as his 'favourite child') marks an interesting extratextual intrusion, diverting the spectator from the usual questions concerning the adaptation's textual fidelity and towards an investment in the personality and aura of Dickens himself as the text's fundamentally authenticating 'ground'. As Thomas Leitch observes, 'textual fidelity is less important than fidelity to the image or idea of a Dickens text, an image that [*Copperfield*] explicitly textualizes, though it does not correspond precisely to any source text.'[5] This is no isolated instance: Graham Petrie notes similar explicit 'framing' evocations of Dickens in four silent Danish Dickens adaptations in the early 1920s.[6] In promoting Selznick's own Dickensian follow-up, *A Tale of Two Cities* (Jack Conway, US 1935), MGM urged exhibitors to 'Remember *Copperfield* and the Literary Influence of the Dickens Name!'[7] Given that Dickens himself does not actually appear onscreen (unlike his impersonation by the Great Gonzo in *The Muppet Christmas Carol* (Brian Henson, US 1992)), this (literally and figuratively) 'authorising' Dickensian presence is ultimately maintained by the 'Dickensian' qualities of the film generally.[8] Thus these qualities are necessarily instantiated *by* the adaptation of a specific Dickens text but not ultimately dependent *on* that text for their validation.

In the critical literature on Dickens's varied multimedia afterlives, it is widely agreed that this generalised sense of the 'Dickensian' is an important dimension of many, perhaps most, mainstream screen Dickens adaptations – including the most celebrated examples, such as David Lean's post-war Dickens diptych *Oliver Twist* (UK 1946) and *Great Expectations* (UK 1948).[9] It is important, too, in sustaining Dickens's continuing currency in the cultural and commercial networks to which literary adaptation contributes: Tony Jordan's 2015 BBC serial drama *Dickensian*, a mash-up of Dickens's characters relocated from their original narrative contexts into a Victorian London itself conceived as generically 'Dickensian', is perhaps the logical fulfilment of this tendency. There is also the question of indirect adaptations or remediations of Dickens that activate temporally and culturally displaced modes of the 'Dickensian' (and maybe also 'Victorian'): numerous reviewers remarked (approvingly or otherwise) on the 'Dickensian' aspects of *Slumdog Millionaire* (Danny Boyle,

UK 2008).[10] This essay will confine itself to considering the (very extensive) canon of direct Dickens adaptations, though even here precisely defining this 'Dickensian' aura, let alone specifying its place and function within the aesthetic economy of Dickens screen adaptations, is elusive. The term, as John Gardiner observes, is all too often 'more casually deployed than considered'.[11] I examine here the persistence of a reified notion of the 'Dickensian' as an operative constraint both in the larger cultural economy within which Dickens adaptations are mounted and promoted, and within the textual procedures of individual adaptations. The 'Dickensian' operates within mainstream Dickens adaptations at a textual level – through dialogue, mise-en-scène, acting style and so forth – as a fundamental unit of meaning which delimits and defines the terms in which the text is both produced and consumed. But the notion of the 'Dickensian' also works through and alongside other conventional representational practices to inoculate commercial Dickens adaptations against some of the more challenging and provocative dimensions of the Dickens text.

By thus taking the measure of the 'Dickensian' in Dickens movies, we might also move closer to answering an embarrassing question concerning the abundant heritage of screen versions of Dickens: namely, why so many of them are so oddly unmemorable?

Dickensian Disappointments

Dickens was, and is, popular with filmmakers: to begin with. There is no doubt whatever about that. As almost every critical discussion of Dickens film and television adaptations observes, Dickens seems to have a particular affinity with the moving image.[12] This affinity, now well over a century old, can be measured purely quantitatively: more films have been made of Dickens's works than those of any other author, with 130 known cinematic adaptations by the end of the twentieth century, including more than thirty versions of *Oliver Twist* and *A Christmas Carol* alone.[13] To this at least another ten can be added since the turn of the millennium, outstripping by a clear and indisputable margin even Dickens's closest 'competitors' in the English literary canon (Austen, the Brontës and Hardy).[14] But beyond sheer numbers, claims have also frequently been made for a fundamental *qualitative* relationship between the particular, and peculiar, properties of Dickens's imagination and novelistic style, and moving image media. Dickens did not live to see the emergence of cinema, but in some ways – it is often argued – he seems to have anticipated it or, as Sergei Eisenstein perceived, supplied a 'connecting link'.[15] Eisenstein famously discerned in Dickens's attention to the lived experience of ordinary men and women, his use of 'montage' (the juxtaposition of sharply contrasting tonal/narrative elements as a stylistic principle), and his deployment of 'shots' densely crammed with concrete and symbolic detail a virtual rehearsal of cinematic techniques subsequently systematised by D. W. Griffith. More recently, Grahame Smith has reiterated and extended the argument that, in its rendering of the multifarious, sometimes phantasmagoric qualities of (especially urban) modernity, Dickens's work possesses 'proto-cinematic' qualities, and additionally asserts that Dickens was 'sufficiently important to the private and public life of nineteenth-century culture [. . .] for his dreamlike anticipation of the form to be a significant factor in the emergence of film'.[16]

As such commentators note, beyond its strongly visual qualities Dickens's work appealed to early twentieth-century filmmakers for its continuing broad popularity and ensuing familiarity, strongly reinforced by a continuing practice of popular theatrical adaptation; the reputational gain of Boz's own iconic 'aura'; and at a very practical level the expiration by 1920 of the copyrights Dickens worked so strenuously to protect, making the entire Dickens canon freely available to filmmakers at just the point (around the time of the Great War) that silent cinema shifted from short subjects and an 'attraction'-led aesthetic towards increasingly complex and ambitious narratives whose frequent literary and/or theatrical patrimony lent both form and cultural respectability to the new medium.[17]

Set against this profusion of productions, however, is a disappointing yet really inarguable truth: bar Lean's two films, very few Dickens adaptations have enjoyed lasting critical esteem. Some Dickens film adaptations have been very commercially successful – the MGM *Copperfield*, *Oliver!* (Carol Reed, UK 1968) and *The Muppet Christmas Carol*, among others (*Oliver!* also won the Best Picture Oscar). But beyond the box office, there is a palpable discrepancy between the sheer number of Dickens movies and the impression they have left on cinematic tradition. Is Dickens then the outstanding instance of Fredric Jameson's 'law' of adaptation: 'A great film can be made from a mediocre novel; most great novels yield only second-rate movie versions'?[18] Major auteur filmmakers have rarely been attracted to Dickens: Lean and Cukor aside, the only major sound-era directors to have tackled his works are Reed, Roman Polanski (a moderately received *Oliver Twist*, US/UK 2005) and perhaps Alberto Cavalcanti (*Nicholas Nickleby*, UK 1948). (Numerous scholars have remarked 'Dickensian' elements in the films of Chaplin, Hitchcock, Welles and other major directors,[19] and a strong case might be made for Frank Capra's *It's a Wonderful Life* (US 1946) – notionally an adaptation of a *Harper's* short story, but manifestly a version of *A Christmas Carol* – as a singularly powerful 'Dickensian' film.)

It is possible, of course, that Dickens's own titanic stature, while making his work an attractive commercial proposition for producers, has simultaneously made him less appealing to filmmakers with strong personal artistic signatures of their own who may experience a certain anxiety of influence – fearing that their vision risks becoming compromised by or even subordinated to that of the 'Inimitable', preferring instead to take on less incandescent writers upon whom they can more easily impress their own stylistic imprint.[20] Nor have the legion of 'second-tier' Dickensian directors generally raised their own game to meet the challenge: for example, Brian Desmond Hurst's version of *A Christmas Carol* (UK 1951), starring Alastair Sim, is fondly remembered and reliably re-broadcast each televisual festive season, yet few would declare it a landmark movie.

Of course, such judgements beg many questions concerning the criteria on which critical evaluations are based, and the social and cultural positions whence they issue; the difference between aesthetic merit and popularity, as measured by commercial success (itself a debatable metric); and – perhaps particularly pertinent in Dickens's case – the relative status of middlebrow and elite opinion formation. Yet, if we do accept at least provisionally the proposition that Dickens's cinematic legacy – sheer volume of adaptations aside – is aesthetically underwhelming, mediocre execution by second-rank talent is an unsatisfactory explanation. Rather, if there is indeed an asymmetry of output to accomplishment, this relates to an important dimension of

Dickens's novels' formal qualities: one not only characteristically 'Dickensian' but that, crucially, both significantly qualifies the chances of his fiction being effectively translated into the stylistic, narrative and representational conventions of mainstream narrative cinema *and*, however paradoxically, simultaneously *confirms* critical arguments for Dickens as a notionally 'cinematic' novelist. For the most influential and widely disseminated representational modes of mainstream commercial cinema have been for much of the past century organised according to formal principles that stand in almost direct contradiction to those that make Dickens's work so distinctive and remarkable – and indeed 'cinematic'.

The Imitable Boz: Shaping the 'Dickensian'

In the Dickens cinematic universe, Dickens's works are not all equal or equally popular with filmmakers or (presumably?) audiences – far from it. Of his fifteen completed novels, four between them comprise almost half the total number of theatrically released Dickens adaptations: pre-eminently *A Christmas Carol* (twenty-one theatrical films since the silent era, including straight dramatic adaptations, musicals, animations and updated versions); followed by *Oliver Twist* (eighteen); *Great Expectations* (nine); and *David Copperfield* (eight). *A Tale of Two Cities*, an immensely popular choice for adaptation in the earlier twentieth century with six versions through 1958, has recently been less favoured, with only TV adaptations since the Ralph Thomas/ Dirk Bogarde version. (In the early silent era – when incidentally *Oliver Twist* was a more popular choice than *Carol* – short vignettes from many Dickens novels were produced; some contained the skeleton of the main plot, but others dramatised only isolated passages from the titular novels: for example the 150-second, single-shot 1903 *Nicholas Nickleby*, which condenses the Dotheboys schoolroom scenes into a single action without any narrative context. Others restaged for the camera scenes from popular contemporary stage adaptations.) By contrast, Dickens's socially panoramic novels of the 1850s and 1860s – the venues for his most ambitious explorations of novelistic form – have rarely attracted filmmakers: there have, for example, been no full-scale feature adaptations of either *Bleak House* (1852–3) or *Our Mutual Friend* (1864–5).[21] The sheer scale of these later novels is clearly an important factor, but is it the only one? Other extremely long (though arguably less complex) nineteenth-century novels have been successfully adapted as features (pre-eminently, Hugo's *Les Misérables*, filmed seven times in English and French in the sound era, not including the 2012 musical); conversely, long-form television serials, too – in which Dickens adaptations have abounded and to which the discursive sprawl of his longer narratives appears better adapted than feature filmmaking – though less avoidant of the later novels, have also strongly favoured the 'big four' novels. True, that list includes Dickens's most generally popular and cherished works (*Twist, Carol, Copperfield*) since his own lifetime. But taste is malleable, not fixed: as Mary Hammond has shown, *Great Expectations* (1860–1) has only relatively belatedly reached its current eminence as a canonically 'Dickensian' text.[22] In repeatedly turning to the same sources, producers do not merely reflect popular taste, they help shape and certainly consolidate it. This applies to Dickens generally: as Juliet John argues, 'Dickens would not have attained his posthumous position as an international [literary] icon whose fame rivals that of Shakespeare were it not for the screen.'[23]

If this small subset of Dickens's fiction has come to constitute, and delimit, our sense of the 'Dickensian' – at least as far as mainstream commercial cinema is concerned – we might note that by thus privileging its earlier and – very broadly speaking – more affirmative and pro-social phases (*Great Expectations* clearly excepted), filmmakers have tended to replicate the reputational arc promoted by many of Dickens's contemporaries – a masterful natural entertainer whose later works were blemished by self-consciousness, failures of taste and excesses of mannerist style.[24] This influential cinematic construction of the 'Dickensian' thus finds itself partly at odds with critical readings in which the proleptically cinematic dimensions of his writing are aligned with a conception of Dickens as a highly self-conscious and formally ambitious literary stylist whose work challenges and meditates (albeit performatively rather than programmatically) the conventions and limits of literary representation even as it renders contemporary social realities in indelibly vivid fashion.[25] No surprise there: the agendas of literary historians and theorists are seldom those of commercial filmmakers. Certainly, film adaptations have rarely demonstrated much awareness of or interest in the experimental, even incipiently 'modernist' Dickens discerned by some scholars.[26] Rather, they have generally preferred to emphasise those elements in Dickens that most closely correspond to received and mutually reinforcing notions of the 'Victorian' and the 'Dickensian' (which, as Sharon Aronofsky Weltman notes – echoing earlier observations by Gordon Marsden and John Gardiner, among others – 'audiences now read as the same thing').[27] The latter is (received as), so to speak, a distillation and encapsulation of the former in stylised form, and the two together constitute a set of representational 'readymades' highly resistant to alternative readings.

In this way the cinematic 'Dickensian' – 'the Dickens movie' – emerges as a robust and durable subgenre of the costume drama/literary adaptation as the conventions of the latter are themselves codified in interwar studio productions both in Hollywood and British cinema. Or if not a genre then perhaps, as Leitch suggests, a 'Dickens franchise': a concept that has the advantage of emphasising material (commercial and marketable) rather than purely aesthetic attributes.[28] In any case, we can quickly arrive at a basic sense of the most canonically 'Dickensian' attributes, both semantic and syntactic.[29] These include colourful, larger-than-life characters; a profound sympathy for the socially marginal and excluded (especially children and above all orphans); stark tonal contrasts of broad comedy and high melodrama; matte shots of the London skyline, dominated by Wren's St Paul's; and, of course, Christmas scenes. Together these elements produce a composite sense of the 'Dickensian' that is in its turn duly reconfirmed and perpetuated by the reiteration of these tropes through the repeated adaptation of the same texts. If such a claim seems overstated or schematic, a glance at the press book for MGM's 1935 *Tale of Two Cities*, released on Christmas Day and encouraging exhibitors to include among their promotional activities 'Dickens Tally-Ho Coach or Sleigh Rides', and goodwill screenings at orphanages, amusingly suggests otherwise.[30]

What these generically Dickensian elements – iconographic, narrative, tonal or stylistic – have in common is their quality of externality – that is, they are *visible* – and this association of the quintessentially Dickensian with the concrete and visual is itself an important element in the further identification of Dickens and cinema. Dickens's characteristic ear for dialogue, eye for telling or extravagant scenic detail, and penchant for starkly contrasted and clearly embodied moral oppositions, are all part of what renders him incipiently cinematic. (Such proto-filmic Dickensian propensities are influenced and subsequently reinforced both by Dickens's own relationship to stage melodrama, and by popular theatrical adaptations of his novels.)[31] In the 1935 *Copperfield*, the notably successful effort by Cukor and his production team to model characterisations on Phiz's illustrations – heavily promoted by the studio as a dimension of the adaptation's authenticity – tends also to emphasise the externally oriented nature of the film's 'Dickensian' aesthetic.

Dickens's ability to render psychological and emotional states via physical and environmental attributes is famous.[32] But onscreen, the inner worlds to which these vividly rendered outer properties metaphorically or metonymically gesture are often highly attenuated, if not missing altogether. In fact, a high degree of psychological inwardness with individual protagonists is not, it seems to me, really a defining attribute of the canon of the 'Dickens movie'. That Dickens was perfectly capable of empathetic psychological realism is not seriously at issue, but nor is it the point. Imaginative inhabitation of psychic trauma and damage arising from abuse and exclusion simply fails to become an ingredient in the Dickens movie's recipe of the typically 'Dickensian': onscreen, Oliver's, or David Copperfield's (or indeed Scrooge's – even if, like George Bailey in *It's a Wonderful Life*, qualified by the self-conscious fairy-tale trappings) ready recovery of robust psychic health and cheerful and productive reintegration into society are far more palatable.

Strange, then, that the 'big four' Dickens novels on film are all notable, though in very different ways, for precisely the intensity of their subjective focalisation. *David Copperfield* and *Great Expectations*, obviously, are first-person narratives; *A Christmas Carol* takes place essentially within the – albeit spatially and temporally expanded – mindscape of Scrooge; while *Oliver Twist*, though the most externally focused of these four novels and in many ways the simplest, nonetheless achieves an almost hallucinatory intensity in its vividly subjective free indirect rendering of Oliver's traumatic passage through the orphanage and Fagin's rookery (as well as, later, Sikes's phantasmagoric guilt after Nancy's murder and Fagin's last night in the condemned cell).

Yet of the various adaptations of this *ur*-Dickensian quartet, only Lean's duo (and, perhaps surprisingly – via the adjusted verisimilitude of the mode which allows for a freer interplay of realism and fantasy, subjective and objective perspectives – Robert Zemeckis's 2009 digitally animated Disney *Carol*) seem to emphasise this dimension of their source texts. Generally, adaptations of the 'big four', like others, prefer to substitute for Dickens's heightened subjectivity an accumulation of 'Dickensian' accoutrements. Returning to Cukor's *Copperfield*, the striking remodelling of the narrative even as it basically follows (with major omissions) the outline of Dickens's plot can in part at least be traced to this de-emphasising of intense subjectivity. That the film opens with an exterior shot of Clara Copperfield's house as we arrive there in the company of Betsey Trotwood on the night of David's birth neatly exemplifies the way in which the film consistently abjures the first-person perspective which many readers since the novel's first publication have found *David Copperfield*'s most striking feature. Generally, Cukor makes no effort to approximate the quality of the novel's early chapters that famously convinced the young George Orwell that 'they had been written *by a child*'.[33]

Although, as David Bordwell notes, the first decade of Hollywood sound cinema was marked generally by a retreat from the sometimes flamboyant expressivity and stylisation that had characterised late silent film in favour of 'the sharp, sober presentation of dialogue and behaviour', Cukor's approach should not be explained away as the default stylistic function of the period. [34] He had other options, as a striking exception to his general rule here clearly illustrates. When David leaves his mother for the last time (in the novel for Salem House, in the film to stay with Peggotty), Cukor deploys a rather unusual travelling shot/reverse shot sequence – the point of view lengthening across the sutures that conventionally bind the participants together – that binds us firmly to David's sensibility without reverting fully to ocular point of view. This eloquently captures in visual form David's lament at this point in the novel, where the sentence's syntactically indeterminate prolongation expresses his undischarged longing: 'So I lost her. So I saw her afterwards, in my sleep at school – a silent presence at my bed – looking at me with the same intent face – holding up her baby in her arms.'[35] *Copperfield*'s departure sequence tends if anything to underscore the spectator's general lack of alignment elsewhere in the film with Freddie Bartholomew as Young David, whose stilted performance throws into relief the skilful work of the character performers, as self-contained 'bits' rather than as integrated elements in the progress of David's 'disciplined heart'.[36] This was therefore a choice on Cukor's part: nor on his part or in his era alone. Consider, for example, how, with the solitary exception of 'Where is Love?', the fourteen songs in Reed's *Oliver!* almost wilfully avoid the unique expressive privileges afforded by the integrated musical. Neither Sikes's guilt, nor Fagin's agonies in the condemned cell (of course, in *Oliver!* he never enters it), find musical/sung expression; indeed, the film is probably best remembered for the large ensemble numbers (among them 'Food, Glorious Food', 'Consider Yourself' and 'Who Will Buy?') that have themselves helped consolidate a sense of the Dickensian as communal, and both literally (the London streets) and figuratively external. (This is not to say that Oliver's subjectivity is wholly absent from either *Oliver!* or Lean's version of *Twist*: indeed, both arguably make Oliver's perspective, externalised or not, more convincing and intense than his two-dimensional presence in the novel.)

These are but two instances of a widespread tendency for the generically 'Dickensian' mode to give rise to film adaptations conceived as incompletely aggregated series of 'Dickensian' routines. Few modern scholars, armed with Dickens's copious and detailed plans and attentive to the associative patterns of imagery, symbol and story in his work, would accept Orwell's infamous aphorism that Dickens is 'all fragments, all details – rotten architecture, but wonderful gargoyles'.[37] Yet the architectonics of the Dickens movie are indeed in this sense Orwellian. William Luhr argues that the 1935 *Copperfield* is fashioned not as a 'formally coherent whole' but as a series of vignettes individually focused on what principally appealed to Selznick: Dickens's characters, conceived as semi-autonomous 'attractions'.[38] Seven decades on, Douglas McGrath's adaptation of *Nicholas Nickleby* (US/GB/Germany 2002) appeared to *New York Times* reviewer A. O. Scott 'a colourful [. . .] collage of Dickensian moods and motifs'.[39]

Dickens film adaptations that resist this externalised model of the 'Dickensian' and rebalance their narratives towards the subjective are much rarer. But they too miss important qualities of the Dickens text. In Delbert Mann's 1969 TV movie of

David Copperfield, for example, Jack Pulman's screenplay stages the action explicitly as David's memory-work, flashback scenes from early childhood and young adulthood cued by various shots of the haunted older David trying and failing to write his life story and wandering beside the restless surf on the beach at Yarmouth. With much modish (for 1969) use of telephoto (aka 'zoom') lenses to mark the interpenetration of inner and outer worlds, the latter ultimately become largely a function of the former: with the result that whereas the Dickensian 'bits' of the 1935 adaptation threatened to become dissociated from David's inadequately rendered psychological and emotional realm, in the 1969 film the contributions of British stage titans including Laurence Olivier (as Creakle), Ralph Richardson (Micawber), Edith Evans (Aunt Betsey) and Michael Redgrave (Peggotty) are so subordinated to the protagonist's mindscape they achieve little independent life at all. Pulman himself judged his adaptation a failure, 'not so much [overly] literary as [. . .] too intellectual', and inferior to the 1935 film (notwithstanding that, as he maintained, there was 'more of Dickens' in his version).[40]

I would suggest that the overstated interiority of Pulman/Mann's *Copperfield*, just as much as the conventionally 'Dickensian' tropes of most Dickens adaptations, should be understood as a legitimate attempt to engage with Dickens's works whose limitations reflect not artistic failure but a misalignment with the Dickens text. These adaptations set themselves, above all, to *contain* Dickens – most often by the application of a veneer of 'Dickensianism' whose ultimate purpose is, precisely, to render the centrifugal energies of Dickens's writing within the essentially centripetal representational strategies of mainstream cinema. They are, one might say, integral halves of an authentic Dickensian text to which they do not, and cannot, add up. In the concluding sections of this essay, I will explain this formulation by means of a brief theoretical digression, and finally suggest an alternative approach for the 'Dickens movie' in the twenty-first century.

Classic Realism, Classical Hollywood and Dickens

In a body of theory and criticism during the 1970s and 1980s, the nineteenth-century novel became identified with the concept of 'classic realism'. Extrapolated from the work of Roland Barthes and other French theorists, 'classic realism' did not address itself primarily to the detailed formal analysis of realist literary techniques, but was fundamentally concerned with the ways in which the reader was ideologically positioned by 'the' (that is, any) realist text. In her slim but influential 1980 volume *Critical Practice*, Catherine Belsey enlisted Dickens – as it might seem today, rather improbably – to the ranks of classic realism alongside other canonical Victorian and early twentieth-century writers. The central proposition of 'classic realism' was that the realist text locates its reader in a position of certainty, foreclosing on contradiction: thus, as a 'closed text', the realist work reassures its readership of the reliable and self-evident nature of the world represented, which mirrors those qualities in the world of the reader herself. Taking as a case study one of Dickens's most formally innovative and ostensibly challenging works, the double narrative of *Bleak House*, Belsey claims that in the ultimate reconciliation of the divided narration (between an impersonal and often ironic third-person narrator and Esther Summerson's gushingly ingenuous first-person account), the novel effectively disempowers, at the level of its supervening discourse, the reader's capacity to question or actively intervene in the world thus rendered: 'initially liberating the reader to produce meaning but finally proving to be a constraint on the process of production'.[41] The argument rests on a crucial distinction (drawn from Tzvetan Todorov and others) between the so-called 'subject(s) of the *énoncé*' (the subordinated voices within the narrative, such as those of individual characters) and the 'subject of the *enunciation*' (the typically impersonal narrative voice that records and transmits these second-order voices – that 'says' 'he said', 'she said', and provides the novel's essential narrative infrastructure, and which remains itself unplaced, indeed unplaceable, thus functionally incontestable as a pre-condition of the text's production of meaning).

Though 'classic realism' was for a while highly influential in Victorian studies, as a blanket category that implausibly claims a monolithic orthodoxy for a richly hetero-geneous literary heritage it has few adherents today. The varieties, tonal nuances and differential perspectives of literary narration make the argument for a 'closed text' unpersuasive in respect of the novel – those of Dickens, perhaps, above all. (Bakhtin-ian dialogism/heteroglossia seems a much more attractive paradigm.) Yet in its inter-rogation of the formal mechanisms whereby narrative, thematic and/or ideological contradictions are reconciled, this hoary debate can yet make a contribution to better understanding the deficiencies in mainstream cinema's version of the 'Dickensian'. As Belsey acknowledged, 'classic realism' drew extensively on essays published in *Screen* during the 1970s where theoretical debates around realism originally referred these to moving image media as well as, or more than, literature.[42] In fact, the 'invisible' or unremarked eye of the camera – that is, the framed shot as the basic cinematic 'lexical unit' – may be a better illustration of the incontestable discursive voice of the 'subject of the *enunciation*' than any nineteenth-century novel. The claim that 'classic realism cannot foreground contradiction'[43] is central to a once-celebrated exchange begun in *Screen* in 1976 between Colin McArthur and Colin MacCabe. This was prompted by the avowedly radical 1975 BBC television drama *Days of Hope*, a por-trayal of the early history of the British labour movement from World War II to the General Strike written by Jim Allen and directed by Ken Loach. Loach's politics not-withstanding, MacCabe criticised *Days of Hope* as a 'classic realist' work which, by claiming a transparency of vision, concealed its own conditions of production, and hence remained ultimately complicit with dominant ideologies. *Days of Hope*, Mac-Cabe maintained, like other 'classic realist' texts, resolved contradictions rather than opening them up for interrogation by the spectator. Defending the series, McArthur responded that *Days of Hope* did expose the contradictions of bourgeois democratic institutions at certain '*obviously* structured moments': for example, a scene where a mine owner lectures striking Durham miners on the British tradition of evolution-ary and peaceful constitutional reform while, in the background of the shot, soldiers brought in to supress dissent in the coalfield undertake bayonet practice.[44] MacCabe responded that McArthur's example was, in fact:

> exactly the classic realist form which privileges the image against the word to reveal that what the mine-owner says is false. In this matter our position of knowl-edge is guaranteed – we may choose to disagree with what the narrative tells us but if it has already placed us in the position where we are sure we are right, it has not questioned the very construction of that position.[45]

For MacCabe here, form trumps, indeed neutralises, ideological content: notwithstanding that Loach's adoption of a part-improvised, documentary-like visual style was intended to distinguish *Days of Hope* from conventional television costume dramas, in MacCabe's view by preserving a hierarchy of discourses the series disables itself from effectively contesting dominant ideologies. However, MacCabe's analysis insists on the formal unity of the realist text itself: it does not account or indeed allow for the destabilisation of discursive hierarchies by competing or conflicting formal or stylistic elements simultaneously present within the text. Contemporary film scholarship has strongly challenged the homogenising tendency of models of classical narrative, noting the persistence of alternative signifying practices that work within and across the notionally composed classical/realist/'classic realist' gaze. Thus, while not dismissing the usefulness of a concept of classical narrative, Rick Altman suggests it should be seen as a 'dynamic, multilevel *system* in which coexisting contradictory forces must regularly clash'.[46] Yet in its legitimate scepticism of levelling notions of 'classicism' and ensuing emphasis on *textual* generic and formal heterogeneity, a heteroglossically minded film theory may understate the importance of conventionalised and conventionalising *practices* in mainstream filmmaking. A degree of formal containment is an undeniable dimension of the particular brand of (modulated) realism associated with studio cinema in the sound era, driven by industrial norms and commercial priorities.[47] This is, perhaps, especially so in the generally stylistically conservative genre of literary adaptation in both Hollywood and British studio filmmaking.

Here we return to Dickens, the problems his work poses for mainstream adaptations – and the 'Dickensian' as a tactic for dealing with (but not resolving) those problems. Ever since Edmund Wilson's famous account of Dickens's 'dualism', the distinctively centrifugal aspects of the Dickens text have been widely recognised and discussed. In a study of how minor characters populate the imaginative spaces of the novel, Alex Woloch argues for an essentially and necessarily irreconcilable productive tension of textual elements between individualised characters and the narrative structures in which they are contained yet into which, at the same time, they are never fully incorporated – a tendency 'always away from a polycentric, or symmetrical, distribution, toward various forms of imbalance: all the characters still retain some position in the narrative discourse (else we could never place them in the story at all), but these are radically differentiated'.[48] No feature of Dickens's works is more celebrated, of course, than his powers of characterisation. What originally drew David O. Selznick to *David Copperfield* was, above all, its retinue of 'brilliant characters [. . .] living, breathing, fascinating people' around the neutral narrative axis of David himself.[49] Woloch, however, argues that the unique vividness of Dickens's secondary characters – and, we might add, the uncanny vitality of his inanimate objects and environments too – helps build 'the peculiar pressures of Dickensian asymmetry'.[50] For Woloch, these are pressures that pose a particular and perhaps unique challenge to the realist projection to reconcile, or at least contain, contradiction because contradiction is not only inscribed at the formal level into the Dickensian text, but also central to its enduring appeal.

The Dickens text is indeed a 'dynamic system' in Altman's terms, much more overtly so than studio cinema: it is a novelistic difference engine, its persistently dialectical elements refusing to coalesce or comfortably resolve themselves. The key drivers of this obstinate difference are the very same quintessentially 'Dickensian' attributes that have traditionally attracted filmmakers. Yet the reification of the 'Dickensian' in the Dickens movie can be seen as the reflexive self-defence of the classical system of film narrative against inherently unclassical, centrifugal qualities in the Dickens text. Generally, Dickens adaptations have striven to preserve those elements of the dialectical Dickens text – narrative closure (however strained), 'Dickensian' good cheer, externality and, above all, Dickens's characters – that help systematise and contain his resistantly un-, even anti-systematic qualities. Hence the inertness of so many Dickens adaptations, strangled so to speak at birth.

Dickens's Network Narratives

In a letter to John Forster of August 1855, during the early stages of work on *Little Dorrit* (1855–7), Dickens discussed his conception of the novel's opening in the quarantine station in Marseille:

> It struck me that it would be a new thing to show people coming together, in a chance way, as fellow-travellers, and being in the same place, ignorant of one another, as happens in life; and to connect them afterwards, and to make the waiting for that connection a part of the interest.[51]

This conception of connections across time, space, nation and class – only dimly and gradually, if at all, apprehended by his characters, but apparent as a governing narrative and thematic principle – was already familiar both to Dickens and to other major nineteenth-century novelists, whether confined to a single work or, as in Balzac and Zola, operating across a linked series of self-contained individual novels. A rhetorical question in *Bleak House* draws Dickens's readers' attention to this structuring device: 'What connexion can there have been between many people in the innumerable histories of this world, who from opposite sides of great gulfs have, nevertheless, been very curiously brought together!'[52]

As outlined to Forster, Dickens's concept previews the trend within contemporary film narrative towards what David Bordwell has called 'network narratives', and has elsewhere variously been termed the multi-protagonist or ensemble picture.[53] Bordwell acknowledges the nineteenth-century novel as a key source of the network narrative, before tracing its episodic cinematic history via *Grand Hotel* (Edmund Goulding, US 1932), *The VIPs* (Anthony Asquith, GB 1963) and, most famously and canonically, *Nashville* (Robert Altman, US 1975), prior to its more widespread adoption in the 1990s in influential independently produced American films including Altman's own *Short Cuts* (US 1994), *Pulp Fiction* (Quentin Tarantino, US 1994) and *Magnolia* (Paul Thomas Anderson, US 1999).[54] Arguably, however, in lumping together as literary antecedents, alongside Dickens, not only *Middlemarch* but also *War and Peace* and dynastic narratives such as Mann's *Buddenbrooks* and time/fate stories like Thornton Wilder's 1927 *The Bridge of San Luis Rey*, Bordwell does a disservice to the more distinctive and innovative aspects of Dickens's approach and its affinity with the most ambitious examples of cinematic 'network narratives' such as *Nashville* itself.

A notable feature shared by Altman and Dickens is the way both organise their narratives through semi-abstract overarching concepts against which, rather than on account of which, the works take form in the reader's or spectator's mind. By contrast, one tends not to find this in novels or films where the apparent randomness of the character set is from the outset mitigated by a unity of action grounded in a shared, consistent and clearly defined location (*Middlemarch*, *Grand Hotel*), family and business relations (*Buddenbrooks*), common struggle (*War and Peace*, *The Thin Red Line* (Terence Malick, US 1998)) or, more strongly still, by a tightly delimited unity of time within and against which the action unfolds (*The VIPs*, *Mystery Train* (Jim Jarmusch, US 1994)). *Bleak House*'s disparate storylines all unfold with a closer or looser connection to a lawsuit teetering on (and ultimately evaporating into) abstraction that is itself a metonym of the abstracted – abstracted from human realities and suffering – realm of the law. *Little Dorrit* is grouped around the large, ironic and impersonal opposition of 'Poverty' and 'Wealth', mirrored within the world of the story by the intangible yet catastrophic, and abstract (in fact, fictitious), wealth circulating through the House of Merdle. *Our Mutual Friend* rings a variety of changes across its personae through the idea of waste in a variety of literal and figurative permutations. *Nashville*, similarly, gathers its characters together not, as it initially seems, through the country music industry (to which several have no connection); nor even the titular city, where all are present as visitors or residents but which itself exists as an absence in a film mostly located in interchangeably impersonal domestic and public spaces; but rather through the idea of community – more accurately, its palpable lack – which itself is metonymically linked to the nation for which 'Nashville' in its various meanings self-consciously stands. Connection, or its absence, is the true connecting tissue or narrative ligament of *Nashville*. Furthermore, beyond its disaggregated narrative form and refusal of definitive closure, *Nashville* is also notable for its inconsistency in handling character. Though the film's broad canvas means we get to know none of them very intimately, *Nashville*'s characters range from the relatively complex and dimensional to the almost cartoon-like: a similarly 'inconsistent' spectrum as, say, the one that contains both Amy Dorrit at one extreme and the melodramatic villain Rigaud at the other.

Multi-strand long-form ensemble television narratives from *Hill Street Blues* onwards are often cited as exemplars of network narrative, and the recent experiments in very long-form television adaptations of Dickens (the BBC's 2005 *Bleak House* and 2008 *Little Dorrit*) might suggest that Dickens adaptations have finally found a congenial form that can accommodate the centrifugal elements and general discursive excess of the Dickensian text. Yet – and notwithstanding the obvious and pleasing rhyme of serial form with Dickens's original mode of publication – the overdetermined and ever-present tension between unavoidable structural discipline and constraints (not least of duration) and super-abundant content in feature-film network narratives seems to me closer still to the particular and peculiar qualities of the Dickens text. Those qualities, which mainstream Dickens film adaptations have only partly acknowledged and futilely tried to contain, await the innovative twenty-first-century adaptation that can engage them fully.

Notes

1. Qtd in Jeffrey Sconce, 'Dickens, Selznick and *Southpark*', in *Dickens on Screen*, ed. by John Glavin (Cambridge: Cambridge University Press, 2003), 172; see 171–80 generally for a detailed account of Selznick's efforts to 'authenticate' his version of Dickens throughout the pre-production and publicity process.

2. For an authoritative overview, see Juliet John, *Dickens and Mass Culture* (Oxford: Oxford University Press, 2010).
3. See Guerric DeBona, 'Dickens, the Depression, and MGM's *David Copperfield*', in *Film Adaptation*, ed. by James Naremore (New Brunswick: Rutgers University Press, 2000), 109–10. See also Paul Davis, *The Lives and Times of Ebenezer Scrooge* (New Haven: Yale University Press, 1990).
4. DeBona, 121–5.
5. Thomas Leitch, *Film Adaptation and Its Discontents: From* Gone with the Wind *to* The Passion of the Christ (Baltimore: Johns Hopkins University Press, 2007), 160.
6. Graham Petrie, 'Dickens in Denmark: Four Danish Versions of His Novels', *Journal of European Studies* 26 (1996), 185–93, 191.
7. *A Tale of Two Cities* press book, 1935, BFI Special Collections PBL-47296.
8. Petrie records that a coda to *David Copperfield* (A. W. Sandberg, Denmark 1922) identifies Dickens himself (impersonated onscreen) as the 'real' Copperfield.
9. See, for example, John Gardiner, 'The Dickensian and Us', *History Workshop Journal* 51.1 (2001), 226–37.
10. See, for example, Ann Hornaday's comment that '*Slumdog Millionaire* plays like Charles Dickens for the 21st century', in 'From "Slumdog" to Riches in a Crowd-Pleasing Fable', *Washington Post*, 12 November 2008 <http://www.washingtonpost.com/wp-dyn/content/article/2008/11/11/AR2008111102775.html> [accessed 4 June 2019].
11. Gardiner, 226.
12. Grahame Smith, *Dickens and the Dream of Cinema* (Manchester: Manchester University Press, 2003) is perhaps the most expansive exploration of this relationship. See also Joss Marsh, 'Dickens and Film', in *The Cambridge Companion to Charles Dickens*, ed. by John O. Jordan (Cambridge: Cambridge University Press, 2001), 204–23.
13. Marsh, 204. See also the listing in Kate Carnell Watt and Kathleen Lonsdale, 'Dickens Composed: Film and Television Adaptations, 1897–2001', in *Dickens on Screen*, 201–16.
14. For a concise summary of the state of play in the field of Victorian literary adaptations, see James Cutler, 'Remembering the Victorians: Cultural Memory, Popularity, Place' (unpublished doctoral thesis, Royal Holloway, University of London, 2017), 10–11. As Cutler notes, certain marginal or non-canonical writers (such as Conan Doyle and Bram Stoker) vie with or outstrip Dickens for pole position.
15. Sergei Eisenstein, 'Dickens, Griffith and the Film Today', in *Film Form: Essays in Film Theory*, ed. and trans. by Jay Leyda (London: Harvest, 1977), 195–25, 224.
16. Smith, 59.
17. On early cinema's 'aesthetic of astonishment', see Tom Gunning, 'A Cinema of Attractions: Early Film, its Spectator and the Avant-Garde', in *Early Cinema: Space, Frame, Narration*, ed. by Thomas Elsaesser (London: BFI, 1990). On Dickens in silent cinema, see Joss Marsh's essay in this volume.
18. Fredric Jameson, 'Afterword: Adaptation as a Philosophical Problem', in *True to the Spirit: Film Adaptation and the Question of Fidelity*, ed. by Colin MacCabe, Kathleen Murray and Rick Warner (Oxford: Oxford University Press, 2011), 215–34, 217.
19. See, for example, Marguerite Rippy, 'Orson Welles and Charles Dickens 1938–1941', in *Dickens on Screen*, 145–54.
20. See Harold Bloom, *The Anxiety of Influence* (New Haven: Yale University Press, 1974).
21. Maurice Elvey's 1920 silent adaptation eliminates everything but the Lady Dedlock narrative.
22. Mary Hammond, *Charles Dickens's* Great Expectations: *A Cultural Life 1860–2012* (London: Routledge, 2015).
23. John, *Dickens and Mass Culture*, 188.

370 BARRY LANGFORD

24. See, for example, the reviews of *Little Dorrit* in *Dickens: The Critical Heritage*, ed. by Philip Collins (London: Routledge & Kegan Paul, 1971), 358–62, 367–8 and 375–7. It is worth noting in this context, however, that *The Pickwick Papers* and *The Old Curiosity Shop*, two early Dickens novels much cherished by his contemporaries but far less so by twentieth-century tastemakers, have proved far less attractive to filmmakers (notwithstanding the obvious melodramatic and actorly appeal of Quilp).
25. Television adaptations have arguably been readier to vary from this normative version of Dickens's career.
26. For a wide-ranging survey of Dickens's 'modernism', see *Charles Dickens, Modernism, Modernity*, ed. by Christine Huguet and Nathalie Vanfasse, 2 vols (Wimereux: Éditions du Sagittaire, 2014).
27. Sharon Aronofsky Weltman, 'Boz versus Bos in *Sweeney Todd*: Dickens, Sondheim and Victorianness', *Dickens Studies Annual* 42 (2011), 55–76, 69. See also Gardiner, 227; and *Victorian Values: Personalities and Perspectives in Nineteenth-Century Society*, ed. by Gordon Marsden (London: Longman, 1998), 49.
28. Leitch, 91.
29. The terms are based upon Rick Altman's influential model: see *Film/Genre* (London: BFI, 2000), 216–26.
30. *A Tale of Two Cities* press book, 1935, BFI Special Collections PBL-47296.
31. See John Glavin, 'Dickens and Theatre', *Cambridge Companion*, 189–203; Juliet John, 'Melodrama', in *Charles Dickens in Context*, ed. by Sally Ledger and Holly Furneaux (Cambridge: Cambridge University Press, 2011), 133–9 – note John's comment that 'it is the fusion of melodrama and narrative in [Dickens's] novels, and not his melodramatic aesthetics alone, that allows them to function as a bridge between melodrama and cinema' (137). For a concise overview of the relationship between popular melodrama and early cinema, see David Mayer, 'Melodrama in Early Film', in *The Cambridge Companion to English Melodrama*, ed. by Carolyn Williams (Cambridge: Cambridge University Press, 2018), 224–44 (including a brief account of *The Only Way* (Herbert Wilcox, GB 1926), a screen version of Frederick Longbridge and Freeman Wills's long-running stage adaptation of *A Tale of Two Cities*).
32. See, for example, Juliet McMaster, *Dickens the Designer* (London: Macmillan, 1987).
33. George Orwell, 'Charles Dickens', *A Collection of Essays* (New York: Harcourt Brace Jovanovich, 1946), 48–103, 80.
34. David Bordwell, *Reinventing Hollywood: How 1940s Filmmakers Changed Movie Storytelling* (Chicago: University of Chicago Press, 2017), 10.
35. Dickens, *David Copperfield*, ed. by Nina Burgis (Oxford: Oxford University Press, 1991), 97, ch. 8.
36. Guerric DeBona, 'A Victorian New Deal: Dickens, the Great Depression, and MGM's *David Copperfield* (1935)', in *Film Adaptation in the Hollywood Studio Era* (Urbana: University of Illinois Press, 2010), 37–63.
37. Orwell, 77.
38. William Luhr, 'Dickens's Narrative, Hollywood's Vignettes', in *The English Novel and the Movies*, ed. by Michael Klein and Gillian Parker (New York: Ungar, 1981), 132–92, 138. Arguably, the various Muppets' character 'turns' in *The Muppet Christmas Carol* deconstruct and send up this concept (I am indebted to Juliet John for this fabulous interpretation).
39. A. O. Scott, 'The Pure of Heart at a Hard-Hearted Boarding School', 27 December 2002, *New York Times* <https://www.nytimes.com/2002/12/27/movies/film-review-the-pure-at-heart-at-a-hardhearted-boarding-school.html> [accessed 3 August 2018].
40. Michael M. Riley, 'Interview with Jack Pulman, English screenwriter', *Southern Humanities Review* 8 (1974), 471–84, 482. The general displacement (compared to cinema) of

visual spectacle by psychological elements in 'serious' TV drama in the 1960s may be an institutional factor in the dramatic choices in this version.

41. Catherine Belsey, *Critical Practice* (London: Methuen, 1980), 80.
42. Ibid., 69–70.
43. Ibid., 82.
44. Colin McArthur, '*Days of Hope*', *Screen* 16 (1975–6), 4, 139–44, 140.
45. Colin MacCabe, 'Memory, Phantasy, Identity: *Days of Hope* and the Politics of the Past', in *Rogue Reels: Oppositional Film in Britain, 1945–90*, ed. by Margaret Dickinson (London: BFI, 1999), 141–5, 143.
46. Rick Altman, 'Dickens, Griffith, and Film Theory Today', in *Classical Film Narrative: The Paradigm Wars*, ed. by Jane M. Gaines (Durham, NC: Duke University Press, 1992), 9–48, 27. Emphasis in original.
47. On the role of craft guilds and Hollywood film industry organisations in standardising film style, see David Bordwell, Janet Staiger and Kristin Thompson, *The Classical Hollywood Cinema: Film Style and Mode of Production to 1960* (London: Routledge, 1985), 250–61.
48. Alex Woloch, *The One vs. the Many: Minor Characters and the Space of the Protagonist in the Novel* (Princeton: Princeton University Press, 2003), 41.
49. David O. Selznick, *Memo from David O. Selznick*, ed. by Rudy Behmer (New York: Viking, 1972), 83–4.
50. Woloch, 178. On Dickens's forceful representation of inanimate objects, see John Carey, *The Violent Effigy: A Study of Dickens' Imagination* (London: Faber, 1973), especially chs 4 and 5.
51. 'To John Forster, [19 August 1855]', *The Letters of Charles Dickens*, ed. by Madeline House, Graham Storey et al., Pilgrim/British Academy Edition, 12 vols (Oxford: Clarendon Press, 1965–2002), VII (1993), 692–3.
52. Charles Dickens, *Bleak House*, ed. by Norman Page (Harmondsworth: Penguin, 1971), 272, ch. 16.
53. David Bordwell, *The Way Hollywood Tells It* (Berkeley: University of California Press, 2006), 97.
54. David Bordwell, 'Mutual Friends and Chronologies of Chance', in *Poetics of Cinema* (London: Routledge, 2008), 189–250, 194.

Further Reading

John Glavin, ed., *Dickens on Screen* (Cambridge: Cambridge University Press, 2003)

Juliet John, *Dickens and Mass Culture* (Oxford: Oxford University Press, 2010)

Joss Marsh, 'Dickens and Film', in *The Cambridge Companion to Charles Dickens*, ed. by John O. Jordan (Cambridge: Cambridge University Press, 2001), 204–23

Grahame Smith, *Dickens and the Dream of Cinema* (Manchester: Manchester University Press, 2003)

24

GLOBAL CINEMA

Marty Gould

APPROPRIATING AND RECONFIGURING DICKENS'S TEXTS TO suit diverse cultural contexts and to address a wide array of modern social and political issues, the cinema has played an important role in making the author a modern, globally recognisable cultural icon.[1] Adapted and readapted, his novels, novellas and stories such as *Oliver Twist* (1837–9), *A Christmas Carol* (1843) and *Great Expectations* (1860–1) cross cultural and linguistic borders, becoming what Paul Davis has termed 'culture-text[s]'. Repeatedly reimagined, Dickens's fictions flow through the collective cultural consciousness: across the globe, Dickens's characters and their stories are recognised and recalled as they have been translated and remediated on stage and screen.[2] Taking cinematic adaptation not only as a powerful vehicle for the international cultural circulation of Dickens but also as a primary site for the perpetual (re-)constitution of Dickens's texts, this essay considers how and why global cinema has reimagined Dickens.

The global circulation of modern cinema – or, perhaps more accurately, Hollywood's domination of global cinema – complicates any effort to discuss non-Western transpositions of Dickens to film. The Bollywood film *Fitoor* (2016), for example, reconceives *Great Expectations* via Alfonso Cuarón's Americanised version (1998), in much the same way that Roman Polanski's *Oliver Twist* (2005) represents its source text as previously reimagined by David Lean (1948) and Carol Reed (1968).[3] Every successive adaptation of a novel intersects with those that came before, and this internationally intertextual adaptive genealogy makes it impossible to completely disentangle non-Western cinematic engagements with Dickens from the Western films that preceded them.[4]

A complete analysis of any film as an adaptation of a Dickens text requires a multi-layered investigation of a sort that the present essay cannot hope to undertake. In this limited space, I aim instead to sketch a bigger picture of cinematic engagement with Dickens outside the more critically familiar Western film adaptations that have achieved a sort of canonical status alongside their originary text, tracing out, in broader strokes, some of the contours of the global landscape of cinematised Dickens.

To begin, then, with what 'counts' as an adaptation of Dickens. This is not an easy question to answer, for, as Thomas Leitch (citing Geoffrey Wagner, Dudley Andrew, Gérard Genette and Kamilla Elliott) has explained, film adaptations exist along a continuum of transmutation, from transpositions, which clearly signal their literary sources and strive to retain as much of the originary text as possible, to freer adaptations, which alter plots, characters and settings, to films that take a literary text as a point of more general inspiration, retaining just enough plot and character to be recognised as bearing some meaningful relationship with it.[5] Beyond the obvious, self-identifying adaptations we can find traces of Dickens even in films that do not explicitly claim a remediating relationship with his work. Alessandro Vescovi, for example, argues that Sergio Runini's *La Stazione* (1990) is drawn from Dickens's short story 'The Signalman' (1866). *La Stazione* modernises Dickens's story and reworks its plot yet retains its originary tale's characterisation, setting and general thematic focus.[6] Similarly, *The Kid with a Bike* (2011) and *Slumdog Millionaire* (2008) do not directly acknowledge origins in specific Dickens texts (and indeed may not self-consciously be engaging with Dickens at all), yet for those familiar with Dickens's work, the echoes of plot and character seem more than coincidental.[7]

From cinema's earliest days, filmmakers have been drawn to Dickens, producing a large – and steadily growing – body of adaptations of his novels. There are any number of reasons for this sustained adaptive interest in Dickens. Firstly, rather ironically, 'The Inimitable' was himself an imitator, regularly reworking his own texts and borrowing the work of other authors: Dickens's novels quite often, and in various ways, adapt other texts, making adaptation, as process and product, intrinsic to Dickens. Secondly, as Sergei Eisenstein famously observed, Dickens's writing exhibits a fundamentally 'filmic' quality, stylistically anticipating the mechanics of cinema: Dickens's novels are thus uniquely suited to representation on screen. Thirdly, published in illustrated volumes and rich in vividly pictorial language, Dickens's novels lend themselves to visual representation: the nineteenth century saw innumerable attempts to adapt Dickens to the stage, and these theatrical adaptations, along with the textual illustrations, provided templates for early film adaptations (which, in turn, served as models for subsequent cinematic remediations). Moreover, Dickens's characters represent recognisable social types and inhabit familiar relationships: when freed from their larger narrative apparatus, many of Dickens's characters are broadly accessible, familiar and relevant. We might add as further considerations Dickens's deep interest in pervasive social issues and his texts' status as canonical 'literary classics'.[8] But if we want to explain why Dickens continues to be adapted to the screen, we might only need to consider how often, and how variously, Dickens has already been adapted to the screen: while a century of remediations has demonstrated the multifarious adaptive potential of his novels, we cannot forget that Dickens is, for many, an author whose work they know primarily (even perhaps solely) through film, and so audiences are prepared, even eager, for further on-screen encounters with Dickens.

Dickens and Early Cinema: The Silent Era

As Joss Marsh notes in this volume, from its very beginnings, cinematising Dickens was a global enterprise.[9] Having been translated into multiple languages and adapted to stages across Europe, Dickens's novels – their characters and plots – were recognisable in areas outside the English-speaking world, and filmmakers could count on their audiences' interest in – if not always first-hand knowledge of – Dickens. With their exaggerated physical markers, Dickens's characters were easily identifiable when they were relocated from the illustrated page to the moving screen, and the novels' strongly melodramatic situations were readily translated into the episodic, pictorial language of early cinema.[10]

Graham Petrie estimates that around a hundred film adaptations of Dickens were produced between 1897 and 1927, and though most of these were American or British productions, there were at least fifteen silent films produced in continental Europe in this period. These films included a Russian (1915) and French (1920) *Cricket on the Hearth*, an Italian *Old Curiosity Shop* (1922), a German *Little Dorrit* (1917), and French (1910), German (1920) and Hungarian (1919) *Oliver Twists*.[11] Condensing their originary novels into a few select scenes, these films, with running times averaging less than an hour, constructed complete, self-contained stories around a set of connected episodes or groups of affiliated major characters. Quite often, the episodes and characters selected for presentation on the silent screen were identical to those that had been most frequently selected for stage dramatisation: when it came to the what and the how of adapting material from Dickens, the early cinema owed an enormous debt to theatrical dramatisations.[12]

In the 1920s, Danish production company Nordisk produced four full-length films drawn from Dickens: *Great Expectations* (1922), *Our Mutual Friend* (1921), *David Copperfield* (1922) and *Little Dorrit* (1924). Directed by A. W. Sandberg and intended primarily for foreign markets, the Nordisk films were meant to challenge the British and American studios that dominated the Dickens-based film industry. The Nordisk films, which Petrie describes as constrained by their 'excessive respect for the original text', relied, to an unusually heavy extent, on dialogic and explanatory intertitles: with between 200 and 450 title cards, fully a third of each film might be taken up by textual clarification. In consequence, the Nordisk films seem little more than an 'endless succession of tableau-like scenes, highlighting major incidents in the story and introduced and explained by lengthy titles'.[13] Perhaps for this reason, the Nordisk films, despite their broad international release, were neither critically nor financially successful.[14]

Aside from the ingenious work of Charlie Chaplin, whose films took a creatively freer approach to remediating Dickens, most film adaptations of the silent era celebrated their faithfulness to their literary origins.[15] In the sound era that followed, a period that witnessed a boom in adaptations of Dickens, claims to textual fidelity formed the cornerstone of advertising campaigns that promoted the extent to which films were true to their literary sources, by which was meant the extent to which they retained the words of the author. This focus on the retention of originary language would come to define the fundamental aim of literary adaptation, and a film's fidelity to its self-acknowledged literary source would be taken as the most important measure of its quality. This fidelity standard would inform the production and reception of film adaptations for most of the twentieth century.[16] Recently, the push against the constraints imposed by fidelity criticism has given filmmakers wider latitude in adapting literary 'classics' with a more interventional and innovative eye, producing adaptations that reinterpret and repurpose Dickens, allowing his novels to speak with an updated voice inflected by diverse cultural dialects.

Around the World with *Oliver Twist*

From the silent *The Kid* (1921) to the orchestral *August Rush* (2007), *Oliver Twist* has appeared in a surprising array of cinematic guises. Of Dickens's oeuvre, only *A Christmas Carol* has inspired more adaptations, appropriations and allusions than

Oliver Twist, and as Juliet John has observed, this active cultural (re-)production has made *Oliver Twist* a powerful culture-text that, untethered from its authorial mast, circulates freely within the wider culture.[17] These adaptations frequently mobilise the novel's radical political energies.[18] *Oliver Twist* offers a frame that can help make visible the plight of children in difficult circumstances, as in Joost Vandebrug's 2018 documentary investigation of a community of children living in Bucharest's sewers under the Fagin-esque guidance of a man named Bruce Lee. In their own ways, films such as *Twist* (2003) and *Boy Called Twist* (2004) update and translocate Dickens's novel to speak to contemporary social issues such as homelessness, prostitution, child exploitation, substance abuse and the HIV pandemic.[19] Among the more than twenty film versions in existence, two dominate the cultural memory: David Lean's iconic 1948 film and Carol Reed's *Oliver!* (1968), adapted from the stage musical.[20] As we will see, more than half a century on, filmmakers continue to engage with *Oliver Twist* via these two classic cinematic renderings, which have become originaries in their own right, arguably as canonical and culturally significant as the novel they adapt.[21]

Polish director Roman Polanski claims he wanted to make a 'children's' version of Dickens's novel; however, with images of London derived from Gustave Doré's prints and subtle suggestions of paedophilia and homosexuality, his *Oliver Twist* (2005) appears to take its cues primarily from David Lean's darker vision of the novel.[22] The lively and light-hearted musical score of Polanski's film arguably offers a redemptive tonal counterbalance.[23]

Oliver Twist seemed a natural choice for Polanski, who grew up in the Kraków ghetto and was left an orphan at age eight when his parents were sent to a concentration camp.[24] In interviews, Polanski noted that he, like Oliver, had been an orphan, familiar with confinement, exhaustion and hunger.[25] On its release Polanski's *Oliver Twist* was generally viewed as an adaptation with a strongly autobiographical turn; however, most critics seemed disappointed by the director's impersonal treatment of the story, lamenting the film's lack of dramatic, emotional impact. Polanski's film ends with Oliver's visit to Fagin in his cell. Awaiting execution, Fagin is mentally distressed, and Oliver offers a prayer for him. Perhaps it is here, in this sombre final scene, that we can find the autobiographical echo critics have persistently looked for in the film, for the fugitive director's identification may not be with the orphan, whose childhood seems so like his own, but with the convicted criminal. Fagin, awaiting a final act of justice he would rather avoid, might be taken as a figure for Polanski himself, who escaped imprisonment in the USA for crimes against a child, a run from justice that led to thirty years' exile in Europe.[26] This personal resonance with the character may partly account for Polanski's efforts to redeem Fagin by counterbalancing his criminality with an acknowledgement of his humanity: though he takes advantage of the orphan boys, he appears to care for them on some level and at least offers them a family, of sorts, and a refuge from the streets.[27]

This somewhat sympathetic treatment of Fagin is also evident in *Twist* (2003), which transports Dickens's story from London to Toronto. Directed by Jacob Tierney, *Twist* may have been inspired by Seth Michael Donsky's *Twisted* (1996), an 'updated' American *Oliver Twist* that reimagined the boys of Fagin's gang as queer hustlers and drug addicts struggling to survive on the streets of New York. The rough criminal/sexual underworld of *Twist* explores what James Kincaid describes as the homoerotic, paedophilic and violent 'urban nightmare' world that Dickens's Oliver has always inhabited.[28] In Tierney's film, a naively innocent young Oliver falls for the emotionally troubled and drug-addicted Dodge, a hustler working for Fagin under the direction of an invisibly off-screen – yet menacing – Bill Sikes. With his curly locks and knotted scarf, *Twist*'s Oliver might be David Lean's orphan at adolescence.

Sexually abused by his father – and, later, brother – *Twist*'s Dodge has become a hardened boy of the streets, well beyond any possibility of redemption. Near the end of the film, Dodge kills Sikes, and as the camera focuses on Dodge's cold, emotionless face, we see how life on the streets has eroded his humanity. The film's closing shot echoes its opening scene, establishing a grim similarity between Dodge and Oliver. In this final moment, Oliver, turning a trick, stares vacantly into the camera, his blank face bespeaking the film's haunting final message about the inescapability of the emotionally eviscerating effects of this urban sexual underworld. There is no suggestion of salvation for *Twist*'s Oliver; there is no lost family waiting to rescue him. But then, as Dodge's backstory shows, in this world the family home offers no refuge from the brutality of the city streets. The hopeless, sexualised world of *Twist* follows the line of James Kincaid's reading of the novel, which sees the Brownlow/Maylie world of the family as not so distant from Fagin's 'criminal world of child-molesting'.[29] In keeping with such a reading, the visual parallels of the first and final scenes of *Twist* suggest that there is no real refuge in a world in which families and criminal gangs similarly traffic in sexual exploitation.

Filmed half a world away but appearing just a year after *Twist*, Tim Greene's *Boy Called Twist* (2004) relocates *Oliver Twist* to Cape Town, where Africa's AIDS epidemic has created a new generation of orphans.[30] *Boy Called Twist* reflects the political aesthetics of modern African cinema, which pushes against colonialist discourses whenever it seeks to adapt canonical Western literature.[31] As Danny Boyle would do in filming *Slumdog Millionaire* (2008), Green cast real-life street kids in order to provide an authentic representation of the solidarity and fraternity of a gang of children struggling to transcend the harsh realities of life in an unforgivingly racially divided country. Like Polanski, who acknowledges Fagin's role as saviour of the abandoned boys, Greene shows how the gang offers Oliver his first taste of freedom, a liberation that is echoed by the film's spacious South African setting which stands in stark contrast to the dark, almost claustrophobic environment of Dickens's novel.[32] Like so many other cinematic adaptions of *Oliver Twist*, Greene's film follows closely in the footsteps of David Lean, acknowledging – and reinforcing – Hollywood's domination of the modern Dickens industry, especially in areas where literary content is more often accessed via the screen than the page.

A less textually faithful transposition, the Dardenne Brothers' film *The Kid with a Bike* ((*Le Gamin au vélo*) 2011) intersects in significant ways with *Oliver Twist*, rearranging the deconstructed elements it quietly but unmistakably borrows from a literary wellspring it refrains from naming. In a review that reveals a sense of what Dickens *is* for modern audiences, Nigel Andrews says *The Kid with a Bike* is 'so Dickensian, [s]o like a fairy tale, with social grit tucked inside its gleaming oyster shell'. He posits that modern filmmakers like the Dardenne Brothers are drawn to Dickens because his stories offer a blueprint for elemental storytelling and a formula for energising realism with an infusion of fantasy.[33]

A ward of the state, Cyril, the 'kid' of the title, is determined to find both his absent father and his missing bike. Cyril meets Samantha, a hairdresser, who becomes his weekend guardian and later arranges a reunion between Cyril and his father, whose brutal rejection makes Cyril easy prey for Wesker, a drug dealer and street thief who quickly wins Cyril's trust and enlists his help in staging an assault and robbery against the local newsagent. As soon as the crime is done, Wesker takes the stolen money and turns his back on Cyril. Seeking revenge, the newsagent's son attacks Cyril in the woods. Closing on a shot of Cyril limping quietly away, the film ends without certain closure, though one imagines Cyril will finally find stability within Samantha's emotionally supportive home.

Wesker (Wes) is the film's most obvious nod to Dickens. A teenage leader of a gang of neighbourhood thugs, Wes bears some resemblance to Fagin: finding a boy on the streets, Wes offers him friendship and takes him home, filling the boy's need to connect with a father figure while training him, as if a game, to be a thief. The quiet and unsettling suggestion of paedophilia that hovers about Dickens's Fagin hovers here as well, as Wes takes Cyril into his bedroom and offers him alcohol while the two sit side by side on Wes's bed playing video games.[34] Unlike the fantastically angelic Oliver commonly seen in most film adaptations, Cyril is an emotionally troubled child with a deep well of anger ever ready to erupt in violence, and this, combined with a desperate longing to find paternal affection and acceptance, makes him easy prey for a confident con artist like Wes. Though he is visibly anxious about robbing the newsagent, Cyril's desire for a paternal figure is so powerful that he is willing to do anything that will secure Wes's approval. It is no accident that in the course of the robbery Cyril smashes the skulls of a father and son, an assault that we might read as a lashing out in anger against a family connection that seems to be denied him.

Wesker, like Fagin, stands as a stark reminder of the very real dangers that lurk beyond the safe circle of the family, waiting to prey on the most vulnerable children. But he is also a fairy-tale figure, conjured up from the darker recesses of the cultural imagination. Anthony Lane likens the bit of wilderness where Cyril discovers Wes's gang to the dark forest of fairy tales, where innocence is assaulted and virtue is tried.[35] In this characterisation, Wes, like Fagin, is the Big Bad Wolf, flattering and seducing the lone child who has ventured into the wider world in a search for family. Cyril's red shirts, as Lane notes, are emblems of the anger he harbours, but they also visually connect him to Little Red Riding Hood, another child who falls victim to vulpine seduction in a forest. These fairy-tale elements suggest that the Dardenne Brothers were accessing Dickens by way of Roman Polanski, who rendered *Oliver Twist* in fairy-tale colours of blues, greens and reds, 'a darkly hirsute Sikes (Jamie Foreman) reminiscent of a big bad wolf and Ben Kingsley as Fagin, beneath his layers of prosthetics, resembling some kind of hobgoblin'.[36] Where Polanski's detailed physical set suggests an impulse towards realism, however, the colours, lighting and costuming of *The Kid with a Bike* resituates this take on *Oliver Twist* within the world of the fairy tale.

Appropriating Pip: *Great Expectations* in Asia and Oceania

A story of identity and development, of desired and unwanted affiliations, of grappling with the traumatic legacies of the past and of forging a new future, *Great Expectations* (1860–1) is teeming with potential political resonance, particularly for countries that grew up under the influence of colonialism. Pip's story can be easily refigured as an allegory of postcolonial political awakening: brought up 'by hand' under an unrelentingly disciplinarian order dedicated to the removal of all traces of savage 'wicious'-ness, the orphaned boy seeks to overcome the traumas of his severed lineage and of the brutality of the regime under which he developed by embracing an aspirational, escapist future for himself. Forging new social connections, the orphan recreates himself in the (Western, capitalist) image of the gentleman. In due course, he discovers that this morally problematic path of progress was, in the end, not properly his.[37] Thus enlightened, he is able to escape the web of expectations that had entrapped him, and from the seeds of his experience springs the promise of a better future. Viewed in this way, Pip's story patterns the paradigmatic developmental trajectory of non-Western nations that have fought to free themselves from the cultural and political domination of Western imperialist powers.[38] Thus has *Great Expectations*, the paradigmatic English Bildungsroman that had served as a cultural implement of Western domination, been appropriated in the service of postcolonial political agendas.

Filmed in Hong Kong and starring Bruce Lee as young Frank (the Pip figure), *An Orphan's Tragedy* ((*Gu Xin Xue Li*) 1955) was shaped by Hong Kong's triangulated relationship with Great Britain and China in the 1950s.[39] While the decision to adapt Dickens reflected and reinforced Hong Kong's colonial cultural identifications with Britain, the film's treatment of its source material was undoubtedly influenced by the changing political relationship between Hong Kong and mainland China: the film's celebration of the values of traditional communities is consistent with the ideological focus of the diasporic Chinese cinema that was developing in the mid-1950s, while its critique of modern, individualistic capitalist greed suggests the lingering influence of mainland filmmakers and their efforts to infuse Hong Kong films with nationalist Chinese politics.[40]

Aside from the suggestively named character 'Dickson Fan', a sly nod in the direction of its textual source, if not its chief intended audience (i.e. 'Dickens Fans'), *An Orphan's Tragedy* does not overtly signal its debt to Dickens, a citational omission that may reflect the film's strongly revisionary approach to its textual source, which is, unmistakably, *Great Expectations*.[41]

Translations of Dickens's novels were available in East Asia as early as 1897, but even if they had never read the novel that inspired it, the film's audiences might have recognised the story from David Lean's iconic *Great Expectations*, which had been shown in Hong Kong in 1948 (followed by the publication of a 'book of the film' in Cantonese).[42] The film's opening scene – which shows a lost woman collapsing on the street before giving birth and then dying – is most certainly borrowed from Lean's *Oliver Twist* (1948), further evidence that *An Orphan's Tragedy* engages Dickens by way of cinematic intermediaries that may, in fact, have formed its own audiences' primary means of accessing British literature.[43]

The novel's Pip becomes the film's Frank, born an orphan and raised by the village blacksmith. Alone in the forest at night, Frank encounters an escaped convict, Dickson Fan, who quickly realises that Frank is his lost son. Without divulging their relationship, Fan advises Frank to go to school to study medicine so that he can help the poor. Frank laments he has no money for school, laying the groundwork for Fan's efforts to become the boy's secret supporter. Years later, having received a scholarship sponsored by an anonymous donor, Frank goes to the city in search of an education.

Everyone believes Dr Toh, the director of the local hospital, must be Frank's mysterious patron, his generous support meant to transform Frank into a suitable match for his daughter, Rainbow. Seduced by the flashy, utterly false world of Dr Toh and his daughter Rainbow, the film's colourful and glammed-up take on Estella, Frank is led astray. He forgets the selfless values of the village in which he grew up; he turns away from his surrogate father, the village blacksmith; and he forsakes the love of Polly, the film's version of Biddy, a sweet village girl who spends much of the film singing about the virtues of hard work. In the end, Dr Toh's offer to set Frank up as the manager of a pharmacy in the city turns out to be the evil doctor's plot to entangle an unwitting Frank in a scheme involving the sale of counterfeit medicines. When this plot is discovered, Frank's long-lost father Fan returns to challenge Dr Toh. The two fight, and Toh is killed. Fan then dies in Frank's arms as the screen fades to black.

Where readers of Dickens expect to find Miss Havisham we encounter, instead, Dr Toh, whose villainous scheme to sell counterfeit drugs has increased his wealth while endangering the health of the local population. There is nothing subtle about Dr Toh: he is every inch the melodramatic villain, scheming, lying, surrounded by spies and toadies. Unlike Miss Havisham, Dr Toh presents us with no psychological mystery, no chilling backstory, and no Gothic darkness. He is a straightforward cinematic bad guy whose only motives seem to be the eradication of his enemy, the amassing of more wealth, and the consolidation of his power.[44]

Having been tempted away from his village by Toh's promises of fortune in the city, Frank comes to understand, by the end of the film, that there is no shame in poverty, but there is honour in honest, hard work. His eyes opened to the false doctrine of individuality preached by Dr Toh, Frank learns that truly great doctors do not just treat the privileged few: they serve their entire community. The film's didactic message reflects the reputation Dickens enjoyed among Chinese critics: that is, as a writer sympathetic to the working classes. When David Lean's *Great Expectations* was screened in China, the press called attention to the film's exposure of the cruelty and selfishness of the upper classes and the elusiveness of love and happiness under Western capitalism.[45] *An Orphan's Tragedy* extends this reading of *Great Expectations* as a text that endorses communal service over individual self-interest.[46] Through this cultural relocation, Dickens's novel is revised by its cinematic intertext.[47]

This effort to, in Leitch's terms, 'revise' or 'colonise' Dickens also informs the Indian film *Fitoor* (2016).[48] Directed by Abhishek Kapoor, *Fitoor* translocates *Great Expectations* to Kashmir, where it turns Dickens's tale to nationalist political purpose. Where most filmmakers follow the footsteps of David Lean in transposing Dickens to the screen, *Fitoor* draws heavily upon Mexican director Alfonso Cuarón's *Great Expectations* (1998). In the first scene, a young boy, Noor, is walking alone by the lake when a man, Moazam, emerges from the water to grab him. This scene strongly recalls the opening scene of Cuarón's film, which has Arthur Lustig (the Magwitch figure) rise from the waters of the Gulf to grab Finn (Pip). The decision to make Noor, like Finn, an artist is further evidence that Kapoor's retelling of *Great Expectations* was inspired by Cuarón's. Noor, like Finn, obsessively paints portraits of the girl he claims to love, though he cannot stop objectifying her. Just as Lustig arranges for Finn to have money and a New York studio, eventually ensuring Finn's 'success' by buying all of his paintings, so too does Noor discover that it was Moazam who set him up with an art scholarship and who has purchased all of his work. As

380   MARTY GOULD

Begum Hazrat Jahaan, Indian actress Tabu invokes the spectre of Anne Bancroft in her interpretation of the Miss Havisham character: like Nora Dinsmoor, Jahaan smokes, moves seductively, travels to New York and even dyes her hair red. If *Fitoor* delivers a Bollywood *Great Expectations*, it does so by way of Cuarón's distinctively Hollywood version.

Even as it borrows American cultural references, *Fitoor* mobilises its Dickensian source materials in the service of a political agenda involving Kashmir's status in relation to India and Pakistan, taking advantage of the allegorical potential of the key relationships in Dickens's novel. Most of the film's political mileage comes from its central romantic triangle: Firdaus's (Estella's) struggle to choose between Noor (Pip), with whom she shares a long history, and Bilal (Drummle), a Pakistani diplomat, almost begs to be read as a representation of Kashmir's position in the tug of war between India and Pakistan. In the end, Firdaus chooses Noor over Bilal, an ending which may endorse Kashmiri independence. At the very least the film's ending disavows terrorism and political violence, a message made most clear where Kapoor departs from Cuarón in his handling of the final meeting between Pip and Magwitch. In Cuarón's film, Finn embraces Lustig as he dies, comforting him in his final moments. *Fitoor* offers no such comfort to its Magwitch figure, Moazam, who is violently rejected by Noor, a rejection that severs the ties between the two men. Only once he is freed from the militant's influence can Noor become a suitable match for Firdaus, similarly liberated from both Jahaan and Bilal. This celebration of freedom is prefigured in an earlier scene, in which Noor uses his new fortune to buy a car. Having spent his childhood being carried in the backseat of Jahaan's Mercedes, Noor becomes the one who determines his own destination.

At the heart of New Zealand novelist Lloyd Jones's novel *Mister Pip* (2006) is a story about how literary characters become a part of our cultural memory and how our experiences are filtered through the texts we share.[49] If Jones's novel is an object lesson in adaptation – how active readerly engagement transforms static texts into portable cultural property – Adamson's film adaptation, *Mr. Pip* (2012), refines that message, taking Jones's novel and Dickens's *Great Expectations* as raw materials from which it constructs something new, something that engages with – but does not seek fully to reproduce – its narrative sources and cinematic predecessors.[50] *Mr. Pip* explores an active form of literacy that figures literary texts as structures through which readers can frame their own life experiences and understand their cultural histories. Matilda and her classmates have access to *Great Expectations* indirectly, first through Mr Watts's abbreviated and altered version and then via their own recreation of the lost text. And it is this multiply adapted, multiply recreated story that grabs imaginative hold over Matilda and that ultimately offers her – in the film – means first to escape and then to return, forming and reforming herself in the process. An adaptation of an adaptation, *Mr. Pip* alters its own immediate source text in order to address the postcolonialist criticism that Jones's novel reinscribes the hegemony of the white, Western literary canon.

Where Jones's novel leaves open the question of whether Matilda manages to return home, succeeding where Pip had failed, the film closes on a picture of Matilda, with her father, walking along Bougainville's beach, near the spot where her shrine to Pip – the inscription that caused so much trouble for her and her village – had stood. The film thus 'fixes' both its originary texts, offering a recuperative closure – the protagonist's

GLOBAL CINEMA 381

successful return home – that they withhold. But Matilda does not simply return to live on Bougainville: like Frank in *An Orphan's Tragedy*, who becomes a doctor who will serve his whole community, Matilda returns to her village in the role of teacher. If Jones's novel concludes with an image of Matilda alone and isolated from any community, Adamson's film closes on the image of communal reintegration.

Crafting a personal biography that interweaves her own experiences with British literature and local folklore, Matilda becomes the emblem for a heterogeneous globalised identity that displaces the traditional centre–periphery binary of postcolonialism.[51] In this way, *Great Expectations* becomes a liberating fiction, transportable and adaptable to multiple cultural environments, the raw material for forging new narratives that address emerging social challenges in diverse locations.

Stylish Fidelity: Botelho and Virzì

Filmed in black and white, João Botelho's *Tempos Difíceis* (1988) captures the dark, moody, melodramatic tones of *Hard Times* (1854) while also approximating the visual texture of silent film.[52] The gritty industrial landscape of the town of World's End visually renders Dickens's stark prose description of Coketown, while the sharply reduced role of Sleary's circus removes most of the originary novel's light comedy, leaving us with scenes dominated by darkness and shadow, as if the characters are moving through a grey Gradgrindian world of fact.[53]

With its contemporary setting, *Tempos Difíceis* casts a cold eye on the mechanical nature of life in the modern city. This is a world in which a good-hearted, hardworking man like Sebastião (Stephen Blackpool) is unceremoniously crushed in the street by a truck, a helpless victim of unstoppable mechanised progress. Among the looming chimneys of the smoky skyline we might almost expect to see the giant clock that opens Charlie Chaplin's *Modern Times* (1936), another Dickens-inspired film obsessed with the industrialisation of time and the mechanical dehumanisation of the modern world. The people of World's End live side by side, but they are separated by the walls of social class and the divisions wrought by the absence of empathy in this industrial world, where time itself is an inescapable mechanical force grinding mercilessly against its inhabitants.[54] In one scene, Tomazhino (Tom) refuses to punch his time card at the factory, an arrogant but pointless attempt to escape the disciplinary surveillance of the industrial system that rules the city. In another scene, Luisa (Louisa) tries to talk her way out of her engagement, but the steady ticking of the clock in the background is a stark reminder that her time is running out.

As the wedding preparations are made, the screen fills with images of factories and smoking chimneys that structurally resemble the spires of the church to which they finally give way, a visual reminder that, in this modern world, marriage – perhaps love itself – is a soulless production. At the end of the film, Cecilia (Sissy) and Luisa gaze out onto an open agricultural landscape. Cecilia asks if Luisa is happy. The camera centres on Luisa's stony white face, her silent stare closing the film with a haunting condemnation of a world in which happiness is not available.[55] This is, indeed, *Hard Times* for these times.

The Dickens of Botelho's *Hard Times* is the stark realist, the unflinching investigator of modern urban life, the outspoken critic of social injustice. But there is another Dickens: the cleverly humorous, wryly observant and autobiographically inspired Dickens, and this is the Dickens that Italian director Paolo Virzì captures in *Ovosodo* (1997).[56] Emiliano Dominici argues that *Ovosodo* is indebted to *Great Expectations*: the film's protagonist, Piero, is, like Pip, an orphan who longs to escape into a better life.[57] Both Piero and Pip neglect their families and friends as they move into a new social orbit, and both experience a reversal of fortunes. Yet, while *Great Expectations* is directly cited at the end of the film, when Piero reads aloud from that novel, *Ovosodo* also engages with *David Copperfield*: like *Copperfield*, *Ovosodo* is a Bildungsroman narrated by its protagonist, who begins with a recollection of his own birth. Piero, like David, becomes a writer and aspires to membership in a higher social class. Born to a wealthy family and wielding his privilege with casual ease, Piero's friend Tommaso is, surely, Steerforth. Worlds tragically collide when Piero introduces his clever, confident friend to his former teacher, Giovanna, a Little Em'ly-like figure who has encouraged Piero's development and functioned as a sort of refuge from the harder realities of his life. Giovanna suffers an emotional breakdown as a consequence of Tommaso's unwanted sexual advances and is confined to an institution before finally committing suicide. Piero, like Copperfield, struggles to come to terms with the emotionally destructive arrogance of the young man he so admires, ultimately deciding it best to forge his own independent path into adulthood.

Although much of its plot is inspired by *David Copperfield*, *Great Expectations* is the novel that the film directly cites: Piero, working in the factory owned by Tomasso's father, entertains his co-workers by retelling them Pip's story.[58] Piero falls for Tomasso's cousin who, like Estella, refuses to return his affections and ends up with another man. Battered but not broken, Piero makes a happy ending for himself, marrying a young woman from his childhood. He earns his diploma, has a job and family, and seems happy. Like Pip, he works hard, and so may be said to be successful. In the end, *Ovosodo* is, strictly speaking, not exactly or entirely an adaptation of either *Great Expectations* or *David Copperfield*, though it unmistakably engages with both novels in multiple, meaningful ways.

Balancing realism with humour, *Ovosodo* does not simply borrow Dickens's plots but also his techniques. Indeed, the film invites its audience to consider the fuller extent of its debts to Dickens. Piero's teacher reads his essay aloud in class so that classmates can see 'what it means for a writer to combine the creativity of a novel with realism of description; that is to combine the fun of story-telling with life's dramatic reality, just like Dickens, Mark Twain and Salinger'. Extending the relevance of Dickens beyond the realm of nineteenth-century literature the film points to Dickens's enduring relevance to the artistic aims of modern cinema, which may, like *Ovosodo*, follow in the tradition of Dickens to tell stories both realistic and inventive, with situations and characters recognisably Dickensian yet creatively reconfigured to reflect fresh artistic aims and to speak to new social issues across diverse cultural contexts.

Notes

Research for this essay was supported by a Marie Curie Fellowship, under the sponsorship of Brunel University.

1. See Michael Pointer, *Charles Dickens on the Screen: The Film, Television, and Video Adaptations* (London: Scarecrow, 1996).

GLOBAL CINEMA

2. Paul Davis, *The Lives and Times of Ebenezer Scrooge* (New Haven: Yale University Press, 1990), 4. On *Oliver Twist* as a culture-text, see Juliet John, *Dickens and Mass Culture* (Oxford: Oxford University Press, 2010), 211–14.

3. *Fitoor*, dir. by Abishek Kapoor (UTV Motion Pictures, 2016). *Great Expectations*, dir. by Alfonso Cuarón (20th Century Fox, 1998). *Oliver Twist*, dir. by Roman Polanski (20th Century Fox, 2005). *Great Expectations*, dir. by David Lean (Cineguild, 1946). *Oliver!*, dir. by Carol Reed (Romulus Films, 1968).

4. Chris Louttit, 'Dickens, David Lean, and After: Twenty-First Century Adaptations of *Oliver Twist*', *Cahiers victoriens et édouardiens* (2012), 91–104, 91–5.

5. Thomas Leitch, *Film Adaptation and Its Discontents* (Baltimore: Johns Hopkins University Press, 2007), 93–126.

6. Alessandro Vescovi, 'Dickens's "The Signalman" and Rubini's *La Stazione*', in *Dickens on Screen*, ed. by John Glavin (Cambridge: Cambridge University Press, 2003), 53–60.

7. *The Kid with a Bike*, dir. by the Dardenne Brothers (Artificial Eye, 2011). *The Kid*, dir. by Charlie Chaplin (Charlie Chaplin Productions, 1921).

8. Deborah Cartmell, *Adaptations in the Sound Era, 1927–37* (London: Bloomsbury, 2015), 56–7; John, 187–97; Martin Meisel, *Realizations: Narrative, Pictorial, and Theatrical Arts in Nineteenth-Century England* (Princeton: Princeton University Press, 1983), 62–3.

9. Cartmell argues that the advent of 'sound brought with it a loss to cinema's global language' (22).

10. For a discussion of the development of early cinema in relation to theatrical history and practice, see Nicholas Vardac, *Stage to Screen: Theatrical Method from Garrick to Griffith* (Cambridge, MA: Harvard University Press, 1949), in particular chs 2, 3, 6 and 8.

11. Graham Petrie, 'Silent Film Adaptations of Dickens. Part I: From the Beginnings to 1911', *Dickensian* 453 (Spring 2001), 7–21, 7–8, 15–16; Pointer, 38–42.

12. Rick Altman, 'Dickens, Griffith, and Film Theory Today', in *Silent Film*, ed. by Richard Abel (Brunswick: Rutgers University Press, 1996), 145–8.

13. Graham Petrie, 'Dickens in Denmark: Four Danish Versions of His Novels', *Journal of European Studies*, 26.2 (June 1996), 185–93. For summaries of these films, see Graham Petrie, 'Silent Film Adaptations of Dickens. Part III: 1920–1927', *Dickensian* 97 (2001), 197–214, 203–10.

14. Mary Hammond, *Charles Dickens's* Great Expectations: *A Cultural Life, 1860–2012* (Farnham: Ashgate, 2015), 93–6.

15. Garrett Stewart, 'Modern *Hard Times*: Chaplin and the Cinema of Self-Reflection', *Critical Inquiry* 3.2 (Winter 1976), 295–314; Joss Marsh, 'The Tramp, the Jew, and the Kid', *Early Popular Visual Culture* 8.3 (August 2010), 315–35.

16. Cartmell, 1, 61–3.

17. Davis, 4; John, 236.

18. John, 210–13.

19. *Bruce Lee and the Outlaw*, dir. Joost Vandebrug (Haiduc Films, 2018). *Twist*, dir. by Jacob Tierney (Strand Releasing, 2003). See also Holly Furneaux, '*Boy Called Twist* and the Social Conscience of Dickens Adaptation in the Twenty-First Century', *Peer English* 2 (2007), 143–7.

20. H. Philip Bolton, *Dickens Dramatized* (London: Mansell, 1987), 107.

21. John, 208–14, 228.

22. Mark Cousins, 'Roman Polanski: The Insider', *Sight and Sound* 15.10 (2005), 20, 2224; Louttit, 97–8; Mario Martino, 'Olivers Twisted: Urban Milieu from Text to Media', *Cahiers victoriens et édouardiens* (2012), 105–18, 108–9, 117–18.

23. Philip Kemp, 'Oliver Twist', *Sight and Sound* 15.10 (2005), 80–2; Anthony Lane, 'Hunting Dickens: Roman Polanski's "Oliver Twist"', *The New Yorker* 81.30 (3 October 2005), 10–7.

24. Benjamin Bergey, 'A Boy's Will', *American Cinematographer* 86.9 (2005), 30–41, 31; Cousins.

25. Michel Ciment, 'Entretien avec Roman Polanski: un film pour mes enfants', *Positif* (February 2011), 102–5.

26. Todd McCarthy, '*Oliver Twist*', *Variety* 400.5 (19–25 September 2005), 62. Cousins similarly interprets Polanski's handling of the rape scene in *Tess of the D'Urbervilles* (1979) as a cinematic apology for his past (24).

27. Ciment, 103–4.

28. James Kincaid, *Child-Loving: The Erotic Child and Victorian Culture* (New York: Routledge, 1992), 389–91.

29. Ibid, 390–91.

30. *Boy Called Twist*, dir. by Tim Greene (Monkey Films, 2004). Ronnie Scheib, '*A Boy Called Twist*', *Variety* 401.10 (23–9 January 2006), 35–6. Louttit, 100–1.

31. Alexie Tcheuyap, 'African Cinema and the Politics of Adaptation', *Post Script* 23.3 (Summer 2004), 36–49.

32. Scheib; Clémence Folléa, 'Persistent Marginality: Deviance as a Travelling Aesthetic', *Études anglaises* 65 (2012), 43–53, 46–8.

33. Nigel Andrews, 'Dardennes' Brighter New World', *Financial Times* (22 March 2012) <https://www.ft.com/content/05260724-740c-11e1-bcec-00144feab49a> [accessed 1 June 2017].

34. Many scholars have pointed to the (racialised) hints of sexual deviance in Fagin's lair. See, for example, John Gordon, *Sensation and Sublimation in Dickens* (New York: Palgrave, 2011), 8–9; and Liora Brosh, *Screening Novel Women: From British Domestic Fiction to Film* (Basingstoke: Palgrave, 2008), 89–91.

35. Anthony Lane, 'Not Child's Play: "The Kid with a Bike" and "Detachment"', *The New Yorker* 88.5 (19 March 2012), 90–1.

36. Benjamin Poore, '"I have been true to you, upon my guilty soul I have!": Negotiating Nancy, "Hyperauthenticity" and "Hyperfidelity" in the 2007 BBC Adaptation of *Oliver Twist*', *Journal of Adaptation in Film and Performance* 3.2 (2010), 157–70, 163.

37. Hana Wirth-Nesher, 'The Literary Orphan as National Hero: Huck and Pip', *Dickens Studies Annual* 15 (1986), 259–73.

38. Neil Lazarus, 'Great Expectations and After: The Politics of Postcolonialism in African Fiction', *Social Text* 13/14 (1986), 49–57.

39. In 1958, shortly before moving to the USA, Bruce Lee starred in *Gu Hong* (The Orphan), an adaptation of *Oliver Twist*.

40. Yingchi Chu, *Hong Kong Cinema: Coloniser, Motherland, and Self* (London: Routledge, 2003), 11–14, 30–5.

41. *An Orphan's Tragedy*, dir. by Ji Zhu (Cinema Epoch, 1955).

42. Kay Li, 'Dickens and China: Contextual Interchanges in Cultural Globalization', *Dickens Studies Annual* 37 (2006), 119–21; Paul Fonoroff, 'Art House: *An Orphan's Tragedy* Takes a Dickensian Twist', *South China Morning Post*, 19 September 2013, <http://www.scmp.com/magazines/48hrs/article/1309116/art-house-orphans-tragedy-takes-dickensian-twist> [accessed 1 June 2017]; Hammond, 169.

43. Louttit, 91–2.

44. Fonoroff.

45. Ting Guo, 'Dickens on the Chinese Screen', *Literature Compass* 8/10 (2011), 802.

46. Guo, 799; Li, 123–9.

47. Dennis Cutchins, 'Bakhtin, Intertextuality, and Adaptation', *The Oxford Handbook of Adaptation Studies*, ed. by Thomas Leitch (Oxford: Oxford University Press, 2017), 74–80.

48. Leitch, 106–11.

GLOBAL CINEMA

49. Annegret Maack, 'Variations on Dickens's *Great Expectations*: Lloyd Jones's *Mr. Pip*', *Zeitschrift für Anglistik und Amerikanistik* 57.4 (2009), 327–38.
50. Dana Schiller, 'The Pleasures and Limits of Dickensian Plot: or "I have met Mr. Dickens, and this is not him"', *Neo-Victorian Studies* 5.2 (2012), 84–103, 94–8; Jennifer Gribble, 'Portable Property: Postcolonial Appropriations of *Great Expectations*', in *Victorian Turns, Neo-Victorian Returns: Essays on Fiction and Culture*, ed. by Penny Gay and Judith Johnston (Cambridge: Cambridge Scholars, 2009), 182–92, 186–7; Linda Hutcheon, *A Theory of Adaptation*, 2nd edn (London: Routledge, 2013), 63–92.
51. Schiller, 98.
52. *Tempos Difíceis*, dir. by João Botelho (Artificial Eye, 1988). Grahame Smith, 'Dickens in Film', in *The Reception of Charles Dickens in Europe*, ed. by Michael Hollington, 2 vols (London: Bloomsbury, 2013), II, 589–94, 591–3.
53. Alan Stanbrook, '*Hard Times* for Portuguese Cinema', *Sight and Sound* 58.2 (Spring 1989), 118–22.
54. Jean A. Gili, 'A Finistère of Feelings', *Positif* 341/342 (July 1989), 115–16.
55. Stanbrook, 120.
56. *Ovosodo*, dir. by Paolo Virzì (Cecchi Gori, 1997).
57. Emiliano Dominici, 'A Low Degree of Transposition: From *Great Expectations* to Paolo Virzì's Film *Ovosodo*', in *Dickens: The Craft of Fiction and the Challenges of Reading*, ed. by Rossana Bonadel, Clotilde de Stasio, Carlo Pagetti and Alessandro Vescovi (Milan: Edizioni Unicopli, 2000), 343–50.
58. Vescovi, 53.

Further Reading

Michael Hollington, ed., *The Reception of Charles Dickens in Europe*, 2 vols (London: Bloomsbury, 2013)

Juliet John, '*Oliver Twist* on Screen', in *Dickens and Mass Culture* (Oxford: Oxford University Press, 2010), 207–39

John O. Jordan, 'Global Dickens', *Literature Compass* 6.6 (2009), 1211–23

Part VI

National and International Dickens

25

TRANSLATIONS

Klaudia Hiu Yen Lee

IN THE PREFACE TO THE 1857 French edition of *The Old Curiosity Shop* (1840–1), *Le Magasin d'antiquités*, Charles Dickens laments the widespread circulation of unauthorised translations in France in his 'Address of the English Author to the French Public':

> Hitherto less fortunate in France than in Germany, I have only been known to French readers not thoroughly acquainted with the English language, through occasional, fragmentary and unauthorized translations over which I have no control, and from which I have derived no advantage.[1]

The 'advantage' that Dickens mentioned in the Preface refers to the remuneration that he should have received as an author had an international copyright law been put in place. As various critics point out, early French translations of Dickens's works were mostly pirated editions for which the author did not receive any compensation. Setting aside the potential profits that Dickens would have made had the pirated editions been curbed, the fact that, in the Preface to the 1857 authorised, translated version, Dickens foregrounds the 'fragmentary' nature of the unauthorised translations clearly indicates his resentment against the disruption, or violation, of the artistic design of his creative work. Underlying this is his doubt as to whether the one who translated his work could master two languages and 'faithfully' re-render his English writings into another language; this concern is made explicit in his praise of the authorised French edition because the translation is supervised by what he described in the Preface as 'an accomplished gentleman, perfectly acquainted with both languages, and able, with a rare felicity, to be perfectly faithful to the English text, while rendering it in elegant and expressive French'.[2] Dickens's emphasis on faithfulness and the elegance of the prose in the target language remains of much relevance to contemporary discussion on the practice and art of translation, even though contemporary translation scholars have increasingly emphasised the 'cultural' turn in translation studies, in that much emphasis has been put on situating any act of translation practices within the wider socio-cultural contexts.[3] As an author who has been widely noted for his authorial control over not only the linguistic text but also the way it is presented (including publication format, use of illustrations, and material embodiment), Dickens's concerns with the way his texts were re-rendered in another language is unsurprising. Yet it does draw attention to the symbiotic relationship between Dickensian texts and their (authorised and unauthorised) translations, ever since they have been circulated in regions and areas where English is not the dominant, everyday language.

Indeed, the 'global' or international image of Dickens that Victorian studies scholars have recently highlighted cannot be fully understood if one does not take account of various acts of translation that help re-envision Dickens, or Dickensian texts, in specific cultural and historical contexts.[4] In this chapter I aim to explore the complexities of the acts of translation and to demonstrate how the attempt to cross linguistic boundaries can become a means not only to re-render the text in another language but also to interpret and at times, reconceptualise, the artistic vision of the author – in this case Dickens.[5] As a form of textual and creative practice, the translated text often embodies different cultural influences; this is manifested not only in the use of language and the cultural connotations that are associated with it during processes of translation but also in the way in which a translated text is situated within a particular literary tradition or trend at specific moments of cross-cultural transmission. Instead of attempting to give a cursory view of every translated version of Dickens's works that exist in different parts of the globe – an impossible task, not only due to language issues but also the incomplete, scattered nature of records of translations – in this chapter I will develop two case studies of selected translations of *A Christmas Carol* (1843) and *Oliver Twist* (1837–9) in different historic periods in China. I aim to show how acts of translation have the potential to destabilise the concept of a stable 'authorial' text, and in the process open up the text for cultural re-envisioning. Such a process of re-envisioning the text, as I shall also demonstrate, involves a complex negotiation or interaction between source and target cultures, to the extent that sometimes a hybrid form of the Dickensian text may emerge.

The plurality of the concept of 'translation' stems from the multi-layered considerations that one needs to engage with before the text can continue its afterlife in another cultural context. The linguistic choices that the translator makes are by nature comparative, in that she or he consistently needs to carry out the act of comparison in order to come up with the most suitable terms and expressions that can re-render, or at least capture, the essence of the original text, which Walter Benjamin describes as 'the echo'.[6] It can also be understood as a form of 'translingual' practice, a term coined by Lydia Liu to refer to the contact or 'collision' between the guest and host languages during cross-cultural encounters. Such contact or collision, Liu contends, can often lead to the creation of new words, meanings or forms of representation.[7] Indeed, the translation strategy that one ultimately adopts often hinges upon the wider socio-cultural, and sometimes political, conditions at a specific historical moment. It is also often affected by the local publication environment. What complicates this process even further is the possibility of absence in the target culture of the culturally specific scenes, events and values that pertain to the source culture. In *Born Translated: The Contemporary Novel in an Age of World Literature*, Rebecca Walkowitz has demonstrated how contemporary writers choose to use less (local) culture-specific diction and syntax when composing their work in order to make their writing more readily translatable.[8] As a writer who is self-conscious about his 'English-ness', it is highly unlikely, or even unthinkable, that Dickens adjusted his prose style because of his awareness of the foreign book markets, though it is well known that his melodramatic aesthetics and the serial publication format that he pioneered aimed at reaching out to a wider audience. As contrasted with some contemporary writers who chose to adapt their writing styles in order to reach a global audience, Dickens maintained his idiosyncratic prose style, his imaginative use of names (of places and people), and his microscopic and mythic representation of culturally specific space and place.[9] The challenge, then, is for translators to render the very culturally specific text into another language and socio-cultural context. Having an awareness of the complexities of translation practices can help one realise that the image of the author or the idea of the Dickensian text has seldom remained stable. While screen adaptation is obviously another creative practice that complicates the idea of the authorial text, as it involves selection and (re)creation of elements of the original, in this chapter I focus on written texts not only because I want to direct attention to the translation practice itself but also because, as the case of China demonstrates, readers of the target culture often first encountered a foreign author through translated versions of the written texts. Of course, further complicating this process of cross-cultural transfer is the potential change in the material embodiment of the text and the print context in which the work appears. For example, changes in the paratexts, a term which Gérard Genette uses to refer to a 'threshold', or 'a zone between text and off-text', such as subtitles, prefaces and notes, will have the effect of directing the audience's attention to specific elements of the novels, while the larger print context (such as publishing in a political or literary magazine) may influence the way in which a text is understood and read.[10]

The complexities of translation can be gleaned from a short article published in *The British Museum Quarterly* in September 1940 about an artefact described as 'perhaps the most remarkable work in the collection—a Kazak translation of Dr Manette's paper (*The Substance of the Shadow*) from *A Tale of Two Cities*, in the form of a crudely illustrated chapbook'.[11] Although it is only a brief note on this particular translation, it does raise questions to do with content and form: are translations of selected scenes of a novel, republished in a chapbook format, a 'translation' of the original text? To what extent can the translated text be seen as a translated version of the original text or, at least, to capture the essence of the original text? How can the act of reissuing a work in another material embodiment or format influence the reading of the text, or the readers' perception of a particular text, and hence the image or even status of a particular author in a target culture? There are, of course, many more questions than these that one can raise in relation to any translated version of a text. Indeed, in some cases, and as I shall demonstrate in this chapter, the line between translation and adaptation or appropriation could become so blurred that the end product often defies an easy categorisation. Besides, one also needs to realise that, even though the decision to translate a particular author may be a political one – for example, a novel may get translated because it is intended for particular political and social causes – the translator still needs to take account of the aesthetic features and the structure, or the narrative design, of the text in order to render it in a language, and very often in a literary style, which aligns with that of the target culture, so that it is accessible to its target audience. When a leading Chinese writer, translator and critic, Qian Zhongshu, heaped praise on Lin Shu, who was credited with over 180 translations of Western literary works, including those by Dickens, H. Rider Haggard and Sir Walter Scott, it is clear that his compliment is to a large extent due to Lin's own literary style and his flair for narrative art.[12] As Lin himself admitted, he did not know any foreign languages, so what he did was mainly to render his collaborator's oral rendering of a particular novel into classical Chinese, or *wenyan*.[13] As such, Lin's translated works very often become hybrid texts that include not only elements of the authorial texts but also Lin's own reinterpretation and imagination of those texts. Recalling his reading of these translated novels, Qian acknowledged their influence on arousing his interest in learning foreign languages. 'Only after I encountered Lin's translations did I realise how appealing Western fiction was,' Qian wrote, while pointing out how Lin would add, delete or change the original text in order to enhance a particular narrative effect, such as characterisation and plot development.[14] Of course, not all would have agreed with Lin's translation methods especially during and after the May Fourth period, as by then translators started placing more emphasis on faithfulness in translation. In what follows I shall first discuss selected translations of *A Christmas Carol* and *Oliver Twist* in order to explore how the process of translation and the attempt to resituate the text within the target culture could transform, and at times subvert, the 'original' text.[15]

A Christmas Carol in China

A Christmas Carol was first released in a book format in China in 1919 when the novella, which was renamed as *Gui Shi* (literally meaning 'A History of Ghosts'), was 'translated and edited' by Wen Yehe (who in the Preface acknowledged that he turned his friend's oral rendering of the story into Chinese) and published by Dongfu Xiongdi Library.[16] My focus on this translated version is because its publication format most resembles the way in which the novella first appeared in Victorian England during the festive period in 1843. Two earlier translations preceded this one: in 1914 Jing Sheng's translated version of the novella, renamed as *Qian Ren Meng* (A Dream of a Frugal Man), was published in *Xiaoshou Shibao*, a Chinese literary journal set up in 1909; a year later Sun Yuxiu again translated the novella, which was then published in *Xiaoshou Yuebao* (Fiction Monthly). *A Christmas Carol* is one of Dickens's works that have constantly attracted attention from translators and publishers. In 1928, for example, the novella was translated by Xie Songgao and renamed as *San Ling* (Three Spirits), and brought out by the Commercial Press in Shanghai. In 1945, the novella was again translated by another translator, Fang Jing, and named *Sheng Dan Huan Ge* (A Christmas Carol), a translated title that resembled that of the original, English one, and one which has been recurrently used since then (though Mi Xingru and Xie Songgao renamed the novella as *A Christmas Dream* when they translated it in 1950).[17]

In the original Preface to the novella, Dickens clearly explains that the purpose of his composition is to promote the Christmas spirit of charity, humour and benevolence:

> I have endeavoured in this Ghostly little book to raise the Ghost of an Idea which shall not put my readers out of humour with themselves, with each other, with the season, or with me. May it haunt their houses pleasantly, and no one wish to lay it.[18]

The translator's Preface in the 1919 Chinese translation, meanwhile, attempts to situate *A Christmas* Carol within the tradition of *zhiguai* (literally meaning 'narratives of the strange') that was rooted in Chinese literary culture. *Zhiguai* was popularised by Po Songling's famous work, *Liaozhai Zhiyi* (Strange Stories from a Chinese

Studio), which was published in seventeenth-century China. By renaming Dickens's novella as *Gui Shi* (A History of Ghosts), the translator foregrounds the important role that historiography plays in the conceptualisation and development of fiction, a genre that was traditionally seen as *waishi* ('unofficial history') and *yishi* ('leftover history').[19] The Preface also serves as a catalyst for translators to reflect upon the (blurred) boundary between human beings and ghosts, and the moral lessons that such stories may deliver:

> It's impossible to know whether ghosts exist. When people talk about ghosts, it is always from their own imaginations. As such, while they make their stories very strange, they end up not being the truth of ghosts, but just expressing something unlike human beings. Today there is no lack of people investigating encounters between humans and ghosts, yet when it comes to solid evidence, all they offer is reverberating sounds and missed glimpses. They try to explain these events with reasoning, but their reasoning fails. And they try to prove their assertions with particulars, but their particulars are not credible. This is because the ghosts are not speaking for themselves, but are being described by human beings. But since it is human beings who talk about ghosts, it would be better if they told ghost stories closer to human sentiments rather than just telling strange ghost tales. If there are no ghosts, that is the end of the matter, but if ghosts do exist, they probably won't be too far removed from humans in sentiment. This is why ghost stories from the past to the present should always aim to encourage good and censure evil.[20]

The moral purpose of the story, as the translator suggests, is conveyed through a humanistic portrayal of ghosts, in that ghosts were seen as sharing experiences that resemble those of human beings. For, it is only through these experiences that their stories are believable and can serve the function of 'encouraging good and censuring evil'. In this sense, then, Christmas becomes more like a backdrop against which the translator reflects upon the purpose of ghost stories and how they can reveal the human condition and experience. This contrasts with the case of Dickens, as he wants to remind the public of the true meaning of Christmas and what individuals should do in order to promote a shared sense of community and benevolence.

The Christmas spirit as promoted in the Preface to the original *A Christmas Carol* is strengthened by the structure of the novella, in that Dickens uses 'staves' – according to the *Oxford English Dictionary*, the use of 'staves' to refer to verses in songs or stanzas in poems was current from the seventeenth to the nineteenth centuries – instead of chapters when breaking down the story into sections. Yet in the translated version, the five staves of the novella, which chronicle the moral transformation of Scrooge, are divided into ten chapters. However, rather than seeing these chapters as a result of some random choices made by the translator, it is clear that the translator has followed the development of the plot when breaking down the original 'staves'. In other words, the translator appears to have taken the structure of the text and plot development into consideration, even though he clearly does not pay heed to, or is perhaps not aware of, the traditional carol form upon which the structure of the novella is based when he translated it. The narrative design of the novella is further transformed in the translated version through the inclusion of the author-commentator, who, in the name of Charles Dickens, literally starts off the story with the following line: 'Charles Dickens said: at the beginning of my book, Marley was already dead.'[21] Charles Dickens as the narrator also appears from time to time to comment on, or interpret, the action of particular characters or significant moments in plot development, a practice which was common in traditional Chinese storytelling and one which was popularised by Sima Qian the 'Grand Historian' and Pu the 'Historian of the Strange' in their respective narratives.[22] The function of Dickens the author-narrator, as a new addition to the novella in this Chinese translated version, can be gleaned from the way in which 'Dickens' comments on Scrooge's demeanour and his preparation for the expected arrival of the second ghost in the middle of the narrative:

> Suddenly he [Scrooge] became very bold and swore that if the ghost appeared again, he would challenge it to a fight. He did not want to let the ghost take action first and be caught off guard, for then his strategy would come to naught. Charles Dickens said: 'Those who read my book need to believe Scrooge's oath. But if the ghost should boldly conjure, its magic would be to no avail.' At this moment, he thought himself well-prepared; the only thing he needed to do was to wait for the arrival of his enemy.[23]

The interaction between the author-narrator and readers is clear from this episode that saw Dickens inviting readers to believe in Scrooge's oath, even though he recognised the futility of it should the ghost use his magic. Translation practice in this instance thus not only makes the text accessible to their target readers in terms of language, but, most significantly, it has the effect of resituating the text within the Chinese literary tradition and in the process destabilises the original form of the narrative.

Changes in Translation Practices

The free translation (as demonstrated from this textual example) that writers and translators such as Lin Shu and Wen practised, and one which I regarded as representing some of the most creative textual practice in China's translation history, was out of favour during and after the May Fourth Movement. Inspired by Western modernisation efforts, the campaign advocated democracy, science and individuality; it also impacted on Chinese literary and cultural practices. In terms of translation practices, Chinese intellectuals by then emphasised fidelity between source and target texts, and they deemed the translation practices adopted by Lin and his contemporaries as obsolete. As Leo Tak-hung Chan points out, 'a dominant trend in translation since 1919 (the year the May Fourth Movement broke out) was to adhere closely to the formal features of source texts and to import, on a huge scale, foreign terms and expressions.'[24] Such a phenomenon, as Chan contends, reflects the Chinese intellectuals' seeking not only for '*literary* modernity' but also '*linguistic* modernity'.[25] After the Communist Party rose to power in the 1940s, the decision to translate Dickensian texts appears to have become more political by nature. If the major impulse that underlined the act of translating Dickensian texts in the first period of the cross-cultural transfer – marked by the translation of seven of Dickens's novels from 1904 to 1914 – is due to Dickens's image as a social reformer and the realistic portrayal of the underprivileged among the working class, then in later periods his works were reframed as ones that foreground the exploitation of the lower class by the bourgeois in a capitalist society.[26] In other words, while early translators and publishers of Dickensian texts were primarily concerned with what they regarded as Dickens's realistic representation of a range of lower-class characters, and, most importantly, the potential of fiction as a literary form to draw the authorities and the public's attention to various social problems in society, in later periods what the translated text highlighted were the problems with a capitalist society and the 'class struggles' that Dickensian narratives purportedly expose. This is clearly reflected by the descriptions of a few of the Dickensian novels that were contained in the *Bibliography of the Publication of Translated Western Classics 1949–1979* (shortened to *Bibliography* in subsequent citations). For example, in the catalogue entry on *The Old Curiosity Shop*, which was translated by Xu Jungyun and brought out by two different publishers in 1955 and 1956, respectively, there is a brief commentary on the novel: 'The work profoundly exposes the capitalist society, and sings an elegy of the destined collapse of small proprietors.'[27] A similar tone is adopted for a few other entries. For instance, the synopsis of *Great Expectations*, translated by Wang Keyi and published in 1979, is written as follows: 'It depicts a rural youth, who, under the influence of a capitalist society, has been changed from being simple to flamboyant, frugal to extravagant, and who blindly pursues life as a dandy and chases after an unhealthy love affair. At the end, his "future" is destroyed.'[28]

Being alert to the changing socio-political setting of China against which acts of translation took place could thus help us reflect upon the influence of the wider socio-cultural context on the choice of literary texts that were to be translated, and, in many instances, the way in which the text was translated and published. This is further demonstrated by Lin's translation of *Oliver Twist*, which was renamed as *Zei Shi* (A Thief's History), in 1908, and Xiong Youzhen's translation of the novel, which was renamed as *Wu Du Gu Er* (An Orphan in a Foggy City), in 1957.

The detailed topographical features, and the specific place names, are some of the recurrent characteristics of Dickens's urban aesthetics which help map out the various social spaces in the novel. From the perspective of the translator, however, the specific place names (except probably London as a general signifier for Britain), with which the translator and his intended readers would be least familiar, were less important than other elements of fiction, such as plot and characterisation. This is testified by the fact that, while Lin's translation reflects his attempt to re-render or reconstruct the general atmosphere of the places that are depicted in the original novel, albeit at times in a modified or condensed form, the specific place names are frequently taken away. This is shown in the two translated passages from the novel. The first one is a comparison between the English original text and the Chinese translation of the beginning of Chapter 12, in which Oliver is taken by Mr Brownlow to his own house by coach. The original passage reads:

> The coach rattled away, down Mount Pleasant and up Exmouth-street: over nearly the same ground as that which Oliver had traversed when he first entered London in company with the Dodger; and, turning a different way when it reached the Angel at Islington, stopped at length before a neat house, in a quiet shady street

near Pentonville. Here, a bed was prepared, without loss of time, in which Mr. Brownlow saw his young charge carefully and comfortably deposited; and here, he was tended with a kindness and solicitude that knew no bounds.[29]

The Chinese translation renders the scene thus:

> The coach arrived at the left-hand side of Pentonville, where the old man's house was located. The old man stopped the coach and asked people to prepare a bed, and put Oliver to bed.[30]

In this instance the original narrative noting the specific places that the coach drove past is much condensed, though on some other occasions the sense of dilapidation and poverty that are often associated with lower-class dwelling places that Dickens frequently depicts are re-rendered in detail. For example, the following is the scene that shows Oliver accompanying Jack Dawkins to the thieves' den run by Fagin:

Original:

> Although Oliver had enough to occupy his attention in keeping sight of his leader, he could not help bestowing a few hasty glances on either side of the way, as he passed along. A dirtier or more wretched place he had never seen. The street was very narrow and muddy; and the air was impregnated with filthy odours. There were a good many small shops; but the only stock in trade appeared to be heaps of children, who, even at that time of night, were crawling in and out at the doors, or screaming from the inside.[31]

Chinese version:

> Although he followed along, he still looked from side to side now and then. The dilapidated and wretched houses were ones that Oliver had never seen in his life. The alleys were narrow and full of mud. The stench in the air assaulted his nose. There were some shops here and there, but they lacked goods. They contained only a few dirty children. Although it already passed 11pm, some passers-by still continued to come and go.[32]

The detailed re-rendering of the aura of the place could be seen as an attempt by the translator to picture the living condition of the poor and the underprivileged; these kind of descriptions, rather than specific place names as discussed earlier, could best serve the social function that Dickensian novels were perceived to perform. While a similar focus on social conditions has largely dominated the Chinese reading of Dickens's novels since their early reception, the influence of Soviet literary culture in China after the Communist Party rose to power is evident in the choice of the source text upon which the 1957 Chinese translated edition was based. According to the Chinese translator Xiong Youzhen, the translation of the novel, renamed as *Wu Du Gu Er* (An Orphan in a Foggy City), was based on the 1953 'simplified version' published by Soviet Educational Publishing. In the afterword to this translated version, Xiong the translator acknowledged the different simplified versions that were in existence though he considered that this Soviet edition was 'comparatively better' because it retained the major plot and writing style of Dickens. The intention of the translation, Xiong wrote, was to give Chinese readers, many of whom still could not read the English texts, an opportunity to acquire some knowledge of world literature, as well as arouse their interest in this area.[33] The translator emphasised that this version was a 'faithful' and a 'direct translation from the original text', though he acknowledged that, because of his level of language proficiency, there would certainly be some 'mistakes' or 'inadequacies' in the translated version.[34] The book condensed the fifty-three chapters into thirty-one chapters (and it should be pointed out here that the elaborate descriptions of the topographical features of specific place and space are largely absent from this edition). It retained most of the illustrations and one which, as the translator mentioned, was based on the 1955 edition published by Moscow Foreign Language Publishing and the 1941 edition published by Dodd, Mead & Co. in New York. The heavy use of illustrations, I suggest, reflects the possibility that the book was intended for the general public, especially young people, as images would possibly be of greater appeal to young people and to those who may not be used to reading dense prose. Translations of foreign literature in China remained vibrant till the ten-year Cultural Revolution, during which such translation activities virtually came to a halt. As Shouha Qi points out, 'The ten-year Cultural Revolution was a period of stifled creativity and silenced voices.'[35] While many artists, writers, translators and other intellectuals struggled to survive, Qi further notes that all journals and magazines devoted to foreign literature translations were shut down during the Cultural Revolution.[36] It was after the Cultural Revolution that translation of foreign literature resumed. Indeed, it is probably no coincidence that *Great Expectations* (1860–1), a rags-to-riches story, was first released in 1979, a year after China adopted the 'Open Door Policy', which signalled a change in the direction of China's economic development.[37]

What complicates the translation history of Dickensian texts in China, especially in the early stages of the cross-cultural transfer, is that the practice of translation was very different from our contemporary conception of what constitutes an act of translation. As both Lin and Wen acknowledged in their prefaces to their respective translated texts, they did not know any foreign languages, so what they did was to turn the oral rendering of the primary texts by somebody who had a certain knowledge of English into Chinese. As such, it is difficult to decide at which stage of this translation process the changes were introduced, and the extent to which the literary network, such as publishers, editors and writers, might impact on the way a text was produced. Even in later periods when a greater affinity has been attached to the original text, especially with the increasingly frequent use of modern Chinese, rather than *wenyan*, to translate the texts, in some instances it is also uncertain which source texts (that is, which version of Dickens's novels) the translators had used, and in what way a shift in ideology and cultural practice might impact on the choice of text to be translated and the way in which the text was re-rendered in the native language.[38]

While this chapter is not primarily concerned with textual editing, it is still important to be alert to the complex editorial processes that help shape the ultimate narrative. Indeed, it is probably no coincidence that on the cover page of the 1919 *A History of Ghosts*, Wen's role as both the translator and editor (*bian yi*) was clearly stated, suggesting that he, or the publisher, was aware of the fact that his role goes beyond simply rendering the English text into Chinese. The trajectory of the translations of Dickens's novels in China, while being situated in a specific cultural and historical context, thus draw our attention to some of the broader issues surrounding acts of translation and their relationship with the representation, interpretation and transformation of Dickens's works in a socio-cultural context that is very different from their original place of production. Ultimately, one may well ask: is there a possibility that there are simply different versions of Dickens that exist in different languages and cultural contexts in different historic periods?

The quick answer to this, as I hinted at the beginning of the essay, is obviously yes, in the sense that a translated text is often both an interpretation of the original text, as well as a textual practice that reveals both the source and the target cultures at specific moments of history. How Dickens's works were translated was often determined both by the prevailing literary style of the target culture as well as by how Dickens was perceived at that particular historic moment. Yet what is particularly striking are the similar challenges and concerns that translators of Dickensian texts across different cultures have shared in their attempt to render Dickensian texts in their native language. While the translation history of Dickens's works in China, as discussed above, serves as an illuminating example of the close relationship between translation practices and the wider socio-cultural contexts, similar situations also occur in places where Dickens's texts have been read in translation. In Germany, for example, translations of Dickens's works quickly appeared after the English originals were released in Britain. The popularity of Dickens's work in Germany at that time, as Antije Anderson points out, was largely due to the symbolic meaning of Dickens's works – that is, they were seen as representing a quintessential Englishness as well as the nation's power and economic might. In Poland, Dickens, who is described by Ewa Kujawska-Lis as 'the most frequently published foreign novelist in 19th-century Poland', was seen as both a humourist and social critic during the period. As Kujawska-Lis suggests, while Dickens was no longer seen as a 'great artist' during the modernist and interwar periods because of a shift in the aesthetic taste of the time, he was refashioned by the new socialist leaders after the post-World War II period into a social critic, rather than a humourist, so that he could be used for their propaganda efforts.[39] In Italy, meanwhile, Paola Venturi uses the example of *David Copperfield* (1849–50) to demonstrate the fact that the novel has been listed as a 'classic' in Italy; such a categorisation, as Venturi demonstrates, 'encourages the adoption of a didactic aim and a duly elevated style for use in translations'.[40] Citing different examples of Italian translations of *David Copperfield*, such as the 1939 version by Enrico Piceni and the 1966 translation by Franco Prattico, Venturi observes that the Dickensian text has been 'embellished and normalised' during the processes of translation.[41] As he notes: 'The Italian translations of *David Copperfield* tend to eschew the lower varieties of language, and pursue a general policy of sanitizing all colloquial traits, even when these are used by Dickens for the purposes of mimesis and characterization.'[42] Indeed, the difficulties of rendering Dickens's idiosyncratic prose into their native language have been documented by translators from different parts of the world. For example, Toru Sasaki highlights the 'syntactic disparity' between Japanese and English when he translated *Great Expectations* in 2011. Sasaki writes: 'Among other things, the syntactic disparity that I most acutely feel as translator is the lack of the relative pronoun in Japanese. As a result, the structure of the translated sentence

TRANSLATIONS 399

sometimes markedly diverges from the original; one long winding sentence may very well be divided into two or three terse sentences.'[43]

Some may readily assume that translating Dickens in a culture and geographical location that is closer to the source culture in which Dickensian texts first emerged may make the task easier. Yet when Sylvère Monod recalls his own experience of rendering the British novels into French, he raises a key question: 'Is Dickens, in fact, translatable at all?' 'A rough-and-ready answer might be that Dickens was a fantastically creative and forceful writer, and that no one can hope to convey all of his style through a foreign translation,' Monod suggests, yet he also highlights the ways in which the essence of Dickens can still be captured and conveyed through a translated text:

> if Dickens's translator lets the spirit of Dickens blow through her or his work and carry him or her along with it, something of the fantastic creative energy that informs and animates the great writer's prose will come through and be put across to the French reader. That creative energy is in fact so powerful that it can never be rendered in its entirety, but neither can it be entirely kept out.[44]

The 'fantastic creative energy' in this sense, then, can perhaps be best understood as a driving force that creates the various 'afterlives' of Dickensian texts in Benjamin's terms, in that the translated texts often carry with them 'echoes' of the source texts.[45] Of course, this creative energy, as has been demonstrated in this essay, is being used and adapted within particular socio-cultural contexts at specific moments in history. It is through these culturally specific, historically contingent practices that different images of Dickens, and diverse translated versions of Dickensian texts, have emerged, circulated and been read in different parts of the world.

Notes

1. Charles Dickens, *Le Magasin d'antiquités*, trans. by Alfred des Essarts, 2 vols (Paris: Hachette, 1857).
2. Ibid.
3. See, for example, Susan Bassnett, *Translation Studies* (London: Routledge, 2002) and Susan Bassnett and André Lefevere, *Constructing Cultures: Essays on Literary Translation* (Clevedon, Avon: Multilingual Matters, 1998).
4. For a discussion of the circulation and publication of Dickens's works in different parts of the world, see Regenia Gagnier, 'The Global Circulation of Charles Dickens's Novels', *Literature Compass* 10.1 (2013), 82–95; *Global Dickens*, ed. by John O. Jordan and Nirshan Perera (Farnham: Ashgate, 2012); and *The Reception of Charles Dickens in Europe*, ed. by Michael Hollington, 2 vols (London: Bloomsbury, 2013).
5. Lefevere and Bassnett famously argue that translation is a 'rewriting' of the original text, to the extent that it is also a form of manipulation: it can either contribute to innovations in new concepts, genres and style, or it can repress and contain them. For details, see the 'General Editor's Preface' at the beginning of Lefevere's *Translation, Rewriting, and the Manipulation of Literary Fame* (London: Routledge, 1992), vii–viii. While my work resonates with Lefevere and Bassnett's broader premise of the close relationship between translation practices and the wider socio-cultural contexts, I do not consider translation in terms of 'manipulation'. This is because in many instances the way a

translator translates a particular work is predicated upon her or his knowledge of the source and target languages, as well as the literary style of the time. In other words, while in some cases a translator may deliberately manipulate the source text for particular political and social purposes in her or his own culture, in many instances the way in which a text is translated can best be understood as reflecting a particular literary and translation culture of the time. I will explore this further with reference to the Chinese translations of Dickens's works.

6. Walter Benjamin, 'The Task of the Translator', in *Illuminations*, ed. by Hannah Arendt, trans. by Harry Zorn (London: Pimlico, 1999), 70–82, 77.

7. Lydia Liu, *Translingual Practice: Literature, National Culture, and Translated Modernity – China, 1900–1937* (Stanford: Stanford University Press, 1995), 26.

8. Rebecca Walkowitz, *Born Translated: The Contemporary Novel in the Age of World Literature* (New York: Columbia University Press, 2015), 1–48.

9. Ibid.

10. Gérard Genette, *Paratexts: Thresholds of Interpretation*, trans. by Jane Lewin (Cambridge: Cambridge University Press, 1997), 2.

11. R. A. Wilson, 'Translations of the Works of Charles Dickens', *The British Museum Quarterly* 14.3 (1940), 59–60, 60.

12. Michael Hill, *Lin Shu, Inc.: Translation and the Making of Modern Chinese Culture* (Oxford: Oxford University Press, 2013), 2.

13. In the Preface to *Xiao Nu Nai'er Chuan: lun li xiao shuo* (The Old Curiosity Shop), Lin openly admitted: 'I don't know any foreign languages. I have managed to struggle my way through to the field of translation through listening to the oral renderings of the original works by a few gentlemen and then writing them down.' See Lin and Wei Yi, *Xiao Nu Nai'er Chuan: lun li xiao shuo*, 3 vols (Shanghai: Commercial Press, 1914), 1.

14. Ibid., 92.

15. I recognise the different 'original' versions of Dickens's texts that were in circulation in Victorian England due to the different publication formats that he adopted. In this chapter, 'original' mainly refers to the texts that were first published in book form in Victorian England.

16. I use the Mandarin pinyin system for Chinese book titles and the names of publishers. Most of the Chinese titles of the primary texts when they first appear in this essay will be accompanied by an English translation.

17. See *Bibliography of Publications during the Republic Period (Foreign Literature) 1911–1949*, ed. by Archival Library of Chinese Publications (Beijing: Zhonghua Book Co., 1980) and *Bibliography of the Publication of Translated Western Classics 1949–1979*, ed. by Archival Library of Chinese Publications (Beijing: Zhonghua Book Co., 1980) for the publication details of the related entries.

18. Charles Dickens, *A Christmas Carol*, in *Christmas Books*, ed. by Ruth Glancy (Oxford: Oxford University Press, 1988), 3.

19. Judith Zeitlin, *History of the Strange: Pu Songling and the Chinese Classical Tale* (Stanford: Stanford University Press, 1993), 2.

20. *Gui Shi*, ed. and trans. by Wen Yehe (Shanghai: Dongfu Xiongdi Library, 1919). Unless otherwise stated, all English translations of Chinese editions of Dickensian texts are my own.

21. *Gui Shi*, 1.

22. See, for example, David Rolston, *Traditional Chinese Fiction and Fiction Commentary: Reading and Writing Between the Lines* (Stanford: Stanford University Press, 1997).

23. *Gui Shi*, 50.

24. Leo Chan Tak-hung, *Twentieth-Century Chinese Translation Theory* (Amsterdam and Philadelphia: John Benjamins Publishing, 2004), 31.

25. Ibid., 25–6.
26. See Klaudia Hiu Yen Lee, *Charles Dickens and China, 1895–1915: Cross-Cultural Encounters* (London: Routledge, 2017) for a discussion of the early translation and circulation of Dickens's novels in China. See also Eva Hung, 'The Introduction of Dickens in China (1906–1960): A Case Study in Target Culture Reception', in *Global Dickens*, 29–43.
27. *Bibliography*, 176.
28. Ibid., 177.
29. Charles Dickens, *Oliver Twist* (Oxford: Oxford University Press, 2008), 83, ch. 12.
30. Lin Shu and Wei Yi, *Zhe Shi* (vol. 1) (Shanghai: Commercial Press, 1915), 54.
31. *Oliver Twist*, 59–60, ch. 8.
32. *Zhe Shi*, 59.
33. *An Orphan in a Foggy City*, ed. by Xiong Youzhen (Beijing: Popular Literature and Art Publishing, 1957), 116.
34. Ibid., 116.
35. Shouhua Qi, *Western Literature in China and the Translation of a Nation* (Basingstoke: Palgrave Macmillan, 2012), 127.
36. Ibid., 125–6.
37. Tong Zhen has provided a brief overview of the association of Dickens with Marxism and socialism in China, especially during the period from the establishment of the People's Republic of China by the Communist Party in 1949 till 1966. See Tong, *Di Geng Si and Zhong Guo* (Dickens and China) (Hunan: Xiangtan University, 2008).
38. As Josephine Guy and Ian Small point out, 'one of the distinguishing features of nineteenth-century literary culture is the variety of formats in which literary works, especially those of prose fiction, were made available to contemporary readers.' See Guy and Small, *The Textual Condition of Nineteenth-Century Literature* (London: Routledge, 2012), 21.
39. Ewa Kujawska-Lis, 'The Transformations of Charles Dickens in Early Socialist Poland', in *Literature Compass* 10.4 (2013), 396–405, 396.
40. Paola Venturi, '*David Copperfield* Conscripted: Italian Translations of the Novel', *Dickens Quarterly* 26.4 (2009), 234–47, 234.
41. Ibid., 241.
42. Ibid.
43. Toru Sasaki, 'Translating *Great Expectations* into Japanese', *Dickensian* 107.485 (Winter 2011), 197–200, 198.
44. Sylvère Monod, 'Translating Dickens into French', in *Dickens, Europe and the New Worlds*, ed. by Anny Sadrin (Basingstoke: Macmillan, 1999), 229–38, 233, 237.
45. Elizabeth Brennan, 'Curiosities of *Le Magasin d'antiquités*', *Études anglaises* 50.3 (1997), 319–27, 324.

Further Reading

Susan Bassnett and André Lefevere, *Constructing Cultures: Essays on Literary Translation* (Clevedon, Avon: Multilingual Matters, 1998)

John O. Jordan and Nirshan Perera, eds, *Global Dickens* (London: Ashgate, 2012)

Klaudia Hiu Yen Lee, *Charles Dickens and China, 1895–1915: Cross-Cultural Encounters* (London: Routledge, 2017)

Lawrence Venuti, ed., *The Translation Studies Reader* (London: Routledge, 2000)

26

GLOBAL DICKENS

Michael Hollington

Dickens the Mythmaker

THERE ARE FEW AUTHORS, HOWEVER GREAT, who can truly be said to enjoy global recognition, that is to say, in language, and out of language. Dickens is certainly one of them, giving his name in many languages to the word 'Dickensian', which often principally connotes poverty and social injustice, and its denunciation.[1] There is also Cervantes, with the adjective 'Quixotic', but in English, I think, the only other writer who can really be thought of as global is Shakespeare. Great writer though she is, and hugely widely read, known and admired internationally, Jane Austen, for instance, does not quite seem to me to fall into this category, existing as she does primarily for literate people, perhaps also chiefly of a certain class.

But from the start Dickens spoke both to literate and illiterate people. We know that illiterate servants, for example, might gather round one of their number who could read, and hear the latest instalment of *The Pickwick Papers* (1836–7) or *Oliver Twist* (1837–9) as they appeared, the illustrations of Cruikshank or Phiz offering a kind of *biblia pauperum* in a visual language they could understand.[2] If they had difficulty following the plot of *Oliver Twist*, they could at least tell from his straight nose in Cruikshank's illustrations that Oliver was fundamentally a 'good'un', and Noah Claypole, with his crooked one, not.[3] The experience, as Gertrude Himmelfarb observes, might well lead them on to become readers themselves:

> those who could not read [might be] listening to the latest instalment read aloud in the servants' hall, lodging house, public house, or tea shop [. . .]. An early review praised him for performing the role of 'moral teacher' to the 'millions who are just emerging from ignorance into what may be termed reading classes.'[4]

Nowadays, not dissimilarly, a Dickens reader in a bus or train might recently have watched a screen version, and been moved to pick up the book of the film.

Even so, the most crucial thing to think about, in my view, in any attempt to understand Dickens's global appeal, is the mythic dimension of his writing – his capacity to create incidents and characters that are so vivid and memorable that they can become universal myths. Scrooge, of course, giving his name to common, everyday misers, Oliver asking for more, and for an earlier generation Little Nell or Paul Dombey dying, Uriah Heep's 'humility', or Sam Weller with his Wellerisms – 'business first, pleasure arterwards, as King Richard the Third said ven he stabbed the other King in the Tower, afore he smothered the babbies'[5] – these are images that have extratextual and extra-contextual as well as textual life.

A number of critics, of course, have emphasised Dickens as myth-maker: I select three. The first is that doyen of Dickens critics, G. K. Chesterton, author of what is still perhaps the most widely read book on the author, in an essay entitled 'The Fairy Pickwick':

> Dickens was a mythologist rather than a novelist; he was the last of the mythologists, and perhaps the greatest. He did not always manage to make his characters men, but he always managed, at the least, to make them gods. They are creatures like Punch or Father Christmas. They live statically, in a perpetual summer of being themselves. It was not the aim of Dickens to show the effect of time and circumstance upon a character; it was not even his aim to show the effect of a character on time and circumstance.[6]

Though one may disagree with the last sentence in the case of the later novels – it was surely most definitely his aim to show the effect of time and circumstance on Pip in *Great Expectations* (1860–1), for example – this is merely to qualify rather than cavil at Chesterton's convincing explanation of why Dickens the mythologist is a writer for all times and places.

The second is another conservative, T. S. Eliot, someone whom one might not initially suspect of being an ardent Dickensian with an encyclopaedic command of his books (he set Dickens examination papers for friends), though the fact that Dickens met his grandfather in St Louis in 1842 and praised him as a 'gentleman of great worth and excellence' doubtless has something to do with it.[7] In one of his two important essays contrasting Wilkie Collins as 'a man of talent' and Dickens as 'a man of genius', he assigns Dickens to a class of myth-makers that includes Shakespeare and Dante, whose figures 'belong to poetry [. . .] in that a single phrase, either by them or about them, may be enough to set them wholly before us'.[8]

And the third is Virginia Woolf, neither conservative in politics nor from a family of Dickens lovers. In her 1925 essay on *David Copperfield*, her favourite Dickens novel, she compares the regular appearance of new Dickens editions to the 'ripening of strawberries [. . .] and other natural processes', and writes that it and *Pickwick* are 'not books, but stories communicated by word of mouth in those tender years when fact and fiction merge, and thus belong to the memories and myths of life, and not to its aesthetic experience'.[9] In other words, she offers an explanation of Dickens's hold on our consciousness by going to non-literate or pre-literate stages of childhood in which myths get implanted in our mind in ways that seem to go deeper than the conscious absorption of language through reading in adult life.

As previously suggested, a lot of Dickens's universal appeal has to do with the visual power, both of the writing itself and the accompanying illustrations, and of later visual versions, films especially, of his work.[10] However, in modern urban culture, the visual sense, as the classic sociologist Georg Simmel suggests, is so dominant (so that some predict that with evolution our sense of smell may atrophy as a result of living in odourless environments in the course of time) that it is worth remembering that Dickens is an artist who deploys all five senses in his work. In the next section I thus attempt to emphasise the extent to which the global dissemination of Dickens's

404 MICHAEL HOLLINGTON

work has taken place through the medium of another of the senses, hearing, that is to say, through the power of the human voice.

Dickens in the Anglophone World

It is obvious that the globalisation of Dickens has much to do with the globalisation of the English language on the one hand, and the global reach of the former British Empire (where his fame at home was replicated) on the other. To illustrate only a fraction of Dickens's imperial impact, I shall concentrate here on the antipodean white settler colonies, Australia and New Zealand, focusing in particular on the case of Katherine Mansfield, a major writer brought up in New Zealand, and immersed from the start in Dickens, in a culture where he was to be encountered at every turn. I shall return later to some other areas of the former British Empire.

At the age of four, even before she went to school, Mansfield moved with her family into a house with a Dickensian name. Such house names were not uncommon in nineteenth-century Australasia: the Australian poet Adam Lindsay Gordon purchased in 1864 a cottage in South Australia, and promptly named it Dingley Dell after the idyllic Kent home in *The Pickwick Papers*. The name of the Beauchamp household in Karore was grander (if gloomier), as befitted Mansfield's father, the governor of the Bank of New Zealand. Chesney Wold, according to a descendant of the man who built it in 1866 (the first mayor of Karore, Stephen Lancaster), was named after a perceived resemblance between the surrounding countryside and that represented in Phiz's engravings of the Dedlock mansion in *Bleak House* (1852–3) – the global importance for literate and illiterate alike of those illustrations on display again.

Not long thereafter, Mansfield came into closer contact with Dickens at school. Her performance as Little Nell in a charity performance of the Mrs Jarley's Waxworks scenes from *The Old Curiosity Shop* (1840–1) brought her initial acclaim as a Dickens performer, and later she took over from her headmistress the role of reading Dickens aloud during sewing classes, remarking in her journal that 'I could make the girls cry when I read Dickens in the sewing class' – in order to beat her elocution rival Jinne [*sic*] Moore, according to Mary Hammond.[11]

It is here that we encounter one of the most important ways in which Dickens circulated freely in colonial society: through the habit (often in isolated settings where few other forms of entertainment were on offer) of reading aloud, often by fathers to their families or teachers to their pupils, or even, in colonial Australia, by prison officers to convicts and prisoners. Through this early exposure to oral Dickens, Mansfield became a mimic and performer throughout her life, so that later Leonard Woolf would remark, 'I don't think anyone has ever made me laugh more than she did.'[12] At its very end, nine months before her death, she talks of hiring the Bechstein Hall to give public performances of her work because 'Dickens used to do it'.[13] Her work, as Holly Furneaux and Angela Smith and myself among others have shown, pays tribute to his considerable influence on the multiple voices in her fiction.[14]

The same phenomenon of reading Dickens aloud is to be observed in Australia and elsewhere. John O. Jordan, for instance, records the evidence of an 1893 memoir by James Demarr, who worked in the Outback on a cattle station in 1841–2. A copy of the latest instalment of *Nicholas Nickleby* (1838–9) arrived and was read round the campfire to an audience of men from far and wide. Not houses here, but 'calves and puppies, and tame pet birds' were named after characters in the book. According to Jordan again, a similar moment of rapture in the California goldfields is the subject of Bret Harte's poem 'Dickens in Camp'.[15]

But perhaps the most comprehensive history of reading Dickens aloud in Australasia currently available is provided in Joy Damousi's study of the diffusion of 'Englishness' and 'English culture' in nineteenth- and early twentieth-century Australia.[16] She argues that Dickens's own practice of reading aloud or indeed 'performing' extracts from his novels was the catalyst for countless similar public elocutionary performances in the colonies: 'the number of evenings given over to recitations of Dickens's work in places like Sydney and Melbourne was seen as a sign that culture was alive and well at the outposts of the empire', and, moreover, that these occasions disseminated 'Englishness' in Australia: 'The circulation of Dickens around the Empire and his connectedness with elocution was an effective form of circulation of ideas of Englishness.'[17] So we may see that Mansfield's urge, when she was desperately ill, to carry on the Dickens tradition by reciting her own work in public is a throwback to her earliest days in New Zealand. In the course of her book Damousi assembles an impressive number of public Dickens readers and impersonators in Australia in the nineteenth and early twentieth centuries – Thomas Hill, Thomas Bentley and James Brunton Gibb among them – and one important political figure for whom Dickens in childhood, as a result of hearing him read aloud, was a source of inspiration throughout his career. This is Alfred Deakin, Australia's second prime minister, who writes in 'Books and a Boy', speaking of himself in the third person, how 'in the winter evenings and many others his father read aloud. A better unprofessional interpreter of Dickens in particular [. . .] he had not and has not heard.'[18]

Dickens in Europe

By contrast, in nineteenth-century Europe the dissemination of Dickens takes place in the main through three centres – Germany, Russia and France – whose print culture dominated that of their respective surrounding geographical and cultural spheres. All of them – particularly the first two – have at times experienced extreme political turbulence in the period since Dickens's emergence, and it is not surprising that his reputation has undergone a number of vicissitudes in that time. Yet at no point in the past did his work lapse into neglect or indifference. Paradoxically, it is only now, with little or no political interference in its publication, that in Russia and Germany in particular there is some tendency to pay less attention to Dickens than before, by relegating him to secondary rank as primarily a writer for children.

Germany was the first in the field in recognising Dickens, and its initial enthusiasm over *The Pickwick Papers* the closest to that in Britain itself. Indeed, as the researches of Antje Anderson have shown, for a good many years Dickens was more popular in Germany than any German writer. German critics were also good at perceiving ways in which his writing stood somewhat apart from the mainstream of the dominant realist tradition, belonging rather to something that they called 'poetic realism' – again, I think, partly in recognition of his capacity for making myths.[19]

Dickens's reputation declined somewhat in Germany after political unification and the rise in the later nineteenth century of a nationalist tendency less open to foreign writers. And, despite the continuation in the early part of the twentieth century of its distinctive 'poetic realist' critical tradition, in figures like Otto Dibelius and Stefan Zweig (the latter, for instance, proclaiming that Dickens's great achievement was to perceive 'the poetic in the prosaic'[20]), we find that Theodor W. Adorno in the 1920s, in his important essay on *The Old Curiosity Shop*, has to begin by arguing against the view that Dickens was chiefly a writer for children.[21] Norbert Lennartz shows how, in the Nazi period of extreme German nationalism, Dickens was definitely relegated to the status of mere entertainer, with the role of Victorian guru given to his friend Thomas Carlyle. But the German military hierarchy always seems to have had a soft spot for him: Helmuth von Moltke the Elder, the chief of staff of the Prussian Army, was reading *Little Dorrit* (1855–7) during the siege of Paris in 1870, and three-quarters of a century later some of the defendants at Nuremberg were still reading him during their trials.[22]

The division of Germany after World War I led to the emergence of two competing distortions of Dickens – as a socialist realist in the East, and as an exponent of the purity and autonomy in literary art then in vogue in the West during the period of the Cold War.[23] But the emphasis on reaching out to the working classes in the German Democratic Republic certainly had at least one positive effect, according to Joachim Möller – a major school of Dickens illustrators, more or less free of political restraint.[24] Reunification has produced some very strong academic writing on Dickens – Matthias Bauer, Norbert Lennartz, Annegret Maack and Stefan Welz are among the names to mention – but there is perhaps a greater cleavage between Dickens's standing with scholars and his reputation among readers in general than elsewhere.

Exploring why Dickens also took Russia by storm in the nineteenth century, and helped produce, in Tolstoy, Dostoevsky, Turgenev and others, an astonishing school of novelists, all of them deep admirers, gives me the opportunity to highlight the role a great translator can play in the global print dissemination of an author. Irinarch Ivanovich Vvedensky is the case in point: he wrote to Dickens in 1849, inviting him to Russia, to inform him that 'from the banks of the Neva to the remotest parts of Siberia you are read with avidity', modestly omitting to mention his own role in this. Although he died in 1855, and so was unable to translate Dickens's last novels, his versions of *The Pickwick Papers*, *David Copperfield* and *Dombey and Son* are described in Igor Katarsky's authoritative *Dikkens v Rossii* (Dickens in Russia) as 'even now unquestionably the *best* Russian translations of these novels'.[25]

It is to be stressed, though, that Vvedensky's versions – as a result of his inadequate command of English – are full of mistakes, and that he 'sings along with Dickens' karaoke-style by inventing numerous 'Dickensian' phrases of his own; which brings to mind Ezra Pound's great mistranslations from the Chinese, the *Cathay* poems, of which T. S. Eliot declared that 'Pound is the inventor of Chinese poetry for our time'.[26] Likewise, Vvedensky in Russia was the inventor of Dickens for his time, of whom Chukovsky writes 'the fact is that without him we would have no Dickens at all. He alone brought us closer to [Dickens's] work, immersed us in his flavour, infected us with his temper', and goes on to claim that many of his additions 'are so much in the spirit of Dickens, are so much in harmony with his general tone [. . .] that one wonders whether Dickens would have crossed them out himself'.[27]

Dickens was also feted in France, although enthusiasm for his work has always perhaps been rather more measured there than in Germany or Russia. It also had to wait somewhat longer to take off, until the mid-1850s, when Hippolyte Taine took up his cause, performing a dissection that deplored some aspects of his work – his sentimentality, poor plot construction and characterisation – while praising others. Like the Germans, Taine emphasises Dickens as a poet of the city, and indeed his conception of the novelist anticipates some of the central modern reasons for admiring his work, such as its ability to represent extreme mental states. Taine took on that very French role of *maître à penser* for several generations of critics content to follow the general outlines of his assessment of Dickens.

But where France differs from Germany or Russia lies in the novelist's fate in more recent times. It too has in Sylvère Monod its great translator, reaching out beyond the academic world to capture a broader readership, though we are now talking about the post-World War II period, the 1950s and beyond. Monod continued to be fully active in the field right up to his death in 2006, not only as a translator but as a major Dickens scholar and critic, recognised as such just as much in the anglophone world as in France (his Norton Critical Edition of *Bleak House*, done in collaboration with another important 'global Dickens' figure, the Canadian George Ford, remains unsurpassed). He and his brilliant pupil Anny Sadrin have inspired a new generation of Dickensians in France, inside and outside academia, that includes Christine Huguet, Nathalie Vanfasse, Marie-Amélie Coste and Georges Letissier.

Before I leave Europe behind, I should like to take a brief glance at some of the reasons why Dickens has circulated so widely in so many countries – that is to say, other than through the influence of these major centres. The general principle might be: to each country or national tradition its own. Though it is not a question of being right or wrong, I am reminded of T. S. Eliot's dictum in 'Shakespeare and the Stoicism of Seneca': 'About any one so great as Shakespeare, it is probable that we can never be right; and if we can never be right, it is better that we should from time to time change our way of being wrong.'[28] Dickens, too, can accommodate all sorts of different emphases and perspectives, some of them, on the face of it, a little incongruous, and these too change with the passing of time. In Sweden, for instance, he has in the past been seen as a feminist, in Catalunya as a model for the Catholic family novel, in the Czech lands as a Symbolist and Decadent.

Even more markedly, he tends to get assimilated in some way or another to the dominant literary tradition of each given country. Thus, in Spain he is linked and compared to Cervantes, in Iceland (where by and large only his short fiction and dramatic scenes from his novels have been translated) to the saga tradition, in Greece to Homer, and so on. He is obviously protean enough, not merely to survive any number of metamorphoses in time and space, but to speak to people everywhere in a multitude of different personae.[29]

Global Dickenses

In August 2012, during the Dickens bicentenary year, *Newsweek* published an article by Jimmy So entitled 'The Charles Dickens of the World: Balzac, Premchand and Others'.[30] It is a cliché-ridden piece of work which provides a random, heterogeneous and unsystematic list of writers who 'have been crowned the Dickenses of Denmark, of Egypt, even of Detroit'. Ten names are offered as examples, and briefly discussed: those of Munshi Premchand of India, Benito Perez Galdos of Spain, Natsume Sōseki of Japan, Honoré de Balzac of France, Lu Xun of China, Martin Andersen Nexø of

408   MICHAEL HOLLINGTON

Denmark, Carlos Fuentes of Mexico, Naguib Mahfouz of Egypt, Elmore Leonard of
the United States and Cyprian Ekwensi of Nigeria.

The interest for my subject here is twofold. First, the very exercise of searching
for and labelling such and such a writer as the 'Dickens' of somewhere implies a
global notion of Dickensian writing as something completely distinctive, a kind of
gold standard for writers everywhere. And second, more interestingly perhaps, it can
be shown that a number of writers on every continent, in and out of the anglophone
world, have indeed been exposed to Dickens, usually at an early age, and later sought
to emulate him in their work.

I am not proposing here to examine this list in any detail at all, but one name, that
of Cyprian Ekwensi, might initially be explored a little before taking on board some
other examples whom So does not name. He is indeed correct in saying that Ekwensi
has been hailed as a new Dickens – by B. Riche and M. Bensemanne of the University
of Algiers who claim in their article 'City Life and Women in Cyprian Ekwensi's *The
People of the City* and *Jagua Nana*' that Ekwensi 'can be described as the Charles
Dickens of modern African literature because he is the first among African writers to
be interested in city life'.[31]

And indeed Ekwensi acknowledges a debt to Dickens. In an interview with Bernth
Lindfors of February 1973 he describes how he began to discover himself as a writer
at school in Ibadan, as a result of an exposure in the classroom to English literature,
in which Dickens played a prominent role:

> I got the impulse to write in my secondary school days at the Government col-
> lege, Ibadan. We had a very good library and teachers who were oriented towards
> literature. Most of the emphasis was on English literature, English history. And
> we used a series of textbooks by Lancelot Oliphant called a Progressive English
> Course, in which the teaching was done by extracts from literature and then the
> grammar and syntax came out of these texts. There were passages from Oliver
> Goldsmith, from 'Abou Ben Adhem', from Dickens' *The Pickwick Papers*, *David
> Copperfield* – famous poetry, famous prose essays and so on. These extracts
> stimulated the appetite and made you want to go to the original source.[32]

And what Ekwensi got from Dickens, he later passed on to another generation of
writers, including Chimamanda Ngozi Adichie. Born in 1977, she describes, in a
Guardian article of February 2008 written three months after Ekwensi's death,
how she discovered Ekwensi and Dickens at the age of fifteen, She admires Ekwensi
because 'he chose not to write about the past as many of his contemporaries did;
instead he engaged with the rapid urbanisation of the new Africa.' He made Lagos
his essential subject, writing (like Dickens) 'unabashed melodrama' because 'Lagos
is, after all, a melodramatic city'. The novel she highlights, *Jagua Nana*, 'widely read
and loved by us 15 year olds', is the story of a stock Lagos character, the whore with
a heart of gold. Its strengths and weaknesses, in her view, stem in part from Dickens:
'Ekwensi may not have consistently written round characters (much like Charles
Dickens, a writer I first read at about the same time)', but in his work Lagos, like
London in Dickens, is itself a character. *Jagua Nana* portrays 'Lagos's hold over the
characters. There is little ambiguity about the corrupting influence of the city in Ekwensi's morality tales.'[33] Another writer, this time not on So's list, whose work has been

GLOBAL DICKENS

bracketed with Dickens – in particular his early novels set in Trinidad and, above all, *A House for Mr Biswas* – is the 2001 Nobel prize-winner V. S. Naipaul. Indeed, at the Jaipur Festival in January 2015 Naipaul is reported to have broken down in tears when Paul Theroux compared him as a writer to Charles Dickens.[34]

This is a particularly telling moment in the history of Naipaul's relation to Dickens because for some years prior to that the writer, grown cantankerous as an old man, as if he were himself a Dickens character, had been on record as a scornful repudiator of the writer he had once revered. According to Robert McCrum, writing in 2001 just after the award of the prize, he held at that time the ludicrous view that Dickens 'died from self-parody', a view on which McCrum comments: 'Where once he had been influenced by Dickens, Naipaul now took on the haughty grandeur and snobbery of Joseph Conrad.'[35] In this he recapitulates a similar evolution in the nineteenth century of the American painter James McNeill Whistler, who as a young man at West Point military academy adored Dickens and, unprompted, sketched seven illustrations to various of his novels (a contemporary of his, William W. Averell, writes, 'He had no equal in art or in the quick and vivid perception and appreciation of the best literature – especially that in which the humorous and pathetic phases of life might be mostly found. Dickens was his nearest favorite').[36] As a mature artist, he ostentatiously turned his back on all that – 'Dickens he could find no excuse for at all,' writes his disciple Mortimer Menpes, adding that Whistler thought Bret Harte 'a far greater literary genius than Thackeray or Dickens'.[37]

But once more in the case of Naipaul the evidence from an earlier phase of his development is completely different. I owe the following testimony of this to John O. Jordan's splendid essay on 'Postcolonial Dickens', reprinted in *Global Dickens*. He quotes first a passage from 'Prologue to an Autobiography' in *Finding the Centre*, about his early years in Trinidad:

> I was too young for newspapers. I was old enough only for stories [. . .] the early chapters of *Oliver Twist*; Mr. Murdstone from *David Copperfield*; Mr. Squeers. All this my father introduced me to [. . .]. It was the richest and most serene time of my childhood.

He continues with passages from *The Enigma of Arrival* that once more testify to the importance of the illustrations by Cruikshank or Phiz as well as the writing itself: 'The London I knew or had imaginatively possessed was the London I had got from Dickens. It was Dickens – and his illustrators – who gave me the illusion of knowing the city.' In *A House for Mr Biswas*, Biswas himself, modelled on Naipaul's father, succumbs to what is described as 'the solace of Dickens [. . .] he transferred characters and settings to people and places he knew. In the grotesques of Dickens everything he feared and suffered from was ridiculed and diminished,' in phrasing that Naipaul echoes in part of himself in *The Enigma of Arrival*: 'I transferred the Dickens characters to people I knew.'[38]

Moving to the Indian subcontinent, the name I want to mention first is not that of Premchand but of Mulk Raj Anand, whose early novel *The Untouchable*, appearing in 1935 when the author was thirty years old with a preface by E. M. Forster, quickly earned for him the well-worn tag of 'India's Charles Dickens'. But yet again, as S. Ramamurthy has shown, Anand was indeed a Dickens disciple, inspired in particular by his profound

410   MICHAEL HOLLINGTON

social criticism of Victorian England. 'As long as the world is poised between the few rich and the many poor,' he writes, 'Dickens will be read as Tolstoy is read in Russia.'[39]

Befriended by Forster, and taken up by other members of the Bloomsbury Group, Anand nonetheless read Dickens in the 1920s against the Bloomsbury grain – he writes of 'the contempt in which he [Dickens] was held in Virginia Woolf's circles'. Ramamurthy goes on to quote his article 'What the Dickens, Do You Mean?' where he describes how this reading fed into his second novel, *Coolie*, of 1936. 'I must confess that my passion for the rejected, which I had imbibed from my own life, certainly gained its intensity, to an extent, from the novels of Charles Dickens,' and again 'I took courage from him to try and bring into writing those underworld characters who had not so far entered polite literature.'[40]

But the most extended and articulate declaration by an Indian writer of homage to Dickens – equal and parallel to another master of the grotesque, Günter Grass – is surely that of Salman Rushdie. Once again, this is more than adequately covered by Jordan, though I begin my own quotation from Rushdie's account of this debt halfway through the passage that Jordan quotes, and extend it further than he, in order to demonstrate the extent to which the fundamental conception of *Midnight's Children* (1981) is modelled on an acute reading of later Dickens:

> In my earlier novels I tried to draw on the genius of Dickens. I was particularly taken with what struck me as his real innovation: namely, his unique combination of naturalistic backgrounds and surreal foregrounds. In Dickens, the details of place and social mores are skewered by a pitiless realism, a naturalistic exactitude that has never been bettered. Upon this realistic canvas he places his outsize characters, in whom we have no choice but to believe because we cannot fail to believe in the world they live in. So I tried, in my novel *Midnight's Children,* to set against a scrupulously observed social and historical background – against, that is, the canvas of a 'real' India – my 'unrealist' notion of children born at the midnight moment of India's independence, and endowed with magical powers by the coincidence, children who were in some way the embodiment of both the hopes and the flaws of that revolution.
>
>   Within the authoritative framework of his realism, Dickens can also make us believe in the perfectly Surrealist notion of a government department, the Circumlocution Office, dedicated to making nothing happen; or in the perfectly Absurdist, Ionesco-like case of *Jarndyce v. Jarndyce*, a case whose nature it is never to reach a conclusion; or in the 'magical realist' image of the dust-heaps in *Our Mutual Friend* – the physical symbols of a society living in the shadow of its own excrement.[41]

There we have it: in the late twentieth century, and still now, in the early twenty-first, Dickens remains a global inspiration and model to writers who, by any standards, are of the very highest class.

But I close with another Nobel prize-winner, this time one who, to the best of my knowledge, has never been compared to Dickens (I met him once, in Toulouse in France, and would have thought him more like Shakespeare). I am indebted once more to Jordan, who opens his 'Postcolonial Dickens' with a roll-call of four quotations, from Amitava Kumar, Ngũgĩ wa Thiong'o, V. S. Naipaul, as well as here from

Wole Soyinka, who declares he does not read novels – with one exception, those of Dickens:

> When I was a child I *devoured* Dickens. I think there is hardly any volume of Dickens' work that I have not read. There was something that fascinated me about the kind of life he depicted and I remember that in school I read literally all Dickens' novels.[42]

Bibliographical Reflections

This essay will be followed by a few titles of essential reading on the subject of 'Global Dickens'. But – having here only scratched the surface of the subject, limited as my coverage has been to work in English and a few related European and Indo-European languages – I should like to reflect here on the difficulties anyone must face in working in this area.

For, if global Dickens is an undoubted fact, its study, for any individual at least, is a virtual impossibility. Indeed, it can be said that the single most important scholar in the field, Ada Nisbet, the absolute pioneer and reference point for anyone who wishes to make worthwhile contribution to it, died on the job, without managing to do more than assemble a useful collection of essays on individual countries by an international array of contributors who, in their turn, in the case, for instance, of the great Russian Dickensian Igor Katarsky, sometimes themselves died during the course of work on it.

The archive containing these essays, and Nisbet's voluminous notes for the project they were meant to form part of – *Charles Dickens: International Guide to Study and Research 1870–1970* – are housed at the University of California at Santa Cruz. In *Global Dickens*, John O. Jordan, himself of Santa Cruz, gives an authoritative account of the massive undertaking they document, which occupied Nisbet for the best part of twenty years between the late 1960s and the mid-1980s, and of the archive itself.[43] He describes in detail both its contents and the history of its use, in which I myself played a part. In Santa Cruz, in the summer of 2006, I met Bob Nisbet, Ada's brother, who had donated the archive to the university after her death. He then expressed disappointment that, as far as he knew, no one had yet made use of it. As if to prove his point, I remember also talking at that time to other distinguished Dickensians who believed that there was no such archive, and that Ada Nisbet had in fact lost it in a London taxi (this was in fact true only of a section of her Dickens bibliography).

By the summer of 2007, when I was first able to spend a week or so examining it, Bob himself had died, and so was unable to witness the steady increase in its use in the last decade or so. In the twenty-first century, 'Global Dickens' is definitely now on the map: a conference with that title was organised at Griffith University in Brisbane in 2012, there is work in the field by a number of prominent Dickensians, including Regenia Gagnier and Dominic Rainsford, and above all there is the volume entitled *Global Dickens* edited by John O. Jordan and Nirshan Perera, on which I draw extensively here.

What for so long hindered the development of such a perspective was the myth of Dickens as a quintessential Englishman – 'our national novelist' according to

R. C. Lehmann.[44] George Augustus Sala's pronouncement in 1894 – 'I doubt whether there has ever been, among modern English writers, a more thoroughly typical example of the plain, downright Englishman than Charles Dickens [. . .] Dickens had, on the whole, a good-humoured contempt for foreigners' – also enjoyed wide currency.[45] Profoundly mistaken though it is, in my view, it held its reputation as canonical truth, up until the late twentieth century: the great Philip Collins, for instance, if I am not mistaken, was given to quoting it with approval.

There were certainly occasional voices, some of them foreign, who found space in surveys of Dickens or Dickens criticism for mention at least of a reception outside the English-speaking world. In this respect, George Ford's 1955 *Dickens and His Readers* is easily the most important precursor of Ada Nisbet's work, and I think Jordan is just a shade ungenerous when he remarks that 'Ford's book limits itself with only a few exceptions to examining the response of British and American audiences'[46] – at any rate, speaking personally, it was the first place where I learnt about the writer's influence on Dostoevsky or Kafka or Strindberg.

But it is only with Ada Nisbet's contribution to Lionel Stevenson's 1964 volume *Victorian Fiction: A Guide to Research* that we find a determined attempt to break out of what she calls the 'Anglo-American club' and provide some kind of systematic approach to surveying Dickens criticism in other languages. She fastens here, for instance, on an important 1957 essay in German on *Our Mutual Friend* by Ludwig Borinski placing Dickens as a proto-Modernist, 'Dickens' Spätstil', that I was able later to translate as 'Dickens's Late Style';[47] I only knew about it thanks to her. And it is worth remarking here that, despite significant advances in the study of global Dickens in recent years, a whole world remains to be done in the sphere of opening up to monoglot English and American Dickensians the impressive array of work on this author written in other languages. A major contemporary case in point is that of Nathalie Vanfasse of Aix-en-Provence, well known internationally as an important specialist in the field, but whose two books on Dickens are written in French, and therefore at present are off limits to all but a few outside the francophone world.[48]

But we are still only dealing with Dickens in Europe, a field to which my own two edited volumes of 2013, *The Reception of Charles Dickens in Europe*, offer a contribution, and Europe, even if the third largest continent in population, is only the sixth largest in size. Nisbet's project was to include all continents, and many important non-European languages. Again, she was way ahead of her time, anticipating the strong emergence of studies in postcolonial literature, which, as Jordan suggests, is one of the forces behind the emergence of the idea of a global Dickens. Their limitation, on the other hand, is that they are commonly confined to literature written in one or more of the colonising languages – English, French, Portuguese and so on – and again Nisbet had a broader vision. Major languages, and major centres of Dickens reception – India, China, Japan, with huge populations – are now de rigueur for any meaningful survey of global Dickens.

A virtual impossibility, then. Jordan is probably right to suggest that Ada Nisbet's project was never completed, at least in part, because of inadequate technology: he mentions the flimsy air-mail letters, through which it was largely conducted, that litter the archive. But this does not mean that – even with the more adequate technology available to us now – a proper, rounded vision of global Dickens is anywhere near to hand. It remains an aspiration.

Notes

1. Following the suggestion of Florian Schweizer, project director of the international Dickens 2012 campaign, the meaning of the word 'Dickensian' formed the subject of the bicentenary travelling Dickens conference (Paris/Boulogne/Rochester/London) in February 2012.
2. See my 'Dickens, "Phiz" and Physiognomy', in *Fantasy on a Long Rein: English Literature Illustrated*, ed. by Joachim Möller (Marburg: Jonas Verlag, 1988), 120–34, and 'Dickens and Cruikshank as Physiognomers in *Oliver Twist*', *Dickens Quarterly* 7.2 (1990), 1–11.
3. On reading character through external bodily features, see also my '"For God's Sake Look at This!": Physiognomy in *Bleak House*', *Cahiers victoriens et édouardiens* 90 (Autumn 2019). <https://doi.org/10.4000/cve.6255>
4. Gertrude Himmelfarb, *The Moral Imagination: From Adam Smith to Lionel Trilling* (Lanham: Rowman & Littlefield, 2012), 56.
5. Charles Dickens, *Pickwick Papers*, ed. by James Kingsley (Oxford: Clarendon Press, 1986), 371, ch. 25.
6. Gilbert Keith Chesterton, 'The Fairy Pickwick', *A Shilling for My Thoughts* (London: Methuen, 1917), 47.
7. Charles Dickens, *American Notes and Pictures from Italy* (Oxford: New Oxford Illustrated Edition, 1957), 175.
8. T. S. Eliot, *Complete Prose: Literature, Politics, Belief 1927–1929*, iii, ed. by Ronald Schuchard, Jennifer Formichelli and Frances Dickey (Baltimore: Johns Hopkins University Press, 2014), 165–6.
9. Virginia Woolf, '*David Copperfield*', in *Collected Essays*, ed. by Leonard Woolf, 4 vols (London: Hogarth Press, 1966), i, 191–5, 191.
10. On the latter, see Juliet John, *Dickens and Mass Culture* (Oxford: Oxford University Press, 2013), particularly ch. 6.
11. Mary Hammond, *Charles Dickens's* Great Expectations: *A Cultural Life, 1860–2012* (Farnham: Ashgate, 2015), 170.
12. Leonard Woolf, *Beginning Again: An Autobiography of the Years 1911–1918* (London: Hogarth Press, 1964), 204.
13. See my 'Mansfield Eats Dickens', in *Katherine Mansfield and Literary Influence*, ed. by Sarah Ailwood and Melinda Harvey (Edinburgh: Edinburgh University Press, 2015), 155–67, 158.
14. Angela Smith, 'Mansfield and Dickens: "I am not reading Dickens idly"', in *Celebrating Katherine Mansfield: A Centenary Volume of Essays*, ed. by Gerri Kimber and Janet Wilson (Basingstoke: Palgrave, 2011), 189–201; Holly Furneaux, '(Re)writing Dickens Queerly: The Correspondence of Katherine Mansfield', in *Reflections on/of Dickens*, ed. by Ewa Kujawska-Lis and Anna Krawczyk-Laskarzewska (Newcastle upon Tyne: Cambridge Scholars Publishing, 2014), 121–37; and Hollington, 'Mansfield Eats Dickens'.
15. *Global Dickens*, ed. by John O. Jordan and Nirshan Perera (Farnham: Ashgate, 2012), xix.
16. Joy Damousi, *Colonial Voices: A Cultural History of English in Australia, 1840–1940* (Cambridge: Cambridge University Press, 2010).
17. Ibid., 87.
18. Ibid., 174.
19. Antje Anderson, 'Dickens in Germany: The Nineteenth Century', in *The Reception of Charles Dickens in Europe*, ed. by Michael Hollington, 2 vols (London: Bloomsbury, 2013), i, 19–34.
20. Ibid., i, 9.

21. See my 'Adorno, Benjamin and *The Old Curiosity Shop*', *Dickens Quarterly* 6.3 (1989), 1–20, which offers a translation and discussion of this essay.
22. Lennartz, 'The Reception of Dickens in Germany, 1900–45', in *Reception*, I, 35–50.
23. See Stefan Welz, 'Dickens's Reception in Germany after 1945', in *Reception*, I, 51–68.
24. See Joachim Möller, 'German Illustrations,' in *Reception*, I, 69–76.
25. See Michael Hollington, 'The Underground Passage: Dickens and Dostoevsky', in *Reception*, I, 93.
26. In the introduction to Ezra Pound, *Selected Poems* (London: Faber & Gwyer, 1928), xvi. For a fuller consideration of the challenges and creativity involved in translating Dickens, see Klaudia Hiu Yen Lee's essay in this volume.
27. Quoted by Maurice Friedberg in *Literary Translation in Russia: A Cultural History* (University Park: Penn State University Press, 1997), 47–8.
28. In *Selected Essays* (London: Faber & Faber, 2014), 107.
29. The material in this and the preceding paragraph is drawn from my 'Introduction' to *Reception*, I, 1–16.
30. Jimmy So, 'The Charles Dickens of the World: Balzac, Premchand, and Others', *Newsweek*, 13 August 2012 <http://www.newsweek.com/charles-dickens-world-balzac-premchand-and-others-64373> [accessed 8 April 2019].
31. B. Riche and M. Benemanne, 'City Life and Women in Cyprian Ekwensi's *The People of the City* and *Jagua Nana*', *Revue Campus* 8 (2007), 37–47.
32. See Bernth Lindfors, 'Interview with Cyprian Ekwensi', *World Literature Written in English* 13.2 (1974), 141–54, 141.
33. Chimamanda Ngozi Adichie, 'Sex in the City', *Guardian*, 2 February 2008 <https://www.theguardian.com/books/2008/feb/02/featuresreviews.guardianreview1> [accessed 8 April 2019].
34. Dean Nelson, 'V. S. Naipaul and Paul Theroux in emotional Jaipur Literature Festival reunion', *Telegraph*, 21 January 2015 <http://www.telegraph.co.uk/news/worldnews/asia/india/11361208/V.S-Naipaul-and-Paul-Theroux-in-emotional-Jaipur-Literature-Festival-reunion.html> [accessed 8 April 2019].
35. Robert McCrum in 'Inimitable and Truly Great', *Guardian*, 14 October 2001 <https://www.theguardian.com/books/2001/oct/14/nobelprize.nobelprize2001> [accessed 8 April 2019].
36. See Gustave Kobbé, 'Whistler at West Point and in the U. S. Coast Survey', [1/20 December 1897], in *The Correspondence of James McNeill Whistler, 1855–1903*, ed. by Margaret F. MacDonald, Patricia de Montfort and Nigel Thorp, online edition, University of Glasgow <https://www.whistler.arts.gla.ac.uk/correspondence/people/display/?rs=2&namemeid=Gilder_1&sr=0&initial=g> [accessed 8 April 2019].
37. Mortimer Menpes, *Whistler As I Knew Him* (Tucson: Hol Art Books, 2009), 50.
38. Jordan and Perera, 187, 198, 199.
39. S. Ramamurthy, 'A Study of Influence and Popularity: Charles Dickens and Mulk Raj Anand', 2 April 2015 <http://srm1948.blogspot.com.au/2015/04/influence-and-popularity-dickens-and.html> [accessed 8 April 2019].
40. Ibid.
41. Salman Rushdie, 'Influence', in *Step Across This Line: Collected Non-Fiction, 1992–2002* (London: Vintage, 2003), 71.
42. Jordan and Perera, 187.
43. Jordan and Perera, xxi–xxii; 45–54.
44. See *Reception*, I, 1.
45. In *Things I Have Seen and People I Have Known* (London: Cassell, 1894), 103.
46. Jordan and Perera, 46.

GLOBAL DICKENS

47. *Charles Dickens: Critical Assessments*, ed. by Michael Hollington, 4 vols (Sussex: Helm, 1995), III, 617–39.
48. See Nathalie Vanfasse, *La Plume et la Route: Charles Dickens écrivain-voyageur* (Aix-en-Provence: Presses universitaires de Provence, 2017) and *Charles Dickens, entre normes et déviance* (Aix-en-Provence: Publications de l'Université de Provence, 2007).

Further Reading

Michael Hollington, ed., *Charles Dickens: Critical Assessments*, 4 vols (Sussex: Helm, 1995)
Michael Hollington, ed., *The Reception of Charles Dickens in Europe*, 2 vols (London: Bloomsbury, 2013)
Juliet John, *Dickens and Mass Culture* (Oxford: Oxford University Press, 2013)
John O. Jordan and Nirshan Perera, eds, *Global Dickens* (Farnham: Ashgate, 2012)
Ada C. Nisbet, 'Charles Dickens', in *Victorian Fiction: A Guide to Research*, ed. by Lionel Stevenson (Cambridge, MA: Harvard University Press, 1964), 44–153

27

EDUCATION

Sarah Winter

WRITING IN 1886, HENRY MORLEY, PROFESSOR of English at University College London and a former contributor to *Household Words*, described Charles Dickens's editorial work as a wide-ranging effort 'to improve society' through publications that would contribute to 'right citizen-building' and 'help one half of the world really to know how the other half lived'.[1] Voiced after the major educational reforms of the 1870s and 1880s, Morley's view suggests in retrospect that Dickens's works purveyed a kind of civics lesson geared towards forging social consensus – a lesson of the kind that public school classrooms would be tasked to convey in twentieth-century representative democracies. Giving evidence that this characterisation was an accurate one, in a February 1844 speech at a banquet in support of the Mechanics' Institution at Liverpool, Dickens proclaimed: 'I look forward from this place, as from a tower, to the time when high and low, and rich and poor, shall mutually assist, improve, and educate each other.'[2] Morley's comments and Dickens's speech exemplify this chapter's focus on the ways that Dickens's writings and authorial persona became associated with an ideal of social solidarity to be achieved through universal education in conjunction with wide public access to literature and the arts. Morley's characterisation, however, fails to capture the ways in which Dickens's vision for education incorporated ideals that could be considered as social democratic, implying a dimension of social justice. For Dickens, universal education would play a socially corrective role, and not simply by enabling individuals to pursue their own self-betterment. More crucially, the spread of education would increase access of the poor collectively to benefits and opportunities for advancement that were generally inaccessible to them, and from which they were unjustly excluded. In recommending universal education, Dickens envisioned a more fully participatory and inclusive society in which the potential for creativity of the poor and their positive contributions to social and cultural life could be more explicitly recognised.

This chapter investigates Dickens's own multifaceted and energetic engagements with educational themes and initiatives in his writings and career. Beginning with a survey of the central themes and frequent social criticism in Dickens's fictional plots related to schooling and education, the chapter also studies Dickens's journalism and public addresses concerning education and the arts. In his speeches, Dickens also advocated for greater public access to the independent and voluntary learning pursued in Mechanics' Institutions and free public libraries. He also supported schools for students engaged in trades, newly founded colleges for women and the working classes, and public arts organisations. Dickens also engaged in many social reform efforts that incorporated educational schemes, including his founding in 1847

EDUCATION 417

with the help of the philanthropist Angela Burdett-Coutts, of Urania Cottage, a home for retraining former prostitutes in domestic tasks and assisting them to emigrate to begin new lives in Australia. Such combined efforts evidence Dickens's sustained commitment to the long-delayed goal of universal, free and mandatory public education in Britain.[3]

After his death, the dissemination of Dickens's canonical image of authorship would take place not only through the global circulation of his novels, but also in school classrooms in Britain and its colonies, and in the United States. In the final section of the chapter, I examine how the inclusion of Dickens's writings in the English literature textbooks and curricula of schools and universities in the United States and in colonial Kenya and Uganda participated in the cultural transmission of Englishness. His pointedly nonpartisan advocacy of the role of popular literature and the arts in fostering the social inclusion of the masses could be incorporated into the 'citizen-building' rationales of the public school system in a twentieth-century representative democracy such as the United States. Dickens's cultivated Victorian reputation as a humanitarian reformer could also be enlisted within textbooks and curricula as a canonical image of English authorship. Anthologies of English literature implemented this image in various ways: to model a civics lesson on democratic participation in an American school or, within colonial school systems in Africa, to provide a cultural rationale for the legitimacy of British imperial rule.[4] In both cases, however, Dickens's stringent criticisms of social exclusion and class prejudices in Victorian society, evident in the novels, were submerged within literature curricula in favour of the consensus-building goals of American public education and justifications of British cultural superiority communicated to students in the Empire. Yet, due to creative teaching, it also became possible for African students to interpret Dickens's novels in an anticolonial light.

Schooling and Social Critique in Dickens's Novels, Journalism and Educational Projects

Beginning with spoofs on schools for young ladies in his early newspaper sketches (collected in the First and Second Series of *Sketches by Boz* (1836)) and *The Pickwick Papers* (1836–7), Dickens's fictional depictions and journalistic opinion pieces were often satirical and sometimes harshly critical of the coercive measures, negligence and reliance on rote learning perpetrated by Victorian schools, particularly those for the poor.[5] In his serial novel *Nicholas Nickleby* (1838–9), Dickens pursued one of his most concerted efforts to link his fiction directly to a social reform project by incorporating into the novel an exposé of a Yorkshire boarding school for boys administered by an incompetent and sadistic schoolmaster, Wackford Squeers. The incidents in the novel are based in part on an investigative trip that Dickens made to Bowes Academy in Gretna Bridge at the end of January 1838, to investigate the notorious Yorkshire schools. These inexpensive schools, remote from major cities, marketed themselves through advertisements to parents with limited incomes, and they were also known as places to send illegitimate children to keep them out of the way.[6] In the novel, after his father's death and the loss of his family's income, Nicholas Nickleby becomes an assistant teacher at Squeers's boarding school, Dotheboys

Hall, and befriends a student, Smike, who has been abandoned there by his relatives. Exemplifying Dickens's developing critique of pedagogies that crush students' spirits and imaginations rather than appealing to their natural curiosity and wonder, the narrator describes the bullied Smike's futile attempts 'to master some task which a child of nine years old, possessed of ordinary powers, could have conquered with ease, but which, to the addled brain of the crushed boy of nineteen, was a sealed and hopeless mystery'.[7] When Squeers and his wife begin to beat Smike in front of all the other boys as a punishment, Nicholas intervenes, snatching away the lash from Squeers and beating him into a stupor in an act of poetic justice praised by neighbours when they learn of it: 'Beatten a schoolmeasther! 'Cod it's the best thing a've heerd this twenty year!'[8] The novel depicts how, after his abuse, the partial restoration of Smike's memory takes place through the dramatic arts. After they flee the school and join a travelling theatre troupe, Smike performs a minor role alongside Nicholas in a production of *Romeo and Juliet*. In his Preface to the 1848 First Cheap Edition, Dickens implies that his novel had played a role in the closing of most of the Yorkshire schools, commenting that: 'Of the monstrous neglect of education in England, and the disregard of it by the State as a means of forming good or bad citizens, and miserable or happy men, this class of schools has long afforded a notable example.'[9] This commentary underscores Dickens's ongoing efforts to leverage fiction into public awareness that could lead to educational reforms.

Other coercive teachers satirised in Dickens's novels include Miss Monflathers in *The Old Curiosity Shop* (1840–1), the proprietor of a provincial school for young ladies. During a walk with her pupils, the schoolmistress encounters Little Nell distributing bills advertising Mrs Jarley's waxworks exhibition. She takes the opportunity to berate Nell for her idle occupation as an instructive lesson in proper class relations for her charges:

> Don't you feel how naughty it is of you [. . .] to be a wax-work child, when you might have the proud consciousness of assisting, to the extent of your infant powers, the manufactures of your country; of improving your mind by the constant contemplation of the steam-engine; and of earning a comfortable and independent subsistence of from two-and-nine-pence to three shillings per week? Don't you know that the harder you are at work, the happier you are?[10]

For a character like Miss Monflathers, who parodies conservative educational writers such as Hannah More, every poor child who is not involved in factory work is subversive of society and nation by existing outside of his or her appointed place. This vignette shows Dickens's disdain in the 1840s for popular education schemes pursued as a means of religious and political indoctrination.

Perhaps Dickens's most famous satire of Victorian schooling for the poor as a vehicle for reproducing docile workers presumed incapable of independent thought appears in *Hard Times* (1854), set in the fictionalised industrial town of Coketown. Dickens launches his critique of Utilitarian political economy in a classroom, through a satire of a system of education that mechanises children's minds on the factory model. As the teacher, Mr M'Choakumchild, interrogates the children on their factual knowledge, Mr Gradgrind MP, patron of the school and propounder of the doctrines of political economy, constantly reminds them that 'You are never to fancy', revealing his goal of evacuating any freedom of thought and imagination that could fuel children's love for the arts and literature and carry them through hard times in the harsh, exploitative environment of the industrial town.[11] The demoralising implications of this pedagogy are revealed when Sissy Jupe, the daughter of a circus performer, recounts to Gradgrind's daughter Louisa how she was quizzed by Mr M'Choakumchild, who asked her to agree to a proposition measuring 'National Prosperity':

> [The teacher asked] 'Now, this schoolroom is a Nation. And in this nation, there are fifty millions of money. Isn't this a prosperous nation, and a'n't you in a thriving state?'
> 'What did you say?' asked Louisa.
> 'Miss Louisa, I said I didn't know. I thought I couldn't know whether it was a prosperous nation or not, and whether I was in a thriving state or not, unless I knew who had got the money, and whether any of it was mine. But that had nothing to do with it. It was not in the figures at all', said Sissy, wiping her eyes.[12]

Through this interchange exhibiting the tendentious and ideological nature of so-called facts and statistics concerning aggregated measures of wealth, the novel extends its critique of Victorian political economy's disregard for the effects of its doctrines on society and individuals and its propagation as a glorified form of rote learning. Sissy's resistance to being taught to ignore the distribution of income in her understanding of national prosperity, and her inability to give up her common-sense perception of injustice, make her a failed student in this kind of indoctrination of the young. Louisa's brother, Tom Gradgrind, ends up stealing money from a bank, showing that stunting the child's imagination also corrupts the moral character. If Dickens often saw education as a means to prevent criminality, the novel's plot depicts how an education of factual cramming and a life of work without leisure and the influence of the arts could actually promote criminal behaviour, and not just among the poorer classes.

Throughout his career as a novelist Dickens also depicted characters among the illiterate as well as the self-taught poor and workers as inventive and resourceful despite their limited means, and as cultural producers and not just consumers. In a brief vignette from *Oliver Twist* (1837–9), the narrator describes a 'miserable shoeless criminal' held at the metropolitan police office in London where Oliver is taken after his erroneous arrest for stealing Mr Brownlow's handkerchief. According to the highly sarcastic narrator, this is a prisoner:

> who had been taken up for playing the flute, and who—the offence against society having been clearly been proved—had been very properly committed by Mr Fang to the House of Correction for one month, with the appropriate and amusing remark that since he had got so much breath to spare, it would be much more wholesomely expended on the treadmill than on a musical instrument.

When Nancy calls out for Oliver during her search through the jail in order to return him to Fagin's gang, the prisoner 'made no answer, being occupied in mentally bewailing the loss of the flute, which had been confiscated for the use of the county'.[13] A critique of the vagrancy laws and arbitrary court proceedings prejudicial to the poor, this scene of injustice and deprivation illuminates the human need for creative self-expression, which knows no class distinctions, and can become a means of livelihood for street performers and authors alike. But such artistic expression can be suppressed or thwarted by institutions exhibiting class and partisan prejudices, especially in the absence of public provision and support for education and the arts.

Similarly, in *Our Mutual Friend* (1864–5), the impoverished and disabled but fiercely independent doll's dressmaker, Jenny Wren, a teenager who supports herself and her alcoholic father, confidently explains how 'We Professors, who live upon our taste and invention, are obliged to keep our eyes always open', and describes her work 'cutting out' replicas of the most popular figures in the London scenes that she observes around her.[14] In this way she becomes a representative of the creative resources to be found among the poorest members of society, whose 'inventions' could foster greater social inclusion and participation in cultural life from the bottom up rather than from the top down. Jenny Wren also stands in for the novelist Dickens's own inventive fashioning of transformative literary art.

As evidenced in the early sketch 'A Visit to Newgate' (in the First Series of *Sketches by Boz*, 1836), Dickens's explorations of schooling in his journalism developed his lifelong concern with the linkage between juvenile delinquency and the lack of educational provision for poor children. The description of certain boys in a school within the prison, who had been 'committed for trial on charges of pocket-picking', is disparaging and pessimistic: 'We never looked upon a more disagreeable sight, because we never saw fourteen such hopeless and irreclaimable wretches before.'[15] However, in 'A Walk in a Workhouse' (*Household Words*, 25 May 1850), based on a visit Dickens made to the Marylebone Workhouse, the narrator notes approvingly that the Infant School is 'a large, light, airy room at the top of the building' with 'two mangey pauper rocking-horses rampant in a corner'. In the boys' school, 'the boys were roaming unrestrained about a large and airy yard', and 'some of them had been drawing large ships upon the schoolroom wall'. These are signs of children's learning through play and by imagining an adventurous way of life that they might pursue when their freedom to roam outside the workhouse would no longer be restricted. Similarly, in the girls' school 'everything bore a cheerful and healthy aspect', and, most importantly, the children generally seem 'robust and well, and apparently the objects of very great care'.[16] This detail is important, because elsewhere in the article, Dickens conveys the cooped-up and hungry adult paupers' poignant pleas, evoking a radical political platform, that they long for 'a little more liberty—and a little more bread'.[17] Both impoverished children's and adults' capacities for creativity and contributing to the larger society require attention to their fundamental right to freedom as well as their health and welfare – with both of these being the responsibility, in Dickens's liberal view, of the state.

In his journalism, Dickens also criticised common instructional methods of rote learning and religious indoctrination, to the exclusion of almost all other subject matter or practical skills, in Victorian schools for the poor, including the Ragged Schools for the street children of London founded by Anglican Evangelicals. A proponent of the Ragged Schools from their beginnings in 1843, Dickens urged readers of *The Daily News* in 1846 to join him in support of them, while voicing both his criticism of their lessons as 'not being sufficiently secular, and as presenting too

EDUCATION 421

many religious mysteries and difficulties, to minds not sufficiently prepared for their reception', and his 'appreciation for the efforts of these teachers'.[18] But *Our Mutual Friend*, published almost twenty years later, includes a harshly critical satire when the narrator describes Charley Hexam's education in a Ragged School-like setting:

> Its atmosphere was oppressive and disagreeable; it was crowded, noisy, and confusing; half the pupils dropped asleep, or fell into a state of waking stupefaction; the other half kept them in either condition by maintaining a monotonous droning noise, as if they were performing out of time and tune, on a ruder sort of bagpipe.[19]

Recognisable as the droning recitation from a spelling-book, the students' efforts seem only an imitation of reading for comprehension, while the teachers, 'animated solely by good intentions, had no idea of execution, and a lamentable jumble was the upshot of their kind endeavours'.[20] For Dickens, the shortfalls in educational provision for London's pauper children had become by the 1860s indicative of a wholly inadequate, partly state-funded system, which standardised and manufactured 'school-buildings, school-teachers, and school-pupils, all according to pattern and all engendered in the latest Gospel according to Monotony'.[21] The system facilitated cramming and conformity but failed to promote individual learning or creativity. Such outcomes were quite the opposite of Jenny Wren's independent artistic inventiveness and her acute social vision, acquired from her struggles to make a living and her experiences, rather than formal schooling.

In *Our Mutual Friend*, the most shocking product of this educational system is the former 'pauper lad' and 'highly certificated stipendiary schoolmaster' Bradley Headstone, a beneficiary of the British Parliament's funding of pupil-teacher training and teacher training colleges, beginning in 1846. In Bradley, Dickens seems to personify the thwarted ambitions of professionalised working-class teachers, whose status as de facto civil servants was repudiated by the free-market educational reforms of the Revised Code of 1862. A money-saving measure, the Revised Code eliminated teachers' stipends for training apprentice pupil-teachers and made their salaries entirely contingent on the number of their students who passed government inspections. Bradley violently assaults and almost succeeds in murdering the urbane, public-school-educated *flâneur* and part-time barrister Eugene Wrayburn, out of rage and jealousy over his upper-class privilege and Lizzie Hexam's rejection of his own attentions in favour of Wrayburn's. Bradley exhibits a psychopathology through which the novel seems to indict the mid-Victorian school system for perpetuating social distinctions and inequalities.[22] Most likely recognising the social privilege that a public school conferred, however, Dickens sent his oldest son Charley to Eton.[23] Henry Fielding Dickens was the only one of Dickens's seven sons to attend university, at Trinity Hall, Cambridge.[24] Dickens's daughters, Mary (Mamie) and Katherine (Katey), were educated at home by governesses, like many upper-middle-class Victorian girls.[25]

Dickens also addressed the social prejudices and material difficulties experienced by working-class writers in response to personal relationships he developed with his readers. For example, he was supportive of the literary endeavours of John Overs, a cabinetmaker, who contacted him in January 1839 about the possibility of publishing his poems in *Bentley's Miscellany*, where Dickens was just winding up his role as editor. The poems were eventually published elsewhere, but the two men kept up a correspondence and a frequent visiting acquaintance until Overs's death from tuberculosis in 1844. Before his death, Dickens supported Overs financially at various times and helped him to publish his book, *Evenings of a Working Man, Being the Occupation of his Scanty Leisure* (1844), a collection of his essays, poems and stories, meant to raise funds to support his family.[26] Dickens also contributed a preface, in which he states of the book: 'While I do not commend it, on the one hand, as a prodigy, I do sincerely believe it, on the other, to possess some points of real interest, however considered; but which, if considered with reference to its title and origin, are of great interest.' Dickens also argues that Overs's example of 'the principle of a working-man turning author' will seem much less unusual when 'the Universal Education of the people [. . .] will effectually swamp any interest that may now attach in vulgar minds, to the few among them who are enabled, in any degree, to overcome the great difficulties of their position'.[27]

Evidence for Dickens's support for cultural enrichment opportunities for factory workers appears in *American Notes* (1842), his account of his travels in the United States in 1842, where he describes approvingly the boarding houses for young women mill workers that he visited in Lowell, Massachusetts, as a model to be emulated in England:

> Firstly, there is a joint-stock piano in a great many of the boarding-houses. Secondly, nearly all these young ladies subscribe to circulating libraries. Thirdly, they have got up among themselves a periodical called THE LOWELL OFFERING, 'A repository of original articles, written exclusively by females actively employed in the mills,'—which is duly printed, published, and sold; and whereof I brought away from Lowell four hundred good solid pages, which I have read from beginning to end.

As in his preface to Overs's book, Dickens refutes the opinion, attributed to narrow-minded English readers, that such cultural attainments by these young women are 'above their station' as mill workers, instead arguing that they 'startle us by their novelty, and not by their bearing upon any question of right or wrong'.[28]

These observations on overcoming prejudices against working people's aspirations towards self-improvement and cultivation pertain as well to Dickens's remarkable project for Urania Cottage, a 'Home' for young women released from London's jails, many of them former prostitutes. Dickens opened Urania Cottage in 1847 at Shepherd's Bush in London, and oversaw it for ten years, with the help of his close friend and collaborator on multiple philanthropic projects, the banking heiress Angela Burdett-Coutts, who funded the initiative. Expressing Dickens's particular variation on the 'duty' and 'self-restraint' central to conventional Victorian middle-class ideals of women's domestic roles, the project nevertheless became a model for non-punitive, small-scale liberal reform institutions.[29] Dickens describes the aim of this 'Home' in a May 1846 letter outlining the project to Burdett-Coutts:

> I would have it written up in every room—that they were not going through a monotonous round of occupation and self-denial which began and ended there, but which began, or was resumed, under that roof, and would end, by God's blessing, in happy homes of their own.[30]

EDUCATION 423

Dickens explained to Burdett-Coutts how he viewed the plight of prostitutes as 'unfortunate women' who are 'constantly in and out of the Prisons, for no other fault or crime than their original one of having fallen from virtue'. He emphasises that, once admitted, if any woman decided to run away, she would be treated with leniency:

> I would pay particular attention to [this tendency among such women], and treat it with particular gentleness and anxiety; *and I would not make one, or two, or three, or four, or six departures from the Establishment a binding reason against the readmission of that person being again penitent*, but would leave it to the managers to decide upon the merits of the case.

Decisions on readmission would be based on each woman's past behaviour while in the home. Dickens thus aligned the asylum's discipline with a forgiving family model, rather than an inflexible disciplinary regime.[31]

Recruited by reform-minded officials at women's prisons who were known to Dickens, the young women (including not just former prostitutes but also former thieves, starving and destitute needle workers, and inmates of workhouses) who chose to accept the opportunity would be trained during their residence at Urania Cottage as domestic servants and then assisted to emigrate to Australia, where they would find employment or marry, and begin new lives.[32] The layout and furnishing of the house, the clothing the residents were to wear, and the highly structured daily and weekly routines were all designed by Dickens himself. They included training in and thereafter carrying out all the cooking, laundry, needlework, and other household chores and, since most of the young women were illiterate, lessons in reading, writing and arithmetic for two hours per day and religious instruction by a clergyman. While the routine was rigorous, there were several hours of free time at different points in the day and in the evening.

Expressing Dickens's belief in the essential role of leisure and pleasurable entertainments, the arts and literature were also a significant component of Dickens's paternalistic aspiration to reform these outcast and poor women. The establishment also had a garden divided into plots for each woman to plant and tend, and a small library stocked by Dickens with poetry by authors such as Crabbe and Wordsworth and novels, which the resident matrons (personally hired by Dickens) would read aloud to their charges in the evenings. The selection of these reading materials may indicate that Dickens shared the views of liberal educational commentators such as John Stuart Mill and Matthew Arnold on the positive effects of poetry across social classes for personal cultivation, emotional renewal, and inculcation of humane moral values.[33] Dickens also arranged for the purchase of a used piano along with a short series of lessons for the women in singing hymns in parts.[34] Through a combination of demanding discipline as well as creative self-expression on a modest scale, Dickens sought to educate these 'fallen women' towards happy and productive lives (by his lights) as 'faithful wives of honest men' in 'a distant country' where they may 'live and die in peace'.[35] These formulations also indicate that Dickens's Urania Cottage project was a reformist contribution towards ameliorating the often dire circumstances that drove the British poor to emigrate to the settler colonies and dominions of the British Empire.

'The Great and Omnipotent Principle of Comprehensive Education Everywhere'

In addition to Dickens's fiction, journalism and social welfare projects, his public speeches reveal particularly clearly how his promotion of universal education was directly linked to his support for expanding public access to the arts and literature. Between 1840 and 1870, Dickens gave numerous addresses, often as the featured speaker or Chair, at fundraising and celebratory events in support of Mechanics' Institutions, public libraries, Athenaeums and other institutions that extended educational and cultural opportunities to the working classes. Several significant themes return repeatedly in these speeches: the social inclusiveness and harmonising effects of such educational institutions, due to their provision of higher learning for working-class members, including women; the non-partisan efforts and civic-minded motives exhibited by such institutions' founders and organisers; and the ways that the spread of education encouraged the growth of popular readership and demand for good literature, thus enabling authors to emancipate themselves from the patronage and political agendas of the wealthy. Dickens makes the latter two points forcefully in one of his earliest extant addresses in 1840 at the Southwark Literary and Scientific Institution in London. He asserts that, 'had institutions similar to this existed long since, that one disgraceful leaf of dedication which formed the blot upon the literature of past ages would have been torn from its pages', and 'Milton might have been appreciated in the age which he adorned, Otway might have lived and dined a few years longer [*a laugh*], and he knew not but that even Wordsworth might have been drawn from the dust of those shelves where until lately he had lain unnoticed and unmarked. [*Hear, hear*]'.[36] In a more politically radical vein, Dickens also points out how such institutions could be models for political cooperation and even democratising electoral reform:

> It was gratifying to find that this was a neutral ground upon which all shades of political opinions might mingle without a political compromise, proving satisfactorily—and a gratifying circumstance it was—the desire of those gentlemen rather to be elected by an enlightened constituency than to be representatives of ignorance and grovelling stupidity. [*Applause*].[37]

Political reform would proceed from more informed and therefore more exigent electors, and not by means of clientelism and condescension. Within such educational institutions, the role of literature and the arts would be to create a more inclusive public that could, in turn, militate against divisive political partisanship.

Dickens was consistently supportive of institutions extending educational opportunities to the working classes, particularly when addressing middle-class audiences. In a speech in honour of the Birmingham Polytechnic Institution in 1844, Dickens pointed to its educational resources as supplying the working classes with 'an opportunity for disproving the stigma and vindicating themselves before the world' against the 'idle and prejudiced' opinion that they are 'wanton and mischievous persons' in their public behaviour, specifically, when visiting such public arts venues as the National Gallery and the British Museum in London.[38] He expresses his approval that:

the resolutions about to be proposed do not contain in themselves anything of a sectarian or class nature; that they do not confine themselves to any one single institution, but assert the great and omnipotent principle of comprehensive education everywhere, and under each and every circumstance.[39]

Here Dickens promotes universal education as a public duty of society and the state. Reinforcing this imperative, in a speech at the Glasgow Athenaeum in 1847, Dickens voiced his approbation for its 'educational example to all Scotland; when I regard it no less as a recognition on the part of everybody here to the right indisputable and inalienable of all those who are actively engaged in the work and business of life to elevate and improve themselves so far as in them lies by all good means', indicating that the pursuit of such inclusive educational goals must be achievable because they represent a 'common cause of right'.[40] Dickens's radical democratic claim for a universal right to education, seeming to invoke the French and American revolutionary declarations, is remarkable here. He may have made such bold assertions in the context of a visit to Scotland in recognition of its much more comprehensive provision of elementary education.

Dickens more frequently embraced certain liberal notions of education as a means of producing social harmony and discouraging class conflict. For example, in a speech on 2 September 1852, at the opening of the Manchester Free Library shortly after the passage of the 1850 Public Libraries Act, Dickens claimed to voice the deepest sentiments of the grateful working-class patron:

how he knows that the books stored here for his behoof will cheer him through many of the struggles and toils of his life, will raise him in his self-respect, will teach him that capital and labour are not opposed, but are mutually dependent and mutually supporting [*hear, hear, and applause*].[41]

Dickens's consistent arguments for horizontal, generalised social empowerment of the masses through education differs from the top-down strategy of implanting a stronger ability to reason in the lower classes articulated by such liberal educational reformers as Sir James Kay-Shuttleworth and John Stuart Mill. In an 1853 speech at a banquet in his honour at Birmingham, Dickens emphasised that 'the people have set Literature free' from any subservience to patrons and non-artistic principles, and consequently, 'that Literature cannot be too faithful to the people in return—cannot too ardently advocate the cause of their advancement, happiness, and prosperity. [*Loud applause*]'. Arguing that literature has improved rather than declined in quality by being made more affordable, Dickens expresses confidence in working-class readers' intellectual interests and appreciation of the arts, including music and painting.[42] In this speech, Dickens also praised the educational institutions of Birmingham more generally, including the 'excellent girls' schools in various parts of the town, which [. . .] I should most sincerely desire to see in every town in England'.[43]

We can see from Dickens's speeches that, in aligning his own success as an author and his aesthetic independence as an artist with the goals of universal education, he developed a distinctive cultural politics built on the idea of expanding access to the arts and education as arenas of social participation with egalitarian and progressively democratising tendencies.[44] In one of his final public appearances before his death, as the prize presenter in his role as president of the Birmingham and Midland Institute on 6 January 1870, Dickens extolled 'the benefits of such an establishment [that] must extend far beyond the limits of this midland county fires and smoke, and must comprehend, in some sort, the whole community'.[45] Such progressive institutions, for Dickens, must be sustained by the broadest possible social inclusiveness, including of women students:

> I hope and believe that the [Birmingham and Midland Institute] will always be expansive and elastic; for ever seeking to devise new means of enlarging the circle of its members, and of attracting to itself the confidence of still greater and greater numbers, and never more evincing any more disposition to stand still than time does, or life does, or the seasons do.[46]

Given the paternalistic ethos of Dickens's Urania Cottage project and his generally conventional views of women's domestic role, it is evident that his support for girls' and women's education did not extend as far as, for example, the progressive views of advocates of women's higher education such as Emily Shirreff, John Stuart and Harriet Mill, or Frances Buss, who promoted women's educational advancement into the professions. However, in a character such as *Bleak House*'s (1852–3) Esther Summerson, whose judgement in things that truly matter is the only sound and reliable one in the world of the novel, we might find a limited prefiguration of the educated domestic woman's capabilities as a fellow citizen.

During the 1840s and 1850s particularly, the goal of universal education was also part of the political platform and social reformist goals of groups whose members came from the working classes, including the followers of Robert Owen, the Chartists, and labour organisations such as the London Working Men's Association, the Miners' Association of Great Britain and Ireland and the Metropolitan Trades Delegates.[47] At the same time, Chartist writers objected to ulterior motives towards building class consensus of organisations for working-class education founded by middle-class reformers and businessmen, especially when working-class members were excluded from leadership roles.[48] Often distrustful of organised labour and its leadership, Dickens nevertheless defended the sincerity of striking workers and admired their sense of solidarity, both in *Hard Times* and his contemporaneous article 'On Strike' (published in *Household Words*, 11 February 1854). His support for institutions such as Mechanics' Institutes therefore comes into focus as liberal reformist, and perhaps more paternalistic than his participatory and inclusive vision for universal education and public access to the arts. Dickens's stringent critiques of the mind-numbing routine of memorisation and the fact-centred curriculum of Victorian elementary schooling also articulate his reformist belief that the imaginations of students in a national education system should be encouraged to expand through creative expression in a curriculum including the arts and literature.

Coda: Reading Dickens in School – Towards Imperial and Global Anglophone Connections

The wide dissemination of Dickens's novels through cheap publications across anglophone countries such as Canada, Australia and the United States as well as other British colonies where English was taught and spoken, made his literary influence into an international and even a global phenomenon. At the same time, Dickens's authorial persona took on a multifarious life of its own. One of the most important locations where Dickens's authorship developed as a global phenomenon was in schoolrooms, textbooks and curricula, where what I have been calling the democratising, participatory cultural politics that he had defined over his career were shifted by the school and university English literature curriculum into a cultural identification with Englishness. Launched during his lifetime, a capsule biography of Dickens as a man of the people who became a world-famous humanitarian advocate for the poor was, through its reproduction in school readers, rendered a canonical image of English authorship. Alongside this cameo, his stories (often abridged) could be taught as touchstones supporting the socially affiliating civic functions of free public schooling in Britain and the United States. But his critiques of exclusionary Victorian institutions and social prejudices that had gained him both attention and notoriety through his fiction do not form a part of this curricular message.

For example, an introduction describing the worldwide influence of *A Christmas Carol* (1843) included in an American school reader from 1919 interprets the story's meaning as follows:

Few stories have ever been written that have made more people really happy than this. Probably it has turned millions of sour-tempered Scrooges into well-wishers and transformed many a bleak Christmas into a joyous time of feasting and loving.

This characterisation of the tale's effect as teaching 'well-wishing' to all is presented by the textbook authors as the result of a vote taken in a coeducational classroom asking students to discuss the story's meaning and to 'name what they considered the very noblest quality that any person can possess'.[49] The choice of 'noblest' suggests that the lesson fosters a subtly hierarchical frame of reference and a kind of heroic individualism attributed to the great English author and his influence. This example of a classroom reading of *A Christmas Carol* conjures an image of Dickens's authorial influence for the purposes of a civics lesson in participatory democracy, but one that celebrates individual achievement. Such a pedagogical use of Dickens's canonical humanitarian persona (as I have shown in greater detail elsewhere), positions the school and the English literature curriculum as the transactional space and frame of reference where social and gender stratification outside the school is transformed and submerged, at least temporarily, into a historically deracinated exercise in consensus and citizen-building.[50]

Novelist and dramatist Ngũgĩ wa Thiong'o's account of his schooling in colonial Kenya provides evidence that a similar view of Dickens's humanitarian influence as transmitted through his authorial persona and writings was accompanied by a more stringent enforcement of Englishness as a cultural hegemony within English literature classrooms in the British colonies. Born into a large peasant family, Ngũgĩ explains that, during the first four years of his elementary schooling during the 1940s and early 1950s, instruction in the missionary school he attended was in his mother tongue of Gĩkũyũ. But after a state of emergency was declared by the colonial government in Kenya in 1952 in response to the armed independence movement referred to by the British as 'Mau Mau', all local schools came under the supervision of District

428   SARAH WINTER

Education Boards administered by English officials, and English became the mandatory language of formal instruction. Ngũgĩ recounts how speaking Gĩkũyũ was pro-
hibited both inside classrooms and on school grounds, and children were encouraged
to report other students for infractions, which were followed by corporal punishment
or shaming in front of the class.

It was within this repressive regime of the English language that Ngũgĩ read
'simplified Dickens', alongside works by Stevenson, Hughes and Haggard in primary school.[51] He reports that 'Jim Hawkins, Oliver Twist and Tom Brown—not
Hare, Leopard and Lion—were now my daily companions in the world of imagination'.[52] Characters spanning the Victorian social and educational spectrum from a
workhouse childhood to public schoolboys at Rugby thus displaced the traditional
oral folktales that Ngũgĩ had learned at home. It would seem that the missionary
school, by importing the imperialist curriculum designed for working-class English
boys in the 1880s, attempted to foster loyalty to the colonial administration.[53] But
such readings, Ngũgĩ suggests, may have elicited confusing identifications among the
Kenyan boys with both disempowered and pauperised children such as Oliver and
the intrepid boy protagonists of imperial adventure tales, starring white male explor-
ers. In a colonial classroom during an anticolonial rebellion, Dickens's depictions of
Oliver's victimisation by cruel Victorian institutions such as the workhouse might
conceivably have led students to question a curriculum intended to promote loyalty
to the colonial state through enforcement of English literacy.

Ngũgĩ describes the purpose of this 'colonialist imposition of a foreign language'
through education as 'domination of the mental universe of the colonised, the control,
through culture, of how people perceived themselves and their relationship to the
world'.[54] Commenting on the English literature curriculum that he studied starting
in 1959 at Makerere University in Kampala, Uganda, Ngũgĩ includes Dickens within
'the great humanist and democratic tradition of European literature', which, however,
'even at its most humane and universal, necessarily reflected the European experience
of history'. This centring of historical consciousness in Western literature created an
alienating effect for African students 'that was not helped by a critical tradition that
often presented these writers [. . .] as if they were mindless geniuses whose only consistent quality was a sense of compassion'.[55] Ngũgĩ nevertheless draws a distinction
between the transmission of these works in an educational setting and the potential
meanings of the works themselves, retrieving what he considers to be a 'democratic
and humane' tradition represented by such novels.[56] According to Ngũgĩ, the effects
of ignoring political critique in nineteenth-century novels by authors such as Dickens,
Balzac and Tolstoy and their historical deracination within the English curriculum
were even more extreme in the African context: 'These writers, who had the sharpest
and most penetrating observations on the European bourgeois culture, were often
taught as if their only concern was with the universal themes of love, fear, birth, and
death.'[57] In a colonial setting, to make Dickens's authorship into a vehicle for the English literature curriculum's self-proclaimed globalisation of universalising humanitarian sympathies, therefore, seems to have involved a sort of travesty of the corrective,
social democratic goals which Dickens had attached to greater access for the Victorian
poor and working classes to education, literature and the arts. Reading Dickens's
novels according to the sanitised and generic tradition promulgated by the colonial
curriculum of English literature became an alibi for the cultural violence of empire.

EDUCATION 429

In his more recent memoir, however, where he recounts his university studies in greater detail, Ngũgĩ seems to draw a distinction between the curriculum and his experience of classroom reading, due to the approach of his teachers. Ngũgĩ explains that his white English professor, Peter Dane, taught Dickens's *Great Expectations*, through methods of close reading and historical contextualisation, as a commentary on empire:

> Dane's delineation of Magwitch's elaborate attempts to create his own gentleman in the Pip character, and the temptation to come back to enjoy, though surreptitiously, the sight of his creation, was moving, and without his saying so, Dane made us see the novel in terms of class exclusion and empire. He brought Dickens closer home to us. Colony and Crown, prison and palace, they produced each other. *Great Expectations* became a favorite, and a group of us adopted the name Pip.[58]

Lane's teaching was particularly important in light of Ngũgĩ's vocation as a writer, and also in the context of his later discovery that some of his teachers upheld white racial superiority. He learned that his professor of philosophy at Makerere, admired by the students for his liberal views, published a book with a British press mocking and disparaging the intellects of his African students: 'They had hugged him as a fellow human; he had embraced them as black objects of his colonial anthropological gaze.'[59]

Trying to decide what to write about after his graduation, Ngũgĩ considers Dickens as a model among the English novelists he admires, and he mentions his fond memories of reading Stevenson in elementary school. Lane's teaching of *Great Expectations* as a novel capable of reflecting critically on the British Empire and its history may have helped his students imagine themselves writing an anticolonial literature. However, Ngũgĩ's more immediate models and inspirations would be the many African and African American novelists and intellectuals whose works he also read in his courses.[60] To enter this specifically African-centred world of critical thought and literary creation, Ngũgĩ realises, he would need to write about his childhood home in the midst of anticolonial violence and repression:

> Write about a village in Kenya. Write about Limuru. Write about my going to school under a hail of bullets. Write about life in an endless nightmare. Write about a community awakening to new life.[61]

Notes

1. Henry Morley, *A First Sketch of English Literature*, 26th edn (1873; London: Cassell, 1890), 1059.
2. Charles Dickens, speech at the Soirée of the Mechanics' Institution, Liverpool, 26 February 1844, in *The Speeches of Charles Dickens*, ed. by K. J. Fielding (Oxford: Clarendon Press, 1960), 54–5.
3. The 1870 Elementary Education Act, known as Forster's Education Act, created the institutional structures for universal schooling in England and Wales between the ages of five to ten but did not require attendance. The 1880 Elementary Education Act required all children to attend school but parents still had to pay fees. Fees were finally abolished in most cases by the Fee Grant Act of 1891. Scotland's educational system remained independent.

4. For a pivotal study of the adoption of English literature in colonial education as a tactic of cultural hegemony, see Gauri Viswanathan, *Masks of Conquest: Literary Study and British Rule in India* (New York: Columbia University Press, 1989).

5. For a helpful chronology of Dickens's educational activities and writings, see the Appendix to Philip Collins's *Dickens and Education* (London: Macmillan, 1963), 222–5.

6. Michael Slater, 'Appendix B: Dickens and the Yorkshire Schools', in Charles Dickens, *Nicholas Nickleby*, ed. by Michael Slater (London: Penguin, 1978), 940.

7. *Nicholas Nickleby*, 210–11, ch. 12.

8. Ibid., 225, ch. 13.

9. Ibid., 47. Slater backs up Dickens's claim about his novel's instrumental role in the closure of the Yorkshire schools, in *Nicholas Nickleby*, 942.

10. Charles Dickens, *The Old Curiosity Shop*, ed. by Angus Easson (London: Penguin, 1972), 308, ch. 31.

11. Charles Dickens, *Hard Times*, ed. by Graham Law (Toronto: Broadview, 1996), 46, bk 1, ch. 2.

12. Ibid., 93, bk 1, ch. 9.

13. Charles Dickens, *Oliver Twist*, ed. by Philip Horne (London: Penguin, 2002), 102, bk 1, ch. 13.

14. Charles Dickens, *Our Mutual Friend*, ed. by Michael Cotsell (Oxford: Oxford University Press, 1989), 734, bk 4, ch. 9.

15. Charles Dickens, 'A Visit to Newgate', in *Sketches by Boz*, ed. by Dennis Walder (London: Penguin, 1995), 240–1.

16. Charles Dickens, 'A Walk in a Workhouse', *Household Words*, 25 May 1850, in *Dickens' Journalism*, ed. by Michael Slater and John Drew, 4 vols (London: Dent, 1994–2000), II (1996), 234–41, 238.

17. Ibid., 241.

18. Charles Dickens, 'Crime and Education', letter to the *Daily News*, 4 February 1846; qtd in Collins, *Dickens and Education*, 90.

19. *Our Mutual Friend*, 214, bk 2, ch. 1.

20. Ibid.

21. Ibid., 218, bk 2, ch. 1.

22. For a more detailed reading of *Our Mutual Friend* in relation to the history of parliamentary funding of education from the 1840s to the 1860s, see Sarah Winter, *The Pleasures of Memory: Learning to Read with Charles Dickens* (New York: Fordham University Press, 2011), 243–54.

23. Michael Slater, *Charles Dickens* (New Haven: Yale University Press, 2009), 296.

24. Ibid., 587.

25. Robert Gottlieb, *Great Expectations: The Sons and Daughters of Charles Dickens* (New York: Farrar, Straus and Giroux, 2012), 60.

26. See Sheila M. Smith, 'John Overs to Charles Dickens: A Working-Man's Letter and its Implications', *Victorian Studies* 18.2 (December 1974), 195–217.

27. Charles Dickens, 'Preface', *Evenings of a Working Man, Being the Occupation of his Scanty Leisure: by John Overs. With a Preface Relative to the Author by Charles Dickens* (London: Newby, 1844), in *Dickens' Journalism*, IV (2000), 416–19, 419.

28. Charles Dickens, *American Notes*, in *American Notes and Pictures from Italy*, ed. by Leonée Ormond (London: Dent, 1997), 79, ch. 4.

29. Jenny Hartley, *Charles Dickens and the House of Fallen Women* (London: Methuen, 2008), 245.

30. Charles Dickens, letter to Angela Burdett-Coutts, 26 May 1846, in *The Heart of Charles Dickens, As Revealed in His Letters to Angela Burdett-Coutts*, ed. by Edgar Johnson (New York: Duell, Sloan and Pearce and Boston, MA: Little, Brown and Company, 1952), 80.

EDUCATION   431

31. Ibid., 81; emphasis in original.
32. *The Heart of Charles Dickens*, 100.
33. See Mill's discussion of Wordsworth in ch. 5 of his *Autobiography* (1873), and Arnold's *Reports on Elementary Schools, 1852–1882*, 2nd edn (London: Eyre & Spottiswoode, 1910).
34. Dickens's arrangements for Urania Cottage are described in Hartley, 89–95.
35. Charles Dickens, 'An Appeal to Fallen Women', enclosed with a letter to Angela Burdett-Coutts, 28 October 1847, in *The Heart of Charles Dickens*, 99. This invitation, written by Dickens as expressing the views of the unnamed benefactress (Burdett-Coutts) who wished to aid them, was shared with the women recruited by prison officials.
36. Charles Dickens, speech at the Southwark Literary and Scientific Institution, 2 December 1840, in *Speeches*, 5.
37. Ibid.
38. Charles Dickens, speech at the Conversazione of the Polytechnic Institution, Birmingham, in *Speeches*, 62–3.
39. Ibid., 60.
40. Charles Dickens, speech at the First Annual Soirée of the Athenaeum, Glasgow, 28 December 1847, in *Speeches*, 86.
41. Charles Dickens, speech at the Opening of the Free Library, Manchester, 2 September 1852, in *Speeches*, 153.
42. Charles Dickens, speech at the Presentation to Dickens and Banquet to Literature and Art, Birmingham, 6 January 1853, in *Speeches*, 157.
43. Ibid., 159.
44. For two important studies of Dickens's cultural politics, see Sally Ledger, *Dickens and the Popular Radical Imagination* (Cambridge: Cambridge University Press, 2007), and Juliet John, *Dickens and Mass Culture* (Oxford: Oxford University Press, 2010).
45. Charles Dickens, speech at the Birmingham and Midland Institute: Annual Inaugural Meeting, Birmingham, 27 September 1869, in *Speeches*, 399.
46. Ibid., 403.
47. Brian Simon, *Studies in the History of Education, 1780–1870* (London: Lawrence & Wisehart, 1960), 340–6.
48. See, for example, Chartist critiques of the middle-class paternalism of Mechanics' Institutions, in Malcolm Chase, *Chartism: A New History* (Manchester: Manchester University Press, 2007), 144.
49. William Iler Crane and William Henry Wheeler, *Wheeler's Graded Literary Readers, with Interpretations: An Eighth Reader* (Chicago: Wheeler, 1919), 154–5.
50. For an expanded account of the ways Dickens's authorship was reshaped in British and American literary histories and school textbooks published between 1873 and 1940, see Winter, 285–311.
51. Ngũgĩ wa Thiong'o, *Decolonizing the Mind: The Politics of Language in African Literature* [1981] (London: James Currey; Nairobi: Heinemann Kenya; Portsmouth, NH: Heinemann, 1985), 12.
52. Ibid.
53. On the imperialist readers designed by the London Schoolboard in the 1880s, see Joseph Bristow, *Empire Boys: Adventures in a Man's World* (London: HarperCollins, 1991), 16–21. Confirming curricular connections between metropole and colony, Regenia Gagnier also reports that missionaries in Africa distributed Dickens's works in pamphlet form in the 1880s, and that secondary school students in mid-twentieth-century Ghana were required to read *Oliver Twist*. See 'Dickens's Global Circulation', in *The Oxford Handbook of Charles Dickens*, ed. by Robert L. Patten, John O. Jordan and Catherine Waters (Oxford: Oxford University Press, 2018), 722–37, 728–9. On the English curriculum in

Ghana, Gagnier cites Stephanie Newell, *Literary Culture in Colonial Ghana: 'How to Play the Game of Life'* (Bloomington: Indiana University Press, 2001).

54. Ngũgĩ wa Thiong'o, *Decolonizing the Mind*, 91.
55. Ibid.
56. Dipesh Chakrabarty influentially characterises such deracination of Western cultural artefacts and accounts of history as a provincialism of Western historicism, in *Provincializing Europe: Postcolonial Thought and Historical Difference* (Princeton: Princeton University Press, 2007).
57. Ngũgĩ wa Thiong'o, *Decolonizing the Mind*, 91. Ngũgĩ groups Dickens together with Aeschylus, Sophocles, Shakespeare, Balzac, Dostoevsky, Tolstoy, Gorky and Brecht.
58. Ngũgĩ wa Thiong'o, *Birth of a Dream Weaver: A Writer's Awakening* (New York: New Press, 2016), Kindle Edition, 37.
59. Ibid., 34.
60. Ibid., 84–6.
61. Ibid., 86–7.

Further Reading

Catherine Robson, *Heart Beats: Everyday Life and the Memorized Poem* (Princeton: Princeton University Press, 2015)

David Vincent, *Literacy and Popular Culture in England, 1750–1914* (Cambridge: Cambridge University Press, 1993)

David Vincent, 'Social Reform', in *The Oxford Handbook of Charles Dickens*, ed. by Robert L. Patten, John O. Jordan and Catherine Waters (Oxford: Oxford University Press, 2018), 420–35

28

POLITICAL ART AND THE ART OF POLITICS

Dominic Rainsford

LITERARY FICTION CAN BE POLITICAL IN many ways, most obviously by expressing views about society through the words of narrators and characters, and by implying judgement of those views; or by constructing fictional communities, plots and scenes that reference the real world, either reinforcing the status quo or implying a need for change. Literature can also be politicised, in the sense of being read in a way that bends it towards specific agendas, irrespective of its original context or its author's intentions. Conversely, politics can be literary, insofar as political positions and projects are conceived, developed, circulated and sold through language of a calculated, artful kind. A vote-winning vision is a type of persuasive fiction. In some quarters, these days, this leads to a cynical or euphoric 'post-truth' indifference to consistency and verifiability, but even some of the most earnest contributors to political debate acknowledge the roles of imagination, rhetoric and storytelling. George Monbiot, for example, sums up what is now a conventional wisdom:

> A string of facts, however well attested, will not correct or dislodge a powerful story. The only response it is likely to provoke is indignation: people often angrily deny facts that clash with the narrative 'truth' established in their minds. The only thing that can displace a story is a story. Those who tell the stories run the world.[1]

This chapter will touch upon all of these aspects of the political in literary art, and of politics *as* literary art – in relation to Dickens, an author whose fictions are packed with political implications; who, beyond his fiction, engaged directly in political debate; who has been enlisted, from the early years of his career until the present, as an ally, a source of examples, or a symbol, epitome or byword, by innumerable politicians at both ends of the political spectrum; and whose work provides extraordinary resources for thinking about the relations between the literary and the political more generally, in his time and ours.

The History of 'Political' Dickens

Dickens famously spent formative years as a parliamentary reporter, observing real politicians at work,[2] and yet, when we think of politicians in his novels, they usually have conspicuously unreal names (like the Boodles and Buffys of *Bleak House* (1852–3)), while their institutional contexts tend to be without direct real-world equivalents (the Circumlocution Office in *Little Dorrit* (1855–7)). Conceptions of Dickens as a political force in the world range from the idea that he was an intellectually lightweight defender of tradition (supposedly offering a good Christmas dinner as the solution to all the world's ills); to Dickens as haphazard proponent of progressive causes, strong on sentiment but weak on ideas; to George Bernard Shaw's theatrical claim that '*Little Dorrit* is a more seditious book than *Das Kapital*.'[3] Such assessments are usually based exclusively on the novels, many of which do indeed emphasise political themes: poverty, social exclusion and crime in *Oliver Twist* (1837–9); class and the sclerotic legal system in *Bleak House*; bureaucracy, finance and corruption in *Little Dorrit*; industrial relations in *Hard Times* (1854); political revolution in *A Tale of Two Cities* (1859). But it is important to set these works in the wider context of Dickens's writing and public presence: not simply because this shows that he had an even greater range of political interests, but also because it shows that he was alive to the complex relations between political position-taking, audience and genre: the conjunction, that is to say, of politics and art.

On 25 July 1842, a committee in the House of Lords met to consider 'An Act to prohibit the Employment of Women and Girls in Mines and Collieries, to regulate the Employment of Boys, and make Provisions for the Safety of Persons working therein'. The potential beneficiaries of the act included six-year-old 'trappers', who operated 'doors or traps for the coal-carriages [. . .] alone [. . .], in the dark, for 12 hours or more a day'.[4] The bill would eventually receive royal assent on 10 August 1842, but not before vigorous opposition in the Lords, led by the Marquis of Londonderry, who had extensive mining interests in Durham. One might expect that the author of *Oliver Twist* and *Nicholas Nickleby* (1838–9) would have feelings about the brutal exploitation of the young, but whereas those novels might be designed to jostle consciences for years to come, Dickens the parliamentary journalist knew that consequential decisions were constantly being made while he wrote. Thus, just hours before the Lords committee meeting, he submits a long letter to *The Morning Chronicle*, writing with a rhetorical verve in which literary and political motives and modes of expression cannot be told apart:

> That for very many years these mines and all belonging to them, as they have been out of sight in the dark earth, have been utterly out of legislative mind; that for so many years all considerations of humanity, policy, social virtue, and common decency, have been left rotting at the pit's mouth, with other disregarded dunghill matter from which lordly colliers could extract no money; that for very many years, a state of things has existed in these places, in the heart and core of a Christian country, which, if it had been discovered by mariners or missionaries in the Sandwich Islands, would have made the fortune of two quarto volumes, filled the whole bench of bishops with emotion, and nerved to new and mighty projects the Society for the Propagation of the Gospel in Foreign Parts, is well known to every one. That the evidence taken by the commissioners wrought (as well it might) an extraordinary impression on the public mind, from the first moment of its diffusion; that the bill founded upon it, passed the House of Commons with the hearty consent of all parties, and the ready union of all interests; that the people of every class, and their representatives of every class, were no sooner made acquainted with the evil, than they hastened to apply the remedy, are recent and notorious facts. It was reserved for the House of Lords alone to discover that this kind of legislation was very bad and odious, and would never do.[5]

Not only does Dickens have the skill with words to ridicule hypocrisy and impel action, he also shows, in this case, a mastery of the facts. He had been well acquainted with the Children's Employment Commission since 1840, and especially with the mover of the Mines and Collieries Bill, Lord Ashley, later 7th Earl of Shaftesbury, who would still be soliciting Dickens's advice on current affairs in 1865.[6] He also knows all about the vested interests of Lord Londonderry and his ilk. This is not the Dickens who is popularly supposed to have disliked or distrusted all politicians. It is a Dickens who can distinguish between different politicians' motives and policies, and ally himself vigorously with one side or the other.

According to Shaw, Dickens 'seems to have regarded all social phenomena as fortuitous and unconnected; he had neither knowledge of science nor science of knowledge'; George Eliot 'often shewed herself a scientific thinker and a trained sympathiser, where [Dickens and Thackeray] were only shrewd guessers and vehement partisans'.[7] This is worth quoting because it still typifies what many critics say about Dickens, especially in contrast to Eliot. Shaw is right to identify vehement partisanship in Dickens's depiction of the Circumlocution Office (or the workhouse system in *Oliver Twist*, or factory management in *Hard Times*), but he makes the mistake of allowing this to stand for Dickens's political understanding as a whole. This is partly the consequence of the long hiatus in Dickens studies, roughly between his death and the 1990s, during which his non-fiction writings received little attention.[8] In Dickens's letter to *The Morning Chronicle* it is quite clear that he is able to see beyond the immediate issue, linking it with other matters that he cares about, so as to begin to generate something that looks like a systemic analysis:

> [I]t was stoutly contended by their collier lordships that [. . .] all labourers in mines are perpetually singing and dancing, and festively enjoying themselves; in a word, that they lead such rollicking and roystering lives that it is well they work below the surface of the earth, or society would be deafened by their shouts of merriment. This is humorous, but not new. Exactly the same things have been said of slavery, factory-work, Irish destitution [. . .]. Show beyond all dispute [. . .] that any class of persons are in especial need of legislative protection and assistance, and opponents of this stamp will instantly arise [. . .]. Now, happiness capers and sings on a slave plantation, making it an Eden of ebony. Now, she dwelleth in a roofless cabin, with potatoes thrice a week, buttermilk o' Sundays, a pig in the parlour, a fever on the dungheap, seven naked children on the damp earth-floor, and a wife newly delivered of an eighth, upon a door, brought from the nearest hut that boasts one—five miles off.[9]

Connected thinking of this kind is present in the novels, too, but requires more work on the part of the reader: absorbing not just the multiple strands of individual novels (linking judicial and sanitary neglect in *Bleak House*, for example, or economic and emotional abuse in *Hard Times*), but also across novels, and between novels and other kinds of writing. Dickens's political identity becomes clearer, the more we consider his textual production as a whole.

There are certainly occasions in Dickens's communication with friends when he seems to dismiss politicians in general. But we know that he admired some of them, not least for their skill with language – Henry Brougham, for example, was 'the greatest

436   DOMINIC RAINSFORD

speaker he had ever heard'.[10] We know, too, that there were people who would have liked Dickens to become an MP, and that he gave the idea serious consideration in both 1841 and 1848.[11] In 1855, the year in which Dickens invented the Circumlocution Office, an Administrative Reform Association was founded, lobbying in the wake of the Crimean War for radical changes in the Army, Navy and Civil Service, opposing nepotism, party-political bias and the unthinking perpetuation of old routines. The leading figure was Austen Henry Layard, Liberal MP, Assyriologist and friend of Dickens. At Layard's invitation, Dickens addressed the association on 27 June 1855.

Just as Dickens had taken aim at Lord Londonderry in 1842, here he goes straight for the prime minister, Lord Palmerston, who had frustrated Layard's efforts in Parliament. Palmerston took advantage of the association's meeting-place, the Drury Lane Theatre, to characterise its activities as 'private theatricals'. Dickens gleefully exploits this feeble jibe: 'I have some slight acquaintance with theatricals, private and public, and I will accept that figure of the noble lord. I will not say that if I wanted to form a company of Her Majesty's servants, I think I should know where to put my hand on "the comic old gentleman".'[12] It is a fine debating manoeuvre, albeit in the opponent's absence; had Dickens been speaking in Parliament, he would no doubt have discomfited the prime minister, received a rebuke from the Speaker, and won 'roars of laughter' from the Opposition – as he did, repeatedly, on this occasion at Drury Lane. But the tone of the speech is not humorous throughout. Dickens makes it clear exactly where his common ground with the association lies, denouncing the mistakes and indifference that led to far more military deaths in the Crimea than occurred in battle: 'the ghastly absurdity of that vast labyrinth of misplaced men and misdirected things, which made England unable to find on the face of the earth, an enemy one-twentieth part so potent for the misery and ruin of her noble defenders as she has been herself'.[13] He does not want his audience to suppose that he is speaking as a professional politician – this is his 'first political meeting' and his 'trade and calling is not politics' – but he goes on complicate this position, with some quite parliamentary equivocation:

> Within my sphere of action—which I shall never change; I shall never overstep, further or for a longer period than I do tonight, the circle of my own pursuits, as one who lives by Literature, who is content to do his public service through Literature, and who is conscious that he cannot serve two Masters—within my sphere of action I have, for some years, tried to understand the heavier social grievances and to help to set them right.[14]

Rectifying 'social grievances' is almost the definition of a political vocation. Dickens presumably means that he does not wish to make a habit of direct political speech-making. Perhaps he needs to make this so clear precisely because he knows that he could have become an MP, and had been tempted to do so.

But 'Literature' was not an alternative to politics for Dickens; it was politics by another means. This is a matter of technique as well as content. He runs with his characterisation of Palmerston as 'the comic old gentleman', referring to Parliament as 'pantomime': the 'public theatricals which the noble lord is so condescending as to manage', 'the *Comedy of Errors* played so dismally like a tragedy that we cannot bear it'.[15] The political wit of hoisting Palmerston with his own petard develops into something bigger here. Dickens's own professional authority, picking up on the setting of the speech, allows him to develop an allegory in which the verbal and performative practices of Westminster and the theatre are linked but also opposed, in terms of their motivation and effect. In the Circumlocution Office, Dickens returns *The Comedy of Errors*, as it were, to comedy – but in a way that depends upon our sense of the culpable insouciance, rhetorical evasiveness and expedient role-playing of the nation's real decision-makers. We can see the satirical parallels of this speech anticipated in *Hard Times*, where the grotesquely utopian and exploitative, sincere and cynical, ideological pact of Gradgrind and Bounderby is opposed to the genial and healing absurdities of Sleary's Horse Riding, in a way that implies that art and entertainment are more fun than professional politics (at least for Dickens and his implied readers), but also that art, entertainment and politics have more in common than practitioners on either side might wish to believe.[16]

Dickens in *Hansard*

A search for 'Dickens' up to the year 2005 in the digital edition of *Hansard*, the proceedings of the British Houses of Parliament, generates 1,673 results.[17] Some of these relate to MPs James and Geoffrey Dickens (respectively Labour, 1966–70, and Conservative, 1979–95), some to the parliamentarily acceptable expostulation 'the dickens!', but the great majority concern the author. 'Dickensian' appears 310 times.

The earliest reference to 'our' Dickens appears to have been made in the Commons on 6 April 1842, by the Whig (formerly Tory) MP Richard Monckton Milnes. Alongside many other accomplishments (suitor of Florence Nightingale; student of parapsychology; distinguished collector of erotica), Milnes was an active patron of literary figures ranging from Swinburne to Emerson. The occasion in question was a debate about copyright. Milnes rose to reply to the radical Thomas Wakley, who had denounced, in Milnes's words, 'a number of persons whom the House had seen coming before them with petitions on this subject as literary quacks. Among these were the names of Campbell, Miss Martineau, Fonblanque, Fox, Leigh Hunt, Carlyle, Dickens, Rogers, and Joanna Baillie.' Milnes robustly counters that these were 'persons who had exalted their country and would ever be held in affectionate veneration', and singles out the 30-year-old Dickens in particular, who:

> was receiving from the Republicans of America such demonstrations of sympathy as perhaps never literary man received from a whole nation before this time; and yet this was just the time at which the hon. Member [Wakley], with his republican bias, and with his love for America, came forward to call such men literary quacks.

The first reference to Dickens in Parliament, therefore, is explicitly political: he is a 'literary man' who will 'ever' be remembered for his achievements as a writer, but he is linked to partisan politics and seen as a cultural-political ambassador: an agent, as we might now say, of soft power.

If we pursue Dickens's relations with the Honourable Members named above, we soon see the intricacy of his entanglement with the political world. Milnes (later 1st Baron Houghton) became a friend whose relations with Dickens can be traced from 1840 to the bitter end, thirty years later: he was apparently the last person to

438   DOMINIC RAINSFORD

look upon Dickens's coffin.[18] We might expect that there would be less to say about Milnes's antagonist in the copyright debate, but here again there is a series of connections, spanning four decades. Wakley was well placed, in a sense, to detect 'literary quacks', being founder, in 1823, and editor of *The Lancet*. At the very beginning of Wakley's parliamentary career as MP for Finsbury (1835–52), Dickens had observed him from the Reporters' Gallery, leading to a rather bland portrait in 'The House', published in *The Evening Chronicle* in March 1835, subsequently revised as part of 'A Parliamentary Sketch' for the Second Series of *Sketches by Boz* (1836). Here, Wakley is merely 'the large man in a cloak with the white lining—not the man by the pillar; the other with the light hair hanging over his coat collar behind'.[19] In January 1840, Dickens was called for jury service and found himself confronted with the painful case of a housemaid who had at best concealed her dead baby and possibly murdered it. In a moving example of his availability to the real people to whom politics is supposed to answer, Dickens successfully argued for lenient treatment of 'the utterly friendless orphan girl', with the support and encouragement of the 'nobly patient and humane' coroner – none other than Thomas Wakley.[20] This was to provide material for both an article in *The Examiner* in 1849, 'The Paradise at Tooting', and a piece in *All the Year Round* in 1863, reprinted in *The Uncommercial Traveller* as 'Some Recollections of Mortality'. Like most politicians, Dickens and Wakley could be on opposing sides on some issues (such as copyright) and the same one on others (decent treatment of the poor and unprotected).

In his own political interventions, Dickens himself often had recourse to Shakespeare. In the 1842 letter to *The Morning Chronicle*, for example, he quotes *King Lear*, while in the 1855 speech to the Administrative Reform Association he references not just *The Comedy of Errors*, but also *As You Like It* and *Julius Caesar*.[21] This, in itself, is a parliamentary game: MPs had begun making references to Shakespeare, for illustrative, comic and self-aggrandising purposes, long before Dickens's birth.[22] From the 1840s onwards, they could deploy Shakespeare and Dickens in similar ways – with which no other author has quite been able to compare. We can trace this not only in the use of 'Dickens' and 'Dickensian', but also through allusions to a range of characters. 'Oliver Twist' – almost invariably 'asking for more' – is probably the favourite, at 440 occurrences; but 'Scrooge' runs him very close at 422. 'Pickwick' (often courtesy of the Fat Boy) is mentioned 147 times; 'Gradgrind', 96; 'Copperfield', 63; and 'Pecksniff', 42. If a character is a byword for a social issue in his own fictional lifetime, so much the better: all 40 instances of 'Jarndyce' betoken 'Jarndyce *v.* Jarndyce', while 'Skimpole' gets the attention he deserves, with a mere 4 hits.

Most of these allusions are formulaic and repetitious, but sometimes a speaker reveals a more advanced familiarity with Dickens. Thus, Neil Kinnock in the Commons on 18 November 1981, moving to oppose cuts to higher education:

> I know that there are Ministers who agree with all of the Government's policies and Ministers who agree with some of them. We now have a Minister [William Waldegrave, Under Secretary of State for Education and Science] who apparently agrees with none of them. He has a role to play which will be familiar to readers of Charles Dickens. The hon. Member was taken on by the Prime Minister in the same way as Oliver Twist was taken on by Mr. Sowerberry, the undertaker because 'there is an expression of melancholy on his face' which will come in useful at the

assorted educational funerals that he will have to attend if the Government carry on with their policies. Some people have been uncharitable enough to ascribe the hon. Gentleman's assumption of office to ambition. I believe that it was masochism.

What distinguishes this contribution is not only its allusion to Sowerberry (only mentioned in the Commons once before, in 1973), but also the way in which its aggressive wit and relish for words fit into a larger comic, literary and political tradition of which both Kinnock and Dickens himself are part. Kinnock has clearly learned from Dickens. But Dickens may have learnt more than we realise from parliamentarians of his own time.

The same tradition continues in 'another place'. Another former leader of the Labour Party (and prime minister), Lord Callaghan, welcomed Baroness Thatcher to the House of Lords on 2 July 1992, perhaps with a touch of *Schadenfreude*, thus:

> I suppose she must have felt quite at home on Tuesday when she was introduced and found herself surrounded by so many of her former colleagues—those whom she had promoted, those whom she had elevated, those whom she had fired [. . .]. It must have made her feel very much at home to see a collection of ghosts like this which cannot have been witnessed since Dickens' *Christmas Carol*, all waiting to strike.

No doubt Dickens has been used and abused by a great many politicians elsewhere in the world, in ways that this chapter cannot hope to cover. A starting point might be the official gift in London in 1987, from Margaret Thatcher's Education Secretary, Kenneth Baker, to Raisa Gorbacheva, wife of the Soviet leader, of a first edition of *Little Dorrit*. This occasioned a semi-earnest debate in Britain about the appropriateness of the novel: would it 'reinforce the prejudices which every Russian schoolchild has already been taught about the capitalist system', or would it rather send the Soviets themselves a sharp message about 'the impact of a dead public bureaucracy upon the lives of ordinary citizens'? Perhaps, given that *Little Dorrit* 'was the big literary hit of the war in the Crimea', 'Mr Baker could say that his was not a "wet" gift [in Thatcherite terms] but a subtly "dry" one—like giving a German politician a set of Vera Lynn records'.[23] The affair would be given an unexpected and dismaying twist four years later, when Gorbacheva returned to London, visited the Great Ormond Street Hospital (of which Dickens had been a powerful supporter), and then lamented to the violinist Yehudi Menuhin that 'hardly any of the staff, the parents or the children had read any Dickens. She said in Russia people continually read Dickens. She was absolutely amazed that in London, the home of Dickens, that great tradition was not being carried on.'[24]

On the evidence of the interventions quoted above, some politicians, such as Kinnock and Callaghan, have resisted the decline that the Soviet First Lady deplored. The same cannot necessarily be said of a more recent Labour leader, as we see in this Commons exchange, of 13 March 1997:

Mr. [Paul] Flynn [Labour]

I wonder whether my hon. Friend, in his wide reading, has read the book by the hon. Member for Havant (Mr. [David] Willetts [Conservative]). It is called

'The Age of Entitlement' [1993]. The hon. Member for Havant may need to be reminded that the book describes the vast exaggeration of the demographic time bomb by a Government who wish to change pensions policy and were taking advantage of it.

Mr. [Jeremy] Corbyn [Labour]

I do read very widely, but not that widely. I often visit the bookstalls at stations such as Waterloo or Euston, and I am always looking for remaindered copies. I am sure that it will not be long before there is a pile of that book selling for £1 along with non-pulped copies of Charles Dickens's novels. I will get both and see which is the most interesting.

It is clear that Corbyn was being uncomplimentary about David 'Two Brains' Willetts, one of the more academically distinguished Conservative parliamentarians of recent years. Quite what attitude concerning Dickens he sought to express, or was assuming in others, is harder to discern ('non-pulped' perplexes) – but it seems, at best, lukewarm. Perhaps Corbyn was holding Dickens's hostility to trade unions (notably in *Hard Times*) against him, but that does not mean that twenty-first century politicians on the Right are necessarily more enamoured. Jacob Rees-Mogg, for example, characteristically embodies a certain kind of Tory historiography and taste when he refers to 'the Victorian age, [. . .] one of the finest ages in British history, when most employers were benevolent, kindly, good and not out of a Dickens novel: they were more Trollope than Dickens by and large' (Commons, 17 June 2011).

The Art and Politics of Disproportion

There may still be no other literary author whose name is invoked as frequently as Dickens's in anglophone (perhaps even global) political debate, even if the references tend to boil down to a loose concept of the 'Dickensian', now largely disconnected from his writing. In the words of Naomi Klein, for example: 'If [the Trump administration's] agenda is fully realized, workers in the United States will find themselves with fewer protections than they have had at any point since the Dickensian nightmares of the Gilded Age.'[25] That is it: 'Dickensian nightmares' seem to require, and receive, no detailed description. We probably know what Klein means, but questions for those interested in taking Dickens seriously as a force in the world must include whether his political role can go beyond uses of his name (or perhaps of 'Oliver Twist', 'Scrooge' or 'Gradgrind') as convenient, comfortably high- *and* mass-cultural markers for bad social conditions; whether there are aspects of the complex inner workings of his texts that still have real political power; whether, in fact, there is any connection between the moral reinforcement that Dickens scholars find in his work and any substantive political activity or change.

According to Martha Nussbaum, 'if I am reading [. . .] *Hard Times* as a blue-print for labor reform, much will elude me. [T]his does not mean that the texture of Dickens' [. . .] language is not profoundly moral and political, aimed at creating a community of a certain sort and at acknowledging certain parts of the human world as worthy of our attention and love.'[26] Dickens's 'political language', as Juliet John says, 'is instinctively and purposely creative, because creative expression, for Dickens, can function politically whilst offering an empowering alternative to more narrowly "political languages".'[27] In other words, there is more to be found in Dickens, morally and politically, not in opposition to, but via, the aesthetic. This is not just a matter of discourse or rhetoric, but also of form. We might consider Dickens's understanding of politics in terms of shapes and movement (or lack of movement): the swell of the mob, the stasis of Chancery, the circular motion of Circumlocution, the ruthless aristocratic impulse of 'Steerforth', the obstruction of 'Dedlock'. Dickens and the aesthetics and politics of freedom and imprisonment is a vast subject in itself. But I will end with a different political/aesthetic nexus.

A sensitivity to disproportion is pervasive or even defining for Dickens, with comic, moral, ontological and, not least, political dimensions. Simple examples of this, at least at first glance, are provided by those scenes that crop up frequently in Dickens's writing, of small children carrying large babies. These go as far back as 'The Black Veil', in *Sketches by Boz*, where 'a little slipshod girl [. . .] contrive[s] to stagger a few yards [. . .] under the weight of a sallow infant almost as big as herself',[28] and exhibit their more classical form in the Preface to *Little Dorrit*, where Dickens describes himself seeking information about the Marshalsea from local residents: 'The smallest boy I ever conversed with, carrying the largest baby I ever saw, offered a supernaturally intelligent explanation of the locality in its old uses, and was very nearly correct.'[29] The underlying reality, in cases such as these, and perhaps in some original encounter in Dickens's early life, presumably involves a child that is small, *for a child*, carrying a baby that is large, *for a baby*. But in later iterations Dickens tends to make it sound as though the baby might actually be bigger than its older companion. In this, lies part of the humour. We can handle the concepts of a gigantic flea or a tiny elephant; *a fortiori*, the small child and the big baby are nothing special in isolation. But they become funny when literally superimposed, making them small and big *relative to one another*, and in reverse of the usual relation. In this way, Dickens makes jokes about children, about what it is to be a consciousness or personality but also a physical object, and also about how we manage matters of scale in general, conceptually and linguistically.

Malcolm Andrews has discussed how Dickens's humour often involves *bisociation*: the same person, thing or idea being viewed simultaneously from two incompatible perspectives. The child/baby situation is a version of this: big and small are each bisociated, seen at once in child and baby terms, and therefore cut loose from their taken-for-granted intelligibility and usefulness. Andrews extends bisociation to the general structure of Dickens's first-person novels, pointing out the humorous effects of the same situation being viewed by two very different versions of the same character: young and old David, young and old Pip. In these cases, two very different points of view are in comic contrast, but nevertheless come to be reconciled in the larger account of a developing life. Andrews links this to Dickens's 'social sympathies', his desire for 'a rapprochement between disparate classes of people'.[30] Dickens's humour of disproportion and incongruity, therefore, tends to promote understanding and humanity. Returning to a much simpler case than the life stories of David and Pip, we could say that the comic predicament of the big baby carried by its little sibling makes us warm to both of them. Both are caught up in the helpless materiality of a young

442   DOMINIC RAINSFORD

human, the arbitrariness of being a particular size. John Forster may have been the first to notice this aspect of Dickens:

> To perceive relations in things which are not apparent generally, is one of those exquisite properties of humour by which are discovered the affinities between the high and the low, the attractive and the repulsive, the rarest things and things of every day, which brings us all upon the level of common humanity.[31]

Both Forster and Andrews are right: Dickens often exposes apparent differences, contradictions, incongruities and disproportions in order to twist them around and represent them as comic evidence of what we share. But there is another side to it, another tone in which the same kinds of observation can be presented, that is tragic and satirical, and that, rather than suggesting that we should all be brothers and sisters, indicates that, with society as it is, we are deeply divided. Disproportion can be political in Dickens, in other words, and generates anger as well as laughter.

A blatantly political case occurs in *Bleak House*, where Lady Dedlock is paradoxically constrained by a web of privilege and deference:

> She supposes herself to be an inscrutable Being, quite out of the reach and ken of ordinary mortals—seeing herself in her glass, where indeed she looks so. Yet, every dim little star revolving about her, from her maid to the manager of the Italian Opera, knows her weaknesses, prejudices, follies, haughtinesses, and caprices; and lives upon as accurate a calculation and as nice a measure of her moral nature, as her dressmaker takes of her physical proportions. Is a new dress, a new custom, a new singer, a new dancer, a new form of jewellery, a new dwarf or giant, a new chapel, a new anything, to be set up? There are deferential people, in a dozen callings, whom my Lady Dedlock suspects of nothing but prostration before her, who can tell you how to manage her as if she were a baby; who do nothing but nurse her all their lives; who, humbly affecting to follow with profound subservience, lead her and her whole troop after them; who, in hooking one, hook all and bear them off, as Lemuel Gulliver bore away the stately fleet of the majestic Lilliput.[32]

Dickens alludes here to the central text of personal/political disproportion in the English-language tradition: *Gulliver's Travels*. Lady Dedlock conceives of herself as a kind of deity, 'an inscrutable Being', a celestial body, with minor stars (rather than astronomically correct planets or moons) 'revolving about her', and indeed as a kind of giant, 'out of the reach [. . .] of ordinary mortals'. But her servants can 'measure [. . .] her physical proportions'. And, at the end of the passage, it is not Lady Dedlock who is the Gulliver who pulls away the fleet, but, in a strange mixture and reversal of the metaphor, it is the 'deferential people, in a dozen callings' who turn out to have oversized powers.

Consciously or not, Dickens has surely been led by Swift to include 'a new dwarf or giant' in the list of things that Lady Dedlock may be persuaded to finance. In fact, these are the only things on the list that it is hard to imagine that the Dedlocks *would* sponsor: they are anachronistic and too pop-cultural or vulgar. And yet, in a much deeper vulgarity, the Dedlocks support the system of *metaphorical* dwarfs and giants that is a hierarchical and unequal society, and are themselves turned upside down by it. Like other characters in *Bleak House* (in other ways), they become the giant babies who weigh down but can also be manipulated by other people who are socially inferior but more effective, or less grand but more responsible. And this might make us look back at the funny vignettes of children bearing the burden of their parents' younger offspring, and realise that there is a continuum: Dickens's scenes of domestic disproportion always reflect human beings stretched too far by socio-economic circumstances, both at the top and the bottom of the social tree, whether by being given status that far exceeds their inner worth, or by being made to bear responsibilities beyond their years.

These preoccupations with the inequities of class, with wealth and poverty, and with the predicament of the young – all clearly political – are tangled up with Dickens's understanding of his own personal history and changing social position, in terms of how he came to be himself (the sickly, neglected child turning into the international phenomenon), and in terms of his sense of what it is to be a successful novelist: an individual who, through his peculiar imagination can create and destroy multitudes on the page and then have a massive impact on far greater multitudes of readers. The essence of the Blacking Warehouse narrative is not just that there is such a kind of dirty, monotonous work, nor even that children are made to do it, but rather the gross disproportion of that work being given to a boy with little Dickens's aspirations, and, retrospectively, with big Dickens's achievements and status. This seems to have given Dickens a permanent sense of what it is to be someone who counts, and what it is to be someone who doesn't, and of the whole system of counting and measurement within which human fates are arranged, registered and understood: so that what might seem an anti-political tendency to focus on a romanticised self actually lends Dickens's work political authenticity, intimacy and power.

Moreover, from a very early stage, these entangled personal and collective issues seem to have been linked, for Dickens, with aspects of literary narration and form, particularly focused on scale and number. Take, for example, his famous recollection of visiting the pub in Parliament Street, as a small boy, on a break from work. Little Dickens asked, as Big Dickens tells John Forster, 'What is your very best—the very best—ale, a glass?' The landlord delivers a beer (perhaps not the very best, and probably diluted) and calls his wife to observe the phenomenon, whereupon the anecdote concludes: 'the landlord's wife, opening the little half-door and bending down, gave me a kiss that was half-admiring and half-compassionate'.[33] Dickens's feelings about himself, in this story (in ways that can be extended to other autobiographical reports and countless incidents involving Oliver, David and Pip), seem also half-admiring and half-compassionate, involving disproportion in both directions: this boy was capable of so much despite his age and size; and yet he was so insubstantial compared with his idea of himself. But what is perhaps most striking about the conclusion of the story is the way that Dickens, in distant retrospect but with the appearance of photographic recall, allows 'half-admiring and half-compassionate' to echo 'half-door' and the bending (the self-halving) of the woman. It is above all this touch of the mechanical and mathematical that saves this and many similar passages from too much pathos.

It is from such beginnings that Dickens develops accounts of conflicted or unstable identity, revolving around issues of counting and comparison, and in particular of one individual coming into focus although he or she feels somehow less than one, or just one among many: Pickwick, Oliver or Nell finding themselves identified as singularly good or innocent, and therefore attracting many forms of peculiar attention; David Copperfield uneasy as the hero of his own life or anyone else's, constantly running into others who might be better heroes; Esther Summerson failing to understand how she came to be so important, or even to be writing these memoirs about herself; Pip sensing that he could so easily have been lying under a sixth tiny tombstone alongside those of his five brothers. All of these cases have a personal, psychological, Dickensian history, but they are also all political: to do with the life chances, even the survival chances, of people in Dickens's world, having a dimension of blind fate, the limits of self-knowledge, and universal mortality, but also determined by factors such as gender and, above all, by class. We can see many of these elements brought together in a late example, the one in which Dickens shows us a protagonist most literally about to be cut down to size, when Sydney Carton waits for his turn at the guillotine:

> He had never seen the instrument that was to terminate his life. How high it was from the ground, how many steps it had, where he would be stood, how he would be touched, whether the touching hands would be dyed red, which way his face would be turned, whether he would be the first, or might be the last: these and many similar questions, in no wise directed by his will, obtruded themselves over and over again, countless times. Neither were they connected with fear: he was conscious of no fear. Rather, they originated in a strange besetting desire to know what to do when the time came; a desire gigantically disproportionate to the few swift moments to which it referred; a wondering that was more like the wondering of some other spirit within his, than his own.[34]

The feeling of disproportion that Carton experiences is a type of self-alienation. He experiences this ironically, intellectually, with curiosity, whereas other Dickens characters are marked by it in unconscious forms, making them hypocrites or victims: Pecksniff warming his hands 'as benevolently as if they were somebody else's'; Mrs Gradgrind's feeling a pain, not exactly in her own body but 'somewhere in the room'.[35] Carton has experienced the unfairness of the way life is run on a range of levels, from the circumstances of birth and opportunity that make him Sydney Carton, whereas another man, physically identical, becomes Charles Darnay, to the state of emergency and disintegration of the Revolution, in which the rights of man are nominally elevated and the rights of the individual casually, even whimsically, abrogated and terminated.

When Dickens thinks about himself, with responsibilities and affectations beyond his years, at the level of the half-door in the Parliament Street pub, or Lady Dedlock unknowingly caught up in a cultural history and current reality of symbolic and economic dwarfs and giants, or Sydney Carton, on the cusp of losing his life, sensing, calmly, how much he doesn't know about the world around him, and how much more there is to being him than the part that he is conscious of and can control, he exerts an extraordinary interdisciplinary suggestiveness. He approaches issues of ontology and epistemology that go back to the Presocratics, making him a leading philosophical thinker of his age, but in ways that are embedded in the real circumstances of personal psychology and social and political organisation. To make the same point in reverse: there is so much local detail in his work, and yet so much that is abstract – literary form understood as much more than a transparent medium for storytelling, but also mathematics understood as a real force in determining lives and interpreting them, which in turn gives his work a much deeper and more provocative relation to the social structures that politics must analyse and address, than if he had merely criticised them explicitly.

What I have offered here are further reflections on the amazingly fruitful mysteriousness, the mixture of autobiographical intimacy and cool alienation, sentiment and irony, the embodied and the abstract, that seems to make Dickens's work so suggestive – doubling, in my own way, points that have been made in recent years by many other critics: John Bowen, for example, on many other forms of measurement and counting in *A Tale of Two Cities*; Rosemarie Bodenheimer on the internal disproportion within a writer who knows so much more than he knows that he knows; the way in which Dickens's most 'poetic' utterances, according to Jeremy Tambling, are grounded on 'the completely groundless'; Leslie Simon on Dickens's engagement, through dust, with a 'loose and baggy world'; Natalie McKnight on Dickens paradoxically completing himself with a truncated final text.[36] To these perspectives must be added an understanding of Dickens the political writer, speaker and activist – so conscious of the individuals suffering within a complex society as well as of the general structures that bring that suffering about; so conscious, too, of the gross disproportion between a Palmerston and a 'trapper' in one of Palmerston's mines, or even between his own sense of himself 'as a faithful servant of the public, always imbued with a sense of duty to them, and always striving to do his best' (again, a self-characterisation one might expect more from a politician than a novelist), and yet as someone uniquely privileged in his chance to speak up and connect with society as a whole.[37]

The disproportionate Dickens is a writer for our political moment. Despite the widespread celebration of unearned privilege and a reversion to cults of the (unworthy) individual – in social media, for example, and populist politics – there may be a change taking place in the ways in which we recognise and deal with inequality, requiring a new sense of number, a paradigm shift that echoes and yet takes further one that took place in the Victorian age of measurement, mapping, counting and comparison. Among other things, this has to do with understanding how inequality on the social/political level connects with disproportion on the personal level. In this respect, the grotesque characterisation that might once have seemed to rule Dickens out as a political author is what really makes him one. Many readers will have made their own parallels between current political leaders and Dickens's procession of all-too-human monsters. Some of the most powerful nations are now led by people no less essentially mismatched to themselves than Pecksniff – or Dickens's Palmerston. Meanwhile, a two-dimensional 'Dickens' still keeps popping up in political discourse. The real politics, however, lie in the depth and complexity of his texts: not just in what they say, but how they work. In this respect, they may inspire new writers seeking to combine artistic freedom with political relevance. They may also serve as a model for humanities scholars struggling to preserve the idea that a politically healthy society is one that cares about literature as both content and form, and where time has to be available for prolonged immersion in complex texts.

Notes

1. George Monbiot, 'How Do We Get Out of This Mess?', *Guardian*, 9 September 2017 <https://www.theguardian.com/books/2017/sep/09/george-monbiot-how-de-we-get-out-of-this-mess> [accessed 28 September 2017].
2. See John M. L. Drew, *Dickens the Journalist* (Basingstoke: Palgrave Macmillan, 2003), esp. 12–38.
3. George Bernard Shaw, 'Foreword to *Great Expectations*' (1937), in *Shaw on Dickens*, ed. by Dan H. Laurence and Martin Quinn (New York: Ungar, 1984), 45–59, 51.
4. *The Letters of Charles Dickens*, ed. by Madeline House, Graham Storey et al., Pilgrim/British Academy Edition, 12 vols (Oxford: Clarendon Press, 1965–2002), III (1974), 281, n. 3. Hereafter *PLets*.
5. *PLets*, III, 279–80.
6. *PLets*, II (1969), 164; XI (1999), 59.
7. George Bernard Shaw, 'Fiction and Truth' (1887), in *Shaw on Dickens*, 99–101, 101.
8. Exceptions include the discussion of *The Uncommercial Traveller* in F. S. Schwarzbach, *Dickens and the City* (London: Athlone, 1979). However, research on the non-fiction was impeded for many years by the unavailability or unreliability of texts. This was finally ameliorated by the publication of Dickens's *Selected Journalism, 1850–1870*, ed. by David Pascoe (Harmondsworth: Penguin, 1997) and *Dickens' Journalism*, ed. by Michael Slater and John Drew, 4 vols (London: Dent, 1994–2000).
9. *PLets*, III, 281.
10. Whitwell Elwin, *Some XVIII Century Men of Letters: Biographical Essays*, 2 vols (London: Murray, 1902), I, 249, qtd in Drew, *Dickens the Journalist*, 37.
11. *PLets*, II, 288; V (1981), 317.
12. *The Speeches of Charles Dickens*, ed. by K. J. Fielding (Oxford: Clarendon, 1960), 200.
13. Ibid., 201.
14. Ibid., 200–1.
15. Ibid., 200.
16. For more on Dickens, Parliament and theatre, see Robert Douglas-Fairhurst, *Becoming Dickens: The Invention of a Novelist* (Cambridge, MA: Harvard University Press, 2011), 79–86.
17. *Hansard 1803–2005* <http://hansard.millbanksystems.com> [accessed 4 October 2017]. All further parliamentary quotations are taken from this source.
18. Edgar Johnson, *Charles Dickens: His Tragedy and Triumph*, 2 vols (London: Gollancz, 1953), II, 1157.
19. *Dickens' Journalism*, I (1994), 154–5. For the identification of Wakley, see W. J. Carlton, 'Portraits in "A Parliamentary Sketch"', *Dickensian* 50 (1954), 100-9, 104.
20. *Dickens' Journalism*, IV (2000), 227.
21. *PLets*, III, 283; *Speeches*, 202, 207.
22. 3,145 instances, 1804–2005 (slightly complicated, as in the case of 'Dickens', by two MPs with the surname in question).
23. 'To Raisa with Love' (leading article), *The Times*, 12 December 1987 <https://global.factiva.com> [accessed 4 October 2017].
24. Jeff Postlewaite, 'A Dickens of a Task for Raisa', *Evening Standard*, 18 July 1991 <https://global.factiva.com> [accessed 4 October 2017].
25. Naomi Klein, *No is Not Enough: Defeating the New Shock Politics* ([London]: Allen Lane, 2017), 107. For a similar case, see Pankaj Mishra, *Age of Anger: A History of the Present* ([London]: Allen Lane, 2017), 115.
26. Martha Nussbaum, *Cultivating Humanity* (Cambridge, MA: Harvard University Press, 1997), 103.

27. Juliet John, *Dickens and Mass Culture* (Oxford: Oxford University Press, 2010), 71.
28. *Dickens' Journalism*, I, 364.
29. Charles Dickens, *Little Dorrit*, ed. by Harvey Peter Sucksmith (Oxford: Clarendon, 1979), lix–lx.
30. Malcolm Andrews, *Dickensian Laughter: Essays on Dickens and Humour* (Oxford: Oxford University Press, 2013), 97.
31. John Forster, *The Life of Charles Dickens*, ed. by J. W. T. Ley (London: Cecil Palmer, 1928), 721.
32. Charles Dickens, *Bleak House*, ed. by George Ford and Sylvère Monod (New York: Norton, 1977), 14–15, ch. 2.
33. Forster, 32.
34. Charles Dickens, *A Tale of Two Cities*, ed. by George Woodcock (Harmondsworth: Penguin, 1970), 378, bk 2, ch. 13.
35. Charles Dickens, *Martin Chuzzlewit*, ed. by Margaret Cardwell (Oxford: Clarendon, 1982), 34, ch. 3; *Hard Times*, ed. by Fred Kaplan and Sylvère Monod, 3rd edn (New York: Norton, 2001), 151, bk 2, ch. 9.
36. John Bowen, 'Counting On: *A Tale of Two Cities*', in *Charles Dickens, A Tale of Two Cities and the French Revolution*, ed. by Colin Jones, Josephine McDonagh and Jon Mee (Basingstoke: Palgrave Macmillan, 2009), 104–23; Rosemarie Bodenheimer, *Knowing Dickens* (Ithaca: Cornell University Press, 2007); Jeremy Tambling, *Dickens' Novels as Poetry* (New York: Routledge, 2015), 75; Leslie Simon, '*Bleak House, Our Mutual Friend*, and the Aesthetics of Dust', *Dickens Studies Annual* 42 (2011), 217–36, 228; Natalie McKnight, 'Dickens and the Post-Modern Self: Fragmentation, Authority and Death', in *Charles Dickens, Modernism, Modernity*, ed. by Christine Huguet and Nathalie Vanfasse, 2 vols (Paris: Éditions du Sagittaire, 2014), II, 137–51.
37. Charles Dickens, 'Farewell Reading' (15 March 1870), *Speeches*, 413.

Further Reading

Monroe Engel, 'The Politics of Dickens' Novels', *PMLA* 71 (1956), 945–74
Sally Ledger, *Dickens and the Popular Radical Imagination* (Cambridge: Cambridge University Press, 2007)
Jeremy Tambling, *Dickens, Violence and the Modern State* (Basingstoke: Macmillan, 1995)

29

New Media and Cyberspace

Emma Curry

IT IS OVER TWENTY YEARS SINCE the first websites dedicated to Charles Dickens were launched, at a time when the World Wide Web was just beginning to be accessible to all.[1] Since then, Dickens's web presence has increased exponentially – today, a simple Google search of his name returns a huge variety of results, including webpages, images, YouTube videos, games, apps, memorabilia shops and a number of spoof social media accounts. As Jay Clayton has observed, this popularity on digital media can perhaps be traced back to Dickens's personal enthusiasm for new technology: as Clayton argues in his seminal study *Charles Dickens in Cyberspace*, Dickens was an 'early adopter' of new publishing techniques and modes of distribution throughout his career, and was keen to utilise these new technologies to create networks of readers around the globe.[2] Just as Dickens consistently sought to increase the size and diversity of his audience during his lifetime, so too does his online presence cross geographical, temporal and cultural boundaries: *The Dickens Page*, an international information repository hosted by Nagoya University in Japan, is still live today, having been set up in 1995, while elsewhere Dickens's name is attached to a range of initiatives with a global reach, from academic and community reading projects to a BBC interactive game, and from concordances of his complete works to virtual tours of Victorian London.[3]

It would, of course, be impossible to document or analyse the full range of multifarious ways in which Dickens has found a home in cyberspace, some of which, as Clayton remarks, seem to place Dickens's work at some distance.[4] However, in this chapter I will bring together several key instances of this online presence which have a close relationship with the original texts, in order to uncover their potential to reframe or reinvigorate assessments of Dickens's language. While the 'newness' of these various digital platforms and projects might seem on the one hand to draw us away from the texts, with the cultural capital of Dickens's name used as a springboard to other creative or commercial endeavours, what I am interested to explore is how certain aspects of Dickens's online presence can return us to his words in new and surprising ways and, in so doing, facilitate fruitful new perspectives on his distinctive literary style. Attention to Dickens's language has been seemingly less popular in criticism of recent years: as Daniel Tyler remarks in his introduction to the 2013 edited collection *Dickens's Style*, work has 'tended to focus on Dickens's relation to culture: to the ideological biases and blinds of his own culture, to Victorian material and popular cultures, and to mass culture today'.[5] While Dickens's online presence has much to tell us about the ways in which his image and cultural brand continue to be marketed globally, in this chapter I seek to trace the prominence of

Dickens's words in cyberspace, and to explore some of the ways digital media makes use of, responds to or transforms those words.

The first section of the chapter touches upon a few of the many online corpora of Dickens's writing, including hyper-concordances, the University of Buckingham's *Dickens Journals Online* initiative, and the CLiC Dickens project, hosted by the University of Birmingham. In considering the illimitable and infinitely adaptable 'space' of Dickensian cyberspace, this section highlights how digital tools and corpus linguistic technologies might allow readers to place extracts of Dickens's writing alongside each other in new and surprising ways, and to trace patterns and stylistic tics across Dickens's career with a detail hitherto unprecedented. The second section considers the concept of 'sharing' Dickens's words in smaller quantities, with reference to serial reading group projects, online discussion fora, and their role in the creation of global 'networks' of Dickensians. This section explores how online communication and collaboration between Dickensians might provide new critical languages with which to approach Dickens's own, as well as a means of reflecting upon Dickens's relationship with his readers, then and now. The final section of the chapter touches upon several creative initiatives of recent years which have sought to transpose or transform Dickens's words, from fan fiction to 'crowdsourced' continuations or rewritings of the original novels. In considering how such projects have brought Dickens's texts into conversation with the unique idioms of online spaces, this section reflects on the ways in which such new languages might supplement or reframe critical approaches to adaptations of Dickens's writing, as well as providing a fresh perspective on Dickens's own linguistic creativity.

While in some ways the breadth and reach of Dickens's cyber presence can make its assessment seem almost overwhelming, what is fundamental to each of the initiatives analysed here is the enduringly potent presence of Dickens's literary invention. In considering the rich variety of forms in which Dickens surfaces online, I would like to suggest that what emerges most clearly throughout is a sense of the continued creative impetus of Dickens's writing, and the ways in which his distinctive language persists in connecting and energising communities of readers across the globe.

Amassing Dickens's Words

One of the most fertile aspects of cyberspace for a writer as prolific as Dickens is the infinite sense of 'space' such a platform provides: unbound as an individual or library collection may be by restrictions of cost or shelving, the internet provides an illimitable, adaptable space that can host every word of Dickens's writing concurrently, from the more familiar novels and short stories to his plays, journalism, letters and even working notes, all free to access. Indeed, several of the first Dickensian spaces online focused upon amassing full corpora: the Victorian Literary Studies Archive's 'Hyper-Concordance', linked to Nagoya University's early *Dickens Page* (1995), hosts the complete works of a range of nineteenth-century authors, not only as a means of making the texts available for free but in order to provide the tools for researchers to perform keyword searches across an author's entire oeuvre. Notably, in the case of Dickens, this early tool also includes the option to search 'all novels' or 'all Dickens', a function which draws in Dickens's letters, as well as biographies or assessments of his work by John Forster, George Gissing, George Orwell and G. K. Chesterton. Even

450 EMMA CURRY

at this early stage of digital Dickensian projects, the impulse to find ways for research-ers to analyse Dickens's words across genres, or even to trace the appearance of his words in other writers' assessments of him, is an interesting one: it suggests the poten-tial of the digital space to provide an intriguingly broad and yet hyper-specific perspec-tive on Dickens's language, both comprehensive and yet concerned with a micro level of detail.

In more recent years, digitised corpora and their search functions have become increasingly sophisticated, and more and more of Dickens's writing has become avail-able online: in 2006 a team at the University of Buckingham embarked upon the *Dickens Journals Online* project, launching a website which hosts the scanned pages of every copy of Dickens's weekly magazines *Household Words* (1850–9) and *All the Year Round* (1859–70), as well as plaintext renderings of the contents.[6] The site places an important emphasis on accessibility, with text-to-speech functions for blind or visually impaired visitors, and it too seeks to make its huge collection of words searchable and analysable, offering the options to trace keywords or phrases across the full archive, as well as, to use Ben Winyard's description, 'using computa-tional stylistics to attempt some new attributions' for the journal's unsigned articles.[7] Similar initiatives include *The Dickensian*'s 'Charles Dickens Letters Project', which hosts searchable copies of all of Dickens's letters discovered since 2002 (and thus not included in the printed Pilgrim Edition); and the V&A's 'Deciphering Dickens' project, which aims to create an online digital archive of Dickens's notoriously densely written manuscripts, thus 'allowing us to see his first thoughts, changes of mind and innumerable refinements of expression'.[8] Perhaps most sophisticated of all, in corpus stylistics terms, is the CLiC Dickens project, hosted by the University of Birmingham, which aims to uncover how 'computer-assisted methods can [. . .] lead to new insights into how readers perceive fictional characters' by providing options to perform complex searches on patterns of text in Dickens's novels, including 'quotes' (speech or other text within inverted commas) and 'suspensions' ('an inter-ruption of a character's speech by narrator text').[9]

Taken together, these tools provide a fascinating sense of the ways in which the internet can function as a kind of mediating space for drawing together and sort-ing through huge quantities of Dickens's writing, and can provide a rich range of new avenues for scholars to detect connections between patterns of language across genres by, to use the words of Mr Inspector in *Our Mutual Friend* (1864–5), 'put-ting this and that together'.[10] While full-corpus searching is, of course, a function available for many authors' work, Dickens is a writer who particularly rewards this kind of reading: as Mahlberg comments of the CLiC project, the sophistication of the searching function is particularly effective in uncovering Dickens's techniques of constructing his characters, especially through his use of repeated phrases of body language.[11] Furthermore, while the letters and journalism remain understudied in perspectives on his literary style, using these digital tools to 'read' Dickens can also demonstrate how certain ideas and images are returned to and revised across mul-tiple genres of his writing. Perhaps one of the most famous examples of this is the character of Inspector Wield, described in 'A Detective Police Party' (a *Household Words* article of 1850), as 'a middle-aged man of a portly presence, with a large, moist, knowing eye, a husky voice, and a habit of emphasising his conversation by the aid of a corpulent fore-finger, which is constantly in juxta-position with his eyes or nose'.[12] Such a description will be familiar to readers of *Bleak House* (1852–3), who know Inspector Bucket to be similarly assembled through the means of a keen eye and a large finger: indeed, for the novel Dickens embellishes this description even further, describing Bucket's eye as being so penetrating that he looks at Mr Snagsby 'as if he were going to take his portrait', while his 'fat forefinger' is an almost magical presence, acting as a 'familiar demon' which 'whispers information' in consultation with him.[13] This ability of a finger to solve mysteries or reveal secrets seemingly becomes too good a creative opportunity to miss for Dickens, returning in Stryver's 'forensic forefinger' in *A Tale of Two Cities* (1859), and in Jaggers's intimidating habit of 'biting his forefinger' at clients in *Great Expectations* (1860–1).[14] With all of these instances hosted in the same digital space, the ability to isolate such examples and make links across texts and genres becomes much quicker; as Mahlberg writes, such moments demonstrate 'the potential of the concordance display to "zoom in"' on otherwise infinite stretches of text 'and group them for close analysis'.[15] In the case of these detecting forefingers, highlighting such repetitions also indicates the significance of such bodily-based images to Dickens's literary style.

Indeed, tracing patterns of language across digitised corpora indicates how certain phrases contribute centrally to the ways characters are conceived by Dickens, or even occur independently of their characters' construction. To take another body-part-based example: Dickens's fondness in his novels for characters with wooden legs has long been noted by critics.[16] When tracked across digital corpora, however, it becomes clear that such a construct infiltrates almost every genre of his writing, with patterns of language shared across a range of texts, enabling critics to add a quantitative, data-driven element to more impressionistic discussions. In Dickens's working notes for the second part of *Our Mutual Friend*, for example, we see how Silas Wegg himself springs from the single phrase 'seems to have taken his wooden leg naturally'.[17] While Wegg's name undergoes shifts – Dickens writes in his notes 'Solomon? Silas? *Yes*' [emphasis in original] – the wooden leg does not, indicating its centrality to the narratorial construction of Wegg's character, and the importance of its repetition in signalling to readers a sense of Wegg's form and personality whenever he appears in the narrative. Indeed, such a stylistic impulse is one Dickens is seemingly both aware of and deeply committed to: just below this note he refers to Mrs Boffin being 'a High-Flyer at Fashion', 'in a hat and feathers', and adds, with a double underline for emphasis, 'this to go through the book'.

The ways in which Wegg's leg is used within the narrative of *Our Mutual Friend* also build upon earlier descriptions outside of Dickens's novels. In a piece titled 'New Year's Day' in *Household Words* in 1859, Dickens describes an odd childhood memory of he and his sister 'secreting' a man with a wooden leg in their coal cellar. Such a task is made more difficult when, as Dickens narrates, the man's wooden leg 'bored itself in among the small coals, and his hat flew off, and he fell backward and lay prone: a spectacle of helplessness'.[18] Such a description here seems to function as a kind of imaginative trial run for the moment in *Our Mutual Friend* a number of years later when Wegg's 'self-willed' leg becomes stuck in the ashes of the Harmon dust heap, and Mr Venus is forced to 'haul [. . .] him from his tether by the collar: [. . .] his head enveloped in the skirts of his coat, and his wooden leg coming last, like a drag' (482, bk 3, ch. 6). Indeed, later in the same scene Venus throws Wegg to the floor, 'knowing that, once down, he would not be up again easily with his wooden leg' (484, bk 3, ch. 6). In each case, Dickens's fascination with the creative and linguistic possibilities of this particular body part is clear. But by reading and making links across corpora, such repeated images also uncover a broader cohesiveness in Dickens's semantic universe, one which is suggestive of the ways in which ideas and forms of imaginative language develop across his career. Such a method can also work to shift or reframe prevailing critical assumptions in Dickens studies about the binary progression of Dickens's writing style, from 'light' to 'dark', or 'comic' to 'melancholic'.

While such examples are very brief initial explorations of digitised corpora, one of the most exciting elements of these particular digital spaces and tools is the range of avenues for new work that they present. Bob Nicholson has written of the possibilities available to scholars if they 'remix' digital archives, drawing material together in new ways and making fresh connections across texts and disciplines.[19] In the case of Dickens, these spaces also present the opportunity for researchers to fully immerse themselves in his language, be it a piece of his travel writing or one of his letters or the notorious 'personal' address he makes in *Household Words* following his separation from Catherine in 1858. In that particular piece, Dickens reflects upon the fact that 'there is a great multitude who know me through my writings, and who do not know me otherwise'.[20] What is intriguing about the corpora of Dickensian cyberspace is the opportunity they present to unsettle what we think we know about Dickens through his writing.

Sharing Dickens's Words

One of the most notable and indeed heartening elements of many of these full-text repositories of Dickens's work is the collaborative nature not only of their assembly, but of their outputs: as Mahlberg highlights, tools and projects 'under the digital umbrella allow [. . .] us to ask new research questions and provide [. . .] new avenues for interdisciplinary work in the humanities' and beyond.[21] This element of collaboration and community is also a prominent feature of other Dickensian projects which use the internet as their shared meeting space. In recent years, a number of groups have sought to read Dickens's texts communally online, most notably as part of the bicentenary celebrations of Dickens's birth in 2012. Initiatives such as the British Council's twenty-four-hour 'read-a-thon' explicitly aimed to bring together and engage a global audience, hosting twenty-four readings of Dickens's work from twenty-four different countries, and inviting responses to the texts from participants around the world through the British Council's various social media channels.[22] This framing of the reading of Dickens's work as a shared and somewhat festive experience has also been an important element of online projects which have read Dickens in his original monthly instalments, artificially reconstructing the temporal rhythms of serial publication. Such initiatives – including the weekly blogs for *A Tale of Two Cities* (hosted by the University of Leicester in 2012) and *Great Expectations* (hosted by the University of Buckingham in 2017), as well as the monthly blogs for *Our Mutual Friend* (hosted by Birkbeck, University of London) and *The Mystery of Edwin Drood* (part of Pete Orford's 'Drood Inquiry' at the University of Buckingham in 2014) – have all capitalised on digitised editions of the texts freely available online, and have all crucially foregrounded the ability for readers to comment upon and discuss the texts with one another in their attached online fora.[23]

NEW MEDIA AND CYBERSPACE · 453

Such an interactive framing of the reading experience is one which can work to reorient perspectives on Dickens's language and the narratorial construction of his stories in a number of potentially fruitful ways. Just as digital search tools allow readers to 'zoom in' on phrases that may be missed or forgotten over the course of reading a complete novel, so too do serial, instalment-focused projects such as these encourage a 'slowed-down' attention to portions of the text over longer periods of time, allowing readers to reflect on the structural mechanics of Dickens's stories as they develop. In recent years, the idea of 'slowness' in all its forms has become an increasingly popular response to the fast-paced, high-stress characterisation of modernity, with the 'slow movement' asserting itself across a range of aspects of culture, from food and fashion to education.[24] In Dickens's case, such 'slowness' of consumption not only ostensibly seeks to mimic a contemporary reader's original experience of the stories, but, in encouraging pause and deliberation, refocuses attention to the fringes or connective tissues of Dickens's narratives, often bringing minor or overlooked characters into new relations with one another.

In Birkbeck's *Our Mutual Friend* project, for example, a great deal of discussion was devoted at a meeting of the reading group to the portion of the ninth instalment (originally published in January 1865) in which Dickens briefly dwells upon the imaginative inner life of Pleasant Riderhood, pawn shop owner and Mr Venus's love interest. At this stage of the narrative Pleasant is chiefly introduced into the story in order to draw out the more narratively significant tale of John Harmon's true fate, and yet this passage is rendered remarkably vividly by Dickens's narrator. He writes of how:

> sometimes of a summer evening, [. . .] she may have had some vaporous visions of far-off islands in the southern seas or elsewhere (not being geographically particular), where it would be good to roam with a congenial partner among groves of bread-fruit, waiting for ships to be wafted from the hollow ports of civilization. (346, bk 2, ch. 12)

Pleasant's 'visions', although 'not geographically particular', are nevertheless remarkably detailed here, constructing an entire alternative location, love and life in just a few phrases. But the way this passage is framed by Dickens's narrator also connects Pleasant's dreams with those of other female characters within the novel: as Holly Furneaux points out, in a piece which partly reflects upon this particular meeting of the reading group, Pleasant's 'vision of exotic wealth, and agency over men and their money, clearly recalls Bella's November instalment imagining of "all sorts of voyages for herself and Pa", [. . .] married to a "merchant of immense wealth"' (315, bk 2, ch. 8), not to mention Lizzie Hexam's fire 'pictures' of a life with Eugene Wrayburn, which occur just a few pages earlier in this monthly instalment (343, bk 2, ch. 11).[25] In this case a brief, seemingly insignificant digression provides a crucial connective link in the narrative, working to highlight one of the novel's broader but potentially overlooked thematic energies.

This relationship between individual details of phrasing and broader structural patterns becomes even clearer when dwelling over time upon the shorter instalments of Dickens's fiction. Much of the online discussion attached to the University of Leicester's weekly *A Tale of Two Cities* reading project in 2012 focused upon the ways in which Dickens organises and marshals his narrative, often by returning to familiar phrases or images, from the 'echoing footsteps' of the various real and imagined crowds in the novel to the repetition of the phrase 'recalled to life'. While Dickens famously complained about the concise, curtailed form of the 'teaspoons' he was forced to write in for the novels he published weekly in *Household Words* and *All the Year Round*,[26] a good deal of the discussion on the blog in the first week explored how the elision of elements of exposition creates a sense of narrative intrigue and momentum, which encourages readers to return. User 'Jill' commented:

> if I'd been a Victorian reader, reading this as a first instalment, I don't know how I could have put up with having to wait for the next chapter. I find I read more slowly and carefully by being limited to instalments, and appreciate the genius of Dickens the better for that.[27]

Another user, 'littledorritfan', noted that:

> I was so engrossed that I read on, and suddenly realised I was now into an article about something completely different! I am now impatient to find out what this nightmare is about, what is the meaning of the mysterious return message [*sic*], [. . .] and will we see Tom, Joe or Jerry again . . .?[28]

Ben Winyard specifically linked these emotional responses to the energetic structure of Dickens's three opening chapters, commenting 'the novel's plot is thrillingly propulsive [. . .] hurtling us back in time and then dashing us forward', from Dickens's famous opening of oppositions to the subsequent scene of the 'lumbering' stagecoach and its gloomy horses, 'mash[ing] their way through the thick mud' in the dead of night (8, bk 1, ch. 2).[29]

The withholding of character information that 'littledorritfan' refers to above is also a narrative impulse on Dickens's part which specifically relates to the weekly instalment, and is one which a 'slowed-down' reading such as this can work to highlight. Susan David Bernstein and Catherine Derose argue that there are deliberate and crucial linguistic differences in the ways monthly and weekly serials are structured by writers of this period, suggesting that 'weekly instalments (more frequently than their monthly counterparts) contain words that reference past events, concrete nouns, and spatial layouts, while simultaneously making fewer direct references to characters' interiority and exteriority'.[30] As the reader responses on the blog make clear, in *A Tale of Two Cities* such a point is realised acutely: indeed, Dickens specifically opens the third chapter of the first instalment by musing on the ways in which 'every human creature is constituted to be that profound secret and mystery to every other' (14, bk 1, ch. 3), foregrounding a sense of elided or obfuscated interiority from the very beginning of the narrative. Such a framing also spills out not only into the literal and figurative darkness of the novel's opening scenes, but the similarly shadowy, indistinct nature of the descriptions of the characters we do meet, from the 'multitude of faces' in Mr Lorry's dream (17, bk 1, ch. 3) to the description of Jerry Cruncher's eyes as being of 'surface black, with no depth in the colour or form' (15, bk 1, ch. 3). What is particularly interesting about the collaborative effort of the project's online discussion forum is that it serves to draw out not only the import of these structural and thematic elements but also their affect, collating reader responses and analyses of Dickens's language as the novel unfolds.

Indeed, the creation of this shared critical forum is a particularly key illuminative outcome of the digital space, providing fresh avenues for reflection on the growing sense of interaction and collaboration in the relationship between text and readers over the course of a novel. Such a point is particularly realised in the posts on the *Tale of Two Cities* blog following Dickens's final weekly instalment, in which the project's participants responded to the famous final words of the novel on a personal and emotional as well as an analytical level. As Holly Furneaux wrote in her last post, '. . . gulp . . . What a pay off for thirty one weeks of loyalty. [. . .] I'm very aware of writing into the poignant hush left by what are surely some of the finest last words on record', while Pete Orford added, 'it expresses itself so perfectly by itself, any commentary can feel a little redundant. This is great for Dickens, but not so great for the academic and critic.'[31]

Such responses to the novel's famous ending are perhaps familiar to many readers, but the reflection on the relationship between Dickens's words and the commenters' own here is an intriguing one. Below these comments, some discussion and light-hearted debate broke out over readers' responses to the novel as a whole, causing Orford to eventually respond, after a delay enabled by the extended timelines of the digital group, 'okay, okay, break it up people. Honestly, I leave the blog for a couple of days and what do I come back to?'[32] Such moments provide a cheering insight into the close and affective communities constructed by these digital reading experiments, but the relative informality of the language and tone that characterises these comments and, indeed, all of those quoted above is also striking and potentially fruitful in considering analyses of Dickens's style. In reflecting upon all of these digital reading projects, there is a sense that, as familiarity grows between the commenting community, they construct and develop together a new, shared critical language with which to think through responses to the novel; one which is perhaps more contemplative, experimental and reflexive than the more formal modes of analysis published in academic presses. By reading, thinking and, most crucially, writing about Dickens together, these digital commenters negotiate different forms of discussion and analysis in the manner of a seminar or book club (albeit one which traverses temporal or geographical boundaries), but in each case these conversations require a linguistic response, which can be prepared, responded to and revisited over a number of hours, days or months. While Dickens famously sought to unite communities of readers with his stories, then, what is striking about this particular aspect of Dickensian cyberspace is that such groups also bring together and create communities of writers. In grappling collaboratively with Dickens's language, these online reading projects can work to produce new critical languages of their own.

Transforming Dickens's Words

The creative impetus of Dickens's writing is a thriving characteristic of Dickensian cyberspace which also inspires more explicitly imaginative or transformative responses. While the internet hosts a diverse, wide-ranging space for individuals to read, analyse and discuss Dickens's work, it also provides them with the tools to create and share adaptations or alternative versions of his stories, without the need for the budget or infrastructure that a formal film or television adaptation would require. Such online reworkings are often much smaller in scale and focus, frequently drawing on memorable scenes or characters in the original texts to create new outputs that are still intriguingly rooted in the 'Dickensian' mode. As Juliet John argues in her introduction to *Dickens and Modernity*, the combined energies of familiarity and innovation present in Dickens's original texts specifically feed this continued prominence in popular culture. As she writes, Dickens's contemporary presence builds upon:

> his ability to bring together [. . .] ways of seeing and feeling that received logic perceives as oppositional. [. . .] In Dickens, a communal, nostalgic, organic view of the world co-exists and indeed grows out of a very modern sense of instability, mobility and radical uncertainty.[33]

Such 'mash-ups' of old and new are a distinctive characteristic of many online creative projects of recent years, from thriving Dickensian fan fiction communities to Birkbeck's '*Our Mutual Friend* Tweets' Twitter project, which ran alongside the university's serial reading group in 2014–15.[34] These creative responses to Dickens frequently draw specifically upon the 'instability' that John identifies in Dickens's texts, explicitly building upon intricacies or overlooked undercurrents in the original novels to draw out and develop alternative energies or trajectories.

One of the most popular elements of the range of online transformations of Dickens's work is the extension or embellishment of the lives of 'minor' characters lurking within the fringes of the main text. This activity was a key element of the '*Our Mutual Friend* Tweets' project, which, in its collaborative role play of the novel's events on Twitter, specifically sought to develop the voices of as many characters within the novel as participants wished to portray, even drawing in the inanimate objects of Mr Venus's shop. Such an impulse is equally popular within fan fiction communities, as Maureen England explores in this volume. The stories in the 'Dickens' section of the website *fanfiction.net* cover a wide range of texts and characters, from musings on Mr Venus and his romantic travails to the marital life of Ernest and Madame Defarge, and even a short piece imagining the marriage of Bertha Plummer to the newly reformed Mr Tackleton in *The Cricket on the Hearth*.[35]

This portability of Dickens's characters across popular culture is one which Alex Woloch famously links to the mechanics of Dickens's language and literary style: in *The One vs the Many*, Woloch suggests that the strange '*over*-significance of minor characters' in Dickens's novels is due to his 'radical stylistics of characterisation', within which so-called 'minor' characters play crucial roles in the linguistic construction of Dickens's fictional universe.[36] Indeed, the detail and vitality of such online reimaginings or developments of these minor characters frequently serve to draw out their intriguing, unexpected prominence within their original narratives. Mr Venus, for example, who is introduced into *Our Mutual Friend* partially to perform some structural space-filling between instalments, discovers a richly imagined life online, which plays upon the significance of his name and of Dickens's brief references to the 'boney light' which impedes his romance with Pleasant Riderhood (90, bk 1, ch. 7).[37] One online fan-written tale amusingly publicises itself with the tagline: 'Mr Venus was only searching for a serviceable parrot. He wasn't expecting to find true love.'[38] Within the '*Our Mutual Friend* Tweets' project, Mr Venus's 'New Year's Resolutions'

NEW MEDIA AND CYBERSPACE

457

include similarly comical plans to 'cultivate a nautical air: maybe a tattoo? Grow a beard perhaps? Remove hand & replace with hook?', as well as to 'pursue my beloved with a renewed ardour, and finally step out of the boney light!' (@OMF_Venus, 4 January 2015). Such moments serve to draw out the 'radical' characterisation Woloch identifies in Dickens's writing, demonstrating not only how much imaginative flesh is on the bones of even the most briefly mentioned individuals, but how apposite or even creatively inspiring these particular bits of flesh can be. The emotional engagement that readers draw from these originally 'marginal' characters is also demonstrably crucial to this process of reimagining. As Melissa Symanczyk writes in reflecting upon her role as Mr Venus's stuffed alligator in the Twitter project:

> I became quite protective of Mr Venus [. . .]: were you to ask me today what the book is about, my first instinct would be to tell you it's about a lonely taxidermist in a dark London shop, trying to do the right thing and trying to find love.[39]

This sense of a vibrant and creative impetus in Dickens's language is also particularly demonstrated in the tweeting 'voice' adopted by many of the characters in the 'Our Mutual Friend Tweets' project. A number of the project's participants specifically drew on Dickens's linguistic innovations, aping styles of speech or behaviour lifted directly from the text in order to create comical juxtapositions with the contemporary idioms of online spaces. Sloppy, for example, whose conversations in the novel are punctuated by his loud, idiosyncratic laugh – Jenny Wren describes him as being 'like the giant' who 'wanted Jack for supper' (787, bk 4, ch. 16) – reimagines this tic on Twitter through the creation of both a distinctive idiolect and the use of imaginative 'hashtags': his first tweet was 'spend ol mornin explainin twitter to @ OMF_Betty . . . got to catch up on me mangling naw! #haaa #mangle' (@OMF_ Sloppy, 30 April 2014). The tweeter Rogue Riderhood similarly drew upon both the personality and speech patterns created by Dickens to imagine new avenues of contemporary villainy, tweeting: '@DickensOMF Your account may be infected by a wirus! Please send me your password so's I can verify your security' (@OMF_Rogue, 8 May 2014). And Bella Wilfer, whose voice and worldview is clearly articulated in the novel's opening monthly instalment, in which she ostentatiously bemoans being 'left to [John Harmon] in a will, like a dozen of spoons' (45, bk 1, ch. 4), was able to explore her developing sense of self over the course of the project by drawing upon the acutely performative nature of the Twitter space. As Beatrice Bazell, who tweeted as Bella, reflects, these performances also served to link up Bella's speech with the broader narratorial fabric: the Twitter monologues 'provide a way of articulating feelings and interests which [Bella] doesn't consciously register, but which Dickens's wry authorial voice accounts for in the written narrative'.[40] In each of these cases the imaginative link between original story and creative reworking is reoriented by the new platform and purpose, but nevertheless remains distinct; indeed, what is striking about these particular creative projects is that movements ostensibly 'away' from the original in fact serve to bring about further returns to, and reflections upon, Dickens's text.

Such an impulse remains potent even when these projects go beyond the flexible bounds of the original. Entirely new or alternative endings to Dickens's texts thrive online, but, as critics have pointed out, these counterfactual energies again take their roots from Dickens's original narratorial frameworks.[41] An alternative ending to *Our Mutual Friend* in which the queer energies of the relationship between Eugene Wrayburn and Mortimer Lightwood are realised alongside Eugene's relationship with Lizzie Hexam can be found in fan fiction texts online, and was similarly played out in the closing stages of the Twitter project, with Eugene cheerfully reflecting, 'a happy ending: @OMF_Lizzie curling one whisker & @OMF_Mortimer carefully combing out the other. #muttonchopsforeveryone #omfcounterfactuals' (@OMF_Eugene, 2 December 2015).[42] As Furneaux comments, this particular counterfactual ending draws upon not only 'the memorable same-sex intimacies of Dickens's work' but the rich creative potential of Dickens's serial form, which in its extension of temporality opens the bounds for alternative trajectories such as this to proliferate. Such a process seems only to be increased by the temporal distance between the original publication and today. Furneaux suggests that these energies reorient 'Dickens and his queer readers' as 'co-producers of fantasies',[43] a term which draws out the affective but also proprietary nature of the relationship between Dickens and his readers and (re)writers. That such creative projects flourish online indicates not only the inclusive imaginative potential of these areas of Dickensian cyberspace, but of the creative stimulus that Dickens's distinctive style continues to represent for his readers.

Concluding Remarks

In her article on 'crowdsourced' Dickensian projects, Juliet John importantly sounds a note of caution regarding the optimism with which many online projects claim to reach and involve large new audiences, highlighting that such extensive influence is generally confined to those projects with '"top-down" infrastructure or finance'.[44] As she argues, however, what is key to many digital initiatives, rather than their critical or commercial 'impact', is instead the sense of communal ownership and affective pleasure that such projects embody. As John writes, in many ways 'the internet has facilitated not an extension of Dickens's audience or new "crowds", but a reconfiguration of communication structures which allows "clubs" to feel newly empowered'.[45] The sense of 'empowerment', which characterises all of the aspects of Dickensian cyberspace surveyed in this chapter, becomes a key element of critical and creative innovation, encouraging and enabling readers of Dickens to do new things with his words, whether by forging fresh analytical tools and communities or by experimenting enthusiastically with their own transformations of his characters and plots.

While there are, of course, other broad facets of Dickensian cyberspace which spool away from the original novels, the continued potency of Dickens's linguistic roots across these forms of 'new' media is striking, and the avenues for new work that such innovations present for a critic are exciting (albeit dizzying). The characteristics and idioms of Dickensian cyberspace continue to change rapidly, as witnessed simply in the shift from the objectivity of the original *Dickens Page* to the carnivalesque exuberance of the '*Our Mutual Friend* Tweets' project. But what remains common to many of these digital projects is a sense of the enduring interactive pleasures of Dickens's language: of the ways in which his words continue to inspire us as readers to think and to talk and to write – crucially, to communicate with one other.

Notes

1. These include *The Dickens Page*, launched by Professor Mitsuharu Matsuoka of Nagoya University in September 1995, and a site with the same title uploaded in the summer of 1995 by Professor George P. Landow of Brown University, who went on to create *The Victorian Web*. See Jay Clayton, *Charles Dickens in Cyberspace: The Afterlife of the Nineteenth Century in Postmodern Culture* (Oxford: Oxford University Press, 2003), 4, 215 n. 1.
2. Clayton, 3.
3. See 'Dickens commemorated in 24 countries over 24 hours with global read-a-thon', *British Council*, 7 February 2012 <http://literature.britishcouncil.org/news/2012/january/readathon>, which can be accessed via the Wayback Machine (2014) <https://web. archive.org/>; *A Tale of Two Cities Reading Blog* (2012) <https://dickensataleoftwocities.wordpress.com/page/15/>; 'Survive Dickens' London', *BBC Arts* (2014) <http://www. bbc.co.uk/arts/multimedia/dickens/>; The Victorian Literary Studies Archive Hyper-Concordance (2003) <http://victorian-studies.net/concordance/dickens/>; 'Charles Dickens's London with Simon Callow', *Guardian*, 7 February 2012 <https://www.theguardian. com/books/video/2012/feb/07/charles-dickens-london-simon-callow-video> [all accessed 26 July 2017]. It is interesting to note that, while some older sites such as *The Dickens Page* endure, elsewhere Dickens's online presence is more unstable, with certain pages (the British Council's 2012 celebrations, for example) now only accessible through internet archiving tools.
4. Clayton, 150–2.
5. Daniel Tyler, 'Introduction', in *Dickens's Style*, ed. by Daniel Tyler (Cambridge: Cambridge University Press, 2013), 1–25, 7.
6. See 'About Us', *Dickens Journals Online* <http://www.djo.org.uk/about-us.html> [accessed 26 July 2017].
7. Ben Winyard, '"May We Meet Again": Rereading the Dickensian Serial in the Digital Age', *19: Interdisciplinary Studies in the Long Nineteenth Century* 21 (2015), 1–21, 5 <http://doi.org/10.16995/ntn.737>.
8. The Charles Dickens Letters Project (2016) <http://dickensletters.com/>; V&A Research Projects: Deciphering Dickens (2016) <https://www.vam.ac.uk/research/projects/deciphering-dickens> [all accessed 2 November 2019].
9. CLiC Dickens (2016) <http://clic.bham.ac.uk/concordances/> [accessed 26 July 2017]; Michaela Mahlberg, Peter Stockwell, Johan de Joode et al., 'CLiC Dickens: Novel Uses of Concordances for the Integration of Corpus Stylistics and Cognitive Poetics', *Corpora* 11.3 (2016), 433–63, 443.
10. Charles Dickens, *Our Mutual Friend*, ed. by Adrian Poole (London: Penguin, 1997), 40, bk 1, ch. 3. Subsequent references are given in the text.
11. Mahlberg, Stockwell, de Joode et al., 455. See also Michaela Mahlberg, *Corpus Stylistics and Dickens's Fiction* (Abingdon: Routledge, 2013), 100–27.
12. Charles Dickens, 'A Detective Police Party (I)', *Household Words* 18 (27 July 1850), I 409–14, 409.
13. Charles Dickens, *Bleak House*, ed. by Stephen Gill (Oxford: Oxford University Press, 2008), 328, ch. 22; 742, ch. 53.
14. Charles Dickens, *A Tale of Two Cities*, ed. by Richard Maxwell (London: Penguin, 2000), 153, bk 2, ch. 12; Charles Dickens, *Great Expectations*, ed. by Charlotte Mitchell (London: Penguin, 2003), 134, ch. 18. Subsequent references are given in the text.
15. Mahlberg, Stockwell, de Joode et al., 450.
16. See John Carey, *The Violent Effigy: A Study of Dickens' Imagination* (London: Faber & Faber, 1973) for a discussion of this trope.

17. See 'Notes for Our Mutual Friend Installment #2' <http://dickensnotes.com/omfno2/> [accessed 26 July 2017].

18. Charles Dickens, 'New Year's Day', *Household Words* 458 (1 January 1859), XIX, 97–102, 98.

19. Bob Nicholson, 'The Victorian Meme Machine: Remixing the Nineteenth-Century Archive', *19: Interdisciplinary Studies in the Long Nineteenth Century* 21 (2015), 1–34 <http://doi.org/10.16995/ntn.738>.

20. Charles Dickens, 'Personal', *Household Words* 429 (12 June 1858), XVII, 601.

21. Mahlberg, Stockwell, de Joode et al., 457.

22. See 'Happy Birthday Charles Dickens' (7 February 2012) <https://www.facebook.com/britishcouncil/posts/happy-birthday-charles-dickens-to-celebrate-the-bicentenary-of-the-authors-birth/236094596474445/> and 'Dickens 2012 Read-a-thon in 24 Countries' (8 February 2012) <https://youtu.be/l09caKqEEyo> [accessed 1 May 2020].

23. See *A Tale of Two Cities Reading Blog* (2012) <https://dickensataleoftwocities.wordpress.com/page/15/>; *Great Expectations* Readalong (2017–18) <https://greatexpectationsreadalong.wordpress.com/>; Dickens *Our Mutual Friend* Reading Project (2014–15) <https://dickensourmutualfriend.wordpress.com/>; and The Drood Inquiry (2014) <http://www.droodinquiry.com/> [all accessed 2 November 2019].

24. See, for example, Carlo Petrini, *Slow Food: The Case for Taste*, trans. by William McCuaig (New York: Columbia University Press, 2001); Maggie Berg and Barbara K. Seeber, *The Slow Professor: Challenging the Culture of Speed in the Academy* (Toronto: University of Toronto Press, 2016).

25. Holly Furneaux, 'Mortimer Lightwood; or, Seriality, Counterfactuals, Co-Production, and Queer Fantasy', *19: Interdisciplinary Studies in the Long Nineteenth Century* 21 (2015), 1–4, 3 <http://doi.org/10.16995/ntn.751>.

26. Michael Slater, *Charles Dickens: A Life Defined by Writing* (New Haven: Yale University Press, 2009), 477.

27. Gail Marshall, 'Week One' <https://dickensataleoftwocities.wordpress.com/2012/04/30/week-one/> [accessed 26 July 2017].

28. 'littledorritfan', 'Week 1 – and it really is my first time!' <https://dickensataleoftwocities.wordpress.com/2012/05/06/week-1-and-it-really-is-my-first-time/> [accessed 26 July 2017].

29. Ben Winyard, 'Week 2' <https://dickensataleoftwocities.wordpress.com/2012/05/07/week-2> [accessed 26 July 2017].

30. Susan David Bernstein and Catherine Derose, 'Reading Numbers by Numbers: Digital Studies and the Victorian Serial Novel', *Victorian Review* 38 (2012), 43–68, 50.

31. Holly Furneaux, 'Week 31: 'A Far, Far Better Thing' <https://dickensataleoftwocities.wordpress.com/2012/11/25/week-31-a-far-far-better-thing/> [accessed 26 July 2017].

32. Ibid.

33. Juliet John, 'Introduction', in *Dickens and Modernity*, ed. by Juliet John (Cambridge: Brewer, 2012), 1–18, 15.

34. For fan fiction see, for example, <https://www.fanfiction.net/book/Charles-Dickens/> or <https://archiveofourown.org/>; for '*Our Mutual Friend* Tweets', see Emma Curry, 'Doing the Novel in Different Voices: Reflections on a Dickensian Twitter Experiment', *19: Interdisciplinary Studies in the Long Nineteenth Century* 21 (2015), 1–19 <http://doi.org/10.16995/ntn.736>.

35. Laura Schiller, 'Reflections of Light' (2014) <https://www.fanfiction.net/s/10291322/1/Reflections-of-Light> [accessed 26 July 2017].

36. Alex Woloch, *The One vs the Many: Minor Characters and the Space of the Protagonist in the Novel* (Princeton: Princeton University Press, 2003), 125, emphasis in original.

37. See Nicola Bown, 'Month 2 (June 1864): There's Animation! Dickens and Taxidermy' <https://dickensourmutualfriend.wordpress.com/2014/05/29/month-2-june-1864-theres-animation-dickens-and-taxidermy/> [accessed 26 July 2017].

38. Wickfield, 'Cupid and Venus' <https://www.fanfiction.net/s/9144753/1/Cupid-and-Venus> [accessed 26 July 2017].
39. Melissa Symanczyk, 'Reflections of a Sawdust-Filled, Six-Foot, Tweeting, Taxidermy Alligator', *19: Interdisciplinary Studies in the Long Nineteenth Century*, 21 (2015), 1–3, 1, 3 <http://doi.org/10.16995/ntn.749>.
40. Beatrice Bazell, 'Being Bella: Adventures in the Dickensian "Twittersphere"', *19: Interdisciplinary Studies in the Long Nineteenth Century* 21 (2015), 1–5, 4 <http://doi.org/10.16995/ntn.748>.
41. See Robyn Warhol-Down, '"What Might Have Been Is Not What Is": Dickens's Narrative Refusals', *Dickens Studies Annual* 41 (2010), 45–59 and Andrew H. Miller, '"A Case of Metaphysics": Counterfactuals, Realism, *Great Expectations*', *ELH* 79 (2012), 773–96.
42. Zlot, 'Two Men in a Boat' and Deanna, 'Sources of Light' <https://archiveofourown.org/tags/Mortimer%20Lightwood/works> [accessed 2 November 2019].
43. Furneaux, 'Mortimer Lightwood', 4.
44. Juliet John, 'Crowdsourced Dickens', *The Oxford Handbook of Charles Dickens*, ed. by John O. Jordan, Robert L. Patten and Catherine Waters (Oxford: Oxford University Press, 2018), 756–73, 757.
45. Ibid.

Further Reading

Carolyn Burdett and Hilary Fraser, eds, 'The Nineteenth-Century Digital Archive', *19: Interdisciplinary Studies in the Long Nineteenth Century*, 21 (2015) <https://19.bbk.ac.uk/issue/114/info/>

Jay Clayton, *Charles Dickens in Cyberspace: The Afterlife of the Nineteenth Century in Postmodern Culture* (Oxford: Oxford University Press, 2003)

Juliet John, *Dickens and Mass Culture* (Oxford: Oxford University Press, 2010)

Part VII

Cultural Memory

30

DICKENS AND SHAKESPEARE

Pete Orford

How Dickens Saved Shakespeare (and Why We Choose to Tell That Story)

IN 2017 THE SHAKESPEARE BIRTHPLACE TRUST in Stratford-upon-Avon ran the exhibition 'Saving Shakespeare's Birthplace' to commemorate the 170th anniversary of its auction. The narrative has the makings of a feel-good movie: P. T. Barnum visited the site in the 1830s and conceived a plan to purchase the building and ship it, brick by brick, to the United States for display. But he was thwarted by a plucky band of British figures working together to raise funds and 'save' the Birthplace, including Dickens at the forefront, armed with his amateur production of *The Merry Wives of Windsor* on 27 June 1848. It provides everything an audience needs: celebrity figures in the role of local underdogs acting with civic pride to fight against commercial and capitalist interests. The story is not untrue, but then nor is it exactly as we have romanticised it. While Dickens was certainly involved in Victorian reclamation of the Birthplace, needless to say when the Birthplace Trust's commemorative exhibition was being promoted in 2017, it was his name above all others that featured in the headlines. Article titles such as *The Guardian*'s 'Tale of Dickens' fight to save Shakespeare house' rather ignore the efforts of fellow committee members Charles Cowden Clarke and John Payne Collier, who, as prominent Shakespeare scholars, can be said to have had just as much investment in keeping the Birthplace in England, but they ultimately lack the celebrity status to warrant a place in a twenty-first century headline.[1] To be fair to *The Guardian*, it is simply repeating what various generations have long done in their own boiling down of the story: to maintain public interest, it has been distilled to the tale of how Dickens saved Shakespeare. The recurrent appearance of 'save' in the various narratives surrounding this event is no coincidence: it is not enough that Dickens and his contemporaries helped to raise funds to buy the Birthplace, but in doing so they were somehow heroically freeing it from 'the dastardly clutches of US showman Barnum', even though Barnum's role has been equally overinflated in the retelling.[2] The story of Dickens saving Shakespeare is not simply a tale of two writers, but a conduit for wider concerns about cultural identity and intellectual ownership, a tale which uses a nineteenth-century British author's identity as the successor of Shakespeare to maintain and tie the playwright to his country through a chain of literary descendants.

In contrast to these headlines, when we investigate the event in the context of Dickens studies, it garners little attention. Michael Slater's biography of Dickens gives little space to his involvement in Stratford, mentioning only in brief how

'A body called the London Shakespeare Committee had recently bought the Stratford Birthplace and Dickens now reactivated the Amateurs to fund-raise for the endowment of a Birthplace curatorship' by staging *Merry Wives* in 1848.[3] Nor was it the first time that Dickens had performed *Merry Wives*, having previously staged it on 19 July 1847 'for the benefit of Leigh Hunt'.[4] The performance the following year was thus not as novel as we might first think, and in a letter to Émile de la Rue, Dickens seems surprisingly unenthusiastic about it, noting how the Shakespeare House Committee was 'imploring and beseeching' him to stage a production that he appears to be less than willing to do: 'I am not particularly anxious to take the needful trouble, and am holding off at present, but it is very possible that the thing may be done, because of the difficulty of getting out of it.'[5] Nor was it so directly linked to saving Shakespeare's house, but, as Slater notes above, to securing a curator for the house, namely James Sheridan Knowles, author of the 1820 play *Virginius* which 'had provided Macready with one of his most acclaimed roles'.[6] The majority of letters which Dickens wrote to his friends seeking support for the production do betray more enthusiasm for the project than the one to de la Rue, but frequently that enthusiasm is primarily for the benefit offered to Knowles over Shakespeare:

> We do not play to purchase the house (which may be positively considered as paid for) but towards endowing a perpetual curatorship of it, for some eminent literary veteran. And I think you will recognise in this, even a higher and more generous object than the securing, even, of the debt incurred for the house itself.[7]

As Emily Smith has noted in her recent doctoral research, if Dickens's primary motivation for restaging *Merry Wives* in 1848 was helping Knowles, rather than Shakespeare, then it repositions his motivation from saving bricks and mortar to helping a struggling playwright secure a living: it becomes an act of compassion rather than national interest, using a venerable dead author to support a living one, but also trusting those who live by the pen to protect the reputation of their forebears.[8] The act has more in common with Dickens's work for the Royal Literary Fund, or General Theatrical Association, both of which sought to aid writers and actors in financial distress. But 'Dickens saves Knowles' is far less likely to grab the attention of most readers in the way that the headline 'Dickens saves Shakespeare' can. And there lies the rub: our fascination with Dickens and Shakespeare is borne out of a singular interest in both that simultaneously encourages exploration of any connection between them and discourages analysis of other mutual connections. Figuring Dickens as a central player in the fight for Shakespeare's birthplace benefits him by defining him as both Shakespeare's inheritor and champion; it equally benefits Shakespeare studies in this instance by providing a known name to amplify interest in a tale of administration and property acquisition some two hundred years after his death.

Our understanding of Dickens's admiration for Shakespeare is awash with other such anecdotes: his annual celebration of Shakespeare's birthday with John Forster, or his acquisition of Gad's Hill, the scene of Falstaff's criminal exploits. But do these stories offer more beyond the initial brief pleasure of seeing these two authors connected? It is satisfying to hear that one great writer admired another, to think that one plays a role in the narrative of the other. But why do people care if Dickens 'saved' Shakespeare's birthplace? What is to be gained by examining and endorsing a relationship between the two writers? Questioning the fascination with the idea of Dickens and Shakespeare reveals underlying insecurities about cultural icons, about the perception and defence of literary quality and the arts, and the curious attempt to connect historical narratives by assuming a line of descent through the ages. Our fascination with Dickens and Shakespeare is mutually beneficial. On one hand, it endorses Shakespeare as ever relevant and universal. On the other, it affords a cultural currency to Dickens as a purveyor of great art, a narrative he himself was just as keen to promote. As early as *Oliver Twist* (1837–9), he defends his work not only as popular fiction, but as having 'precedents [. . .] in the noblest range of English literature'; and while Dickens does not name Shakespeare specifically in this defence, his use of Shakespeare throughout his work dovetails with this acknowledgement of literary predecessors.[9] The narrative of Dickens saving Shakespeare is linked to a parallel story of Shakespeare inspiring Dickens; a mutually beneficial literary heritage narrative which legitimises the latter while reinforcing the durability of the former.

How Shakespeare Inspired Dickens (and How We Have Interpreted That Inspiration)

While biographical moments like the Birthplace auction offer colour to the narrative, the most explored aspect of Dickens's reliance on Shakespeare is through his writing, and the regular allusions, both direct and indirect, which he makes to Shakespeare's plays. Daniel Pollack-Pelzner defines Dickens's engagement with Shakespeare as 'a relationship founded on quotation'.[10] This may be direct quotations, or the appropriation of characters, but together they create an undeniable sense that Dickens knew his Shakespeare, either choosing deliberately at points to quote from him (such as his decision to name his journal *Household Words* after the famous St Crispin's Day speech in *Henry V*), or otherwise simply having it there in his consciousness to draw upon when looking for an apt phrase or description. It is no surprise to know that Shakespeare's complete works are listed in Dickens's borrowing history at the Reading Room in the British Museum, nor that a copy was subsequently in his library at Gad's Hill.[11] And yet as much as we can be certain that Dickens read Shakespeare, it is equally important to note how on occasion Dickens refrains from referring specifically to the act of doing so, such as the famous passage from *David Copperfield* (1849–50) in which the young David's bookshelf is widely seen as a projection of Dickens's own childhood reading. For our purposes, it is illuminating to see what the quotation does *not* tell us:

> From that blessed little room, Roderick Random, Peregrine Pickle, Humphrey Clinker, Tom Jones, the Vicar of Wakefield, Don Quixote, Gil Blas, and Robinson Crusoe, came out, a glorious host, to keep me company. They kept alive my fancy, and my hope of something beyond that place and time, – they, and the Arabian Nights, and the Tales of the Genii.[12]

Among this host of characters called upon to support David, not one is from Shakespeare. Falstaff offers him no cheer, nor does Hamlet offer a model in melancholy. Nor is this moment unique; young Scrooge's imaginary encounter with Ali Baba and others is also a Shakespeare-free zone.[13] The omission of Shakespeare's characters from association with these literary figures might suggest how, for Dickens, Shakespeare is more synonymous with theatre and performance, not solitary reading, querying the extent to which Dickens perceives Shakespeare as literary predecessor or a theatrical presence. Sylvère Monod suggests that Dickens's understanding of Shakespeare:

> has to be placed fairly close to the popular theatre, because Dickens became acquainted with his works in the same way he came to know the lower forms of drama – on the stage. Such is the conclusion one is inevitably led to by studying the Shakespearean quotations and references in his works.[14]

We know that Dickens certainly read Shakespeare, both in the British Library as a young man and from his personal library in his maturity, but the question remains as to what extent Dickens read Shakespeare in relation to seeing the plays performed. Indeed, quite often those that *do* read Shakespeare in Dickens's works are viewed with mistrust or ridicule, such as the insufferable Uncle Tom in 'Mrs Joseph Porter' (1834), whose 'pride [was] that he remembered all the principal plays of Shakespeare from beginning to end' and who actively disrupts a performance of *Othello* with his slavish reverence for the text.[15] While the humour in this sketch is focused mainly on the failing amateur performance, there is an implicit criticism being made of Tom himself. He cannot enjoy or engage with the performance as he should, but is instead compelled to bind it to the text, noting any deviations. Uncle Tom epitomises the idea of Shakespeare as art more than entertainment, but it is not a flattering portrayal; he prioritises strength of recollection over emotive reading. Having read Shakespeare, Uncle Tom feels compelled to ensure everyone *knows* that he has read Shakespeare. There is an inherent snobbishness being exposed here by Dickens of the armchair Shakespeare fans of that time, and their misguidedly condescending perception of those who 'merely' see Shakespeare performed instead of reading him intently. Monod's perception of Dickens's enthusiasm for Shakespeare is certainly in line with this:

> Dickens was a Shakespearean only in the sense that he never tired of attending new performances of the great plays; but he was not one of those who know Shakespeare's works inside out; he despised scholarly research devoted to the playwright's biography, and it can be shown that he did not feel the true Shakespearean reverence.[16]

Monod draws on the parodic multivolume titles displayed on the dummy shelves of Dickens's study in Gad's Hill, such as *Was Shakespeare's Mother Fair?*, *Had Shakespeare's Uncle a Singing Face?* or *Was Shakespeare's Father Merry?*, which point to the worst type of myopic biographical criticism. But what Monod does not note is the actual critical works also present in the Gad's Hill library. Stonehouse lists seven purely critical works on Shakespeare in Dickens's library at the time of his death, five of which were presentation copies gifted to Dickens.[17] Seven works of criticism do not confirm Dickens as a Shakespeare scholar, and the extent to which Dickens relied on these, if at all, is difficult to determine, but what they do show is that many of his friends perceived him as someone who would be interested in Shakespearean criticism. As much as Dickens might scorn Uncle Tom, there may yet be some small element of the author in this bookish character. But this needs to be balanced against Dickens's regular attendance at the theatre and the impact of experiencing these works primarily through performance. While the abundance of Shakespearean quotations within Dickens's works speak of his familiarity, it does not determine how much of that familiarity arises from reading or watching the plays.

The tension between criticism and performance of Shakespeare taps into the larger Romantic debate, stimulated by critics such as Charles Lamb who believed the plays were best experienced on the page rather than on the stage, but it equally alludes to a broader snobbery in the nineteenth century that belittled popular theatre compared to the intellectual delights of reading.[18] This tension centred around the distinction between art and entertainment, and it is an issue on which Dickens frequently argues for both sides. In 'The Amusements of the People' (1850), for example, he provides a half-mocking, half-endearing portrayal of Joe Whelks, a man who does not read but instead absorbs all his culture from the theatre, prompting Dickens's open question of whether his 'education is at all susceptible of improvement, through the agency of his theatrical tastes'.[19] While Dickens recognised the importance of theatre as the popular medium for those who could not, or would not, read, he was not averse to ridiculing the bizarre theatrical practices applied to Shakespeare. In 'Private Theatres' (1835), Dickens takes great delight both in the egotism driving productions of *Richard III* and the antics behind the curtain in the run-up to a pitiful production of *Macbeth*:

> The boy of fourteen who is having his eyebrows smeared with soap and whitening is Duncan, King of Scotland; and the two dirty men with the corked countenances, in very old green tunics, and dirty drab boots, are the 'army'.[20]

Dickens is specifically laughing at the actors and the production, not the play-text itself, just as he mocked Uncle Tom rather than the play he systematically memorised. Shakespeare's works are not objects to mock, but rather a standard by which those who try to perform those works, and fail, are ripe for mockery instead. It was a theme Dickens stuck with, and one which resurfaces in the gloriously parodic performance of *Hamlet* by Mr Wopsle in *Great Expectations* (1860–1), in which 'The late king of the country not only appeared to have been troubled with a cough at the time of his decease, but to have taken it with him to the tomb, and to have brought it back.'[21] Here, and in 'Private Theatres', the performance of Shakespeare is the conscious focus, but there are many more references in Dickens's work where they appear as incidental details. For example, take the dinner at Mr Grewgious's house in *The Mystery of Edwin Drood* (1870), when a waiter's mode of exit is described in terms which allude to *Macbeth*:

> And here let it be noticed, parenthetically, that the leg of this young man, in its application to the door, evinced the finest sense of touch; always preceding himself and tray (with something of an angling air about it), by some seconds: and always lingering after he and the tray had disappeared, like Macbeth's leg when accompanying him off the stage with reluctance to the assassination of Duncan.[22]

Once again the reference is to a performance of Shakespeare – the action of Macbeth leaving the stage – rather than Shakespeare's text. Nor is *Macbeth* being invoked here to add gravity to the waiter's exit, but to mock it: the performance of Shakespeare becomes a conduit for absurdity. Though John Carey reads a vein of 'constant ridicule' in Dickens's references to Shakespearean tragedies, he misses a vital distinction: when Dickens does offer ridicule, it is always at the expense of those interpreting Shakespeare, never directly at Shakespeare himself – whether that be through preposterous performance or self-congratulatory reading.[23] If there is a consistency in Dickens's attack, it is that it is directed at pomposity.

Contrast this attack on theatre's more ridiculous practices with Dickens's review of William Charles Macready's *Much Ado about Nothing*. In it he commends Macready specifically for playing 'Shakespeare's Benedick [*sic*] – the real Benedick of the book, not the conventional Benedick of the boards'.[24] Dickens is not praising reading over performance here, but arguing for sincerity and simplicity in our treatment of Shakespeare. Speak the speech, sparingly, as Hamlet would argue. For a man who would go on to request a simple burial, with no memorial (proclaiming, 'I rest my claims to the remembrance of my country upon my published works'), there is a consistency in the way Dickens chooses to approach Shakespeare and the mistrust he has of those who would be his interpreter.[25] There is a great irony then that Dickens should widely be recognised for his own appropriation of Shakespeare. Valerie Gager argues that quotation offers authority: 'just as prior criticism is generally relied upon by scholars to substantiate their academic theses, so past literature is often summoned forth by authors to support their creative works.'[26] Following Gager's logic, the recognition of Shakespearean traits in Dickens's works bestows artistic authority upon them, raising them from popular novels to high art. It may seem quite a leap, or a simplification, to suggest that Shakespeare's passing presence in a work raises its quality, but the authority Gager speaks of is a perceived authority, and as such even passing references can present the appearance of higher cultural engagement – if the reader in turn is able to recognise those allusions.

King Lear in particular has often been upheld as a fundamental inspiration to Dickens. Paul Schlicke writes convincingly of how Macready's performance of *Lear*, just a few years prior to the writing of *The Old Curiosity Shop* (1840–1), can be seen as a significant influence, extending beyond characterisation and into the wider thematic tone of pathos.[27] The parallel with Cordelia and Lear is not to be found solely in Nell and her grandfather, but has been spotted among a host of Dickens's novels: Florence Dombey, Little Dorrit and Lucie Manette are just some of the Dickens heroines who fill the role of dutiful, patient daughters to fathers who are proud, lacking self-knowledge or cognitively failing. Alexander Welsh concludes that 'Dickens, in fact, cannot be said ever to have completed the study of *King Lear* inspired by Macready's production of 1838'.[28] In the instance of *The Old Curiosity Shop*, the proximity of events cements the likelihood of correlation, but can we still say the same of, for instance, Mr Boffin and Bella Wilfer in *Our Mutual Friend* (1864–5) some twenty years later? Even if we do, what precisely are we proposing as the inspiration: Shakespeare's *Lear*, Macready's *Lear*, or an amalgamation derived from reading and watching several productions, and does it matter? The binary of the phrase 'Dickens and Shakespeare' encourages ideas of a direct link between the two, but an indirect link via theatrical productions and practitioners need not devalue the impact of Shakespeare on Dickens, nor Dickens's engagement with the arts. The innocent and pure daughter figure was by no means exclusive to Shakespeare; 'the angel in the house' was a predominant theme in Victorian literature, and it could be justly argued that this is not an instance of Shakespeare influencing Dickens, but of contemporary trends influencing what Dickens and Macready chose to use from Shakespeare. The audience interest in the 'angel in the house' created the right atmosphere for the return of Shakespeare's *Lear*, and Cordelia's death. In this light it could well be that Dickens is not citing Shakespeare, but rather drawing on the same cultural ideology which in turn had led to the restoration of Shakespeare's play on the popular stage.

Returning to Gager's argument that citing our forebears offers authority, identifying Shakespeare specifically as Dickens's spectral mentor offers the Victorian writer the cultural respectability of his early modern tutor.[29] But this framing of the relationship asserts a hierarchy between the two, and belittles the achievements of Dickens to reduce him merely to a follower of another writer rather than praising his originality. Determining the level of autonomy and control in the relationship between Shakespeare and Dickens also begs the question of which writer benefits most from the connection. Schlicke suggests that the frequency of Shakespearean references in Dickens's writing 'seem[s] to indicate that Dickens uses Shakespeare's lines as vehicles for his own thought', while Alfred Harbage charges the death of Nell to 'Forster and Dickens, with Shakespeare, Tate, Lamb and Macready as their unwitting accomplices'.[30] Both writers position Dickens as someone who commands Shakespeare, rather than being indebted to him. Schlicke and Harbage both position Dickens as the one in control, not standing in the shadow of Shakespeare, but freely engaging with him to suit his needs. This elevates Dickens from follower to innovator.

However, the question is not 'Did Shakespeare influence Dickens?' but rather 'Why do we look for Shakespeare's influence on Dickens?' What is it that drives our interest in this topic and influences the conclusions we seek to make? There is not a universal consensus on what a discussion of Shakespeare and Dickens should be. Consider, for example, the contrasting responses to two monographs on the topic from different eras: Robert Fleissner's 1965 book, *Dickens and Shakespeare*, and Valerie Gager's 1996 book, *Shakespeare and Dickens*. When Fleissner's book first came out, Philip Collins wrote scathingly that he 'shows the book needs to be written, and he is emphatically not the man to write it'.[31] Collins's issue was that Fleissner did not ground his ideas sufficiently, which resulted in 'zany logic' where 'one may indeed wonder anything'.[32] For Collins, the book was too speculative, yet when Gager wrote her book on the topic three decades later, John Glavin felt that it was not speculative enough: Gager's decision to 'credit as influence only unmistakeable literal overlap' results in 'too pale an ale'.[33] Whether reviewing Fleissner or Gager, all agreed that this was a topic that needed to be written about, but they also agreed that the book in front of them was not the book they wanted.

While Collins's aggressive review of Fleissner reads as extraordinarily critical, in itself it reveals a great deal about the status of Dickens in the twentieth century and the role that Shakespeare plays in that. The review of Fleissner's work coincides with the year in which Collins was playing a 'pivotal role' in founding the Victorian Studies Centre at the University of Leicester, and a time when the predominant perception of Dickens as a popular author threatened the idea of him as a serious literary figure.[34] Consequently, while Collins and his contemporaries were keen to celebrate Dickens's popularity, he also had to be aggressive, to an extent, to challenge overly subjective and uncritical praise, and usher in a new, more objective criticism of Dickens.

His review of Fleissner opens with Edmund Wilson's reflection on the 'old duffer' in Dickens studies who likes to write gentle pieces about topography or *Pickwick*, with Collins condemning Fleissner precisely for being merely 'a new duffer' of the same mould.[35] There were enough of such pieces being written about Dickens; Collins wanted something new. Hence, when he writes that *Dickens and Shakespeare* is a book that needs to be written, but that Fleissner is not the man to write it, he is not only condemning Fleissner, but everything that he stands for. A book investigating the Shakespearean traits and influence in Dickens could have been an enormous boon to Collins at a time when he was trying to establish Dickens's literary credentials, but the genial approach of Fleissner, more enthusiastic than academic, not only failed to deliver that precise vision but worse exacerbated the prevailing view that Collins was trying to demolish. Thus Collins's review tells us as much about Collins as it does about Fleissner. Dickens's use of Shakespeare has in turn been used by others, consciously and subconsciously, as a means to define precisely what kind of writer Dickens is and how we are supposed to read him.

Dickens, Shakespeare and Populist/Elitist Perspectives

Collins's anger at 'the old duffer[s]' evidences the aggressive divide which once existed between enthusiasts and academics; thankfully, with time, the relationship between the two is proving to be more nuanced. Initiatives such as the UK Research Excellence Framework have encouraged academics to consider public engagement and impact, while museums in turn are encouraged to evidence the research potential and productivity of their archives as much as appealing to enthusiasts and encouraging visitor footfall. The celebration of Dickens and Shakespeare as cultural icons, as much as great writers, requires navigation of the spheres of popular culture as well as academic criticism. At times these can appear to be in conflict; at other times they can actively inform and encourage one another.

In *The Great Tradition*, F. R. Leavis noted what he felt was an unwarranted move to recognise popular authors as critical heavyweights: 'one after another the minor novelists of [the Victorian] period are being commended to our attention, written up, and publicised by broadcast, and there is a marked tendency to suggest that they not only have various kinds of interest to offer but that they are living classics.'[36] Leavis subsequently warns against succumbing to hype, and finds it 'necessary to insist, then, that there are important distinctions to be made, and that far from all of the names in the literary histories really belong to the realm of significant creative achievement'.[37]

If Leavis was concerned about contemporary authors getting undue attention, Thomas Carlyle made a similar warning about the writers of past generations. In his 1840 series of lectures, *Heroes and Hero Worship*, he notes 'what an enormous *camera-obscura* magnifier is tradition!'[38] Even the greatest writers achieve that reputation over generations as much by our reception of them as by the inherent quality of their writing. Shakespeare, and Dickens after him, has reached a level of literary fame that is self-perpetuating: in 2013, the UK Secretary of State for Education, Michael Gove, changed the school syllabus in favour of 'traditional' works, namely Shakespeare's works (and classic nineteenth-century texts), 'as part of a wide-ranging plan to drive up education standards', following 'criticism of the existing curriculum amid claims pupils can leave school without studying anything more than bite-sized extracts of Shakespeare's most famous plays'.[39] Critics sarcastically noted Gove's 'ambitions to return schools to the good old days', reducing the number of international works in favour of Shakespeare and the pre-twentieth-century British novel.[40] In this instance, popular awareness of Shakespeare and the associated image of him as a canonical writer has directly influenced the school syllabus. As Sarah Olive notes, 'The criteria for Shakespeare's superiority in these statements draw on, and prioritise, a moral and educational agenda which is imposed on these children, and extends beyond their classrooms to pastimes and entertainment'; the drive to promote Shakespeare relies upon an assumption of his cultural and intrinsic value.[41]

There are obviously connotations of patriotism, even nationalism in this. Shakespeare and Dickens are both tremendous cultural exports for the UK, often associated with England in particular. Carlyle, for example, effects this association in praising Shakespeare's importance as a spokesman for all Englanders, and therefore greater than other Englanders. Thus Carlyle argues for the value of Shakespeare in terms of millions of others from the same nation:

> Which Englishman we ever made, in this land of ours, which million of Englishmen, would we not rather give up than the Stratford peasant? There is no regiment of highest dignitaries that we would sell him for. He is the grandest thing we have ever done.[42]

The 'we' in that final sentence speaks more truth than Carlyle realises. Shakespeare's fame and legacy – like Dickens's – is the product of a group effort. Michael Dobson has argued convincingly how the construction of Shakespeare as a national poet was a conscious construction by successive generations, elevating him above his contemporary position of one among several playwrights to an isolated genius, while Juliet John shows the way in which Dickens pervades mass culture.[43] For Dickens, like Shakespeare, his literary reputation has been built upon conceptions of popular and great literature, with mid-twentieth century scholars conceding his appeal, while questioning his canonical status. Leavis, who compared Dickens unfavourably to Henry James as 'a writer at the other end of the scale from sophistication', argued that Dickens was first and foremost a popular author, and not a great one:

> That Dickens was a great genius and is permanently among the classics is certain. But the genius was that of a great entertainer, and he had for the most part no profounder responsibility as a creative artist than this description suggests.[44]

It is not simply that Leavis thinks Dickens was only a popular author, but rather that it was precisely *because* he was a popular author – 'a great entertainer' – that he was not part of the great tradition of writers, relegated instead to an appendix in a later edition. To prove Dickens belonged in this tradition, early defenders of his critical weight used Shakespeare to further their argument. Alfred Harbage wrote that 'a critic who put his mind to it could prove that Wilkins [Micawber] is as complex and enigmatic as Hamlet'.[45] Harbage's comment is not intended to detract from Shakespeare, but to expand the power of Dickens. The direct comparison to Shakespeare justified study of Dickens by piggybacking on the extensive foundations of

Shakespearean criticism and the gravitas attached to our perception of his characters. Though Harbage suggests that he may have gone too far, he still uses the point to stress that Dickens's creations should not be underestimated or dismissed:

> Perhaps I have exaggerated a little the infinite variety of this friend of Copperfield's youth – or was it the other was around? His complexity may not be as challenging as Hamlet's, but his creation was no simple matter: we should never patronize the creations of the great.[46]

Dickens's and Shakespeare's positions in popular and elite culture often inform one another, and recent merchandise has taken particular delight in subverting our notion of a serious tribute. Accoutrements, since renamed Archie McPhee Wholesale, has been producing action figures of both Shakespeare and Dickens since 2008 and 2012, respectively, while Yarno has been producing novelty rubber ducks 'Drakespeare' and 'Charles Duckens' since 2012 and 2018, respectively. Given Dickens's concerns about monuments, it is questionable how he might feel about being remembered as a rubber duck. Both these and the action figures mock the pomposity of cultural status, by reducing iconic figures to the least pompous of merchandise, while simultaneously celebrating their wide social appeal: ultimately, if the manufacturers did not have confidence that people would buy these things, they would not make them. The action figure is tongue in cheek; while traditionally such figures come equipped with various weaponry, the box for the Charles Dickens action figure declares that it 'comes with quill pen and removable hat!'[47] This announcement is equally sarcastic and excited: it can be read as a mocking takedown of the author by equipping an 'action' figure with items requiring little physical exertion; or it can be read as mocking the action hero trope by offering a more cerebral figure for idolatry, like a twenty-first-century kitsch critique of Carlyle's philosophy.

Dickens and Shakespeare exist beyond both the classroom and the novel/theatre, and this wider presence in the general zeitgeist speaks as much of their positioning in cultural tourism and national identity. Both have at times featured on UK banknotes, of course, and both were called upon in 2012 as part of the cultural Olympiad to coincide with the Olympics in London as a source of patriotism and – more commercially – tourism. Peter Kirwan and Charlotte Mathieson note how the celebration of both writers 'continued to assert the prominence of London as cultural centre and privileged this space as the location of authorial meaning'.[48] Thus the framing of a dynasty, in which Shakespeare and Dickens are key figures, serves an additional purpose of reinforcing patriotic narratives of Englishness. Dickens and Shakespeare are connected by their nationality as much as by their professions. It allows for the idea that Shakespeare endures in all of us, his 'genes', in this sense literary rather than literal, passing through generations and emerging in Dickens. Harbage waxes lyrical on the sense of a literary dynasty:

> At the moment there is no playwright or novelist who serves as common bond among us, to whom people of widely varying social and educational backgrounds can turn year after year in happy expectation, knowing that they will be conducted into a world of wonderful words, absorbing events, fascinating people, good fun, and restorative human warmth. However, we wish there were, and that

is a good omen. Seasons change, and we should not mistake each wintry one for the beginning of an ice age. Writers like Shakespeare and Dickens do not appear in every generation or even every century. The one appeared 248 years after the other, and if a third appears in the year 2060 he will still be on schedule.[49]

Dickens stands as the successor of Shakespeare – the comparisons made between them stand as pseudo-genealogical links in a literary family tree, with the expectation that there will be further generations to come. Robert Sawyer speaks similarly of his hope that 'the greatest appropriator of Shakespeare has yet to be heard from or discovered'.[50] Shakespeare, and after him Dickens, stands there ready for any of us to invoke. To view them as isolated figures strips them from their culture and society and denies the opportunity to use them as a way of celebrating nationhood. But if the idea of future bearers of the torch is like a family tree, there is also a sense of a ruling dynasty here; note how Harbage writes '*he* will still be on schedule' (my emphasis); he assumes the 2060 successor will be a male, another king to rule over literature. For all his waxing lyrical of 'happy expectation', Harbage's conception of a 'common bond' still maintains a point of exclusivity.

Indeed, the familiarity of 'Dickens and Shakespeare' as a concept is one borne from exemption as much as inclusion, be that through nationhood or gender. As much as it can be used to suggest that there are yet more writers to follow in future generations, isolating Shakespeare and Dickens as two great writers from across the ages threatens to erase the many other writers working in both their lifetimes and the interim. However, there is sufficient evidence to suggest a counternarrative to this concept of a special relationship. As I have said, the link between Dickens and Shakespeare profits both. It offers validity to Dickens as a writer of art, and endorses the perception of Shakespeare as timeless and universal. But the advantages of using Shakespeare and Dickens to bolster one another are tempered by the resulting restrictions that these perceptions place upon them. Even if we allow the relationship to be mutually beneficial, it comes at a cost to other writers. Dickens's use of Shakespeare is strikingly less remarkable when viewed in the context of both Shakespeare's wider influence among other nineteenth-century novelists and Dickens's admiration for other early modern playwrights. As Gary Taylor suggests, 'Shakespeare's reputation peaked in the reign of Queen Victoria', and recent book-length studies have looked at the relationship of Shakespeare not only with Dickens, but also Hardy, Scott, Eliot and several more.[51] The recognition that so many Victorians are quoting Shakespeare lessens the significance of Dickens doing so. It raises the question of whether Dickens was directly or indirectly influenced by Shakespeare, and whether he was quoting and appropriating Shakespeare as a personal choice, or rather as part of a wider cultural habit.

But if Shakespeare is not exclusively to be found in Dickens, nor is Dickens exclusively using Shakespeare. The obvious connection to another early modern playwright is Dickens's 1845 amateur production of Ben Jonson's *Every Man in His Humour* in which he played Captain Bobadil, immortalised by C. R. Leslie's engraving. Less obvious, but requiring consideration, is the inclusion in Dickens's library at Gad's Hill of works by Beaumont, Fletcher and Webster. In her work, Gager presents a catalogue of Shakespearean references across Dickens's works. This is certainly a helpful tool, but could be developed further if read in the context of references to other authors. This would be an ambitious task, certainly, but as advances in computational corpus studies continue, it may yet prove possible.[52] For now, when we talk of Dickens and Shakespeare, or Shakespeare and Dickens, or even Shakespeare versus Dickens, we should resist the popular narrative of a special relationship, and instead maintain an awareness of the wider view beyond the relationship between these two writers.

There is a danger, then, in isolating these two for consideration, as this very chapter has done. Having placed them in a literary hall of fame, two writers divided by nearly three centuries have become unlikely roommates, with comparisons drawn between them which extend beyond those which Dickens might have hoped for. Furthermore, by placing them as great artists above their contemporaries, an expectation is raised that their legacies will endure. Shakespeare's reputation stands as a model to Dickens scholars as much as his work does: he has developed from one writer among many to a praised author, idolised figure and scholarly subject. So too, in a shorter space of time, Dickens has emerged from his contemporary position as popular author to one with an assured place in academic study. Rubber ducks and action figures may raise a passing smile, but do not directly prompt engagement with the books from a first-time reader. Ironically, given the condescending treatment of Dickens by the academy in the early twentieth century, there is a danger that many will only read Shakespeare and Dickens through set texts in the classroom, rather than reading by choice. Placing these authors on a pedestal as artists both secures their fame and threatens to alienate their popular base.

Notes

1. Maev Kennedy, 'Tale of Dickens' Fight to Save Shakespeare House Retold in Exhibition', *Guardian*, 3 April 2017 <https://www.theguardian.com/culture/2017/apr/03/story-dickens-fight-save-shakespeare-house-retold-exhibition> [accessed 16 April 2017]. Dr Paul Edmondson, Head of Research at the Shakespeare Birthplace Trust, provides a more balanced account of the events in 1847, in 'The 19th-century Auction That Saved Shakespeare's Birthplace', *History Extra*, 15 September 2017. <https://www.historyextra.com/period/elizabethan/the-19th-century-auction-that-saved-shakespeares-birthplace/> [accessed 4 June 2018].
2. Kennedy.
3. Michael Slater, *Charles Dickens* (New Haven: Yale University Press, 2009), 275.
4. See 'To W. B. Hodgson, 12 June 1847', *The Letters of Charles Dickens*, ed. by Madeline House, Graham Storey et al., Pilgrim/British Academy Edition, 12 vols (Oxford: Clarendon Press, 1965–2002), v (1981), 87. Hereafter *PLets*.
5. 'To Émile de la Rue, 29 February 1848', *PLets*, v, 255.
6. Slater, 275.
7. 'To Mrs Cowden Clarke, 14 April 1848', *PLets*, v, 278–9.
8. Emily Smith, 'Charles Dickens and Literary Tourism: His Experiential Encounters and Legacy' (unpublished doctoral thesis, Royal Holloway, University of London, 2022).
9. Charles Dickens, 'The Author's Introduction to the Third Edition (1841)', in *Oliver Twist*, ed. by Philip Horne (London: Penguin, 2003), 456–60, 459.
10. Daniel Pollack-Pelzner, 'Dickens and Shakespeare's *Household Words*', *ELH* 78.3 (2011), 533–56, 535.
11. For Dickens's borrowing history, see Leon Litvack, 'Dickens's Lifetime Reading', in *The Oxford Handbook of Charles Dickens*, ed. by John O. Jordan, Robert L. Patten and

Catherine Waters (Oxford: Oxford University Press, 2018), 25–42, 30. For his private library, see *Reprints of the Catalogues of the Libraries of Charles Dickens and W. M. Thackeray*, ed. by J. H. Stonehouse (London: Piccadilly Fountain Press, 1935), 100.

12. Charles Dickens, *David Copperfield*, ed. by Nina Burgis (Oxford: Oxford University Press, 1997), 53, ch. 4.

13. Charles Dickens, *A Christmas Carol and Other Christmas Books*, ed. by Robert Douglas-Fairhurst (Oxford: Oxford University Press, 2006), 31–2.

14. Sylvère Monod, *Dickens the Novelist* (Norman: University of Oklahoma Press, 1968), 41–2.

15. Charles Dickens, 'Mrs Joseph Porter', *Monthly Magazine* (January 1834), in *Dickens' Journalism*, ed. by Michael Slater and John Drew, 4 vols (London: Dent, 1994–2000), I (1994), 405–14, 409.

16. Monod, 42.

17. The works as listed in Stonehouse are: Henry G. Bohn, *Biography and Bibliography of Shakespeare* (1863), gifted by the author; Lord Campbell, *Shakespeare's Legal Acquirements Considered* (1859), gifted by the author; J. C. Bucknill, *The Medical Knowledge of Shakespeare* (1860); J. C. Bucknill, *The Psychology of Shakespeare* (1859), gifted by the author; *Shakespeare Society's Publications* (1841–53); John Conolly, *A Study of Hamlet* (1863), gifted by the author; Charles Knight, *Studies of Shakespeare* (1849), presented by the author. Of these, the forty-nine volumes of Shakespeare Society's Publications seem the most significant entry, both for the series' size and for it not being gifted by someone else. See Stonehouse, 101 for further details.

18. Charles Lamb, 'On the Tragedies of Shakespeare', 1811, reprinted in Charles Lamb, *Selected Prose*, ed. by Adam Phillips (London: Penguin, 2013).

19. Charles Dickens, 'The Amusements of the People (I)', *Household Words* (30 March 1850), in *Dickens' Journalism*, II, 179–85, 181.

20. Charles Dickens, 'Private Theatres', *Evening Chronicle* (11 August 1835), in *Dickens' Journalism*, I, 120–6, 125.

21. Charles Dickens, *Great Expectations*, ed. by Margaret Cardwell and Kate Flint (Oxford: Oxford University Press, 1994), 250, ch. 31.

22. Charles Dickens, *The Mystery of Edwin Drood*, ed. by Margaret Cardwell (Oxford: Oxford University Press, 1982), 91, ch. 11.

23. John Carey, 'Review: *Shakespeare and Dickens: The Dynamics of Influence*', *Modern Philology* 96.4 (May 1999), 541–3, 543.

24. Charles Dickens, 'Theatre Review: Macready as Benedick', *The Examiner* (4 March 1842), in *Dickens' Journalism*, II (1996), 55–9, 57.

25. 'The Will of Charles Dickens', in John Forster, *The Life of Charles Dickens*, ed. by J. W. T. Ley (London: Cecil Palmer, 1928), 857–60, 859.

26. Valerie Gager, *Shakespeare and Dickens: The Dynamics of Influence* (Cambridge: Cambridge University Press, 1996), 174.

27. Paul Schlicke, 'A "Discipline of Feeling": Macready's *Lear* and *The Old Curiosity Shop*', *Dickensian* 76 (1980), 78–90.

28. Alexander Welsh, *From Copyright to Copperfield: The Identity of Dickens* (Cambridge, MA: Harvard University Press, 1987), 104.

29. The potential authority offered by literary forebears is explored in more detail in T. S. Eliot's seminal text 'Tradition and the Individual Talent', collected in *The Sacred Wood and Other Essays* (London: Methuen, 1920).

30. Paul Schlicke, 'Dickens and Shakespeare', *The Japan Branch Bulletin of the Dickens Fellowship* 27 (2004), 84–98, 94; Alfred Harbage, 'Shakespeare and the Early Dickens', in G. B. Evans, ed., *Shakespeare: Aspects of Influence* (Harvard: Harvard University Press, 1976), 109–34, 127.

31. Philip Collins, 'Review: *Dickens and Shakespeare*', *Nineteenth-Century Fiction* 21.4 (1967), 401–3, 403.
32. Ibid., 402; 401.
33. John Glavin, 'Review: *Shakespeare and Dickens: The Dynamics of Influence*', *Nineteenth-Century Literature* 52.2 (1997), 265–7, 266.
34. Gowan Dawson and Joanne Shattock, 'Celebrating Dickens: The Victorian Studies Centre at 50', *Dickensian* 114 (2018), 15–25, 15. For an overview of Dickens's critical reception, see Laurence W. Mazzeno, *The Dickens Industry: Critical Perspectives, 1836–2005* (New York: Boydell & Brewer, 2012).
35. Collins, 401.
36. F. R. Leavis, *The Great Tradition: George Eliot, Henry James, Joseph Conrad*, 2nd edn (London: Chatto & Windus, 1960 [1948]), 2.
37. Leavis, 2.
38. Thomas Carlyle, *Sartor Resartus and On Heroes and Hero Worship*, ed. by W. H. Hudson (London: Dent, 1908), 262.
39. Graeme Palton, 'National Curriculum Overhaul; Pupils to Study More Shakespeare', *The Daily Telegraph*, 8 July 2013 <https://www.telegraph.co.uk/education/education-news/10166697/National-Curriculum-overhaul-pupils-to-study-more-Shakespeare.html> [accessed 5 May 2020].
40. Peter Wilby, 'Education Review 2013: Michael Gove Continued to Promote "Traditional Schools"', *Guardian*, 17 December 2013, <https://www.theguardian.com/education/2013/dec/17/education-review-2013-year-zealot-vision-past> [accessed 5 May 2020].
41. Sarah Olive, 'Shakespeare in the English National Curriculum', *Alluvium* 2.1 (2013). Web. 12 January 2013. <http://dx.doi.org/10.7766/alluvium.v2.1.01>.
42. Carlyle, 344.
43. Michael Dobson, *The Making of the National Poet: Shakespeare, Adaptation, and Authorship, 1660–1769* (Oxford: Clarendon, 1992); Juliet John, *Dickens and Mass Culture* (Oxford: Oxford University Press, 2010).
44. Leavis, 18, 19.
45. Alfred Harbage, *A Kind of Power: The Shakespeare-Dickens Analogy* (Philadelphia: American Philosophical Society, 1975), 45.
46. Harbage, 49.
47. Blurb from the packaging for 'Charles Dickens Action Figure', Accoutrements Ltd (now Archie McPhee Wholesale), 2012.
48. Peter Kirwan and Charlotte Mathieson, 'A Tale of Two Londons: Locating Shakespeare and Dickens in 2012', in *Shakespeare on the Global Stage*, ed. by Paul Prescott and Erin Sullivan (London: Bloomsbury, 2015), 227–52, 229.
49. Harbage, 72–3.
50. Robert Sawyer, *Victorian Appropriations of Shakespeare* (Madison: Fairleigh Dickinson University Press, 2003), 145.
51. Gary Taylor, 'Afterword: The Incredible Shrinking Bard', in *Shakespeare and Appropriation*, ed. by Christy Desmet and Robert Sawyer (London: Routledge, 1999), 197–205, 197. For more on Shakespeare and the Victorians, see, for example: Robert Sawyer, *Victorian Appropriations of Shakespeare: George Eliot, A. C. Swinburne, Robert Browning and Charles Dickens* (Madison: Fairleigh Dickinson University Press, 2003) and *Great Shakespeareans Volume Five: Scott, Dickens, Eliot, Hardy*, ed. by Adrian Poole (London: Bloomsbury, 2014).
52. This level of engagement with corpus linguistics is becoming ever more possible thanks to initiatives such as the University of Birmingham's CLiC Dickens <clic.bham.ac.uk> organised by Michaela Mahlberg, Peter Stockwell and Viola Wiegand.

Further Reading

Valerie Gager, *Shakespeare and Dickens: The Dynamics of Influence* (Cambridge: Cambridge University Press, 1996)

Gail Marshall, ed., *Shakespeare in the Nineteenth Century* (Cambridge: Cambridge University Press, 2012)

Laurence W. Mazzeno, *The Dickens Industry: Critical Perspectives, 1836–2005* (New York: Camden House, 2008)

Adrian Poole, ed., *Great Shakespeareans Volume Five: Scott, Dickens, Eliot, Hardy* (London: Bloomsbury, 2014)

Robert Sawyer, *Victorian Appropriations of Shakespeare: George Eliot, A. C. Swinburne, Robert Browning and Charles Dickens* (Madison: Fairleigh Dickinson University Press, 2003)

31

DICKENSIANA

Ryan D. Fong

To stand in front of a shelf that holds Charles Dickens's many novels is to view a set of objects that can intimidate even the most enthusiastic of readers. While his corpus is not the largest of those generated by some of his Victorian contemporaries, his fourteen completed novels (and half-finished final novel) nevertheless comprise considerable heft, containing thousands of pages of written text. Combined with his journalism, short fiction and other writing, his oeuvre spills across multiple shelves. Given this prodigious output, even the most ardent Dickens fan might have more than enough to satiate their desire for the Great Inimitable. And yet, as we well know, this has not been the case. From images that depict the author's likeness to numerous figurines and ceramic collectibles that pay homage to famous characters and scenes, there is a huge array of items associated with Dickens. Collectively known as Dickensiana, these items have been produced across the centuries and continue to be consumed with great fervour. Forming an even larger mass of material for enthusiasts to read, engage with and collect, these objects of Dickensiana illustrate an intensity in the public's appetite for the author that has been powerfully enduring and shows very few signs of being satisfied or even waning.

In this essay, I analyse the relationship between this investment in consuming, possessing and collecting objects of Dickensiana and the representational work that Dickens undertakes in his fiction. The essay is divided into four sections, the first of which situates the production and consumption of Dickensiana within the body of work on 'thing theory' in Victorian studies, as well as within prominent theories of collection. The essay then shifts to focus on three specific case studies, each of which illustrates an undergirding desire and fantasy that motivates the collection of Dickensiana. The first is Frederic G. Kitton's 1886 compendium, *Dickensiana: A Bibliography of the Literature Relating to Charles Dickens and His Writings*. Published just sixteen years after Dickens's death, Kitton's book uses the taxonomic processes inherent in the project of bibliography to address the recent loss of Dickens himself. In aspiring to collect all known texts associated with the deceased author into a single book, Kitton's project not only marks an early and prominent use of the term, but it also dramatises fantasies of recovery and completeness that are often active in the collection of Dickensiana more generally. The second object, a letter opener made from the paw of Dickens's cat, offers an example of the special status that personal effects have for collectors of Dickensiana (as they do for all collectors of author memorabilia), since they serve as artefacts and evidence of his textual production as a lived process. The letter opener's singularity and, more significantly, its use of taxidermy uncannily literalise the collector's desire to establish a tangible connection to Dickens's body through the act of possession, in ways that use the cat's corpse to enable fantasies of interacting with the author himself. Finally, the essay turns to the Royal Doulton character jug of Sairey Gamp as a more typical example of Dickensiana and the many forms that it takes within the decorative arts. As one of the most popular products within the company's line of ceramic collectables, the character jug transforms the iconic Dickens character into a material object that allows collectors to indulge in fantasies of narrative immersion and to imaginatively cross the line that separates them from the fictional world. Throughout each of these readings I assert that the material things that comprise Dickensiana and the processes of their collection are fundamentally linked to the desires that Dickens's novels themselves powerfully and palpably activate, drawing upon examples from *Bleak House* (1852–3), *Our Mutual Friend* (1864–5) and *Martin Chuzzlewit* (1843–4). Ultimately, this essay argues that objects of Dickensiana and their collection provide a vital mechanism for the function of Dickensian 'thingness' not only within the world of his texts but also within the worlds of his readers, focusing in particular on affective experience.

The Desire for Dickensian Things

In recent years, much critical attention has been paid to the 'thingfulness' of Victorian literature, with Dickens's fiction often functioning as an exemplary case in point. Indeed, to state that Dickens's novels are full of things is in many ways to state the obvious, as his fictional worlds are famous for their clutter of objects, including the numerous nautical items strewn about The Midshipman in *Dombey and Son* (1846–8) and the bric-à-brac-filled rooms of the eponymous structure in *The Old Curiosity Shop* (1840–1). Drawing on Bill Brown's path-breaking work on 'thing theory', this body of scholarship sought to respond to an earlier trend within criticism that read objects largely through the Marxist framework of the commodity, in which objects were understood to accrue meaning through the processes of exchange and consumption and, thus, were framed as symptomatic of an ascendant middle-class and an increasingly global marketplace.[1] Providing an alternative approach, proponents of thing theory, some of whom I discuss below, prioritise the literal qualities of these circulating objects, in advocating for a mode of interpretation that could better think 'with or through the physical object world', in order to establish how these objects allow us 'to make meaning, to remake ourselves, to organise our anxieties and affections, and to sublimate our fears and shape our fantasies'.[2]

For Elaine Freedgood, who has been one of the most influential critics to use thing theory in Victorian studies, the mahogany furniture that appears in *Jane Eyre* (1847) and the 'Negro head' tobacco that Magwitch smokes in *Great Expectations* (1860–1) need to be reckoned with in terms of their materiality, in order to properly understand how they function as metonyms embedded within the larger history that surrounds and conditions their presence.[3] Additionally, John Plotz has highlighted the need to index a thing's movement both within and beyond the market. Using the concept of 'portability', Plotz traces the value(s) that things gather outside the systems of capitalist exchange, exploring alternative forms of relationality.[4] In this way, for Freedgood, Plotz and the various critics who have followed them, the turn to things within Victorian studies offers a new form of historicising that could recuperate materiality and the literal as important, if mundane, sources of interpretive meaning.[5]

As various critics have pointed out, thing theory's fixation on tangibility and materiality has led to a de-emphasising of the issues of representation and figuration, which fundamentally mediate the objects featured within Dickens, as well as in other works of literature. After all, as Juliet John succinctly puts it, 'things in Dickens's writing are not things but words representing things'.[6] As such, literary things must be understood as functioning differently from the items that actually took up space in the Victorian world and, thus, must always be read within the signifying system that a given text establishes. Although characters might interact with things in their story worlds, readers can interact only with their linguistic constructions. At the same time, Dickens was intensely 'fascinated by how things mean', and his writing frequently dramatises the relationship between things and words – relationships which he consistently subjected to 'conspicuous and self-conscious scrutiny'.[7] In this way, while Dickens's language, through its very nature *as* language, creates a gap between the thingfulness of his textual worlds and the material world of his readers, his writing also frequently calls attention to this space by thematising things, by rendering them so palpably and vividly, and by cataloguing them so thoroughly.

This critical context helps to illuminate why the production and collection of Dickensiana is such a notable Dickensian phenomenon. Indeed, in following the insights that both thing theorists and their critics offer, I argue that the enthusiasm for Dickensiana demonstrates the intensity of the investment that many readers have in the bountiful thingfulness of Dickens's texts. Instantiated and activated by the specific features of his fictional world-making and his penchant for descriptive detail, the desire to possess the represented things within Dickens by acquiring the literal things of Dickensiana imbricates reading and collection as interpretive practices, with each providing what the other lacks. Thus, as material objects that can be owned and grasped, Dickensiana makes concrete what can only be concretised in the processes of reading, or, at the very least, galvanises those fantasies. As such, it offers material objects as a bridge that reader-collectors can use to move imaginatively across the various levels of narrative reality, in a metaleptic gesture made possible by the literal thingness that Dickensiana provides and by its reference to the represented thingfulness in his novels and other texts.

In addition to addressing this gap, created by the intrinsic qualities of literary representation, the collection of Dickensiana also works to ameliorate an additional form of absence: the temporal distance that separates the collector's present from the historical past, as well as from Dickens himself. Coming into prominence as a named category of object only after the author's death, as the next section will show, Dickensiana thus offers reader-collectors a mode of imaginatively constructing a tangible relationship with the absent Dickens, in ways that attempt to collapse disparate moments in time and to recuperate a lost past. As such, the activities of the collector of Dickensiana resemble those of the book collector famously described by Walter Benjamin in 'Unpacking My Library' (1931), whose 'relationship to objects [. . .] does not emphasise their functional, utilitarian value' but rather is animated by a 'profound enchantment' with the concept of history itself, in which 'everything remembered and thought, everything conscious, becomes the pedestal, the frame, the base'.[8] Captivated by the literal and material qualities of a collection's objects and endowing them with the supernatural qualities of relics, the collector reads the signs of 'the period, the region, the craftsmanship, the former ownership' within an item as a 'magic encyclopedia', forging an imagined link to a 'distant past'.[9] In this respect, the collection of Dickensiana aspires to materialise time and history itself, cultivating an experience of synchronicity by gathering objects and treating them as the fragments of history.

Furthermore, in emphasising the corporeal processes of collecting, Susan Stewart adds to Benjamin's understanding of collection by foregrounding the haptic interactions that take place with objects in a collection in the here and now. Underscoring how a collection's spatialising of time and history works not only as a cognitive process, but as a set of embodied activities, she outlines how the processes of possession, categorisation and arrangement imbricate the subjectivity of the collector with the collection itself. As she states:

> To arrange objects according to time is to juxtapose personal time with social time, autobiography with history, and thus to create a fiction of the individual life, a time of the individual subject both transcendent to and parallel to historical time. Similarly, the spatial organization of the collection, left to right, front to back, behind and before, depends upon the creation of an individual perceiving and apprehending the collection with eye and hand.[10]

Bearing out Benjamin's insight that 'ownership is the most intimate relationship that one can have to objects' and his famous statement that it is not objects that 'come alive in [the collector]' but '[the collector] who lives in them',[11] Stewart's description of collection as a profoundly corporeal process thus illustrates why it carries such a potent affective charge. By constructing a complex, if particularised, set of relationships between the past and the present, collectors not only posit possession, accumulation and arrangement as privileged routes to accessing and inhabiting the past, but they also use these actions to constitute themselves as embedded within time and history itself.

In this way, the act of collecting contains within it a utopian strain that strives to achieve the plenitude of making the past materially present, while also being shot through with a profound melancholy, in its inevitable failures to provide this full sense of presence or communion.[12] And while this tension runs through all forms of collection, according to Stewart and Benjamin, the three objects that I explore stage these processes with particular salience. As the case studies underscore, each object attests to the power and, indeed, pleasure of the fantasies that Dickensiana activate – of recuperating the presence of a lost past, of interacting with Dickens himself, and of being immersed within the worlds created in his fiction – even as their fulfilment is inevitably impossible. Indeed, these tensions and pleasures are central to the affective force that Dickens's fiction exerts on its readers through its richly populated object-worlds, and are just as central to the production and collection of Dickensiana in the world of its readers.

Object I: Frederic G. Kitton's *Dickensiana*

According to the *Oxford English Dictionary*, the term 'Dickensiana' emerges in 1842, in a brief *New York Herald* article that names the growing 'fever' surrounding the author. Although he was not the first writer to have the suffix '-iana' attached to his name, the coining of the term registered an enthusiasm that would only continue to grow within and beyond his lifetime. With the 1886 publication of Frederic G. Kitton's *Dickensiana: A Bibliography of the Literature Relating to Charles Dickens and His Writings*, the term took on a new saliency, marking a moment in Dickens's celebrity when even the objects and texts that had been generated around his work were deemed significant enough for notation, collection and collation.[13] And while it was not the first bibliography of Dickens's texts to be generated – Kitton cites Richard Herne Shepherd's *Bibliography of Dickens* (1880) and James Cook's *Bibliography of the Writings of Charles Dickens* (1879) as important resources in one of his footnotes – *Dickensiana* nevertheless appears to have been among the earliest, if not the first, effort to create a comprehensive list of the myriad writings about and associated with Dickens in a single source.[14]

Trained as an engraver, which paved his way into the world of Victorian art periodicals, Kitton came to be best known for his work editing and writing several books on Dickens and his circle during the late nineteenth and early twentieth centuries. One of the earliest biographers of Dickens, following John Forster, Kitton also served as one of his initial anthologisers and helped to found the Dickens Fellowship. As a work of reference bibliography, *Dickensiana* is fairly unremarkable, containing lists of citations along with brief annotations and descriptions of items that are, in a few selective instances, accompanied by short excerpts. Divided into several categories, the book arranges these references and categorises them according to types, which include: Personal, Critical, Poetical, Anthological, Musical, Dramatic, Plagiaristic, etc., Testimonies, 'Notes and Queries' and Omniana. In each case, the work that Kitton performs is not ground-breaking, and its organisation is very much in accordance with what has become standard in this form of bibliography.

What is notable about Kitton's work in *Dickensiana*, however, is how he frames his project and its relationship to the author. In his introduction, Kitton begins with a long epigraph from Christopher North, the nom de plume of Scottish essayist John Wilson. Although North was not writing about Dickens per se, Kitton connects North's contemplation of literary genius and the question of an author's 'posthumous fame' to the Victorian author (ix). As North argues, for the 'common lot of man', death is a consignment to 'oblivion', whereas, for geniuses, their work, 'however small its sphere, if conversant with the conditions of the human heart', comes to be 'vivif[ied] with indestructible life' when it is 'held dear by successive sorrowers in this vale of tears' (ix). Subsequently emphasising that this indestructibility relies on the emotional impact of the work, North suggests that it is the feelings of 'love and sympathy' that the genius inspires in 'the hearts of not a few who never saw his face' that allow 'his memory' to be regarded 'with something of the same affection as his remains' (ix).

For Kitton, these words 'could not be more appropriately associated than with the name and fame of Charles Dickens', and the opening paragraphs of *Dickensiana*'s introduction chronicle how Dickens had been 'vivified with indestructible life' and recognised as a genius by his many readers and devotees (ix). This summation leads Kitton to repeat Thackeray's anecdote about a woman who stopped Dickens in the streets of York to ask if he would 'let [her] touch the hand that has filled [her] home with many friends', as well as an instance in Belfast where a reader similarly sought to shake hands with the author. Asking then 'To what mortal man has been meted out fame and honour, and personal affectionate regard, in greater measure than this?', Kitton closes the opening paragraph of the introduction by stating that these interactions signal a popularity for Dickens that has been 'hitherto unparalleled in the history of literature' (x).

Kitton's choice to open his book in this way is made all the more poignant given its publication in 1886, just sixteen years after Dickens's death. Indeed, to recount episodes of various readers' treasured interactions with the living Dickens calls attention to the striking absence of Dickens at the time of Kitton's writing. As such, the bibliography and the collection of Dickensiana that it assembles are framed by a sense of loss. From the invocation of death and remains in the epigraph to Kitton's speculations at the end of the introduction that Dickens's 'popularity must inevitably decline as the manners he describes become obsolete, and the scenes of English life he depicts disappear' (xxxi), it is clear that Kitton conceives of *Dickensiana* as a way to secure the author's legacy and express his mournful longing for the author's presence. Although his fears about Dickens's enduring fame would prove to be unfounded, his worry marks how his bibliographic acts of collection and accumulation can be read as a desire to memorialise and secure the 'posthumous fame' for Dickens that North names as the standard for genius. Indeed, this desire would define the rest of Kitton's life and career: he would go on to publish four more bibliographies of Dickens's works in the next eighteen years, along with various anthologies that collected Dickens's lesser-known writings, illustrations of his work, and descriptions of the places that served as models for his fiction.[15]

The fact that Kitton would turn to bibliography to achieve these goals speaks to significant developments that were taking place at the time in the history of bibliography as a discipline. As various historians of bibliography have noted, the term did not come into wide use to describe formally organised booklists and catalogues of printed materials until the nineteenth century, when it became an important tool to conceptualise and manage the period's explosion of print culture.[16] Bolstered by the rapid availability of new cheaper methods for reprinting texts, this meteoric rise in the sheer number of books and the rapidly expanding range of their circulation led, as G. Thomas Tanselle has noted, to the establishment of bibliography as an institutionalised practice that sought to comprehensively trace these flows of information and to systematically account for the material differences between various editions and printings.[17] As such, bibliography aspires to capture and contain, precisely through the establishment of rules that could govern, the processes of collection and classification.

In this respect, Kitton's aims in *Dickensiana* to capture the 'nature and extent' of Dickens's popularity, to present 'a complete list of the published writings relating to the novelist and his works', and to 'chronicle all such writings whether biographical or critical, both in England and abroad', reflect an investment in totality that dominate the concerns of bibliographers more generally (x). But as a project that must be understood in the context of Dickens's death, Kitton's language also shows that his embrace of bibliography, with its methods of accumulation and collation and its fantasies of containment and completeness, is undergirded by a parallel desire to recover Dickens by constructing a comprehensive volume that could substitute for the lost presence of the author himself. Understood, then, as a set of techniques for gathering and ordering sources as well as for managing grief, Kitton's project of bibliographic collection seeks to amass the disparate materials of Dickensiana as a scholarly exercise and contain them within an exhaustive object, in ways that posit the tangible thingness of the book itself as a remedy, however partial, for the lack of Dickens himself.

To imagine Kitton tracking down every possible scrap of Dickensiana conjures up images of Krook sitting in his Rag and Bottle Shop in *Bleak House*, with its piles of paper and rubbish, obsessively gathered as the detritus of that ceaseless generator of text, the Court of Chancery. At the same time, the ordered and orderly catalogue that Kitton produces in *Dickensiana* manifests the exact opposite of Krook's hoard, which similarly aspires to contain everything but in a way that embraces chaos and disorder rather than aspiring to the tight taxonomic structure of the bibliography.[18] In this sense, given the melancholic tension between the bibliographic production of totality and order and the constitutive absence of Dickens created by his death, Kitton's closest avatar in Dickens's oeuvre is Esther Summerson, whose copious keys and careful housekeeping stand in stark contrast to the overwhelming sense of lack created by her lost mother. As John O. Jordan argues, the order and coherence provided by Esther's retrospective narration is one that is always shot through with the grief that the narrating Esther feels in the wake of her mother's death – a wake that emerged in Lady Dedlock's abandonment of Esther at the time of her birth.[19] As such, Esther's trauma and loss always linger at the margins of her portions of the novel, like the ghost of Lady Dedlock herself, in a way that destabilises Esther's careful ordering of her account.

Thus, in considering the similarities between Esther's project to narrate her own life and Kitton's project to create a bibliographic monument to Dickens, the former's intimate relationships with things and even her occasional depiction of herself as an object take on an increasing poignancy – such as in her early attachment to her doll or when she imagines herself at the height of her illness as 'one of the beads' of a 'flaming necklace [. . .] strung together somewhere in great black space'.[20] As material encapsulations of her traumas, these objects become a means for expressing the continuing resonance of her pain in the narrating present. Furthermore, despite her relatively happy ending, her account's coherent ordering famously breaks off as her narration comes to a close, signalling an open-endedness to her story and to the still-looming gulf that separates her from her lost mother and from the lost past that her mother represents. The same sense of loss looms over *Dickensiana*; more than five hundred pages of citations attest to the acute uncertainty and contingency that the bibliographer felt about his beloved author's fate and reputation. Although his work could not restore Dickens himself to presence through the accumulation of bibliographic plenitude in the object that is *Dickensiana*, his careful chronicling of the proliferating texts of Dickensiana nevertheless attests to the power and, perhaps, genius of Dickens's work, helping to secure the author's posthumous fame – much like the power of Esther's narration in the object that is *Bleak House*, which has ensured that Lady Dedlock has remained neither dead nor locked away, but alive and active in the memories and imaginations of readers.

Object II: Dickens's Letter Opener

If Kitton's introduction attests to the intense feelings of loss that Dickens's death inspired for the enthusiasts who lived during the author's lifetime, then the status that Dickens's personal effects continue to have as especially prized objects of Dickensiana provides evidence for the long endurance of these emotions. Indeed, for most present-day collectors of Dickensiana, the desire to possess things that Dickens owned or used is one that is impossible to satisfy, given their extreme rarity in today's market and their likely cost, should any item become available. Nevertheless, the fascination that they generate as objects in museums speaks to the affective force that even beholding these items commands, suggesting an experientially based mode of consuming Dickensiana that works through spatial proximity, rather than through actual ownership.

In her analysis of the rise of literary tourism to various author's 'home and haunts', Alison Booth argues that 'things in writer's houses, like saints' relics, have a fetish-like animation'.[21] In creating a sense of immediacy, these objects have a 'magical effect' on the viewer, in which 'the poet's walking stick implies the hand that held it, and extends to us the virtual grasp of the ghostly "hand" that created the works'.[22] In this way, as items of Dickensiana that bear the closest material relationship to the author, Dickens's personal effects can activate fantasies of interaction in an acutely corporeal sense, in their ability to act as contact relics and as metonyms of his lived presence. These imaginings become especially vivid in the case of objects that bear testament to his writing as an embodied act – such as his desk or chair, which are displayed at the Charles Dickens Museum in London. But even in items that are more banal and less dignified, such as his lemon squeezer and commode chair (which the museum also possesses), there remains a sense of heightened significance that stems from their relationship to a living Dickens.[23] Additionally, since several of the museums dedicated to Dickens are located in former residences, these objects are often situated within sites already freighted with meaning, amplifying the illusion of presence that Booth describes.

The ivory letter opener that Dickens had made from the preserved paw of a favourite cat, Bob, is displayed at the New York Public Library, as part of its Henry W. and Albert A. Berg Collection, rather than one of Dickens's homes. Nevertheless, it saliently illustrates the dynamics that Booth identifies. As an object that was once literally grasped by Dickens's hand, the letter opener activates multiple fantasies: of reaching magically across time to shake hands with Dickens himself and of stepping into Dickens's place, all created by simply touching what he once touched.[24] Not only does the letter opener possess certain auratic properties as an object made and handled by Dickens, it is also imbued with Dickens's own delight in the cat's playful and mischievous nature – particularly his determined efforts to be pet and stroked. In *My Father as I Recall Him*, Mamie Dickens describes:

> One evening [. . .] 'the master' was reading at a small table, on which a lighted candle was placed. Suddenly the candle went out. My father, who was much interested in his book, relighted the candle and stroked the cat, who was looking at him pathetically he noticed, and continued his reading. A few minutes later, as the light became dim, he looked up just in time to see puss deliberately put out the candle with his paw, and then look appealingly toward him. This second and unmistakable hint was not disregarded and puss was given the petting he craved.[25]

Given the centrality of Bob's paw in this anecdote, it is perhaps not surprising that it became the part of the cat's body that Dickens had preserved in his keepsake. Recalling Bob's snuff of the candle, the paw, in functioning as the letter opener's handle, also offers Dickens the opportunity to memorialise Bob's life – he inscribes the blade with the words 'For Bob' – and to sustain a form of touch and attention, which Bob sought out.[26] Thus, as a testament to the tender affection that Dickens and his cat once shared, the object speaks to the collector's similar desire for touch and proximity, and to the fantasy of sharing a similarly embodied and tactile experience of interacting with the departed Dickens, in a way that uses Bob and his paw as a vehicle for undertaking this imaginative work.

Of course, because the object incorporates the body part of the formerly living cat, it also functions as an inevitable reminder of Bob's death and, by extension, Dickens's. Indeed, given that the blade is made from ivory, the object is quite literally made up of animal corpses, which have been carefully preserved and reshaped. As such, while these parts of the letter opener activate fantasies of reanimation and living interaction, as all relics do, they nevertheless remain stubborn in their inertness. In this way, the likely inability of the taxidermy paw to provide the same level of comfort to Dickens as the living one echoes the letter opener's failure to provide the touch of Dickens's living hand, even if one can imagine the lingering traces of his fingers and palm.[27] For neither Bob nor Dickens are living or able to be grasped in their full vitality, separated as they are from the present by the gulf of time and by the threshold of life and death. Thus, even if admirers could wrap their fingers around the taxidermy handle, which now sits behind the glass, it would only allow them to touch the cold, unnaturally firm surface of the cat's stuffed skin and fur, not the warm touch that they likely wish for, from either the cat or from Dickens.

In reading the cat's paw within the context of Dickens's long interest in taxidermy, Jenny Pyke argues that the letter opener represents the author's desire for stillness, which could provide 'a space that is neither work nor laziness' that would interrupt or at least pause the frenzied processes of writing and creation.[28] While this may have been true of Dickens himself, the investment that the consumer of Dickensiana has in the object is one that is far more active, in the way that it instantiates this desire for material interaction. Thus, although the object is one that might seem macabre, the interest that it garners from visitors to the New York Public Library speaks to a greater degree of comfort with the 'porousness of the life/death boundary' manifest in the letter opener and, as Deborah Lutz argues, in Dickens's fiction more generally.[29] Indeed, as an author who had a 'lifelong fascination with the thing-ness of the body', his novels frequently probe 'the way that animation could move smoothly, both ways, along a continuum: from vitality into matter and from dead matter into a kind of liveliness'.[30] In this sense, the letter opener can be understood as an object embedded within a larger cultural sensibility that treated death in emphatically material and often physically intimate terms, with the object itself attesting to Dickens's personal belief in the body's 'availability for becoming a thing'.[31] And in generating a range of multiple and often contradictory affective responses – from recoil to amused wonder – the letter opener functions in a similar way to death objects in Dickens's work, which 'seem to be teaching the reader not to be fixed, but to be [. . .] comically fluid even in the midst of sorrow'.[32]

This ability of the taxidermied paw to signify across so many different emotional registers is especially apt given the way Dickens depicts his famous taxidermist Mr Venus in *Our Mutual Friend*. Although Silas Wegg, who longs for the bones of his amputated leg, is constructed as a villain in the novel, Mr Venus is treated with a lighter gloss, despite the objects of death that he traffics in. In the early chapters where readers first meet Venus and are allowed a glimpse at the items that clutter his shop, the catalogue works in a largely comic register:

> Let me show you a light. My working bench. My young man's bench. A Wice. Tools. Bones, warious. Skulls, warious. Preserved Indian Baby. African ditto. Bottled preparations, warious. Everything within reach of your hand, in good preservation. The mouldy ones a-top. What's in those hampers over them again, I don't remember. Say, human warious. Cats. Articulated English baby. Dogs. Ducks. Glass eyes, warious. Mummified bird. Dried cuticle, warious. O, dear me! That's the general panoramic view.[33]

The dark humour continues when he tells Wegg that, 'if you was brought here loose in a bag to be articulated, I'd name your smallest bones blindfold equally with your largest, as fast as I could pick 'em out, and I'd sort 'em all, and sort your wertebrae, in a manner that would equally surprise and charm you.'[34] As a source of pleasure, however grotesque, the act of articulation deals with the substances of death but is nevertheless elevated in Venus's hand as an act of personal creation, if not art.

In this sense, although many critics have looked at Venus's taxidermy in its Victorian context, to think about it in terms of Dickensiana and the letter opener, in particular, allows for a more acute perception of the creative and enlivening energy that stems from it, even as it simultaneously signals death and the impossibility of reanimated life.[35] In Venus's hands and in his hyperbolic speech and extensive cataloguing, items that would more likely inspire horror provide 'surprise' and 'charm' instead, due to the skilful articulation of Dickens's prose. As such, Venus's work helps to frame the collection of Dickens's personal effects – and the especial uncanniness of the letter opener as an object – as not just a reminder of pain, lack and loss, but a source of pleasure and enchantment, however vexed, in allowing the viewer-collector to articulate their own imaginings of embodied interaction and intimate, if unsettling, touch.

Object III: Sairey Gamp Character Jug

The collectable ceramics of the Royal Doulton Company in many ways possess the exact opposite qualities of Dickens's letter opener, in the wide-ranging set of objects that comprises Dickensiana. Ubiquitous and mass produced, the ceramics contain nothing of the singular rarity that personal effects do. They bear no material relationship to Dickens's life and embodied presence and are thus comparatively inexpensive in their ready availability. Indeed, it is possible to amass an army of figurines, jugs and commemorative plates that either represent iconic characters from the novels or render well-known scenes. As such, owning an item that depicts Pickwick, Oliver or Sairey Gamp is achievable for most collectors of Dickensiana, including those with limited means.

Furthermore, in their focus on the characters and worlds of his novels rather than on the person of Dickens himself, these ceramics represent a different investment in the thingness of Dickensiana and speak to a different set of animating desires and fantasies. Instead of endeavouring to reach across the gap of time and historical distance towards the author, as the last two objects did, these ceramic collectables offer an imaginative breach across the boundaries that separate the depicted story worlds of the novels and the lived reality of the collector. In this sense, the undergirding fantasy in the collection of these objects is about becoming immersed within the richness of Dickens's story world, rather than recovering a lost past or the departed author himself. By turning a vividly imagined and beloved set of characters into concrete objects, Royal Doulton allows collectors to relish the idea of bringing a piece of Dickens's distinctive fictional world into their own.

The origins of what was to become the Royal Doulton company emerged in 1815, when John Doulton formed a commercial pottery works in Lambeth. Doulton and Watts grew alongside a burgeoning ceramics industry in the area, and specialised in the production of utilitarian goods, including salt-glazed stoneware bottles and other jars.[36] Achieving commercial prominence when it became the main supplier of the ceramic sewer and water pipes for London's growing sanitation system, the company expanded its products to include fine pottery in the 1860s, which were 'enthusiastically received' by attendees at the Paris Exhibition in 1867 and the International Exhibition of London in 1871.[37] While it would be Edward VII who would grant the company permission to use the title 'royal' in its name, the company had already garnered the attention and patronage of Queen Victoria, who placed orders for several items to decorate Windsor Castle. Increasing in popularity over the subsequent decades among a growing number of consumers, Royal Doulton's products have since become synonymous with fine ceramic collectables, with its international collectors' club boasting over 25,000 members across the world at the end of the twentieth century.[38]

Among the most popular Royal Doulton products are its Toby and character jugs, which depict famous figures, both contemporary and historical, and numerous fictional characters, including many of Dickens's. Although the Toby jug was first introduced in the mid-eighteenth century and various versions were produced throughout the nineteenth century, the modern character jug was developed under the influence of Charles Noke in the 1930s, who was then artistic director at Royal Doulton.[39] Along with designers Leslie Harradine and Harry Fenton, he created an extensive line of character jugs that would eventually come in four sizes: full, small, miniature and tinies.[40] Among these were a host of characters from Dickens, since Noke was a particular fan. The company went on to produce various products inspired by Dickens's creations and prized by collectors, including character jugs, figurines and decorative plate ware. In fact, in the sought-after best-selling line of character jugs created in 1940, the 'Original Twelve Tinies', five of the figures are Dickens characters, including Pickwick, Sam Weller, the Fat Boy, Micawber and Sairey Gamp. Royal Doulton's Dickens line-up has grown to include twenty-four character jugs and a jug of Dickens himself. Of these, the Sairey Gamp character jug has proved to be one of the most enduring pieces, as one of only two jugs in Royal Doulton's history in continuous production for over fifty years.[41]

That the character jug of Mrs Gamp would be so popular among collectors of Dickensiana is not wholly unexpected, given that ardent readers of Dickens's work would know her as one of his most remarkable creations and as a prime example of the comedic exuberance that his prose can display. Although she does not feature in most of *Martin Chuzzlewit*'s chapters, she nevertheless dominates the scenes in which she appears, both literally, in the unfolding action of the plot and her interactions with other characters, and figuratively, in the attention she demands of the reader. Much of this dominance comes through her relationship with objects and things – in addition to the effects of drinking – and through her particular relationship with her umbrella, which at one point in the novel is called 'indispensable' and described with particular detail.[42] Used several times as a weapon and shaken threateningly at various characters, the umbrella is never far from her grasp. In this sense, the object forms an essential part of her being and becomes one of her most identifiable characteristics, to the extent that 'gamp' became a synonym for 'umbrella' in British slang during the first half of the twentieth century.[43]

For these reasons, it is unsurprising that the Sairey Gamp jug incorporates the umbrella into its handle design, in one of the first instances when this portion of a jug featured such an elaborate and distinctive shape. As the Royal Doulton line of character jugs expanded, these decorative handles became important sites of creative expression for ceramic designers. But, more importantly, in thinking about the jug as an object that captivated the attentions of the Dickensiana collector, the umbrella handle recreates the same playful slippage between thing and character that makes Sairey Gamp's depiction such a comic tour-de-force.[44] By taking her treasured object and making it an integral part of her rendering as an object, the handle is what most clearly marks the jug as Mrs Gamp, and allows her to be easily distinguished from the other jugs that feature depictions of working-class women, such as the generically named character 'Arriet', who was one of the seven non-Dickensian figures in the 'Original Twelve Tinies'.

Furthermore, for the collector of the Sairey Gamp character jug, to admire and potentially grasp the handle as umbrella is to recall the memorable scenes when the character, too, reaches anxiously and repeatedly for it, moving it so often 'in the course of five minutes, that it seemed not one umbrella but fifty'.[45] Or, likewise, to remember the moment when the 'tremendous instrument' and its 'hooked handle' are caught around the throat of Tom Pinch, having first been 'made known to him by a painful pressure on the windpipe'.[46] In these instances, which are some of the funniest moments in the entire novel, the tactile and the material force of Mrs Gamp is powerfully foregrounded, in ways that can be palpably imagined when admiring or holding the jug. Moreover, as with the handle of Dickens's letter opener, the ability to wrap one's hand around the umbrella activates fantasies of interacting with Mrs Gamp herself. By having the ability to hold a material object that represents and concretises her beloved object, the possessor can indulge in acts of imaginative substitution, in thinking of her and her umbrella as real things that have a tangibility outside the text.

Of course, as a character, Sairey Gamp is just as fictive for the reader-collector as her imaginary friend Mrs Harris, but possessing and holding the jug can momentarily suspend that reality. The pleasures that this act of imagining can provide are made even clearer when the collector owns multiple pieces. Thus, the ability to behold Mrs Gamp as one among a host of Dickensian characters in a curio cabinet dramatises the desire to be surrounded by, and enfolded within, the world of Dickens's texts, as each additional piece adds to a sense of being embedded within a vibrant community of distinctive and memorable characters while remaining in one's own home. In this sense, the character jugs, like all of Royal Doulton's ceramic collectibles, activates and relies upon the very pleasures of being immersed in the experience of reading a

Dickens novel by providing an object that, however partially and however briefly, can literalise those worlds and the memorable characters that inhabit them.

Concluding Remarks

In examining these three objects and analysing their various material qualities, this essay has argued that the production and collection of Dickensiana provides a critical mode for engaging with Dickens's work. In particular, these processes provide a material mechanism that allows enthusiasts of the Inimitable to grapple with and manage the constitutive gaps that are created by his beloved texts – gaps that separate readers from the author himself, from the historical world in which he lived and which he represents, and from the fictional realms where this representative work takes place. And while each of these case studies has shown how any effort to fully reach across these divisions is destined to fail, their attempts to do so must not be seen as a break or departure from Dickens's novels and the work that they undertake. Rather, they are testament to the cultural power and enduring salience of the desires and fantasies that Dickens's writings instantiate and encourage. In this respect, to seek out and to collect Dickensiana is to seek out and find the very thing that animates his fiction: their ability to make readers reckon with the weight of loss, to imaginatively articulate and create new worlds, and to laugh uproariously at those worlds' idiosyncratic inhabitants. Such is the power of a Dickens text, and such is the power of seeing those texts manifested and organised in new material forms through the production and collection of Dickensiana.

Notes

1. See Andrew H. Miller, *Novels behind Glass: Commodity Culture and Victorian Literature* (Cambridge: Cambridge University Press, 1995) for an example of this type of criticism.
2. Bill Brown, *A Sense of Things: Object Matter in American Literature* (Chicago: University of Chicago Press, 2004), 3–4.
3. Elaine Freedgood, *The Ideas in Things: Fugitive Meaning in the Victorian Novel* (Chicago: University of Chicago Press, 2006). See also Freedgood's 'Commodity Criticism and Victorian Thing Culture: The Case of Dickens', in *Contemporary Dickens*, ed. by Eileen Gillooly and Deirdre David (Columbus: Ohio State University Press, 2009), 152–68.
4. John Plotz, *Portable Property: Victorian Culture on the Move* (Princeton: Princeton University Press, 2008). Plotz returns to thing theory in 'Materiality in Theory: What to Make of Victorian Things', in *The Oxford Handbook of Victorian Culture*, ed. by Juliet John (Oxford: Oxford University Press, 2016), 522–38. Here Plotz asserts the importance of understanding materiality as both a medium for and subject of representation.
5. For examples, see the essays included in 'Special Issue: Denotatively, Technically, Literally', *Representations* 125.1 (2014), 1–126, which was co-edited by Freedgood and Cannon Schmitt, and Deborah Lutz's *Relics of Death in Victorian Literature and Culture* (Cambridge: Cambridge University Press, 2015). See also Hannah Lewis Bill, '"The World Was Very Busy Now, In Sooth, And Had a Lot to Say": Dickens, China and Chinese Commodities in *Dombey and Son*', *Victorian Network* 5.1 (2013), 28–34; and Mark Celeste, 'Metonymic Chains: Shipwreck, Slavery, and Networks in *Villette*', *Victorian Review* 42.2 (2016), 343–60.

DICKENSIANA

6. Juliet John, 'Things, Words and the Meanings of Art', in *Dickens and Modernity*, ed. by Juliet John (Cambridge: D. S. Brewer, 2012), 115–32, 117. See also David Trotter, 'Household Clearances in Victorian Fiction', *19: Interdisciplinary Studies in the Long Nineteenth Century* 6 (2008), 1–19 <https://doi.org/10.16995/ntn.472>.

7. John, 117.

8. Walter Benjamin, *Illuminations*, trans. by Harry Zohn (New York: Schocken, 1968), 60.

9. Ibid., 61. Freedgood compares the thing theorist to the Benjaminian collector in *The Ideas in Things*, 2–3.

10. Susan Stewart, *On Longing: Narratives of the Miniature, the Gigantic, the Souvenir, the Collection* (Durham, NC: Duke University Press, 1993), 154–5.

11. Benjamin, 67.

12. For an analysis of the utopian strain, see Rey Chow, 'Fateful Attachments: On Collecting, Fidelity, and Lao She', *Critical Inquiry* 28.1 (2001), 286–304. For an analysis of the melancholic strain, see Peter Schwenger, *The Tears in Things: Melancholy and Physical Objects* (Minneapolis: University of Minnesota Press, 2006).

13. Frederic G. Kitton, *Dickensiana: A Bibliography of the Literature Relating to Charles Dickens and His Writings* (London: Redway, 1886). Subsequent references are given in the text.

14. According to Duane DeVries, the first bibliography of Dickens was completed by John Forster and featured as an appendix to the third volume of his *Life* of Dickens, published in 1873. Like Cook's and Shepherd's bibliographies, its contents focused almost exclusively on materials written by Dickens himself, although Shepherd's included a very brief section on 'Ana'. Other short bibliographies appeared in the early 1880s and were mostly written for collectors of Dickens's works, with Charles P. Johnson's 1885 *Hints to Collectors of Original Editions of the Works of Charles Dickens* including a short list of dramatisations, portraits of Dickens and other Dickensiana. At only fifty-six pages, however, its assembled list is cursory compared to the copious materials assembled by Kitton. See Devries, 'A Survey of Bibliographical and Textual Studies of Dickens's Works', *Dickens Studies Annual* 33 (2003), 239–350.

15. See Laurence W. Mazzeno, *The Dickens Industry: Critical Perspectives, 1836–2005* (Rochester, NY: Camden House, 2008), 38–9. Kitton's papers are held at the Charles Dickens Museum in London, and his collection of Dickens's works and Dickensiana formed an important part of their early library. See Devries, 244.

16. Luigi Balsamo, *Bibliography: History of a Tradition*, trans. by William A. Pettas (Berkeley: Rosenthal, 1993), 3.

17. G. Thomas Tanselle, *Bibliographical Analysis: A Historical Introduction* (Cambridge: Cambridge University Press, 2009), 9–14.

18. For an extensive analysis of the distinction between hoarding and collecting in Dickens and nineteenth-century literature and culture, see Nicole Lobdell, 'The Hoarding Sense: Hoarding in Austen, Tennyson, Dickens and Nineteenth-Century Culture' (unpublished dissertation, University of Georgia, 2013).

19. John O. Jordan, *Supposing Bleak House* (Charlottesville: University of Virginia Press, 2011), 3–5.

20. Charles Dickens, *Bleak House*, ed. by Nicola Bradbury (London: Penguin, 1996), 556, ch. 35.

21. Alison Booth, *Homes and Haunts: Touring Writers' Shrines and Countries* (Oxford: Oxford University Press, 2016), 56.

22. Ibid., 58.

23. See also Clare Pettitt, 'On Stuff', *19: Interdisciplinary Studies in the Long Nineteenth Century* 6 (2008), 1–12 <https://doi.org/10.16995/ntn.474>.

24. Helena Michie discusses these fantasies of becoming Dickens in the context of drinking, in 'Drinking in Dickens', *The Oxford Handbook of Charles Dickens*, ed. by John O. Jordan, Robert L. Patten and Catherine Waters (Oxford: Oxford University Press, 2018), 597–612.
25. Mamie Dickens, *My Father as I Recall Him* (New York: Dutton, 1896), 80–1.
26. Dickens's emotional investment in his pet cat speaks to the rise of pet culture more generally in the Victorian period. As Harriet Ritvo has noted, organised cat fancy developed over the course of the nineteenth century, with breeding practices becoming increasingly codified by the century's end. See *The Animal Estate* (Cambridge, MA: Harvard University Press, 1987), 115–21.
27. The blurring of Dickens and Bob here speaks to the more general ontological slippage that occurs between the categories of human and animal, especially in the case of companionate species. For the definitive exploration of this topic, specifically in the case of cats, see Jacques Derrida, *The Animal Which Therefore I Am*, ed. by Marie-Louise Wallet, trans. by David Willis (New York: Fordham University Press, 2008).
28. Jenny Pyke, 'Charles Dickens and the Cat Paw Letter Opener', *19: Interdisciplinary Studies in the Long Nineteenth Century* 19 (2014), 1–12, 4 <http://doi.org/10.16995/ntn.701>. For more on the history of taxidermy and its collection in the nineteenth century, see Rachel Poliquin, *The Breathless Zoo: Taxidermy and the Cultures of Longing* (State College: Penn State University Press, 2012).
29. Lutz, 80.
30. Ibid., 80.
31. Ibid., 81.
32. Ibid., 101.
33. Charles Dickens, *Our Mutual Friend*, ed. by Adrian Poole (London: Penguin, 1997), 86–8, bk 1, ch. 7.
34. Ibid., 89, bk 1, ch. 7.
35. For more on Dickens, taxidermy and *Our Mutual Friend*, see Conor Creaney, 'Paralytic Animation: The Anthropomorphic Taxidermy of Walter Potter', *Victorian Studies* 53.1 (2010), 7–35; and Verity Drake, 'Reading the Body-Object: Nineteenth-Century Taxidermy Manuals and *Our Mutual Friend*', *19: Interdisciplinary Studies in the Long Nineteenth Century* 24 (2017), 1–24 <http://doi.org/10.16995/ntn.779>. On this scene and the commercialisation of death in *Our Mutual Friend*, see Claire Wood, *Dickens and the Business of Death* (Cambridge: Cambridge University Press, 2015), 131–56.
36. Michael Doulton, *Discovering Royal Doulton* (Shrewsbury: Swan-Hill Press, 1993), 8–9. Doulton also notes that the early Doulton and Watts company actually supplied the stoneware bottles for Warren's Blacking Warehouse, where the young Dickens worked as a child in 1824 (56).
37. Gregg Whittecar and Arron Rimpley, *Royal Doulton: A Legacy of Excellence, 1871–1945* (Atglen: Schiffer, 2002), 2.
38. Doulton, 8.
39. A Toby jug refers to a vessel made in the shape of a full-bodied standing or sitting figure, whereas a character jug features only the face, head and sometimes shoulders. For more on the origins of the Toby jug and its naming, see The American Toby Jug Museum, 'Origins and Development', <https://www.tobyjugmuseum.com/origins-development> [accessed 4 May 2020].
40. Doulton, 53.
41. The American Toby Jug Museum, 'The Royal Doulton Story', <https://www.tobyjugmuseum.com/royal-doulton-story> [accessed 4 May 2020].
42. See Charles Dickens, *Martin Chuzzlewit*, ed. by Patricia Ingham (London: Penguin, 1999), 712, ch. 49; 300, ch. 19.

DICKENSIANA   495

43. The *Oxford English Dictionary* entry for 'gamp' cites usages of this term from 1855 to 2003, while noting that it is 'now somewhat archaic'. It is also used as a term to describe a 'woman resembling Mrs Gamp', especially negligent or unqualified nurses.

44. For an extensive reading of this slippage as an indicator of Dickens's style more generally, see John Bowen, 'Dickens's Umbrellas', in *Dickens's Style*, ed. by Daniel Tyler (Cambridge: Cambridge University Press, 2013), 26–45. For a discussion of umbrellas in Victorian culture more generally, see Maria Damkjaer, 'Awkward Appendages: Comic Umbrellas in Nineteenth-Century Print Culture', *Victorian Literature and Culture* 45.3 (2017), 472–92.

45. Dickens, *Martin Chuzzlewit*, 444, ch. 29.

46. Ibid., 587, ch. 40.

32

PLACING DICKENS

Charlotte Mathieson

THE RELATIONSHIP BETWEEN DICKENS AND PLACE has long played a central role in his legacy: whether it is through the wealth of scholarly writings on place in Dickens's work, or the cultural practice of visiting the locations of his life and writing, the association between Dickens and place is both a critical and cultural commonplace. This chapter explores the latter phenomenon of how, from his death to the present day, generations of readers have sought to bring themselves closer to Dickens and his characters through visiting the places associated with his life and works. Recent years have witnessed a resurgence of interest in Dickens and place: amid the host of activities to mark the bicentenary of Dickens's birth in 2012, literary tourism formed a strong focal point of activities in London, around the UK and across the world. Further to this, digital initiatives utilised Dickens and place as their theme, engendering forms of virtual literary tourism that provoke new ways of conceptualising Dickens and place.

The bicentenary focus upon Dickens and place provides a starting-point from which to re-evaluate the history of cultural interest in Dickensian tourism, and to consider the avenues that it opens up for future critical enquiry. In the first section of this chapter I examine the historical context, tracing the rise of Dickensian tourism in the years after his death and drawing out dominant tropes of literary tourism that were established in this period. Subsequently, I explore how Dickens and place became a prominent focal point of the bicentenary year, with literary tourism appearing both in the traditional form of walking tours, as well as being reinvigorated by digital technologies such as apps and podcasts.

This section, focused upon the UK and especially London, raises implicit questions about cultural nationalism in the contemporary globalised era. These questions are further explored in the final part of the chapter which looks at how the connections between Dickens and place were explored in international contexts in the bicentenary year. Here, the act of placing oneself in Dickens's landscapes was rethought through creative and digital projects which sought to recreate the experience of literary tourism in ways that were globally accessible. I suggest that the act of 'placing Dickens' within his landscapes became reconceptualised as a global, portable concept in the digital age in ways that offer scope for understanding the history of Dickens and place anew, and open up new directions through which to continue to place Dickens in future scholarship.

'Something in the Place': The History of Dickensian Literary Tourism

I find I take so much more interest in his plays, after having been to that dear little dull house he was born in! [. . .] I don't know how it is, but after you've seen the

PLACING DICKENS 497

place and written your name in the little book, somehow or other you seem to be inspired; it kindles up quite a fire within one.[1]

Mrs Wititterly's account of her visit to the Shakespeare birthplace in Stratford-upon-Avon in *Nicholas Nickleby* (1838–9) provides a less than auspicious start to a consideration of Dickens's connections with literary tourism. Through her overly enthusiastic reminiscence, Dickens creates a lightly mocking tone which conveys an irreverence towards the practice of visiting writers' houses and invites the reader to humour those who insist upon an emotional investment in place. While Mrs Wititterly is supported by Mrs Nickleby, who is similarly adamant that 'there must be something in the place', the reader is called upon to side with Mr Wititterly's retort that 'there is nothing in the place, my dear – nothing, nothing!'[2] Dickens's own experience of visiting Shakespeare's birthplace in 1838 similarly locates him as an ambivalent literary tourist, the episode acknowledged in his letters in the understated line: 'we went thence to Stratford-upon-Avon, where we sat down in the room where Shakespeare was born, and left our autographs and read those of other people and so forth.'[3]

Nonetheless, the *Nickleby* passage indicates that, by the time Dickens was writing, the custom of visiting writers' houses was well established enough that a supposed temperament of literary tourists would be familiar to readers. The practice of literary tourism had emerged in Britain during the eighteenth century, and throughout the nineteenth century there was a growing trend, as Nicola Watson writes, towards 'reinventing whole regions of the national map': the landscapes of 'Brontë country', 'Wordsworth's Lake District' and 'Hardy's Wessex' took shape, and by the late nineteenth to early twentieth century, literary tourism had reached the height of popularity with a wealth of guidebooks providing for the eager tourist.[4] Dickens's readers, evidently not deterred by their reading of *Nickleby*, followed suit: after his death in 1870, a landscape of 'Dickens country' began to form, intersecting with the coterminous formation of 'Literary London' as a tourist terrain, and expanding to the surrounding regions of Kent and southern England.[5]

Dickens's houses formed one point of touristic interest. Upon his death, Gad's Hill Place became the immediate focus of memorialisation: this was not only Dickens's final and longest residence but also, as Catherine Malcolmson writes, a key location in 'the self-mythologized version of Dickens's past'.[6] In the years that followed, Dickens's birthplace in Portsmouth and the numerous houses he inhabited during his lifetime formed points of interest on Dickens tours. Only one, 48 Doughty Street, came close to the venerated status afforded to the likes of Shakespeare's birthplace. Hailed as the 'veritable Dickens shrine', 48 Doughty Street was purchased by the Dickens Fellowship in 1922 and opened to the public as the Dickens House Museum in 1925 (today, the Charles Dickens Museum).[7] The birthplace itself was purchased by Portsmouth Town Council in 1903 'for preservation as a Dickens memorial, and with the intention of adapting it for the purposes of a Dickens Museum', but never achieved quite the same iconic status, perhaps due to its more peripheral location and lack of resonance with Dickens's London association, as well as the Fellowship's active promotion of Doughty Street as the house with most symbolic resonance with Dickens's creative output.[8] In addition to the houses, a landscape of 'Dickens Land' took shape through a plethora of publications: these range from books designed for the armchair traveller that take a biographical journey through the places of Dickens's life, or detail the locations of each novel in turn, to guidebooks mapping routes through London, Rochester and beyond.

Dickens also features prominently in literary tourist books with a broader focus on author countries.[9]

While Dickens was not unique in being the subject of the formation of a 'country', the phenomenon differs somewhat from that of other authors through the dispersal across multiple sites: Brontë country focuses around Haworth Parsonage, Wordsworth's upon Dove Cottage and Walter Scott's on Abbotsford, but 'Dickens country' has always been harder to locate precisely, scattered across numerous houses and even more numerous locations detailed in his works. Yet, while Dickens's places are numerous, their appeal is no less strong. Watson posits that the crucial factor in establishing literary tourism is the work of the source text that 'invents and solicits tourism': 'no author or text can be successfully located to place unless their writings model or cue tourism in one way or another'.[10] The embeddedness of Dickens's writing in the materiality of locatable places is consistent throughout his works, from the detailed plotting through the city streets in novels such as *Bleak House* (1852–3), to the fictionalisation of sites such as Millbank Prison into the Marshalsea in *Little Dorrit* (1855–7): as Juliet John writes, 'Dickens is remarkable for the extent to which he literally willed the association between the artist's image and material things and/or places.'[11] This is a trait which attests to his commodifiable appearance across mass culture more broadly and, it may be further inferred, to the strength of appeal surrounding Dickens's places. Dickens's places may unfold a large map, but it is one which is readily laid out in detail in his works for the tourist.

The appeal of placing Dickens within his literary landscapes was thus established in the half century after his death. Looking more closely at a selection of literary tourist publications from the late nineteenth century that set out journeys around Dickens country, we find a set of tropes that persist to the present day. The first of these is the conflation of author and work: the literary tourist moves fluidly through a landscape in which fact and fiction, and different fictions, jostle up against one another. On one of Robert Allbut's *London Rambles 'en zig-zag' with Charles Dickens* (1886), which maps out tours around the city, successive calling-points go from the Rowland warehouse of *Nickleby*, to Mr Waterbrook's establishment in *David Copperfield* (1849–50), and on to Thavies Inn from *Bleak House*.[12] Similarly, Malcolmson notes that 48 Doughty Street became imagined in the 1920s discourse around the Dickens Fellowship's purchase of the house as a space where, as per the title of Charles Buchell's 1926 illustration, 'Mr Dickens and Mr Pickwick Meet on the Door Step of 48 Doughty Street'.[13] In accounts of literary tours, characters are brought vividly to life in imaginative recreations of familiar scenes: in *Little Journeys to the Homes of Good Men and Great* (1895), Elbert Hubbard becomes animated as he walks along the riverside and sees 'Bob and several other boys, grimy with black, chasing each other across the flat boats'; a few minutes later he continues, 'we saw just ahead of us David Copperfield and Mr Peggotty following a woman whom we could make out walking excitedly a block ahead. It was Martha intent on suicide.'[14] This last sentence attests to the appeal of 'dark tourism' to which some Dickens literary tourism lends itself.[15] Moreover, it is noticeable that there is an inherent mobility in this passage, which is illustrative of much of Dickens's writing, making it particularly amenable to the touristic exploration.

For others, it was the invocation of the author himself that became a prominent trope. In Christian Tearle's *Rambles with an American* (1910), the fictional literary tourist Mr Fairchild is questioned as to why he takes such delight in the act: he replies that it is because 'Charles Dickens has been in that room', with 'so much reverence' that the British narrator is 'abashed'.[16] His words recall Mrs Nickleby's insistence that there is 'something in the place': Alice Newcomer's 1923 article on 'London's Dickens Shrine' echoes this when she writes 'Think how we women will thrill our clubs back home with accounts of how WE have walked on the very floors which Dickens feet had trod.'[17] In this, literary tourism takes on the status of a religious pilgrimage that brings the tourist into a spiritual communion with the author: as John writes, even among tourists today the idea persists 'that a visit to Dickens's former home is a pilgrimage' signified as involving an 'almost spiritual investment' by the tourist.[18] In these early writings, the house becomes signified as a sacred space, as in the invocation of Doughty Street as 'the Dickens shrine'.

This spiritual reverence centres upon the specific act of 'tracing' or 'following' in the author's footsteps: Tearle elaborates, 'it isn't so much because Dickens has described these places that I take an interest in them [. . .] It's because I know he went over every inch of the ground himself. And that being so, when I see these places, they seem to bring me near *him*.'[19] In the act of treading in the author's footsteps, the spiritual investment of the tourist culminates in an attempt to solidify the connection between tourist and writer through the embodiment of their past presence: as Watson suggests, this is a way of 'coping with the precariousness of immersion in a fictive experience by constructing a personal relationship with the author'.[20] At the same time, the attempt to bring the author closer is underscored by the knowledge of their inevitable absence such that, as Booth writes, 'a literary walk doubles as a ghost walk', every step in the shadow of the long-dead author iterating the futility of trying to reclaim their presence.[21] This, Watson continues, is nonetheless part of the appeal: in this form of 'tourist gothic', tourists 'actively seek out the anti-realist experience of being haunted, of forcefully realizing the presence of an absence'.[22]

Yet not only does the act of 'treading in the footsteps' reveal the absence of the author, but it also foregrounds the presence of the tourist. As the tourist calls attention to the author's absent ghost, they draw attention to their own, embodied presence within and movement through the space. In so doing, these writers are recording the intrinsically experiential, spatial and mobile quality of the touristic act, feeling themselves part of the place they are moving through and creating their own embodied-spatial relationship to the place around them. In this, they are not just forging a connection with the author but also enacting a placing of *self* within Dickens's places; inhabiting, occupying, understanding place through the placing of the self. This enactive role of tourists in constructing their account of space is briefly expressed in these writings, but will become more acutely realised in recent iterations of Dickens tourism explored later in this chapter.

The ghost-hunting of the author's presence also raises questions about the temporal negotiations that are foregrounded in literary tourism, which at once suggests the past is there to be retraced in the present moment, while simultaneously reinforcing the distance between past and present as the tourist encounters changed landscapes to those that the author knew. Allbut's *Rambles*, first published in 1886 and then reissued thirteen years later, negotiates this very tension in its republication: an introductory note by Gerald Brenan optimistically announces that 'no far away foreign country is Dickens' Land. It lies at our doors.' But Allbut's following preface decries the disappearance of many buildings since the first edition of the work: 'Thus it comes to pass that only the memory of what has been remains, in regards to many of these Dickensian localities and landmarks.'[23] Interestingly, this transience of the physical landscape is replicated in the transitory nature of the digital resources that we will see in the next section, many of which have not had a lasting digital presence.

Literary tourism also acquired a wider national significance in the early years of its formation. As Watson writes, the nineteenth-century rise of literary tourism 'emerged as a side-effect of cultural nationalism, with the emerging national literary canon seized upon in order to effect a sort of interiorised national mapping'.[24] In the case of Dickens, the connections between author, place and nation are evident in fleeting moments throughout the tourist guides and further coalesced around the time of the 1912 centenary of his birth. As Claire Wood has discussed, the tone of the centenary was 'reverential', with a 'focus on securing the legacy of an author whose place in the canon was not yet certain'.[25] This securing of legacy was in part solidified through a literal anchoring of Dickens to place, and specifically national place: as Karen Laird writes of the film adaptation chosen to mark the year, *David Copperfield*, the focus of directors Thomas Bentley and Cecil Hepworth was upon 'making visible Dickens's ties to the English landscape', for example through emphasising the on-location shooting of the film, 'thereby crystallising the writer's reputation as a national treasure'.[26] The film – one of several Dickensian adaptations by Thomas Bentley in the years surrounding the centenary – not only tied Dickens to Englishness and to English place but also, in a move anticipatory of more recent activities, worked to commodify the relationship between Dickens and English place as a global export, creating 'a timely form of virtual literary tourism for an international audience primed to eulogise Dickens's life and works'.[27]

In the late nineteenth- to early twentieth-century development of literary tourism, key themes thus emerge around the relationship between Dickens and place: in particular, the role of the tourist in negotiating the Dickens landscape and the placing of 'Dickens Land' within a wider national landscape and as a globally exportable form are themes that continue to evolve in the more recent iterations of Dickensian tourism.

Placing Dickens in 2012

The bicentenary of Charles Dickens's birth on 7 February 2012 prompted a year-long commemoration of his life and works, coordinated under the umbrella of 'Dickens 2012' by the Charles Dickens Museum and Film London in association with the Dickens Fellowship. Official partners ranged across cultural institutions and universities, while a website catalogued a huge number of smaller-scale activities including exhibitions, reading groups and talks.[28] Throughout the diverse activities on offer, a recurrent theme was a focus on Dickens and place: many events and activities centred on the houses, streets and other physical places associated with his life and works, as well as situating his characters within these. Interest in Dickens's places had continued through the twentieth century, with the museum at 48 Doughty Street remodelled several times, and 'Dickens World' – a theme park imagining of Dickensian locations and spaces – in Kent in operation between 2007 and 2016.[29] The resurgence of focus upon Dickens's places in 2012 took familiar form in literary tourist routes around London and Kent as well as abroad, and became reinvigorated through the introduction of digital technologies that generated new ways to experience Dickens's places.

In its simplest form, literary tourism was evident in the familiar form of walking tours led by experienced guides taking groups around locations that Dickens had lived in, written about or visited – many of them in London and south-east England.[30] These tours speak to how, as Watson writes, 'nowadays literary tourism is so naturalised as a cultural phenomenon', and the simple act of retracing an author's routes holds an enduring appeal, albeit one of relatively niche interest.[31] Moreover, familiar forms of literary tourism were rethought through digital technologies such as podcasts, apps and interactive maps. A number of digital walking tours were available which provided audio guides accompanied by a map of the route, either downloadable from a website or integrated into a mobile phone app: *The Guardian*'s five-part series of Dickens audio walks and Southwark Council's 'Dickens in Southwark' tour provide two examples of this.[32] The Dickens House Museum similarly created an app of 'Dickens Trails' which traced four routes onto a digital map, with descriptive text to be read at each site; the routes were themed around Dickens characters, thus building on the museum's historical focus on the house as 'the birthplace, or home, of many of Dickens's most celebrated characters' and taking this into the surrounding streets of London.[33] Indeed, a feature of all the digital tours was the fluid movement across a landscape composed of author biography and fictional scenes, thus using new technologies as a means to access familiar tropes of literary tourism.[34]

The 2012 focus on 'placing Dickens' was also prominent in the Museum of London's initiatives to celebrate the bicentenary: an exhibition on 'Dickens and London', accompanied by a mobile app and a short film. Each of these, while not classifiable as literary tourism as such, was interesting for the way in which it drew on the discourse of literary tourism in the presentation of the Dickensian city. The exhibition marketing promised that, 'Evoking the atmosphere of the streets of Victorian London and the river Thames, visitors will follow in Dickens' footsteps and be taken on a memorable and haunting journey, discovering the places and subjects which sparked his imagination.'[35] The accompanying mobile app 'Dickens [*sic*] Dark London' similarly took users 'on a journey through the darker side of Charles Dickens' London'[36] using an interactive audio-visual format that centred upon traversing the streets through a Dickensian lens. A film commissioned by the Museum of London, 'The Houseless Shadow', again foregrounded these themes through a reading of Dickens's 'Night Walks' in which the viewer is taken on a tour through a series of locations, such as three scenes around Westminster Bridge from nightfall to sunrise, the reading accompanied by the persistent sound of footsteps that situate the viewer as a mobile tourist within the scene.[37]

Throughout each of these projects the recurrence of the idea of taking visitors 'on a journey' that 'follow[s] in Dickens's footsteps' reiterates the tourist tropes established in the nineteenth century; the use of 'haunting' in the museum publicity material is especially evocative of how, as Booth writes, 'a literary walk doubles as a ghost walk' that both pursues the author's embodiment while simultaneously revealing proof of the author's absence.[38] The recreation of this trope within the space of the museum hall, where 'Victorian London' was an artificial projection of sound and lighting effects, arguably becomes emptied of meaning, although at the same time it encourages critical reflection upon what exactly *is* the meaning held by the 'authentic' spaces that literary tourism attempts to recapture.[39] Moreover, although characters did feature within the body of these walks, it is the focus upon the author rather than the works or characters that takes precedence, further emphasising the sense of the absence of the living presence, rather than the enduring quality of the works.

In other instances, the trope of 'haunting' was used to traverse the Dickensian landscape of the city today, coming into convergence with older tropes of literary tourism. The Southwark Dickens trail 'leads you in the footsteps of Dickens' and further promises that the visitor will travel *with* Dickens himself: 'During this guide [. . .] we will journey with the penniless young boy through the workhouses and slums.'[40] At subsequent stops, the tourist is called upon to 'picture the scene' that Dickens may have seen as he watched from a favoured vantage-point on London Bridge, and later to step back a few paces so that 'you'll be standing exactly where John Dickens spent his prison days'.[41] This invocation of the author's ghost recalls the nineteenth-century tourist's reverence at knowing that 'Charles Dickens has been in that room' and the excitement that 'WE have walked on the very floors which Dickens feet had trod'. Implicit in each of these is the suggestion of a temporal collapse between past and present, through which the tourist is called upon to make an imaginative leap from the present into inhabiting the past: this reflects how, as David Lowenthal writes, 'collapsing the entire past into a single frame is one common heritage aim [. . .] stressing the likeness of past and present is another'.[42]

Yet Dickensian tourism, particularly in its 2012 form, also encouraged more enactive, critical reflection on the supposed continuities of past and present. I suggested earlier that the trope of treading in footsteps be read as a placing of *self* within Dickens's place, with an emphasis on the embodied, interactive negotiations of the tourist within the landscape. In a similar vein, others have suggested that literary tourism be read as a process in which tourists 'actively participate in the production of meaning'.[43] Sarah Tetley and Bill Bramwell caution against the common assumption made about literary tourism, that 'people are not in active negotiation with their material and symbolic environment, but are passively shaped by it', and they argue that 'when people visit a literary destination they make their own sense and value their own knowledge, albeit negotiated within a myriad of influences'.[44]

In calling upon the tourist to imaginatively embody the scene, the Southwark walks cited above undertake this foregrounding of the role of the tourist and encourage them to think actively about the space they are inhabiting, embodying and moving through. This was a prominent theme of *The Guardian*'s Dickens walks, which frequently encouraged the tourist to engage with the dual temporality of the touristic landscape. The tours draw attention to features of present-day London that have changed since Dickens's time: for example, they note that Warren's Blacking Factory is now the rather foreboding black building of PricewaterhouseCoopers, and reflect upon the changed space of the surrounding Embankment. As I noted in my own undertaking of the tours:

> at times, too, the city threw in its own chance happenings [. . .] a passage from *Dombey and Son* about the destructive building of the railway line was sharply echoed by the cavernous space that had recently been created by a huge building site opposite the station. These and many other instances, were ordinary, everyday

features that I'd otherwise have paid little attention to, but which suddenly became re-perceived, refocused, in the context of the tour.[45]

My experience echoes how, as Susan Bennett writes, rather than offering an absorbing process of 'reliving the past', tourism can offer a 'productive perspective that moves us, albeit temporarily, out of otherwise prescriptive spatial dynamics of the city'.[46] Whereas texts such as Allbut's 1899 *Rambles* decried the loss of Dickens's places, the 2012 tours self-consciously engaged with the changing landscape and encouraged the tourist to look for the discontinuities in place as much as the continuities, to inhabit and explore the productive juxtapositions between past and present that the city unfolded. In doing so, they suggested a new way of understanding Dickens and place as a concept: that it might not only be a passive reclaiming or recreating of the places of the past through the invocation of the author, but that Dickens might also provide a lens through which to perceive the city anew, to gain an alternative vision of place today. In this, the act of retracing Dickens's footsteps became less about reclaiming the author, characters or writing, and more about the process of observation and interpretation, a thread developed further in the final section.

Literary tourism in 2012 thus offered opportunities to think about the practice as one that is perhaps more enactive and involved on the part of the tourist than we might initially assume, moving into a more critical engagement with the notion of 'Dickens and place'. This was also true of the ways in which the individual relationship between tourist and place was situated within a wider national context. The year 2012 was not only that of Dickens, but a year of national celebration for Britain: the concurrent events of Queen Elizabeth's Jubilee, the Olympic Games and the accompanying Cultural Olympiad prompted an assertion and revaluation of British cultural identity, culminating in Danny Boyle's 'Isles of Wonder' that commenced the Olympic Games, widely lauded as 'a byword for a new approach, not only to British culture but to Britishness itself'.[47] Dickens 2012 was not officially part of these celebrations, and indeed Dickens was notably absent from the stage of the Olympic Opening Ceremony but, as Charlotte Boyce and Elodie Rousselet note, official services to mark the bicentenary 'implicitly co-opted [Dickens] as a symbol of "Britishness"'.[48]

Dickensian tourism similarly became implicitly co-opted into the national landscape of the city that year. The literary tourist in London in 2012 negotiated a multitude of national cultural markers as they traversed Dickens routes: a 100-metre-wide picture of the Royal Family spread along the banks of the Thames, Union Jack flags waving throughout the city in support of Team GB, 'London 2012' logos proliferating on Olympic merchandise. These signs, while not consciously part of Dickens tours, were an inescapable part of the cityscape and thus implicitly served to reiterate Dickens's place in the national landscape. Just as in 1912 the securing of Dickens's legacy was achieved through attachment to national place, in 2012 Dickens became drawn into a national narrative that was visibly being created in the space of the city: walking Dickens's London was implicitly walking Dickens in Britain. This national narrative by no means went unchallenged, however: constructed in an international context, and performed on a global stage, the London narrative of Dickens existed as coterminous with 2012 ventures that sought to productively re-examine the concept of 'Dickens and place' from a variety of national perspectives.

Dickens's Global Places

In turning finally to the global engagements with Dickens in 2012, these acts of national locating raise further questions. Does the emphasis upon Dickensian literary tourism reify the connection between Dickens and Britain in a way that insists upon the privilege of nation-place as a requisite to understanding Dickens's works? Do the digital iterations of Dickensian tourism function as acts of national cultural export that seek to authenticate and reassert Dickens's Britishness while responding to the impetus for globality in the digital age? While a focus solely on British productions might initially suggest as much, a number of international projects allowed for the idea of 'Dickens and place' to be reconsidered from a variety of national perspectives.

The international interest in celebrating Dickens 2012 included both location-based and digital forms. The author's visits to the United States and France were celebrated: Washington, DC, held a Dickens walk, and UMass Lowell commemorated 'Dickens in Lowell' with a seven-month programme of events and an exhibition.[49] Dickens's connections with France were explored in a symposium on 'Dickens in the New Millennium' in Aix-en-Provence, and 'A Tale of Four Cities' conference travelled across four significant places in Dickens's life – Paris, Condette near Boulogne, Rochester and Chatham, concluding in London – to explore 'Dickens's ideological pliability in different national contexts'.[50] These events transported the idea of 'Dickens and place' away from London and south-east England to open up the concept to new nationally specific contexts. The British Council's Dickens 2012 activities took a slightly different approach, working to resituate the reading and interpretation of Dickens's works as a truly international project through the use of digital and online technologies: the cornerstone of this was a twenty-four-hour global read-a-thon spanning twenty-four countries on 7 February 2012, in addition to which the British Council worked with over sixty-eight countries on two hundred and eight global activities to celebrate the bicentenary.[51] As Claire Wood writes, the digital component allowed for 'a connected international community of Dickens enthusiasts' and, in turn, the discovery of 'a more complex and interesting Dickens, who had relevance to contemporary concerns and a profound influence on modern culture'.[52]

One of the most interesting facets of this international engagement was how it enabled new perspectives on and experiences of 'Dickens and place' as a concept. This was evident in two British Council projects that utilised digital technology to productively resituate Dickens in new national contexts: 'Sketches by Boz: Sketching the City' and 'The Uncommercial Traveller' turned to the streets of cities including Karachi, Beijing, Shanghai, Buenos Aires and New York, using Dickens as an inspiration to create new urban narratives. 'Sketches by Boz: Sketching the City' was a creative competition that invited school children, young adults and professional writers to respond to the local environment through the lens of Dickens's writing, producing podcast recordings of the winning entries. 'The Uncommercial Traveller' had a similar aim of writing about cities around the world via Dickensian modes of observation and narration, developing 'a creative and reflective tour in each location by using Dickens's approach of seeking out forgotten places and uncovering hidden stories'.[53] The resultant audio journeys recreate the experience of an urban tour, taking the listener on an 'immersive journey' through the city.[54] In both projects, cities thus became contact zones in which the idea of Dickens and place became rethought as a mode of perception, and in turn rewritten into the local landscape to create a new 'Dickensian' locale.

These projects drew upon themes that run throughout the history of Dickens and place: they emphasised the experiential qualities of literary tourism, with the listener occupying the place of the literary tourist being taken on a narrated journey through the city; they captured vibrant, animated scenes that demonstrated a minute attentiveness to the places being described, recalling how Dickens's writing 'invents and solicits tourism' through its embeddedness in place; and they reiterated 'Dickens and place' as a largely urban concept, transported from London to international cities. At the same time, this detached Dickens from the national contexts into which the British, and especially London-based activities, of 2012 were implicitly co-opted: rather than simply dis-place or export Dickens into new national spaces, they instead relocalised Dickens through creating narratives that pertained to each specific locality. Having untethered Dickens from his local roots, these localised narratives were then located within the global sphere, taking the form of podcasts made available on the British Council website and thereby freely accessible across the world. These projects thus disrupted the idea of 'Dickens and place' as a national cultural construct, and demonstrated that this concept might be rethought from international perspectives to result in productive creative outlets.

Furthermore, in these urban rewritings 'placing Dickens' becomes rethought *as* a concept, and a portable one at that: it becomes a mode of observation, a way of perceiving and narrating locality that seeks to capture a 'Dickensian' sense of writing place; it is at once heavily localised, invested in the particularities of place, yet is not about Dickens's 'original' places themselves, and can be readily detached and resituated into a new locale – Karachi, Melbourne, Shanghai. 'Placing Dickens' here become more than *Dickens's* places, instead reconfigured as an idea that is about the process of observation, perception and interpretation of locality, and that can thus be dis-placed and rethought in new places – albeit specifically urban environments, suggesting the continuing resonance of Dickens's London. This suggests that there is a core notion inherent in 'placing Dickens', yet untethers this from the authenticating privileges that literary tourism might traditionally seek to iterate through an insistence upon place as a site of access to the author. It also opens up a means of 'placing Dickens' that seeks to expand engagement beyond the streets of London, and is more expansive in its creative possibilities, readily transported and readapted into new international spaces.

These new modes of engaging with Dickens's places return us to reconsider how it is that Dickens's places have come to have meaning, and why the idea of 'placing Dickens' endures today. If, as Nicola Watson writes of literary tourist locations, 'no author or text can be successfully located to place unless their writings model or cue tourism in one way or another [. . .] it is the text itself that invents and solicits tourism',[55] then Dickens's texts can arguably be seen to solicit a particularly portable, relocatable form of tourism that extends beyond the bounds of his actual locations and can be transferred into a multitude of places around the world. This reflects how, as John writes, 'A distinctive feature of Dickens's mass cultural impact is his "portability", the ability of his novels and indeed his image, even during his lifetime, to travel across various media and national boundaries, and after his death, across historical periods.'[56] This, I would suggest, applies also to his construction of place which can finally be read as portable and relocatable, transcending national and historical boundaries. Dickens's places might be found first in the actual locations written into his works, but the legacy of Dickens and place is also more than this: a transportable mode of vision or way of understanding place, a means of perception that can travel into new locations, and continue to be made meaningful in different contexts.

Concluding Remarks

The impulse to locate Dickens has long-held popular appeal as a way of accessing the author and his works through the places in which he lived and which he wrote about; embedding the tourist in a Dickens landscape allows the tourist to imaginatively embody the scenes of Dickens's life and works, creating a sense of proximity and distance that brings one closer to, as well as reinforcing the distance from, the past. The centrality of place in Dickens's legacy has allowed generations of readers, from his death to the present day, to access Dickens through place, to form a personal connection that places the self within Dickens's places. The recent interest in 'placing Dickens' further suggests that however and wherever we read his works, the impulse to 'place' Dickens remains strong, evolving with the technologies available while continuing to reiterate familiar and well-established tropes that have been present in literary tourism from its origins to the present day.

Yet while literary tourism has continued in its traditional form, digital and global iterations have provided scope for more critical reflection on the practice of Dickensian literary tourism, and for questioning what it is about place that holds such significance in the cultural idea of Dickens. Digital forms of global engagement have engendered ways of re-placing Dickens in the international sphere and, in so doing, call on us to reflect upon what is meant by 'placing Dickens' as a concept. Through digital technologies, 'Dickens and place' is refigured as a portable concept, one that suggests that placing Dickens is about more than the locations with which he is associated, and also about identifying the ways in which place is experienced, observed and narrated in his works; at once rooted in the specifics of the locale, but detachable to become meaningful in new contexts. This finally suggests that 'placing Dickens' will continue to be part of his legacy for years to come, travelling across national and international contexts, and evolving as it does to allow us to continue to place Dickens in new ways.

Notes

1. Charles Dickens, *Nicholas Nickleby*, ed. by Mark Ford (London: Penguin, 2003), 340, ch. 27.
2. Ibid.
3. Charles Dickens, *The Letters of Charles Dickens*, ed. by Mamie Dickens and Georgina Hogarth (London: Macmillan, 1893), 17.
4. Nicola J. Watson, *The Literary Tourist* (Basingstoke: Palgrave Macmillan, 2006), 5. In addition to Watson's seminal study of the rise of literary tourism, see also Harald Hendrix, *Writers' Houses and the Making of Memory* (New York: Routledge, 2008) and Alison Booth, *Homes and Haunts: Touring Writers' Shrines and Countries* (Oxford: Oxford University Press, 2016).

PLACING DICKENS

5. Watson, *Literary Tourist*, 5; see also Booth, *Homes and Haunts*, 262–4, for discussion of Dickens in the context of other author countries. On Dickens and London, see Nicola J. Watson, 'Rambles in Literary London', in *Literary Tourism and Nineteenth-Century Culture*, ed. by Nicola J. Watson (Basingstoke: Palgrave Macmillan, 2009), 139–49.

6. Catherine Malcolmson, '"A veritable Dickens shrine": Commemorating Charles Dickens at the Dickens House Museum', *19: Interdisciplinary Studies in the Long Nineteenth Century*, 14 (2012), 1–21, 4 <http://doi.org/10.16995/ntn.604>. See Booth, *Homes and Haunts*, 259, on visitors to Gad's Hill Place.

7. Malcolmson, 10.

8. Frederic George Kitton, *The Dickens Country* (London: Black, 1905), 3.

9. The biographical approach is evident in Henry Snowden Ward and Catharine B. Ward, *The Real Dickens Land: With an Outline of Dickens's Life* (London: Chapman & Hall, 1904) and Kitton, *The Dickens Country*. A focus on each novel is taken in T. Edgar Pemberton, *Dickens's London: or, London in the Works of Charles Dickens* (London: Tinsley, 1876), E. Beresford Chancellor, *The London of Charles Dickens: Being an Account of the Haunts of His Characters and the Topographical Setting of His Novels* (London: Richards, 1924), and B. W. Matz's *The Inns and Taverns of Pickwick* (London: Cecil Palmer, 1921) and *Dickensian Inns and Taverns* (London: Cecil Palmer, 1922). Guidebooks include Robert Allbut, *London Rambles 'en zig-zag' with Charles Dickens* (London: Curtice, 1886) and *Rambles in Dickens' Land* (London: Freemantle, 1899), Duncan Moul, *Week-ends in Dickens Land: A Bijou Handbook for the Rambler with Map* (London: Homeland Association, 1901), and Albert A. Hopkins and Newbury Frost Read, *A Dickens Atlas, Including Twelve Walks in London with Charles Dickens* (London: Spurr & Swift, 1923). Literary tourist books with a broader focus include Elbert Hubbard, *Little Journeys to the Homes of Good Men and Great* (New York: Putnams, 1895) and Christian Tearle, *Rambles with an American* (London: Mills & Boon, 1910).

10. Watson, *Literary Tourist*, 12.

11. Juliet John, *Dickens and Mass Culture* (Oxford: Oxford University Press, 2011), 241.

12. Allbut, *London Rambles 'en zig-zag'*, 38–9.

13. Malcolmson, 1.

14. Hubbard, 272, 282.

15. Dickens himself engaged in dark tourism: see John Edmondson, 'Death and the Tourist: Dark Encounters in Mid-Nineteenth-Century London via the Paris Morgue', in *The Palgrave Handbook of Dark Tourism Studies*, ed. by Philip R. Stone et al. (London: Palgrave Macmillan, 2018), 77–102.

16. Tearle, 13.

17. Alice Newcomer, 'London's Dickens Shrine', *Dickensian* 19 (1923), 14–15, 14.

18. John, 252. The spiritual dimensions of literary tourism have been much discussed: a useful overview is provided in Lorraine Brown, 'Treading in the Footsteps of Literary Heroes: An Autoethnography', *European Journal of Tourism, Hospitality and Recreation* 7.2 (2016), 135–45.

19. Tearle, 13.

20. Watson, *Literary Tourist*, 174.

21. Alison Booth, 'Time-travel in Dickens' World', in *Literary Tourism and Nineteenth-Century Culture*, ed. by Nicola J. Watson (Basingstoke: Palgrave Macmillan, 2009), 150–63, 151.

22. Watson, *Literary Tourist*, 7.

23. Allbut, *Rambles in Dickens-Land*, xii, xxvi.

24. Watson, *Literary Tourist*, 14.

25. Claire Wood, 'Dickens 2012: Recording Commemorative Events in the Digital Age', 5 <http://www.archives.org.uk/images/documents/news/Dickens_2012_Recording_Commemorative_Events_in_the_Digital_Age.pdf> [accessed 26 September 2017].

26. Karen Laird, 'The Posthumous Dickens: Commemorative Adaptations, 1870–2012', *Neo-Victorian Studies* 5.2 (2012), 12–34, 20.
27. Laird, 21.
28. Full partners are listed on the Dickens 2012 website <http://www.dickens2012.org> [accessed 26 September 2017].
29. For discussion of the Charles Dickens Museum see Booth, *Homes and Haunts*, 266–9. 'Dickens World' was a theme-park style amalgamation of Dickens scenes located in Kent; for discussion, see Marty Gould and Rebecca N. Mitchell, 'Understanding the Literary Theme Park: Dickens World as Adaptation', *Neo-Victorian Studies* 3.3 (2010), 145–71; see also Booth, *Homes and Haunts*, 269–74; and John, 273–89.
30. For example 'The Dickens Connection' <http://www.dickens2012.org/event/dickens-connection> and 'Tour of Dickens London Locations' <http://www.dickens2012.org/event/tour-dickens-london-locations-sandra-shevey> [accessed 26 September 2017].
31. Watson, *Literary Tourist*, 5.
32. The *Guardian* walks included *Oliver Twist*, Rochester, *David Copperfield*, The Heart of the City, and the Dickens Birthplace Museum at Portsmouth: see 'Charles Dickens at 200 + London Walks Podcast' <https://www.theguardian.com/books/series/charles-dickens-at-200+travel/series/cityguides> [accessed 26 September 2017]. Southwark Council created 'Self-guided Trails through Dickensian Southwark', along with other heritage information on Dickens and Southwark at <http://www.2.southwark.gov.uk/news/article/723/charles_dickens_in_southwark> [accessed 26 September 2017].
33. 'Dickens Trail App' <https://dickensmuseum.com/pages/dickens-trail-app> [accessed 26 September 2017].
34. A more recent iteration of the use of digital technologies to experience a composite landscape of 'Victorian London' in which Dickens has a presence is evident in the video game *Assassin's Creed*: Syndicate: see Francesca Orestano 'Dickens as Icon and Antonomasia in *Assassin's Creed*: Syndicate', in *Reading Dickens Differently*, ed. by Leon Litvack and Nathalie Vanfasse (Chichester: Wiley Blackwell, 2020), 207–22.
35. Museum of London press release, quoted in 'Dickens and London exhibition opens in London', *Museum Publicity* <http://museumpublicity.com/2011/12/10/dickens-and-london-exhibition-opens-in-london/> [accessed 26 September 2017].
36. 'Dickens Dark London', Museum of London <https://www.museumoflondon.org.uk/Resources/app/Dickens_webpage/index.html> [accessed 26 September 2017].
37. 'The Houseless Shadow', directed by William Raban (2011); the full twenty-minute film was displayed as an art installation at the Museum of London's 'Dickens and London' exhibition and can be viewed at <https://player.bfi.org.uk/rentals/film/watch-houseless-shadow-2011-online>; a shortened version can be viewed on YouTube <https://www.youtube.com/watch?v=SlPPgmPPE4c> [accessed 26 September 2017]. The project is discussed on the Museum of London blog <http://blog.museumoflondon.org.uk/take-a-cinematic-voyage-through-night-time-london-inspired-by-charle-dickenss-night-walks> [accessed 26 September 2017].
38. Booth, 'Time-travel in Dickens' World', 151.
39. The Dickens World theme park similarly raises such issues around authenticity and recreation: see Booth, 'Time-Travel in Dickens' World'.
40. Stop 0, 'Dickens Walk – Acoustiguide app' <https://itunes.apple.com/gb/app/dickens-walk-acoustiguide/id555953092?mt=8&ign-mpt=uo=2%20> [accessed 26 September 2017]. Quotations are from the audio of version 1.1 of the app and reference the 'stop' from which the quote is taken.
41. 'Dickens Walk', stop 1, stop 11.
42. David Lowenthal, *The Heritage Crusade and the Spoils of History* (Cambridge: Cambridge University Press, 1998), 139.

PLACING DICKENS

43. Eveline Kilian, 'Exploring London: Walking the City – (Re-)Writing the City', in *The Making of Modern Tourism: The Cultural History of the British Experience, 1600–2000*, ed. by Hartmut Berghoff, Barbara Korte, Ralf Schneider and Christopher Harvie (Basingstoke: Palgrave Macmillan, 2002), 267–83, 267.

44. Sarah Tetley and Bill Bramwell, 'Tourists and the Cultural Construction of Haworth's Literary Landscape', in *Literature and Tourism: Essays in the Reading and Writing of Tourism*, ed. by Mike Robinson and Hans-Christian Andersen (Andover, Hampshire: Cengage, 2011), 155–70, 157.

45. Charlotte Mathieson, 'Walking Dickens's London', *Journal of Victorian Culture Online*, 6 October 2012 <http://blogs.tandf.co.uk/jvc/2012/10/06/walking-dickenss-london> [accessed 15 September 2017].

46. Susan Bennett, 'Universal Experience: The City as Tourist Stage', in *The Cambridge Companion to Performance Studies*, ed. by Tracy C. Davis (Cambridge: Cambridge University Press, 2008), 76–90, 87.

47. Jonathan Freedland, 'Danny Boyle: Champion of the People', *Guardian*, 9 March 2013. I have written further about the interaction of Dickens 2012 with the Olympics in 'A Tale of Two Londons: Locating Shakespeare and Dickens in 2012', Peter Kirwan and Charlotte Mathieson, in *Shakespeare on the Global Stage: Performance and Festivity in the Olympic Year*, ed. by Paul Prescott and Erin Sullivan (London: Arden/Bloomsbury, 2015), 227–52.

48. Charlotte Boyce and Elodie Rousselot, 'The Other Dickens: Neo-Victorian Appropriation and Adaptation', *Neo-Victorian Studies* 5.2 (2012), 1–11, 1.

49. In Washington, DC, 'A Dickens of a Tour' still runs today <http://www.historicstrolls.com/a-dickens-of-a-tour.html>; 'Dickens in Lowell' programme <https://www.uml.edu/conferences/dickens-in-lowell> [accessed 26 September 2017].

50. See Nathalie Vanfasse, 'A Historical Survey of French Criticism and Scholarship on Dickens', in *The Reception of Charles Dickens in Europe*, ed. by Michael Hollington, 2 vols (London: Bloomsbury, 2013), I, 123–41, 136; and Juliet John, 'Global Dickens: A Response to John Jordan', *Literature Compass* 9 (2012), 502–7, <doi:10.1111/j.1741-4113.2012.00895. x>. See also 'Dickens fans sought to celebrate author's bicentenary' <http://www2.le.ac.uk/offices/press/press-releases/2012/january/dickens-fans-sought-to-celebrate-authors-bicentenary> [accessed 26 September 2017].

51. Much of the British Council's online resources have now been archived and are no longer accessible online; a summary is provided in 'Charles Dickens goes global in British Council's bicentenary festival', *Guardian*, 6 October 2011 <https://www.theguardian.com/books/2011/oct/06/charles-dickens-bicentenary-british-council> [accessed 26 September 2017].

52. Wood, 9–11.

53. 'The Uncommercial Traveller', <https://theatreanddance.britishcouncil.org/projects/2012/the-uncommercial-traveller/> [accessed 26 September 2017].

54. The audio files for these projects are no longer centrally located: Melbourne and Karachi are available on the British Council's Soundcloud page <https://soundcloud.com/bc-literature>, and London tracks can be found on Arcola Theatre's Soundcloud page <https://soundcloud.com/arcolatheatre> [accessed 26 September 2017].

55. Watson, *Literary Tourist*, 12.

56. John, *Dickens and Mass Culture*, 15.

Further Reading

Juliet John, *Dickens and Mass Culture* (Oxford: Oxford University Press, 2011)
Nicola J. Watson, *The Literary Tourist* (Basingstoke: Palgrave Macmillan, 2006)

33

COMMEMORATION

Claire Wood

That great novelist, Charles Dickens by name,
Death! thou hast called in the midst of his fame,
Now that our friend from life has departed,
Thousands are left who are near broken-hearted.

–Joseph Gwyer, 'Death of Mr Charles Dickens'[1]

THE DEATH OF CHARLES DICKENS ON 9 June 1870 inspired dozens of verse tributes on both sides of the Atlantic. In the immediate aftermath, newspapers and periodicals eulogised Dickens's humour and pathos, iconic characters and advocacy for the poor. Further tributes appeared in the months and years that followed, in the press and in various poetry collections. Among the tributes are many written by 'amateurs', such as the former potato salesman Joseph Gwyer quoted in my epigraph. Irritated by the bathos and trite phrasing, Ralph Straus, one of Dickens's twentieth-century biographers, dubbed Gwyer's poem 'the *worst* set of verses ever written about Dickens'.[2] Yet, despite the indifferent versification, the sentiment rings true. Gwyer expresses plainly the grief shared by 'thousands' at the death of a public figure, which is experienced like the loss of a 'friend'. The poem as a whole strikes many of the same chords as other post-mortem tributes in noting Dickens's 'genius', social conscience and affective power.[3] More distinct is Gwyer's emphasis on the 'strict propriety' that Dickens's works 'teach', an ambition restrained within 'proper bounds', and Dickens's love of the Bible.[4] The poem's version of Dickens is thus familiar and subtly distorted, refracted through Gwyer's own values as an artisan poet who 'make[s] no pretension', and whose purpose is explicitly evangelical.[5] While poems like 'Death of Mr Charles Dickens' are often dismissed on grounds of artistic merit, they play a role in shaping the commemorative subject nonetheless, and raise questions about who gets a voice in public remembrance of a popular figure.

This essay explores poetic commemoration: a largely neglected niche within the scholarship dedicated to Dickensian afterlives and cultural memory.[6] Although often associated with the elite tradition of canonical elegy, represented by poems such as Alfred, Lord Tennyson's *In Memoriam* (1850), poetic commemoration can encompass a more varied selection of poetry and poets, both 'professional' and 'amateur'. Linda K. Hughes, Natalie M. Houston and Daniel Karlin have, in different ways, sought to broaden understanding of nineteenth-century poetic culture.[7] Building on their work, I propose to take seriously the unruly body of verse that commemorates Dickens and explore how poetic commemoration works differently when criteria other than artistry and originality are privileged. My corpus is 'Poetical Tributes to Charles Dickens', a series of 168 poems published in *The Dickensian* between January 1905 and December 1918. The collection comprises verse spanning an eighty-year period, from 1838 to 1918, including poems written during Dickens's lifetime, on his death and in the decades that followed. Approximately three-quarters of the tributes are reprinted from British, North American and Australian newspapers, periodicals and poetry collections, creating a scrapbook-like assortment of Dickensiana. The remaining tributes tend to be contributed by members of the Dickens Fellowship and are original to *The Dickensian*. This dual aspect is what makes 'Poetical Tributes' such a compelling record of how Dickens's image was shaped in the early twentieth century: in addition to curating tributes from past friends, colleagues and admirers, we see contemporary readers expressing what Dickens means to them against a changing historical backdrop.

This exploration is necessarily selective. As the series is little known, I begin with some context on 'Poetical Tributes' and its place in *The Dickensian*, before examining the effects of gathering together new and reprinted material by different authors in a non-chronological sequence. Subsequently, I explore how the poetic medium enables readers to deepen their relationship with Dickens and his works. My approach considers the ways in which individual tributes commemorate Dickens and the cumulative work of the collection; in keeping with the comprehensive principles of the series, I avoid value judgements and aim to sample widely. I argue that 'Poetical Tributes' affectively stages Dickens's loss, renewal and endurance, broadly consolidating a sanctioned version of the author while allowing different facets of his life and work to be celebrated.

Contextualising 'Poetical Tributes to Charles Dickens'

The first issue of *The Dickensian* was published in January 1905, under the editorship of B. W. Matz (1865–1925), three years after the foundation of the Dickens Fellowship in 1902.[8] Each monthly issue contained approximately twenty-eight pages of news, reviews, original articles, reprinted criticism, image reproductions, poems, branch reports and a bibliography of 'Dickensiana Month by Month'. Subtitled a 'Magazine for Dickens Lovers', *The Dickensian* cultivated a modest but dedicated readership under Matz, maintaining 'a steady circulation of about 2,000 copies' at an annual subscription rate of four shillings.[9] In January 1919, due to rising production costs, *The Dickensian* became a quarterly of approximately sixty-four pages, retaining many of its original features. But while new and reprinted poems about Dickens continued to appear, these were no longer styled 'Poetical Tributes to Charles Dickens' as part of a titled and numbered series.

Within the magazine, the placement of tributes varies. Never a lead feature, poems generally appear after original articles and before branch reports. However, deviations indicate a pragmatic approach to fitting the poetry around items of differing length. 'Poetical Tributes', as opposed to the unaffiliated poems that feature intermittently, are distinguished by the capitalised series title and a roman numeral. Where the poem has a title, this is given next, followed by the verse itself. Citational practice is inconsistent: sometimes the author's name is provided, as well as the original publication date, place and venue.[10] More commonly, one or more of these elements is missing. With reprinted material, this is likely because newspaper poetry often appeared unsigned and Matz sometimes worked with press clippings from correspondents, which may not have included full attribution information.[11] Poems original to *The Dickensian* are undated and occasionally anonymous or pseudonymous, although other contributors proudly include their name, location and Fellowship branch. In addition to irregularities born of the diversity of material, Matz did not approach 'Poetical Tributes' in the spirit of a critical edition; six poems appear twice, apparently inadvertently, and there are occasional misattributions. Where possible I have traced reprinted verse back to source and established Fellowship credentials by cross-referencing contributions to *The Dickensian*. However, some unknowns remain and the scrapbook – guided by enthusiasm, eclecticism and eccentricity – is closer to Matz's model than the ordered and authoritative mode of the critical edition.

The principle that underpins the 'Poetical Tributes' series is explained in the 'Foreword' to the first issue. Alongside original articles and Fellowship news, the inclusion of reprinted material and reproduction images promised subscribers the opportunity to 'gather together a library of Dickensiana on a scale practically impossible to acquire in the ordinary way by the isolated collector'.[12] To some extent, *The Dickensian* worked in tandem with major bibliographic projects, such as F. G. Kitton's *Dickensiana* (1886), discussed by Ryan Fong in this volume. While Kitton was restricted to citational information and some brief extracts, the magazine could reproduce poems in full.[13] Essentially, *The Dickensian* makes a form of collecting more accessible to readers by reprinting rare sources, 'hitherto unavailable to the public'.[14] Instead of hoarding material and knowledge, the magazine promotes sharing and collaboration. Comprehensiveness is the primary consideration in creating a personal 'library of Dickensiana' at 'scale', rather than the quality of tributes or coherence of the series. This accounts for some of the quirkier selections, including ten acrostics extracted from 'the very rarest of Dickensian pamphlets', *Charles Dickens: Sketches in Acrostics* (1874), on subjects ranging from 'Childhood and Boyhood' to 'Style'.[15]

The comprehensive nature of 'Poetical Tributes' results in a series that is many-voiced and eclectic in coverage. Formally and tonally varied, the collection includes sonnets, elegies, acrostics, ballads and light verse. The sequence of poems disregards cultural hierarchies, with Swinburne's elegiac sonnet for Dickens sandwiched between a contemporary tribute in ballad metre by Leeds Fellowship member Ethel Kidson, and an undated acrostic by Dickens's friend Charles Kent.[16] Contributors hail from various countries – primarily Britain, America, Canada and Australia – and while the diversity of the collection should not be overstated, there are moments when voices historically marginalised, in terms of class and disability, are represented. For example, sonneteer and factory-hand William Dowsing provides a working-class perspective on the 'biographer of poor men's misery'.[17] Elsewhere, Harriet Bradley, 'a resident of the Blind Girls' Home' in St Louis, writes a poem from the perspective of Bertha Plummer, ahead of a character ball to celebrate the centenary of Dickens's birth.[18] From the poem alone, it is difficult to know what inhabiting this character, in costume and in verse, meant to Bradley. However, it is interesting that, while she registers her exclusion from some aspects of the party ('while the gay ones are dancing', 'though beaux I'm denied'), her focus is on including others by planning to socialise with Jenny Wren, Tiny Tim and 'the rest of the poor ones, | Not skipping a name on the list'.[19] The poems cover a vast range of Dickens-related topics: some celebrate individual characters or stories, with *The Pickwick Papers* (1836–7) and the *Christmas Books* particularly well represented; others explore places associated with Dickens's life (London, Gad's Hill), death (Poets' Corner) and fiction (Jacob's Island). Dickens's qualities as a man and an author are lauded, and his loss mourned. Increasingly, as the proportion of contemporary tributes grows, the contributor's own life and experiences are centred.

'Poetical Tributes' has received scant critical attention, in part because of the obscurity of the series as a niche feature in a specialist magazine. When the tributes are noted, they tend to be disparaged on the grounds of scholarly and literary value, which points to a wider issue about the status of non-canonical poetry – particularly poems written by 'amateurs'.[20] Examining the state of Dickens studies in the early twentieth century, Sylvère Monod defended *The Dickensian*, while acknowledging it had its 'weaker sides'.[21] For Monod, the 'poetical tributes [. . .] present in each issue' made for 'dreary reading' and were a prime example of the magazine's preoccupation with 'matter of limited interest and value (at least as serious Dickens studies)'.[22] This comment hints at an underlying tension between 'professional' scholarship and 'amateur' enthusiasm within the Dickens community, of particular concern at the time of Monod's centenary review.[23] Yet, the unique character of the Fellowship and its magazine has long stemmed from an ability to span these different interest groups.[24] Indeed, *The Dickensian* has benefited significantly from 'amateurism', defined by Edward W. Said as 'literally, an activity that is fuelled by care and affection rather than by profit, and selfish, narrow specialization'.[25] As Philip Collins argues, 'probably no other major author has benefited so much, [. . .] from so much good amateur scholarship'.[26]

Other types of amateur contribution to *The Dickensian*, including verse tributes by Fellowship members, are still to be fully appreciated. However, approaches rooted in reader-response and fan studies allow reconsideration of amateur creative engagement with Dickens, as Maureen England argues in this volume. Juliet John rightly identifies the ways in which present-day enthusiasm for Dickens differs from mainstream fandoms, noting that 'the internet is not in fact awash with Dickens fans'.[27] Instead, she argues, the digital age has 'given us new groups or even new clubs – small, localized special interest groups who are able to build their own "world" through their interest in Dickens and to delight in the literal ec-centricity of that world'.[28] Nonetheless, the dynamics of fan culture can illuminate aspects of 'Poetical Tributes', especially in terms of 'fan' or 'enthusiast' engagement with a writer and their works. Corin Throsby's consideration of Lord Byron's nineteenth-century female fans is suggestive in this respect, positioning practices of collection, extraction and poetic response as active forms of engagement that, in Byron's case, 'not only created an illusion of a connection between the reader and author, but generated a collective intimacy that belied the mechanisms of mass consumption'.[29] In particular, we need to pay attention to the affective and personal dimensions of 'Poetical Tributes' and how they operate in relation to the Fellowship's primary aim to 'knit together in a common bond of friendship lovers of the great master of humour and pathos, Charles Dickens'.[30]

Plurality, Temporality, Preservation

Unsurprisingly, given the Fellowship's dedication to preserving Dickens's memory and the framing of these poems as 'Tributes', the series presents Dickens positively.[31] Dickens's humour and pathos, social concerns and vibrant characters are praised repeatedly; there is also a marked emphasis on the 'purity' of Dickens's writing and the author as a role model, which emerges first in the post-mortem poetry and extends into the early twentieth century.[32] Another recurrent theme post-1870 is Dickens's standing among the greatest writers in the Western tradition. Dickens is likened to the father of English literature, Geoffrey Chaucer ('Old Chaucer was his prototype: | But Geoffrey's verse in Charles's prose grew ripe'), and the father of the novel, Miguel de Cervantes ('He gave us "Pickwick," Quixote of the day— | Weller, the Sancho Panza | Of a new extravaganza—').[33] There are also numerous comparisons with William Shakespeare (tributes 15, 16, 35, 45, 123, 125 and 150) in terms that position Dickens as the Bard of the Victorian period ('Thou Shakespeare of our day, farewell').[34] Other contributors reflect upon Dickens's burial in Poets' Corner to establish, figuratively and literally, his place alongside the nation's foremost representatives of the arts. For instance, with a touch of the macabre, *Punch* urges Dickens's artistic predecessors to shuffle up and embrace the author:

> Make room, oh tuneful Handel, at thy feet;
> Make room, oh worthy Sheridan, at thy head;
> Shift, Johnson, till thou leave him grave-space meet;
> Garrick, whose art he loved, press to him dead.[35]

At a series level, these keynotes position Dickens as a pure-hearted and benevolent genius. However, the variety of poems means that individual tributes present a more multifaceted picture. At times, the Inimitable appears a remote and semi-mystical figure, likened to a wizard, a king or a hero from chivalric romance, 'Whose pen was mightier than the sword to smite', 'He rode, Sir Galahad like, nor knew defeat'.[36] Elsewhere, Dickens appears in spiritualised forms, as an angel or Christlike figure. Edward H. S. Terry, with biblical intonation, sees Dickens continuing Christ's legacy on earth: 'And thou became a saviour unto man, | And He, in turn, gave immortality.'[37] Other poems emphasise Dickens's humanity and cast him in a succession of roles with the power to shape the reader's life. For example, a memorial tribute published in *Putman's Monthly Magazine* compares Dickens to a mother, spiritual leader, and teacher:

> As little children, by their mother seated,
> Group softly round
> To hear her stories o'er and o'er repeated,
> With awe profound,
>
> While memory brings back dreams of joy and sweetness,
> Even as he willed,
> We gathered at his feet—from his completeness
> Our store he filled.
>
> We loved the author, who so loved the true,
> So hated wrong;
> We loved the teacher, whose great soul we knew,
> Tender and strong.[38]

The experience of reading Dickens is aligned initially with the *ur*-storytelling scene, of listening to nursery tales that fire the imagination.[39] While the simile suggests a certain lack of sophistication, likening Dickens's work to oral tales rather than densely plotted serial fiction, this familial image indicates Dickens's power as a storyteller. This scene is also studiously removed from the commercial context in which audiences could have heard Dickens tell his own stories at the public readings. The next verse repeats the scene of eager listeners 'gathered at his feet', this time for spiritual wisdom, evoking Christ addressing his disciples. Finally, Dickens is likened to a 'tender' teacher of morality, capable of discerning what is 'true' from what is 'wrong'. Even when Dickens's death renders the author less familiar and knowable, he remains in communication with the terrestrial world: 'And, like the seraphs in the old-time vision, | Still, to and fro, | His thoughts, like spirits from yon world elysian, | Will come and go.'[40]

Essentially, the plurality of voices and perspectives across the series enables different versions of Dickens to coexist. Thus, Swinburne can claim Dickens for the nation, 'Chief in thy generation born of men | Whom English praise acclaimed as English-born', while F. Lock (a member of the Longwood Branch of the Fellowship in Victoria, Australia) celebrates Dickens having 'everywhere [. . .] found renown', including 'Beneath Australia's skies' where 'his lovers meet'.[41] The author is lauded as a young man, at the start of his career, and revered as a sage-like figure in later years; he is a social reformer and an entertainer; serious and humorous; angel and man. In this way, the Dickens of the 'Poetical Tributes' is akin to the Ghost of Christmas Past: 'a strange figure—like a child: yet not so like a child as like an old man' that 'fluctuated in its distinctiveness: being now a thing with one arm, now with one leg, now with twenty legs, now a pair of legs without a head, now a head without a body'.[42]

Apart from the plurality of Dickenses that readers meet across the series, one of the most striking features of 'Poetical Tributes' is the series' non-chronological arrangement. *The Dickensian* provides little information about the selection of individual tributes, although some conventions, tied to the Dickens calendar, can be intuited: a memorial poem marks the death anniversary every June and there is a Christmas-themed tribute in December. Sometimes verse selections are topical, reflecting recent events in the Dickens community or the world at large. For example, a poem published in *Truth* on the August 1909 opening of a Dickens exhibition was reprinted in October's issue of *The Dickensian* to coincide with the exhibition's close, while tribute 87 reproduces the rhyming toast delivered by A. W. Edwards at the Fellowship's tenth anniversary supper the previous month.[43] More poignantly, several tributes from the war years reflect upon the developing situation, urging courage and optimism. In January 1915, after it had become clear that the war would not be 'over by Christmas', Dutch Fellowship member C. C. Remmerswaal positioned Dickens as a source of hope: 'A Lighter of Life's dismal, gloomy night', 'Still pleads thy voice: one day all will be good!'[44] Elsewhere, reprinted tributes – such as Thomas Hood's exuberant toast to Dickens ahead of his 1842 voyage to America – draw the reader back to the nineteenth century. Hood's poem conveys immediacy in the act of toasting Dickens 'Ere his vessel leaves our river', as well as an irony for later readers, aware that Dickens's visit was not the unmitigated success that Hood pledged.[45]

When the tributes are read in sequence, the temporal dislocations become even more apparent; month by month readers move between poems in which Dickens is

516   CLAIRE WOOD

newly buried, long dead and in the prime of life. Chronological arrangement would
favour the pattern that Seamus Perry identifies in elegy: 'a dealing with despair' that
'moves towards, or around' consolation.[46] However, this commemorative project is
melancholic in the Freudian sense, because the work of mourning cannot be completed.[47] Instead, the non-chronological sequence and preponderance of verse written
in the immediate aftermath of Dickens's death causes the loss to be repeatedly experienced afresh. There is an intensity to the grief expressed in some of the memorial
poems, which readers of *The Dickensian* experience second-hand. An anonymous
poem in *The Graphic*, for instance, concludes that it does not matter where Dickens
is buried because:

> Thy resting-place is in the people's heart,
>> Which throbbed with sorrow when the tidings came
>> That all now left to England is the name
> Of him who nobly used a noble art.[48]

The tribute echoes *In Memoriam* in its abba rhyme scheme (although it adopts
iambic pentameter, rather than the tetrameter that distinguishes the *In Memoriam*
stanza form), strengthening the association with Tennyson by selecting lines from
the Laureate's elegy, 'To J. S.' (1833), for the epigraph. The imagery unites the nation
in grief through a shared 'throb' of sorrow, while entertaining a 'fantasy of *incorpo-
ration*' as the 'people's heart' becomes Dickens's tomb.[49] The abba rhyme marks a
return to the beginning of the verse and a transformation: 'people's *he*art' becomes
'noble art', a loss of 'he' that allows artistic transcendence. On a series level, also,
the non-chronological organisation of 'Poetical Tributes' bears similarities with the
progress of *In Memoriam*, which 'does not so much *evolve* as *revolve* [. . .] marked
by moments of repetition that draw us back to where we started'.[50] Just as Tennyson's
speaker moves backwards and forwards through time and memory, in a poem structured around three Christmases, so too are readers of the tributes prompted to reflect
non-sequentially upon Dickens in life, death and the future life, while returning
to Dickens's grave each June.[51]

    'Poetical Tributes' also works to preserve ephemeral or quasi-ephemeral texts
that might otherwise be lost, by reprinting poems from obscure publications and
minor newspapers, and circulating oral tributes, such as A. W. Edwards's rhyming toast, noted above. The logic of the scrapbook, which imbues materials with
new meaning and value in the act of gathering them together, informs the series.
Although *The Dickensian*'s formatting imparts a degree of uniformity and erases
the aesthetic variation that traditional scrapbooks conserve, the words of the tribute
are saved. The sources are often poised between ephemerality and permanence in
form and content. For example, tribute 109, 'An Acrostic Epitaph', originates '*From
a photographic memorial card*'.[52] In evoking the epitaph, the verse positions itself
as a lasting monument; although made of cardboard, private memorial cards were
designed to be treasured by recipients, while commercially produced cards memo-
rialising public figures were highly collectible.[53] The longevity of other tributes is
more dubious. Tribute 139, for instance, consists of a four-line poem submitted to a
1916 competition, hosted by *To-day*, for the 'Best Appreciation of Charles Dickens
on a Postcard':

As glistening rain refresheth thirsty earth,
    As dew brings sweeter life unto the flowers,
    So, unto hosts of lives, thy varied powers
Have given to heart and mind a better birth.[54]

The context of this poem's composition on the back of a postcard, and the fact that it was not the winning entry, renders it doubly ephemeral. Yet the text, which speaks to Dickens's endurance through an influence on 'hosts of lives', endures through its preservation as part of the 'Poetical Tributes' series.

In her discussion of the souvenir, Susan Stewart discusses the resonance of objects such as scrapbooks and memory quilts, noting that:

> while the personal memento is of little material worth, [. . .] it is of great worth to its possessor. Because of its connection to biography and its place in constituting the notion of the individual life, the memento becomes emblematic of the worth of that life and of the self's capacity to generate worthiness.[55]

The 'Poetical Tributes', of course, are primarily about Dickens's life. Nonetheless, some of the poems become entwined with the personal history of individual contributors, explicitly in the content, or implicitly through paratext; in commemorating Dickens, the life of the individual contributor is also preserved. Thus tribute 66, 'The Grave of Dickens', offers an eight-verse meditation on visiting the author's tombstone in Poets' Corner. At the conclusion of the poem, the editor notes:

> the above poem was written by Mrs Snowden Ward when a young girl, in competition for a gold medal, which she won. It was published in the newspapers of her native town, Albany, N.Y., at the time, and in magazines in America. It is reprinted here with Mrs Ward's permission.[56]

Mrs Snowden Ward's husband was a founding, active member of the Fellowship, and the inclusion of this poem, as the June memorial tribute in the fifth year of the series, speaks both to the comprehensive principle that underpinned 'Poetical Tributes' and the bonds of friendship that bound the Fellowship together. Credited under Mrs Snowden Ward's maiden name, followed by her married name in brackets, the poem preserves the contributor's reverence, as a 'young girl', for Dickens but also suggests the endurance of these feelings in the present. Commemoration is entwined with hints of personal aspiration, as the young Catharine Weed Barnes imagines wandering through Westminster Abbey to Poets' Corner: 'Regal honour, warlike glory, | Tempt me not to turn aside; | I can see in farther distance | Where *my* soul would fain abide'.[57] This pattern, in which Dickens's life becomes bound up in the lives of contributors, is increasingly pronounced as time passes – a point that I will return to in concluding.

Intimacy, Endurance, Entwinement

In this final section, I explore how the poetic medium enables contributors to, and readers of, the series to develop their relationship with Dickens and his works. 'Poetical Tributes' mirrors the Fellowship's rhetoric of friendship by cultivating an intimacy

518   CLAIRE WOOD

between the reader, the author and the works in different ways – a repetition of Dickens's intimacy with his readers.[58] The initial prevalence of tributes to Dickens during his lifetime from friends and colleagues, including T. N. Talfourd, Caroline Norton, John Forster and Leigh Hunt, enables readers to experience their proximity to the author second-hand.[59] The language of hearts and hands appears frequently, as in Chauncy Hare Townshend's 1861 dedication of *The Three Gates* to Dickens, which models a growing intimacy:

> I saw thee from afar compel
>   The crowd with magic art;
> Beneath the power that wove the spell
>   I found the genial heart.
> [. . .]
> Then, when that hand to mine its free
>   Warm welcome doth extend,
> I thank kind Heaven who granted me
>   To grasp it as a friend.[60]

In instances where contributors never had the opportunity to meet Dickens, poetry creates a space for communion. Hence Leigh Mitchell Hodges, an American writer born after Dickens's death, can still conjure the author's presence: 'First of the heart's high friends, to-night it seems I I see your face across the vanished years, I And hear your voice amid the chiming tongues', '[. . .] I feel I As if I grasped your kind, creative hand'.[61] Hodges's meditation begins with Dickens's image, familiar enough from photographs and engravings, but moves swiftly towards a multisensory encounter that restores Dickens to life. '[I]t seems' and 'I feel' facilitate an imagined intimacy, allowing the poet to not only hear Dickens's voice and touch his hand, but to know him well enough to distinguish his tones 'amid the chiming tongues'. In the second part of the tribute, Hodges grounds this intimacy in a knowledge of Dickens's work:

>   [. . .] You are yet
> Chief guest in homes uncounted, welcome friend,
>   Whose presence is as constant as the love
> Which seems to cast a light along the shelf
>   Where is your seat of honour. [. . .][62]

In this slippage between author and works, body and books, Dickens lives on as a tangible presence that 'cast[s] a light' in numerous homes.

Tributes focused on Dickens's novels and characters often encourage a playful engagement that tests the poet's ingenuity and the reader's knowledge. For example, tribute 36 incorporates intertextual references and embedded quotations without attribution, giving Dickens enthusiasts the pleasurable thrill of recognition.[63] Elsewhere, tribute 51 takes the form of an abecedarian acrostic. 'A Dickens Alphabet' jumbles together major and minor characters from different novels, with the form of the poem emphasising the euphony of Dickens's names and embracing the virtuosic love of language that is a hallmark of Dickensian style: ''Ivens (Jemima), who visits the Eagle, I Jingle did grossly Miss Wardle inveigle'.[64] The final letter merges the

COMMEMORATION 519

world of Dickens's characters with the world of the Dickensians who love them, concluding 'Zigzag's for Rambles with Allbut and Dickens'.[65] Here the poet references Robert Allbut and his topographical guidebooks *London Rambles 'en zig-zag' with Charles Dickens* (1886) and *Rambles in Dickens' Land* (1899). Fitting Dickens's characters into a mnemonic, in which they are associated with particular traits ('Bumble's the Beadle, the Bumptious, the Big; | C is for Chadband, sham-pious and oily') helps recall them to mind.[66] However, this alphabet is also unashamedly idiosyncratic ('Rosa (dear Rosebud!) loved sweet stuff in lumps'), encouraging readers to consider their own Dickensian A to Z.[67] This subset of poems offers another way to keep Dickens's world alive, through creativity and playfulness.

One final tribute serves to draw the threads of this discussion together: Wilmot Corfield's 'Memories', which is among the most moving poems in the series.[68] Wilmot Corfield (1859–1919) was a renowned philatelist, committed Dickensian and occasional poet, publishing two verse collections: *Dâk Dicta: A Selection from Verses Written in Calcutta, 1907–1910* (1910) and *More Dâk Dicta* (1911). 'Memories' appears in *The Dickensian* undated, consisting of nine quatrains written in ponderous iambic heptameter with alternating rhyme. Essentially the poem is a piece of lifewriting, in which Corfield recalls his feelings on hearing the news of Dickens's death while still a child at school in Edgbaston, Birmingham. While there are glimpses of a longer and larger historical framework (Dickens's burial place prompts a brief digression on the legend concerning the foundation of Westminster Abbey; the Battle of Sedan is referenced), the focus is on personal history. The first-person retrospective style captures poignantly the gulf between the poet's feelings as a child and his mature reflections, particularly the regret that the adult speaker experiences at having turned down his father's offer to buy tickets for what would turn out to be one of Dickens's last public readings: '"A ticket or the price of it?" I straightway [*sic*] took the cash— | For I was but a little lad and neither of us knew: —' (lines 15–16). However, the affective centre of the poem is the announcement of Dickens's death by Corfield's grief-stricken teacher:

> That morn still lives for me at least, the hush of sunlit room,
> 　　The Georgian house, the creepered wall—a fig-tree in the court,
> The school was glad, the school was sad, some laughter broke the gloom—
> 　　A dead man and a holiday! A most confusing thought.
>
> 'You'll ne'er forget to-day!' her words, ah me! I mind her well,
> 　　The gentle face, the tutor'd grace, the aged and manner'd mien—
> ('Twas just before Sedan was fought, before Napoleon fell)
> 　　And I was but a little lad—Lord, keep her memory green! (lines 29–36)

There is a frankness to the ambivalence with which news of Dickens's death is greeted by the schoolchildren, and it is through recalling the teacher's emotion ('her eyes abrim' (line 24), 'she sobbed' (line 27)) and the poet having subsequently developed a relationship with Dickens's works that the impact of the author's loss is felt. This 'Poetical Tribute' to Dickens is simultaneously, perhaps primarily, a memorial to Corfield's teacher, and, to some extent, a memorial to the poet's naive child-self. This is emphasised by the accompanying footnotes, which offer a potted history of the teacher, Miss

Ryland, and the poet's later attendance at another school 'in the house since accepted by universal consent as that which the author of "Pickwick" had in mind as the home of Mr Winkle, the elder'. In this way, the tribute becomes more about the place of Dickens in the lives of his admirers, which enables him to endure.

In 1913 Corfield proposed a scheme for 'A Perennial Dickens' in *The Saturday Review*. He suggested that the author's works should be continually reissued in serial parts, 'prefacing each with chapters giving what is known [. . .] of general interest concerning places, persons, and associations' so that 'we should thus be always going forward [. . .] garnering [. . .] all Dickensian knowledge otherwise left floating in space'.[69] Importantly, Corfield saw this as a collective and inclusive enterprise: '*Everybody* could help to make it interesting and ultimately hope to add something *personally*.'[70] Demonstrating the same generous, comprehensive impulse that underpinned curation of the 'Poetical Tributes' series, Corfield's project suggests that the best way to commemorate Dickens is via a perennial and perpetual process of rereading. This is not a new idea, having been anticipated by the terms of Dickens's will: 'I conjure my friends on no account to make me the subject of any monument, memorial, or testimonial whatever. I rest my claims to the remembrance of my country upon my published works."[71] However, in Corfield's vision of the ultimate Dickens edition, it is significant that the paratextual material supplied by Dickens's admirers has an increasingly important role to play in enhancing readers' experiences of the original texts and keeping Dickens's memory green.

Notes

1. Joseph Gwyer, 'Death of Mr Charles Dickens', in *Sketches of the Life of Joseph Gwyer (Potato Salesman); with his Poems* (London: Millard, 1875), 80–1, lines 5–8. Gwyer is referred to as 'amateur national laureate' in an 1874 review by *The World*, reprinted in this volume (141).
2. Ralph Straus, 'The World on Dickens', *Dickensian* 43.233 (1947), 150–1, 150. Original emphasis.
3. Gwyer, 'Death of Mr Charles Dickens', lines 22–3 and 27.
4. Ibid., lines 28, 29–6 and 44.
5. 'We send this book out as the record of the thoughts and doings of a man whose heart beats for his fellowmen, and who sees in the prince or the peasant the fellow sinner who needs [. . .] the saving grace of Christ.' Joseph Gwyer, 'Preface', *Poems and Prose, by Joseph Gwyer, with a Short Autobiography* (London: Perraton, 1895), n.p.
6. On cultural memory and Dickensian afterlives, see Juliet John, *Dickens and Mass Culture* (Oxford: Oxford University Press, 2010); Catherine Malcolmson, '"A Veritable Dickens Shrine": Commemorating Charles Dickens at the Dickens House Museum', *19: Interdisciplinary Studies in the Long Nineteenth Century* 14 (2011), 1–21 <https://doi.org/10.16995/ntn.604>; Sarah Winter, *The Pleasures of Memory: Learning to Read with Charles Dickens* (New York: Fordham University Press, 2011); Karen Laird, 'The Posthumous Dickens: Commemorative Adaptations, 1870–2012', *Neo-Victorian Studies* 5.2 (2012), 12–34; Emily Bell, 'The Dickens Family, the Boz Club and the Fellowship', *Dickensian* 113.503 (Winter 2017), 219–32; and Lucy Whitehead, 'Restless Dickens: A Victorian *Life* in Motion, 1872–1927', *Journal of Victorian Culture* 24.4 (2019), 469–91.
7. Hughes argues for greater recognition of the poetry that appeared in Victorian periodicals in 'What the *Wellesley Index* Left Out: Why Poetry Matters to Periodical Studies', *Victorian Periodicals Review* 40.2 (2007), 91–125. Houston suggests that anonymous

COMMEMORATION 521

newspaper poems 'illuminate important questions about [. . .] poetry's function in the public sphere', in 'Newspaper Poems: Material Texts in the Public Sphere', *Victorian Studies* 50.2 (2008), 233–42, 234. Elsewhere, Karlin explores 'mediocre' poetry published in *The Athenaeum* and 'bad' poetry by major poets, in '"The Song-Bird Whose Name is Legion": Bad Verse and Its Critics', in *The Oxford Handbook of Victorian Poetry*, ed. by Matthew Bevis (Oxford: Oxford University Press, 2013), 834–52.

8. On the early history of the Dickens Fellowship, see J. W. T. Ley, 'The Dickens Fellowship, 1902–1923: A Retrospect', *Dickensian* 19.4 (October 1923), 178–95.

9. Leo Mason, '*The Dickensian*: A Tale of Fifty Years', *Dickensian* 51 (January 1955), 4–12, 7. There was a one-shilling discount for Fellowship members.

10. In referencing 'Poetical Tributes' I have indicated original publication information in square brackets after the title, where available.

11. Evidence for the latter practice is seen in the 1908 special American number: 'When Found' thanks 'Mr E. S. Williamson, of Toronto' for having 'furnished copy for the Poetical Tribute by Sam Kent'. *Dickensian* 4.8 (August 1908), 199–200, 199. On another occasion, Matz records '*The above poem was sent us by Mr W. Glyde Wilkins of Pittsburg. [sic] who found it in an old scrapbook with no author's name given*'. [Anon.], '[97] 'Broken Off', *Dickensian* 9.1 (January 1913), 18–19. Original emphasis.

12. [B. W. Matz], 'Foreword', *Dickensian* 1.1 (January 1905), 1.

13. See the 'Poetical' section of *Dickensiana: A Bibliography of the Literature Relating to Charles Dickens and His Writings* (London: Redway, 1886), 340–8. Eight of the twelve 'Poetical Tributes' in *The Dickensian*'s first year are listed in Kitton's bibliography.

14. [Matz], 'Foreword', 1.

15. Bertram Dobell, 'Dickens in Acrostics', *Dickensian* 9.10 (October 1913), 263–5, 263. Dobell's tongue-in-cheek review supports the idea that rarity trumps literary merit in the selection of tributes.

16. Algernon Charles Swinburne, '[15] [Untitled]', [*Tristram of Lyonesse and Other Poems*, 1884] *Dickensian* 2.3 (March 1906), 62; Ethel Kidson, '[14] [Untitled]', *Dickensian* 2.2 (February 1906), 46; Charles Kent, '[16] [Untitled]', *Dickensian* 2.4 (April 1906), 100.

17. William Dowsing, '[73] The Question', [*Sonnets Personal and Pastoral*, 1909], *Dickensian* 7.1 (January 1911), 6, line 3.

18. Harriet Bradley, '[163] "Bertha Plummer" at a Ball', [*St Louis Times*, 20 April 1912], *Dickensian* 14.7 (July 1918), 191.

19. Ibid., lines 17, 31 and 25–6.

20. For insightful discussion of these wider issues, see Brian Maidment, *The Poorhouse Fugitives: Self-taught Poets and Poetry in Victorian Britain* (Manchester: Carcanet, 1987), and Mike Sanders, *The Poetry of Chartism: Aesthetics, Politics, History* (Cambridge: Cambridge University Press, 2009).

21. Sylvère Monod, '1900–1920: The Age of Chesterton', *Dickensian* 66.361 (May 1970), 101–20, 118.

22. Ibid.

23. See Ella Westland, 'The Making of Dickens: Conflicts in Criticism, 1940–70', *Dickens Quarterly* 10.4 (December 1993), 208–18 and, for a longer history, Laurence W. Mazzeno, *The Dickens Industry: Critical Perspectives 1836–2005* (Rochester, NY: Camden House, 2008).

24. Malcolm Andrews notes that *The Dickensian* 'positioned itself precisely' on the 'fault-line' between 'lay readers' and 'professional scholars' in '"I Will Live in the Past, Present, and the Future": Time, Place and Dickensians', *Dickens Quarterly* 12.4 (December 1995), 205–12, 206. Elsewhere, Michael Slater commends B. W. Matz, Walter Dexter and Leslie Staples for maintaining the magazine's appeal to different audiences in '*The Dickensian* at Ninety: A Celebration of the First Three Editors 1905-1968', *Dickensian* 91.437 (Winter 1995), 165–70, 170.

25. Edward W. Said, 'Professionals and Amateurs', in *Representations of the Intellectual: The 1993 Reith Lectures* (London: Vintage, 1994), 49–62, 61. For more recent discussions of the role of 'amateurism' in art, craft and theatre, see Glenn Adamson, *Thinking through Craft* (London: Bloomsbury, 2013), 139–63; Stephen Knott, *Amateur Craft: History and Theory* (London: Bloomsbury, 2015); and Nadine Holdsworth, Jane Milling and Helen Nicholson, 'Theatre, Performance, and the Amateur Turn', *Contemporary Theatre Review* 27.1 (2017), 4–17.

26. Philip Collins, '1940–1960: Enter the Professionals', *Dickensian* 66.361 (May 1970), 143–61, 146.

27. Juliet John, 'Crowdsourced Dickens: Adapting and Adopting Dickens in the Internet Age', in *The Oxford Handbook of Charles Dickens*, ed. by Robert L. Patten, John O. Jordan and Catherine Waters (Oxford: Oxford University Press, 2018), 756–73, 769.

28. Ibid., 769–70.

29. Corin Throsby, 'Byron, Commonplacing and Early Fan Culture', in *Romanticism and Celebrity Culture, 1750–1850*, ed. by Tom Mole (Cambridge: Cambridge University Press, 2009), 227–44, 241.

30. Ley, 'The Dickens Fellowship', 179.

31. On the Fellowship's role in guarding Dickens's reputation, see Bell, 'The Dickens Family'.

32. For example, consider the following lines from an 1870 tribute: 'His myriad mind was pure as bright, | A pattern for our age! | [. . .] His steadfast hand refused to write | One sullied page', [Anon.], '[76] Boz', [*Chambers's Journal*, 23 July 1870], *Dickensian* 7.4 (April 1911), 99, lines 7–8 and 11–12. Compare 'And in the general atmosphere of dinkiness and dirt | The purest soul may read him through and not receive a hurt'. E. Mackinnon, '[149] An Appreciation', [from a Sydney paper], *Dickensian* 13.5 (May 1917), 121, lines 15–16. While the poem is undated, it must have been written in 1908 or afterwards, as it references a novel from this time.

33. [Anon.], '[105] [Untitled]', [*The Period*, 25 June 1870], *Dickensian* 9.9 (September 1913), 236, lines 13–14 and 15–17.

34. Edwin Tomlin, '[35] [Untitled]', [*The Jewish Record*, 5 August 1870], *Dickensian* 3.11 (November 1907), 292, line 1.

35. [Anon.], '[54] [The Grave of Charles Dickens]', [*Punch*, 25 June 1870], *Dickensian* 5.6 (June 1909), 153, lines 25–8.

36. J. Hudson, '[102] [Untitled]', *Dickensian* 9.6 (June 1913), 153, lines 9 and 12.

37. Edward H. S. Terry, '[63] [Untitled]', *Dickensian* 6.3 (March 1910), 64, lines 13–14.

38. [Anon.], '[38] Boz', [*Putman's Monthly Magazine*, August 1870], *Dickensian* 4.2 (February 1908), 45, lines 13–24.

39. Dickens discusses the power of tales heard in childhood to fascinate and horrify in 'Nurse's Stories' (1860).

40. [Anon.], '[38] Boz', lines 37–40.

41. Swinburne, '[15] [Untitled]', lines 1–2; F. Lock, '[74] Lines on his Birthday', *Dickensian* 7.2 (February 1911), 42, lines 20–1.

42. Charles Dickens, *A Christmas Carol*, in *A Christmas Carol and Other Christmas Books*, ed. by Robert Douglas-Fairhurst (Oxford: Oxford University Press, 2006), 28.

43. [Anon.], '[58] On the Dickens Exhibition at New Dudley Gallery, Piccadilly', [*Truth*, 18 August 1909], *Dickensian* 5.10 (October 1909), 272; A. W. Edwards, '[87] A Toast to His Immortal Memory', *Dickensian* 8.3 (March 1912), 69.

44. C. C. Remmerswaal, '[121] An Acrostic Sonnet', *Dickensian* 11.1 (January 1915), 18, lines 3 and 14. On public opinion about the duration of the war, see Stuart Halifax, '"Over by Christmas": British Popular Opinion and the Short War in 1914', *First World War Studies*, 1.2 (October 2010), 103–21. In Chapter 3 of *The Dickens Industry*, Mazzeno notes Dickens's use as 'a tool to boost morale' during the war (62).

COMMEMORATION 523

45. Thomas Hood, '[2] On his Proposed Voyage to America', [*The New Monthly Magazine*, February 1842], *Dickensian* 1.2 (February 1905), 51, line 7.

46. Seamus Perry, 'Elegy', in *A Companion to Victorian Poetry*, ed. by Richard Cronin, Alison Chapman and Antony H. Harrison (Malden: Blackwell, 2002), 115–33, 116.

47. See Sigmund Freud, 'Mourning and Melancholia', in *The Penguin Freud Reader*, ed. by Adam Phillips (London: Penguin, 2006), 310–26, especially 311–12.

48. [Anon.], '[19] In Memoriam – June 9th, 1870', [*Graphic*, 18 June 1870], *Dickensian* 2.7 (July 1906), 188, lines 21–4.

49. Developing and refining Freud's work, Nicolas Abraham and Maria Torok explore 'introducing all or part of a love object or a thing into one's own body, possessing, expelling or alternately acquiring, keeping, losing it' as a response to 'the situation of a loss sustained by the psyche'. *The Shell and the Kernel*, ed. and trans. by Nicholas T. Rand (Chicago: University of Chicago Press, 1994), 126. Original emphasis.

50. Anna Barton, *Alfred Lord Tennyson's* In Memoriam: *A Reading Guide* (Edinburgh: Edinburgh University Press, 2012), 156. Original emphasis.

51. Alfred, Lord Tennyson, *In Memoriam*, ed. by Erik Gray, 2nd edn (New York: Norton, 2004). There is limited space here to consider the subset of 'Poetical Tributes' that imagine Dickens in heaven, although tribute 65 offers an interesting comparison with Tennyson's anguished speculations on the nature of death and the dead. In the tribute, the poet's main interests lie in whether Dickens is still writing and if his characters are present: 'I turn his pages o'er, | And question what this hand will do | Upon the other shore; | And in a mist of dreams I sigh, | As I his deathless names recall, | "I wonder if he there has met | With Nell and little Paul?"' Hattie Tyng Griswold, '[65] [Untitled]', [Columbus, Wisconsin, 1870], *Dickensian* 6.5 (May 1910), 120, lines 34–40.

52. S. W., '[109] An Acrostic Epitaph', *Dickensian* 10.1 (January 1914), 15. Original emphasis.

53. See 'Memorial Card', in Maurice Rickards, *The Encyclopaedia of Ephemera: A Guide to the Fragmentary Documents of Everyday Life for the Collector, Curator and Historian*, ed. and completed by Michael Twyman with the assistance of Sally De Beaumont and Amoret Tanner (New York: Routledge, 2000), 157.

54. Charles F. Ingham, '[139] [Untitled]', [*To-day*, 27 May 1916], *Dickensian* 12.7 (July 1916), 184. Details of the competition are recorded in 'Tabloid Appreciation of Dickens' on page 192 of the same issue, indicating that this was a contemporary paper, not to be confused with the British weekly *To-Day* (1893–1905).

55. Susan Stewart, *On Longing: Narratives of the Miniature, the Gigantic, the Souvenir, the Collection* (Durham, NC: Duke University Press, 1993), 139.

56. Catharine Weed Barnes, '[66] The Grave of Dickens', *Dickensian* 6.6 (June 1910), 153–4.

57. Ibid., lines 25–8. My emphasis.

58. See Susan L. Ferguson, 'Dickens's Public Readings and the Victorian Author', *Studies in English Literature, 1500–1900* 41.4 (2001), 729–49, and John, *Dickens and Mass Culture*, 5.

59. Compare the appeal of projects such as Frederic G. Kitton's *Charles Dickens by Pen and Pencil: Volume I* (London: Sabin, 1890). As Kitton puts it in the Introduction, 'The direct personal interest imparted to the work by [. . .] Anecdotes and Recollections from the pens of some of Dickens's friends and contemporaries will, no doubt, be appreciated' (v).

60. Chauncy Hare Townshend, '[7] [Untitled]', [*The Three Gates*, 1861], *Dickensian* 1.7 (July 1905), 183–4, lines 17–20 and 49–52. Dickens dedicated *Great Expectations* to Townshend.

61. Leigh Mitchell Hodges, '[75] [Untitled]', [*The Optimist*, Philadelphia, USA], *Dickensian* 7.3 (March 1911), 69, lines 1–3 and 5–6.

62. Ibid., lines 32–6.

63. See, for example, Z. B. Buddington, '[36] The Voice of Christmas Past', [*Harper's Magazine*, January 1871], *Dickensian* 3.12 (December 1907), 336. The poem quotes 'rare old plant' from 'The Ivy Green' in *The Pickwick Papers* (1836–7) and paraphrases the refrain 'Lord keep my memory green', from *The Haunted Man* (1848).
64. F., '[51] A Dickens Alphabet', *Dickensian* 5.3 (March 1909), 74, lines 9–10.
65. Ibid., line 26.
66. Ibid., lines 2–3.
67. Ibid., line 18.
68. Wilmot Corfield, '[91] Memories', *Dickensian* 8.7 (July 1912), 183–4. Line references are given in the text.
69. Wilmot Corfield, 'A Perennial Dickens', *Saturday Review* 116 (22 November 1913), 653.
70. Ibid. My emphasis.
71. John Forster, *The Life of Charles Dickens*, ed. by J. W. T. Ley (London: Cecil Palmer, 1928), 859. See also Emily Bell's suggestive discussion in her Introduction to *Dickens after Dickens*, 1–13.

Further Reading

Emily Bell, ed., *Dickens after Dickens* (York: White Rose University Press, 2020)

Emily Bell and Claire Wood, eds, 'Dickens, Death, and Afterlives', Special Issue, *Victoriographies* 10.3 (2020)

Juliet John, *Dickens and Mass Culture* (Oxford: Oxford University Press, 2010)

Laurence W. Mazzeno, *The Dickens Industry: Critical Perspectives, 1836–2005* (Rochester, NY: Camden House, 2008)

Notes on Contributors

Malcolm Andrews is Emeritus Professor of Victorian and Visual Studies at the University of Kent, and a former editor of *The Dickensian*, the journal of the Dickens Fellowship. He has written on Dickens and on landscape art: his *Landscape and Western Art* was published in the Oxford History of Art series in 1999. His most recent book was *A Sweet View: The Making of an English Idyll* (2021).

Sharon Aronofsky Weltman is Professor and Chair of English at Texas Christian University (TCU) and co-editor of *Nineteenth-Century Theatre and Film*. Widely published on Victorian literature, theatre and culture, her books include *Victorians on Broadway: Literature, Adaptation, and the Modern American Musical* (2020, winner of the 2021 SCMLA book prize), *Performing the Victorian: John Ruskin and Identity in Theater, Science, and Education* (2007) and *Ruskin's Mythic Queen: Gender Subversion in Victorian Culture* (Outstanding Academic Book, *Choice* magazine, 1999). Her 2011 *NCTF* special issue is a scholarly edition of George Dibdin Pitt's 1847 melodrama *Sweeney Todd*. In 2014 she directed an NEH Summer Seminar: 'Performing Dickens: *Oliver Twist* and *Great Expectations* on Page, Stage, and Screen'. Her current book project is on Elizabeth Polack, the first Anglo-Jewish woman playwright.

Paul Baines teaches literature in the Department of English at the University of Liverpool. He has published several books, editions and articles in the area of eighteenth-century studies, including *The House of Forgery in Eighteenth-Century Britain* (1999), *Five Romantic Tragedies, 1768–1821* (2000), *The Complete Critical Guide to Alexander Pope* (2000), *Edmund Curll, Bookseller* (with Pat Rogers, 2007) and *The Collected Writings of Edward Rushton, 1756–1814* (2014). He is one of the editors of the Longman Annotated Edition of *The Poems of Alexander Pope, Volume 1* (2019) and of a volume of Pope's *Early Prose* in the Oxford University Press edition of Pope's *Works*, for which he is also a general editor.

526 NOTES ON CONTRIBUTORS

Jonathan Buckmaster was an Honorary Research Fellow at the University of Buckingham from 2016 to 2018, and a Visiting Lecturer at Royal Holloway from 2012 to 2015. He was awarded his doctorate for his thesis on Charles Dickens and the pantomime clown in February 2013 and published *Dickens's Clowns: Charles Dickens, Joseph Grimaldi and the Pantomime of Life* with Edinburgh University Press in 2020. His other research interests include Dickens's afterlives in cinema and television, the influence of Dickens's work on Salman Rushdie, and Wilkie Collins. Outside academia, he has been a technical author for nearly twenty years.

Emma Curry completed her PhD thesis in 2016 at Birkbeck, University of London. From 2014 to 2015 she spearheaded the '*Our Mutual Friend* Tweets' digital engagement project at Birkbeck, and has published articles on the project's outcomes in the *Journal of Victorian Culture* and *19: Interdisciplinary Studies in the Long Nineteenth Century*. From 2017 to 2018 she co-ran a *Great Expectations* blog and tweet-along with colleagues at the University of Buckingham, and from 2020 to 2021 she was a Research Fellow on the 'Deciphering Dickens' project at the Victoria and Albert Museum in London.

Jim Davis was Professor of Theatre Studies at the University of Warwick. His major research interest was in nineteenth-century British theatre, and his most recent books are *Comic Acting and Portraiture in Late-Georgian and Regency England* (2015) and *Theatre & Entertainment* (2016). He is the editor of *Victorian Pantomime: A Collection of Critical Essays* (2010) – the first academic book devoted exclusively to this topic – and *Lives of Shakespearian Actors: Edmund Kean* (2009). He is also joint author of a prize-winning study of London theatre audiences in the nineteenth century, *Reflecting the Audience: London Theatre-going, 1840–1880* (2001). He produced a two-volume edition of nineteenth-century dramatisations of Dickens (with Jacky Bratton) and was also an editor of *Nineteenth Century Theatre and Film*.

David Ellison is Senior Lecturer in the School of Humanities, Languages and Social Science at Griffith University. His research focuses on the literary and cultural histories of Victorian domesticity. Among his publications are *On Discomfort: Moments in a Modern History of Architectural Culture* (2016, with Andrew Leach) and *Sound, Space and Civility in the British World, 1700–1850* (2016, with Bruce Buchan, Karen Crawley and Peter Denney).

Maureen England is an independent researcher who completed her PhD on the afterlives and cultural memory of Charles Dickens's characters at King's College London in 2017. She has previously been a curatorial volunteer and exhibition assistant with the Charles Dickens Museum in London and Royal Holloway. In her spare time, she collects odd Dickensian memorabilia and enjoys Dickens adaptations. She currently works as a bookseller.

NOTES ON CONTRIBUTORS

Ryan D. Fong is Associate Professor of English at Kalamazoo College and is also an affiliated faculty member in the Women, Gender, and Sexuality programme. Ryan's essays and articles have appeared in *Victorian Studies, Victorian Literature and Culture, Nineteenth-Century Gender Studies* and *Studies in the Novel*. One of the founding co-editors of the digital humanities project *Undisciplining the Victorian Classroom*, Ryan is finishing a book manuscript on indigenous literatures of the nineteenth century from across the British Empire, which seeks to build better and more ethical relations between Victorian studies and critical indigenous studies.

Christine Geraghty is Honorary Professorial Fellow at the University of Glasgow. She is internationally known for her work on film and television drama, with a particular interest in narrative, genre and performance. Her publications on adaptations include *Now a Major Motion Picture: Film Adaptations of Literature and Drama* (2008), *Bleak House* (BFI TV Classics, 2012) and an overview article, 'Filming with Words: British Cinema, Literature and Adaptation', in *A Companion to British and Irish Cinema* (2019). She was among the first to examine the issue of diverse casting, publishing an article on colour-blind casting in period drama in *Adaptation* (14.2.2021). She is on the advisory boards of *Adaptation, Journal of British Cinema and Television* and *Screen*.

Marty Gould is Associate Professor of English at the University of South Florida. He is the author of *Nineteenth-Century Theatre and the Imperial Encounter* (2011). His latest work in the areas of Victorian literature and adaptation studies appears in *Charles Dickens in Context* (ed. Sally Ledger and Holly Furneaux, 2011), *The Oxford Handbook of Adaptation Studies* (ed. Tom Leitch, 2016) and *The Cambridge Companion to Melodrama* (ed. Carolyn Williams, 2017).

Michael Hollington is a retired professor of English and Comparative Literature living in Scotland. He has held Chairs in Australia and France and taught as Visiting Professor on every continent. He is the author of *Dickens and the Grotesque* (1984; reissued 2014) and editor of *Charles Dickens: Critical Assessments* (1995) in four volumes and *The Reception of Charles Dickens in Europe* (2013) in two. His current Dickens research project is entitled *Dickens among the Modernists*.

Matthew Ingleby is Lecturer in Victorian Studies at Queen Mary, University of London. He has published widely on aspects of nineteenth-century culture, including the monographs *Bloomsbury: Beyond the Establishment* (2017) and *Nineteenth-Century Fiction and the Production of Bloomsbury: Novel Grounds* (2018), and several articles and chapters. Co-edited collections include *Coastal Cultures of the Long Nineteenth Century* (2018) and *G. K. Chesterton, London and Modernity* (2013). He is writing a book about the cultural history of landlord–tenant relations.

Mary Isbell is Associate Professor of English at the University of New Haven. Her research explores how human creative work interacts with the ever-fluctuating concept of the amateur. This includes theatrical productions mounted in living rooms, hand-written newspapers circulated at sea, and open educational resources published on the internet. Her work has been published in *Leviathan: A Journal of Melville Studies*, *Victorian Literature and Culture* and *Scholarly Editing: The Annual of the Association for Documentary Editing*.

Juliet John is Vice President, Education, at City, University of London and Professor of English Literature. She was previously Head of Humanities and Head of English at Royal Holloway, University of London, where she held the Hildred Carlile Chair of English Literature. Before that, she was Professor of Victorian Literature at the University of Liverpool. She has published widely on Dickens and Victorian studies; her work ranges beyond literary studies to media and film studies, theatre studies, digital humanities, cultural geography, and heritage and tourism studies. Among her books are *Dickens's Villains: Melodrama, Character, Popular Culture* (2001), *Dickens and Mass Culture* (2010), (ed.) *Dickens and Modernity* (2012) and (ed.) *The Oxford Handbook of Victorian Literary Culture* (2016). She was the founding editor-in-chief of *Oxford Bibliographies Online: Victorian Literature*, which she edited for a decade.

Melisa Klimaszewski is Professor of English and Director of the Black Diaspora Studies minor at Drake University, Des Moines. In addition to Victorian studies, she specialises in South African literature, critical race studies and women's/gender studies. Dr Klimaszewski has authored brief biographies of Wilkie Collins and Charles Dickens for Hesperus Press and has edited nine of Dickens's collaborative works for publication, restoring important contributions from women authors and other marginalised writers. Her monograph *Collaborative Dickens* (2019) examines all eighteen of Dickens's collaborative Christmas numbers in their entirety and argues for a conversational model of collaboration. She is currently researching representations of multiracial characters in Victorian literature.

Barry Langford is Professor in Film Studies at Royal Holloway, University of London. His major publications include *Film Genre: Hollywood and Beyond* (Edinburgh University Press, 2005), *Teaching Holocaust Literature and Film* (with Robert Eaglestone, 2007) and *Post-Classical Hollywood: Film Industry, Style and Ideology since 1945* (Edinburgh University Press, 2010). He is currently writing *Darkness Visible*, a study of Holocaust cinema, and has published on a wide variety of subjects in film and television history, theory and aesthetics. He is also a professional screenwriter and most recently co-created and co-wrote the drama serial *The Frankenstein Chronicles* (ITV 2015).

Klaudia Hiu Yen Lee is Associate Professor at the Department of English, City University of Hong Kong. Her research and teaching interests include Charles Dickens, Victorian literature and culture, spatiality and the city, comparative and world literature. She is the author of *Charles Dickens and China: Cross-Cultural Encounters,*

1895–1915 (2017). Her forthcoming works include her second monograph, *Spatial Stories and Intersecting Geographies: Hong Kong, Britain, and China, 1890–1940*, and two co-edited volumes, the first focusing on cities and fantasy across cultures and the second on the approaches, practices and pedagogy of world literature.

Brian Maidment is Emeritus Professor of the History of Print at Liverpool John Moores University and an ex-President of the Research Society for Victorian Periodicals. He has published widely on nineteenth-century print culture, especially on illustration, popular literature and mass-circulation periodicals. His most recent book is *Robert Seymour and Nineteenth-Century Print Culture* (2021).

Joss Marsh is a Victorianist and Dickensian who has always also been a cinema and pre-cinema critic and historian. She took early retirement from Indiana University, Bloomington, in 2013 to build Kent Museum of the Moving Image with her research and magic-lantern performance partner, film archivist David Francis. Her best-known works are *Word Crimes: Blasphemy, Culture, and Literature in 19th-Century England* (1998), 'Dickens and Film' (in *The Cambridge Companion to Charles Dickens*) and 'Dickensian "Dissolving Views"' (in *Comparative Critical Studies*). At Kent MOMI, with David Francis, she has created exhibitions on Ealing films and film posters (2018–), the History of Shadows, magic-lantern 'Dissolving Views' (2022–), Victorian multimedia (2018–20) and World War I on film (2022–). Forthcoming exhibitions include 'Production Design' and 'Dickens, Cinema and Pre-Cinema'.

Charlotte Mathieson is Senior Lecturer in Nineteenth-Century English Literature in the School of Literature and Languages at the University of Surrey. Her publications include *Mobility in the Victorian Novel: Placing the Nation* (2015), the edited collections *Sea Narratives: Cultural Responses to the Sea, 1600–Present* (2016) and *Mobilities, Literature, Culture* (co-edited with Marian Aguiar and Lynne Pearce, 2019), and articles in journals including *European Journal of English Studies* and *Nineteenth-Century Contexts*. She is a co-editor of Palgrave Studies in Mobilities, Literature and Culture.

Ben Moore is Assistant Professor in English Literature at the University of Amsterdam. He is the author of *Invisible Architecture in Nineteenth-Century Literature: Rethinking Urban Modernity* (Edinburgh University Press, 2024) and *Human Tissue in the Realist Novel, 1850–1895* (2023), as well as articles on Dickens and related topics in journals including *Dickens Quarterly*, *Victorian Literature and Culture* and the *Journal of Victorian Culture*. He is co-editor of the *Gaskell Journal* and a Trustee of the Dickens Society (2022–5). His new project looks at money's relationship to space in nineteenth-century literature and culture, including in Dickens.

Goldie Morgentaler is Professor Emerita of English at the University of Lethbridge, where she taught nineteenth-century British and American literature, as well as modern Jewish literature. She is the author of *Dickens and Heredity* (1999), and of numerous articles on Dickens and Victorian literature, including one on translations of Dickens into Yiddish. She is a past president as well as a former trustee of the Dickens Society. Her translations from Yiddish to English of Chava Rosenfarb's fiction and essays have won several prizes including an MLA Book Award and two Canadian Jewish Literary Awards. Once upon a time, she dreamed of being a dancer.

Daniel A. Novak is Associate Professor of English at the University of Alabama. He is author of *Realism, Photography, and Nineteenth-Century Fiction* (2008) and co-editor with James Catano of *Masculinity Lessons: Rethinking Men's and Women's Studies* (2011). He has published essays in *Representations, Victorian Studies, Novel, Criticism, Nineteenth-Century Theatre and Film* and other venues.

Francesca Orestano taught English literature at the University of Milan. She is the author of books on John Neal, on William Gilpin and the picturesque, on visual culture and nineteenth-century literature. She has edited three books on children's literature, *Dickens and Italy* (2009), *History and Narration* (2011), *New Bearings in Dickens Criticism* (2012), *Not Just Porridge* (2017) and *Some Keywords in Dickens* (2021). Her wide-ranging work covers garden studies, Hogarth and Dickens, *fin de siècle* taste and chemistry, Walter Pater, John Ruskin and meteorology, Thomson and Dante, Virginia Woolf, Dada in England, Joyce and D'Annunzio, Tomasi di Lampedusa, Etruscans in modern art, and Giovanni Arpino. Her latest book, *The Giardiniere: semi, radici, propaggini, dall' Inghilterra al mondo* (2021), was published in English translation as *Lady Gardeners: Seeds, Roots, Propagation* in 2023.

Pete Orford is Senior Lecturer in English Literature at the University of Buckingham, course director of the MA in Charles Dickens studies, and academic associate of the Charles Dickens Museum in London. He has published numerous articles and books on Dickens, the most recent being *The Life of the Author: Charles Dickens* (2024) and *The Mystery of Edwin Drood: Charles Dickens' Unfinished Novel and Our Endless Attempts to End It* (2018). He is the editor of *Pictures from Italy* (2024), *Dombey and Son* (forthcoming) and *The Plays of Charles Dickens* (Edinburgh University Press, forthcoming).

Gillian Piggott is Associate Professor of English and Humanities at the American University of Afghanistan. She is an expert on Dickens and current research includes decolonising Dickens, Dickens in Afghanistan and teaching in emergencies; Victorian representations of Afghanistan; and global Dickens. Other interests in teaching and research are Walter Benjamin, critical theory, British theatre, Shakespeare and performance history, film studies, Dickens's afterlives in adaptation and silent cinema, the Gothic novel, detective fiction and neo-Victorianism. Publications include: *Dickens and Benjamin* (2012/2016), 'Dickens in Arabia: Going Astray in Tripoli', in *E-Rea* 13.2 (2016), and 'Dickens Touches the Sky: London's Greatest Novelist and Urban

NOTES ON CONTRIBUTORS 531

Exploration', in *Reading Dickens Differently*, edited by Leon Litvack and Nathalie Vanfasse (2020).

Dominic Rainsford is Professor of Literature in English at Aarhus University, Denmark, having previously taught at universities in England, Wales, Poland and the United States. His publications include *Authorship, Ethics and the Reader* (1997), *Literature, Identity and the English Channel* (2002), *Literature in English: How and Why* (2nd edn, 2020) and many articles. Most of his research concerns Dickens and/or the relations between literature, ethics and quantification. He is the General Editor of *Dickens Quarterly*.

Jeremy Tambling was Professor of Comparative Literature at the University of Hong Kong, and Professor of Literature at the University of Manchester until retirement and is now Professor of English at SWPS University, Warsaw. He is author of over twenty books, some on Dickens, some on literary theory, his latest being *The Death Penalty in Dickens and Derrida: The Last Sentence of the Law* (2023). He is currently writing on Shakespeare.

Julia Thomas is Professor of English Literature at Cardiff University. She has published widely on aspects of Victorian visual culture, including *Pictorial Victorians: The Inscription of Values in Word and Image* (2004), *Shakespeare's Shrine: The Bard's Birthplace and the Invention of Stratford-upon-Avon* (2012) and *Nineteenth-Century Illustration and the Digital* (2017). She is a leading figure in the field of illustration studies and directs the AHRC-funded *Database of Mid-Victorian Illustration* (www.dmvi.org.uk) and *The Illustration Archive* (http://illustrationarchive.cardiff.ac.uk).

Carolyn Williams is Distinguished Professor and Kenneth Burke Chair in English at Rutgers University in New Brunswick, New Jersey. In addition to essays on Victorian theatre, poetry and the novel, she is author of *Gilbert and Sullivan: Gender, Genre, Parody* (2011) and editor of *The Cambridge Companion to English Melodrama* (2018). Earlier books are *Transfigured World: Walter Pater's Aesthetic Historicism* (1989) and the co-edited collection of essays (with Laurel Brake and Lesley Higgins), *Walter Pater: Transparencies of Desire* (2002). She is currently working on a study of Victorian melodrama, under the title 'Melodramatic Form'. Her most recent publication on Dickens was 'Stupidity and Stupefaction: *Barnaby Rudge* and the Mute Figure of Melodrama', in *Dickens Studies Annual* (2015).

Sarah Winter is Professor of English and Comparative Literary and Cultural Studies at the University of Connecticut, Storrs. She is the author of *Freud and the Institution of Psychoanalytic Knowledge* (1999) and *The Pleasures of Memory: Learning to Read with Charles Dickens* (2011) and co-editor of *From Political Economy to Economics through Nineteenth-Century Literature: Reclaiming the Social* (2019). Her current book project in legal and literary history identifies the human rights narratives that have emerged from activists' uses of habeas corpus to contest slavery and colonial violence in the British Empire.

Claire Wood is Associate Professor in Victorian Literature at the University of Leicester. She is the author of *Dickens and the Business of Death* (2015) and has published on epitaphs, material culture, adaptation and Dickens's ghost stories. She currently serves as Secretary of the Dickens Society (2021–4) and, with Hugo Bowles, led the award-winning 'Dickens Code' project, which explored Dickens's undeciphered shorthand writing.

Index

Illustrations are shown by a page reference in *italics* and plates are indicated with a P.

actors
Amateurs and Actors, 101, 104–5
Black and ethnic minority actors in
television adaptations, 348–53
classical style of acting, 136–8, 139, 146
n.49
Fanny Kelly's theatre, 106, 107, 108–9
as a precarious profession, 84, 466
professional-amateur distinctions, 97–9,
105
publicity photographs, 277
in stage adaptations, 115, 120–4, 127,
132
William Macready, 67, 101, 116, 125,
226–7, 466, 470, 471
see also amateur theatricals
adaptation
of culture-texts, 189, 359
of Dickens, 180–1
by Dickens of Dickens, 124–6, 373
the 'Dickensian' in, 357
fidelity to source texts, 188, 374
the knowing audience, 343
performative public readings, 115, 119,
125–6
romanticisation of upper-class privilege,
187–8
similarities with parody, 84
Victorian culture of, 85
see also film; musical theatre; silent film;
stage adaptations; television drama

Adichie, Chimamanda Ngozi, 408
Adorno, Theodor, 2, 68, 406
aesthetics
Dickens's aesthetic value judgements,
8
Dickens's political language, 441
empty signifiers of cultural capital, 5, 7
idealism's separation of the aesthetic and
economic, 2, 4–5
picturesque, 260, 261
the sublime, 263–4
transcendent aestheticism, 5, 7
Agyeman, Freema, 348–50
Ainsworth, William Harrison, 23
Alken, Henry, 244, 245, 248
All the Year Round, 450
Allbut, Robert, 498, 499–500, 519
Altman, Rick, 366, 367
amateur, term, 98
amateur music-making
amateur choral singing, 164–5
in *Bleak House*, 168
creative self-expression, 419–20
in Dickens, 164–5, 168
Dickens's aptitude for, 165–6
in *Dombey and Son*, 168
in *Little Dorrit*, 165, 169–70, 171,
172–3
in *Sketches by Boz*, 168–9
social harmony through, 164, 165,
169–70

INDEX

amateur theatricals
    Amateurs and Actors, 101, 104–5
    'Amusements of the People' and, 99–100
    aristocratic amateurs, 99, 101
    audiences, 109–10
    in Austen, 100
    charity performances, 97, 105, 106–7, 109
    deliberate amateurism, 98–101, 104, 106
    Dickens's company members, 102
    Dickens's hire of Fanny Kelly's theatre, 105–6, 107, 108–9
    Dickens's involvement in, 97–8, 100, 101, 114
    effect of the aggregate, 100–1, 106
    Every Man in His Humour, 107–8, 110, 475
    The Frozen Deep, 101, 107, 111 n.5, 114
    in *Great Expectations*, 98
    home theatricals, 101–5
    of Katherine Mansfield, 404
    The Merry Wives of Windsor, 465, 466
    play selection, 101–3
    playbill for *Clari*, 101, *102*
    public theatricals, 105–10
    rehearsal/backstage play trope, 104
    sanatorium performance, 107–10
    scholarship, 98
    in *Sketches by Boz*, 98
American Notes
    the American Prairies, 263
    dissections of identity via clowning, 69
    landscape in, 294
    magic lanterns, 37
    Niagara Falls, 263–4
    tap dance, 152
    working-class cultural enrichment, 422
Anand, Mulk Raj, 409–10
Anderson, Gillian, 341–2
Andrews, Malcolm, 441, 442
architecture
    anti-architecture in Dickens, 304, 305, 306
    architectural uncanny, 304–5, 312
    blacking warehouses, P4, 303, 304, 316
    in *Bleak House*, 304, 305–6, 307–8
    body-building doubling, 308
    books-buildings relationship, 314
    Church Building Society, 311
    Crystal Palace, 311–12
    in *Dombey and Son*, 307
    dreams-buildings relationship, 312–13, 315

    as an expression of national character, 311–12
    at Gad's Hill, 306, 307
    Gothic, 305, 309, 314, 315–16
    in the illustrations, 309–11, *310*
    language of in Dickens, 305, 306, 316
    in *Little Dorrit*, 308, 315
    in *Martin Chuzzlewit*, 309–12, 314
    moral principles and, 309, 311–12
    motifs and narrative function, 303–4
    in *The Mystery of Edwin Drood*, 315–16
    ornamentality, 305–6
    in *Our Mutual Friend*, 307, 308
    Palladianism, 307
    picturesque in, 307–8
    professionalisation, 309
    as reproducible commodity, 303–4, 314, 316
    ruined buildings, 307–8
    the simulacral of, 304
    St Paul's on Peggotty's work-box, 303–4, 316
    Tavistock House, Bloomsbury, 306–7
    of Venice, 312–15
Archive of Our Own (AO³)
    Dickensian-Harry Potter crossover, 47, 49, 51, 56–7
    frequency of reference to and use of particular Dickens stories, 50
    'In the Quiet', 55
Armstrong, Alun, 139
Armstrong, Nancy, 275, 280, 281
Arnold, Matthew, 2, 423
art criticism, 7–8
arts, the
    the Baroque, 295–9
    death motifs, 298–9
    definitions, 5
    Dickens and the arts, 1–10, 289, 300
    in Dickens's works, 1
    humanitarian aesthetic vision, 10
    lightning-sketch artists, 328
    in *Pictures from Italy*, 289–90, 291
    for the public good, 9–10
    rejection of idealism, 4
    see also painting
audiences
    Dickens's *theatrum mundi*, 134
    emotional connections with television dramas, 342
    the knowing audience, 343

INDEX

reading Dickens aloud, 402, 404–5
silent films, 324
ventriloquial narration and, 135–6
Austen, Jane, 100, 358, 402
Austin, Henry, 306–7
Australia, 404–5, 423
authorship
  author-artist relationship, 223–4, 230–2, 242
  cultural capital of the author, 232
  in *David Copperfield*, 3, 19
  Dickens push for the professionalisation of, 3–4
  dramatic authorship, 114
  education and freedom from patronage systems, 424
  popular authors within the great tradition, 472–3
  reader-author relationship in poetic commemoration, 513, 518
  shared authorship in fanfiction, 48, 51–2, 53–9
  see also copyright; fanfiction

Baker, Kenneth, 439
Barbauld, Anna Laetitia, 16, 17, 18
Barnaby Rudge
  eighteenth-century setting, 15–16
  illustrations, 226
  silent films, 332, 334
  stage adaptations, 116
Barnard, Frederick, 326, 327
Barnes, Catharine Weed, 517
Baroque, the
  in *A Christmas Carol*
  Dickens as a baroque artist, 41, 297–9
  the grotesque and, 296
  of the Italian Tour, 291
  of Murillo's influence in *Oliver Twist*, 290
  in *Pictures from Italy*, 295–7
Bart, Lionel, 180, 189, 190, 198, 201
Battle of Life, The, 117–18, 154–6
Baudrillard, Jean, 304
Beadnell, Maria, 101
Bear, Jordan, 276, 280
Belsey, Catherine, 364–5
Benjamin, Walter, 142, 296, 304, 305, 313, 390, 399, 482, 483
Bentley, Thomas, 326, 332–4, 500
Bergonzi, Bernard, 33
bibliography, 485–6, 512

bicentenary celebrations
  BBC adaptations for, 341
  British Council's twenty-four-hour global read-a-thon, 452, 504
  commemorative stamps, 235
  cultural nationalism, 503
  David Copperfield (film), 500
  'Dickens 2012', 500
  'Dickens World' theme park, 500
  focus on Dickens and place, 500–1, 504, 505–6
  global Dickens, 504–6
  literary tourism and, 496
  at the Museum of London, 235, 501
  re-placed Dickens in the global context, 504–6
  'Sketches by Boz: Sketching the City', 504–5
  trope of 'haunting', 501–2
  'The Uncommercial Traveller', 504–5
  virtual literary tourism, 496, 500, 501
Bleak House
  allegory, 298
  amateur music-making, 168
  architecture's function in, 304, 305–6, 307–8
  artists and paintings, 291, 292–3, 297
  as a classic realist text, 364–5
  clowning, 71
  commodity status of art, 292–3
  conflicted identities, 444
  dance in, 156, 157, 158–9
  eighteenth-century literary references, 24–5
  Esther's curated narrative, 486
  the Fine Arts, 9
  as the first detective novel, 42
  historical and psychological haunting, 89–90
  illustrations, 228, 230, 297, 404
  influences on Hitchcock films, 330
  landscape tourism, 261
  locatable places, 498
  melodrama, 87–90
  MPs, references to, 438
  patrimony of literary inheritance, 18
  photography and Dickens's realism, 274–5
  physical characterisations, 451
  political themes, 434, 442–3
  role of memory, 38

536 INDEX

Bleak House (cont.)
satirisation of opera, 167
silent films, 326
stage adaptations, 123
the tableau in, 88–9
television adaptations, 341, 342, 343, 368
transcendent aestheticism critiqued, 7, 9
women's education, 426
Bloomsbury Christening, The, 183
'The Boarding House', 290
Bolton, H. Philip, 127, 180, 181, 182, 183
Booth, Alison, 487, 501
Bordwell, David, 367
Botelho, João, 381–2
Boucicault, Dion, 277, 281
Bourdieu, Pierre, 5, 8
Bowen, Elizabeth, 265, 266
Bratton, Jacky, 68, 97, 117–18, 181
Brereton, Austin, 122
Brewer, David, 51, 60
Britten, Benjamin, 175
Britton, John, 262, 289, 309
Brontë sisters, 39, 188, 267, 358, 497, 498
Brooks, Peter, 92, 227
Brown, Bill, 303, 481
Brown, Daniel, 273
Browne, Hablot K. ('Phiz')
Bleak House illustrations, 297, 404
caricature, 223
'Damocles' for *Little Dorrit*, P5
as a Dickens's illustrator, 224, 230, 232, 233, 289, 326, 402, 409
Dombey and Son illustrations, 357
frontispiece for *The Pickwick Papers*, 228
Martin Chuzzlewit illustrations, 357
'Our Pew at Church', 226, 227, 228, 235
Bulwer Lytton, Edward, 4, 23, 175
Burdett-Coutts, Angela, 312, 417, 422–3
Burke, Edmund, 307
Bush-Bailey, Gilli, 105, 106, 108
Buss, Robert William, 235–6
Busse, Kristina, 52, 54
Byron, Lord, 513

Caird, John, 131, 132, 133, 134
Calè, Luisa, 245, 254–5
Callaghan, James, 439
Calvino, Italo, 29–30, 41
caricature
association with photography, 278
'The Club' (Seymour), 240, *241*

comedies of manners, 244, 245
comic strips, 243–4
in Dickens, 232, 276
Dickens-Hogarth parallels, 30, 31, 32
Dickens's comic visual imagination, 30, 241–3, 246, 254–5
Dickens's rejection of Georgian satire, 216–18
graphic origins of Samuel Pickwick, 239, 240
graphic tropes, 239, 240
graphic-verbal relationship, 239, 245
John Leech's prints, 216
multi-image plates, 244–5
of Napoleon, 214–16
new narrative forms, 239, 243–5, 246–7
sequential organisation of images, 243
serial formats for, 245, 246–7, 248–9, 255
single-plate caricatures, 244, 246
small scale, wood-engraved images, 244–5
'Starting for Cheltenham', P1, 240
transformation in comic art, 243–5
visual narrative, 243–5
visual sources for illustrations, 239–41, 254
Carlson, Marvin, 100–1
Carlyle, Thomas, 2, 4, 125, 472, 473
Carroll, Rachel, 348–9
Cattermole, George, 309
Céleste, Céline, 115, 118, 120, 127
Chaplin, Charlie, 35, 330, 335, 359, 374, 381
characterisation
authorial control, 134
Dickensian characterisations on stage, 114, 117, 120–1, 127, 132
Dickens's melodramatic poetics of, 137
filmic identifiability of Dickens's characters, 362
'flat' and 'round' characters, 33, 41, 275, 276
identifiability of Dickens's characters, 362
individualised characters and the narrative structure, 366
larger-than-life characters in clowning, 78
melodramatic modes, 280
minor characters in fanfiction, 456
in music hall versions of Dickens, 328
mythic appeal of Dickens, 402–3
physical portrayals, 138–9, 217, 241, 441, 451
portability of Dickens's characters, 51–2, 456–7, 505–6

as puppet-like, 208
realism in Dickens's characterisation, 275–6
Sairey Gamp character jug, 481, 490–2
in silent films, 324, 328
Charles Dickens Museum, 487, 493 n.15, 497, 500; *see also* Dickens House Museum
Chesterfield, Philip Stanhope, 4th Earl of, 16
Chesterton, G. K., 42, 73, 76, 78, 164, 165, 175, 403, 449
Chimes, The, 117, 261, 332
China
  A Christmas Carol, 390, 392–4
  Oliver Twist, 390, 395–7
  An Orphan's Tragedy (Ji), 378–9
Christmas Books, The see *Battle of Life, The*; *Chimes, The*; *Christmas Carol, A*; *Cricket on the Hearth, The*
Christmas Carol, A
  baroque sensibility of, 298
  Chinese translations, 390, 392–4
  classroom reading of *A Christmas Carol*, 427
  as a culture text, 189, 372
  dance in, 152–4, 185
  death motifs in art, 298
  in fanfiction, 49–50, 55, 61 n.14
  films, 358, 359, 360, 362, 374
  global Dickens and, 427
  illustrations, 228
  magic lantern versions, 325
  MPs references to, 438, 439
  The Muppet Christmas Carol, 357, 359
  as musical theatre, 185–6
  in poetic commemoration, 512
  preface, 392–3
  silent films, 324, 327, 329, 360
  stage adaptations, 117, 125
  staves in, 393–4
'A Christmas Tree', 209–10, 211, 217
class
  pretensions of the middling classes, 69
  realism and class dynamics, 93
  romanticisation of upper-class privilege, 187–8
  working-class cultural and educational enrichment, 416, 419–22, 424–5
Clayton, Jay, 448
Clipse featuring Ab-Liva, 196, 202–3

clowning
  bodily disproportion, 75–6
  the clown's identity, 70–1
  communitas creation, 71, 72, 73, 76
  in *David Copperfield*, 76, 77
  Dickens's appreciation of, 67
  Dickens's conception of the clown, 67–8, 78
  disruptions of social hierarchies, 68, 71–3
  dissections of identity, 68–71
  Grimaldi's pantomime clown, 67, 68, 69, 70–1, 72, 73, 76, 77
  in *Hard Times*, 70, 74, 76, 78
  Harlequin, 67
  in *King Lear*, 67
  larger-than-life characters, 78
  literary criticism and, 68
  in *Martin Chuzzlewit*, 69–70, 74
  in *The Mystery of Edwin Drood*, 68
  in *Nicholas Nickleby*, 73, 74–5, 76, 77
  in *Old Curiosity Shop, The*, 69, 71, 76
  in *Oliver Twist*, 71, 72, 76
  outcasts, 68, 75–8
  in *The Pickwick Papers*, 69, 72, 73–4, 75–6, 77
  pleasures of the flesh, 73–4, 77
  pretensions of the middling classes, 69
  the Shakespearean clown, 67, 75, 76, 78
  slapstick violence, 74–5
  social taboos exposed, 68, 73–5
  in *A Tale of Two Cities*, 75
Cohen, Jane R., 223, 224, 247
Cohn, Elisha, 279
collections
  bibliographic practices, 485–6
  completeness, 480, 483
  of Dickensiana, 512
  haptic qualities, 483
  recovery, 480, 482–3
  see also Dickensiana
Collins, Philip, 125, 471–2, 513
Collins, Wilkie, 31, 116, 118–19, 125, 262, 290, 403
colonialism
  Dickens in colonial education, 427–9
  Dickens in the settler colonies, 404–5
  imposition of English, 428
comedy
  bisociation of points of view, 441
  commedia dell'arte, 134
  critical laughter, 68

comedy (*cont.*)
Dickens's comedic songs, 165–6
in Dickens's works, 138
humour of disproportion, 441–2
in Lewis's *The Wild Body*, 35
Proust-Dickens parallels, 37, 38
in television adaptations, 347
see also caricature
comic strips, 243–4
commemoration
memorial cards, 516
personal mementos, 517
see also poetic commemoration; 'Poetical Tributes to Charles Dickens'
commercialism
of Dickens, 59
idealism's separation of the aesthetic and economic, 2, 4–5
Coppa, Francesca, 51
copyright
debates in Parliament, 437, 438
Dickens's copyright law campaign, 3, 85
Dickens's on serial piracies alongside his works, 53–4
expiration of, 359
fanfiction and copyright infringement, 48, 55–6, 59
for international translations, 389
Corbyn, Jeremy, 439–40
Corfield, Wilmot, 519–20
Costello, Dudley, 207, 210, 217
Craig, Edward Gordon, 122
Cricket on the Hearth, The
dance in, 154
fanfiction, 456
opera, 175
silent films, 128 n.21, 328–9, 374
stage adaptations, 117, 121, 181
crime
Bleak House as a detective novel, 42
in Dickens's works, 22–3
in the eighteenth-century novel, 22–3
Cruikshank, George
affiliative interplay in the works of, 229
author-artist relationship, 242
Dickens's correspondence, 107
as a Dickens's illustrator, 223, 232, 234, 241, 289, 326, 402, 409
within the graphic comic tradition, 241, 242, 243, 244
illustrations for *Oliver Twist*, 225, 229–30, 235, 239, 402

as the originator of *Oliver Twist*, 223–4
Scraps and Sketches, 245
stock figures, 242, 243
Universal Songster, 239–40, *240*
visual sources for illustrations, 239–41, 242
Cruikshank, Robert, 239
Cuarón, Alfonso, 372, 379
Cukor, George, 356–7, 359, 362–3, 366
culture
the art/culture of everyday life in *Pictures from Italy*, 5–7
Britishness of Dickens, 411–12, 503–4
cultural nationalism, 474–5, 496, 503
Dickens's liking for popular culture, 84, 132–3, 141
global appeal of Dickens, 402–3
high/low culture divide, 132–3, 141–2, 468–9, 470, 472–4
mass cultural appeal of Dickens, 59–60, 473
in the nineteenth century, 2–3
opportunities for the working classes, 416, 419–22, 424–5
Cumberland, John, 102
cyberspace
bicentenary celebrations, 452, 504–6
CLiC Dickens project, 449, 450
collaboration and community, 449, 452–5
communal online readings, 452–3
crowdsourced Dickensian projects, 458
Dickens Journals Online, 449, 450
Dickens Page, 448, 449, 458
Dickens's works in, 448–50
hyper-concordances, 449–50
language patterns across genres, 450–2, 453
new avenues for scholarship, 452, 458
new perspectives on Dickens's language, 448–9
'*Our Mutual Friend* Tweets' project, 456–7, 458
re-placed Dickens, 496, 504–6
searchable digital archives, 449–50, 453
serialised, slowed down reading projects, 452–4
text-reader relationship, 455
transformations of Dickens's works, 455–6
virtual literary tourism, 496, 500, 501
see also fanfiction

INDEX

539

Damousi, Joy, 404
dance
  in *American Notes*, 152
  ballet, 159, 160, 213–14
  in *The Battle of Life*, 154–6
  in *Bleak House*, 156, 157, 158–9
  the Carmagnole, 118, 155
  in *A Christmas Carol*, 152–4, 185
  country dancing, 153–4
  courtship via, 155–6
  in *The Cricket on the Hearth*, 154
  Dickens's love of, 151, 157
  in Dickens's works, 151
  female desirability and, 156
  feminisation of, 158–9
  in *Hard Times*, 159, 160
  as life-affirming, 152–3, 155
  in *Little Dorrit*, 159–60, 161, 170
  as a male activity, 156–7, 158
  in *Nicholas Nickleby*, 159, 160
  in *The Old Curiosity Shop*, 153
  performance, 151
  in *The Pickwick Papers*, 182
  polkas, 151, 153, 156
  professional female dancers, 159–61, 170
  in prose, 151–3
  the shawl dance, 151
  sinister qualities of, 154–5
  Sir Roger de Coverley (reel), 153
  in *Sketches by Boz*, 151, 158
  society balls, 156
  symbolic duality of, 154–5
  in *A Tale of Two Cities*, 155
  tap dance, 152
dance of death, 76, 162 n.1, 299–300
dance masters, 151, 156–7, 158;
David Copperfield
  clowning, 76, 77
  Copperfield (Cukor), 356–7, 359, 362–3,
    366
  Copperfield (musical theatre), 182,
    186–7, 188
  David's bookshelf, 17, 467
  David's model of authorship, 3, 19
  Dickens's public readings, 125
  eighteenth-century literary influences, 20
  the fallen woman figure, 20
  films, 356–7, 359, 360, 362–4, 366, 500
  illustrations, 226, 226, 227, 228, 234, 235
  lack of the arts in, 1
  landscape descriptions, 265
  legacy of *Crusoe*, 19–20

locatable places of, 498
the masculine, eighteenth-century novel
  in, 17–18, 19–20
MPs, references to, 438
patrimony in, 19
Peggotty's work-box, 303–4, 316
role of memory, 38
silent films, 323, 324, 329, 331–7, 374
stage adaptations, 119, 126
translations, 398
Davies, Andrew, 344, 346, 348
Davis, Paul, 49, 186, 359
Defoe, Daniel
  crime in the works of, 22
  Farther Adventures, 21
  Moll Flanders, 20, 22, 23, 24
  references to in Dickens's works, 21–2
  Robinson Crusoe, 16, 18, 19–20, 25
Dickens, Catherine, 151
Dickens, Charles
  anti-Catholicism, 5–6, 293–4, 311
  career, 232
  in Chatham, 216–17, 262
  childhood experiences of the blacking
    factory, 303, 305
  childhood hardship, 3, 4
  death, 510
  financial carefulness, 3
  oeuvre, 480
  portraits, 235–6
  sense of self, 443
Dickens, Katey, 151
Dickens, Mamie, 151, 180, 487
Dickens Fellowship, 48, 333, 356, 484, 497,
  498, 500, 511, 512, 515
Dickens House Museum, 501; *see also*
  Charles Dickens Museum
Dickensian
  as a global term, 402
  MPs, references to, 438–40
Dickensian, The, 450, 511–13, 515; *see also*
  'Poetical Tributes to Charles Dickens'
Dickensian tourism
  bicentenary celebrations, 500–3
  dark tourism, 498
  Dickens country, 497–8
  Dickens within his literary landscapes,
    497–8
  embodied presence of the touristic act, 499
  the figure of the author, 498–9
  48 Doughty Street (Charles Dickens
    Museum), 497, 498, 500

540   INDEX

Dickensian tourism (*cont.*)
  Gad's Hill Place, 497
  legacy consolidation, 500, 503
  rise of, 496
  temporal negotiations, 499–500, 502
  walking tours, 501–2
Dickensiana
  acts of possession, 481, 487
  cat's paw letter opener, 480–1, 487–9
  collections of, 512
  Dickensiana (Kitton), 480, 483–6, 512
  haptic qualities, 483, 487
  literalisation of the imaginary world,
    489–90, 491–2
  mass-produced objects, 489–90
  personal effects, 480, 486–7
  relationships with Dickens, 482, 484–5
  as relics, 482–3
  rubber ducks and actions figures, 474, 476
  Sairey Gamp character jug, 481, 489–92
  term, 483–4
  thing theory, 480, 481
  thingness of, 481–2, 486, 489–90
  see also collections
digital media *see* cyberspace
Dixon Hunt, John, 242–3, 247
Dobson, Michael, 98, 473
Dombey and Son
  amateur music-making, 168
  architecture, 307, 313
  Dickens's public readings, 125
  eighteenth-century literary references, 24
  illustrations, 228, 357
  landscape descriptions, 265
  landscape tourism, 261
  magic lantern versions, 325
  melodrama of, 83
  painting, 297
  the railroads, 259
  visions and character change, 37
Donsky, Seth Michael, 375
Dowsing, William, 512
drama
  acting style and, 131–2
  drama criticism, 131
  in philosophy, 143 n.4
  photography in, 277–8
  stage adaptations as, 132
  the tableau in, 82, 182
  term, 131
  see also amateur theatricals; melodrama;
    television drama; theatre

Eagleton, Terry, 7
Edgar, David, 131, 132, 133, 135, 141
Edison, Thomas, 325, 327, 331
education
  in *Bleak House*, 426
  in the colonial setting, 427–9
  creativity of the poor, 419–20
  in Dickens's journalism, 416, 417, 420–1
  in Dickens's speeches, 416, 424–6
  Dickens's vision for, 416–17
  global Dickens, 317
  in *Hard Times*, 418–19
  juvenile delinquency and the lack of
    education, 420
  Mechanics' Institutes, 416, 424, 426
  in *Nicholas Nickleby*, 417–18
  in *The Old Curiosity Shop*, 418
  public libraries, 416, 425
  Ragged Schools, 420–1
  role of dance schools, 156–7
  satires of Victorian schooling, 417–19,
    420–1
  Shakespeare in the contemporary British
    curriculum, 472–3
  social critique of education provision,
    416, 417–23
  social harmony through, 424, 425
  teacher training, 421
  universal education, 424–6
  Urania Cottage, 27 n.25, 312, 417,
    422–3, 426
  wider literary benefits of, 424
  for women and girls, 416, 420, 422, 424,
    426
  working-class cultural and educational
    enrichment, 416, 419–22, 424–5
  Yorkshire schools, 417, 418
Edwards, A. W., 515, 516
Edzard, Christine, 174–5, 187, 335
Egan, Pierce, 246–7, 252, *252*
eighteenth-century
  criminal world, 22–3
  Defoe's literary influence, 21
  in Dickens's journalism, 16
  Dickens's novels set in, 15
  the fallen woman figure, 20
  literary influences in Dickens, 18–19, 25
  the masculine, eighteenth-century novel
    in, 17–20
  Newgate novels, 23
  objects of, 23–5
  Robinson Crusoe, 21–2

INDEX 541

as a time of unrule, 15–16
true-crime writing, 22, 23
Eisenstein, Sergei, 31, 86, 128 n.21, 287 n.67,
  329–30, 358, 373, 374
Ekwensi, Cyprian, 408
Eliot, George
  Adam Bede, 9
  critique of Dickens, 2, 275–6, 294
  Daniel Deronda, 166
  'The Natural History of German Life',
    275, 294
  political understanding, 435
  realism and, 31
Eliot, T. S., 42, 403, 406, 407

fanfiction
  alternative endings, 457–8
  alternative universes, 47
  amateur creative engagement, 513
  archontic principles, 51, 52
  author's notes (A/N), 56–7
  A Christmas Carol, 49–50, 55, 61 n.14
  comments sections, 57
  copyright infringement and, 48, 55–6, 59
  The Cricket on the Hearth, 456
  cultural memory practices, 47–50, 51, 52,
    54–5, 59–60
  culture-texts, 49–50
  Dickensian–Harry Potter crossover, 47,
    49, 51, 56–7
  Dickens's established characters, 50–2
  Dickens's potential for, 48, 59–60, 449,
    456–7
  Fanfiction.net, 50, 456
  filling in the blanks (FIB), 50–1
  Great Expectations, 49, 50
  interactivity of text/user/community, 48,
    51–2, 53–9, 455–6
  Little Dorrit, 55
  on minor characters, 456–7
  Nicholas Nickleby, 61 n.14
  Oliver Twist, 52
  as 'other', 59–60
  Our Mutual Friend, 456
  post-object fandom, 48
  published authors' stance on, 48, 55–6
  serial formats, 54, 56
  slash fiction, 58, 61 n.14
  source material, 47–9
  source text extensions, 58–9
  A Tale of Two Cities, 50, 61 n.14
  'What if?' principle, 52

Farren, Nellie, 123
Fechter, Charles, 115, 119, 120
Fielding, Henry, 16, 18, 22, 23, 25
film
  A Christmas Carol, 358, 359, 360, 362, 374
  the cinematic 'Dickensian', 356–8, 360–2,
    363, 366–7
  classic realism, 366–7
  Copperfield (Cukor), 356–7, 359, 362–3,
    366
  cultural currency of Dickens, 356, 360
  David Copperfield, 360, 362–4
  Dickens in global cinema, 372
  Dickensian influences in non-Dickens
    films, 329–30, 359
  of Dickens's works, 372–3
  Dickens's works affinities for, 358–9
  disappointing adaptations, 358–60
  Great Expectations, 360, 362
  Great Expectations (Lean), 357, 359, 362,
    378, 379
  identifiability of Dickens's characters, 362
  illustrations as templates for, 362, 373
  international versions, 357, 362
  It's a Wonderful Life, 359, 362
  Little Dorrit (Edzard), 174–5, 187, 335
  The Muppet Christmas Carol, 357, 359
  network narratives, 367–8
  Oliver! 359, 363, 375
  Oliver Twist, 358, 362
  Oliver Twist (Lean), 357, 359, 362, 375
  proto-cinematic qualities of Dickens, 358,
    362, 373
  remediations of Dickens, 357–8
  the subjective in, 363–4
  A Tale of Two Cities, 357, 360, 361
  textual fidelity, 357, 374
  see also global cinema; silent films
Fiske, John, 58
Flaubert, Gustave, 166
Fleissner, Robert, 471–2
Ford, George, 407, 412
Forster, E. M., 33, 78, 409, 410
Forster, John, 18, 21, 37, 110, 115, 216, 289,
  312, 367, 442, 449, 466, 484, 518
Forsyth, William, 278, 279
Fox Talbot, Henry, 272
France
  bicentenary celebrations, 504–6
  Dickens's reputation, 406–7, 412
  silent films, 374
  translations into French, 399, 407

Freedgood, Elaine, 303, 481
Freud, Sigmund, 313
Futurism, 34

Gabriel Grub, 325
Gad's Hill Place, 306, 307, 466, 467, 497
Gager, Valerie, 470, 471, 475–6
Gainor, J. Ellen, 100
Gay, John, *Beggar's Opera*, 18, 22, 23
Genette, Gérard, 372, 391
Germany, 374, 405–6
ghosts
    A Christmas Carol, 152, 285 n.12, 298,
        325, 392–3, 394, 439
    in fanfiction, 49, 50
    ghosting and spectatorship in the theatre,
        100–1
    historical and psychological haunting in
        Bleak House, 89–90, 266–7, 486
    literary tourism walking tours and,
        499–501, 502
Gilbert, W. S., 122, 123–4, 126
Gillray, James, 216, 217, 241, 243, 299
Gilpin, William, 307–8, 311
Gissing, George, 32–3, 449
global cinema
    Boy Called Twist (Greene), 376
    Dickens's works in, 372–3
    Fitoor (Kapoor), 372, 379–80
    The Kid with a Bike (Dardenne Brothers),
        373, 376–7
    Mr. Pip (Adamson), 380–1
    Oliver Twist, 374
    Oliver Twist (Polanski), 372, 375
    An Orphan's Tragedy (Ji), 378–9
    Ovosodo, 382
    postcolonialism and *Great Expectations*,
        377–8
    silent films, 373–4
    Tempos Difíceis (Botelho), 381–2
    Twist (Tierney), 375–6
    Twisted (Donsky), 375
global Dickens
    in the Anglophone world, 404–5, 426–7
    appeal of Dickens, 402–3
    bicentenary celebrations, 504–6
    A Christmas Carol, 427
    in the colonial setting, 427–9
    the 'Dickens' of other countries, 407–8
    Dickensian, term, 402
    Dickens's 'Englishness' and, 411–12, 503–4

education, 317
    in Europe, 407, 412
    the illustrations and, 409
    in India, 409–10
    in Kenya, 410, 427–9
    in Nigeria, 408
    postcolonial Dickens, 377–8, 409,
        410–11
    reading Dickens aloud, 404–5
    in Russia, 406
    scholarship, 411
    see also translations
Goldsmith, Oliver, 18–19, 21, 36
Gorbacheva, Raisa, 439
Gothic, the
    architecture, 314, 315–16
    medieval Gothic, 309
    melodrama, 88, 89
    tensions with Classical architecture, 305
Great Expectations
    amateur theatricals in, 98
    'architectooralooral' ornamentality, 303,
        305, 306
    blacking warehouses, P4, 303, 304, 305,
        316
    body-building doubling, 308
    conflicted identities, 444
    eighteenth-century literary references, 24
    fanfiction, 49, 50
    films, 357, 359, 360, 362, 372, 377–81, 382
    Handel's 'Hallelujah' chorus, 165
    illustrations, 237 n.13
    the masculine, eighteenth-century novel
        in, 18
    musical theatre, 185
    mythic qualities, 403
    performance of *Hamlet*, 469
    photography in, 273
    physical portrayals, 451
    role of memory, 38
    silent films, 374
    stage adaptations, 122–4, 126
    television adaptations, 341–2, 346, 347
    translations, 396, 398–9
    visions and character change, 37
'The Great Wingleberry Duel', 124–5
Greene, Tim, 376
Griffith, D. W., 128 n.21, 323, 329–30, 334,
    358
Grimaldi, Joseph, 67, 68, 69, 70–1, 72, 73,
    76, 77

INDEX

543

Grotesque, the
  as baroque, 296
  in comic art, 244
  Death as, 298
  in *Pictures from Italy*, 296
Guild of Literature and Art, 4
Gwyer, Joseph, 510

Hall, Peter, 132, 145 n.30
Halliday, Andrew, 119, 126
Hammond, William James, 115–16, 120
Handel, George Frederick, 164–5
Harbage, Alfred, 471, 473–4
Hard Times
  as an allegory for the industrial era, 2
  circus performers, 2, 3, 16, 34, 159, 160
  clowning, 70, 74, 76, 78
  dance in, 159, 160
  Defoe and Goldsmith in, 21
  films, 381–2
  idealism, 3
  illustrations, 237 n.13
  landscape descriptions, 266–7
  marginalised forms of entertainment, 84
  MPs, references to, 438
  in photography, 273
  political themes, 42, 434, 435, 437
  reviews, 208
  satire of Victorian schooling, 418–19
Harley, John Pritt, 124–5
Harvey, John Martin, 115, 123, 126–7
  see also Martin-Harvey, Sir John
Haydon, Benjamin, 289
Heath, Henry, 245
Heilmann, Ann, 343, 353
Hellekson, Karen, 52, 54
Herzog, Alexandra, 56, 59
hierarchies of privilege
  artistic production, 5–6
  the arts and, 2, 4, 7
  idealism and, 5
  patrimony of literary inheritance, 18
  photography and, 275
  satirisation of opera, 166–7, 170–1
  society balls and, 156
Himmelfarb, Gertrude, 402
Hitchcock, Alfred, 330, 359
Hodges, Leigh Mitchell, 518
Hogarth, William
  Dickens-Hogarth comparisons, 30–1, 43
  Dickens's knowledge of, 297

Dickens's references of, 290
within the graphic comic tradition, 242
influence on illustrations in Dickens, 228,
  234, 241
moral parables, 31
prints owned by Dickens, 31
Satire on False Perspective, 32
visual satire, 35
Holbein the Younger, Hans, 299; *see also*
  dance of death
Holman Hunt, William, 293–4, 297
Holmes, Oliver Wendall, 272
Holmes, Rupert, 180, 187, 189, 190,
  191
homoerotic desire, 19
Hood, Tom, 234
Horne, Richard Henry, 261, 262
Household Words
  'Amusements of the People', 10, 84,
    99–100, 166, 470
  'A Detective Police Party', 450–1
  Dickens as 'Conductor' of, 164
  in the *Dickens Journals Online*, 450
  in Dickens's works, 165
  Henry V reference, 467
  'Home for the reclamation and
    emigration of women', 312
  'Insularities', 259
  melodrama-opera relationship, 166
  'New Year's Day', 452
  'One Man in a Dockyard', 262
  'Our Watering Place', 260
  'Out of Town', 269
  'The Pedigree of Puppets' (Costello &
    Wills), 207, 210, 217
  'A Walk in a Workhouse', 420
Houston, Natalie M., 510
Hughes, Gwyneth, 350, 351
Hughes, Linda K., 510
Hugo, Victor, 314, 360
Hunt, Leigh, 466, 518
Hutcheon, Linda, 186

idealism
  hierarchies of privilege and, 5
  of the Romantics, 4
  separation of the aesthetic and economic,
    2, 4–5
illustrations
  affiliative interplay between, 228–9
  in architectural books, 309

544 INDEX

illustrations (*cont.*)
  author-artist relationship, 223–4, 230–2, 242
  Barnaby Rudge, 226
  Bleak House, 228, 230, 297, 404
  A Christmas Carol, 228
  collections, 228
  complexities of, 224
  criticism of the illustrated format, 230–1
  David Copperfield, 226, 226, 235
  'Dickensian' style of, 228
  in Dickens's works, 232, 236
  Dombey and Son, 228, 357
  extra illustrations, 244
  foreshadowing effects, 225–8
  by Frederick Barnard, 326
  global impacts of, 409
  Hard Times, 237 n.13
  Hogarth's influence, 228, 234, 241
  illustrated novels, 225, 231
  influence on film adaptations, 362, 373
  influence on silent films, 326–7, 336
  by James McNeill Whistler, 409
  lack of in *Great Expectations*, 237 n.13
  Little Dorrit, 225–6
  Martin Chuzzlewit, 357
  memorialisations of Dickens, 235
  memories of, 234–6
  multi-images, P2, 251, 252–3
  Nicholas Nickleby, 235
  The Old Curiosity Shop, 226–7, 309–11, 310
  Oliver Twist, 225, 228–9, 234, 235, 239, 243, 402
  Our Mutual Friend, P2, 223, 252
  'Our Pew at Church' in *David Copperfield*, 226, 226, 227, 228, 235
  performative readings, 233–4
  'At the Piano' in *The Mystery of Edwin Drood*, 191
  The Pickwick Papers, 223, 225, 227, 228, 230–1, 233, 235, 243, 244, 247–8, 249
  in print culture, 223
  the public readings and, 233–4
  reader-illustration relationship, 224–6, 227–30, 236
  reading Dickens's novels as illustrated works, 225–6, 227–30, 236
  reviewers' comments, 230
  the serial format and, 225, 226
  sporting art, 248

  as templates for film adaptations, 362, 373
  textual dynamics and, 227
  in translated texts, 397
  variety of art forms, 223, 228
  visual sources for, 239–41, 242
  word-image relationship, 225, 227, 230–2, 402
  see also Browne, Hablot K.; Cruikshank, George; Seymour, Robert
India
  Anand's work and Dickens influence, 409–10
  Dickens's influence on Salman Rushdie, 410
  Fitoor, 372, 379–80
integrationism, 2–4, 5
Irving, Henry, 115, 121, 122
Is She His Wife? 258

James, Henry, 2, 17, 39, 228–9, 473
Jameson, Fredric, 279, 359
Jay-Z
  'Anything', 196, 198–200, 202
  on the sonnet form in rap, 203
Jefferson, Joseph, 121
Jenkins, Henry, 55, 59, 60
John, Juliet, 48, 50, 51, 137, 141, 276, 279–80, 281, 343, 360, 374, 441, 456, 457–8, 473, 482, 498, 499, 513
Johnson, Samuel, 16, 17, 18
Jonson, Ben, 107–8, 116, 475
Jordan, John O., 88, 89, 409, 410–11, 412, 486
Jordan, Tony, 60 n.2, 354 n.23, 357
journalism
  Dickens as a parliamentary journalist, 433, 434–5
  on education, 416, 417, 420–1
  eighteenth-century in, 16
  see also All the Year Round; *Household Words*; *Sketches by Boz*
Joyce, James, 2, 35–6, 39
Judge, Elizabeth F., 60

Kaplan, Deborah, 51, 52
Kapoor, Abhishek, 372, 379–80
Karlin, Daniel, 510
Keats, John, 5
Keeley, Mary Ann, 115, 116–17, 118, 120, 123, 124, 127
Keeley, Robert, 115, 116–17, 118, 120, 127

INDEX 545

Kelly, Fanny, 105–6, 107, 108–9
Kenya, 410, 427–9
Kinnock, Neil, 438–9
Kitton, Frederic George, 223, 224, 480, 483–6, 512
Klein, Naomi, 440
Knowles, James Sheridan, 466
Kucich, John, 54

Laird, Karen, 500
Lamb, Charles, 469
landscape
    in *American Notes*, 294
    the American Prairies, 263
    in Dickens's works, 258
    evocations of mood, 267–9
    in *Hard Times*, 266–7
    human associations with, 261–3
    kinetic energy, 269–70
    in *Little Dorrit*, 268
    in *Martin Chuzzlewit*, 265–6, 294
    narrative functions, 265–6
    Niagara Falls, 263–4
    in *The Old Curiosity Shop*, 258, 264–5
    in *Oliver Twist*, 264–5
    painting, 295
    in *The Pickwick Papers*, 265, 266
    the railroads intrusion into, 258–9
    the sublime, 263–4
    tourism to, 258–9
    see also Dickensian tourism; literary tourism; picturesque, the
language
    of architecture, 305, 306, 316
    characterisation through repetition of body language, 450–2
    classical acting's focus on, 136–8, 139
    corpus linguistic technologies, 449
    dialogue and emotional legibility in television drama, 346–8
    of Dickens in cyberspace, 448–9
    Dickens's political language, 440–1
    digital tools for analysis of, 449
    imposition of English in the colonies, 428
    language patterns across genres, 450–2, 453
    literary things, 482
    loss of in silent films, 324
    object-word relationship, 482
    in *Oliver Twist*, 306

the rhythms and motions of dance in prose, 151–3
    see also characterisation; style; translation
Las Case, Emmanuel de, 214, 215
Lawrence, D. H., 35
Lazy Tour of Two Idle Apprentices, The, 31, 262
Lean, David, 357, 359, 362, 375, 378, 379
Leavis, F. R., 2, 3, 59, 472, 473
Leavis, Q. D., 59
Ledger, Sally, 6, 7, 181, 239, 243, 244
Lee, Jennie, 115, 124, 127
Leech, John, 216, 228, 289
Leitch, Thomas, 189, 357, 361, 372, 379
Lewes, G. H., 2, 33, 59–60, 209, 275, 281, 289, 294
Lewis, Wyndham, 34, 35, 39
Lin Shu, 391–2, 394, 396
Lipsitz, George, 200–1
Lisle, Joe, 244, 245
literary criticism
    on Dickens's clowns, 68
    Leavis's exclusion of Dickens, 59
    popular authors within the great tradition, 472–3
    on the Shakespeare-Dickens relationship, 471–4
literary tourism
    Allbut's guidebooks, 498, 499–500, 519
    bicentenary celebrations and, 500
    cultural nationalism, 500, 503
    Dickens's ambivalent stance on, 497
    figure of the author, 487, 499, 501–2
    locatable places for, 498, 505
    in *Nicholas Nickleby*, 496–7, 499
    objects of, 487
    rise of, 487, 497, 500
    temporal negotiations, 499–500, 502
    virtual literary tourism, 496, 500, 501
    walking tours, 501–2
literature
    Calvino's literary values, 29–30
    commercialisation, 3
    value systems, 8–9
Little Dorrit
    amateur music-making, 165, 169–70, 171, 172–3
    architecture, 308, 315
    artists and paintings, 291, 295
    associations with photography, 278
    'Compagnons de la Marjolaine', 171

Little Dorrit (*cont.*)
  eighteenth-century literary references, 18, 24, 25
  fanfiction, 55
  film, 174–5, 187, 335
  in Germany, 406
  Gowan's exploitation of the arts, 9
  illustrations, 225–6
  Italy in, 171, 172, 173
  landscape descriptions, 268
  landscape tourism, 261
  locatable places of, 498
  melodrama, 83, 90–3, 278
  musicality of Cavalletto's Italian identity, 171–2, 174–5
  the novel's opening, 367
  political themes, 434, 435, 436
  professional female dancers, 159–60, 161, 170
  professional musicians, 172–3
  realism of, 93
  role of memory, 38
  satirisation of opera, 170–1
  silent films, 326, 329, 334, 374
  staring and fixation in, 91–3
  the tableau in, 90–1
  television adaptations, 341, 343, 344, 347–50, 368
Litvack, Leon, 273, 277
Liu, Lydia, 390
Llewellyn, Mark, 343, 353
Lloyd, Frank, 323, 327, 328, 331
Locke, John, 157, 158
Lowe, Joseph, 156, 157–8
Ludacris, 196, 198, 201–2
Lutz, Deborah, 488

McArthur, Colin, 365
Macaulay, Thomas Babington, 15, 259
MacCabe, Colin, 365–6
Macready, William, 67, 101, 116, 125, 226–7, 466, 470, 471
magic lanterns
  lantern versions of *A Christmas Carol*, 325
  lantern-slide lectures, 333
  magic lantern imagery, 37
  in Victorian visual culture, 30, 269, 273
magic realism, 33, 42
Mahlberg, Michaela, 450, 451, 452
Malcolmson, Catherine, 497, 498

Mansfield, Katherine, 34, 404, 405
Marinetti, Filippo Tommaso, 34
Martin Chuzzlewit
  architecture, 309–12, 314
  clowning, 69–70, 74
  Defoe references in, 21
  illustrations, 357
  landscape in, 265–6, 294
  MPs, references to, 438
  photography and Dickens's realism, 274, 275
  Sairey Gamp character jug, 490–2
  silent films, 327, 328
  stage adaptations, 117, 120
  visions and character change, 37
Martin-Harvey, Sir John, 123, 326–7;
  see also Harvey, John Martin
Master Humphrey's Clock, 54, 226–7, 262
Mathews, Charles, 126
Matz, B. W., 511–12
Maxwell, Richard, 314
Mayhew, Henry, 69
Mechanics' Institutes, 416, 424, 426
Mellor, Kay, 342, 348
melodrama
  in *Bleak House*, 87–90
  comic form, 83, 84, 86–7, 90–1
  in Dickens's works, 82–3, 132–3, 137, 181, 276
  the Gothic and, 88, 89
  historical dimension, 84
  in *Little Dorrit*, 83, 90–3, 278
  melodramatic rhythm, 82, 86–7
  motif of fixation, 91–3
  in *Nicholas Nickleby*, 83, 84–6, 139–40
  non-parodic uses, 82–3
  in *Oliver Twist*, 86–7, 181, 280, 281
  opera-melodrama relationship, 10, 166
  parody and adaptation in, 82, 83–6
  pictorial dramaturgy, 82
  realism-melodrama opposition, 83, 86–7, 93
  RSC's adaptation of *Nicholas Nickleby*, 139–40
  in silent film, 324
  soundscapes of, 82
  stage adaptations, 126–7
  the tableau in, 82, 88–9, 90–1, 134, 146 n.36, 277, 279–80, 282
  television adaptations of Dickens, 343
  television soap operas, 342, 343–4

INDEX   547

memory
  associational memory, 54–5
  cultural memory practices of fanfiction,
    47–50, 51, 52, 54–5, 59–60
  in Dickens's works, 38
  of illustrations, 234–6
  in Proust, 37–8
Mendelssohn, Felix, 165, 166
Mill, John Stuart, 2, 423, 425
Millais, John Everett, 293, 294, 296
Milnes, Richard Monckton, 437–8
modernism
  engagement with Dickens, 1, 33–4, 41–2
  rejection of nineteenth-century fiction,
    38–9
  see also Joyce, James; Mansfield,
    Katherine; Woolf, Virginia
Monbiot, George, 433
Moncrieff, W. T., 45 n.52, 85, 115–16
Monod, Sylvère, 399, 407, 468, 513
morality
  art's moral mission, 32
  moral legibility in television drama, 342,
    343–6
  moral parables in Hogarth and Dickens,
    31
  moral principles and architecture, 309,
    311–12
  music-making in *Little Dorrit*, 165, 173
  parodies of moral superiority, 69
  in stage adaptations, 132
Morley, Henry, 416
'Mrs Joseph Porter', 468
Murillo, Bartolomé Esteban, 296–7
music
  Chesterton's 'chorus' metaphor, 164, 165
  'Compagnons de la Marjolaine' in *Little
    Dorrit*, 171
  dialogic approach, 200–1
  Dickens's appreciation of professional
    musicianship, 166
  Handel's 'Hallelujah' chorus, 164–5
  professional musical performance, 166–8,
    172–3
  soundtrack to *Little Dorrit* (Edzard),
    174–5
  street musicians, 172
  see also amateur music-making; opera;
    rap music
music halls, 328
musical theatre

burlettas, 181, 183, 190
  A Christmas Carol, 185–6
  Copperfield, 182, 186–7, 188
  Dickens adaptability for, 180–1, 191
  failed adaptations, 186–9
  fidelity to source texts, 180
  Great Expectations, 185
  The Mystery of Edwin Drood, 180, 181,
    182, 187, 190–1, *191*
  Oliver! 180, 181, 182, 184, 186, 189–90,
    198–9, 200, 201, 202
  in *Oliver Twist*, 181
  The Pickwick Papers, 183–5
  the tableau in, 182
  A Tale of Two Cities, 189
Mystery of Edwin Drood, The
  amateur choral singing, 165
  architecture, 315–16
  the clown figure, 68
  crime in, 22–3
  as musical theatre, 180, 181, 182, 187,
    190–1, *191*
  painting, 297
  'At the Piano' illustration, *191*
  professional musical performance, 167–8
  Shakespearean references, 469–70
  silent films, 324
  slowed down reading projects in
    cyberspace, 452
  stage adaptations, 191
  television adaptations, 341, 350–3
  writing of, 270

Nabokov, Vladimir, 30
Naipaul, V. S., 409
Napoleon, 214–16
narrative
  caricature's new narrative form, 239,
    243–5, 246–7
  discontinuity and temporal stasis, 279
  Esther's curated narrative in *Bleak House*,
    486
  graphic narrative form, 247–8, 249–50, 255
  individualised characters and the
    narrative structure, 366
  narrativisation of architecture, 303–4
  network narratives, 367–8
  perspective as narrative device, 32
  realism's immobility, 276–7, 279
  for serial formats, 454
  ventriloquial narration, 135–6

548 INDEX

neo-Victorian fiction, 33–4, 42
New Zealand, 380–1, 404
Ngũgĩ wa Thiong'o, 410, 427–9
Nicholas Nickleby
  Chesterton's 'chorus' metaphor, 164
  clowning in, 73, 74–5, 76, 77
  as a cultural text, 133–4
  dance, 159, 160
  Dickens's public readings, 125
  eighteenth-century literary references, 23
  fanfiction, 61 n.14
  illustrations, 235
  literary tourism, 496–7, 499
  marginalised forms of entertainment,
    84–5
  melodrama, 83, 84–6, 139–40
  opera, 167
  RSC adaptation, 131, 132, 133–42, 187
  satire of Victorian schooling, 417–18
  scepticism over the 'novel', 17
  silent films, 327–8, 360
  stage adaptations, 115, 116
  transcendent aestheticism critiqued, 7
Nigeria, 408
Nisbet, Ada, 411, 412
No Thoroughfare, 116, 118–19
North, Christopher, 484, 485
novel genre
  British Novelists, 16–17, 18
  in *David Copperfield*, 17–18
  Dickens's career as a professional
    novelist, 111 n.6, 114
  Dickens's eighteenth-century heritage, 18
  Dickens's scepticism of, 17
  emergence of, 16
  genre parody and, 84
  illustrated novels, 225, 231
  the masculine, eighteenth-century novel, 18
  Newgate novels, 23
Nunn, Trevor, 131, 132, 133, 134, 136, 137
Nussbaum, Martha, 440–1

Obama, Barack, 196
objects/things
  Dickensiana's mass-produced objects,
    489–90
  of the eighteenth-century, 23–5
  literary tourism, 487
  object-word relationship, 482
  post-object fandom in fanfiction, 48
  thing theory, 32, 35, 480, 481–2

thingness of Dickensiana, 481–2, 486,
    489–90
  of Victorian literature, 481
Okonedo, Sophie, 348–9
Old Curiosity Shop, The
  Adorno's essay, 406
  clowning, 69, 71, 76
  conflicted identities, 444
  dance in, 153
  death of Nell, 57
  eighteenth-century literary references, 24
  illustrations, 226–7, 309–11, *310*
  landscape descriptions, 258, 264–5
  marginalised forms of entertainment, 84
  parallels with *King Lear*, 470
  pre-industrial countryside idyll, 23–4
  the Punch play, 207, 210–12
  Quilp's affinity with Punch, 212
  satire of Victorian schooling, 418
  silent films, 328, 332, 374
  stage adaptations, 116, 126
  translations, 389, 396
'Old Lamps for New Ones', 32
Olive, Sarah, 473
Oliver!
  the BBC adaptation of *Oliver Twist* and,
    353
  film, 359, 363, 375
  musical theatre, 180, 181, 182, 184, 186,
    189–90, 198–9, 200, 201, 202
  rap music's adaptation of, 198–9, 200,
    201, 202
Oliver Twist
  Chinese translations, 390, 395–7
  clowning, 71, 72, 76
  conflicted identities, 444
  crime in, 23
  as a culture-text, 189, 372, 375
  Dickens's public readings, 125
  eighteenth-century literary references, 18,
    22
  fanfiction, 52
  films, 357, 358, 362, 374, 375–7
  foundling *topos*, 18
  in global cinema, 372, 374, 375–6
  illustrations, 225, 228–9, 234, 235, 239,
    243, 402
  landscape descriptions, 264–5
  language, 306
  melodrama, 86–7, 181, 280, 281
  MPs, references to, 438–9

INDEX

Murillo's paintings and Fagin's gang, 290
musical theatre in, 181
need for creative self-expression, 419–20
Oliver Twist (Polanski), 372, 375
photographic imaginary of, 273, 280–4
political themes, 434, 435
Preface, 9, 18, 22
rap music adaptations, 196, 197–9, 200, 201, 202
realism of, 280–1
silent films, 323, 324, 326, 327, 329, 330, 332, 360, 374
stage adaptations, 115, 116, 121, 327
'streaky bacon' passage, 10, 86–7, 139, 281
success of and Dickens's professional status, 111 n.6
the tableau in, 282
television adaptations, 341, 343, 344–7, 348–9, 353
Twist (Tierney), 375
opera
adaptations of Dickens's works, 165, 175–6
in *Bleak House*, 167
burlettas, 183
Clari, or The Maid of Milan, 102
The Cricket on the Hearth adaptations, 175
Dickens's love of, 166
in Flaubert, 166
Italian audiences, 212–13
melodrama-opera relationship, 10, 166
national vernacular opera, 175
in *Nicholas Nickleby*, 167
The Pickwick Papers adaptations, 184
satirisation of in Dickens, 166–7, 170–1
A Tale of Two Cities adaptations, 175–6
Verdi in *Litte Dorrit* (Edzard), 174–5
Orford, Pete, 452, 455
Orwell, George, 42, 69, 72–3, 78, 449
Our Mutual Friend
architecture, 307, 308
creativity of the poor, 420, 421
eighteenth-century literary references, 24, 25–6
illustrations, 223
minor characters in fanfiction, 456
'*Our Mutual Friend* Tweets' project, 456–7, 458
parallels with *King Lear*, 470

patrimony, 26
photography in, 278
physical portrayals, 452
satire of Victorian schooling, 421
satirisation of opera, 166–7
silent films, 326, 334, 374
slowed down reading projects in cyberspace, 452, 453
title pages, P2, 252
Venus's taxidermy shop, 451–2, 453, 456–7, 488–9
Overs, John, 421–2

painting
allegory, 297–8
in *Bleak House*, 291, 292–3, 297
Dickens's art criticism, 295
Dickens's comments on Haydon, 289
Dickens's dislike of the Pre-Raphelites, 293–4
Dickens's Dream (Buss), 235–6
Dickens's knowledge of, 289–93
landscape, 295
realism in, 294, 296
Sickert-Dickens comparisons, 42
see also arts, the
Palmerston, Henry John Temple, 3rd Viscount, 436–7, 445
parody
definitions, 83
melodrama and, 82, 83–6
and the novel genre, 84
similarities with adaptation, 84
Parry, John Orlando, P1, 240
Pate, Alexs, 197
Patten, Robert, 31, 247
Peake, R. B., 243, 248
performance
artificiality of in *Nicholas Nickleby*, 159, 160
Cassell's Penny Readings, 234
Dickens's performative public readings, 115, 119, 125–6, 233, 404, 515
drama criticism and, 131
illustrations and performative readings, 233–4
Penny Readings, 233–4
of photography, 276
reading Dickens aloud, 402, 404–5
see also actors; dance
Perry, Imani, 198, 202

550 INDEX

Perry, Seamus, 516
Petrie, Graham, 357, 374
Phelps, Sarah, 344–6, 347, 353
Phiz *see* Browne, Hablot K. ('Phiz')
photography
  advent of, 31–2, 272, 273
  as analogous for realism, 273–6
  association with caricature, 278
  bodily reproducibility, 272, 280, 281–4
  cartes de visite, 272
  in Dickens's works, 273
  in *Great Expectations*, 273
  illusion and performance, 276
  images of Dickens, 273, 277
  inspired by Dickens's works, 273
  in *Our Mutual Friend*, 278
  photographic imaginary, 273–4
  photographic imaginary of *Oliver Twist*,
    273, 280–4
  and realism in *Bleak House*, 274–5
  realism in Dickens's characterisation,
    275–6
  and realism in *Martin Chuzzlewit*, 274,
    275
  seeing-reading relationship, 278–9
  social hierarchies and, 275
  the theatre and, 277–8
Pickwick Papers, The
  clowning, 69, 72, 73–4, 75–6, 77
  conflicted identities, 444
  dance in, 182
  Defoe references, 22
  eighteenth-century literary influences, 18
  in Germany, 405
  graphic origins of Samuel Pickwick, 223,
    224, 239, 240
  illustrations, 223, 225, 227, 228, 230–1,
    233, 235, 243, 244, 247–8, 249
  influence on Joyce, 35
  landscape descriptions, 265, 266
  landscape tourism, 259–60
  melodrama of, 83
  MPs, references to, 438
  as musical theatre, 183–5
  operatic adaptation, 184
  painting in, 290
  plagiarisms of, 54
  in poetic commemoration, 512
  Seymour's illustrations and, 223, 224,
    239, 244, 247–8, 249
  silent films, 325

stage adaptations, 115–16, 121–2, 123,
  182–3
success of and Dickens's professional
  status, 111 n.6
Pictures from Italy
  the art/culture of everyday life, 5–7
  the arts in, 289–90, 291
  audiences at the opera, 212–13
  critique of the Baroque, 295–6
  critique of the judgement of taste, 8
  Dickens's humanitarian vision of the arts,
    10
  'Genoa' chapter, 207, 212–15, 217
  marionette theatres, 213–18
  poverty in Naples, 261
  puppetry references, 207
  'St. Helena, or the Death of Napoleon',
    214–15, 217
  the suffering underpinning artistic labour, 6
  Venice, 312–13, 314
picturesque, the
  aesthetics, 260, 261
  in architecture, 307–8
  The Beauties of England and Wales, 262,
    289
  definition, 307
  in Dickens's works, 259–61
  landscape tourism, 258–9
  Master Humphrey's Clock, 262
  in *The Pickwick Papers*, 259–60
  poverty in, 261
  term, 260–1
Piggott, Gillian, 35
place
  bicentenary focus upon Dickens and
    place, 496, 500–1
  literary tourism, 487, 496
  materiality of Dickens's locations, 498
  portability of Dickens's characters, 51–2,
    456–7, 505–6
  see also literary tourism
Plotz, John, 481
poetic commemoration
  'Death of Mr Charles Dickens' (Gwyer),
    510
  genre, 510
'Poetical Tributes to Charles Dickens'
  amateur contributions and scholarship, 513
  bibliographic practices, 512
  celebration of Dickens's genius, 513–14
  collection, 510–11, 512–13

INDEX 551

comparisons with Shakespeare, 514
comprehensive nature, 512, 514–15
Corfield's 'Memories', 519–20
in *The Dickensian*, 511–13
Dickens's place within literary heritage, 514
ephemeral texts, 516–17
focus of, 513–14
intertextual references, 512, 518
non-chronological arrangement, 515–16
parallels with the scrapbook, 512, 516–17
personal histories and, 517, 519–20
reader-author relationships, 513, 517–18, 520
referencing *A Christmas Carol*, 512
referencing *The Pickwick Papers*, 512
relationships with Dickens, 517–20
scholarship, 513
Polanski, Roman, 372, 375
Polhemus, Rob, 69, 74
politics
agitprop theatre, 141–2
and art, 434
Bleak House, 434, 442–3
Dickens as a political thinker, 433, 434–7, 445
Dickens in *Hansard*, 437–40
Dickens's dislike of politicians, 435–6
Dickens's political language, 440–1
in Dickens's works and speeches, 436–7
disproportion as political, 442–4
Hard Times, 434, 435, 437
in literary fiction and, 433
Little Dorrit, 434, 435, 436
Mines and Collieries Bill, 434–5
MPs Dickensian references, 438–40
Oliver Twist, 434, 435
post-truth, 433
rap music and African American cultural politics, 197, 202
Shakespearean references, 437
A Tale of Two Cities, 434
translation's political contexts, 390, 391, 394–5
Pope, Alexander, 20, 24, 25
popular entertainment
Dickens's love of, 132–3, 138, 141, 208
historical forms, 134, 141
puppetry, 211–12
theatrical forms, 141–2
violence in, 211

postcolonialism, 377–8, 409, 410–11
postmodernism, 4
Potter, Russell, 204
Pound, Ezra, 406
print culture
bibliographic practices, 485–6
illustrated novels, 225, 231
new technologies, 448
see also illustrations
Proust, Marcel, 37–8
public libraries, 416, 425
Pugin, A. W. N., 309, 311
Punch, 108, 216, 336, 514
puppets
'A Christmas Tree', 209–10, 211, 217
in Dickens, 207–10
Dickens as puppet-master, 208–9
Dickens's puppet-like characterisation, 208
marionette theatre, 213–18
'A Modern Frankenstein' (anon), 207–8
The Muppet Christmas Carol, 357, 359
'The Pedigree of Puppets' (Costello & Wills), 207, 210, 217
in popular entertainment, 211–12
the Punch play in *The Old Curiosity Shop*, 207, 210–12
puppet motion, 209, 212, 213, 215, 217
realism and, 209, 210
'St. Helena, or the Death of Napoleon', 214–15, 217
Pyke, Jenny, 488

Qian Zhongshu, 391–2

rap music
African American cultural politics and, 197, 202
'Anything' (Jay-Z), 198–200, 202
as an art form, 197–8
dialogic approach, 200–1
Dickensian references, 196–7, 204–5
'Large Amounts' (Ludacris), 198, 201–2
literary and historical conversations of, 202, 203–4
Oliver! 197, 198–9, 200, 201, 202
Oliver Twist in, 196
redefined Black masculinity, 197, 204
'Ride Around Shining' (Clipse), 202–3
scholarship, 196, 197
sonnet form, 203
within wider culture, 196

readers
childhood reading and silent films, 329
communal online readings, 452–3
Dickens as puppet-master, 208–9
on digital media, 449
the idle reader, 230–1
illiterate people's access to Dickens, 402
the knowing/unknowing audience, 343
reader-author relationship in poetic
commemoration, 513, 517–18, 520
reader-illustration relationship, 224–6,
227–30, 236
and the realist text, 364
seeing-reading relationship, 278–9
slowed down reading projects in
cyberspace, 453–5
text-reader relationship in cyberspace,
455
at Urania Cottage, 423
realism
class dynamics and, 93
classic realism, 364–6
as detailism, 275
in Dickens's characterisation, 275–6
immobility in narratives, 276–7, 279
melodramatic modes of characterisation,
280
of *Oliver Twist*, 280–1
in painting, 294, 296
photography as analogous for, 273–6
the Pre-Raphelites, 294
puppets and, 209, 210
realism-melodrama opposition, 83, 86–7,
93
television drama, 342
Rees, Roger, 136–7
Rejlander, Oscar, 273
Reynolds, Frank, 336
Romanticism, 4
Rose, Tricia, 197
Rowlandson, Thomas, 216, 217, 241, 247,
260, 289
Royal Doulton company, 489–90
Royal Shakespeare Company (RSC), 131,
133–42
Rushdie, Salman, 410
Ruskin, John, 2, 156, 296
on architectural ornamentation, 305
architecture and national character,
311–12
the Baroque, 296

on caricature in Dickens, 276
dislike of Murillo's paintings, 290, 296–7
on landscape in Dickens, 258, 264
on landscape in fiction, 267–8
Modern Painters, 294
on urban architecture, 315–16
on Venice, 312, 313–14, 315
Russia/Soviet Union
The Battle of Life, 118
Dickens's reputation, 405, 406, 439
Russian translations, 406
Sergei Eisenstein's works, 31, 86, 128
n.21, 287 n.67, 329–30, 358, 373, 374
silent films, 328–9, 374
Rylance, Rick, 2, 4, 9, 10

Said, Edward W., 513
Sala, George Augustus, 272, 275
Sandberg, A. W., 323, 334–7, 374
Schlicke, Paul, 132, 211, 470, 471
Schweizer, Florian, 3
Selznick, David O., 356, 357, 363, 366
serial formats
for comic art, 245, 246–7, 248–9, 255
communal online readings, 452–3
Dickens on pirated versions of his works,
53–4
Dickens's success due to, 54–5, 59
fanfiction, 54, 56
green wrappers, 225, 226, 237 n.13
illustrations, 225, 226
narrative practices, 454
reading of as a collective activity, 133
title pages, 252
see also television drama
Seymour, Robert
career, 247, 248
'The Club', 240, *241*
development of graphic narrative forms,
247–8, 249–50, *255*
as a Dickens's illustrator, 229, 232, 233,
239
'Fisherman Dozing Against a Tree', 249,
250
within the graphic comic tradition, 244,
247
The Heiress, 250–2, *251*
Humorous Sketches, 247, 248–9
influence on *The Pickwick Papers*, 244,
247–8, 249
multi-image title pages, P2, 252–3, *253*

INDEX

as the originator of *The Pickwick Papers*, 223, 224, 239
Pierce Egan's Book of Sports and Mirror of Life, 252, 252
Pilgrims of the Thames, 253, 253
The Schoolmaster Abroad, P3, 253–4
sporting art, 247, 248, 249
Shakespeare, William
 association with the theatre, 468–9
 classical performances, 136
 clown figures, 67, 75, 76, 78
 The Comedy of Errors, 436, 437, 438
 in the contemporary British curriculum, 472–3
 criticism-performance tensions, 468–9
 within cultural and national identity, 474–5
 'Dickens and Shakespeare' as a cultural unit, 474–6
 Dickens as the literary inheritor of, 465, 466–7, 471–2, 474–5
 Dickens compared to in poetic commemoration, 514
 Dickens's *Merry Wives of Windsor*, 465, 466
 Dickens's on stagings of, 469–70
 in the Gad's Hill library, 467, 468
 global status, 402
 Hamlet, 469
 Julius Caesar, 438
 King Lear, 67, 438, 470–1
 literary tourism to his birthplace, 496–7
 Macbeth, 469–70
 in 'Mrs Joseph Porter', 468
 Much Ado about Nothing, 470
 mythic qualities, 403
 popular-elite, 473–4
 Shakespearean references by Dickens, 7, 437, 466, 467, 469–71, 475–6
 story of Dickens saving Shakespeare's birthplace, 465–6, 467
 Verdi operas based on, 175
 As You Like it, 438
Shaw, George Bernard, 68, 114, 434, 435
Shelley, Percy Bysshe, 4, 5
Sickert, Walter, 42
Siddons, Sarah, 105
silent films
 adaptation and faithfulness, 323–4, 332
 American versions, 328, 330, 331, 332
 audiences, 324
 Barnaby Rudge, 332, 334
 Bleak House, 326

characterisation, 324, 328
childhood reading and, 329
The Chimes, 332
A Christmas Carol, 324, 327, 329, 360
The Cricket on the Hearth, 128 n.21, 328–9, 374
David Copperfield, 323, 324, 329, 331–7, 374
The Death of Nancy Sykes, 323
Dickensian film as illustration, 326–7, 336
Dickensian influences in non-Dickens films, 329–30
Dickensian settings, 331, 333–4
of Dickens's centenary, 330–1
of Dickens's works, 323, 324–6, 373–4
Great Expectations, 374
Hepworth Company films, 323, 324, 326, 327, 331, 332–4
international versions, 328–9, 334, 374
intertitles, 324, 374
Little Dorrit, 326, 329, 334, 374
loss of language, 324
magic lantern versions, 325
Martin Chuzzlewit, 327, 328
melodrama in silent film, 324
The Mystery of Edwin Drood, 324
Nicholas Nickleby, 327–8, 360
Nordisk Films, 323, 331, 334–7, 374
The Old Curiosity Shop, 328, 332, 374
Oliver Twist, 323, 324, 326, 327, 329, 330, 332, 360, 374
Our Mutual Friend, 326, 334, 374
The Pickwick Papers, 325
references to stage adaptations, 326–7
sound film and, 324, 325
A Tale of Two Cities, 326
Sketches by Boz
 amateur music-making in, 168–9
 amateur theatricals in, 98
 critiques of education, 417
 dance in, 151, 158
 'The Dancing Academy', 151
 description of 'Gin-Shops', 31
 Dickens's comic visual imagination, 246
 melodrama of, 83
 precarious survival in, 15–16
 'Private Theatres', 106, 469
 scepticism of the 'novel', 17
 stage adaptations, 183
 'A Visit to Newgate', 420
 visual images, 289

INDEX

Slater, Michael, 165, 465–6
Small, Helen, 8–9
Smith, Albert, 117, 181
Smith, Emily, 466
Smollett, Tobias, 17, 18, 19, 22, 299
So, Jimmy, 407, 409
social reform
  arts, potential for, 9
  of Dickens, 5
  in *Hard Times*, 42
  see also education
Sontag, Susan, 272
Soviet Union *see* Russia/Soviet Union
Soyinka, Wole, 411
stage adaptations
  acting style and, 131–2
  the actors and the success of, 115, 120–4,
    127, 131, 132
  audience prior knowledge, 114–15, 123
  Barnaby Rudge, 116
  The Battle of Life, 117–18
  Bleak House, 123
  The Bloomsbury Christening, 183
  centrality of the text, 133, 136
  The Chimes, 117
  The Christmas Books, 117, 125
  A Christmas Carol, 117, 125
  The Cricket on the Hearth, 117, 121, 181
  cross-dressed performances, 116, 120,
    123–4
  David Copperfield, 119, 126
  Dickens as producer, 117, 118
  by Dickens of Dickens, 124–6
  Dickensian characterisations on stage,
    114, 117, 120–1, 127, 132
  Dickens's collaboration in, 116–20, 181
  of Dickens's works, 114–15, 132–3, 137
  as drama, 132
  ensemble creativity, 133–4
  Great Expectations, 122–4, 126
  'The Great Wingleberry Duel', 124–5
  the high/low cultural divide, 132–3, 141–2,
    468–9, 470
  influence on silent films, 326–7
  Martin Chuzzlewit, 117, 120
  of the melodramas, 126–7
  moral aspects of the novels, 132
  The Mystery of Edwin Drood, 191
  No Thoroughfare, 118–19
  The Old Curiosity Shop, 116, 126
  Oliver Twist, 115, 116, 121, 327

physical comedy, 138–9
The Pickwick Papers, 115–16, 121–2,
  123, 182–3
professional actors, 136–8, 139
rough theatre approach, 134–5
RSC's adaptation of *Nicholas Nickleby*,
  131, 132, 133–42, 187
Sketches by Boz, 183
staging, 119
A Tale of Two Cities, 118, 123, 126–7,
  326–7
theatricality of Dickens's works, 114
Steig, Michael, 224
Sterne, Laurence, 17, 19, 24, 299
Stewart, Susan, 483, 517
Stirling, Edward, 115, 116, 117, 182
Stone, Marcus, 223, 232
Stott, Geroge, 208
Straus, Ralph, 510
style
  'flat' and 'round' characters, 33, 41, 275,
    276
  plurality of Dickens's, 32–3, 40–1
  visibility in Dickens's style, 33, 40
  see also characterisation; language;
    narrative
Swift, Jonathan, 18, 22, 24, 442

Taine, Hippolyte, 30, 31, 406–7
Tale of Two Cities, A
  the Carmagnole (dance), 118, 155
  clowning, 75
  disproportion in, 444
  eighteenth-century setting, 16
  fanfiction, 50, 61 n.14
  films, 357, 360, 361
  musical theatre, 189
  operatic adaptation, 175–6
  physical portrayals, 451
  political themes, 434
  silent films, 326
  slowed down reading projects in
    cyberspace, 452, 453–5
  stage adaptations, 118, 123, 126–7,
    326–7
Tambling, Jeremy, 306, 309
Taylor, Tom, 118
Tearle, Christian, 498–9
television drama
  BBC adaptations of Dickens, 341–2, 343,
    353

Bleak House, 341, 342, 343, 368
  comedy in, 347
  Days of Hope, 365–6
  dialogue and emotional legibility, 346–8
  Dickensian, 47, 49, 51, 56, 60 n.2, 354
    n.23, 357
  diversity, 341, 351–3
  emotional connections with audiences,
    342
  Great Expectations, 341–2, 346, 347
  integrated casting, 341, 348–50
  Little Dorrit, 341, 343, 344, 347–50, 368
  melodrama and, 342–4
  moral legibility, 342, 343–6
  The Mystery of Edwin Drood, 341, 350–3
  network narratives, 368
  Oliver Twist, 341, 343, 344–7, 348–9,
    353
  realism, 342
  soap operas's influence on, 341, 343–4,
    347, 349, 350–1, 353
  visual technology, 342, 344
temporality
  discontinuity and temporal stasis, 279
  of literary tourism, 499–500, 502
  realism's immobility, 276–7, 279
Tennyson, Alfred, Lord, 267, 510, 516
Ternan, Ellen, 107
Thackery, William Makepeace, 3, 15, 16,
    23, 38, 125, 208, 209, 291–2, 484
Thatcher, Margaret, 438
theatre
  Adelphi Theatre, 115, 116, 117, 118,
    119, 120, 121, 182, 183
  agitprop, 141–2
  in 'Amusements of the People', 99–100
  challenges of making a living in, 84
  cloth and stick theatre, 134
  Dickens's early involvement with the
    professional stage, 97, 114, 132
  Dickens's mockery of private theatres,
    106, 469
  Dickens's *theatrum mundi*, 134
  as a dignified profession, 105, 114
  Fanny Kelly, 105–6, 107, 108–9
  materiality of, 134–5
  non-patent (minor) theatres, 183
  photography and, 277–8
  professional actors, 136–8, 139
  Shakespeare's association with, 468
  the tableau in, 134, 146 n.36, 279–80, 282

toy theatres, 210
  ventriloquial narration, 135–6
  Your Likeness – One Shilling, 277–8
  see also actors; musical theatre; puppets
thing theory, 32, 35, 480, 481–2; *see also*
    objects/things
Throsby, Corin, 513
Tierney, Jacob, 375–6
Tolstoy, Leo, 4, 9
Toole, J. L., 115, 121, 122, 127
tourism
  dark tourism, 498
  landscape tourism, 258–61
  see also Dickensian tourism; literary
    tourism
Tramp, The, 34
tramp figures, 34, 35
translations
  'Address of the English Author to the
    French Public', 389
  into Chinese, 390, 392–7
  as a creative and textual practice, 390–1,
    398–9
  cultural re-envisioning of the text, 390
  the 'cultural' turn in, 389
  of Dickens's works, 328–9
  in East Asia, 378
  fidelity to source texts, 389, 391–2, 394,
    395–7
  free translation practices, 391–4, 406
  into French, 399, 407
  into German, 398
  Great Expectations, 396, 398–9
  into Italian, 398
  local publication environment, 390
  The Old Curiosity Shop, 389, 396
  Oliver Twist, 390, 395–7
  into Polish, 398
  political contexts, 390, 391, 394–5
  prose in the target language, 389, 390–1
  into Russian, 406
  socio-cultural contexts, 390–1, 397–8
  unauthorised translations, 389
true-crime writing, 22, 23
Trump, Donald, 440
Turner, J. M. W., 293–4, 295
Tyler, Daniel, 448

Uncommercial Traveller, The, 16, 21, 34
Urania Cottage, 27 n.25, 312, 417, 422–3,
    426

INDEX

urban life
architecture, 315–16
cityscapes in Dickens, 258
Lagos in Ekwensi's works, 408
London as Dickens's world, 38, 39, 269
London as the magic lantern, 37
in the modern novel and Dickens, 36
urban tours for the bicentenary
celebrations, 501, 504–5
Utilitarian philosophy, 2

Vanfasse, Nathalie, 412
ventriloquism, 135–6
Victoria, Queen, 156, 157–8, 275, 490
Vidler, Anthony, 304, 312
Virzì, Paolo, 382
visual technology
Dickens's interest in, 30, 448
magic lantern imagery, 37
photography, 31–2, 272, 273
television adaptations, 342, 344
visuality
the cinematic 'Dickensian', 361
in Dickens's style, 33
in Dickens's works, 30, 36
as a literary value, 29
perspective in painting, 32
use of the tableau, 82, 88–9, 90–1, 134,
146 n.36, 182, 277, 279–80, 282
visual power of Dickens, 403
Vogler, Richard, 242, 243
Vorticism, 34
Vvedensky, Irinarch Ivanovich, 406

Wakley, Thomas, 437, 438
Walkowitz, Rebecca, 390
Walpole, Hugh, 356
Ward Black, Rebecca, 48–9, 57
Watson, Nicola, 496–7, 498, 499, 500, 501,
505

Wattpad, 50, 52
Wen Yehe, 392, 394, 397–8
Whistler, James McNeill, 409
White, Miles, 197, 204
Willetts, David, 439–40
Williams, Bransby, 328
Williams, Carolyn, 279, 280
Williams, Raymond, 2, 6, 9, 131, 136
Williams, Rebecca, 48
Wills, W. H., 207, 210, 217, 261
Wilson, Edmund, 37–8, 366, 472
Winter, Sarah, 54–5
Wolfreys, Julian, 304
Woloch, Alex, 78, 282, 366, 456, 457
women
angel in the house trope, 470–1
dance and female desirability, 156
education for, 416, 420, 422, 424, 426
professional female dancers, 159–61
Urania Cottage, 27 n.25, 312, 417, 422–3,
426
Wood, Claire, 212, 500, 504
Woolf, Leonard, 404
Woolf, Virginia
Bloomsbury Group's dislike of Dickens, 410
on character in Dickens, 40–1
'A Conversation about Art', 42
Dickens's influence in the works of, 41
on Dickens's style, 40
expression of the visible world, 38
as a Londoner, 39
mythic appeal of Dickens, 403
re-reading of the Victorian novelists, 39
Woolf-Dickens relationship, 38–9
Wordsworth, William, 4, 22, 258–9, 265,
423, 424, 496–7, 498

Xiong Youzhen, 396–7

Yates, Edmund, 277